IN DEPENDENT TR..

THAILAND

MALAYSIA & SINGAPORE

THE BUDGET TRAVEL GUIDE

Other titles in this series include:

SHARE YOUR EXPERIENCE

Have you had a great, interesting or even awful experience while travelling in Thailand, Malaysia or Singapore? Or do you have a helpful tip to pass on, that no guidebook seems to mention? We'd love to hear from you – and if we publish your experiences in the next edition we'll be happy to send you a free copy of the guide!

Write to the Series Editor, *Independent Travellers Thailand, Malaysia and Singapore*, Thomas Cook Publishing, PO Box 227, The Thomas Cook Business Park, 15–16 Coningsby Road, Peterborough PE3 8SB, UK, or e-mail books@thomascook.com.

INDEPENDENT TRAVELLERS

THAILAND

MALAYSIA & SINGAPORE

THE BUDGET TRAVEL GUIDE

Sean Sheehan and Pat Levy

Thomas Cook
Publishing

Published by Thomas Cook Publishing,
a division of Thomas Cook Tour Operations Limited
PO Box 227
The Thomas Cook Business Park
15–16 Coningsby Road
Peterborough
PE3 8SB
United Kingdom

Telephone: 01733 416477
E-mail: books@thomascook.com

ISBN 1 841574 23 6

Head of Publishing: Chris Young
Series Editor: Edith Summerhayes
Text design: Tina West
Production/DTP Editor: Steven Collins
Project Administrator: Michelle Warrington
Cover design: Liz Lyons Design, Oxford
Cover layout: Studio 183, Thorney, Peterborough
Proofreader: Jan Wiltshire
Maps prepared by: RJS Associates
New maps prepared by: Lovell Johns Ltd,
    Witney, Oxfordshire

Text typeset in Book Antiqua and Gill Sans
    using QuarkXPress
Layout and imagesetting: Z2 Repro, Thetford
Text revisions: Fakenham Photosetting Ltd,
    Fakenham, Norfolk
Printed and bound in Italy by Legoprint S.P.A.

Mini CD design and revisions: Laburnum
    Technologies PVT Ltd, New Delhi, India
CD manufacturing services: ODS Optical Disc Service
    GmbH, Dassow, Germany

First edition (2001) written and
researched by:
Sean Sheehan
and Pat Levy

First edition edited by:
Jane Egginton

Update research for 2005 edition:
Andrew Forbes, CPA Media
Susie Lunt
Sean Sheehan

With thanks to:
Tan Hong Boon

Mini CD written and updated by:
Sean Sheehan

Transport information:
Peter Bass, Editor,
and **Reuben Turner**,
Thomas Cook Overseas Timetable

THE AUTHORS

Sean Sheehan was born and brought up in London and worked as an English teacher before visiting Thailand and Malaysia in 1986. Since then he has made many return trips and lived in the region for over six years. Sean now has his home in Ireland.

Pat Levy worked and studied in Singapore for many years and spent much of her time travelling around the region. Pat now lives in London but the lure of South-East Asia often draws her back and she is a still a regular visitor.

ACKNOWLEDGEMENTS

Pat Levy and **Sean Sheehan** would like to sincerely thank the following people who gave their time to help in the research work for this book.

THAILAND
Sutat Praesurin in Udon Thani
Yupaporn Chaisatit and **Nares Puangthonthip** in Khorat
Surachai Yomchinda in Ban Phe
Dumrongsak Nokbunjong, Kanokros Wongvakin, Natchanok Chundasuta, Panita Leongnarktongdee, Paveenatat Boonnop, Surapan Somthai, Srima Chaturansomboon, Israporn Posayanond and **Thurdsak Suksasilp** in Bangkok
Lieutenant Colonel Terry Beaton in Nam Tok
Vorapong Muchaotai, Sawatdiwatana Chaikuna and **Surachai Leosawasthiphong** in Chiang Mai
Duncan Jamieson in Chiang Saen
John Stall, David Good, Frederic Simmen, Naruemoi Thierkarochanakul and **Chompunute Hoontrakul** on Ko Samui
Petcharat Atiset in Phuket
Pierre-Andre Pelletier in Pattaya
Sreerat Sripinyo in Ko Chang

MALAYSIA
Ann Victor and **Daulat M Jethwani** in Kuala Lumpur
Sarren Michael Atu at the Sarawak Tourist Board
Manfred Kurz, Doris Ong and **Layla Leeza Bolek** in Kuching
Calixtus James Laudi in Lahad Datu
Alice Yap and **Noreadah Othman** at the Sabah Tourism Promotions Corporation
Farizal Jaafar, Koh Teck Guan, Annie Chung, Faizul Hassan and **C L Chang** in Kota Kinabalu

UK
Razally Hussin at Tourism Malaysia in London
Last, but not least, **Deborah Parker** and **Edith Summerhayes** at *Thomas Cook Publishing*, without whose support and hard work this guide would never have appeared. Thanks also to **Linda Bass**.

Thomas Cook Publishing would like to thank Spectrum Colour Library for supplying the photographs, with the exception of those otherwise credited below (and to whom the copyright belongs).

p. 155 Chiang Mai photo supplied by CPA Media
Colour section pp. 192–193 (i) gold-leaf Buddha, ffotograff/Mary Andrews
pp. 288–289 (i) Petronas Twin Towers, Tourism Malaysia
pp. 384–385 (i) climbing Mount Kinabalu, Tourism Malaysia; (ii) Danum Valley canopy walkway; orang-utan; traditional Malay house, all Tourism Malaysia

Cover photograph: Floating market, Bangkok, Peter Adams/Alamy

Historical illustrations supplied by the **Thomas Cook Archives**.

Legend for Town Maps

Motorway & slip road	
Main road & mall	VULCAN LANE
Other road	
Footpath	
Railway	
Underground	
One-way street	↖
Bus station/Airport	🚌 ✈
Ferry route/Pier	– – – 🚢
Shopping centre	Ⓢ
Place of interest	🏛 ● Art Gallery
Information centre	ℹ️
Hospital	⊕
Police station	●
Post office	✉
Hotel	CARLTON Ⓗ
Park	
Library	📖
Golf course	⌐
Temple	⛩
Other place of worship	△

Legend for National Park Maps

Major route	═4═
Minor road & track	
Footpath	========
State boundary	———
National park	
Place of interest	●
Peak	▲ 466 m

HELP IMPROVE THIS GUIDE

This guide will be updated each year. The information given in it may change during the lifetime of this edition and we would welcome reports and comments from our readers. Similarly we want to make this guide as practical and useful as possible and are grateful for any comments, criticisms and suggestions for improving future editions.

A free copy of this guide will be sent to all readers whose information or ideas are incorporated in the next edition. Please send all contributions to the Series Editor, *Independent Travellers Thailand, Malaysia and Singapore*, Thomas Cook Publishing, at: PO Box 227, The Thomas Cook Business Park, 15–16 Coningsby Road, Peterborough, PE3 8SB, United Kingdom, or e-mail: books@thomascook.com.

CONTENTS

CONTENTS

INTRODUCTION

'To live in one land, is captivitie
To runne all countries, a wild roguery'

John Donne's third *Elegie*

A journey to Thailand, Malaysia and Singapore — three countries in South-East Asia joined by railway and road — is a traveller's version of the pick and mix system that operates for some types of goodies in supermarkets. The basic procedures are undemanding and easy to learn, and the enjoyment comes from considering the choices and selecting what appeals to you as an interesting combination. This is just what Thailand, Malaysia and Singapore offer to the traveller — easy accessibility, undemanding procedures, plenty of choices and the freedom to tailor-make an itinerary without paying out good money for fancy wrapping and presentation.

It really is as simple as this, and there is absolutely no need to incur the extra cost of having your holiday organised and planned by a tour company. Visas are not required for European and North American citizens, and a host of international airlines are competing vigorously for passengers so that the cost of the long-haul flight is kept within reason. Accommodation is equally easy to arrange and all it takes is an e-mail or a fax to secure a reservation for your first couple of nights. After that, you can either make it up as you go along or have planned every night's accommodation in advance. As for meals — a trip to South-East Asia could change your life as far as food is concerned. British and American cities may seem increasingly cosmopolitan in their range of international restaurants and fusion menus, but this will all seem rather banal after experiencing the incredible diversity of authentic tastes on offer in the orient.

To cap it all, a trip to South-East Asia is not prohibitively expensive. The airfare is going to be the largest compulsory expenditure because once you have arrived there are options to suit all budgets, and they all offer better value for money now than ever before. The cost of meals can account for a sizeable proportion of a travel budget, but in South-East Asia this can easily be kept to a minimum without having to eat food that tastes cheap even when it isn't. A delicious lunch in Bangkok or Kuala Lumpur can cost not much more than the price of a bar of chocolate and a bottle of mineral water back home, while the bill for a three-course meal in an elegant restaurant will amount on average to about one-third of what you might expect to pay in any half-posh establishment in Europe or North America.

Similarly with accommodation, a clean room in a hotel with a bathroom, air-conditioning and a telephone will cost between £10 and £15/$16 and $25 in Thailand or Malaysia, and a lot less for a room in a guesthouse with a fan (perfectly adequate in the tropics, where air-conditioning is not as essential as many think). A stylish room in a luxury five-star hotel can cost the equivalent of a mid-range hotel back home, and the level of pampering will be in a class of its own. Singapore is an exception in the money department and your budget will largely determine the length of stay there.

So, to get back to the pick and mix, where do you go and what are the choices to be considered?

SIAM

Thailand, called Siam until 1939, stretches from the Golden Triangle in the far north, where it is enveloped by Myanmar (Burma), Laos and Cambodia, to a southern border with Malaysia. Thai islands are found off the west coast and along the east coast, which stretches to a border with Cambodia.

MALAYSIA AND BORNEO

Peninsular Malaysia, called Malaya under the British, is the land mass that stretches from Thailand in the north to a narrow causeway in the south that can be crossed in ½ hour on foot to reach Singapore. Part of the huge island of Borneo, separated by sea from peninsular Malaysia, is also part of Malaysia and consists of the two states of Sarawak and Sabah.

SINGAPORE

The island of Singapore is a mere 42 km long and 23 km wide, and it is situated just over 10 km north of the equator. For two years in the 1960s it was part of the Federation of Malaysia but in 1965 was booted out in the wake of Malay fears of Chinese domination. It is now an independent republic.

The promise of sun and sand is easy to satisfy in the tropical heat of South-East Asia and the coastal beaches and islands of Thailand and Malaysia. Popular Thai islands like Ko Samui and Phuket have highly developed beach resorts and plenty of bars and discos for an active nightlife. Lesser-known but equally alluring islands, like Ko Samet, Ko Chang and Ko Lanta, welcome visitors who wish to laze and sun-bathe on their white-sand beaches but without the hype. Move south to Malaysia and the entire east coast is one long sandy beach stretching for 200 km and includes the beautiful island of Tioman, which first came to fame when it was chosen for idyllic scenes in the film *South Pacific*. There are also the tranquil Perhentian islands off the north-east coast and Pulau Pangkor's tropical beaches on the west coast.

When it comes to activity and adventure holidays, the traveller is spoilt for choice. The largest mountain in South-East Asia, Mount Kinabalu, is in the state of Sabah on the island of Borneo (part of which belongs to Malaysia), and every year thousands of people from the age of eight upwards make it to the summit at 4101 m, half the height of Everest. It involves sleeping a night on the side of the mountain and a dawn start next morning to reach the top for the sunrise. Back at sea level, watersports have been developed to a fine art in areas of Thailand and Sabah and there is nowhere better to learn scuba diving. Opportunities for snorkelling, enriched by a polychromatic marine life, occur so often along the coasts and islands of Thailand and Malaysia that it is worth finding luggage space for your own gear. The most fulfilling activity holidays are likely to be ones that combine the adventure with elements of trekking and opportunities to observe the astonishing wildlife of the region.

There are unique trekking possibilities, the best of which are only now starting to come into their own, although northern Thailand has a well-developed tradition of hill walks that combine water-rafting and elephant rides with overnight sojourns in the villages of ethnic hill tribe people. Not so well known are the options for trekking in the jungles of Borneo in the Malaysian state of Sarawak. These start with one- and two-day trips that can be extended for up to ten-day real-life adventures involving climbing hills, crossing rivers on fallen timbers, sleeping in longhouses of the indigenous tribes, and crossing into Indonesian territory when the jungle shrugs off borders that cannot be regulated deep in the steamy jungle.

Shorter treks and boat rides often feature in trips undertaken to observe the compelling natural wildlife of the region. The proboscis monkey, unique to Borneo, is not difficult to find and orang-utans can be seen at survival school in a rehabilitation centre. Pitcher plants, usually spotted while climbing the lower regions of Mount Kinabalu, are common in Bako National Park in Sarawak, while neighbouring Sabah is home to the world's largest flower, the rafflesia. The tropical forests of Malaysia — even Singapore has a very small but highly significant area of primary rainforest — are rich in wildlife, and visitors can hope to see gibbons, orang-utans, monkeys and an increasing succession of colourful birdlife that culminates in the spectacular hornbills. Taman Negara, Malaysia's greatest natural asset, is a national park in the heart of the country where visitors can trek through primary rainforest, sleep in the jungle, and experience the painless thrill of having some blood taken by a harmless leech.

When it comes to the cultural landscape, every bit as diverse and appealing as the natural world, it is difficult not to start with the Thai people, whose ancient cultural forms, imbued with the spirit of Buddhism, are a constant source of fascination. Malaysia and Singapore are multicultural societies where Malays, Chinese and Indians, not to mention the rich ethnic groupings of Borneo, live together without sacrificing their cultural traditions. All three countries covered in this guide are deeply traditional and yet they embrace aspects of the contemporary world with a bewildering adaptability. E-mails are easier to send than in Europe, the work of post-modern architects runs riot in city skylines, while inside a temple in Bangkok rests a carved sculpture of the British footballer David Beckham, placed there by a devout Buddhist soccer fan with the blessing of the senior monk.

The various traditional cultures help account for the rich array of arts and crafts that make shopping so inescapably a part of a visit to South-East Asia. Fabrics, clothes and cultural artefacts are a constant shopper's temptation in Bangkok and Chiang Mai, while computer software, music CDs, brand-name watches and designer clothes, both pirated and original, throng the street markets of Bangkok, Kuala Lumpur and Penang. Singapore itself can be imagined as one giant shopping mall devoted to planet-wide consumerism, and a wide range of products can be bought for less than back home.

This gives only a taste of what awaits the visitor who travels through Thailand, Malaysia and Singpore. Every day will be different because the history of these lands has produced complex, evolving societies where tradition and modernity rub shoulders, and where the traveller is welcomed one moment and healthily ignored the next as people go about their daily lives. There is nowhere else like it in the world. Start picking and mixing.

Sean Sheehan and Pat Levy

HOW TO USE THIS BOOK

PRICES

Current costs are indicated throughout the book by a rating system.

Accommodation

Based on the average cost of a double room, prices are listed in Thai baht (**B**), Malaysian ringitt (**RM**), or the Singapore dollar (**S$**).

$	under 350**B**
	under **RM**40
	under **S$**40
$$	350–600**B**
	RM40–60
	S$40–60
$$$	600–1500**B**
	RM60–100
	S$60–100
$$$$	1500–2000**B**
	RM100–150
	S$100–150
$$$$$	over 2000**B**
	over **RM**150
	over **S$**150

Food

Based on the average cost of a meal for two people, excluding drinks.

$	under 200**B**
	under **RM**15
	under **S$**10
$$	200–400**B**
	RM15–40
	S$11–30
$$$	400–700**B**
	RM40–80
	S$31–60
$$$$	700–1200**B**
	RM80–120
	S$61–100
$$$$$	over 1200**B**
	over **RM**120
	over **S$**100

Other costs

Based on admission for one person to a museum or place of interest.

$	under 30**B**
	under **RM**8
	under **S$**3
$$	30–60**B**
	RM8–20
	S$3–10
$$$	over 60**B**
	over **RM**20
	over **S$**10

This guide covers the very best of what Thailand, Malaysia and Singapore have to offer the traveller. It is written by two authors who between them have spent over 15 years living and working in South-East Asia and travelling extensively by train, bus, boat and air throughout Thailand, Malaysia and Singapore. The chapters are route based and vary in approach to suit the appeal and attractions of each particular route.

Each route chapter gives detailed information on transport, accommodation, eating, tourist offices and places of interest along the way. Large cities like Bangkok, Kuala Lumpur and Singapore have their own chapters covering the same essential information for the visitor.

The Thailand routes start in Bangkok and radiate out to the north, west, east and south of Thailand. The last southern route, Ko Samui to Hat Yai, arrives at the Malaysian border and covers cross-border travel. The routes in Malaysia start in Kuala Lumpur and cover the west and east coasts before moving across the sea to east Malaysia and the states of Sarawak and Sabah in Borneo. Sometimes a train suggests itself as the best mode of travel. At other times it will be a bus, boat or plane ride or a combination of these.

KEY TO ICONS

RAIL	Rail
	Bus
	Car
	Songthaew
	Ferry services
	Airports
i	Information
	Accommodation
	Food and drink

PUBLIC TRANSPORT DETAILS

Timetables for the routes have been extracted from the *Thomas Cook Overseas Timetable* (OTT). The timetables were accurate at the time of going to press, but may change slightly during the year. For details of how to obtain the latest edition of the OTT, see p. 62.

Symbols used in the timetables are explained below.

①	Monday
②	Tuesday
③	Wednesday
④	Thursday
⑤	Friday
⑥	Saturday
⑦	Sunday
ex	except, e.g. 'ex 6' means does not operate on Saturdays
Ⓐ	Monday to Friday
Ⓒ	Saturday, Sunday and holidays

BANGKOK — AYUTTHAYA
OTT Tables 7060/7071

Service	RAIL	🚌	🚌	RAIL	RAIL	⛴	RAIL	RAIL	RAIL	RAIL	RAIL	RAIL
Days of operation	Ⓐ	Daily	Daily	Daily	Daily	Daily	Daily	Daily	Daily	Daily	Daily	Daily
Special notes		A	B			D		C				
Bangkok..............d.	0420	0530	0540	0600	0700	0800	0905	1115	1430	1905	1940	2010
Bang Pa-In ....a.	0534	0700	|	0720	|	|	1002	1247	|	2010	|	2110
Ayutthaya ....a.	0547	0730	0710	0742	0845	D	1027	1300	1604	2034	2111	2146

Special notes:
A–Additional services about every 30 mins to 1830.
B–Additional services about every 20 mins to 1920.
C–Additional services 1400, 1610Ⓐ, 1615Ⓒ, 1715Ⓐ, 2045, 2200.
D–Several operators run trips along Chao Phraya River to Ayutthaya.

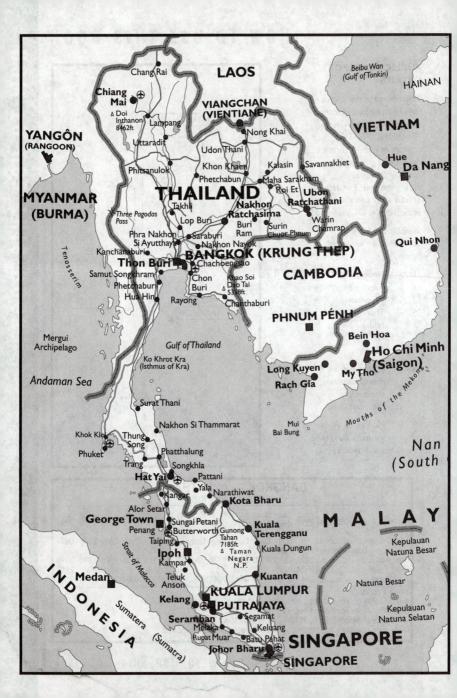

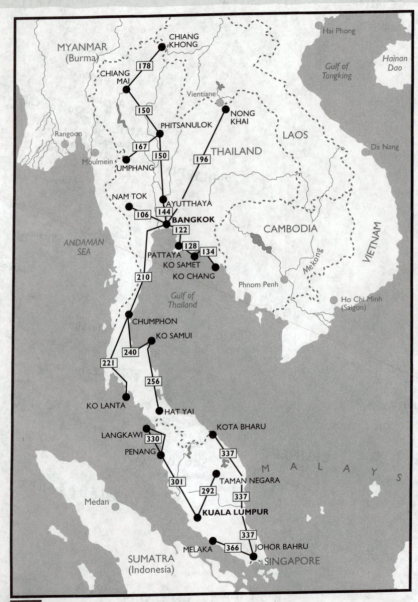

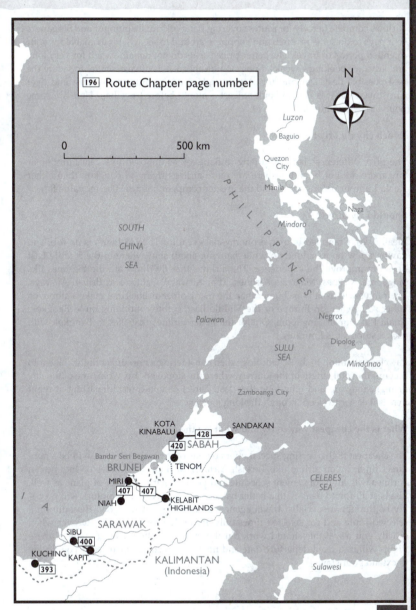

196 Route Chapter page number

0   500 km

SOUTH

CHINA

SEA

Luzon

Baguio

Quezon
City

Manila

Mindoro

Naga

PHILIPPINES

Palawan

Negros

SULU
SEA

Dipolog

Mindanao

Zamboanga City

KOTA
KINABALU   SANDAKAN
          428
420   SABAH

Bandar Seri Begawan

BRUNEI   TENOM

CELEBES
SEA

MIRI
407   407
NIAH   KELABIT
          HIGHLANDS

SARAWAK

SIBU
400
KUCHING
393   KAPIT

KALIMANTAN
(Indonesia)   *Sulawesi*

REACHING THAILAND, MALAYSIA & SINGAPORE

Airlines compete fiercely for routes covering Bangkok, Kuala Lumpur and Singapore so it pays to do some research and shopping around to see what is available for your intended period of travel. The better-priced seats do not remain vacant for very long and advance booking – weeks if not months ahead — is often essential to secure the best possible deal. Demand for seats is highest during July and August and over Christmas, and it is best to book at least a month before travelling. Here are some points to bear in mind.

Which city do I fly to first?

The price differences between flying to Bangkok as opposed to Kuala Lumpur or Singapore are not huge but there are more airlines flying to Bangkok than either Kuala Lumpur or Singapore, and the greater competition means better value fares.

Should I fly direct?

Ideally, yes. Crammed into an economy-class seat for 11 to 13 hours is no fun, and having a few hours added on while hanging about somewhere in the Middle East does not improve the experience. The airlines that fly direct are the big ones like Singapore Airlines, Malaysia Airlines, Thai Airways, Qantas and British Airways. Their fares will usually be higher than the many other airlines that make a stopover, either somewhere in Europe or the Middle East, before continuing on to Bangkok, Kuala Lumpur or Singapore. One of the better airlines that flies to Bangkok with such a stopover is Emirates.

Pay close attention to the scheduling when considering a non-direct flight. Take into account the total length of the journey, where the stopovers are, what time of the day or night they are and how long they last. Direct or non-direct, departing at night makes it easier to sleep through the long journey.

What is the cheapest way to fly and what are the catches?

The cheapest flight, barring special offers by one of the major airlines, will be a non-direct flight by an airline like Turkish Airlines, Sri Lankan Airlines or Indonesian Airlines with an inconvenient schedule and perhaps with a change of plane as well. The best all-round deal, with a better balance between cost and comfort, will probably be through a specialist travel agent who has negotiated a good discount on a selected route and for selected times only. If you have some flexibility over when exactly you travel this should work out the best deal. The catch on many of these flights will be a fixed departure date and time, with a charge incurred if you decide to extend your stay.

REACHING THAILAND, MALAYSIA & SINGAPORE

MALAYSIA AIRLINES

The best reason for flying with Malaysia Airlines (MAS), apart from their generally very competitive fares, is the fact that without an international ticket from them it is not possible to purchase the Discover Malaysia Air Pass (see p. 32). The same restriction does not apply to Thai Airways and their internal travel pass ticket (see p. 29).

FLYING FROM THE UK

Unless you are a student or under 26 expect to pay around £500 and upwards for a direct flight to Bangkok from London. A reputable company like Emirates flying to Bangkok with one stopover along the way will charge around £400. Fares that are significantly less than £400 should be looked at carefully to determine where the saving is being made. Return direct flights to Kuala Lumpur and Singapore start at around £550, dropping to below £400 on the cheaper airlines with stopovers.

MAJOR AIRLINES IN THE UK

British Airways
 tel: (0345) 222-111

Emirates
 tel: (020) 7808-0033

EVA Air
 tel: (020) 7380-8300

Malaysia Airlines
 tel: (0870) 607-9090

Qantas
 tel: (0345) 747-767

Singapore Airlines
 tel: (020) 7439-8111

Thai Airways
 tel: (0870) 606-0911

Students and travellers under 26 should start by getting a quote from STA Travel, tel: (0870) 1 600 599, www.statravel.co.uk. Their fares will not always be the cheapest but they should be able to offer a discounted fare on a major airline with good in-flight service and flexibility about changing the date of return.

Two travel agents that are worth contacting by telephone when you start researching fares are Trailfinders, tel: (020) 7938-3939, www.trailfinders.com and tel: (0161) 839-6969; and Bridge the World, tel: (020) 7911-0900, www.bridgetheworld.com. Online enquiries can be made at flynow.com and online bookings at www.buzzaway.com. The weekend travel sections of newspapers like the *Guardian* and the *Independent* are good sources of information for travel agents and discounted fares. Some companies, like Travel Mood, tel: (08705) 001-002, offer flight and accommodation packages that are worth considering.

FLYING FROM THE USA

It is less expensive to fly from the west coast than the east coast. At peak times expect to pay somewhere in the region of US$1000 for a flight to Bangkok from a west coast city and up to US$200 more from the east coast. There is not much difference between the cost of flights to Kuala Lumpur as opposed to Singapore. Prices are around US$850 from the west coast and up to US$200 more from the east coast.

Major Airlines in the USA

Air Canada
tel: 1-800-776-3000

Air France
tel: 1-800-237-2747

Cathay Pacific
tel: 1-800-233-2742

Delta Air Lines
tel: 1-800-241-4141

Malaysia Airlines
tel: 1-800-552-9264

Singapore Airlines
tel: 1-800-742-3333

Thai Airways
tel: 1-800-426-5204

United Airlines
tel: 1-800-538-2929

Newspapers like the *New York Times* and the *San Francisco Examiner* have hefty weekend travel sections that carry all the contact numbers you need to start checking out fares. A good source of low fares, which can be as little as US$500 from the west coast during low season, is Avia Travel, 1029 Solano Avenue, Suite E-Albany, California 94706. Tel: (510) 558-2150, toll-free tel: 1-800-950-2842, fax: (510) 558-2158, www.aviatravel.com, e-mail: sales@aviatravel.com.

TRAVELLING BETWEEN THAILAND, MALAYSIA & SINGAPORE

TRAIN

This is the most comfortable and enjoyable way of travelling between Thailand, Malaysia and Singapore, but not the fastest. Between the State Railway of Thailand (SRT) and the privatised Keretapi Tanah Melayu Berhad (KTMB) of Malaysia it is possible to travel by train between Bangkok and Singapore, via Kuala Lumpur and Butterworth. Bookings should be made as far in advance as possible. This is essential during peak holiday periods like the middle of April in Thailand and around the Chinese New Year in all three countries. Remember that there is a 1-hour time difference between Thailand and Malaysia (see p. 67).

FROM THAILAND TO MALAYSIA AND SINGAPORE Padang Besar is the border crossing for trains between Thailand and Malaysia. Passengers get off the train with their luggage and clear immigration and customs before reboarding. At Butterworth there is a change of train for Kuala Lumpur and onward travel to Singapore. The immigration procedures for entry into Singapore are conducted on board the train and on arrival at Singapore.

FROM SINGAPORE OR MALAYSIA TO THAILAND Immigration formalities from Singapore are handled at the station in Singapore.

BANGKOK–BUTTERWORTH–BANGKOK: TRAIN TIMES (ALL THAI TIME)

OTT TABLES 7013/7055

Station	Train IE/35			Train IE/36	
Bangkok	departs	1420		arrives	0955
Hat Yai		0724			1820
Padang Besar		1000			1800
Butterworth	arrives	1255		departs	1410

BUTTERWORTH–KUALA LUMPUR–SINGAPORE: TRAIN TIMES (MALAY TIME)

OTT TABLE 7005

Station	Train 7		Train ER/1		Train ER/2		Train 8	
Butterworth	departs	2130					arrives	0545
Ipoh		0150						0113
Kuala Lumpur	arrives	0711	departs	1500	arrives	1458	departs	2010
Johor Bahru			arrives	2030	departs	0921		
Singapore			arrives	2155	departs	0830		

Travelling Between Thailand, Malaysia and Singapore

At Butterworth there is a change of train for onward travel to Thailand, with the train stopping at the border station of Padang Besar for immigration procedures.

Thailand Train Fares The train fare from Bangkok to Padang Besar is 767B for 1st class and 360B for 2nd. Supplementary charges include 100B for a special express train, 60B for an express train and between 250B and 350B for air-conditioning. Sleeping berths cost from 100B (from 220B with air-conditioning) for a 2nd class upper berth in a rapid train and up to 520B per person for a 1st class double cabin.

Malaysia and Singapore Train Fares The train fare from Padang Besar to Butterworth is RM27 in 1st class and RM14.50 in 2nd class. Fares on express trains from Butterworth to Kuala Lumpur are RM79 in 1st class, RM37.50 in 2nd class and RM17 in 3rd class. Butterworth to Singapore fares are RM147 in 1st class, RM71.50 in 2nd and RM51 in 3rd class. These fares are for upper berths, fares are slightly higher for lower berths.

TRAIN AND BUS/TAXI

There is another train route from Bangkok that doesn't actually cross the border with Malaysia but stops within a mile of it at Sungai Kolok (Rantau Panjang on the Malaysian side), south-west of Hat Yai (OTT table 7055). The crossing point is 1 km away at Kolok Bridge and there are motorbikes and *trishaws* (motorised tricycles) waiting at the station to take you there. On the other side of Kolok Bridge, in

Information and Bookings

For general information on Thai railways see www.amazing-thailand.com; for more details and booking online go to www.thaifocus.com/travel/train. For train enquiries, telephone SRT in Bangkok on (02) 223-3762, 224-7788, 225-0300 ext. 5200, fax: (02) 225-6068.

KTMB are well organised and efficient but their train schedules are subject to change, so times and fares should always be checked in advance. For up-to-date information and bookings, tel: (03) 2273-8000 and (03) 2272-2828, www.ktmb.com.my, e-mail: passenger@ktmb.com.my. You can make online reservations 30 days before the date of travel and pay for the tickets online by Visa or Mastercard.

Tickets can be booked in advance at the central train station in Bangkok, at most railway stations in larger cities and from travel agents in Bangkok who will add a surcharge of around 100B. Tickets can also be booked in advance in Kuala Lumpur and other large cities as well as from the train station in Singapore.

Malaysia, it is another 1 km to Rantau Panjang — again transport waits to take passengers there. From here buses and taxis go to Kota Bahru and other Malaysian destinations. Sungai Kolok is a grotty town but fortunately train schedules mean there is no need to spend a night there.

From Thailand The Rapid 171 train departs Bangkok at 1300 and stops at Hat Yai the next morning before departing at 0642 for Sungai Kolok. It arrives at Sungai Kolok at 1020, giving plenty of time to make the crossing on foot and travel on to Kota Bahru the same day. The same arrangement works with the Express 37 train that departs Bangkok at 1515, stops at Hat Yai before departing at 0710 and reaches Sungai Kolok at 1040.

From Malaysia You need to cross the border at Kolok Bridge in the morning in order to catch the Rapid 172 train that departs Sungai Kolok at 1150. This train goes on to Hat Yai and departs at 1525 before steaming up north to arrive at Bangkok at 0755 the next morning. The same arrangement works for the Express 38 train that departs Sungai Kolok at 1405, leaving Hat Yai at 1740, and getting into Bangkok at 0935 the next morning.

BUS

Buses travel on a daily basis between Thailand and Malaysia, between Malaysia and Singapore and even between Thailand and Singapore.

Thailand — Malaysia — Thailand Although there is also a road border crossing at Padang Besar (where the cross-border trains stop), most buses between Thailand and the west coast of Malaysia cross the border at Bukit Kayu Hitam, on the main north–south Highway between the two countries. Buses run regularly in both directions between Hat Yai and Georgetown (Penang), taking about 4 hrs, and travel between Hat Yai and Kuala Lumpur in around 12 hrs.

It is also possible to travel between Hat Yai and Alor Setar on Malaysia's north-west coast. This involves taking a bus from Hat Yai to the border post at Bukit Kayu Hitam, walking across the border and handling the immigration and customs formalities before catching a bus on the other side to Alor Setar. The same journey can be done from Malaysia by taking a bus to the border crossing from Alor Setar.

A less common way of using a bus to cross between Thailand and Malaysia is via the border crossing at Sungai Kolok (Rantau Panjang on the Malaysian side). This is covered in the previous section and involves taking a 90-minute bus journey from the border to Kota Bahru.

Travelling Between Thailand, Malaysia and Singapore

Malaysia – Singapore – Malaysia The Causeway that links Johor Bahru in southern Malaysia with Singapore handles bus transport, with the train line running alongside, between the two countries. Bus number 170 runs every 15 minutes during the day between Johor Bahru (from just before the Causeway) and Singapore. Passengers jump off with their luggage to go through immigration before reboarding the same bus (or the next one that comes along) that waits just beyond the passport control offices.

There is also an express bus that runs between Johor Bahru's bus station, 6 kilometres outside town and Singapore. If you are travelling from Singapore just to Johor Bahru this is still the fastest bus, but do not rejoin it after getting off for passport control. Just walk into town, or you will be whisked away to the bus station outside town.

Long-distance buses travel daily between Singapore and Kuala Lumpur, Melaka, Ipoh and Butterworth on the west side of Malaysia and to Mersing, Kuantan and Kota Bahru on the east coast. It is worth noting that you can save a significant amount of money by taking the express bus from Singapore to Johor Bahru's bus station and catching a bus from there to another destination in Malaysia. As well as being cheaper, there is a wider choice of bus routes and times, which means you shouldn't have to wait long for a connection.

Thailand – Singapore – Thailand The buses used for long-distance travel between Thailand, Malaysia and Singapore are modern and comfortable with air-con, a toilet and television. Nevertheless, you would have to be a masochist to stay on one all the way from Bangkok to Singapore, even though a daily service does run between the two cities. It would make more sense to combine bus and train for such a long journey.

AIR

There are any number of flight connections between the three countries. Thai Airways connects Bangkok with Kuala Lumpur (35 flights a week), Penang (daily) and Singapore (49 flights a week). From Kuala Lumpur, Malaysia Airlines flies up to seven times daily to Bangkok. There is a shuttle bus service, operated by Malaysia Airlines and Singapore Airlines, between Kuala Lumpur and Singapore that costs S\$129 from Singapore or RM222 from Kuala Lumpur. Singapore Airlines also flies regularly between Singapore and Bangkok. If you are planning to fly to Sarawak from Singapore, you can save money by taking Malaysia Airlines' shuttle bus to the airport at Johor Bahru and flying from there.

Travelling Between Thailand, Malaysia and Singapore

As well as the three national airlines, there are smaller airlines that operate flights between the countries. Bangkok Airways, www.bangkokair.com, have daily flights between Bangkok and both Ko Samui and Krabi. Silk Air, the regional wing of Singapore Airlines, tel: (065) 6223-8888, fax: (065) 6221-2221, www.silkair.com, fly between Singapore and Krabi, Langkawi, Chiang Mai and Phuket. AirAsia, www.airasia.com, also fly between Singapore and Bangkok and Berjaya Air, www.berjaya-air.com, fly between Kuala Lumpur and Ko Samui and Krabi. Two new budget airlines worth checking out are www.onetwo-go.com and www.nokair.com. ValuAir is another new budget airline scheduled to start operation in late 2004, and Tiger Airways is due to be launched by Singapore Airlines in conjunction with Ryanair.

There is a 500B international departure tax from airports in Thailand. A RM40 departure tax is levied at Malaysian international airports. Airport departure tax from Singapore is S$5 to Malaysia and Brunei, and S$15 to all other countries.

THAILAND

TRAIN Thailand's rail network covers most of the routes in this guide and travelling by train is the most enjoyable and safest way of getting around the country, if not always the quickest. It is also very affordable. Travelling by night, of course, saves the cost of a night's accommodation.

There are three classes of train travel, but 3rd class travel is not recommended except for the short journey between Bangkok, Kanchanaburi and Nam Tok. Seats in 2nd class travel are comfortable and perfectly adequate for long journeys, though for night journeys a berth is highly recommended. Seats convert into a bed, clean linen is provided and there is a curtain to ensure privacy. Some 2nd class trains have air-con sleepers but are hardly worth the extra money because at night the train's fans are sufficient. First class comes in the form of private cabins for one or two people. All fares can and should be booked as far in advance as possible (up to 60 days), and at Hualamphong station in Bangkok there is a special advance booking office (see p. 24 for advance bookings from abroad).

Meals are available in 1st and most 2nd class trains. On long or overnight journeys staff will take orders for evening meals and breakfast and bring them to your seat. Meals are overpriced at between 90B and 200B, so it's well worth bringing your own food.

Examples of 2nd class fares from Bangkok are 281B to Chiang Mai, 238B to Nong Khai and 345B to Hat Yai. There is a 40B/60B/80B surcharge for rapid/express/special express trains. Prices for a 2nd class sleeper range from 100B/150B for an upper/lower berth to 250B/320B for an upper/lower berth with air-con in a special express train.

Bangkok's central Hualamphong station is well geared up for travellers and a condensed timetable with schedules for all the main routes should be available. To ease traffic congestion, some trains now depart from Bang Sue station (north of Hualamphong), and more are likely to move to Bang Sue in future. By mid-2004 a new subway line will link Hualamphong and Bang Sue. All train stations have a left luggage facility, but always confirm their operating hours because they do vary.

THAILAND RAIL PASS

A rail pass, only purchasable at Bangkok's Hualamphong station, offers 20 days of unlimited, 2nd class travel for 3000B. The pass includes the supplementary charges for rapid and express trains, sleeping berths and air-con.

TRAVELLING AROUND THAILAND, MALAYSIA & SINGAPORE

Bus Government buses connect with every town in Thailand. They run reliable long-distance routes using modern, comfortable vehicles and charge very reasonable fares. Government buses on long distance routes are air-conditioned (to the point of requiring something warmer than a T-shirt) and seats are allocated by ticket number. Local government buses are orange. They are not air-conditioned, but wonderfully cheap.

For popular routes the system is in competition with a range of private bus companies that tend to charge more for their vehicles — both modern coaches and minibuses. Private buses can be OK but passengers are at the mercy of a private company that may cut corners by using inferior drivers and vehicles. Some of the companies operating from Khao San Road in Bangkok have been known to offer some very bad deals for travellers. When there is a choice the government bus service is usually a more comfortable and safer ride.

Tickets are normally bought on the bus, but larger bus stations have ticket offices and advance booking is possible, and recommended, for popular routes.

Air There is an extensive domestic air service, managed primarily by Thai Airways and supplemented by Bangkok Airways. Nearly all the routes in this guide are covered by an air link, except for east Thailand and the Pattaya—Ko Samui and Ko Samet—Ko Chang routes. A journey by air can save a lot of time and avoids the hassle of sometimes having to return to Bangkok. It only takes 2 hrs to fly to Phuket from Chiang Mai, but this journey will take up two days by train and bus.

AIR PASS

Thai Airways issues an air pass that covers any three domestic flights for £100. All three routes must be fixed in advance but you can change the day or time of travel subject to availability. To make the Pass cost effective you need to be planning a fair degree of travel around the country as a whole, and be in a position to utilise some of the longer trips like the Chiang Mai to Phuket flight which normally costs 4600B one way. Unlike the Malaysian air pass, you do not need to use Thai Airways for your international flight and the Pass can be purchased with your international ticket or in Thailand through Thai Airways.

Road No one would want to drive a hired car around traffic-congested Bangkok but in other parts of the country it is a viable means of transport, and an excellent way to get off the beaten track and visit some out-of-the-way places. The far north of the country is especially suitable for driving because there is little traffic and fewer crazy drivers.

Travelling Around Thailand, Malaysia & Singapore

On popular islands like Ko Samui and Phuket and tourist destinations like Chiang Mai it is easy to rent a jeep or motorbike. It is common to be asked for your passport as a deposit for a motorbike. This should be strenuously resisted as in the event of a dispute you would have very little bargaining power. Offer your international driving licence instead. When hiring a car, which normally involves leaving a cash deposit, be very careful about checking your liability in the event of an accident. People will glibly assure you that insurance is included, but check exactly what that means and ask to see it in writing.

To hire a Honda or Toyota saloon car will cost from around 2000B a day, including insurance, from a reputable company like Avis. On Ko Samui a jeep can be hired for 800B a day and a motorbike without insurance for between 150B and 200B per day. When buying petrol, currently about 17B a litre, stick to the modern petrol stations with electric pumps. The antiquated hand-operated systems that simply run a tube into a petrol barrel may look quaint but the fuel will cost between 50% and 70% more.

Rules of the Road in Thailand

Driving is on the left. Bear in mind that bigger vehicles expect to have the right of way and will drive accordingly. There are national speed limits – 50 km per hour in built-up areas and 80 to 120 km per hour on the highways – though, like most rules of the road in Thailand, they are subject to liberal interpretation. Police checks and speed traps are not unknown and military road checks pop up when you least expect them. Foreign drivers must have a valid international driver's licence, obtainable through motoring organisations back home for a small fee.

Taxis and Songthaews   Taxis are metered in Bangkok but not in the rest of the country. This means that it is essential to establish the fare before departure, and it is a good idea to ask staff in your hotel or guesthouse about the standard price for a particular journey. Fares are usually very reasonable but the temptation to rip off an unknowing foreigner is often too difficult for drivers to resist. You should expect to pay a little over the local rate.

In parts of southern and eastern Thailand shared taxis are common and usually congregate at fixed places around town. Motorbike taxis can be found in cities like Bangkok and remote rural areas.

Tuk-Tuks

A *tuk-tuk* is a motorised, three-wheeled taxi vehicle that takes its name from the sound of its engine. As with any form of non-metered taxi it helps to have a rough idea of the local rate before departure. Drivers in tourist areas will sometimes try to charge an exorbitant fee but friendly discourse should bring it down to an acceptable level.

A *songthaew* is a pickup truck with two benches (*songthaew* literally means 'two rows') which can be hailed anywhere along its route. The fare is paid at the end of the journey and passengers can get off anywhere by ringing the bell that is usually installed in the seating area. The routes for *songthaews* are flexible and a fare can always be negotiated for a special journey. As with taxis it helps enormously to know what the fare should be to avoid being cheated. In rural areas the *songthaew* operates as a local bus.

MALAYSIA

TRAIN As in Thailand, trains provide the most enjoyable and comfortable way of getting around the country. Although there are only two main lines, they cover most of the main west coast route in this guide as well as accessing Kota Bahru on the east coast. The main railway line runs between Singapore and Butterworth via Kuala Lumpur and Ipoh and the second line branches off at Gemas and heads north-east to Kota Bahru. In Sabah there is one train line, from Kota Kinabalu to Tenom.

MALAYSIAN RAIL PASS
The KMB Rail Pass allows unlimited travel on intercity trains in Malaysia and through to Singapore. A 15-day pass costs US$70, 10-day pass US$55, 5-day pass US$35. The pass, obtainable from the station in Singapore or from the stations in Kuala Lumpur, Johor Bahru, Butterworth, Penang, Padang Besar and Wakaf Bahru, does not include berth charges on night trains. You will need to show your passport when buying a pass.

The train company Keretapi Tanah Melayu Berhad (KTM Berhad) is well run. You can travel from Kuala Lumpur to Singapore in a 2nd class express train for RM34, for example. From Singapore to Wakaf Bahru (the station for Kota Bahru on the east coast) the fare is RM41.

For overnight trains the cost of the berth is included in the ticket price. Advance bookings can be made in Malaysia at any of the main stations or at Singapore railway station, and online bookings can be made up to 30 days before the date of travel (see p. 24).

BUS Getting around Malaysia by bus is every bit as easy as it is in Thailand and equally affordable. Government buses cover countless local routes as well as long-distance travel between all large towns, and tickets for long journeys can be booked in advance. The public buses are in competition with a host of private companies but the private firms are on the whole safer and more reliable than some of their Thai equivalents.

MALAYSIAN AIR PASS

Malaysia Airlines' Discover Malaysia Pass costs US$199 for up to five flights. The Pass can only be purchased by passengers holding an international ticket with Malaysia Airlines. This includes flights between Thailand and Malaysia but *not* between Singapore and Malaysia.

Changing your route after purchasing the Pass is possible at US$25 per change, but altering the time of any of the five routes doesn't cost anything. The Pass can be purchased from Malaysia Airlines abroad or in Malaysia within 14 days of arrival.

AIR Malaysia Airlines handles all domestic routes within Malaysia. In Sarawak and Sabah a plane is sometimes the only way to travel. Bario in the Kelabit Highlands, for example, can only be reached by plane. A short flight to Gunung Mulu National Park from Miri saves a whole day on buses and boats, and doesn't cost much more. Because air travel is the only quick way to get about in Sarawak and Sabah, fares are heavily subsidised and are well worth considering. Malaysia Airlines are very helpful when it comes to making changes to tickets; any of their offices can amend a ticket for no charge. For the potentially cheaper flights within Malaysia, check out www.airasia.com.

ROAD Car rental is more common than in Thailand. A selection of familiar companies have their cluster of desks at airports, and most four- and five-star hotels can arrange car hire. Expect to pay at least RM150 per day for a standard saloon car, although cheaper rates are available through some local companies, and especially if the car is rented for longer than just a few days. Drivers need an international driving licence and must be over 23 years of age. Driving in Kuala Lumpur is not as hair-raising as in Bangkok but a car is not a great advantage because the road system is complicated. Outside the capital driving is usually a breeze and most Malaysians drive with care. Driving is on the left. Using the horn when overtaking is common.

TAXI

City Taxis: Taxis are mostly metered in Kuala Lumpur but not elsewhere. This means establishing the fare before setting off on a journey. As with Thailand, try to establish the going rate from a third party and then act as if you are an old hand.

Long Distance Taxis: Shared taxis for long-distance travel is more widespread in Malaysia than in Thailand. Most towns have an area where taxis wait to fill their vehicles with passengers. If you turn up early in the morning you should have no trouble finding a taxi waiting to take off on a regular route. Over-charging is relatively uncommon. Fares are fixed on the basis of one charge for the whole taxi which is then divided by four when full. The taxi can be chartered by one, two or three people as long as they cough up the full charge.

SINGAPORE

Singapore is justly famed for its public transport system. There is no other city in South-East Asia where it is so easy to get around. The modern Mass Rapid Transit (MRT) subway system is comfortable and quick, and using it is simplicity itself. There are machines in every station that issue rechargable, single-trip tickets, or stored value tickets that can be used for any journey.

The public bus system is comfortable and reliable. An increasing number of buses have a fixed fare and do not issue change, so you need to have the right money. The stored value card can be used on both the MRT and on buses equipped to read the card. Explorer tickets are also available for three days of unlimited bus travel.

Taxis are plentiful in Singapore and all are metered, with a 50% surcharge between midnight and 0600 and a variable surcharge on all trips into the Central Business District (CBD) during rush hour.

Car rental is readily available but of limited value. There is a surcharge for entry into the CBD during rush hour, little free parking and severe policing to boot. Cars rented in Singapore are not normally insured for travel in Malaysia and, given the difference in cost, it makes sense to travel over to Johor Bahru and hire a car there.

ITINERARY SUGGESTIONS

The following are some suggestions additional to the routes described in the book, offering more options that can be incorporated into your own individual itinerary.

BANGKOK–NAKHON RATCHASIMA–BURIRAM–SURIN–UBON RATCHATHANI OTT TABLE 7065

A journey along Thailand's famed 'Khmer Culture Trail'. The train line takes you all the way through to Ubon, but you can break the journey at Nakhon Ratchasima to visit the Angkor-period Prasat Hin Phimai National Historical Park, then at Buriram to visit the equally magnificent Phanom Rung Historical Park – arguably the best Khmer ruins outside Cambodia, both lovingly restored. Beyond Ubon you have the option of visiting the stunning Khmer temple across the Cambodian frontier at Khao Phra Viharn. All temple visits are easily arranged by local transport.

NONG KHAI–SI CHIANG MAI–CHIANG KHAN–LOEI

One of the most peaceful and visually stunning journeys in Thailand, north along the Mekong River through the predominantly Vietnamese town of Si Chiang Mai, overnighting in the quiet riverside logging town of Chiang Khan, before swinging into the mountains to the isolated town of Loei, once considered Thailand's 'Siberia' because of the cold winter nights. A simple journey by local bus or minibus.

HAT YAI–PATTANI–NARATHIWAT–KOTA BHARU

A trip down Thailand's remote south-east coast through the predominantly Muslim provinces of Pattani and Narathiwat, the former a busy fishing port and market town, the latter a laid-back place of mango trees and long white beaches. Then by local ferry across the Tak Bai River to the most Malay of all Malaysian towns, Kota Bharu. Journey by local bus and ferry.

HAT YAI–YALA–SUNGAI GOLOK–PASIR MAS–KUALA LIPIS–KELUANG–SINGAPORE OTT TABLES 7055, 7006, 7005

The alternative way to get from Thailand to Singapore. By train from Hat Yai through the predominantly Chinese town of Yala to the busy border settlement of Sungai Golok. A taxi will take you to the Malaysian railway terminal at Pasir Mas, then catch the famed 'jungle railway' through unspoiled central Malaysia, past the sleepy town of Kuala Lipis, and on to Singapore.

SANDAKAN–LAHAD DATU–TAWAU

Head south-west out of Sandakan, stopping to visit the huge swiftlet caves at Gomantong, and then on to the isolated oil-planters port of Lahad Datu. Continue southwards to the chocolate-producing town of Tawau and visit Tawau National Park. From here arrange a boat tour to Pulau Sipadan, Malaysia's most celebrated dive spot. Local bus or private transport all the way.

ACCOMMODATION

Between them, Thailand, Malaysia and Singapore offer every kind of accommodation, from the ultimate in luxurious five-star hotels with spoil-yourself-rotten 'hotel within a hotel' floors and comfortable mid-range hotels right down to rooms with a fan and a mattress for a few dollars. Singapore is not in the same category as Thailand or Malaysia when it comes to budget accommodation and the extra cost of staying in Singapore should be taken into account.

The room rate is usually just that — the rate for the room — though sometimes it is possible to obtain a cheaper rate for single occupancy. It is not usually a problem for young children to share a room without having to pay any extra. Outside of expensive hotels, it is normal practice to be shown a room before paying any money and with budget accommodation this should be done as a matter of course.

It makes sense to have accommodation for your first couple of nights booked in advance (see the CD), and with all but budget places it should be possible to arrange this by fax or e-mail from your home country. There are a few websites (see p. 36 and the CD) where hotels can be booked online. Although these sites invariably exclude budget accommodation, they very often offer attractively discounted rates that make the hotels they feature surprisingly affordable.

THAILAND Thailand has a bountiful supply of accommodation options to suit most people's preferences and wallets, but at peak times, especially between December and February, it wouldn't be wise to turn up at Ko Samui or Phuket without something booked in advance. The cheapest accommodation in Thailand is usually in a guesthouse, hostel or beach bungalow with shared bathroom facilities. Such places tend not to take advance bookings over the phone, and at peak periods it is a matter of arriving early in the morning with money in your hand.

Apart from the cost, there are advantages to staying in inexpensive accommodation. Good budget places offer the chance to meet fellow travellers and exchange travelling tips. Most are geared to travellers' needs, providing safety boxes, e-mailing, notice boards with travel news, and often a travel desk for arranging onward travel and tours. These places usually have an affordable café or restaurant on the premises.

Mid-range hotels cover upmarket guesthouses where rooms have a fan or air-con and their own bathroom, as well as a range of hotels that offer rooms of varying quality, sometimes with a choice of air-con or fan, usually with attached bathrooms. Luxury hotels abound in Bangkok and other major tourist destinations, and they always cost a lot less than their counterparts in the West. The rack rates are impressively expensive but many can be booked online with substantial discounts.

A–Z of Travel Basics

General

www.hostels.com

www.hostelworld.com

www.hihostels.com   Online booking for beds and rooms through Hostelling International

Thailand

www.2camels.com/budget_accommodation/thailand.php3   General budget accommodation

www.khaosanroad.com   Online booking for some hotels in the backpacker area of Bangkok

www.chiangmai-online.com   Accommodation in Chiang Mai

Malaysia

www.tourism.gov.my/destination/accommodation.htm   Tourism Malaysia's directory of accommodation

www.malaysia-hotels.ws   Online hotel booking

Singapore

www.hostelsingapore.com   Hostels and budget hotels

www.kasbah.com/hostels/hostels.asp?search=Singapore   More budget accommodation

www.holidaycity.com/singapore90/index.html   Hotels under S$85 a night.

MALAYSIA Malaysia has a range of accommodation options fairly similar to Thailand, and most towns have places to suit a variety of budgets. Backpacker-friendly budget places are not as common or as well organised as their Thai counterparts, but more English is spoken around Malaysia and it is easier to sort out travel arrangements and other matters. The kind of guesthouses that in Thailand would rarely have staff with a smattering of English are relatively uncommon in Malaysia and most places can be telephoned to establish rates and availability of rooms. Malaysia excels in good value mid-range hotels, like those belonging to the Seri Malaysia chain that offer clean and comfortable rooms, but without the extras of more expensive hotels. Kuala Lumpur and Penang have their fair share of luxury hotels, and other large towns or tourist areas will usually have one or two above-average hotels.

SINGAPORE Singapore is more expensive than Thailand or Malaysia and the cost of accommodation reflects this. There are budget travellers' areas around Beach Road and elsewhere, and mid-range places are growing in number even though it is the plush international-style hotels that make an emphatic visual statement in Singapore. As with Thailand and Malaysia, these hotels are very pricey if you ask for their room rates at reception, but substantial discounts are often available when booked through a travel agent from home or online.

CLIMATE

See under **When to Go** (p. 69) and the mini CD for information on climate and weather conditions.

CULTURE

The concept of saving face, fairly common in South-East Asian societies, involves avoiding confrontation in social situations. What this means at a practical level is that shouting and overt displays of emotion are shunned, something that a visitor may misinterpret as indifference. Raising the voice and getting angry is seen as churlish behaviour and is often counter-productive for this reason.

When entering someone's home in Thailand, Malaysia or Singapore, observe the custom of leaving your footwear outside. The same custom of removing footwear applies to any Buddhist temple or mosque, though not to Chinese Taoist temples.

> **TEMPLE ETIQUETTE**
> As well as removing shoes before entering a Buddhist temple, visitors are also expected to dress and behave appropriately. Skimpy skirts and shorts are not acceptable and, although this is only strictly enforced at the Grand Palace in Bangkok, this dress code should be observed when visiting any temple in Thailand. Women should not touch a Buddhist monk.

THAILAND In Thailand, the wish to save face is reinforced by the influence of Buddhism, which values discretion and modest behaviour and shies away from aggressive confrontation. Topless bathing shocks Thais, even though it is common on Phuket and Ko Samui, and overt displays of immodesty are deprecated.

The traditional Thai form of welcome is the folding of the palms of your hand together in a prayer-like gesture to the other person. This way of greeting, called the *wai*, is traditionally extended only to people who are older or more revered than you.

Thai monarchy is highly revered and criticism of the king is not welcomed; in fact it is against the law. The national anthem is played daily at 0800 and 1800 in public places like bus and train stations, and everyone, visitors included, is expected to stand in silence. The anthem is also played in cinemas before the start of the film.

MALAYSIA In cosmopolitan Kuala Lumpur, multicultural Penang and Sarawak and Sabah, where Malays are not the majority, the influence of Islam is not as directly felt as it is on the east coast, from Kuantan northwards. Here it is difficult to purchase alcohol, there are separate queues in supermarkets for men and women, and women travelling alone, as well as women generally whose dress is not viewed as sufficiently modest, are judged unseemly by many men. Topless bathing, needless to say, is not advisable.

TROUBLESOME FILMS

The remake of *The King and I*, starring Jodie Foster and Chow Yun-Fat, was banned in Thailand on the grounds that it is both insulting and inaccurate. The 19th-century King Mongkut employed an English governess to care for his 50-odd children and the film suggests their relationship was very close. The official view is that the relationship was very formal and everything was above board.

The 1956 version of the film with Yul Brynner was also banned, partly because it showed the king eating with common chopsticks when he should have been using a spoon. In the new film, the censors objected to a scene showing the king looking like 'a cowboy who rides on the back of an elephant as if he is in a cowboy movie.'

Hollywood recently faced legal action from environmentalists who accused the makers of *The Beach* (see p. 225) of ruining a beautiful beach in order to create a set for the film.

CUSTOMS

THAILAND The duty-free allowance on entering Thailand is 200 cigarettes and a litre of spirits or wine. To export any antique or religious figure a licence has to be granted by the Fine Arts Department. Any reputable company selling artefacts that come under this category should be able to help organise this permit. Strictly speaking, any Buddha image would require such a licence but the regulation is not generally enforced for the mass-produced Buddhas sold across the country.

MALAYSIA The duty-free allowance on entering Malaysia is 200 cigarettes and a litre of alcohol.

SINGAPORE The duty-free allow-ance is one litre of alcohol but there is no duty-free allowance on cigarettes, and even the alcohol allowance does not apply if you are arriving from Malaysia. For all the regulations see www.customs.gov.sg.

DISABILITIES, TRAVELLERS WITH

Thailand and Malaysia, and Singapore to a lesser extent, present challenges for travellers with disabilities. The cities are wheelchair-hostile in many respects, including public transport and the nature of budget accommodation, but there are ways and means of coping (see the mini CD for more information).

ELECTRICITY

In all three countries 220 volts AC is standard and extends to the remotest villages.

E-MAIL AND INTERNET ACCESS

The Web can be accessed and e-mails sent and collected from all three countries using the growing number of small shops that set themselves up as cyber cafés and cyber shops. They can also be found at the international airports of Bangkok, Kuala Lumpur and Singapore.

Only a couple of years ago, a travel guide would need to indicate where exactly internet access was possible but that is no longer necessary. Thailand is the most developed country in this respect and in every town and city it is easy to find shops where e-mails can be sent or received. The rate is also the cheapest of all three countries, usually 1B or 2B per minute. Malaysia doesn't have as many outlets but they are there in every big town, in both peninsular Malaysia and Sarawak and Sabah, and the number is increasing. Singapore has state-of-the-art cyber cafés.

EMBASSIES

Thai embassies abroad (www.thaiembassy.org)

UK: 29–30 Queen's Gate, London SW7 5JB; tel: (020) 7589-2944
USA: 1024 Wisconsin Ave NW, Washington DC 20007; tel: (202) 944-3600
Malaysia: 206 Jalan Ampang, Kuala Lumpur; tel: (03) 248-1341
Singapore: 370 Orchard Rd, Singapore 238870; tel: 6737-3060

Malaysian embassies abroad (www.kln.gov.my)
UK: 45/46 Belgrave Square, London SW1X 8QT; tel: (020) 7235-8033
USA: 2401 Massachusetts Ave NW, Washington DC 20008; tel: (202) 328-2700
Singapore: 301 Jervis Rd; tel: 6235-0111
Thailand: 35 South Sathorn Rd, Bangkok; tel: 0-2679-2190

Singaporean embassies abroad (www.mfa.gov.sg)
UK: 9 Wilton Crescent, London SW1X 8SP; tel: (020) 7235-8315
USA: 3501 International Place NW, Washington DC 20008; tel: (202) 537-3100
Malaysia: 209 Jalan Tun Razak, Kuala Lumpur; tel: (03) 2161-6277
Thailand: 129 South Sathorn Rd; tel: 0-2286-2111

EMERGENCIES

Useful emergency phone numbers are given below.

Thailand   Tourist Police tel: 1699

Malaysia   Police tel: 999
                Ambulance/Fire tel: 994

Singapore   Police tel: 999
                Ambulance/Fire tel: 995

ENTRY FORMALITIES

IS YOUR PASSPORT VALID FOR THE NEXT SIX MONTHS?
To enter Thailand or Malaysia your passport must be valid for six months from the time of arrival.

THAILAND Most nationalities can enter Thailand without a visa for 30 days. Your passport will be stamped for the 30 days and there is nothing to pay. Your visit can be extended for up to ten days on payment of 500B at an immigration office. It is also possible to hop over to Malaysia and return the same day in order to get a stamp for another 30-day visit. A 60-day tourist visa is also available for US$15 but this should be obtained in advance from the Thai embassy or consulate in your home country.

MALAYSIA Most nationalities are automatically granted a 30-day or 60-day visa upon arrival in Malaysia. Extensions for up to three months can usually be obtained through an immigration office. Sarawak and Sabah have their own immigration control and most nationalities are granted a 30-day visa upon arrival.

SINGAPORE Most nationalities do not require a visa and visitors are normally granted a 14-day or 30-day permit upon arrival. Extensions for up to 14 days are easily obtainable at the immigration office.

FESTIVALS AND EVENTS

Hardly a week passes without a festival or special holiday taking place somewhere in Thailand, Malaysia or Singapore. Multicultural Malaysia, and Singapore to a lesser extent, are blessed with a profusion of religious and state holidays. The downside is that they always seem to occur when you need a bank open or an empty seat on a bus. More positively they present wonderful opportunities to catch colourful celebrations, and learn something about the rich cultural traditions that go to make up life in South-East Asia.

The Chinese New Year festivities affect Thailand, Malaysia and Singapore. It is a lunar-based festival and so the time changes from one year to the next. It takes place in either January or February. Chinese shops and businesses close down for days and the demand for seats on railways and flights is at an all-time high. The impact of Chinese New Year is more keenly felt in west Malaysia and Singapore than in Thailand, or along the east coast of peninsular Malaysia or in Sarawak and Sabah. Wherever there is a Chinese community, though, look out for colourful dragon dances.

Ramadan, the ninth month of the Islamic calendar, is marked by fasting between dawn and dusk. Since the Islamic calendar stretches for only 360 days, Ramadan falls at a different time each year, and makes itself felt on the east coast of peninsular Malaysia, where restaurants will be closed during the day. It is more of an inconvenience than a hindrance because food is still available in hotels and it is usually possible to find a non-Muslim Indian or Chinese place open.

In May, a public holiday in all three countries commemorates the birth, death and enlightenment of the Buddha, known as Visakha Day in Thailand and Vesak Day in Malaysia and Singapore.

FESTIVALS CALENDAR

THAILAND

Chiang Mai Flower Festival in February.

Songkhran, the Thai New Year, is celebrated across the country but especially in Chiang Mai, where locals take great delight in soaking foreigners with water as part of the festivities.

Loi Krathong marks the end of the rainy season in November, and is celebrated by floating small vessels (*krathongi*) laden with a candle, incense and flowers down the river.

River Kwai Bridge Festival starts at the end of November and continues into December, with a light and sound show at the infamous bridge at Kanchanaburi.

MALAYSIA AND SINGAPORE

Thaipusam is an important Hindu festival, usually at the end of January or early February, and is best experienced in Singapore when a spectacular street procession marks the event.

Hari Raya Puasa marks the end of Ramadan and for the next year or so takes place in late November/early December. It is the only day of the year when Malay royal palaces are opened to the general public.

Harvest Festivals: at the end of May and early June in Sarawak and Sabah there are celebrations and family gatherings; a great time to visit a longhouse.

Deepavali is a Hindu festival in November celebrating the triumph of light over dark and marked by the lighting of small oil-lamps.

FOOD AND DRINK

The food and drink of Thailand, Malaysia and Singapore are reason enough to confirm that flight reservation and take off for South-East Asia immediately. Unless you have an acutely sensitive stomach or very strict food taboos, there are some wonderful food experiences in store for you. New arrivals to Thailand and Malaysia are inclined to worry too much about hygiene in informal restaurants and hawker stalls.

Remember that the food has usually been cooked to order and at temperatures that will kill any bacteria. As long as you avoid tap water there is not too much to worry about. Some of the best food in these countries is not going to be found in expensive

Western-style restaurants and sooner rather than later you should head for a night market and order food from a stall being patronised by other customers.

THAILAND Fresh ingredients, seafood, coconut milk, lemon grass, galangal, ginger, coriander, tamarind, basil, lime juice, chillies and fish sauce are just some of the characteristic features of Thai cuisine. Thai food can be very hot but if you stay too long in tourist ghettos — of the five-star kind as well as budget beach huts — you may not notice how the kitchen tones down the cooking to suit Western palates. When a long-distance bus pulls in for a pit stop at a roadside restaurant, you will notice with nose-running alarm just how hot a plate of Thai food can be. Knives are rarely used to eat a meal — bite-sized portions of everything make them unnecessary — and a fork and spoon or chopsticks are the standard cutlery.

Thai food can be very basic, but it can also be very luxurious. Royal Thai cuisine, served up in expensive restaurants, is delicately seasoned with lemon grass, galangal, whole fresh peppercorns, coconut, holy basil and kaffir lime leaves. A typical popular dish all over Thailand is *tom yam* soup, a fiery soup based on fish sauce with kaffir lime, lemon grass and galangal flavouring and often containing prawns.

EATING THAI STYLE

A Thai meal ideally consists of a selection of small dishes shared by a small group. Rice is ladled on to each individual plate, with all the other dishes arranged on the table. To achieve a sense of balance between sweet and sour, hot and cool, fried and steamed, start by ordering one or two appetisers and one plate of salad. Order rice, soup, one curry and one main dish. All of this should arrive together, with perhaps a very short interval between the appetisers and the rest. Dessert is always ordered separately after the meal. Two good books of Thai recipes for when you get home are *Vatch's Thai Street Food*, Vatcharin Bhumichitr, published by Pavilion, and *The Food of Thailand*, published by Murdoch Books. Two others are *Thai Cooking* and *Vegetarian Thai*, by Jackum Brown, published by Hamlyn, offering an excellent introduction to Thai cuisine.

MALAYSIA AND SINGAPORE Both countries have a multi-cultural food scene, including Western food. The least expensive way to enjoy good local food is to visit a hawker centre or food centre. Chinese and Malay food monopolise these places but there is always at least one Indian Muslim stall, and fresh fruit drinks are usually available from more than one outlet. There is always a common seating area and the food ordered from one or more stalls is brought to your table.

Chinese Regional Cuisines: Stir-fried **Cantonese** dishes, originally from the province of Guangdong, are common in Chinese restaurants and food stalls in both Malaysia and Singapore. A version of Cantonese cuisine popular in the West, they are characterised by very fresh bite-sized pieces of food fried very quickly and then coated in often quite sweet sauces. In both Singapore and Malaysia this tends to be much more chilli influenced than it would be in Hong Kong.

A traditional Cantonese lunch is made up of a number of *dim sum* — literally 'little heart'. These small snacks are wheeled around on a trolley for customers to choose what they like from a whole variety of different kinds. *Pau* are steamed rice dumplings which arrive in cane steamers. The filling may be sweet, such as red bean paste, or savoury. Other items might include deep-fried pastry cases filled with prawn or crab, or even deep-fried chicken claws served with mustard.

Sichuan cooking is very popular in both countries. Its style is said to have evolved because chilli is a preservative which also disguises the taste of food, and Sichuan province is a long haul from the sea. Again, bite-sized pieces are stir-fried but this time they are presented without the sauce and are strongly flavoured with chilli. With some, huge pieces of dried chilli are served beside the meat or seafood. Sesame oil and garlic are other strong flavours often used. Often a dish will be made up of contrasting textures — such as soft, fast-cooked meat, crispy dried chillies and crunchy cashew nuts.

Beijing Style Cooking is the cuisine of the North and can be quite expensive. Beijing cooks like to think of their style as the haute cuisine of the genre. Whereas other cuisines are based on rice this is based on wheat. Typical of Beijing food are noodles, steamed buns or the pancakes used in the famous Beijing dish Peking duck. Here the duck is highly roasted until crispy and rolled in pancakes with plum sauce.

Teochew is less popular although there are some places dedicated to the style in Singapore. The cuisine comes from a southern China region called Shantou. Food is cooked longer and in its own juices rather than in fat.

There is a long tradition of **vegetarian** cooking among the Chinese and lots of Chinese people often eat only vegetables on certain days of the lunar calendar. It is associated with Buddhism, and there are often vegetarian restaurants in or near Buddhist temples. One style of vegetarian cooking that is very tasty and a good introduction to Chinese vegetarian food is *yong tau fu*, which originates from Hainan. Stalls have rows of vegetables, deep fried and steamed tofu, beancurd skin, green vegetables like water convolvulus or *pak choi* and huge vats of soup.

Customers collect a pile of vegetables and take them to the stall owner who cuts them up and dips them for a few seconds in one of the vats of soup. Noodles are also dipped and the resulting lightly cooked melange is served up with some of the soup. Rows of condiments can be added to heighten the taste and soups can be plain or thick. Strict vegetarians should take care at *yong tau fu* stalls as some of the vegetables are stuffed with fishcake and not tofu.

MOCK MEAT

Some vegetarian restaurants are dedicated to making their customers feel like they are eating meat when they aren't, creating fake meat dishes that are often very convincing. Tofu in its various states can be twisted and strangled into the texture of meat or sinew and beancurd skin becomes chicken skin or the ingredients for vegetarian Peking duck. Wooden stakes take the form of chicken bones and gluten balls imitate other meats.

Singaporean Chinese Cuisine: Singaporean Chinese cooking has evolved its own special style, which is seafood-based and includes such classic dishes as pepper crab. Part of the fun of eating this dish is getting to the crabmeat in the first place, using what looks like a set of woodworking tools. Don't dress up to eat pepper crab and keep a wary eye out for pieces of flying shell. Drunken prawns is a bloodthirsty dish where live prawns are dipped into a glass of brandy. The creature drowns on the brandy but sucks it into whatever it has instead of lungs as it dies. The head of the prawn, flavoured with the brandy, is regarded as a delicacy.

STEAMBOAT

Another Singaporean favourite is steamboat. Each table is given a metal contraption with charcoal inside an inner section (or now more often a little gas burner) and bubbling stock in the outer part. Diners collect raw pieces of food from a buffet. They are then dipped in the stock and cooked. As the meal progresses the soup becomes more and more tasty until it is the last thing to be eaten. Some competitively priced steamboat restaurants have warning notices about fines for leftover food.

Malay Cuisine: Malay food is basically home cooking and very few people open restaurants dedicated entirely to this cuisine. It is most often seen in hawker centres and food courts with *nasi padang* or *nasi kampur* written above the stall. It consists of a vast range of meat, fish and vegetable dishes, often deep-fried or cooked in thick curry gravy. Customers pick their dishes and add them to a plate of rice. In some areas this is *nasi lemak*, rice cooked in coconut milk with a much richer more glutinous texture. The sauces are dominated by lemon grass, chilli, and garlic and thickened with tamarind. Often fish or meat dishes are wrapped on pandan or banana leaves and cooked slowly. If you enjoy Malay cuisine, look out for *The Book of Malaysian Cooking* back home, by Hilaire Walder, an affordable collection of more than 80 step-by-step recipes.

Fusion Dishes: What has happened to Singaporean palates over the years is that the Chinese have grown to love Malay style chilli flavoured food while the Malays have come to appreciate the quick stir fry. The fusion of these two cooking styles has resulted in the stalls most often found in hawker centres in Singapore. Noodles are

Chinese in origin but *mee goreng* (fried noodles) has a Malay name and is strongly flavoured with Malay ingredients. Other fusion dishes include *tahu goreng* (deep-fried tofu). Chinese in origin, it is served with spicy peanut sauce and chopped raw vegetables, which is Malay in style. *Mee rebus* (noodles served with coconut sauce and other toppings) is again a mixture of the two cuisines. Another popular dish in Singapore which draws in the region's third cooking style — Indian — is *roti John* (French bread dipped in egg and minced meat with chillies and fried).

Indian Food: For many people not used to the fiery nature of Malay food stalls, Indian food will come as a godsend while they are travelling, although it is very far from the rather watered down versions common in Western countries. Singapore and Malaysia have three basic Indian cooking styles. Most common all over Singapore and Malaysia are *daun pisang* coffee shops — very inexpensive fan-cooled places where men in dhotis wander around dishing up curries and sauces onto banana leaves instead of plates alongside pappadoms and unusual chutneys. Customers eat with the right hand (or you can ask for cutlery) and after the meal the leaf is folded over, hiding any leftovers.

Many banana leaf places are strictly vegetarian but others serve up meat and fish curries, which are hotter than most westerners are used to. As well as the banana leaf curry these places also often serve wonderful breakfast dishes such as *masala dosa*, rice flour pancakes served with spicy mashed potato filling and coconut sauce. Some places such as the vegetarian Woodlands in Singapore have about 15 different breads, which are served up with small pots of curry.

A small proportion of the Indian communities in the region is Muslim. Known locally as Chettiars or Chittys, their style of cooking is very spicy. These places often have hot plates full of curry dishes as well as griddles to cook multilayered dough pancakes, called *roti prata* in Singapore or *roti canai* in Malaysia. Variations on this pancake include stuffing it with chicken (*roti ayam*), beef (*roti dagang*), egg (*roti telor*) or vegetables (*roti sayur*). In Singapore the stuffed version is called *murtabak*. Often common in these restaurants is an Indian version of chicken rice, cooked in a huge vat in a mildly flavoured cinnamon and cardamom sauce (*biryani*).

North Indian food is the one most likely to be familiar to westerners and is usually served up in air-conditioned restaurants, although there are some north Indian hawker stalls. The cooking is characterised by thick nutty sauces, yoghurt side dishes called raita and flat leavened breads cooked in a tandoor.

Nyonya cuisine: Nyonya cuisine is currently flavour of the month in Singapore and Malaysia. It is basically Malay style food with some Chinese influence. Meat dishes are served up in sauces flavoured with lemon grass and lots of coconut (in the Melaka version) and chilli (in the Penang version). The most common Nyonya dish, found in every hawker centre, is *laksa*, a noodle based dish with prawns, other seafood and vegetables served in a rich coconut sauce and topped with boiled egg. In Penang *laksa* has less coconut and the fish stock is stronger, making a rather sourer soup.

DESSERTS AND SWEETS These are not a big part of life in Malaysia and Singapore and when they are found they are barely recognisable to Western eyes as dessert. In Chinese cuisine dessert is often tapioca or red beans while Malay desserts might be very sticky cakes made with rice flour and flavoured with equally un-dessert like ingredients. Sweetcorn features in many dessert dishes in both cuisines. Common all over is the hideous looking dessert called *ais kacang*, which is a mountain of shaved ice covered in syrupy, brightly coloured sauces and topped with sweetcorn, red beans, pandan jellies or black beans and condensed milk.

DRINKS There are a few drinks that might be unfamiliar to westerners. Chinese tea is found everywhere in Chinese restaurants and takes many different forms. The basic tea ingredient is often flavoured with other things such as jasmine. Herbal teas are sold in shops dedicated to the drink from strange shaped pots containing the ready-made brew. They also often sell soybean milk, as do most drinks stalls in hawker centres. In addition these places sell fresh juices such as guava or water apple juice — both are worth a taste. Chrysanthemum tea is sold everywhere.

Stalls that crush sugar cane and sell the very sweet, olive green juice are less common than they once were. In Malaysia you can also get fresh young coconuts. The stall owner will hack off the top so you can drink the delicious milk and then scoop out the jelly. Traditional coffee shops — rather than expensive designer coffee bars — sell thick black coffee, often with an inch of undissolved white condensed sweetened milk at the bottom. Tea arrives in a similar state, although you can ask for these drinks without milk. Indian Muslim places 'stretch' their tea and coffee by pouring it from a great height from one pot to another until it is ready to drink, looking very pale and milky and covered in froth.

FOOD GLOSSARY

birds' nest	Chinese medicinal swiftlet nest soup
biryani	North Indian spiced rice with meat or vegetables
cendol	Malay dessert of ice shavings, red beans, coloured syrups, jelly and coconut milk
chapatti	Indian flat, thin wholewheat bread cooked on a griddle
chicken rice	chicken with rice cooked in chicken stock, originally Chinese
dim sum	various small Chinese dishes served for breakfast and lunch
fish head curry	a fish head floating in curry, in Singaporean Indian restaurants
gaeng	Thai for curry

galangal (Th. *kha*)	aromatic root of an Asian plant of the ginger family, used in Thai cuisine
garoupa	white fish popular in South-East Asia
halal	food prepared according to Muslim custom
idli	Tamil steamed rice cakes
ikan	Malay for fish
laksa	spicy soup of noodles, prawns, bean curd and vegetables
mee rebus	yellow noodle, potato and hard-boiled egg soup, popular Malay dish
maekhong	Thai whisky
murtabak	Indian Muslim pancake bread filled with meat and/or vegetables
nasi goreng	Malay for fried rice
nasi lemak	rice boiled in coconut milk, a Malay dish
roti	thin, flaky Indian pancake bread available in all three countries
roti canai	type of pancake consisting of many layers achieved by a complex series of foldings and cooked on a griddle until the outside is crisp. It is sometimes made with eggs, and often served for breakfast with a small bowl of curry in Indian and Muslim restaurants
tohu goreng	fried soya bean and bean sprouts in peanut sauce, Malaysian and Singaporean vegetarian dish

HEALTH

It is highly recommended that you organise health insurance in your home country before you leave. A good policy will cover theft of money and belongings, and provide full cover in the event of illness or an accident. If you are planning to engage in activities like scuba diving or even trekking it is worth clarifying whether they are included in your policy. Similarly, check where you stand in the event of an accident involving a hired motorbike or other vehicle. Remember that in order to make a claim for the theft of belongings you will need some documentation to show you have reported the matter to the police, usually within 24 hours.

HEALTH INFORMATION ONLINE

Two useful websites for current information and advice on health matters affecting travel in South-East Asia are: www.masta.org and www.tmb.ie.

Visit your doctor well before departure to discuss what inoculations you might need. You should be protected against hepatitis A, polio and typhoid. There is a risk of developing malaria in parts of Thailand and Malaysia, although if you stick to tourist areas the danger is slight. Border areas in Thailand that are close to Myanmar (Burma), Laos and Cambodia have a higher risk. If planning to travel in these areas you should discuss with your doctor the pros and cons of taking an anti-malaria prescription drug.

Mosquitoes can spread dengue fever and Japanese B encephalitis as well as malaria, and precautions should be taken to avoid being bitten. There are various mosquito repellents on the market. Hotels in mosquito-prone areas often provide nets, although you may want to bring your own.

Small cuts can become infected quite quickly and it pays to reduce the risk by wearing plastic shoes while swimming. The most common health problem encountered by travellers is a bout of diarrhoea brought about by poor hygiene on the part of someone handling your food. So much food is stir-fried using fresh ingredients that the risk of catching something from a food stall or restaurant is not as great as you might think. If you are vegetarian the risk is very low indeed. Tap water should never be drunk, and although in good hotels there should not be a problem using tap water to brush your teeth many people prefer to use bottled water for everything.

Diarrhoea is best treated by drinking plenty of fluids and taking it easy for a couple of days. Medicines like Imodium are readily available in pharmacies, and while they only relieve the symptoms they may be useful if a journey or some other activity is unavoidable. If symptoms continue for more than 48 hrs consult a doctor.

Sunburn is always a danger if precautions are not taken. Use sun lotion, avoid being exposed to the sun for long periods during the hottest part of the day, and wear sunglasses and some form of headwear. Prickly heat is a common ailment but can usually be dealt with by using prickly heat powder, which is available throughout all three countries.

Aids is a real risk, especially in Thailand, and no chances should be taken. Under Singapore's Immigration Act, amended in 1998, foreigners suffering from Aids or infected with HIV are classified as prohibited immigrants.

Talking about the kinds of illnesses that could happen to you while visiting Thailand and Malaysia (it's tempting to say that all germs and viruses have been officially banned from ultra-clean Singapore) can sound alarming and off-putting. In reality, the chances are that you will come home feeling healthier than ever before.

A–Z of Travel Basics

Sunshine, fresh fruit every day and fresh ingredients in meals are a tonic in themselves and the most likely mishap is a stomach disorder that lasts one or two days at most. Equally reassuring is the fact that all three countries have excellent hospitals and medical services.

MEDICAL KIT

Unless you have a specific problem there are no essential medicines that need to be brought with you. In all three countries there is usually no problem finding a pharmacy that can supply any of the items in this list over the counter without a prescription. If, however, you like to be prepared and especially if you are planning to travel in out-of-the-way places, such as hiking in northern Thailand or trekking in the jungle in Sarawak, then the following might be useful: **aspirin**, **paracetamol** or other **mild painkiller** for general ailments; **antihistamine** for known allergies and for the relief of itching caused by insect stings or bites; **antiseptic** for general cuts; **band-aids** for small cuts and scraped skin on the feet from wearing new sandals; **Immodium** or **Lomotil** for treating the symptoms of diarrhoea and perhaps a **rehydration salt mixture** as well; **insect repellent**; **sun lotion** and something for chapped lips; **travel sickness tablets**.

LANGUAGE

It really pays to learn a few words and phrases in Thai and Malay because the pleasure it will cause and its immediate gain in breaking down barriers far outweighs the time spent memorizing them. Your first efforts in situ will probably sound way off the mark but take note of the corrections offered and you will soon have a few phrases off pat.

THAI
GENERAL

hello	sawat-dii
thank you	khawp khun
I don't understand	mai khao jai
where is the ...?	yuu thii nai ...?

GETTING AROUND

bus station	sathaanii khon song
train station	sathaanii rot fai
left	saai
right	khwaa

ACCOMMODATION

how much is it per night?	kheun-la thao rai?
toilet	hawng naam
towel	phaa chet tua
hot	rawn

SHOPPING

how much?	thao rai?
too expensive	phaeng pai

EMERGENCY

a doctor is needed	tawng-kaan maw
go away!	bai si!
stop!	yut!

FOOD

tea	chaa
curry	gaeng
chicken	kai
rice	khaaw/khao
egg	khai
toast	khanom pang ping
salt	kleua
crab/prawn	bu/kung
knife	meet
pork	muu
bottled water	nam kuat
sugar	nam taan
milk	nom
vegetables	phak
fish	pla
sweet and sour	priaw waan
salad	yam
I am vegetarian	phom/dii chan (male/female) kin jeh

MALAY
GENERAL

good morning	selamat pagi
good night	selamat malam
thank you	terima kasih
I don't understand	saya tidak faham
where is the ...?	di mana ...?

GETTING AROUND

what time does the bus leave?	pukul berapakah bas berangkat?
train	keretapi
left	kiri
right	kanan

ACCOMMODATION

how much is it per night?	berapa harga satu malam?
toilet	tandas

SHOPPING

how much?	berapa?
too expensive	mahal

EMERGENCY

a doctor is needed	panggil doktor
go away!	pergi!
stop!	berhenti!

FOOD

tea	teh
chicken	ayam
fried rice	nasi goreng
boiled rice	nasi putih
pork	babi
sugar	gula
milk	susu
vegetables	sayur-sayuran
fish	ikan
beef	daging lembu
crab	ketam
prawns	udang
fried noodles	mee goreng
I don't eat...	saya tidak mau ...

GENERAL GLOSSARY

bot	main hall in Buddhist temple (Thai)
chedi	see *stupa* (Thai)
dada	drugs (Mal)
farang	a European (Thai)
hat	beach (Thai)
gunung	mountain (Mal)
isaan	north-east Thailand
jalan	road (Mal)
kampung	village (Mal)
ko/koh	island (Thai)
kota	city, fort (Mal)
KTMB	Malaysian Railways System
kuala	river mouth (Mal)

lorong	lane, narrow street (Mal)
MAS	Malaysia Airlines
masjid	mosque (Mal)
mat mee	technique of tie-dying silk or cotton before weaving (Thai)
MRT	Singapore railway system (Mass Rapid Transit)
muay thai	Thai boxing
noi	little (Thai)
Nyonya/Nonya	*Peranakan* (see below) women and cooking style (Mal, Sin)
padang	central grassed square of a town (Mal)
pantai	beach (Mal)
Peranakan	culture resulting from intermarriage of Chinese immigrants in Singapore, Penang and Melaka with Malays (Mal)
PIE	Pan-Island Express, Singapore's main highway
prang	temple tower (Thai)
pulau	island (Mal)
samlor	three-wheeled bicycle taxi (Thai)
sampan	small boat (Mal)
shop-houses	domestic houses with the ground floor given over to a shop
soi	lane, side street (Thai)
songthaew	taxi: pick-up truck with two benches (Thai)
stupa	monument housing a Buddha or holy relic, also *chedi*
sungai	river (Mal)
thanon	road, shown on road signs, abbreviated to Th. (Thai)
trok	alley (Thai)
tuk-tuk	three-wheeled motorised taxi (Thai)
viharn	temple assembly hall, home of the main Buddha image (Thai)
wai	Thai greeting; palms together at chest level
wat	temple (Thai)
wisma	shopping centre, office building (Mal, Sin)
yai	big (Thai)

MAPS

THAILAND Nelles Maps and Bartholomew Maps both publish useful country maps of Thailand. For more detail, Periplus publish a series of maps on Bangkok, Chiang Mai, Phuket and Ko Samui. The quality of free tourist maps varies a lot, depending on the location. Heavily visited areas like Bangkok, Ko Samui, Phuket and Chiang Mai are well provided for, and excellent maps showing a range of tourist-oriented facilities are readily available in tourist offices, hotels and other places. The TAT office in most other towns will have a map of some kind or other.

A–Z of Travel Basics

MALAYSIA Nelles and Periplus publish good country maps of Malaysia, and Periplus also produce a series of regional maps that cover Kuala Lumpur, Melaka, Penang, Sarawak and Sabah. Tourism Malaysia offices around peninsular Malaysia have free maps of their areas, which are fine for general purposes but often lack detail. The tourist offices in Sarawak have excellent free town maps of Kuching, Sibu and Miri, and the Sabah Tourism Promotion Corporation distributes a brochure with handy maps of the state and main towns.

SINGAPORE There are good maps of Singapore published by Nelles and Periplus but for most visitors' needs the free maps available at the airport and from the tourist offices will be fine.

Where to Buy Good Maps

UK **Stanfords**, 12–14 Long Acre, London SW1H OQU, tel: 020 7836-1321, www.stanfords.co.uk. Mail order or over the phone. A branch is also located at Campus Travel, 52 Grosvenor Gardens, London SW1W OAG, tel: 020 7730-1314, and at British Airways, 156 Regent St, London W1R 5TA, tel: 020 7434-4744. Another good source of maps is **The Travel Bookshop**, 13–15 Blenheim Crescent, London W11 2EE, tel: 020 7229-5260, www.thetravelbookshop.co.uk. There is also the **National Map Centre**, 22 Caxton St, London SW1H OQU, tel: 020 7222-2466, www.mapsworld.com.

USA **Rand McNally**, tel: 1-800-333-0136, www.randmcnally.com, has shops across the country and maps can be ordered by mail. Other sources include **Distant Lands**, tel: 1-800-310-3220, www.distantlands.com.

MONEY AND BANKS

There is no black market in the exchange of Thai, Malaysian or Singaporean currencies. At the time of writing exchange rates were stable for all three currencies and the Malaysian ringitt had been officially pegged to the US dollar at the rate of RM3.80=US $1. Current exchange rates are posted in banks and money exchange offices in all three countries, as well as appearing daily in the national newspapers. It is worth keeping an eye on them because rates tend to change a little on a daily basis and you may as well catch a good day to exchange your money.

There are exchange offices and ATM facilities at the international airports of all three countries so there is no need to bring foreign currency with you. Traveller's cheques are the safest way to carry money and exchange rates are often marginally better for traveller's cheques than for cash. Try to bring mostly large denomination traveller's cheques to save on the commission charge for each individual cheque, as well as a couple of smaller ones for last-minute cash needs. Bringing some pounds sterling or US dollars in cash is also useful for small exchanges, emergencies and in out-of-the-way places where there may not be official exchange facilities. Money can be changed at banks and money exchange offices. Try to avoid using hotels because their rates are always the poorest.

Check with your bank or credit agency before you leave home about using your card to obtain cash advances from a bank machine in Thailand, Malaysia or Singapore. If you think you may be using your cash for some large purchases you may want to have your credit allowance raised for this purpose. The more expensive hotels in all three countries expect guests to settle their bills with a credit card, and will ask for details when you are checking in. Guests without a credit card are almost regarded with suspicion and a cash payment upfront may be requested.

THAILAND The currency is the baht (B) and coins come in 1B, 5B and 10B. Banknotes come in 10B, 50B, 100B, 500B and 1000B, and increase in size as their value goes up. At the time of writing the pound sterling was worth between 65B and 68B, and the US dollar between 40B and 43B. If you are planning to cross into Laos or Cambodia from Thailand it helps to have some US dollars with you in cash.

SENDING MONEY WORLDWIDE

MoneyGram is a quick international money transfer service, offered by a number of Thomas Cook offices. It operates in Thailand and Singapore but, inexplicably, not yet in Malaysia. Money can be sent or received using a credit card or with cash.

UK	tel: 008-008-971-8971
USA	tel: 1-800-543-4080
Thailand	tel: 001-800-12-066-0542
Singapore	tel: 800-1100-560.

Western Union, tel: 0800-833-833, operates in Malaysia.

MALAYSIA The currency is the ringitt (RM) and coins come in RM1, RM5, RM10 and RM20. Banknotes come in RM2, RM5, RM10, RM20, RM50, RM100, RM500 and RM1000. At the time of writing the pound sterling was worth approximately RM6.9 and the US dollar was worth RM3.8.

SINGAPORE The currency is the Singapore dollar (S$) and coins come in 1c, 5c, 20c, 50c and S$1. Banknotes come in S$2, S$5, S$10, S$100, S$500 and S$1000. At the time of writing one pound sterling was worth S$3 and the US dollar was worth S$1.7. The Singapore dollar is easily the most stable of the three currencies and the one least likely to experience volatile shifts in value.

A–Z of Travel Basics

TIPPING   Tipping is not normal in Thailand or Malaysia and even more unusual in Singapore. Top hotels and expensive restaurants will add local tax and a service charge onto the bill and unless there is some special reason there is no obligation to tip on top of this. Taxi drivers do not expect a tip though rounding up the fare is not uncommon, especially in Thailand where a few baht does not amount to a lot of money.

BARGAINING

Bargaining is commonplace in Thailand and Malaysia, and not just in obvious places like markets and street stalls. As a general rule anything that doesn't carry a marked price may be open to negotiation. In Thailand, apart from shopping, the most likely situation where bargaining is necessary is when taking a taxi. This is also true, though to a lesser extent, in Malaysia. In both countries, it is sometimes worth bargaining for a hotel room. Instead of straightforward bargaining, suggest a reason for a discount (staying more than one night? arriving late?) and then make an offer. This can work even in more expensive hotels when business is slow.

OPENING TIMES

In Thailand, Malaysia and Singapore, large shops and department stores tend to open around 1000 until 2000 or later, seven days a week. Shop hours are more variable, either opening early in the morning and closing by 1800 or, and especially so in tourist areas, staying open until 2000 or later.

THAILAND   Government offices, which usually includes national museums, open Mon–Fri 0830–1630, and generally close for lunch 1300–1400. Banks open on weekdays 0830–1530. All banks and government departments are closed on national holidays. Mainstream businesses tend to follow similar hours, though they are less likely to close for lunch.

MALAYSIA   Government offices usually open Mon–Fri 0800–1615, often closing for lunch 1300–1400, and Sat 0800–1245. Friday is different and the lunch hour is extended to 1445 to allow for a visit to the mosque. Life is a little different in the more Islamic states of Kedah and Perlis in the north-west, and Kelantan and Terengganu on the east coast. Friday takes the place of Sunday and the working week runs from Sunday to Thursday, and Saturday morning.

SINGAPORE   Government offices are usually open Mon–Fri from 0800 to between 1600 and 1700. Saturday closing time is around 1200. Banks open Mon–Fri 0930–1500 and Sat 0930–1130.

PACKING

Take as little as possible. Apart from special medicines, vital documents and bank cards there is nothing really essential that you need. Spare clothes should be kept to a minimum, but pack one warm garment if you plan to climb Mt Kinabalu in Malaysia or head into northern Thailand during the cool season. Tampons are readily available in Malaysia and Singapore but are less common in Thailand outside of Bangkok.

Some items that could be brought with you are just as easily obtained in Thailand, Malaysia or Singapore and will often be cheaper. These include sunglasses, sun lotion, a small torch and a lighter for lighting mosquito coils if staying in beach huts, and maybe ear plugs for noisy neighbours and overnight journeys. If swimming and snorkelling is on your agenda it may be worth bringing your own gear, although again this kind of equipment is easy to purchase in Kuala Lumpur or Bangkok. Suitcases are a nuisance if a lot of travelling is planned and a backpack or travelpack makes a lot more sense.

POSTAL SERVICES

Efficient and reliable postal services operate in Thailand, Malaysia and Singapore. Sending a parcel home by sea is an affordable way of lightening the load of goodies picked up whilst travelling. In all three countries the cost of parcel post is determined by whether it goes by air, taking about ten days on average, or by much cheaper surface mail but taking up to two months to arrive home, and whether it is insured and for how much.

THAILAND Airmail letters cost 17B to Europe and 19B to North America. Registered and express mail services are available and there is also a way of sending home parcels that combines sea, land and air travel. Post offices sell boxes suitable for packing and tape and string is usually available free of charge. Large post offices may also have an inexpensive packing service.

MALAYSIA Airmail letters cost 90c to Europe and RM1.10 to North America. Large post offices sell boxes and packaging materials.

SINGAPORE Airmail letters cost S$1 to Europe and North America. Singapore being what it is, there is a postage rate helpline tel: 165.

PUBLIC HOLIDAYS

THAILAND

1 January	New Year's Day
February (day of full moon, variable)	Buddhist holiday
6 April	Chakri Day
13–15 April	Songkhran (New Year)
Early May	Royal Ploughing Day
May (day of full moon, variable)	Visakha Day, Buddhist holiday
July (day of full moon, variable)	Buddhist holiday
12 August	Queen's Birthday
23 October	Chulalongkorn Day
5 December	King's Birthday
10 December	Constitution Day
31 December	New Year's Eve

MALAYSIA

1 January	New Year's Day (except in Johor, Kedah, Perlis, Kelantan and Kuala Terengganu)
Early Feb	Chinese New Year
October/November	Hari Raya Puasa (end of Ramadan)
February (variable)	Hari Raya Haji
Early April	Easter Friday (only in Sarawak and Sabah)
February (variable)	Muslim New Year
1 May	Labour Day
May (variable)	Vesak Day
June (first Sat)	King's Birthday
1 and 2 June	Gawai Dayak (Sarawak only)
Late February (variable)	Maal Hijrah (Mohammed's journey to Medina from Mecca)
31 August	National Day
November	Deepavali (except in Sarawak)
25 December	Christmas Day

SINGAPORE

1 January	New Year's Day
October/November	Hari Raya Puasa
	(end of Ramadan)
Early Feb	Chinese New Year
February (variable)	Hari Raya Haji
April	Easter Friday
1 May	Labour Day
May (variable)	Vesak Day
9 August	National Day
November	Deepavali
25 December	Christmas Day

READING

As well as offering an insight into the region, the following books are all worth reading in their own right. It is a good idea to try and get hold of them before you leave. Bookshops are not common in Thailand, Malaysia or Singapore and when you do find one the price of their books will astonish you. Taxes push up book prices and a cynic might think the governments are happy not to encourage reading.

GENERAL *Southeast Asia*, Mary Somers Heidhues, is a concise history of the region and its current dilemmas and conflicts. *Lords of the Rim*, Sterling Seagrave, is a populist account of the economic power of the Chinese in South-East Asia and elsewhere.

End of Empire, Brian Lapping, has a chapter on Malaya that provides a very accessible account of the decline and fall of the British Empire in this part of the world.

The Practical Encyclopedia of Asian Cooking, Sallie Morris and Deh-Ta Hsivng. Everything you need to know and over 100 recipes to get your taste buds going.

THAILAND *The Railway Man*, Eric Lomax, and *The Bridge on the River Kwai*, Pierre Boulle, are two books for any trip west of Bangkok to Kanchanaburi and the Kwai River. Both are available on audiotape from Chivers Press, www.chivers.co.uk.

Arts and Crafts of Thailand, Warren and Tettoni, and *The Grand Palace Bangkok*, Naengnoi Suksri, are two richly coloured illustrated books published by Thames and Hudson.

MALAYSIA *The Malay Dilemma*, Mahathir Mohamad. It is easier to pick up this book in Kuala Lumpur than at home. Written in 1970 by Malaysia's Prime

Minister before he was a name to reckon with, it continues to offer a remarkable insight into how many still regard the country's Malay-Chinese matrix.

The Malay Archipelago, Alfred Russel Wallace, republished by Oxford. This is the book for anyone with an interest in nature to take to Sarawak and Sabah.

For a more modern adventure try *Into the Heart of Borneo*, Redmond O'Hanlon, also available on audiotape. See p. 419 for other books on wildlife in Borneo.

Alfred Russel Wallace, Peter Raby. This is a new biography about the courageous and unconventional explorer who worked out a theory of natural selection, arising from his travels in Borneo, and informed an aghast Darwin who had yet to publish anything on the subject.

Taman Negara Visitor's Guide, David Bowden, is well worth using if planning a trip to Malaysia's great national park.

For 1950s Malaya, *The Long Day Wanes*, Anthony Burgess, is a fascinating trilogy of novels.

A World Within, Tom Harrison, is indispensable reading if visiting the Kelabit Highlands in Sarawak. This true-life adventure tells the story of a scholar who organised resistance to the Japanese during World War II while studying Kelabit culture.

For humorous insights into multicultural Malaysia, look for the collections of **Lat** cartoons – *The Kampong Boy* and *Town Boy* especially – that are readily available in Kuala Lumpur and Penang.

SINGAPORE In Joseph Conrad's *Lord Jim*, Singapore is the novel's 'great Eastern port'. It also features in Conrad's *The Shadow Line*, which has period descriptions of the area around St Andrew's Cathedral and the Padang.

King Rat by former POW James Clavell is set in Singapore's POW camp under the Japanese. *The Singapore Grip* by J G Farrell is set on the eve of the Japanese invasion.

Paul Theroux was a teacher in Singapore and his *Saint Jack* is set in the city. He also wrote an essay on Singapore in *Sunrise with Seamonsters*. Philip Jeyaratnam is an interesting Singaporean writer.

Lee Kuan Yew, T J S George, is still the best account of Lee's rise to power and how he kept it. *Rogue Trader* is Nick Leeson's personal account of his fall from grace.

A–Z of Travel Basics

TIMETABLES   Referred to throughout this guide as the OTT, the *Thomas Cook Overseas Timetable* is published every two months, price £10.50 per issue (see p. 61). Indispensable for independent travellers using public transport in Thailand, Malaysia and Singapore, it contains timetables for all the main rail and bus services, plus details of local and suburban services. It is available from UK branches of Thomas Cook or by mail order, tel: (01733) 416477 in the UK. In North America, contact SF Travel Publications, 3959 Electric Rd, Suite 155, Roanoke, VA 24018; tel: 1 (800) 322-3834; www.travelbookstore.com; e-mail: sales@travelbookstore.com. A special edition of the *Overseas Timetable* – the *Thomas Cook Overseas Timetable Independent Traveller's Edition* – is available from bookshops and from the outlets given above. It includes bus, rail and ferry timetables, plus additional information useful for travellers (see p. 381). Please note that the OTT table numbers very occasionally change – but services may easily be located by checking the index at the front of the *Overseas Timetable*.

SAFETY

THE LATEST SAFETY INFORMATION

For up-to-the-minute travel safety advice and information on Thailand, Malaysia and Singapore contact the website of the UK Foreign and Commonwealth Office's travel section: www.fco.gov.uk/travel/.

At the time of writing, the deep south of Thailand, bordering Malaysia, was experiencing sporadic incidents of political violence. If you plan to spend time here, check out the current situation.

All three countries are generally very safe for travellers and there are few areas that are even remotely dangerous. Sensible precautions should always be taken against thieves — fellow travellers in some cases — and in crowded tourist areas you should always be aware of pickpockets. You can carry a doorstop in your luggage to help make you feel safe at night in budget places where the door lock seems inadequate.

THAILAND   Travellers on their own, especially women, should take extra care if arriving at Bangkok airport or Hualamphong station late at night. Don't use unofficial taxis. In 2000 there was a case of a visitor being robbed at gunpoint, and shot when he resisted, in an unofficial taxi taken at the airport in the early hours of the morning.

Take particular care over your luggage on buses and trains, especially on the popular runs between Bangkok and Chiang Mai and Bangkok and Ko Samui. Train staff will often show you a warning printed in English about the risk of accepting drinks or food from strangers, which is based on cases of passengers being drugged and waking to find all their valuables stolen. Thailand has its share of touts and scams but use common sense and a polite but firm refusal and they should not too troublesome.

MALAYSIA Generally Malaysia is a very safe country. Sensible precautions should still be taken, especially at night, and there have been isolated cases of handbags being snatched at Batu Ferringi in Penang. On the east coast peninsula of Malaysia the influence of Islamic fundamentalism has, in the last few years, begun to make itself felt in an unpleasant way. Western women unaccompanied by a man may be deemed as loose and treated with a lack of respect.

SINGAPORE Singapore is probably the safest country in the world and the chances of being mugged or the victim of a crime are very low indeed.

SAFETY TIPS

Carry photocopies of your passport and air ticket separately from the documents themselves. Details of traveller's cheques should always be kept in a different place from the cheques themselves. Keep a record of contact telephone numbers in the event of losing your traveller's cheques or bank cards, and the contact number for your health insurance policy. Useful numbers can be kept safe in cyberspace using your e-mail account. Budget travellers may benefit from a small but sturdy padlock to supplement those used to lock the doors of beach huts and chalets. A small padlock for backpacks is also a good idea.

Travelling in Safety

A little bit of planning goes a long way in safe travelling. Before anything else, consider whether you want to **travel alone or with a companion**. Having a friend will reap more advantages in Thailand and Malaysia than in compact, ultra-safe Singapore and, given the kind of world it is, this is especially pertinent to female travellers.

Think of those you are leaving behind – they will worry and reassurance helps. Write down your itinerary for them, however vague, and agree beforehand on how you **plan to keep in touch**. Don't promise to telephone every few days and then make two calls in a month. It might be more practical to agree to telephone once a week and then stick to it. Consider obtaining a call charge card from your telephone company that bills your home account (or your parents' home account!). Shops from where e-mails can be inexpensively sent and received are to be found all over South-East Asia, and not just large cities, so keeping in touch this way is recommended. If you don't have an e-mail address, contact www.hotmail.com or www.yahoo.com and sign up for free.

When it comes to **packing**, the really essential items are passport (with at least six months to run), tickets, money and a bank card. Once you have arrived, these same vital items need their own security. Some kind of a money belt is worth considering, especially the kind of large wallet that fits behind the belted waistband of trousers or shorts. Photocopies of documents and traveller's cheques are worth keeping in a separate place in your luggage, and leave a spare set at home as well. Other items worth packing include a small padlock for luggage, and perhaps another one for extra security on the inside door of your room at night. A small Maglite-style torch can be useful on beaches.

As a general rule, don't – literally – leave **credit or bank cards** out of your sight. Check with your bank beforehand about what facilities they offer in Thailand, Malaysia and/or Singapore and have relevant PIN numbers memorized. Bring with you the relevant phone number for reporting a lost or stolen card.

Thefts are not as common in Thailand, Malaysia or Singapore as you might think but if something does go wrong be ready to deal with it calmly and don't let it spoil your holiday. You should have travel insurance and you will need some record of having reported it to the police. Have a back-up plan just in case the very worst happens and your documents and money are stolen. Embassies can replace a stolen passport (having a photocopy of the lost one is a great help) and money can be wired from home through companies like MoneyGram.

If you are unlucky, something belonging to you will be stolen. Always keep a close eye on your luggage and do not make the mistake of assuming that your fellow nationals can always be trusted. Budget guesthouses may have the odd impecunious traveller who is not averse to rifling through your rucksack. It may be as trivial as a fellow traveller stealing your alarm clock from beside your dorm bed. Certain routes, especially Bangkok to Chiang Mai and the train between Malaysia and Thailand, have attracted professional thieves. Try not to carry anything

TRAVELLING IN SAFETY (CONT.)

valuable in your luggage and use a good padlock if you are carrying something you would hate to lose.

You will be very unlucky to be the victim of **violence** in either Thailand, Malaysia or Singapore. There was a highly-publicized case of a female backpacker murdered in Chiang Mai in 2000 but this was high-profile news simply because it was so unusual. Sexual stereotyping, and the consequent low-level harassment it tends to bring, is busy at work in parts of Malaysia. The eastern coast of peninsular Malaysia, where Islamic fundamentalism has a voice, can be uncomfortable for a female travelling alone but it is usually nothing more than a mild nuisance.

There is more risk of **culture shock** than theft or violence in South-East Asia. After all, you probably don't speak the language and yet you will be immersing yourself in various aspects of a culture that is not your own. When you are in a good mood culture shock can be stimulating and educational but every now and again, and it happens to everyone somewhere along the line, you will feel yourself beginning to snap because someone isn't dealing with your problem in a way that is culturally acceptable. For example, you could find yourself getting extremely annoyed at the constant smile of a hotel receptionist as she tries to explain why there is no bed available for you at 10 o'clock at night — not the lost reservation, but that smile … Even in far less stressful situations than this, there will be times when the Asian way of doing things causes consternation. It is usually trivial matters, concerning bureaucracy or an apparent lack of haste, but just try to think how aspects of your culture probably cause them to raise their eyebrows. Yet usually they don't, so try to act likewise. This is part of what world travelling is all about.

One good piece of advice for coping with culture shock is to take time off and just do something very ordinary for a few hours or more. Go read a book in the shade or visit the local cinema and enjoy a Hollywood film, having first established that it has not been dubbed into the local language. Usually you can take this for granted but you could find yourself settling down to watch *The Beach* and hearing Leonardo DiCaprio speak fluent Thai...

For **more information on safe travel**, there are a number of websites worth checking out. Rec.travel.asia is a useful usenet newsgroup. For the latest information on official travel advice contact the Foreign and Commonwealth Office on www.fco.gov.uk and/or the US State Department travel information service on www.travel.state.gov. A very useful little book for travellers is *Your Passport to Safer Travel* by Mark Hodson, published by Thomas Cook and costing £7.99 (see p. 63). The directory of country information it provides is also available on the web at www.brookes.ac.uk/worldwise. (See also the CD.)

DRUGS AND THE DEATH PENALTY

Malaysia and Singapore both have mandatory death penalties for possession of what would be considered fairly small quantities of drugs in the West. Even more alarming is that judges do not make the distinction between soft drugs like marijuana and hard drugs like heroin and cocaine. In Thailand it is illegal to use any kind of drugs and the fact that the police seem to be inconsistent in the application of the law only adds to the risk. There is no shortage of Westerners languishing in Bangkok prisons for drug offences and there are heavy fines – you won't be let out of jail until the fine is paid in cash – for the possession of small amounts of marijuana and other soft narcotics. The death penalty also exists in Thailand for serious cases.

TELEPHONES

The telephone country code for Thailand is 66, for Malaysia 60, and for Singapore 65. If making an international call from Thailand, dial 001 before the number. The access code for international calls from Malaysia and Singapore is 00. Don't forget to drop the 0 from the area code you are ringing.

THAILAND Domestic calls are made from public red phone boxes (for local calls) or blue phone boxes (local and long-distance). Local calls cost 1B for 3 mins. Phone cards are available in units of 50B, 100B, 200B and 250B.

International calls can be made from private telephone offices, found in all the major tourist areas, or from a public CAT (Communications Authority of Thailand) phone office attached to the main post office in every town.

Home Direct service is available at Bangkok's main post office, and at airports and CAT phone offices in all the major tourist towns. To use the service, dial 001-999 followed by the appropriate country phone number: for the UK, tel: 44-1066; for the USA, tel: 1111 (AT&T), 12001 (MCI) or 13877 (Sprint). For operator-assisted international calls, dial 100.

MALAYSIA Domestic calls, 10c for 3 mins, can be made using coins or telephone cards, and international calls can also be made from public phones. Phone calls to Singapore are regarded as long-distance, using area code 02, rather than international. There are three phone systems, Telekom (the most common), Uniphone and Cityphone, and they each issue their own phone cards. Some Telekom phones, and fewer Uniphone ones, allow the user to swipe their credit cards for the payment of international calls.

Home Direct service is available from public phones, dial 102 for assistance. To use the service, dial 1-800-80 followed by the appropriate country phone number: for the UK, 0044; for the USA 0011 (AT&T), 0012 (MCI) or 0015 (Sprint). For assistance with international calls, tel: 103.

SINGAPORE Domestic calls, costing S$0.10 for 3 mins, are usually made using phone cards, although phone boxes accepting coins are still around. Local calls made inside Changi airport terminal are free. International calls can also be made from public phones. Phone cards come in S$2, S$5, S$10, S$20 and S$50 units and are available from 7–11 stores, some supermarkets and small stores.

TIME

Thailand's time zone is 7 hours ahead of Greenwich Mean Time (GMT), 6 hours ahead of British Summer Time. Malaysia's and Singapore's time zones are 8 hours ahead of GMT (7 hours ahead of British Summer Time).

When it is 1200 in Malaysia and Singapore, or 1100 in Thailand, it is the following times elsewhere:

London	0400
New York	2300 (previous night)
San Francisco	2000 (previous night)
Sydney	1400

TOURIST INFORMATION

THAILAND The **Tourism Authority of Thailand (TAT)** has offices around the country and overseas.

UK 3rd Floor, Brook House, 98–99 Jermyn St, London SW1Y 6EE, tel: (020) 7925-2511, fax: (020) 7925-2512, e-mail: www.thaismile.co.uk.
USA 61 Broadway, Suite 2810, New York, NY 10006, tel: (212) 432-0433, fax (212) 269-2588, e-mail: info@tatny.com, tatny@tat.or.th; 611 North Larchmont Blvd., 1st Floor, Los Angeles, California 90017, tel: (323) 461-9814, fax: (323) 461-9834, e-mail: tatla@ix.netcom.com.
Thailand 1600 New Phetchaburi Rd, Makkasan, Ratchathewi, Bangkok 10400, tel: 6602 250 5500 (120 automatic lines), fax: 6602 250 5511, e-mail: center@tat.or.th.
Singapore Royal Thai Embassy, 370 Orchard Rd, tel: (065) 6235-7694. e-mail: tatsin@mbox 5.singnet.com.sg.

MALAYSIA **Tourism Malaysia** is the national tourist board that covers the whole country. Although there are separate organisations handling tourism in Sarawak and Sabah, Tourism Malaysia is the only one with offices overseas.

A–Z of Travel Basics

UK 57 Trafalgar Square, London WC2N 5DU, tel: 020 7930-7932, fax: 020 7930-1998, e-mail: info@malaysia.org.uk.
USA 595 Madison Ave, Suite 1800, New York, NY 10022, tel: (212) 754-1113, e-mail: mtpb@aol.com; 818 West 7th St, Suite 804, Los Angeles, California 90017, tel: (213) 689-9702, fax: (213) 689-1530, e-mail: info@tourismmalaysia.com.
Thailand Unit 1001 Liberty Sq., 287 Silom Rd, tel: (02) 631-1994, fax: (02) 631-1998.

SINGAPORE The **Singapore Tourism Board (STB)** has offices in the city and overseas.

UK Carrington House, 1st Floor, 126–130 Regent St, London, tel: (020) 7437-0033, fax: (020) 7734-2191.
USA 590 Fifth Avenue, 12th Floor, New York, NY 10036, tel: (212) 302-4861, fax: (212) 302-4801; 4929 Wilshire Boulevard, Suite 510, Los Angeles, CA 90010, tel: (323) 677-0808, fax: (323) 677-0801.

Tourist and Travel Information Online

Any search engine will turn up a wealth of pages on Thailand, Malaysia and Singapore, and some addresses for booking accommodation online have already been mentioned (see p. 36). What follows is only a selection of some of the better sites currently available; more are provided on the mini CD.

General
www.travel-guide.com/navigate/sea.asp Good general site
www.asia-hotels.com Excellent for cheap hotels
www.airasia.com Cheap flights in and around Malaysia

Thailand
www.tourismthailand.org Official Thailand tourist board site
http://www.thailand.com/index.php Lots of menus with good links
www.thaisite.com Good general information
www.sawadee.com/index.html Index of sites covering every region of the country
www.thaifocus.com/north/chiangrai.htm Chiang Rai plus links for the north

Malaysia
www.tourism.gov.my and www.visitmalaysia.com Official Malaysia tourist board sites
www.sabahtourism.com Official Sabah tourist board site
www.sarawaktourism.com Official Sarawak tourist board site
www.tourism.gov.my/TRC/resource.asp?cat=BROCHURE Tourism Malaysia's Resource Centre
www.geographia.com/malaysia A site packed with general information

SINGAPORE
www.visitsingapore.com Singapore Tourism Board
www.travel-singapore.com Good site for general information
www.sg Background information

WEIGHTS AND MEASURES

For conversion tables, see p. 474.

WHEN TO GO

THAILAND Thailand can be visited any time of the year but there are seasonal variations to bear in mind. The cool season — November to February — is the most pleasant time but also the busiest in terms of visitor numbers. During these months international travel to Thailand is at its peak and a flight needs to be booked as far in advance as possible. The demand for sleepers on the train from Bangkok to Chiang Mai and the route south to Ko Samui and on to Malaysia dramatically increases, and the price of accommodation in popular tourist destinations like Phuket and Ko Samui is at its highest.

The impact of the hot season — March to May — is most keenly felt in the north-east when temperatures approaching 40°C are not unknown. The rainy season, roughly May or June to October, is not severe enough to prevent travel. Even though a lot of rain falls in the south you can still expect an average of 5 hrs of sunshine each day. During this time the amount of rainfall in any one week is purely down to luck.

MALAYSIA Expect a temperature somewhere between 25°C and 30°C most of the time in most of Malaysia. The amount of rainfall is more variable and affects a visit to the east coast between November and February when the north-east monsoon makes itself felt. It is not going to rain non-stop for days on end, and an hour or two of rain is invariably followed by a period of sunshine. But heavy rainfall and high winds mean that boat transport to the Perenthian Islands becomes uncertain, and as a result nearly all the accommodation closes for a few months. Many resorts along the east coast also close down during these months.

SINGAPORE There are no significant changes in the climate and the temperature is somewhere between 25°C and 30°C every day of the year. Singapore is virtually on the equator and so the sun rises and falls at roughly the same time every day of the year.

WORKING IN THAILAND, MALAYSIA AND SINGAPORE

The best opportunities for work in Thailand are in the teaching of English; not all jobs insist upon an academic qualification. Such work is more difficult to obtain in Malaysia and Singapore though not impossible, especially if you can show proof of an academic teaching qualification. Outside of teaching, work in any of the three countries is difficult to obtain although there may be opportunities (more so in the tourist hotspots of Thailand), if you enquire, to assist in the administration at backpacker accommodation places in return for board and lodging. For information on volunteer work, see the mini CD.

Thailand is a destination to conjure with. Two recent Hollywood films have only increased its deserved popularity with visitors. *The Beach*, starring Leonardo DiCaprio, explores the country's backpacking phenomenon and the search for an exotic paradise. *The King and I*, starring Jodie Foster, shows shining gold temples and a playful but contemplative royal court in the land of Siam — as Thailand was called until 1939. Both movies depict distinctive aspects of modern Thailand that most visitors soon recognise, but no film can capture the surprises waiting to be encountered and enjoyed whilst travelling around the country.

In the south and east of Thailand are idyllic islands splashed with beachside bungalows and affordable restaurants looking out to sea against a backdrop of palm trees and banana plants. Beautiful islands like Ko Samet and Ko Chang are off the coast that stretches from Bangkok east to Cambodia, while directly to the south the land mass of Thailand narrows to a thin strip of territory squeezed between the Andaman Sea and the Gulf of Thailand. The waters here are filled with famed resort islands like Ko Samui and Phuket, superb coral reefs and small, relatively unknown islands that welcome visitors.

The north of Thailand has a very different kind of appeal. Comfortable towns like Chiang Mai and Chiang Rai serve as rest and recreation centres as well as filtering the streams of curious visitors who come to explore the rich local cultures on treks and elephant rides into the countryside. A short way north lies the border with Myanmar (Burma) and Laos, where it is very safe to travel despite the proximity of the infamous Golden Triangle. Far fewer tourists make it to the north-east of Thailand, which is equally rich in culture and benefits from a lack of commercialism.

At the heart of Thailand is vibrant Bangkok, a world city that embraces modernity and tradition in such a way that bewilders and astonishes visitors, whether arriving for the first or tenth time. The capital city is another experience, another part of a complex country that opens its arms to visitors with a smile.

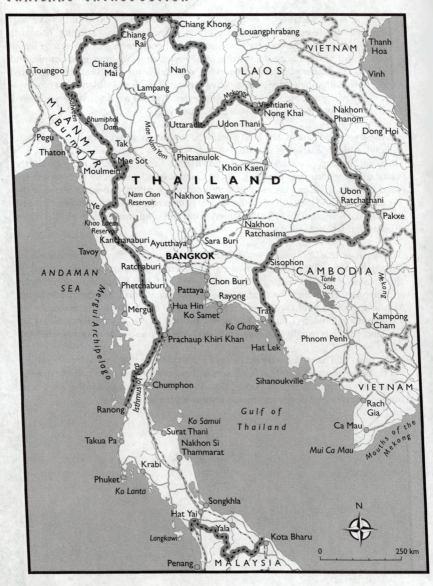

THAILAND: OUR CHOICE

Bangkok
Grand Palace
Wat Po
National Museum
Khao San Rd
Chinatown
Patpong

Kanchanaburi
Bike rides
Bridge over River Kwai
Train to Nam Tok

Ko Chang

Ayutthaya

Chiang Mai
National Museum
Night Bazaar
Shopping

Mae Sot

Chiang Rai
Hill trekking
Trip to Laos
Excursion to Mae Salong

**Ko Samui and
Ko Pha-Ngan**

Krabi and Ko Phi-Phi

HOW MUCH YOU CAN SEE IN A ...

WEEK (7 DAYS)
Option 1
Days 1–2: Bangkok
Days 3–7: Chiang Mai and Chiang Rai (excursion to Chiang Khong or hill trek)

Option 2
Days 1–2: Bangkok
Days 3–4: Kanchanaburi (train to Nam Tok)
Days 5–7: Fly to Ko Samui

FORTNIGHT (14 DAYS)
Bangkok, with excursions to Kanchanaburi and/or Ayutthaya.
North to Chiang Mai and Chiang Rai, hill trekking, excursion to Mae Salong or Mai Sot.
Fly south to Phuket, Krabi or Ko Samui (and Ko Pha-Ngan)

MONTH (28 DAYS)
Bangkok
Trip westwards to Kanchanaburi
Trip eastwards to Ko Chang
Journey north towards Chiang Mai, stopping off at Ayutthaya, with a hill trek out of Chiang Rai and time in the Golden Triangle region
North-east to Nong Khai, with a short trip over the bridge and into Laos.
Journey south to Krabi or Ko Samui for a sand-and-sun experience
Back to Bangkok

BANGKOK

Like many Asian capitals Bangkok is a beguiling mixture of the non-Western and the ultra modern, where urban chaos sits amid shimmering skyscrapers. But no other city accomplishes this balancing act with such abandon. The neurotic noise of *tuk-tuks*, the sheer number of bodies, poverty rubbing shoulders with gold-leaf Buddhas and sex shows put the city in a class of its own. You know you are fully experiencing Bangkok when one day you think you could live here and the next you want to leave instantly.

There are three major cultural buildings, the Grand Palace, Wat Po and the National Museum, which first-time visitors feel obliged to see, but once these have been visited the real sightseeing begins. Find time for a trip on the Chao Phraya River which, apart from being a hassle-free way of travelling through the city, opens up a fresh vista rich in history and culture.

Shopping and eating can easily monopolise time, but there are so many options, from shopping malls to street merchants, the amazing weekend and night markets, and fine dining to pavement stalls, that allow you to see a cross-section of Bangkok's social and cultural richness.

> **MUST SEE/DO IN BANGKOK**
> Hang out on Khao San Road
> The Grand Palace
> Check out Wat Po's reclining Buddha
> A walk through Chinatown
> Chatuchak Weekend Market
> Experience Patpong
> Watch Thai boxing

ARRIVAL AND DEPARTURE

Bangkok's Don Muang international airport is 25 km north of the city. Tel: 0-2535-1111 for arrival and departure information.

Taxis should be booked at one of the taxi counters; there is a booth just outside Arrivals. You have a choice of a metered or a flat-rate fare in a licensed taxi. Expect to pay around 250B for a metered taxi or 650B flat rate. Ignore any touts.

The airport has an information office, exchange counters, left-luggage facilities, a post office, an e-mail café and various places to eat. The cheapest place to eat is the Food Centre half way along the walkway between the domestic and international terminals. A coupon system operates and the menus are not in English. At the international terminal end of the walkway there is a 24-hr convenience store.

AIRPORT BUS

The airport bus runs daily 0430–0030, tel: 0-2645-0555, and is far more comfortable and convenient than the public bus. Four routes depart at regular intervals from directly outside the arrivals hall. Leaflets explain the routes and the major hotels passed on the way. The airport bus stops at the domestic terminal after first dropping off or collecting passengers at the international terminal. The fare is 100B.

Route AB1 goes to the bottom of Silom Rd, passing Amari Watergate, Grand Hyatt Erawan, Regent, World Trade Centre, Oriental and Shangri La.

Route AB2 passes Victory Monument, Democracy Monument and Banglamphu (for Khao San Rd).

Route AB3 runs along Sukhumvit Rd to the Eastern Bus Terminal.

Route AB4 goes to Ploenchit Rd, Siam Square and Hualamphong railway station.

To catch a bus to the airport you need to hail one from a bus stop on the route. Choose a bus stop which gives a clear view of approaching traffic. Buses tend not to stop unless it is clear you are flagging them down.

TRAIN Trains arrive in Bangkok at the centrally located Hualamphong station, tel: 0-2223-0314. It has a range of facilities, including a left-luggage office on platform 12, an advance booking office near platform 3, an information counter and a tourist office, tel: 0-2613-6725, on the walkway above the main concourse. There is also a café and a place for sending e-mails. (Note that some trains are being moved to Bang Sue; see p. 28.)

For transport to/from Hualamphong station, a useful bus that shuttles between Siam Square (for a Skytrain connection) and the railway station is no. 73, sometimes with air-conditioning and sometimes not. Come out of the station and cross the busy junction and take the one-way road heading east, to your left, and the bus stop is outside the 7-11 store. Another useful bus is the no. 53, which goes to Khao San Rd; the stop is reached by taking the station exit near the KFC. Bus no. 75 connects the railway station with Charoen Krung Rd in the Silom Rd area.

CHEAP FARES

Bangkok is one of Asia's great centres for cheap air fares. Major airlines like Malaysian, Qantas, Singapore and Thai offer steep discounts in or out of Bangkok, especially if you buy your ticket through a consolidator. Less familiar airlines like Asiana (Korea) or EVA (Taiwan) offer even better consolidator deals. The best value is EVA's Evergreen Deluxe class, business-class seats (but economy-class food) for less than economy prices on larger carriers.

A sure way of reaching the station from town is to take a skytrain to Chit Lom and catch the no. 73 bus to the station from opposite the World Trade Centre building.

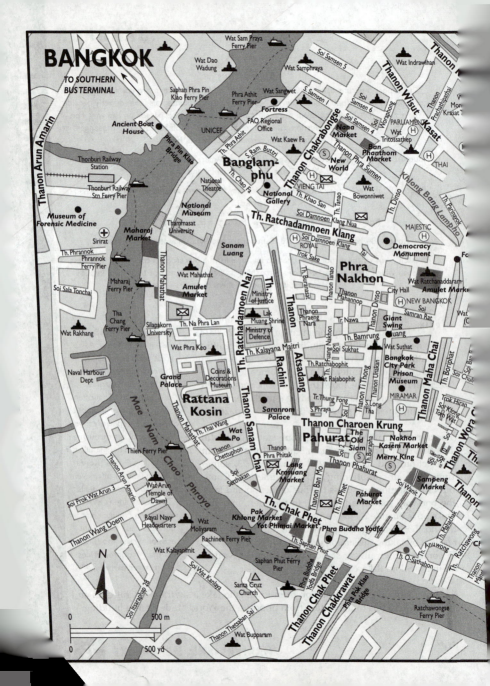

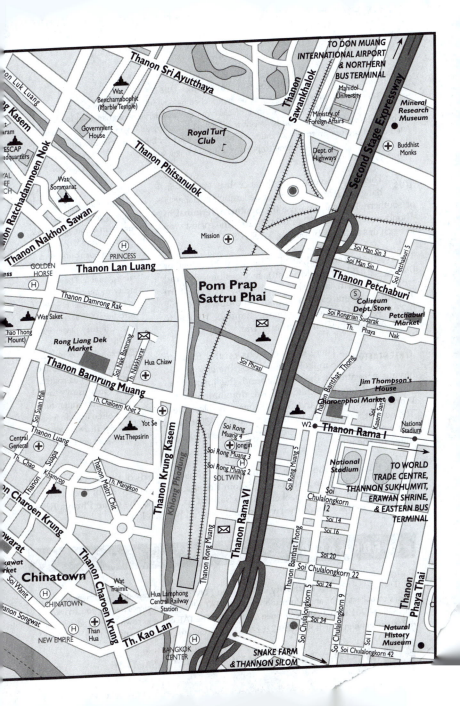

THE HELPFUL TOUT: PART ONE

At the railway station you are likely to be approached by obvious taxi touts but also watch out for the well-dressed solicitous 'official' who carries a large name badge with a photograph and the words 'tourist information'. Don't be surprised if you find yourself being led out of the station to one of the travel agent shops across the road where attempts are made to press you into buying a tour.

BUS There are several long-distance bus stations in Bangkok. If arriving from or departing for Malaysia or southern Thailand you use the **Southern Terminal** in Thonburi, tel: 0-2434-7192 or 0-2434-1200. The easiest way to reach this station is by bus no. 7 (see p. 81).

The **Northern Terminal**, at Mo Chit, tel: 0-2936-3660 or 0-2936-2841 (Skytrain: Mo Chit), services buses to and from the north and the north-east. The **Eastern Terminal**, at the eastern end of Sukhumvit Rd, tel: 0-2391-2504 (Skytrain: Ekamai), handles routes to Pattaya, Rayong, Chantaburi and Trat.

ORIENTATION There is no obvious central focus to Bangkok. The nearest the city gets to having a centre is the area around the junction of Ploenchit Rd and Ratchadamri Rd, dominated by the **World Trade Center** and Siam Square one block west. The nearest Skytrain stations are Siam and Chit Lom, and a number of bus routes converge on the roads that make up the junction.

BANGKOK MAPS

If staying in the capital for more than a couple of days then a good city map showing bus routes and the Skytrain stations is indispensable. There are plenty to choose from, all in colour and all claiming to be 100% accurate (although they never are). Our favourite is the Bangkok Groovy Map & Guide, with colour-coded but selected bus routes. Good hotels usually have a rack of tourist literature and often include free maps like Thaiways with its detailed area maps.

Taking this area as the centre, **Sukhumvit Rd** runs eastwards out of the city, while to the south lies the more commercial **Silom Rd** area. Over to the west of the city is the railway station, the backpackers' **Khao San Rd** (p. 81), and the **Chao Phraya River**. Thonburi, to the west of the river, is rarely visited by travellers.

INFORMATION

ⓘ There is no **Tourist Authority of Thailand (TAT) Office** conveniently located in the city. It pays to collect maps and information from the TAT office at the airport when you arrive, tel: 0-2504-2701 or 0-2535-2669, open 0800–2400. The TAT office in town is situated at 4 Ratchadamnoen North Rd, tel: 0-2282-9773, www.tat.or.th, open daily 0830–1630.

CREDIT CARD COMPANIES For lost or stolen cards: Visa, tel: (001) 80044-13485 (toll-free); Mastercard, tel: (001) 80011-887-0663 (toll-free); American Express, tel: 0-2273-0022 or 0-2273-0044.

DIRECTORY ENQUIRIES Dial 1113 for Bangkok numbers and for the rest of Thailand.

E-MAIL AND INTERNET Shops and cafés offering e-mail and internet access are found in all the main visitor areas of the city. The cheapest rates are around Khao San Rd and Sukhumvit Rd.

EMERGENCIES The tourist police, who speak English, can be reached on 1155. The emergency services phone lines are in Thai. Police, tel: 191 or 123; ambulance, tel: 0-2255-1133/6; fire, tel: 199.

EMBASSIES AND CONSULATES

Australia, tel: 0-2287-2680 Canada, tel: 0-2636-0540 Cambodia, tel: 0-2253-7967

France, tel: 0-2266-8250 Germany, tel: 0-2287-9000 Laos, tel: 0-2539-6667

Malaysia, tel: 0-2679-2190 Nepal, tel: 0-2391-7240 Singapore, tel: 0-2286-2111

UK, tel: 0-2305-8333 USA, tel: 0-2205-4000

EXCHANGE Cash and traveller's cheques can be changed any time of day or night at the airport or in five-star hotels. Exchange booths stay open until around 2000 in tourist areas like Sukhumvit Rd, Silom Rd and Khao San Rd.

HOSPITALS There are lots of excellent hospitals in Bangkok, as well as countless clinics that can deal with minor ailments. The top hotels as well as the European embassies can provide details of English-speaking doctors. Some of the more centrally located hospitals include the Bangkok Adventist Hospital, 430 Phitsanulok Rd, tel: 0-2281-1422, the Bangkok Christian Hospital, 124 Silom Rd, tel: 0-2233-6981, and Bumrungrad Hospital, 33 Soi 3, Sukhumvit Rd, tel: 0-2267-1000.

IMMIGRATION OFFICE Visa extensions are available from the immigration office on Soi Suan Phlu off Sathon Tai Rd, tel: 0-2287-3101/10. Open Mon–Fri 0830–1630. Bring two photos and a photocopy of your passport details.

POSTAL SERVICES The GPO, 1160 Charoen Krung Rd, (River Express: Wat Muang Kae), has a poste restante and a packaging service.

THAILAND

TELEPHONES A good place to find plenty of phones for international calls, and an extensive Home Direct service (for reverse charge calls), is in the grounds of the GPO, 1160 Charoen Krung Rd (River Express: Wat Muang Kae).

BANGKOK'S MAIN AREAS

These are the main areas of Bangkok that are used in this guide to structure the accommodation, eating and shopping sections. If staying in the city for more than a couple of days, you should end up with a nodding acquaintance with most of them.

WORLD TRADE CENTER AREA This area is formed by the junction of Ploenchit Rd and Ratchadamri Rd. Dominated by the giant block of the World Trade Center building, it is a few minutes on foot from the Skytrain Chit Lom station. There are lots of restaurants here, including an excellent food centre, and plenty of shops. Many buses stop outside the World Trade Center, including no. 73 from the train station. Close to all this traffic mayhem is the serene Erawan temple. One of Bangkok's better five-star hotels, the Grand Hyatt Erawan, is located right next to the temple.

SIAM SQUARE AREA Only a short distance west of the World Trade Center the futuristic Siam Square is all concrete and glass, aglow with shopping and entertainment centres and popular with impressionable Bangkok teenagers. Skytrain has a station here and most of the time you find yourself walking under its concrete structure. From a shopping point of view, the Skytrain station further west (Skytrain: National Stadium) is more useful because it has a walkway to the MBK shopping centre.

SILOM RD AREA Silom Rd in the south-west of the city runs from close to the Chao Phraya River (Skytrain: Saphan Taksin and Surasak; River Express: Sathorn) up to Rama IV Rd (Skytrain: Sala Daeng) near to the infamous but very touristy Patpong area. Silom Rd has its fair share of hotels and restaurants but it is primarily a commercial and financial area with lots of banks and airline offices. Half way up Silom Rd (Skytrain: Chong Nonsi) is a Thai Airways office. The Silom Rd area also covers the stretch of Charoen Krung Rd near the river where the famed Oriental Hotel rubs shoulders with good-value budget Muslim restaurants.

SUKHUMVIT RD AREA Sukhumvit Rd is a major road running eastwards from the city centre and heading out of town towards Pattaya. The tourist area, full of mid-to-top-range hotels and restaurants, is the stretch between the skytrain stations Nana and Phrom Phong.

KHAO SAN RD AREA The area is Banglamphu, synonymous with cheap accommodation and its defining thoroughfare, Khao San Rd. Many budget travellers never leave the area, which means they miss much of the excitement and variety Bangkok has to offer.

GETTING AROUND

The horror stories you may have heard about Bangkok's traffic congestion say more about the past than the present. It can still be a nightmare trying to get somewhere in a hurry, and when a road floods or something snarls up the traffic flow the consequences can be dire. With a degree of planning, however, and the use of buses, boats and skytrains it is possible to get around the sprawling mass of the city in reasonable time.

BUS It would take a lifetime to fathom all the bus routes that weave their way through the city but it certainly makes sense to master a few key routes relevant to the area you are staying in. The same bus number on the same route can be a comfortable air-conditioned vehicle or a sweaty, bumpy non-air-con version. Buses are often crowded so you need to have some idea of where to get off. Bus maps of the city are readily available in hotel shops, bookshops and along Khao San Rd, but try to check the route with your hotel first. Here is a list of some of the more useful routes around town.

SKYTRAIN

Bangkok's overhead light railway system, the Skytrain (or BTS, as it is officially known), may not add anything to the capital's aesthetic appeal but it has made a tremendous improvement to the task of getting around the city. It does not cover all of Bangkok but where it does run it offers an inexpensive, clean and reliable alternative to buses and taxis.

There are two lines; one runs from Mo Chit in the north to the east of the city along Sukhumvit Rd. The other runs from the National Stadium to the river at the bottom end of Silom Rd at Saphan Taskin. A new cross-river line may open in 2004. The lines interconnect at Siam station and operate 0600–2400.

A subway system is due to open in 2005. Skytrain, subway and bus tickets will not be interchangeable, but the three transportation systems will connect at several stations. The system will provide a link between the central Hualamphong and Bang Sue railway stations.

No. 7: Connects the Southern Bus Terminal with Sukhumvit Rd, via Sanam Luang (for Khao San Rd) and Hualamphong railway station.

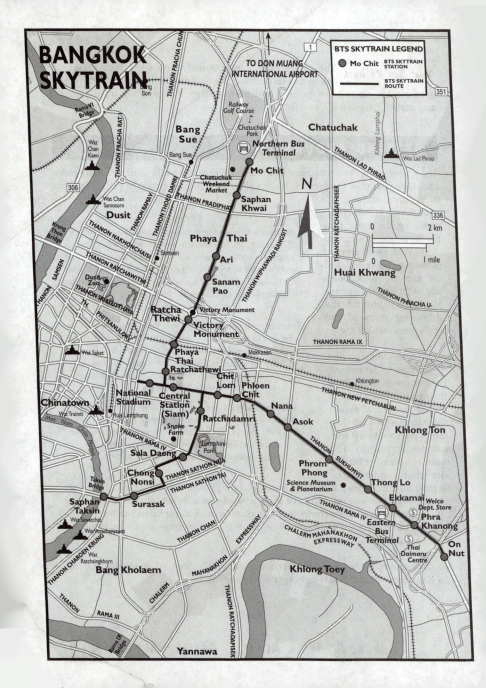

No. 11: Connects the Eastern Bus Terminal with the Southern Bus Terminal, via Sukhumvit Rd, Democracy Document, and Ratchadamnoen Klang (for Khao San Rd).

No. 73: Connects the World Trade Centre, Siam Square and the railway station.

No. 75: Travels between the railway station and Charoen Krung Rd (for Silom Rd).

BOAT The Chao Phraya Express Boat is a very useful boat service that runs up and down the river daily 0600–1840 for 5–15B. It is reliable and makes a welcome change from road transport. The standard boat doesn't carry a flag, which means it will stop at any pier on the route. Between 0600 and 0900, and 1200 and 1900, there are special boats with either a yellow or an orange flag. These boats only stop at the main piers and certain stops indicated by the colour of the flag. Listed below are some of the more useful stops:

Banglamphu: The closest pier to Khao San Rd and the budget accommodation area. Also useful for the restaurants along Tha Pra Athit, the National Museum and the National Theatre. Standard boat only.

Railway Station: This is the Thonburi (Bangkok Noi) station, on the west side of the river, from where trains to Kanchanaburi depart. Standard boat only.

Tha Chang: A short walk from this pier to the Grand Palace. Standard, green and red and orange flag boats.

Tha Thien: For Wat Po. Standard boat only.

Rachavongse: The stop for Chinatown. All boats.

Wat Muang Kae: The stop for the General Post Office. Standard boat only.

Oriental: For Silom Rd and Oriental Hotel. Standard and green flag boat.

Sathorn: Next to the Saphan Taksin skytrain station and the Shangri La Hotel.

TAXI Metered, air-conditioned taxis can be flagged down anywhere and there are plenty of them. Fares start at 35B, athough there is a surcharge for traffic congestion of around 70B for a 10 km journey. Avoid unlicensed cabs that don't use a meter. Taxis can be booked for an extra 20B, tel: 0-2435-0090, 0-2880-0888. Taxis that loiter near the main hotels often charge more.

Motorcycle taxis are used mostly by locals for short journeys. Helmets are usually provided. Agree on a price beforehand.

THAILAND

TAXI FARES

For the first 2 km   35B
2–12 km   4.50B per km
13–20 km   5B per km
21 km plus   5.50B per km

When the taxi moves no faster than 6 km per hour, 1.25B is added per minute.

TUK-TUK The quintessentially Thai form of transport in Bangkok is the *tuk-tuk*, a three-wheeled buggy with open sides that weaves its kamikaze way through the traffic. They are incredibly nippy and can beat the jams that hold up taxis and buses. Most of the drivers don't speak much English so you need an obvious destination or a map, and the fare has to be settled beforehand. The usual rate for a short hop, say from the World Trade Center to Pantip Plaza, is around 40B.

CAR Renting a car for city travel is not advisable. The pace is hectic, traffic etiquette non-existent and the complexity of roads and junctions is mind-boggling, never mind the problem of finding somewhere to park.

AIRLINES

Air France Vorawat Bldg, 849 Silom Rd; tel: 0-2635-1199

Bangkok Airways Ratchadaphisek Tat Mai Rd; tel: 0-2229-3434

British Airways Abdulrahim Place, 990 Rama IV Rd; tel: 0-2636-1700

Canadian Airlines Maneeya Centre, 518 Ploenchit Rd; tel: 0-2251-4521

Cathay Pacific Ploenchit Tower, 898 Ploenchit Rd; tel: 0-2263-0606

Eva Airways Green Tower, Rama IV Rd; tel: 0-2367-3388

Garuda Lumphini Tower, 1168 Rama IV Rd; tel: 0-2285-6470

KLM Charnwattana Rd, Pakkred; tel: 0-2573-0095

Lufthansa Soi 21, Sukhumvit Rd; tel: 0-2264-2400

Malaysia Airlines Ploenchit Tower, Ploenchit Rd; tel: 0-2263-0565

Northwest Peninsula Plaza, 153 Ratchadamri Rd; tel: 0-2254-0789

Qantas Abdulrahmin Place, 990 Rama IV Rd; tel: 0-2636-1700

Singapore Airlines Silom Centre 2 Silom Rd; tel: 0-2236-0222

Thai International 485 Silom Rd; tel: 0-2232-8000. Lan Luang Road, tel: 0-2280-0100

United Airlines 14th Floor, Sindhorn Building, 130–132 Witthayu Road tel: 0-2253-0559

Vietnam Airlines Ploenchit Centre, Ploenchit Road; tel: 0-2656-9056

HIGHLIGHTS

It is easy to visit most of the city highlights on your own rather than by city tour. You will save money and, by going at your own pace, avoid the *wat* syndrome – when exhausted tourists exclaim 'Not another *wat*! *Wat* for?' It is possible to take in the three major sites, the **Grand Palace**, **Wat Po** and **National Museum**, in one day by starting early at Wat Po, then walking north to the Grand Palace and finally the National Museum. But don't expect to remember anything beyond the first few hours. If time allows, start at the Grand Palace when it opens, then move on to Wat Po to see the temple and enjoy a massage – by mid-afternoon, you'll need it! Save the National Museum for a second day.

The Grand Palace is not to be missed. Despite the crowds and queues it's unlikely you won't be bowled over by the shimmering play of light on the golden structures and its sheer magnificence. The sprawling complex started life in 1782 and now occupies over 60 acres of land. Guided tours at regular intervals help make sense of the various royal buildings – the king and his family reside elsewhere and only turn up for special occasions. Some visitors prefer just to wander around, goggle-eyed at the psychedelic surfeit of golden orange, mosaic-rich walls and pillars, shining spires, intricate murals, and the astonishingly pristine mix of the garish and the grand.

The chief attraction within the Palace is **Wat Phra Kaeo**, the Temple of the Emerald Buddha, the first temple constructed within the Grand Palace. Another notable structure is **Chakri-Mahaprasad Hall**. Visitors cannot enter the hall, which functioned as the royal harem, but the exterior is a fairly unique combination of European and Thai styles. Rama V commissioned an English architect in the 1880s who thought of bringing the Renaissance to Siam and got as far as the roof, which would have been a Western-style dome, when he was prevailed upon to add traditional Thai spires instead.

Another highlight is the airy **Amarindra Vinichai Hall**. This was the main audience hall and court of justice where people petitioned the king. Today its gilded interior is reserved for important ceremonial occasions involving the king.

The **Grand Palace**, **$$$**, Naphralan Rd, is open daily 0830–1530. Admission includes a brochure with indigestible text but a handy map. Wearing shorts, sarongs, flip-flops and other casual or revealing clothes is not allowed (appropriate attire can be hired). Bus no. 8 from Siam Square (Skytrain: Siam) is an easy way to reach the Grand Palace, or arrive by water (Express Boat: Tha Chang). There are English language tours at 1000, 1030, 1100, 1300, 1330 and 1400. Without a guide, it can be difficult to make sense of all you see.

THAILAND

The royal palace's website is at: www.palaces.thai.net. A good book on the palace, which has lots of illustrations, is *The Grand Palace Bangkok* by Naengnoi Suksri (Thames and Hudson).

Wat Po is most famous for its colossal **Reclining Buddha**, but it is also home to a noted massage school, tel: 0-2622-1687, 0-2225-4771, as well as novice and experienced monks who are often found strolling in the grounds away from the star attraction. The gold-leafed 46-m-long Buddha may be all brick and plaster inside, but its serene smile registers the mystical journey into the state of nirvana. The statue's feet are inlaid with mother-of-pearl, depicting 108 auspicious marks that belong to the true Buddha.

Wat Po, $, Maha Rat Rd, is open daily 0800–1700, tel: 0-2222-0933 (River Express: Tha Thien). From the pier, turn right onto Mahathat Rd and left into Soi Chetuphon. From the main entrance/exit of the Grand Palace, turn left on Nha Phra Lan Rd, then left onto Mahathat Rd and Soi Chetuphon. It takes about 15 mins to walk from the Grand Palace.

WAT PHRA KAEO

The temple is home to the diminutive **Emerald Buddha**, a mere 60 cm tall but looming large in the Thai cultural consciousness. It came to life, so to speak, in the 15th century when a bolt of lightning split open an ancient *stupa* in northern Thailand and the figure rolled out. Said to have been cut from a single block of jade, it rapidly acquired a reputation as an auspicious image but was taken as booty to Laos, where it remained for two centuries.

The capture of Vientiene towards the end of the 18th century saw its return to Thailand and Rama I duly placed it in his palace as a symbol of national pride. The king had two royal robes especially made to clothe the image and a third costume was commissioned by Rama III. Even today only the king is allowed to change the costume. It has become the most important Buddha emblem in the country.

Surrounding Wat Phra Kaeo, in the welcome shade of its cloisters, are 178 murals depicting the story of the ancient Hindu epic, the *Ramayana*. Go to the north wall for the first panel at the central gate and proceed in a clockwise direction from here.

The **National Museum** is the largest museum in South-East Asia, and like all large museums there is too much to take in on a single visit. One approach is to arrive on a Wednesday or Thursday morning before 0930 and join the free English language tours. They focus on a selection of the more interesting exhibits and serve as a useful introduction to varied aspects of Thai culture and religion.

Without a tour, you have to choose between a vast collection of sculptures and artefacts from all periods of Thai history, and the overall impact can be bewildering. It may be worth selecting just a few of the galleries. The main collection follows a chronological approach, starting on the ground floor where there is a rare example of an early Buddha figure from India. It was found at Gandhara, one of the most easterly outposts founded by Alexander the Great, and clearly reveals the influence of ancient Greek artistic forms.

The museum compound also houses the **Buddhaisawan Chapel**, built in the late 18th century to house the **Phra Sihing Buddha**. This highly venerated statue, like the Emerald Buddha in Wat Phra Kaeo, has a legendary history that begins with its miraculous creation in Ceylon. Experts, however, tend to regard it as a classic northern Thai figure. The chapel is also home to a set of well-preserved murals, depicting scenes from the Buddha's life, that date back to the 1790s.

The **National Museum**, $$, Na Phra That Rd, is open Wed–Sun 0900–1600, tel: 0-2224-1370. Admission includes a very basic sketch of the various galleries.

Jim Thompson's House is actually a group of six traditional Thai teak houses built for the American expatriate Jim Thompson. Their sloping walls channel away hot air and there is an enchanting garden. He furnished them with an eclectic collection of rare antiques and fine examples of craftsmanship from around South-East Asia. Thompson came to Thailand during World War II as an officer in the Organization of Strategic Services, a precursor to the CIA.

He became so earnestly involved in the promotion of Thai silk that he is credited with having resuscitated the industry. During the 1950s he milked his expatriate image to such an extent that famous people coming to the city could feel slighted if dinner with Jim Thompson could not be arranged.

The address is 6, Soi Kasemsan 2, Rama 1 Rd, tel: 0-2215-0122, open Mon—Sat 0900-1630. Admission **($$$)** includes a compulsory guided tour but you can wander around the grounds at will. Take a skytrain or bus to Siam Square and walk westwards along Rama 1 before turning right into Soi Kasemsan 2.

WHATEVER HAPPENED TO JIM THOMPSON?

Thompson was acquainted with some of the liberal Thai politicos of the 1960s which became grist to the rumour mill when he dramatically disappeared on Easter Sunday in 1967. He was in the Cameron Highlands in Malaysia (see p. 303) when he went out for a walk and was never seen again. Extensive searches never found his body. Was he murdered for his political sympathies? Was he still working for American intelligence? Was he eaten by a tiger? Conspiracy theories were never in short supply and an amateur detective recently unearthed fresh evidence suggesting that he was run down in a traffic accident and the frightened driver buried his body.

A CHINATOWN WALK

Bangkok's Chinatown is squeezed in between the river and Charoen Krung Rd, with Hualamphong railway station to the east and the small Indian enclave of Phahurat to the west. This walk through Chinatown is not a shopping trip. It is a fascinating look at Bangkok street life and the perfect antidote to flashy Siam Square.

A good way to reach Chinatown is by the River Express to Tha Ratchawong from where you can walk up **Ratchawong Rd** to the junction with **Sampeng Lane** (Soi Wanit 1). This main commercial artery is one long rambling outdoor market, selling a vast range of everyday goods from silk pyjamas and other clothes to electronic toys and spices.

Turn right at this junction and wander along the congested Sampeng Lane to **Mangkon Rd**. This junction is fronted by old commercial buildings that date back to the end of the 19th century and are well worth a closer look, both inside and out. Continue walking along Sampeng Rd until you reach **Soi Issaranuphap** (Soi 16) and take a left turn here up this narrow lane. On the right you will pass the entrance to a wet fish market before reaching a crossroads with the main Yaowarat Rd and its countless gold and jewellery shops.

Continue walking up Soi Issaranuphap to the main junction with Charoen Krung Rd and turn left for the entrance to **Wat Mangkon Kamalawat**. If you associate

Buddhism with other-worldly mysticism and abstract meditation, then a visit here will be educational. This is one of the city's busiest temples, with people dropping in whenever they can snatch an hour from work.

You may be exhausted by now, in which case the best way out is to catch a taxi. Alternatively, retrace your steps to the pier. If you're up for more, then continue walking along Charoen Krung Road for nearly ½ kilometre to Chakrawat and **Nakhon Kasem (Thieves' Market)**. This labyrinthine bazaar comes into its own after dusk and while it no longer stocks the illicit goods that gave rise to its name, it is always busy with evening shoppers.

Lumpini Park, the largest park in downtown Bangkok, is at the end of Silom Rd, across the road from Robinson's department store (Skytrain: Sala Daeng). An early morning (before 0900) visit to the park (named after the Buddha's birthplace in Nepal) is reco-mmended for a peek at Chinese residents performing t'ai chi in balletic slow motion.

Later in the day, Chinese men play chess and families row boats on the lake. Look out too for the vendors who slice up snakes for their supposedly medicinal blood and bile. Tables for picnics and an inexpensive restaurant make it a good place to relax after an exhausting session in the Silom Rd shops.

What used to be a military parade ground just west of Lumpini Park has become Bangkok's newest shopping attraction, the **Suan Lum Night Market**. The sprawling market is Bangkok's biggest daily shopping opportunity with hundreds of vendors, semi-permanent shops, food stalls, restaurants, a beer garden and the exquisite Joe Louis Puppet Theatre with the finest traditional puppet performances in Thailand. Suan Lum's website is www.thainightbazaar.com.

A visit to the **Snake Farm ($$$)** sounds more worthy if you refer to it by its proper title, the Queen Saovabha Memorial Institute run by the Thai Red Cross. The Snake Farm is located at the corner of Rama IV Rd and Henry Dunant Rd, tel: 0-2252-0161 (Skytrain: Sala Daeng). Arrive before 1030 or 1400 (1030 only at weekends) to catch the ½ hour slide show that precedes the live demonstration. Trained handlers extract deadly poison from some of the world's most venomous snakes, with disarming ease to make snake bite antidotes.

The **Erawan Shrine** to the four-faced Brahma god, Than Tao Mahaprom, has a remark-able setting on the busy corner of Ploenchit Rd and Ratchadamri Rd (Skytrain: Chit Lom), diagonally across from the World Trade Center.

From morning to night Thais turn up to make ceremonial offerings of floral garlands and fruit. Shrines to hedonism are all around in the form of five-star hotels and design-er-label shops and there is a constant roar of traffic, yet in the midst of this worship-ers carry out their rituals oblivious to all, even intrusive tourists with camcorders.

ACCOMMODATION

One reason why more and more travellers are coming to Bangkok is the availability of rooms to suit all budgets. The prices here reflect official rack rates which in the case of budget and mid-range guesthouses and hotels remain fairly constant. In the case of four- and five-star hotels it is usually possible to get discounted rates through an agent, either in your own country or in Bangkok, such as Thai Travel Trade, 557, Silom Rd; tel: 0-2631-0221, fax: 0-2234-0563, e-mail: thaitr@samart.co.th or websites such as www.asiatravel.com.

WORLD TRADE CENTER AND SIAM SQUARE AREA

Bangkok Palace Hotel $$$ 1091/336 New Petchburi Rd; tel: 0-2253-0510; www.bangkokpalace.com. Its location near Siam Square makes the Palace a favourite with regional travellers on a shopping holiday.

White Lodge $$ 36/8 Soi Kasem San 1, tel: 0-2216-8867. Clean, basic and friendly with a good café.

A-One Inn $$ 25/13 Soi Kasem San 1: tel: 0-2215-3029, e-mail: aoneinn@thaimail.com. Around for some time but standards are maintained.

If these two mid-range places are full there are plenty of viable alternatives in the neighbourhood.

SILOM RD AREA

Silom City Inn $$ 72 Soi Prachum (Silom 22), Silom Rd; www.silomcityinn.com. Calls itself a business hotel, but discount web rates make it a bargain for all.

Silom Village Inn $$$ 286 Silom Rd; tel: 0-2635-6810, e-mail: silom-village-inn@thai.com. Not in the quietest corner of town but discounted rates make it good value. Clean, comfortable rooms.

Niagara Hotel $$ 26 Soi 9 (Suksavithaya); tel: 0-2233-5783. One of the few budget places in this area. Long bleak corridors and basic rooms, but clean and with air-con.

SUKHUMVIT RD

Ruamchitt Plaza & Hotel $$ 199 Sukhumvit Rd (near Soi 15); tel: 0-2254-0205. This newish hotel can be noisy late at night from the busy basement bar, but it's clean and good value.

Majestic Suites $$$ 110–110/1 Sukhumvit Rd, between Soi 4–6; tel: 0-2656-8220; www.majesticsuites.com. Good value, but ask for a room at the back to escape street noise.

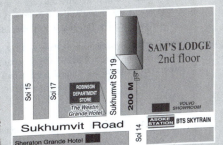

Atlanta $$ 78 Soi 2, Sukhumvit Rd; tel: 0-2252-1650. Hard to beat in terms of location and value. Old-style hotel with excellent restaurant and impecunious but sophisticated atmosphere. Rooms to suit different budgets, and evening videos.

Miami Hotel $$ 2 Soi 13, Sukhumvit Rd; tel: 0-2253-5611. Decent rooms, a pool and a café.

THE ORIENTAL

$$$$$ 48 Oriental Ave; tel: 0-2236-0400, www.mandarin-oriental.com, e-mail: reserve-orbkk@mohg.co.com (Skytrain: Saphan Taksin River Express Oriental).

Because it is hidden away down a traffic-clogged road, The Oriental's history is more apparent when viewed from the river. Even if you are not a guest, a visit to the place where writers such as Joseph Conrad, W Somerset Maughan, Graham Greene and Noël Coward once stayed is a 'must see' for many visitors to Bangkok. Established in 1876, the hotel soon became *the* place for European travellers to reside and to be seen, and its reputation remains undiminished. The original Italianate building survives as the Authors' Residence, with a new wing added in the 1950s and another nearly 20 years later.

It's not quite true that shorts or sleeveless shirts are not allowed in the lobby but in the evening a dress code is an expected part of the ritual here. The lobby is unspectacular but the small lounge area in the Authors' Residence helps create a sense that if Thailand had ever been colonised The Oriental would have adapted to its role with consummate ease.

Joseph Conrad, a young marine officer in 1877, would not have been able to afford the room rates today. They start at US$250 and climb to an astronomical US$2200 for one of the four authors' suites. There are cultural programmes and a Thai cooking school, which is open to non-residents for the resident rate of US$120.

KHAO SAN RD AREA

This is the famed territory of the Bangkok backpacker and features in the opening scene of *The Beach*, when Leonardo DiCaprio's character arrives in the city looking for somewhere to stay (the scene was actually filmed in a studio set in Phuket).

Nana Plaza Inn $$$ off 202 Khao San Rd; tel: 0-2281-6402. A pleasant enough place and its air-conditioned rooms are at the bottom end of the $$$ range. There are lockers, e-mail and internet access and a pool table.

Khaosan Palace Hotel $$ 139 Khao San Rd; tel: 0-2282-0578. Rooms come in all sizes, with air-con or fan, and although basic they are fine for the rates charged. No advance bookings are taken.

Running parallel with Khao San Road to the south is Trok Mayom, a narrow lane with some decent guesthouses that enjoy a relatively quiet and relaxing atmosphere. **7 Holder Guest House $** Spartan but clean rooms, some with their own shower. For half the room rate you can stay until 1800. No telephone bookings.

Sawasdee Guest House $–$$ in the same road has singles, doubles and dorm beds, with and without air-conditioning.

Sugar Guest House $ Trok Mayom at the top end of Khao San Rd, close by the Gaylord restaurant; tel: 0-2282-8396. A typical example of the rock-bottom accommodation available in this area. Rooms with fan and shared showers. International phone calls can be made here for the lowest price in Bangkok.

GOING DIVING?

If you're at all interested in diving off Thailand's southern islands, it's worth making a visit to **Larry's Dive** 8 Soi 22, Sukhumvit Rd; tel: 0-2663-4563; www.larrysdive.com. There are good deals for those booking in Bangkok, including first-hand information and dive gossip at Larry's beach bar, restaurant and grill, and it takes the hassle out of dealing with the touts down south.

FOOD AND DRINK

Finding a place to eat is never a problem in Bangkok. The quality of the food is astonishingly good, usually regardless of price. There is also a huge variety of cuisines. In many food centres you can enjoy a tasty lunch dish for under 50B and most of the real quality restaurants are remarkably affordable. The skytrain has made many more eating places accessible, and where a restaurant is within easy walking distance of a station this information is given in the entry.

WORLD TRADE CENTER AREA

Thai On 4 $$$$ Amari Watergate Hotel, 847 Petchburi Rd, tel: 0-2653-9000. Speciality dishes from all parts of Thailand. Sleek, non-traditional setting with modern art and suave sevice gives it a post-modernist feel.

FOOD COUPONS

Some of the best food centres in Bangkok use a coupon system and no cash is exchanged. Buy coupons from the counter, in various denominations, to pay for food and drink from any of the stalls. Any coupons left over can be exchanged back for cash, although only on the same day of purchase.

Felice $$$$ The Arnoma Hotel, 99 Ratchadamri Rd; tel: 0-2255-3410. Comfortable enclave offering pizzas, other mainstream European dishes and a fair wine list. Across the road, on the 6th floor of the World Trade Center, **Vegeta $$$** tel: 0-2255-9569, has vegetarian salads, noodles and curries.

On the street opposite the World Trade Centre, look for a signpost for the **NP Food Centre $–$$** pointing down a lane that leads to a car park. An excellent place for a quick salad or noodle dish while in the throes of shopping. A coupon system operates and most of the stalls have English menus. The coffee counter is first-rate.

DINING BY THE CHAO PHRAYA RIVER

Salathip $$$$ Shangri-La Hotel, Soi Wat Suan, Charoen Krung Rd; tel: 0-2236-7777 (Skytrain: Saphan Taksin, River Express: Sathorn). Reserve an outdoor table for riverside views, Thai classical dancers performing 1945–2100 except Mon, and delicate Thai food.

Horizon Cruise II $$$ is on the expensive side, but offers the best food on the Chao Phraya River and a great way to enjoy the sound and light show at the Grand Palace and Wat Arun. Shangri-La Hotel, 89 Soi Wat Suan Plu, New Rd; tel: 0-2236-7777 (Skytrain: Saphan Taksin).

Supatra River House $$$$ 266 Soi Wat Rakhang, Arunamarin Rd; tel: 0-2411-0305 (River Express: Wang Lang). Old Thai residence opposite the Grand Palace, with indoor and outdoor tables and cultural dance evenings on Friday and Saturday nights.

SIAM SQUARE AREA

Siam Square's reputation for yuppie (or tuppie for the home-grown Thai version) materialism means it's no surprise to find it chock-a-block with American fast food joints. More interesting possibilities include Vietnamese food at **Pho Restaurant $$–$$$** tel: 0-2251-8900, 2nd floor, AlmaLink Building, 25 Soi Chidlom (Skytrain: Siam).

Sarah-Jane's $$–$$$ Sindhorn Building, 130 Witthayu Rd; tel: 0-2650-9992 (Skytrain: Ploenchit). Two stops east on the skytrain from Siam Square and worth the trip for fiery Isaan cuisine from the north-east of Thailand.

MBK Food Centre $–$$ 7th floor, MBK building (Skytrain: National Stadium). All Thai food, cooked in front of you. For Western-style food there are plenty of outlets in MBK and there is a smaller food centre on the 2nd floor.

PUB FOOD

Bobby's Arms $$$$ Carpark Building, Patpong 11, tel: 0-2233-6828 (Skytrain: Sala Daeng), has a menu with roast beef and Yorkshire pudding, fish and chips, and a set lunch. Ex-pats congregate at the **Bull's Head** on Sukhumvit Soi 33/1, with a British pub atmosphere.

Not far away, **Shenanigans $$$$** Sivadon Building, 1–5 Convent Rd, tel: 0-2266-7161 (Skytrain: Sala Daeng), offers competing fare from Ireland. The oak beams may be plastic but the beef and Guinness pies are for real; Guinness and Kilkenny on draught.

Another Irish pub just up the main road is **O'Reilly's $$$$** 62 Silom Rd; tel: 0-2632-7515 (Skytrain: Sala Daeng). Shrimp cocktail followed by Irish stew or cod and chips are firm favourites here. Both these pubs often have live music in the evenings.

SILOM RD AREA

There is a wealth of value-for-money places to eat which cater for the many middle-class Thai office workers in the area. Around Charoen Krung Rd there are clusters of inexpensive Indian and Pakistani restaurants. Also in this part of town are farang-frequented pub-restaurants that serve reasonable grub from mid-morning until the early hours (see above).

These pubs are at the Patpong end of Silom Road where you will also find **Trattoria Da Roberto $$$** Plaza Arcade, Patpong 2; tel: 0-2234-5987 (Skytrain: Sala Daeng). No surprises here but reliable staples like fresh pizza, *pollo alla cacciatoria* and *spaghetti alla Bolognese.*

The Barbican $$–$$$ Thaniya Plaza, off Silom Rd, tel: 0-2234-3590 (Skytrain: Sala Daeng) is a British-owned bar and restaurant that is surrounded by Japanese hostess bars. It's worth a visit, if only to see the bizarre location.

V9 $$$ is a trendy wine bar and restaurant at the top of the Sofitel Silom Bangkok Hotel, 188 Silom Rd; tel: 0-2238-2992 (Skytrain: Chong Nonsi). View and wine prices are the best of any restaurant in Bangkok.

Silom Village Food Centre $$$ has a brightly lit array of restaurants offering seafood and international dishes.

On the other side of Silom Rd, look for a blue signpost to 13 (trok number) almost opposite the Narai Hotel. Down this small street lurks the spartan but good **Madras Café $** 31/10–11 Trok Vaithi, tel: 0-2233-2128, serving tasty curries, *masala dosai* and *roti.*

For the real centre of Indian food just walk to the bottom of Silom Rd (Skytrain: Surasak) and turn right into Charoen Krung Rd to the **Muslim Restaurant $** at no. 1356, near Soi 42. On the other side of the road, pass the few fading antique shops. The alley on the right with a signpost for the Centaur Inn is home to the **Indian Biryani Restaurant $–$$**. Tasty vegetarian and non-vegetarian Muslim food is served at its small four tables. Next door, the similar **Madina Restaurant $$** is a little plusher.

ALL-YOU-CAN-EAT BUFFETS

All-you-can-eat buffets are usually offered by the top hotels. Assuming you have a healthy appetite they can provide great value for money. Check the *Bangkok Post* for details and prices of buffets featuring special promotions.

Teio $$–$$$ Sofitel Silom Bangkok Hotel, 188 Silom Rd, tel: 0-2238-1991 (Skytrain: Chong Nonsi). A traditional Japanese restaurant with a lunch buffet that doesn't skimp on the raw fish, or the green-tea ice cream. At weekends and on Friday nights the buffet is more expensive, but still worth considering.

The Dining Room, lunch **$$$$**, dinner **$$$$$**. Grand Hyatt Erawan, 494 Ratchadamri Rd, tel: 0-2254-1234 (Skytrain: Chit Lom), delivers a feast of international, seafood, Thai, Asian and Japanese food for gourmands.

Atrium Café $$$ Landmark Hotel, 138 Sukhumvit Rd; tel: 0-2253-4259 (Skytrain: Nana). This place has one of the city's best breakfast buffets and an all-you-can-drink beer bash at lunch and dinner.

SUKHUMVIT RD AREA

You can hardly walk 100 m along this road and its adjoining sois without finding a pleasant restaurant of one kind or another. Starting from the top of Sukhumvit Rd near the JW Marriott Hotel and heading eastwards, turn down Soi 3 (Nana Nua) for a couple of middle-of-the-road Indian and Pakistani restaurants: **MehMaan $$$** 69 Soi 3, tel: 0-2253-4689, and **Akbar $$$** Soi 3, tel: 0-2253-3479 (Skytrain: Nana). Other good Indian places can be found up and down Soi 11. If you want to splash out, consider Vietnamese food at the elegant **Le Dalat Indochine $$$$** 14 Soi 23, Sukhumvit Rd, tel: 0-2661-7967 (Skytrain: Asok). Go for cocktails at Le Lotus bar before settling into the plush golden-hued dining room. Across the road, **Le Dalat $$$** 47/1 Soi 23, Sukhumvit Rd, tel: 0-2260-1849, is its less expensive sister restaurant. What could justly be described as Bangkok's best Indian restaurant is the **Rang Mahal $$$$$** Rembrandt Hotel, Soi 18,

HOTEL RESTAURANTS

Bangkok is teeming with top quality five-star hotels, all boasting fine restaurants that compete fiercely to attract domestic and foreign customers. Standards are high but prices are not as frightening as one might think, and some of the restaurants offer tremendous opportunities to experience and enjoy a variety of cuisines with a high degree of comfort and style.

(Skytrain: Nana) At the **White Elephant** $$$$–$$$$$ JW Marriott Hotel, 4 Sukhumvit Rd, tel: 0-2656-7700, a serene atmosphere accompanies the authentic Thai cuisine, and with sackfuls of ingredients on display this is a place to learn about the food as well as to enjoy eating it. (Skytrain: Asok) **Kisso** $$$$–$$$$$, **Westin Grande Sukhumvit**, 259 Sukhumvit Rd, tel: 0-2651-1000, has a number of set menus that make Japanese food affordable for two people.

Spasso $$$$$ Grand Hyatt Erawan, 494 Ratchadamri Rd, tel: 0-2254-1234 (Skytrain: Chit Lom), is an Italian restaurant serving buffet lunches and a dinner menu of pasta, pizza, fish and meat dishes. Later in the evening there is a live band and dancing. For a quieter Italian-style meal try the **Hibiscus** $$$$ on the 31st floor of The Landmark, 138 Sukhumvit Rd, tel: 0-2254-0404, (Skytrain: Nana).

A non-five-star hotel serving top-notch vegetarian food is the art-deco **Atlanta** $–$$ Atlanta Hotel, 78 Soi 2, Sukhumvit Rd, tel: 0-2252-1650 (Skytrain: Nana).

SHOPPING

Shopping is one of Bangkok's great attractions, but it can be a tiring business and is best staggered over the length of your stay. The size of the city and the diversity of goods on offer are what makes shopping so exhausting. For helpful hints on out-of-the-way shops and obscure markets, it pays to buy a copy of *Nancy Chandler's Map of Bangkok*.

WORLD TRADE CENTER AREA The advantages of shopping centres are the comfort of air-conditioning and the fixed price policy which operates in many of the stores. The disadvantage is that prices tend to be higher, which is not unrelated to the fact that more expensive shops, like brand name stores and designer boutiques, tend to predominate in many of the shopping centres. A good example is the **World Trade Center** (Skytrain: Chit Lom) itself, where there are eight floors of expensive consumer merchandise and clothing, including a fairly useless Duty Free store that is nothing of the sort. Tower Records have a large outlet on the 7th floor.

Sukhumvit Rd, tel: 0-2261-7100 (Skytrain: Asok). Reservations are recommended. Ask for a table by the window or at least take your cocktails on the outdoor terrace. Ecstatic live Indian music every night except Monday, buffet brunch on Sunday, and always lots of superbly subtle dishes like the black lentils, *hara kebab* (spinach, cottage cheese, herbs) and chicken tikka.

Bourbon St Bar & Restaurant $$$ Soi 22 Sukhumvit Rd; tel: 0-2259-0328; www.bourbonstbkk.com (Skytrain: Phrom Phong). Thai ingredients are used to conjure up the most authentic tasting Cajun and Creole food this side of New Orleans. Chicken, pork, shrimp and beef, all with a distinctive Louisiana sizzle.

Old Siam $$ just at the end of Soi Cowboy, 4/6 Soi 23 Sukhumvit Rd; tel: 0-2259-5673 (Skytrain: Asok). Some of Bangkok's most authentic and distinctive Issan-style dishes from north-eastern Thailand – spicier, saltier and more bitter than southern-style Thai cuisine.

KHAO SAN RD AREA

Not only the prime area for budget accommodation, this area also has some very affordable places to eat. Most of the guesthouses have cafés serving much the same kind of food, and when you tire of these, there are lots of good, unpretentious restaurants.

For Indian and Pakistani food, try the **Gay Lord Restaurant $$** 71 Chakrapong Rd, at the top end of Khao San Road, where it forms a T-junction with Chakrapong Rd. *Thali* meals and other dishes can be enjoyed in the comfort of air-conditioning and if you're staying in the area, home deliveries are free.

Easy to reach by boat, **Phra Athit Rd** (River Express: Phra Athit) has a string of continental-style cafés and restaurants that attract young Thais as much as Europeans. Typical are **C & Restaurant $$** 92 Phra Athit Rd, which offers a variety Thai dishes in an art gallery setting, **indy Pub & Restaur $$** 64 Phra Athit Rd, Thai food surrounded by the work rent Bangkok photographers, or **Ton Pho $$** 43 Phra with wonderful soups and occasional jazz.

FOOD AND DRINK GUIDES

Look out for *Bangkok Dining & Entertainment*, a free publication and one of th guides. *Big Chilli* is a listings magazine with the lowdown on the newest and around the city. *Bangkok Metro* is a Western-style city magazine with occas articles and extensive food, drink and entertainment listi

A shopping centre that is well worth a visit is the **Thai Craft Village** on the ground floor of the President Tower Arcade of the Le Royal Meridien Hotel, 973 Ploenchit Rd (Skytrain: Chit Lom). Numerous shops are attractively structured around a series of stalls heavily laden with wood-carvings, silk garments, hand-woven fabrics, ceramics, jewellery, and a range of knick-knacks and souvenirs. Prices are marked, but you can usually get a 10–15% discount off the price just by asking. What's wonderful here is the sheer quality of the merchandise, which far excels most of what is found in the art and crafts shops out on the street. And despite the upscale hotel location, prices are extremely reasonable.

Just next door is **Gaysorn Plaza**, a shopping arcade with 80-plus stores and every upmarket designer name you've ever heard of from Aigner to Lacroix, Prada and Zenith.

SHOPPING: WHERE TO GO FOR WHAT

Arts and crafts: Thai Craft Village (above), Central Department Store (below), River City and Oriental Place (p. 101)

Music CDs: Tower Records in the World Trade Center (p. 98)

Computer hardware and software: Pantip Plaza (p. 100)

Jewellery: Department stores like Central on Ploenchit Rd (below), the Emporium Shopping Complex (p. 101) and the bottom end of Silom Road (p. 101)

Japanese: Tokyu department store in MBK (p. 100) and Zen department store in the World Trade Center (p. 98)

Silk: Jim Thompson's Thai Silk Company (p. 101)

Original designer and brand names clothes: Peninsula Plaza, between the Grand Hyatt and Regent hotels on Ratchadamri Rd, the Emporium Shopping Complex (p. 101), and Siam Centre and Siam Discovery Centre in Siam Square (p. 100)

Atmosphere: Chatuchak Weekend Market (p. 100), Chinatown (p. 88) and Suan Lum Night Market (p. 89)

Around the corner from Gaysorn Plaza, on Phloenchit Rd right by the skytrain station (Skytrain: Chit Lom) is the **Central Department Store,** where middle-class Bangkokians shop for clothes and consumer items. It is not huge but there is a fair selection of brassware, bamboo work, clothes and decorative items, all at fixed prices. There is also a handicrafts section on the 6th floor. This is a good place to check out standard prices before considering a purchase elsewhere where some bargaining is necessary.

Endless computer hardware and software, including video CDs and music compilations for PCs, fills every available inch of space at the **Pantip Plaza** on Petchburi Road. Computer hardware and software (usually pirated) is cheaper here than in the UK and US. From outside the World Trade Center (Skytrain: Chit Lom), it is a 5-min journey by bus or *tuk-tuk*.

A short walk further up Petchburi Rd, past the Indonesian embassy, leads to newly opened **Hollywood Plaza** which is also dedicated to computer technology. Computer games are less expensive here. Pantip Plaza has a terribly overcrowded food centre but for a more restful repast cross the road to the **First Hotel** where the 24-hr Rendevous Café serves a tasty *pad tai goong sod* (fried noodle and shrimp).

SIAM SQUARE AREA

While **Siam Centre** is a very modern shopping centre full of designer clothing stores, a far more versatile shopping centre lies within walking distance to the west, or one stop on the skytrain (Skytrain: National Stadium). The huge **MBK Plaza** (Mahboonkrong) is probably the best shopping plaza in Bangkok for shoes, watches, clothes and portable electronic goods, and computer software on the top floor. The ground floor has artists who produce some uncannily life-like portraits.

A neat little shop specialising in traditional fabrics from all corners of Thailand, sold by the metre or ready-to-wear, is the **Prayer Textile Gallery**, 197 Phaya Thai Rd; tel: 0-2251-7549 (Skytrain: Siam).

SHOPPING TIP

Department stores, open 1030–2100, are a good place to begin shopping. They offer a comfortable environment, hassle-free staff (unlike Malaysia they don't follow you around as if you're a suspect shoplifter), genuine sales and fixed prices that provide useful benchmarks when shopping in stores where nothing is priced. This is particularly useful when it comes to jewellery because the different prices do reflect genuine differences in quality, something you cannot always take for granted elsewhere.

CHATUCHAK WEEKEND MARKET

It used to be a long bus ride out to the Chatuchak market but now the skytrain stops right outside (Skytrain: Mo Chit), and no first-time trip to Bangkok is complete without a visit here. Arrive on a Sunday or Saturday morning around 0900 and you will have a good couple of hours before it gets too crowded. There are around 8000 stalls to wander past, and while some of them sell handicrafts clearly aimed at the tourist, the vast majority, like the stalls specialising in second-hand Levis, are aimed squarely at money-conscious Thais.

The stalls are thematically divided into pets, food, plants, clothes, etc., making it easy to lose your bearings. Make a note of some markers – like the central clock tower – when you first enter the fray. Food and drink stalls are dotted around inside, providing essential pit stops.

SILOM RD AREA Silom Road is not for general purpose shopping, though for arts, crafts and jewellery there are some very good shops.

Along Charoen Krung Rd (Skytrain: Surasak) there are a few antique shops which never seem busy. **U-Thong Antiques**, on the corner of Silom Rd and Charoen Krung Rd, tel: 0-2234-4767, is stuffed with Buddhas and assorted objets d'art. **Asisra Gallery**, 6 Oriental Ave (River Express: The Oriental), has some beautiful Buddha statues and, while many are too large to fit into a suitcase, shipping can be arranged.

For upmarket art and craft items, paintings and antiques, have a look at **Silom Galleria** next to the Holiday Inn Crowne Plaza hotel on Silom Rd (Skytrain: Surasak). This end of Silom Rd also has a cluster of reputable jewellery shops, like **Rama Jewelery** on the corner of Silom and Mahesak Rd.

For quality arts and crafts consumerism the place to go is **Oriental Place**, Soi 38, Charoen Krung Rd; tel: 0-2266-0186, one block north of the Oriental Hotel. Antiques, carpets, leather, jewellery, silk, paintings, souvenirs and various handicrafts populate this upmarket shopping arcade. A similar establishment is **River City** (River Express: Harbour Department), which is packed with luxury arts and crafts and fabric stores but has few fixed prices.

Surawong Rd runs parallel to Silom Rd, one block to the north and easily reached by walking down any of the interconnecting *sois*. At no. 9, **Jim Thompson's Thai Silk Company**, tel: 0-2234-4900, is an excellent place to check out Thai fabrics. Silks and cottons are sold by the length or in ready-to-wear garments, and there are little household items for sale that make great souvenirs or presents.

SUKHUMVIT RD AREA Sukhumvit Road is home to a good run-of-the-mill department store, **Robinsons**, next to the Westin Grande Sukhumvit Hotel near Soi 19 (Skytrain: Asok).

Bangkok's most trendy and upmarket mall, **Emporium Shopping Complex** near Soi 24 (Skytrain: Phrom Phong), is also in the area. As well as genuine designer fashion the sleek Emporium mall also has a very good bookshop.

Sukhumvit Rd, especially around Soi 11 (Skytrain: Nana), is the breeding ground for tailors offering apparently amazing deals on made-to-measure garments for men. The more lavish the deal, such as those with half a dozen shirts and various extras thrown in, the more suspicious you should be. Once you have committed yourself to a deal and paid over some money there is not a lot you can do about the final outcome. Insist on at least two fittings, get everything in writing, especially the price, and know exactly what kind of material is being used. It is probably worth paying more at one of the tailors' outlets in a five-star hotel where at least the proprietor wants to avoid complaints.

Tucked away down a *soi* off Sukhumvit Rd is **Rasi Sayam**, 32 Soi 23, tel: 0-2258-4195 (Skytrain: Asok), one of the better independent art and craft shops in the city. Although nothing here is cheap the merchandise is all good quality.

STREET SHOPPING **Sukhumvit Rd** (Skytrain: Nana or Asok) is packed with pavement stalls stretching from around *soi* 3 near the Marriott Hotel to around *soi* 30. Best at night, there are the usual clothes, copy watches, belts, dangerous-looking knives and whatever battery-operated gadgets happen to be around at the time.

Patpong (Skytrain: Sala Daeng): The hard-to-miss turning off the top end of Silom Rd has more than just sex shows, and for atmosphere the pavement stalls have more going for them than Sukhumvit Road. The vendors, who have seen tourists of every national character, bear the nightly tumult with dignity, and as long as you bargain hard their prices are competitive. It's all here: clothes, fake watches, CDs, leather goods…

Khao San Rd: The usual mixture of the useful and the useless, including print shops that will produce high quality fake student cards, press cards and even TEFL certificates. The quality of the consumer merchandise is generally poor and there are better places to shop.

ENTERTAINMENT

PATPONG Everyone soon hears about Bangkok's red-light district, also home to a thriving night market, off the top end of Silom Road, focused around two *sois*, **Patpong 1** and **Patpong 2**. Some of the sex bars are flamboyantly lit in neon but the less brazen ones are hardly difficult to find. Discretion is not the name of the game. Passing pedestrians are cajoled by small choruses of skimpily clad girls and insistent touts who brandish sex show menu cards as if they were promoting special offers at a burger joint. The theatricality of the spectacle can be disarming and tourists come here in their droves to be titillated by the illicit performances. But behind — or more literally on the floors above — the standard floor shows, prostitution is common and AIDS awareness comes tragically late for many young women. The other tourist red-light 'hot spots' are **Soi Cowboy**, at Sukhumvit Rd Soi 23, and **Nana Plaza**, at Sukhumvit Rd Soi 4.

BARS   There are thousands of bars in Bangkok and the trick is to find one that suits your temperament. The big brand-name joints are easy to find but expect to pay up to 200B for a small bottle of local beer in a place like **Hard Rock Café**, Soi 11, Siam Square; tel: 0-2251-0797 (Skytrain: Siam), about triple the rate in less pricey watering holes.

In the Amari Watergate Hotel's **Henry J. Bean's Bar and Grill**, 847 Petchburi Rd, tel: 0-2653-9000, live bands perform in a more relaxed atmosphere, and during happy hour you get two drinks for the price of one. The Henry J. Bean outlet at the **Amari Airport Hotel**, tel: 0-2566-1020, has a similar set-up with live music from Thursday to Saturday and a happy hour.

Irish pubs like **Shenanigans** and **O'Reilly's** (see p. 95), but not Bobby's Arms, have live bands most nights. They all have happy hours when the cost of a beer becomes more bearable.

The large **Saxophone Pub**, at the top of Phayathai Road near Victory Monument, tel: 0-2246-5472, has a longer history than most popular bars in the city. The music is mostly jazz, R&B, blues and reggae. There is no cover charge. A pool table is on one of the three floors, and beer is more reasonably priced than in any of the other bars mentioned. One of the newest hot spots is **Gullivers**, 6 Soi 5 Sukhumvit Rd; tel: 0-2655-5340 (Skytrain: Nana), a slightly upscale cousin to the original on Khao San Rd. Beer, pool tables, food, and air con inside, but the soi-side tables offer a better view.

SELLING SEX

There are three main haunts for sex tourists of which only Patpong has become a tourist attraction in its own right.

The area around *sois* 21 and 23 off Sukhumvit Road is known as Soi Cowboy, described by one tourist publication as offering a more 'authentic environment than Patpong'.

The third area is down Soi 4 off the same road, in and around Nana Plaza, a favourite hang-out for expatriate males and not so well known to visitors.

Prostitution is endemic in Thailand, and was so long before the war in Vietnam led to American soldiers fuelling the sex industry. Many young country girls are sold into prostitution by their poor families and work as little more than sex slaves for their 'owners'.

If you want to observe the rampant sleaze of Soi Cowboy territory then head for the enclave provided by **The Old Dutch**, Soi 23, Sukhumvit Rd (Skytrain: Asok). Dark stained wood gives this pub and restaurant a reassuring air (the profiteroles have been recommended), without blocking views of the busy soi.

THAILAND

For some of the best jazz in the city it is still hard to beat **Brown Sugar**, 231/20 Soi Sarasin, tel: 0-2250-1826 (Skytrain: Ratchadamri), on the north side of Lumpini Park. Drinks are expensive but the atmosphere is just right and the music ain't bad. If you prefer rock music, pop around the corner to **Round Midnight,** 106/2 Soi Langsuan.

KHAO SAN RD This is a good place to meet fellow travellers and feel cool about being in Bangkok. Lots of bars show up-to-date video films from early afternoon onwards. This is also the place to catch a live English premiership soccer game, get your hair plaited and find the cheapest rates for internet connection. There are a few massage places and reflexology clinics peppered about the place. Trok Mayom, the lane running parallel to the south of Khao San Rd, has some pleasant little cafés, bars and hairdressers along a pedestrianised section of the road.

THAI BOXING

Watching Thai boxing live is a million times more enjoyable than on television, not least because as a real spectator you have the opportunity to be part of the audience. Often the antics of the crowd are much more entertaining than the performance in the ring, and when a lot of money is riding on a bout the temperature rises accordingly.

It is easy to get tickets and there is no need to go through an agent or a tout. Mon, Wed, Thur and Sun, turn up at the **Ratchadamnoen Stadium**, Ratchadamnoen North Rd; tel: 0-2281-4205. Bus no. 3 from Ratchadamnoen Klang near Khao San Rd runs past the stadium. On Tues, Fri and Sat evenings the venue is the **Lumpini Stadium**, Rama IV Rd; tel: 0-2251-4303.

The boxing starts around 1800, sometimes an hour earlier, and it is just a matter of turning up and buying a ticket from one of the windows. Tickets start at around 200B and climb to over 800B for front row seats. The less expensive tickets are just as worthwhile in terms of audience participation.

THAI DANCE Some restaurants, like the Salathip (p. 94) and Supatra River House (p. 94), feature sessions of Thai dancing as part of the evening's entertainment. The best place to watch traditional Thai dance is the **National Theatre**, Chao Fa Rd, tel: 0-2221-0174 (River Express: Phra Athit), which shows full-length performances as well as more tourist-oriented programmes. Two other theatres worth phoning for their programmes are the **Chalermkrung Royal Theatre**, 66 Charoen Krung Rd, tel: 0-2222-0434, and the **Thailand Cultural Centre**, Ratchadapisek Rd; tel: 0-2247-0028. At the **Erawan Shrine** (p. 89) grateful worshippers constantly sponsor short performances of Thai dance with live music.

THAI MASSAGE

Thai massage, *real* Thai massage, is a treat not to be missed. Developed as a medical discipline, traditional massage combines kneading, stretching and twisting that sends clouds of endorphins racing through the body in a haze of pleasure that may be the most blissful experience you can have this side of nirvana – massage junkies liken it to yoga without the effort.

The problem is that many massage parlours practise more sex than massage. The difference is in the name. If it just says 'massage', sex is on the menu. If it says 'traditional massage' or 'ancient massage', massage is all you get. If the word *spa* is in the name, expect spa treatments, not Thai massage.

Massage parlours are usually large open rooms with hard mattresses on the floor that can be separated by curtains. Most traditional massages start with a foot bath, then the massagee takes off his or her outer clothing and puts on loose pajama-like pants and top. Underwear generally stays on, though it's a good idea to remove your bra to prevent chaffing. Massages come in one- or two-hour increments for around 250B per hour, plus a 20–50B tip. Two hours is far more relaxing than one.

The best masseuses and masseurs are trained at the College of Traditional Thai Medicine at **Wat Po** (see p. 86) or a similar institution in Chiang Mai. Students give the cheapest and some of the best massages around, but there is neither privacy nor air-con. **Buathip Traditional Thai Massage**, 4/1-2 Soi 5 Sukhumvit Rd; tel: 0-2251-2627 (Skytrain: Nana), and **Suk Sawasdee Traditional Thai Massage**, 15 Soi 33/1 Sukhumvit Rd; tel: 2258-5035 (Skytrain: Phrom Phong), offer the best of Wat Po plus air con and a calmer atmosphere.

EXCURSIONS FROM BANGKOK

Good ideas for day trips from Bangkok, with the option of an overnight stay, include a visit to the **Damnoen Saduak floating markets**. This requires an early morning 2-hr bus ride from Bangkok (see p. 109). Easier to reach, and return from, is the town of **Nakhon Pathom** and its famous *chedi* (see p. 108), connected to Bangkok by bus and train. Nakhon Pathom is 60 km north of the floating markets and the two places could be taken in on one excursion with an overnight stay, preferably at Damnoen Saduak.

The most popular day trips from Bangkok are to **Ayutthaya** (see p. 146) and **Kanchanaburi** and the **Bridge on the River Kwai** (see pp. 109–110). Both Ayutthaya and Kanchanaburi have inexpensive guesthouses as well as hotels, and an overnight stay is well worth considering, especially if you want a break from Bangkok.

WHERE NEXT?

Visit the wats of Phetchaburi (see p. 212), 40 km to the south. You could take in Nakhon Pathom on the way, stop at the seaside resort of Cha-am (see p. 213) and continue on the route to Chumphon (see pp. 218–219).

BANGKOK — NAM TOK

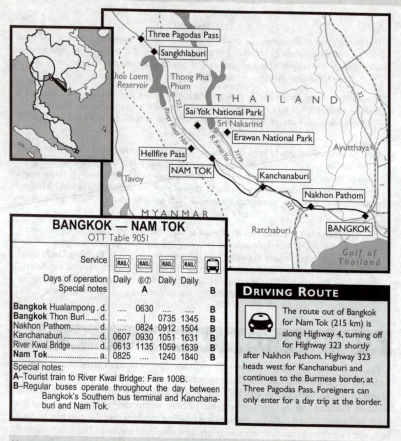

BANGKOK — NAM TOK
OTT Table 9051

Service	🚃 RAIL	🚃 RAIL	🚃 RAIL	🚃 RAIL	🚌
Days of operation	Daily	⑥⑦	Daily	Daily	
Special notes		A			B
Bangkok Hualampong . d.	....	0630	....	....	B
Bangkok Thon Buri .... d.	....	|	0735	1345	B
Nakhon Pathom.............. d.	....	0824	0912	1504	B
Kanchanaburi .... d.	0607	0930	1051	1631	B
River Kwai Bridge .... d.	0613	1135	1059	1639	B
Nam Tok...................... a.	0825	....	1240	1840	B

Special notes:
A–Tourist train to River Kwai Bridge: Fare 100B.
B–Regular buses operate throughout the day between
   Bangkok's Southern bus terminal and Kanchana-
   buri and Nam Tok.

DRIVING ROUTE

The route out of Bangkok for Nam Tok (215 km) is along Highway 4, turning off for Highway 323 shortly after Nakhon Pathom. Highway 323 heads west for Kanchanaburi and continues to the Burmese border, at Three Pagodas Pass. Foreigners can only enter for a day trip at the border.

NOTES
Train
Trains between Bangkok and Kanchanaburi cannot be booked in advance in either direction. On Saturday, Sunday and public holidays there is a special tourist train at 0630 from Bangkok's Hualamphong station for Nam Tok, stopping at Nakhon Pathom and Kanchanaburi. Unlike the trains from Bangkok Thon Buri, this journey can be booked in advance.
Bus
For Nakhon Pathom and Kanchanaburi (leaving from Bangkok's Southern Bus Terminal), be sure to board a non-stop bus or your journey will be considerably lengthened by stops along the way. From Khao San Rd in Bangkok it is possible to book a dedicated minibus service to and from Kanchanaburi. It costs more and may be crowded but it saves the hassle of getting out to the Southern Bus Terminal.

WESTERN THAILAND

Western Thailand stretches to the border with Myanmar (Burma), a route which during World War II attracted the Japanese who planned an invasion of India through Burma. They began building a railway line between Kanchanaburi and the Burmese border, using slave labour and prisoners of war captured after the fall of Singapore. The legacy of this painful period in history draws a large number of visitors but it is not the only reason for considering a journey westwards from Bangkok. The town of Kanchanaburi, despite having no beaches, is gradually acquiring a reputation as a relaxed place to hang out.

The territory beyond Kanchanaburi used to be Thailand's Wild West, dangerous to travel through because of various groups of insurgents operating in the region. But in the last 20 years this has all changed and the risk factor today is zero. This accounts for the growing popularity of the region with Thais and overseas Asians who are attracted to the rugged beauty of the forest-clad mountains that form the borderland with Burma. Population density in this part of Thailand is the lowest in the country, farming follows traditional methods and there is no industrialisation or pollution.

TEMPLE ARCHITECTURE

The walled compound of a temple is called a **wat**. Often two walls form a cloistered area where monks have their quarters. In larger temples this may be decorated with Buddhist images and serve as a meditation area for monks.

The inner courtyard area contains the **bot**, also called the *uposatha* or *ubosoth*, a square-like building with sloping tiled roofs. This is a holy area where monastic ordinations take place. There is also likely to be a **viharn**, a building which often looks like a bot and serves as a home for Buddhist relics. Traditionally both the bot and viharn should face water, emulating the position of the Buddha who sat facing water under the bodhi tree whilst achieving enlightenment.

The most conspicuous of the other structures found within a temple is the **chedi**, or **stupa**, recognisable by its typical bell-like shape but subject to a variety of forms in different parts of the country. The chedi is often thought to contain some relic, in the form of a bone, of the Buddha himself.

To make the most of western Thailand beyond Kanchanaburi, it helps to have your own transport. The use of a car or motorbike will overcome problems caused by gaps in the public transport system. Trains and buses all stop at the town of Nakhon Pathom, and if you arrive in the morning it is worth stopping off to visit the notable *chedi*. But there is nothing else to see and an overnight stay is unnecessary unless you are planning an early morning trip to the floating markets at Damnoen Saduak.

NAKHON PATHOM

It is hard to miss seeing Nakhon Pathom's claim to fame – the shining, gold and ochre, bowl-shaped **Phra Pathom Chedi**. A Buddhist shrine was first built on the site in the early 6th century but it was destroyed in warfare in the 11th century. Building work on the present *chedi*, enveloping the ruins of the ancient shrine, did not begin until 1853, and even though it took 17 years of building to complete the structure there has been more than one rebuilding programme since then. Its height is variously given as 120 m and 127 m, and a bot and other structures have been added to the complex.

An 8-m-high Buddha greets visitors approaching the *chedi* from the main entrance's stone staircase. As you walk around the *chedi* you encounter four *viharns* situated at the four points of the compass. Murals, Buddha figures and a model of the original *chedi* are found inside. Wandering around outside can be a peaceful experience in itself.

There are two **museums** on the site. The one most worthy of the name is on the south side of the chedi, $, open Wed–Sun 0900–1200 and 1300–1600. Inside, there is a fair collection of Buddhist statues and artefacts. The other museum, near the east *viharn*, contains a motley assortment of undistinguished finds.

ORIENTATION The railway and bus stations are close to each other and luggage can be safely left at the railway station. It is a short walk from the stations to the single but singular place of interest, Phra Pathom Chedi.

ACCOMMODATION AND EATING If you do plan to spend a night in Nakhon Pathom – and it only makes sense if making an early morning visit the next day to the Damnoen Saduak floating markets – then head for Rachwithi Rd, which begins south-west of the *chedi*. Along this road there are two good hotels, which also offer the most comfortable environment for a meal:
Nakhon Inn $$$–$$$$ Soi 3, Rachwithi Rd, tel: 0-3425-1152, offers the best accommodation in town.
Whale Hotel $$$ 151/79 Rachwithi Rd, tel: 0-3425-1020, has lots of facilities but less character than the Nakhon Inn.
Mitrsampant Hotel $$ 2/11 Lang Phra Rd, tel: 0-3424-1422. A quiet budget place, best reached by taking Ratchadamnoen Rd, which starts at the west side of the *chedi*, and turning right into Lang Phra Rd after about 50 m.

For an inexpensive meal before getting back on a train or bus the **fruit market** is conveniently situated between the railway station and the *chedi*, on your right when walking due south from the station.

FLOATING MARKETS – AN EXCURSION

About 60 km south of Nakhon Pathom are the **floating markets** of **Damnoen Saduak**, a series of canals laden with boats from which women sell their fruit and vegetables each day between 0600 and 1100. Tourist touts will try to insist that you join one of their motorised boat tours and this is the way most visitors experience the market. But it is just as much fun to wander up and down the narrow walkways and take in the bustling scene as it unfolds. The commercial impact of tourism on these markets is inescapable, and if any place in Thailand could serve as an attraction for the post-tourist then this would be it.

This is a popular day trip for tour groups from Bangkok, but their buses do not usually arrive until about 0900 and it is easy to arrive earlier by taking a public bus from Nakhon Pathom. If you are staying on Rachwithi Road you can pick up a bus here without having to go to the bus station. To get there under your own steam from Bangkok, get to the Southern Bus Terminal as close to 0600 as possible and catch bus no. 78 to Damnoen Saduak. From the bridge near the bus terminal it is a 15-min walk along the canal to the floating market, but arrive in style by taking one of the cheap water taxis from the pier at the bridge.

The best way to experience the markets from dawn onwards is to spend the night in Damnoen Saduak. A convenient little hotel, **Little Bird Hotel $–$$** tel: 0-3225-4382 or 0-3224-1315, is signposted from the bridge near where the bus stops.

KANCHANABURI

Kanchanaburi receives bus- and train-loads of tourists every day, but the vast majority are just passing through and once they have 'done' the **Bridge over the River Kwai** they're off again. The bridge – its iconic status makes it one of the more photographed sites in Thailand – is especially popular with Asian tourists, while an increasing number of Western visitors are discovering Kanchanaburi as a relaxing destination for a couple of nights' stay in its own right.

Apart from the bridge itself, the main places of interest are the war museums and the war cemeteries. The older of the two war museums, the **JEATH War Museum ($)** open daily 0830–1630, tel: 0-3451-5203, is by the Mae Klong River at the bottom of Wisuttarangsi Road. JEATH is an acronym for six of the countries involved: Japan, England, America and Australia, Thailand and Holland. The museum building is a reconstructed *atap* (woven palm thatch) and bamboo hut of the type lived in by the POWs which houses a small collection of old photographs and drawings. As museums go, it is not particularly special, but it is a far more heartfelt homage to the past than the newer **World War II Museum ($)** near the bridge itself, open daily 0900–1800, tel: 0-3451-2556. The section devoted to the war contains an assorted collection of memorabilia but most of the museum is glossy, tacky and uninspiring.

The **Bridge on the River Kwai** is just over 3 km north of Kanchanaburi and if you stay on the train for Nam Tok you will actually travel across it. You can reach the bridge by hopping on the Nam Tok train at Kanchanaburi or by catching a *songthaew* on Saeng Chuto Road.

The original bridge, the wooden one constructed by prisoners and forced labourers, was completed early in 1943 and a second bridge, built of steel, was added a few months later. Allied bombers attacked the bridges and the one you see today was rebuilt after the war, using parts of the original structure that survived the bombing. The bridge you see today has become a premier attraction for sightseers of all nationalities and the tourist razzmatazz of the place may put you off. For a more authentic insight into the history of the railway, a visit to the town's war museum and cemeteries is worthwhile, and for a very moving and informative introduction to what took place a trip to the Hellfire Pass Memorial Museum is highly recommended.

There are two war cemeteries. The one in town is the **Kanchanaburi Allied War Cemetery**, also known as Don Rak. It is off Saeng Chuto Road, not far from the railway station, and reachable on foot or by any *songthaew* heading in that direction along Saeng Chuto Road. The other cemetery, **Chungkai**, is across the river and best visited as part of a bicycle ride (see p. 114).

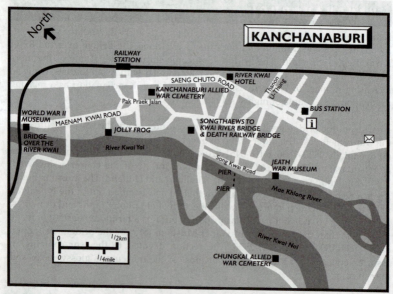

KANCHANABURI

North

RAILWAY
STATION

RIVER KWAI
HOTEL

SAENG CHUTO ROAD

KANCHANABURI ALLIED
WAR CEMETERY

Pak Praek Jalan

Thanon U-Thong

BUS STATION

WORLD WAR II
MUSEUM

MAENAM KWAI ROAD

SONGTHAEWS TO
KWAI RIVER BRIDGE
& DEATH RAILWAY BRIDGE

BRIDGE
OVER THE
RIVER KWAI

JOLLY FROG

River Kwai Yai

Song Kwai Road

PIER

PIER

JEATH
WAR MUSEUM

Mae Khlong River

River Kwai Noi

CHUNGKAI ALLIED
WAR CEMETERY

0   1/2km
0   1/4mile

ORIENTATION Kanchanaburi is not a large town and it is possible to get around most places on foot, but this will soon prove exhausting in the heat. There are two main areas for travellers where you will find accommodation, restaurants, internet cafés, tour agents and places to rent bicycles and motorbikes.

One area, around the River Kwai Hotel on Saeng Chuto Rd, is very central and on the same road as the train and bus stations. Banks are mostly found on and around this road and here too, at the Bangkok end of the road, you will find the tourist office and post office. *Songthaews* run along Saeng Chuto Rd, passing the war cemetery and heading towards the river and the bridge along Maenam Kwai Rd.

FICTION AND NON-FICTION

The Frenchman Pierre Boulle, who made the bridge at Kanchanaburi so famous, was never there himself. This helps to explain his mistake in thinking this part of the Mae Klong River was the River Kwai in the first place. The name has stuck, however, and is now officially called the Kwai Yai River. (This is to distinguish it from the Kwai Noi, the actual river which the main part of the railway line followed and which the Kwai Yai joins just west of Kanchanaburi.) If you want to see the film of the book, drop by the No Name bar (see p. 113), where it is shown most evenings.

Boulle's book, *The Bridge on the River Kwai*, tells the fictional story of Colonel Nicholson and his men who were ordered to build the bridge. Another book worth bringing with you if visiting Kanchanaburi is *The Railway Man* by Eric Lomax. This tells the true and heart-rending story of how Eric Lomax survived two years of torture and distress after being caught with an illicit radio while working on the railway. He never forgot the voice and face of his interrogator and half a century later discovers the man is still alive.

The other area that is fast developing a modest tourist infrastructure is along Maenam Kwai Rd down by the riverside. Accommodation and restaurants are geared towards budget travellers, bikes can be hired, tours arranged, e-mails collected and travel news exchanged in the guesthouses and bars.

Arriving at Kanchanaburi bus or train station you are likely to be accosted by an armada of *tuk-tuks* and *samlors* all willing to take you to a guesthouse for a low fare. The commission they get from the guesthouse owner will be added to the cost of your room so it is worth insisting on a regular fare to the guesthouse of your choice.

TRAIN AND BUS The **railway station** is a couple of kilometres from the centre of town on the main Saeng Chuto Rd. Turn left to walk towards the town centre or take one of the *songthaews* that ply their way up and down the road. The **bus station** is on Saeng Chuto Rd but closer to the town centre. Hotels are centrally located while the budget guesthouses are mostly close to the river, within walking distance of the train station but a little further from the bus station.

THE DEATH RAILWAY

The railway line was laid down during World War II by forced labour and prisoners of war under the control of the Japanese. Creating a rail link between Burma and Japan was considered essential because it would avoid the risk of travelling by sea, but a 415 km stretch between Burma and Kanchanaburi had to be built completely from scratch. Japanese engineers calculated it would take five years to complete the line: the fact that it was completed by the end of 1943 gives some idea of the forced pace.

The route chosen followed the river valley of the Kwai Noi, and, starting in 1942, some 60,000 Allied POWs worked on the line. Around 20% died as a direct result of the harsh conditions. Food rations were insufficient for the back-breaking work, medical facilities were horrendously inadequate and the treatment of prisoners was often brutal. Around 80,000 civilian labourers are also thought to have died before the railway line was finished in late 1943.

i The **TAT Office** is at the Bangkok end of Saeng Chuto Rd, tel: 0-3451-1200, open daily 0830–1630. Here you can get a free town map, information on places to stay and useful advice on transport. The **Tourist Police**, tel: 0-3451-2795, also operate from the tourist office.

River Kwai Hotel $$$ Saeng Chuto Rd, tel: 0-3451-3348, fax: 0-3451-1269. OK, it's not by the river but it does offer the most comfortable accommodation in town and there is a small swimming pool.

River Inn $$ Saeng Chuto Rd, tel: 0-3462-1056, is directly in front of the River Kwai Hotel and although a little past its sell-by date, this centrally located place has affordable rooms with air-conditioning.

VL Guesthouse $ Saeng Chuto Rd, tel: 0-3451-3546, has clean, tidy rooms with fan and telephone.

Nita Raft House $ 27/1 Pak Phraek Rd, tel: 0-3451-4521. One of the least expensive riverside guesthouses, close to the JEATH war museum but definitely not in the quietest part of town. At weekends, especially, the racket from nearby raft discos will keep you awake, but then the rooms are very cheap.

Further up the river, around Maenam Kwai Rd, there is a better choice of accommodation.

Sugar Cane Guest House $ 22 Soi Pakistan, off Maenam Kwai Rd, tel: 0-3462-4520 One of my favourite places, Sugar Cane is small and friendly and enjoys great views of the river. Bike hire and competitively priced tours can be arranged here.

Jolly Frog Backpackers $ 28 Soi China, off Maenam Kwai Rd, tel: 0-3451-4579. A well-known and relatively large guesthouse with a range of bamboo huts close to the river.

⊤◎ **River Inn $–$$** Saeng Chuto Rd has very good value meals, like noodle soup with duck for 30B. There are plenty of other inexpensive restaurants along this stretch of the main road.

Punnee Café $–$$ Ban Neura Rd, tel: 0-3451-3503. Cornflakes, muesli, toast and marmalade, and a host of Western and Thai meals feature on the menu of this expatriate-run restaurant. It is a good source of information, and bicycles and motorbikes can be rented here and tours arranged. Next door is a useful second-hand bookshop with an exchange service.

Sabaijit Restaurant $ Saeng Chuto Rd. A short way past the River Kwai Hotel there is a cardboard sign in English announcing the inexpensive, clean restaurant, directly opposite the conspicuous Apache Bar. It has large fans and an extensive menu in English.

By the river, places to eat can be found along Maenam Kwai Rd and all the guesthouses have affordable restaurants.

ENTERTAINMENT A few bars are beginning to spring up along Maenam Kwai Rd near the riverside, and the area has all the signs of developing into the town's hip ghetto for travellers. Look out for **No Name** bar, where you can expect a warm welcome, Aussie style. Open during the evenings for beers, cocktails and snacks, there is a snooker table and photos of inebriated travellers litter one of the walls.

THAILAND

TOURS AND TRIPS It is possible to see some of the sights around and beyond Kanchanaburi on your own, but public transport is limited and without your own wheels it may be worth considering an organised tour through a Kanchanaburi company.

A BICYCLE RIDE

Bicycles are easily hired in Kanchanaburi and they open up some of the sights on the other side of the Kwai Noi. There are two ways of fording the river: either by ferry (which takes bicycles) from Song Kwai Rd, or over the bridge further north up the road. Once over the river, stay on the main road for a little over 2 km and you will come to the **Chungkai war cemetery**. The graves occupy the site of a former POW camp and, like the cemetery in town, there is a quiet dignity about the place that belies the manner in which these men suffered and died.

Stay on the main road and you will encounter the ostentatious cave temple, **Wat Tham Khao Poon**. Fairy lights guide the way through the cave and past a hotchpotch of gaudy images before arriving at the central Buddha figure surrounded by flashing lights. It is all fairly bizarre but anyone prone to claustrophobia will not appreciate the confined space of the cave interior.

Westours, 21 Tha Makhan Rd and Song Kwai Rd; tel: 0-3451-3654 or 0-3451-3655, is typical of the longer-established and more reliable companies offering a variety of tours. These include popular one-day trips that cover various activities involving an elephant ride, bamboo rafting, visits to a waterfall and Hellfire Pass, and a hot spa. Prices range between 600B and 950B, and include the train ride between Kanchanaburi and Nam Tok, and lunch. Other one-day trips include the floating market at Damnoen Saduak and the Erawan waterfalls, as well as longer hiking trips.

There are quite a few tour companies in Kanchanaburi offering similar trips to Westours. Because a minimum of four persons is often needed, it is well worth shopping around to find a trip that suits you that is actually going to take place.

Other companies to try include **BT Travel Centre**, tel: 0-3462-4630, and **AS Mixed Travel**, tel: 0-3451-4958 or 0-3451-2017. The owner of the **Punnee Café** in Neura Road, tel: 0-3451-3053, is also worth checking out for a variety of tours, especially war-related trips and adventure rafting.

SEVEN WATERFALLS

Erawan National Park is about the same size as Sai Yok (see p. 117) but the waterfalls here are more impressive and enjoy a premier status amongst nature-loving Thais. The acclaim is not unwarranted because the seven falls, spread over 1500 m, are a beautiful sight and ideal for a splash and a swim, but avoid weekends and holidays if you want to enjoy them all to yourself. There is only one walking trail within the park which leads to the waterfalls, and if you want to reach the higher levels you need decent footwear, not just sandals or flip-flops.

Buses for Erawan depart Kanchanaburi on a daily basis: the journey takes a couple of hours so start early if returning the same day, because the last bus back leaves Erawan at 1600. During peak periods, especially between November and January, minibuses for Erawan depart daily from Kanchanaburi and will collect passengers from the riverside guesthouses.

NAM TOK

The train ride between Kanchanaburi and Nam Tok, at the end of the line, is both dramatic and historical. It begins by crossing the famous girdered bridge on the River Kwai and continues for well over an hour through rural landscapes with knobbly mountains in the background. The train uses the line that was built by the POWs and Asian slave labourers and there is more than one reminder of just how backbreaking their work must have been. At one point the train chugs through an incredibly narrow cutting in the solid rock and a little further on it gingerly makes its way over a trestle bridge that looks as if it could have been built 60 years ago.

The station at Nam Tok, whose name literally means waterfall, was not the original station. The present station is situated at the village of Thasao but the station originally lay 1 km further along the line at a waterfall. It was moved to its present location because part of the line was damaged by heavy rains.

There is nothing to do or see in Nam Tok itself; it is merely the end of the line. Visitors either return to Kanchanaburi – the same train begins the return journey after 10 minutes – or travel on to either the museum and Hellfire Pass or the Sai Yok National Park. Some make the scenic journey to the Burmese border.

HELLFIRE MEMORIAL MUSEUM

The memory of those who died working on the Japanese railway line is preserved at the **Hellfire Memorial Museum**, free admission, tel: (01) 754-2098, open daily 0900–1600, 18 km from Nam Tok station. If you walk 500 m from the station through the village of Thasao and onto the main road, Route 323, you can catch an orange-coloured bus to the museum. Apart from arriving on a tour, you could also hire a motorbike in Kanchanaburi or take a *songthaew* from Nam Tok.

The museum has various exhibits, archive photographs and a 7-min video that tells the story of the railway line using war footage and testimonies from prisoners who survived the ordeal.

Two paths, a concrete stairway and a path through a bamboo forest, lead the way to **Hellfire Pass**, only 250 m from the museum entrance. Take the forest path because this follows the route that POWs took and also offers a memorable view looking down on the narrow channel cut through the solid limestone and quartz.

From the Pass there is a 4-km walking trail that follows the line laid down by the POWs. It passes a vantage-point from where the prisoners could view the whole valley and the various sections where prisoners worked like ants digging and shifting the soil with primitive tools. In places it is still possible to see the mounting bolts for the timber beams and the embankments that were constructed. The trail also passes the site of the Pack of Cards Bridge, named by the prisoners because it was such a precarious structure and collapsed on them more than once.

HELLFIRE PASS

One of the largest cuttings that had to be made through solid rock during the construction of the railway line has come to be known as Hellfire Pass. A crew of 400 Australian POWs began the work in April 1943, supplemented by British, Tamil and Malay groups. The men worked for up to 18 hrs a day, digging the 17-m-deep and 110-m-long cutting in only 12 weeks. They nicknamed it the Hellfire Pass because of the eerie lighting effects created at night by the carbide lamps, bamboo torches burning oil and the open fires that illuminated the construction site. Nearly three-quarters of the men who built this pass died in the undertaking.

DEATH TOURISM

The rail journey between Kanchanaburi and Nam Tok, with its camera-toting tour groups charging on and off the train for a short hop before rejoining their coaches, is the closest you will get in Thailand to the unpalatable phenomenon of 'black spot tourism', or 'death tourism'. These attractions – the sites of mass killings or deaths of celebrities – include Auschwitz, the highway junction in California where James Dean was killed, and the Paris underpass where Diana, Princess of Wales, died.

SAI YOK NATIONAL PARK A few miles further up Highway 323 is the start of the 500 sq km Sai Yok National Park, which stretches as far as the Burmese border. Its main attractions are the Sai Yok Yai waterfall, limestone caves, and short walking trails that begin from outside the visitor centre. The chilling scene in *The Deer Hunter* involving a game of Russian roulette was filmed here.

Tour companies in Kanchanaburi organise visits to the park and use a stretch of the river here for rafting trips (see p. 114). Alternatively, take a bus in Kanchanaburi going to Thong Pha Phum and ask to be dropped off at the park entrance. From here it is a 3-km walk to the visitor centre. There are also direct buses from Kanchanaburi.

Accommodation in the park is available in Forestry Department bungalows, most suitable for small groups, and in floating guesthouses by the river.

🛏 **Pung-Waan Resort $$$$$** Thasao (Nam Tok), tel: 0-3459-1017, fax: 0-3459-1017, e-mail: pungwaan@samart.co.th. There are a surprising number of resorts tucked close to the banks of the River Kwai Noi, around Nam Tok. Pung-Waan enjoys one of the most tranquil settings, with waterside rooms with balconies, a pool and restaurants.
Kitti Raft $$ tel: (034) 591-106. Pleasant floating rooms with bathrooms. You could walk here from Nam Tok station but it's worth calling for a pick-up.
Saiyok View Raft $$ tel: 0-3451-4194. The nicest place in the park and good value as rooms have air-con and bathrooms. At weekends rooms are often at a premium. Other places to try include **Kwai Noi Rafthouses** and **Ranthawee Raft**.

🍽 All of the places above have their own small restaurants and there are lots of food stalls near the visitor centre.

THE BURMESE BORDER Beyond Nam Tok, Highway 323 continues all the way to the **Burmese border** at Three Pagodas Pass, reaching the market town of Thong Pha Phum after 30 km. The last town on Highway 323 is actually Sangkhlaburi and a couple of miles before it a road branches off for the 20-km trip to Three Pagodas Pass. To be truthful, there is precious little to see or occupy one's time at Three Pagodas Pass and seeing the pagodas themselves is certainly not worth the journey but, as is the case with many terminal points, it is the journey itself that provides the justification for going there. An overnight stay is required and **Sangkhlaburi**, 200 km from Kanchanaburi, is the place to head for in this respect.

THAILAND

The dramatic scenery on the route is the highlight of the journey, especially along the 70-km stretch between Thong Pha Phum and Sangkhlaburi. The road skirts the huge Khao Laem reservoir and opens up an alien landscape of submerged trees with forested mountains gathered in the background.

The human landscape, made up of a mix of Thai, Karen and Mon people, is also an attraction, and there are a number of Mon refugee camps around Sangkhlaburi. The Mon straddle the Burmese-Thai borderlands and for long have been the victims of persecution directed by the Myanmar military regime. A stopover in Sangkhlaburi is recommended because it provides an opportunity to wander around the town's morning market where you are more likely to hear Burmese being spoken than Thai. There is also an elongated wooden bridge that leads across the lake to a visitor-friendly **Mon settlement**.

Sangkhlaburi has some reasonable accommodation, and some of the guesthouses can arrange day trips into the surrounding countryside with elephant ride and rafting options.

BUSES There are daily buses between Kanchanaburi and Sangkhlaburi, including some air-conditioned vehicles, with the journey taking anything from 4 to 6 hrs. The speediest way to reach Sangkhlaburi is by a 3-hr minibus ride from Kanchanaburi. The minibuses travel fast and stops are infrequent. It is best to reserve your seat the day before travel because they often fill up, especially the morning ones from Kanchanaburi. Non-air-conditioned buses for Sangkhlaburi can also be picked up in Nam Tok. To reach Three Pagodas Pass you need to hop on a *songthaew* in Sangkhlaburi. They run regularly throughout the day, but bear in mind that the last one back to town departs around 1800. Confirm the time when you arrive.

🛏 **Somjaineuk Hotel $–$$$** Thong Pha Phum, tel: 0-3459-9067. Centrally located, this hotel has two wings: an older quarter with fans and a new wing with air-con, showers, and a degree of comfort.
Burmese Inn $–$$ Sangkhlaburi, tel/fax: 0-3459-5146. Not far from the wooden bridge to the Mon settlement, less than 1 km from the bus station, with a variety of rooms. The English-speaking proprietors know the local area well and can advise and arrange tours into the countryside.
P Guest House $–$$ Sangkhlaburi, tel: 0-3459-5061, fax: 0-3459-5139. Another well-run operation with a variety of rooms in a scenic location overlooking the lake. Tours can also be arranged and bicycles and motorbikes hired.

Three Pagodas Pass Resort $$$ Three Pagodas Pass, tel: 0-3459-5316. The only place to stay here. The wooden bungalows are pleasant enough and a very good room rate can sometimes be negotiated.

EATING There is nothing wrong with the food at either of the Sangkhlaburi guest-houses, although the restaurant at the **P Guest House** $-$$ has a more attractive setting. In Sangkhlaburi itself the air-conditioned restaurant at the **Phornphalin Hotel** $-$$ is not bad, and there are a few inexpensive restaurants down the same street.

DAY TRIP TO BURMA

Until quite recently it was not possible for foreigners to cross into Burma. This was a sensible precaution on the part of the Thai authorities at a time when the Burmese military were engaged in fighting with Mon and Karen rebels very close to the border. The rebels are no longer trying to capture the Burmese side of the border and, unless the situation changes dramatically (which it can do, so always check before making any plans), it is now quite safe to venture across.

At Three Pagodas Pass it is possible to cross the border and enter the Burmese village of Payathonzu (literally, three pagodas) for a payment of US$5 or the baht equivalent. Payathonzu is hardly a village and more an excuse to set up stalls and indulge in a spot of cross-border shopping. There are places to eat and a varied selection of Burmese handicrafts and fabrics on sale, as well as Burmese face powder, inexpensive jewellery, and cheroot cigars. Bargaining is usual and no one expects you to pay the first asking price.

WHERE NEXT?

Head north-east to Suphan Buri to visit Don Chedi, a huge stupa erected to celebrate King Naresuan's victory over the Burmese in 1582. The annual Don Chedi Fair takes place here on 23–31 January. From here you can continue eastwards to Ayutthaya (pp. 146–149) and then head north to Phitsanulok and Chiang Mai (pp. 150–154).

RELIGION

RELIGION

BUDDHISM

Buddhism is the main religion of Thailand and one of the main religions of the Chinese in Malaysia and Singapore. Well over 90% of Thais follow Theravada Buddhism, introduced from Sri Lanka (Ceylon) in the 13th century. It is not nearly so metaphysical as the popular stereotype portrays it and your average Thai is not going about on a daily basis seeking some ultimate, transcendental state of being. Good acts are practised and bad ones avoided in order to increase the odds of a decent life in the next world. Good *karma* (deed or act) means a better life in the next world but it is not governed by fate and people act with free will.

Every village community has its *wat*, a cross between a temple and a monastery. The number of monks attached to a *wat* can range from one or two to well over 500 in the case of a large and prestigious *wat*. Every young male Thai expects to spend some time as a monk, averaging a few months, which helps explain why there are nearly half a million monks in the country at any one time. Apart from the spiritual and social merit that accompanies this period of monkhood, for many Thais from poor, rural backgrounds a spell in a *wat* is an opportunity to gain an education beyond the primary level. This mixture of motives, and the impact of the modern world on traditional beliefs and practices, accounts for the occasional tales of sexual peccadilloes and other scandals associated with some monks. A little astray from the aim of seeking enlightenment, *nirvana*, where all desire is transcended . . .

ISLAM

Islam is the religion of Malays in Malaysia and Singapore as well as about 4% of Thailand's population. The Muslims of Thailand are nearly all to be found in the southern part of the country. Islam is based on the observance of five pillars: the creed, prayer, the giving of alms, the observance of fasting during Ramadan, and the endeavour to make a pilgrimage to Mecca. The religion includes a belief in angels and prophets as messengers of God. The Koran, the holy book of Islam, names Jesus as one of the prophets and the Gospels of the New Testament are viewed as prophetic revelations of God.

The influence of Islam is not keenly felt in the east Malaysian states of Sabah and Sarawak but in the rest of the country it is a potent force, political as well as social. In cities like Kuala Lumpur and Penang the religion does not have the same impact for visitors as it does on the east coast of peninsular Malaysia. In this area you will see Malay children learning Arabic in order to study the Koran in its original language. There is also a Malay religious language, Jawi, which is written in the Arabic script.

In Malaysia and Singapore, nearly every Malay is a Muslim and Indians in both countries may also be Muslim. The Muslim day of prayer is Friday and in every town across the country the mosques will be full and lunch hour is extended. Along the east coast, Friday operates like a traditional Sunday in the West and banks and other offices will be closed.

TAOISM

Taoism is the religion of the Chinese in Thailand, Malaysia and Singapore. Taoism, like Buddhism, shows the influence of earlier animist beliefs and practices. Taoism includes an element of ancestor worship and a form of animism lies behind the Taoist belief in *feng shui*. Worship takes place at a temple but most homes will also have a small altar display. Taoism is a very down-to-earth religion that concerns itself with the practical side of life. A person will go to a temple to pray for success in school exams or for luck at a forthcoming job interview.

There is a keen element of plain, old-fashioned superstition and particular gods are worshipped because of their association with specific professions or areas of life. Trying to divine the future can become a preoccupation in the search to avoid bad luck and fortune-tellers are often found around a temple complex.

HINDUISM

The majority of Indians in Malaysia and Singapore are Hindus. The Hindu religion shares with Buddhism a belief in reincarnation, both sets of adherents seeking a state of understanding that escapes the endless cycle of birth and death. There is the same notion of *karma*, a belief that what you do in this life will have consequences for a future existence. *Dharma* is the set of rules to be followed by those who seek to live a good life. Traditional Hinduism carries with it a caste system but this is not so observable in Malaysia or Singapore. When the British were keen to attract Indians to Malaya and Singapore they only wanted unskilled labourers to work on rubber plantations and the like. The result was that most Hindus who came were from the lower classes and caste never became an issue.

The multiform variety of Hindu gods is often baffling to monotheistic Westerners. The different gods are best viewed metaphorically, as manifestations of particular aspects of the one omnipresent god. The one central god has three main forms: Vishnu, Shiva and Brahma. All three are usually depicted as having four arms but Brahma, the creator, also has four heads.

TRADITIONAL RELIGION

Most of the ethnic groups living in Sarawak and Sabah practise forms of animism, also called traditional religion. Ancestor worship is another key characteristic of the religion of the Dyaks, the Ibans, the Bidayuh and the various smaller tribes that make up the population of east Malaysia. A factor that is having a negative effect on these traditional religions is the proselytizing activities of evangelical Christians. In peninsular Malaysia, such groups are kept firmly under control and would not dare to encroach on Muslim sensibilities but in east Malaysia it is a different story.

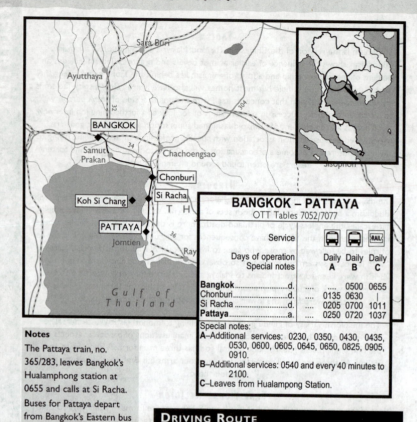

BANGKOK – PATTAYA
OTT Tables 7052/7077

Service				RAIL
Days of operation		Daily	Daily	Daily
Special notes		A	B	C
Bangkok..................d.	....	....	0500	0655
Chonburi...................d.	....	0135	0630	|
Si Racha ....d.	....	0205	0700	1011
Pattaya....................a.	....	0250	0720	1037

Special notes:
A–Additional services: 0230, 0350, 0430, 0435, 0530, 0600, 0605, 0645, 0650, 0825, 0905, 0910.
B–Additional services: 0540 and every 40 minutes to 2100.
C–Leaves from Hualamong Station.

Notes

The Pattaya train, no. 365/283, leaves Bangkok's Hualamphong station at 0655 and calls at Si Racha.

Buses for Pattaya depart from Bangkok's Eastern bus terminal, best reached by the skytrain. Ekkamai station is right outside the bus station.

There are no flights between Bangkok and Pattaya but Bangkok Airways do have a daily 1-hr service between Ko Samui and U-Tapao airport, which is a little under 30 km south of Pattaya.

DRIVING ROUTE

Highway 3, leading to Pattaya from the capital (147 km), is the continuation of Sukhumvit Rd in Bangkok, and is often still called Sukhumvit Rd as it weaves its way through towns along the east coast. Traffic is heavy from Bangkok until Samut Prakan; there is little scenery to admire along the way and the only place worth stopping at is Si Racha. If you are keen on exploring east Thailand by car it might be more worthwhile to hire a car in Pattaya. Avis, tel: 0-3836-1627, have an office at the Dusit Resort Hotel and there are plenty of smaller companies offering car hire.

EASTERN THAILAND

The eastern region of Thailand stretches over 400 km from Bangkok to the town of Trat close to the Cambodian border. The most popular destination remains the beach resort of Pattaya, first made famous during the Vietnam War when it served as a major getaway for American troops. When the soldiers left the resort evolved into a sleazy destination for mostly sex tourists. Now, as a result of the robust and partly successful attempts to improve this image, Pattaya enjoys a wider range of visitors than ever before.

Ko Samet, like Pattaya, is close enough to Bangkok to attract jaded city visitors during weekends and public holidays. Even on Ko Chang, further east and close to the Cambodian border, the atmosphere is very different at weekends and holiday periods. If you want a peaceful time, travel during the week and avoid public holidays.

SI RACHA

Nearly all travellers in Si Racha are passing through on their way to or from the offshore island of Ko Si Chang, but as small Thai towns go there is nothing wrong with spending a night here. Affordable and pleasant hotels and seafood restaurants are strung out attractively along the seafront, called Choemchomphon Rd, and there is a long causeway north of the ferry pier that leads out to an islet, Ko Loi, with a modern Thai-Chinese temple perched on it. As with Ko Si Chang, Si Racha receives its fair share of visitors from Bangkok at weekends and holidays, but during the week the place is invitingly relaxed and unhurried.

🛏 **Samchai $$$$** Soi 10, Choemchomphon Rd, tel: 0-3831-1134 has a choice of aircon rooms. **Srivichai $** Soi 8, Sukhumvit Rd, tel: 0-3831-1212, and the adjacent **Sri Wattana $** tel: 0-3831-1037 are equally good budget hotels but without air-con.

🍽 All the best restaurants are spaced out along the seafront. Current favourites can be judged by their number of customers. Prices $–$$ are competitive and what you pay has more to do with the kind of fish you choose than the actual restaurant. Whatever you eat, be sure to try the chilli-flavoured ketchup, *nam phrik Si Racha*. It is found all over Thailand but is made right here in Si Racha, and will most certainly be on your table.

KO SI CHANG

The first of Thailand's east coast islands, Ko Si Chang would have been quickly passed over as a possible location for *The Beach*. DiCaprio could hardly be seen cavorting on a rocky beach with cargo ships sulking in the offshore, not-quite-turquoise waters. Ko Si Chang has its own charms, though, and plenty of nooks and crannies to explore. The island has enough of a range of reasonable accommodation to make it worth considering as a lazy excursion from Bangkok, or as the first stop on a route that ends with the most easterly island of Ko Chang, near the Cambodian border.

A surfaced road rings the island and motorised *samlors* are easy to find for short trips (**$**) or for a leisurely tour of the island (**$$$**). The only beach with a decent bit of sand is **Hat Sai Kaew**, reached by taking the road south from Tiew Pai Guest House. You pass a Marine Research Centre before following a path west to the ruins of a summer palace built by Rama V at the end of the 19th century. The site was soon deserted, after trouble with the French who occupied the island, but what couldn't be dismantled and taken back to Bangkok was left to nature. Renovation work of sorts is going on, but visitors can wander at will amongst the frangipani-clad ruins. From here, a path heads south to the beach at Hat Sai Kaew.

Boats for Ko Si Chang depart from the pier at the end of Soi 14, Jermjophon Rd in Si Racha from early morning until 1700. The last return boat is at 1630. If you are planning to catch this, confirm whether it can be boarded at one or both of the island's piers.

Si Chang Palace $$$–$$$$ Atsadang Rd; tel: 0-3821-6276. A first-rate place, within walking distance of the piers, with a pool and rooms with superb sea views.

Tiew Pai Guest House $–$$ Atsadang Rd; tel: 0-3821-6084. The best-known guesthouse on the island, with a range of air-con and non-air-con rooms and a reasonable restaurant.

PATTAYA

American GIs looking for more than a suntan turned the name of what was a sleepy fishing village in the early 1960s into a synonym for sex holidays by the beach. The war in Vietnam came and went but the legacy for Pattaya remains the dense concentration of raunchy bars, discos and 'massage parlours' peopled by prostitutes and fuelled by planeloads of sad men from Europe and elsewhere.

Surprisingly, Pattaya also caters for families and regular tourists, and the result is a bizarre mix of the downright seedy and trappings of a conventional holiday resort. There are tattooists, gyms, countless stalls selling fake watches and other goods, and bars and eating places everywhere. Watersports are popular in Pattaya and numerous agents and specialist shops cater for the excellent offshore diving opportunities. All this rubs shoulders with the non-stop sex industry that bedevils the town's attempt to reinvent its image as a more wholesome destination for foreign visitors.

ORIENTATION Beach Rd, which follows the curve of crescent-shaped Pattaya beach, is linked by a series of *sois* to the parallel Pattaya 2 Rd. Central Pattaya, occupying the area between *sois* 5 and 12, is the main commercial area, while the area to the south of *soi* 12 is the red-light district which comes into its own after dark. Jomtien Beach, lying south of Pattaya, is a far more sedate area, dedicated to watersports rather than sex.

GETTING AROUND *Songthaews* ply Beach Rd and Pattaya 2 Rd. It's best not to ask the fare if you are only going a short distance; just hand over 10B at the end of the journey.

> *i* | The **TAT Office**, tel: 0-3842-7667, on Beach Rd between *sois* 7 and 8. Open daily 0830–1630, it is well organised, with maps and accommodation information.
>
> **Pattaya Taxi Centre** offers a 24-hr taxi service with English-speaking drivers. Tel 0-3842-7523 or 0-3836-1075.
>
> **Malibu Travel**, 485 Pattaya 2 Rd, tel: 0-3842-3180, fax: 0-3842-6229, website: www.malibu-travel.com, e-mail: malibu@chonburi.ksc.co.th. Situated next to the Vientiane restaurant, at the top of Soi 13, this is a well-established and reliable travel agent for tours, transport and hotel reservations.
>
> The Soi **Post Office**, Soi 15, is the main post office and a telephone office for international calls, although better rates are often obtainable from private phone offices around town.
>
> First-rate **hospital** treatment is available at the 24-hour Pattaya Memorial Hospital on Central Pattaya Rd, tel: 0-3842-7742, and the Pattaya International Hospital on Soi 4, tel: 0-3842-8374.
>
> The **Tourist Police** can be contacted on Pattaya 2 Rd, near Soi 6, tel: 0-3842-9371.
>
> **Motorbikes**, **scooters** and **jeeps** can be hired from any of the countless touts along Beach Road. **Cars** can be rented from Avis in the Dusit Resort Hotel, tel: 0-3836-1627.

🛏 The **Amari Orchid Resort $$$$$** Beach Rd, tel: 0-3842-8161, fax: 0-3842-8165, e-mail: orchid@amari.com. One of the best hotels in town, situated at the quieter north end of Beach Road, with ten acres of grounds, tennis courts, a large pool, and good restaurants.

Lek Hotel $$$ 284 Soi 13, on corner with Pattaya 2 Rd, tel: 0-3842-5550, fax: 0-3842-6629. A reliable mid-range hotel, with its own small pool, rooms with fridges and phones. Centrally located for shopping and tour agents.

A.A. Pattaya Hotel $$$ 182 Soi 13, tel: 0-3842-8656, fax: 0-3842-9057. Rates drop if you're staying more than one night. Comfortable clean rooms and a small outdoor pool; well, more of a large bath really.

There is no real budget accommodation in Pattaya but the *sois* in central Pattaya are chock-a-block with the cheapest guesthouses.

Apex Hotel $$ 216 Pattaya 2 Rd, between *sois* 10 and 11, tel: 0-3842-9233, fax: 0-3842-1184. This remains a firm favourite with travellers because its air-con rooms are inexpensive. The place is clean and well run and even has a small pool. The nearby **Diana Inn**, tel: 0-3842-9675, e-mail: dianagrp@loxinfo.co.th, is fine if the Apex is full.

🍽 Finding Western food is no problem in Pattaya. The difficulty lies in finding places serving interesting Thai cuisine. Restaurant prices are noticeably higher than most other parts of Thailand, especially the seafood places in south Pattaya and Jomtien. **Vientiane $$** 485 Pattaya 2 Rd, tel: 0-3841-1298, is centrally located not far from Soi 13. The large menu featuring dishes from Laos and Thailand is available daily 1100–2400. Another alternative to fast-food joints and overpriced western meals is **PIC Kitchen $$** Soi 5, which serves excellent Thai dishes in an attractive setting. On the top floor of the Royal Garden Plaza, mid-way along Beach Road, there is a pleasant food centre using a coupon system.

SHOPPING At night Beach Rd and Pattaya 2 Rd are packed with stalls selling the usual mix of fake watches, wallets, fashion and souvenirs. **Royal Garden Plaza** in Beach Rd is a modern shopping plaza with boutiques, a Tower Records store, a cinema and a Boots chemist. On Pattaya 2 Rd there is the similar **Central Festival Centre**.

ENTERTAINMENT Transvestite cabaret shows are very popular at two establishments in north Pattaya: **Tiffany's**, tel: 0-3842-1700, www.tiffany-show.com, opposite Amari Orchid Resort, and **Alcazar**, tel: 0-3842-8746, 78 Pattaya 2 Rd. These colourful shows are decidedly unraunchy and attract families with children as well as tour groups seeking titillation.

South Pattaya is ablaze with **bars and discos** and awash with young Thai girls waiting to attach themselves to a European male. **Hopf**, on Beach Rd just south of Soi 13, is a huge bar and restaurant with comfortable seating and a salubrious atmosphere. A little further south a left turn into South Pattaya Rd brings you to the lively **Bamboo Bar** where the live band thumps out a nightly session.

OUTDOOR ACTIVITIES IN PATTAYA

Pattaya is full of surprises, not least in its provision for sports and outdoor activities. For watersports head for **Jomtien Beach** where windsurfing, parasailing, jet-skiing and sailing with Hobie Cats, Prindles and Lasers all are fully catered for. Pattaya's off shore islands provide good opportunities for scuba diving and snorkelling. There are a number of professionally run and PADI-licensed dive centres like **Mermaid's Dive Centre** on Beach Road, tel/fax: 0-3871-0918, e-mail: divesite@loxinfo.co.th. These places offer courses for novices, as well as experienced divers seeking speciality training in areas such as wreck or deep-sea diving.

Land-based activities include a safe go-kart circuit at the **Thai Palace Hotel**, tel: 0-3842-3062, good bowling and snooker at the **Pattaya Bowl** near Soi 5 on Pattaya 2 Rd and horse-riding at the **Pattaya Riding Club**.

WHERE NEXT?

Visit Nong Nooch Village about 15 km south of Pattaya to enjoy exhibitions of traditional dancing, Thai boxing and an elephant show (daily 0900–1200 and 1330–1700). From here continue along the south-east coast towards Ko Samet (pp. 128–133).

PATTAYA – KO SAMET

Notes

Buses for Rayong and Ban Phe, with and without air-conditioning, depart from Bangkok's Eastern bus terminal, which is best reached by skytrain to Ekamai station.

Tour agents in Bangkok and Pattaya run package deals to Ko Samet, with or without accommodation on the island. These cost more but offer the convenience of being picked up from your hotel and driven to Ban Phe for the ferry.

PATTAYA — KO SAMET
OTT Tables 7068a/7077

Service	🚌	🚌	🚌	🚌	⛴
Days of operation Special notes	Daily **A**	Daily **B**	Daily **C**	Daily **D**	Daily **E**
Bangkok .... d.	....	0330	0500	0500	....
Pattaya .... d.	0250	|	0720	|	....
Rayong .... d.	0405	0610	....	|	....
Ban Phe .... d.	....	....	....	0830	0800
Ko Samet Na Dan beach.. d.	....	....	....	....	0830

Special notes:
A–Additional trips: 0330, 0450, 0545, 0550, 0630, 0700, 0720, 0800, 0805
B–Additional trips: 0400 and about ½ hourly to 1930, 2010, 2100, 2200.
C–Additional trips: 0500 and every 40 mins. to 2100.
D–Additional trips: 0600 and hourly to 2000.
E–Additional trips: hourly throughout the day. There are also ferry services to other beaches on Ko Samet.

There is little to detain the traveller between Pattaya and Ko Samet. Commercial activity, especially around the deep-sea port of Sattahip to the south of Pattaya, has left its blot on the landscape. The Thai military also has a strong presence in the area and there was an incident in 2000 when a couple of their jets accidentally strafed a length of beach and its holiday bungalows. The town of Rayong is famous for its fish sauce, *nam pla*, which is bottled and destined for just about every dining table, public or private, across Thailand. From Rayong it is 17 km by road to the village of Ban Phe, the jumping-off point for the ferry ride to Ko Samet. The destination island of Ko Samet, with clear, clean sand and an absence of crowds, is well worth the short hop from either Pattaya or Bangkok.

RAYONG

There is little reason to stay in Rayong, but the town does have a usefully frequent bus link with Khorat that connects with the Bangkok–Nong Khai route (see p. 196). Also, given that boats from Ban Phe stop around 1600–1700, you may wish to stay a night in Rayong and reach Ko Samet the next morning. There are a few inexpensive hotels close to the bus terminal, and the **Rayong Otani $–$$**, 59 Sukhumvit Rd, tel 0-3861-1112, is typical of what's available. Turn left outside the station onto Sukhumvit Road. Alternatively, if you miss the last boat to Ko Samet, there is also accommodation at Ban Phe itself.

BAN PHE

Ban Phe is the ferry point for Ko Samet and most travellers see little more of the fishing port than the pier that takes them to a waiting boat. There is a bank west of the pier, with better rates than those available on the island, and shops to stock up on perishables for Ko Samet, where everything costs more. If your accommodation on the island has not been arranged in advance, you may be assailed by touts offering various deals and contradictory information. It makes sense to have made a phone call ahead and have somewhere in mind for the first night at least.

ACCOMMODATION Last departure for most boats is 1600–1700. If an overnight stay is unavoidable there are budget hotels $ close to the pier. One good mid-range hotel metres from the pier is the **Diamond Phe Hotel $$**, 286/12 Moo 2, Tambon Phe, Amphur Muang; tel: 0-3865-1826, fax: 0-3865-1757. If you are travelling in style, chill out at the well-run though expensive **Rayong Resort $$$$$**, 186 Laem Tarn, Ban Phe; tel: 0-3865-1000, fax: 0-3865-1007, e-mail: rayongrr@infonews.co.th. From Ban Phe, where there is a free pick-up, it is 10 minutes by road to the resort with its private beach, evening cruises, day trips to Ko Samet, and the best European-style restaurant east of Pattaya.

KO SAMET

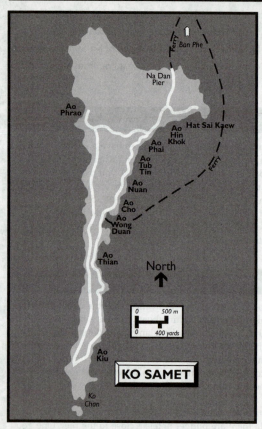

Lovely Ko Samet remained firmly off the tourist track until well into the 1980s, but now this tiny island – only 6 km long – receives daily boatloads of both domestic and foreign visitors. During Thai public holidays (see p. 58), especially over long weekends, there are more visitors than hotel rooms, and the island feels grossly overcrowded. Even ordinary weekends attract busloads of stressed-out Thais looking for a break. By avoiding these times Ko Samet can offer a relaxing getaway for a couple of days, but it does partly depend on which beach you choose for your stay.

GETTING THERE Boats ply their way between Ban Phe and more than one beach on Ko Samet. As well as the regular scheduled services a number of resorts have their own boats, which will also take passengers not staying with them. **Na Dan pier** in the north-east of the island is the main arrival point and from here *songthaews* run south as far as Ao Wong Duan. Boats to Na Dan depart from Saphaan Nuan Tip pier in Ban Phe 0800–1600, $.

Boats also go direct to **Ao Wong Duan** and two of the resorts on this beach also run their own boats here. Boats for **Ao Phrao** depart from Saphaan Sri Ban Phe pier, as do some of the other resort boats as well.

From Khao San Road in Bangkok, and other tour agents in the capital, it is easy to book a combined bus and boat ticket **($$$)** to Ko Samet. In Pattaya, Malibu Travel, tel: 0-3842-3180, runs a daily bus and boat service **($$)**.

DEPARTURE Boats depart regularly for Ban Phe from Na Dan, but unless you are staying at Hat Sai Kaew or one of the other nearby beaches it is more convenient to catch one of the resort boats that depart from Ao Wong Duan, Ao Chao and Ao Phrao. It is also possible to book bus trips to Bangkok or Pattaya through some of the bungalow operators.

BEACHES The best known beach is **Hat Sai Kaew** in the north-east of the island. It is within walking distance of Na Dan Pier, which makes it the most overdeveloped on the island. Bungalows are cheek by jowl, there are noisy videos in the restaurants at night, lots of bars and discos, and a plethora of plastic tables and deckchairs which do their best to disfigure what is a truly beautiful stretch of soft, sandy beach. Definitely worth avoiding at busy times, but fine if you want to be in the thick of the action.

Due south, and separated by a low rocky promontory that is easily walked around, **Ao Hin Khok** offers another very attractive, though smaller, beach. Good budget accommodation can be found here, the food is much better than at Hat Sai Kaew and there is a post office service from one of the bungalows.

The next beach south is **Ao Phai.** With resorts catering specifically for westerners, the place is rarely free from crowded pockets of sun-seekers clustered around umbrella shades. South of here is a string of three small beaches, separated by rocky patches with a trail through them, before you reach the larger Ao Wong Duan beach.

Ao Tub Tim, the first of the three beaches, is the busiest. **Ao Nuan** and **Ao Cho** are delightfully peaceful and free of upmarket resorts. You can stay here and enjoy the tranquility during the day, while a short tramp with the help of a torch at night will take you to the more sociable nightlife of the beaches to the north and south.

Ao Wong Duan is the second most developed beach on Ko Samet and boasts some of the plushest accommodation anywhere on the island. The resorts have their own boats that pull in to the beach daily, and the place does become crowded at times.

Further south is another string of small, very quiet beaches with limited, budget accommodation. **Ao Thian**, usually called Candlelight Beach, is a 5-min walk from

Ao Wong Duan. Along with Ao Nuan this is the most convenient location for a secluded getaway. If you want to feel really isolated head for **Ao Kiu,** the most southerly beach; a short walk over to the west side leads to views of the setting sun.

ACCOMMODATION The cost of a room on Ko Samet can vary enormously, depending on supply and demand. The price ranges indicated here refer to normal times and not holiday weekends, when prices can easily double or even treble. The telephone numbers are mobiles and use the prefix 01.

HAT SAI KAEW	It is hard to distinguish between one bungalow and the next as most of them offer a similar choice, between rooms with a fan and those with air-conditioning. **Diamond Beach $$** tel: 0-1239-0208 and **Coconut House $$** tel: 0-1943-2134, are typical of the better places.
AO HIN KHOK	There are three bungalow operations on the beach. **Naga $** tel: 0-1218-5372, **Tok's Little Hut $** tel: 0-1218-5195 and **Jep's Inn $$** no telephone. All three places serve excellent food.
AO PHAI	Budget accommodation is offered at **Ao Phai Hut $** tel: 0-1353-2644. **Sea Breeze $–$$** tel: 0-1239-4780 and **Samed Villa $$–$$$** tel: 0-1494-8090 offer more comfortable rooms in attractive bungalows.
AO TUB TIM, AO NUAN AND AO CHO	**TubTim Resort $–$$** tel: 0-3861-5041, e-mail: office@tubtimresort.com has a range of bungalows. Buses for Bangkok and Pattaya can be booked here, and cash advances on credit cards are available. **Tiewe $** Ao Nuan is a quiet little retreat, shaded by greenery, offering budget rooms and shared showers.
AO WONG DUAN	Perhaps the best bungalows on the island's east coast, with air-conditioning and hot water, are at **Malibu Garden Resort $$$–$$$** tel: 0-3865-1292, fax: 0-3842-6229.
AO THIAN	There is a choice between **Candle Light Beach $$$** tel: 0-1218-6934 which has doubles with fan right by the beach and **Lung Dum Bungalow $$** tel: 0-1458-8430, with better value rooms.
AO KIU	The only place to stay is at **Coral Beach $$–$$$** tel: 0-3865-2561 or 0-1218-6231. When you phone check when their boat departs from Ban Phe; otherwise it's an hour's walk from Ao Wong Duan.
AO PRAO	The only beach on the west coast, good for snorkelling. It boasts the upmarket **Prao Resort $$$$$** tel: 0-2438-9771, www.aopraoresort.com, with bungalows and watersports.

FOOD   All the bungalows and resorts have their own restaurants. It's just a matter of wandering from one to another and seeing what takes your fancy. The menus, all in the $-$$ range, are very similar, offering fresh fish waiting to be barbecued, steaks, Thai curries, salads, soups and sandwiches. Ao Wong Duan has a far more laid-back atmosphere at night than Hat Sai Kaew. The **Vongduern Villa** restaurant at the southern end of the beach has an attractive night-time setting over the rocks, while the Malibu restaurant has some tempting desserts. **Naga's** at Ao Hin Khok has a well-deserved reputation for above-average food.

WHERE NEXT?

Visit the Vietnamese shop-houses and Catholic cathedral of Chantaburi (pp. 135–136) before continuing through the relatively uninteresting town of Trat to Laem Ngop, the ferry point for beautiful Ko Chang (pp. 138–143).

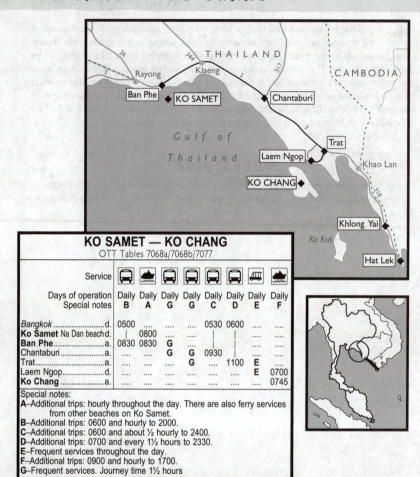

KO SAMET — KO CHANG
OTT Tables 7068a/7068b/7077

Service	🚌	⛴	🚌	🚌	🚌	🚌	🚐	⛴
Days of operation	Daily	Daily	Daily	Daily	Daily	Daily	Daily	Daily
Special notes	B	A	G	G	C	D	E	F
Bangkok ....d.	0500	....	....	....	0530	0600	....	....
Ko Samet Na Dan beach d.	|	0800	....	....	....	....	....	....
Ban Phe.........................a.	0830	0830	G	....	....	....	....	....
Chantaburi ....a.	....	....	G	G	0930	....	....	....
Trat...................................a.	....	....	....	G	....	1100	E	....
Laem Ngop.......................d.	....	....	....	....	....	....	E	0700
Ko Chang ....a.	....	....	....	....	....	....	....	0745

Special notes:
A–Additional trips: hourly throughout the day. There are also ferry services
   from other beaches on Ko Samet.
B–Additional trips: 0600 and hourly to 2000.
C–Additional trips: 0600 and about ½ hourly to 2400.
D–Additional trips: 0700 and every 1½ hours to 2330.
E–Frequent services throughout the day.
F–Additional trips: 0900 and hourly to 1700.
G–Frequent services. Journey time 1½ hours

Notes

Getting to Ko Chang from Bangkok in a day is possible, but only if you get to the Eastern Bus terminal before 0800 for a bus to Trat to catch the last boat from Laem Ngop at 1700. If departing from Ko Samet, catching an early boat to Ban Phe is also recommended. Both Chantaburi and Trat suggest themselves as places to bed down for a night.

As well as the above routes, there are also daily buses between Chantaburi and Khorat (6 hrs) which offer a useful link with the Bangkok–Nong Khai route (see p. 196) while avoiding a return to the capital.

While the Pattaya–Ko Samet route is now well travelled, the number of visitors continuing east to Ko Chang is a trickle by comparison. But the trickle is an interesting one because the route attracts more independently minded travellers seeking unspoilt corners of the country. Ko Chang itself is rapidly developing its tourist potential – in five years' time it may even be a place to avoid – but the area around Trat has an inviting laid-back character. There is a lot to do in terms of conventional tourist attractions but it is an enjoyable area to explore in a lazy kind of way. Adventurers will be drawn to the narrow strip of Thai territory between the Gulf of Thailand and Cambodia. The tourist infrastructure is virtually non-existent as one approaches the Cambodian border and you need your own transport to visit the small beaches dotted along the coastline. Ko Chang, on the other hand, has a host of white sand coves and beaches and new accommodation and visitor facilities are being developed all the time.

CHANTABURI

Chantaburi does not receive a lot of tourists but the town has enough character to justify a half-day visit. Although there are no 'must see' sights the town has retained an appealing sense of its social history. Chantaburi's charm comes from its ethnic mix, its vernacular architecture, and the buzz of specialist activity from the gem trading that dominates the town's commerce.

CHANTABURI'S GEMS

Rubies and sapphires are mined around Chantaburi but the town's fame as a gem-trading centre now goes well beyond the local market. Mynamar (Burma) is the most important source, as well as Cambodia and Vietnam, and the men seen peering intently through a magnifier at their heap of coloured stones are usually engaged in the fine art of classifying each and every gem.

Rubies and sapphires are varieties of the mineral corundum. Subtle variations in colour are caused by impurities like chromium, titanium or iron in the aluminium oxide that mostly constitutes the corundum. Less prosaically, the gemstones are among the most valuable precious stones on the planet and are far more expensive than diamonds of an equal size. While all rubies are red, the most sought after colour is a deep purplish hue known as pigeon's blood. All other non-red gemstones of corundum are sapphires, although the classic sapphire is a deep cornflower blue.

HIGHLIGHTS From the bus station walk along Sartidet Road until it comes to an end on the west bank of the Chantaburi River. Turn right and wander along Rim Nam Road as it follows the course of the waterway. This is the most interesting and **photogenic part of town**, with dilapidated and occasional ornate shops and houses that reflect the mixed cultural influences of China and Vietnam. The

Vietnamese presence in Chantaburi is pervasive, dating back to the end of the 19th century and continuing into the 1970s, when a fresh wave of refugees decided life in communist-controlled south Vietnam was not to their liking.

The French have also made their presence felt in Chantaburi, having occupied the town for ten years at the tail end of the 19th century, when the borders between Siam and her neighbours were open to 'negotiation' and some coercion. As you walk along the river you will soon reach the footbridge that leads directly to the French-designed **cathedral** built in 1880. Remarkable simply by being here, the cool interior is far more aesthetically pleasing than the outside of the building.

The **gem-dealing area** is not far away, back on the west side of the river around Sri Chan Road, which runs parallel with the river one block inland. This is not the place to go shopping for sapphires and rubies, unless you can really assess their worth, but observing the gem-dealing scene can be fascinating. The gem shops are open to the street and the plainly dressed people who patronise them, like the undistinguished-looking experts who sit nonchalantly at a table before a small pile of precious gems, are masters of understatement.

GETTING THERE Buses from the east, west and north-east of Thailand all pull in at Chantaburi's bus station on Sartidet Rd, less than 1 km west of the town centre. If coming from Ko Samet, the easiest way to reach Chantaburi is by *songthaew* from Ban Phe to Rayong and then a regular bus from there.

🏨 **Kasemsan I $** 98/1 Benchama-Rachutit Rd, tel: 0-3931-2340. The easiest budget guesthouse to get to from the bus station. Walk along Sartidet Rd and, one block before the river, turn right at the main junction with Benchama-Rachutit Rd. Air-con rooms are in the quieter part of the building. For standard hotel accommodation **K.P. Inn $$–$$$** Trirat Rd, tel: 0-3931-1756, delivers creature comforts at a moderate price.

🍽 Chantaburi's local food includes the delicious Vietnamese spring rolls (*chao gio*). The best place to find them is down by the river where **food stalls** next to the river serve them piping hot. The riverside stalls also sell the town's famous noodles with a variety of seafood. Standard Thai and Chinese dishes can be found in the **Chanthon Phochana** restaurant at the Kasemsan guesthouse, although reports of the quality of the food here are mixed.

TRAT

Nearly every traveller in Trat is on their way to or from Ko Chang. The town serves mainly as a transit point for the journey to Laem Ngop from where the boats depart. It is also a useful place to stock up on provisions because everything costs a little more on Ko Chang. There are banks on Trat's main road with a far better exchange rate than anywhere on the island. A night's stay may be necessary here if you miss the last boat to Ko Chang at 1700.

HIGHLIGHTS There is not a lot to do in the town although the budget guesthouses can arrange a river trip and one of them, the Windy Guesthouse, has free canoes for paddling up and down the canal. With time to spare, a more recommended activity is an excursion to Khlong Yai near the Cambodian border (see box on p. 138).

ARRIVAL AND DEPARTURE There are a few companies running buses between Bangkok and Trat but they all have their stations along Trat's main road, still called Sukhumvit Rd, with their timetables and prices clearly marked. There are VIP buses, regular air-con buses, and ordinary non-air-con buses. There are also buses between Trat and Chantaburi, Ban Phe, Rayong and Pattaya. *Songthaews* for Laem Ngop depart from behind the shopping centre in Trat.

There are two good budget places, close to one another, and both reached from the bus stations by walking south down Sukhumvit Road in the opposite direction from Bangkok. After 200 m, before the canal, turn left down Thoncharoen Rd. **Windy Guest House $** 64 Thoncharoen Rd, tel: 0-3952-3644 is on the right, and almost opposite is **Foremost Guest House $** 49 Thoncharoen Rd; tel: 0-3951-1923. Owned by the same family, both guesthouses offer simple, clean rooms with shared bathrooms. Best of all, these are excellent places for picking up current information about accommodation on Ko Chang and onward travel across the border to Cambodia. If both are full ask directions to the nearby **NP Guest House $** Soi Luang Aet, tel: 0-3951-2270. This is another friendly place to stay, with a convenient small restaurant. For more comfort and a shorter walk, turn left off Sukhumvit Road by the night market building. On the corner a sign points to the Trad Hotel, which is in fact the **Trat Hotel $$–$$$** Meuang Trat; tel: 0-3951-1091. There is a choice of rooms, some with air-con and all with their own bathrooms.

The **Trat Hotel restaurant $**, only open 0600–1730, but is conveniently close to the bus stations and enjoys air-con. The menu is an unexciting list of rice, noodle and fried chicken dishes; few locals eat here because of the proximity of the day and night markets. Next door, the **Jiraporn's** small menu in English is about half the price of the hotel restaurant. The best places for good local food are undoubtedly the markets. The night market is north of the Trat Hotel, while the day market is one block to the south beneath the town's shopping centre.

EXCURSION TO THE BORDER

A slither of Thai territory slips down to the south-east of Trat as far as Hat Lek at the border with Cambodia, reaching the fishing town of Khlong Yai along the way. *Songthaews* (**$**) depart regularly to Khlong Yai from behind the shopping centre in Trat, and from Khlong Yai there are *songthaews* and motorbikes that continue on to the border.

There is little to do at Hat Lek but the journey to Khlong Yai is worth the trip because of the spectacular beauty of the Cambodian mountains and forests, and the deep blue sea of the Gulf of Thailand. The **Suksamlan Hotel $–$$**, tel: 0-3958-1109, in Khlong Yai has decent rooms.

TRAVELLING TO CAMBODIA

It is currently legal and safe to travel across the border into Cambodia at **Hat Lek**. However, this was not the case until quite recently and circumstances may change. A visa for Cambodia may be obtained in Bangkok (see p. 79) but it is currently possible to travel into Cambodia and return to Thailand on your Thai visa, as long as it is still valid when you return.

Unless you are planning onward travel to Vietnam it is not necessary to obtain a Cambodian visa; just pay the border police at Hat Lek. The budget guesthouses in Trat are excellent sources of up-to-date information on travel into Cambodia.

LAEM NGOP

Laem Ngop, 17 km south-west of Trat, is the departure point for Ko Chang and there is no other reason to travel here. There used to be only one pier in the town itself but two new piers have now been completed outside of town.

i The **TAT office** is near the town pier, tel: 0-3959-7255, open daily 0830–1630. All the piers have 'tourist information offices' which are just fronts for particular resorts on the island. If you arrive in high season with no accommodation they can serve a purpose.

A favourite with travellers is **Chut Kaew $** on the main road, 5 mins on foot from the pier, tel: 0-3959-7088. Rooms are basic and bathroom facilities are shared, but it is a friendly place. The **restaurant** is worth a visit in its own right while waiting for a boat: the food is fine and information on Ko Chang is available from the owner and guests.

KO CHANG

Considering its size – it is Thailand's second largest island after Phuket – Ko Chang has been a late developer on the tourist scene. Proximity to Cambodia and previous lack of safety probably contributed to the island's isolation, but it is now rapidly establishing itself as an idyllic island retreat. It boasts beautiful sandy beaches and, compared to Phuket and Ko Samui, remains unspoilt.

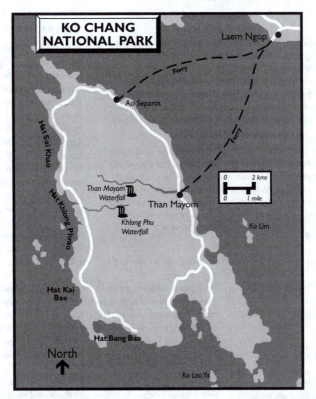

KO CHANG NATIONAL PARK

Laem Ngop

Ferry

Ao Separot

Ferry

Than Mayom Waterfall

Than Mayom

Khlong Phu Waterfall

Hat Sai Khao

Hat Khlong Phrao

Ko Lim

0   2 kms
0   1 mile

Hat Kai Bae

Hat Bang Bao

North

Ko Lao Ya

HIGHLIGHTS Compared to Ko Samui and Phuket, the nightlife is low-key. In fact, whatever the time of day, there is not a lot to do but relax, enjoy a massage on the beach, swim, snorkel (snorkelling trips to nearby islands can be arranged through some of the bungalows) and let time pass idly by. Having said that, when the road that winds its way around the island has been completely paved there will be easier access to some of the more isolated beaches, and new developments will spring up.

GETTING THERE **Boats ($$)** leave from Laem Ngop throughout the day from 0900 until 1600 or 1700, with the most frequent service between December and April. Most boats go to Ao Saparot on the island's north-east coast and from here there are *songthaews* **($)** waiting to take passengers to any of the west-coast beaches. There is also at least one boat a day to Than Mayom on the east coast.

THE BEACHES

The main beach is **Hat Sai Khao**, White Sand Beach, with the largest cluster of bungalows and resorts, and the only nightlife to speak of. This is the most convenient resort in terms of having a good choice of places to stay and eat. The next beach, 5 km south, is the lovely, quiet **Hat Khlong Phrao**, while further south again **Hat Kai Bee** has a beautiful stretch of sand which unfortunately shrinks to a narrow strip at high tide.

On the south of the island the most attractive sandy beach is **Hat Bang Bao** but unless the road has been paved this far south it is a 5 km walk from Hat Kai Bee. Occasionally, there is a boat from Laem Ngop but don't bet on it. The east coast has no beach to compare with those on the west coast, which is reflected in a paucity of accommodation and an infrequent *songthaew* service.

ACCOMMODATION

While budget accommodation tends to be more expensive than on Ko Samui or Ko Samet, accommodation for most budgets means there is a good mix of travellers. Twelve years ago, when the first beach huts appeared, there was no paved road or electricity, but now the best resorts have rooms with a mini-bar, telephone, hot water and air-conditioning. Weekends and public holidays are always the busiest times, and it is worth trying to arrive during the week.

HAT SAI KHAO

NO ANSWER?

Making an advance booking for accommodation on Ko Chang can prove frustrating because of the possible problems encountered when trying to get a mobile phone to answer: awful reception, no one to answer, phone bill unpaid. If you have the time, try using a TAT office on the mainland; if you're banjaxed, consider just turning up (but see Accommodation above).

New places are springing up all the time but the following gives a good idea of what is available. As the *songthaew* reaches the white sand of Hat Sai Khao one of the first places on the right is the venerable **KC $** tel: 0-1833-1010. A pioneer in Ko Chang's tourist development, KC has simple thatched huts virtually on the beach with shared facilities and no electricity.

On the other side of the road **Jinda Bungalow $** has rooms with a fan and indoor bathroom, and discounted rates for stays of more than a couple of nights. There are lots of other budget joints dotted around this stretch of beach and it is easy to walk from one to the other checking them out.

Mac Bungalows $$$ tel: 0-1219-3056, an example of the good mid-range accommodation available right on the beach.

One of the nicest places to stay has to be **Banpu Koh Chang Hotel $$$$$** tel: 0-3954-2355, fax: 0-3954-2359. The bungalows, popular with Germans, are set in tropical gardens with carefully crafted rooms and stone-decorated bathrooms.

Moonlight Resort $$$ tel: 0-1212-6036 or 0-3959-7198, on a rocky beach but within walking distance of a sandy stretch and a choice of rooms.

Another nearby place with a stony beach, and a good 5 minute walk to the sand of Hat Sai Khao, is **Changtong Resort $** tel: 0-1823-0991. Its wooden huts only have a fan but are adequate considering the price.

HAT KHLONG PHRAO   The northern stretch of Hat Khlong Phrao, called Chaiyachet Beach, is the location of the upmarket **Koh Chang Resort $$$$$** tel: 0-1948-8177, fax: 0-1912-0738, e-mail: rooksgroup@hotmail.com. Further south there are a few budget choices like **KP Bungalows $** tel: 0-1219-1225 and **Magic $** tel: 0-1219-3408.

HAT KAI BEE   Once a remote location, the beach area is developing fast. **Coral Resort $$** tel: 0-1219-3815 now has a spread of wood and concrete bungalows close to the sea.

Siam Bay Resort $–$$ tel: 0-1829-5529 at the southern end of the beach has a wider range of bungalows and huts.

Koh Chang Lagoon $$$ tel: 0-1848-5052, fax: 0-3951-1429. Finishing touches were being put to this new operation at the time of writing and it looks like it is going to be a smart place to stay. Substantial reductions for stays of four days or more will bring it into the $$ category. Worth checking out.

HAT BANG BAO   At the moment there are only a few places to stay, though this will soon change. **Bang Bao Blue Wave $,** tel 0-1439-0349, has huts with shared facilities and some larger ones with their own shower. During the low season (May–Oct) telephone ahead to make sure it is open.

🍴 Virtually every resort or bungalow operation has its own restaurant and it's easy to wander from one to another checking out their menus. Some places which look drab during daylight come into their own at night, especially those close to the water's edge. Look for fresh seafood on display in layers of crushed ice waiting to be selected and grilled on the spot.

At Hat Sai Khao the **Little Miss Naughty Restaurant $–$$** serves the usual Thai stir-fried fare, as well as fried tofu with sweet peanut sauce and a choice of pizzas.

The Banpu Koh Chang Hotel restaurant $$–$$$ has a large choice of soups, sandwiches, noodles, salads, fried meat dishes and tempura, as well as Thai favourites like *tom yam* and curries.

On the left side of the road, approaching Hat Kai Bee from Hat Sai Khao, **Piggy's Delight $$** is a pleasant vegetarian restaurant serving tofu dishes and lots of salads.

At Hat Kai Bee the restaurant at the Coral Resort has a well-chosen site on the rocks and an above-average menu featuring some Thai specialities among more commonplace dishes.

ENTERTAINMENT Compared to Ko Samui or Phuket, the entertainment infrastructure is in its infancy on Ko Chang. This can be a blessing for those who enjoy quiet evenings undisturbed by noisy videos, and anyway there is usually a sociable bar within walking distance. At the time of writing the bar next to Mac Bungalows was the liveliest place at night. At Hat Hai Bei the **Kai Bei Pub**, with music, food, pool table, and cocktails, has a grand entrance off the main road.

SHOPPING There are no real shops on Ko Chang, although on Hat Sai Khao, opposite the Banpu Koh Chang Hotel, there is a minimarket with a small selection of garments and beachwear. There is also a small bookshop with a second-hand exchange facility. E-mail and internet access is available upstairs, although the rate is high due to the use of a satellite connection.

DIVING AND SNORKELLING
At the Banpu Koh Chang Hotel **Eco-Divers** tel: 0-1982-2744 offers PADI diving courses and trips out to sea. A four-day open water course with four dives is US$280. The average cost of a diving trip by boat with a dive-master is US$45, including equipment and two dives. A snorkelling trip by boat is US$15.

HIGHLIGHTS Motorbikes, scooters and bicycles can be hired from a few places at Hat Sai Khao. This is the best way of exploring the island and reaching some of the pretty waterfalls in the interior. **Than Mayom waterfalls** could be the focus of a trip to the east side of the island. It is about an hour's walk from the settlement of Than Mayom to the first of the three falls. The stones, inscribed with initials, are said to be the calling cards of Rama VI and Rama VII. If you go on to the furthest fall, another hour's walk, the initials of the more energetic Rama V, King Chulalongkorn, await you.

On the west coast the **Khlong Phu waterfalls** can be reached by taking the turn-off signposted Nam Tok Khlong Phu on the main road south of Hat Sai Khao. Hard work on a bicycle, easier with a motorbike, a rough track leads up to the falls through tropical trees, and your reward is a sparkling pool safe for swimming.

Most of Ko Chang is undisturbed **primary forest,** and there are numerous paths that head into the interior, including a trail that leads across the centre of the island. However, it is easy to get lost on the trail and locals recommend the use of a guide.

ISLAND EXCURSIONS Ko Chang is the largest island in the Ko Chang National Park, but there are other smaller islands, mostly off the south coast, which are mostly visited for their snorkelling and diving opportunities. The **Island Hopper** ferry service operates a daily round-trip from Ko Chang Oct–May, dropping off at Ko Wai, Ko Khan, Ko Mak, Ko Rayang and Ko Kut in the morning and picking up from the same islands in the afternoon. They also offer a range of 'mini hopper packages'. Their office is at Apple Bungalows, Bang Bao Pier, Hat Khlong Phrao; tel: 0-1865-0610/0-9086-3-64; www.koh-chang.ch/IslandHopper/home.htm; e-mail: islandho@tr,ksc.co.th. Other ferry services are indicated with the island descriptions below.

Ko Mak can be reached by a daily boat service from Laem Ngop that only operates regularly during the dry months (Nov–May). Most of the island is devoted to rubber and coconut plantations, but there are beautiful white sand beaches and a handful of places offering accommodation. An affordable and fun place to spend a night is **Ko Mak Resort $–$$,** tel: 0-2319-6714 or 0-1219-1220.

If you want a really small island, head for **Ko Kham** off the north coast of Ko Mak. There is only one place to stay, **Ko Kham Resort $–$$$,** tel: 0-3959-7114. Their boat leaves daily each afternoon from Laem Ngop, but only during the dry months (Nov–May).

The largest island after Ko Chang is **Ko Kut**. Most of the accommodation is handled by upmarket resorts, like **Ko Kud Sai Khao Resort $$$$,** tel: 0-3951-1824, that manage their own transport. To visit the island on your own take one of the boats from Ko Mak that make the journey each day in the dry season. The beaches are sparkling white and the water an inviting transparent turquoise.

Boat trips from Ko Chang can be organised through some of the bungalows. Piggy's Delight restaurant at Hat Kai Bei takes bookings for a twice-weekly trip. Other tour organisers, tel: 0-3959-7242 or 0-1868-2648, offer a night camping on one of the tiny islands before moving on to another island on the second day.

WHERE NEXT?

You could return to Bangkok cross-country directly to Chonburi, taking in the Sun Tha Ten Waterfalls just 10 km south of town. From here continue back to Bangkok and take the historical tour to Bang Pa-In (pp. 145–146) and Ayutthaya (pp. 146–149).

BANGKOK — AYUTTHAYA

Notes

If hopping between Bang Pa-In and Ayutthaya, the buses and *songthaews* are a lot more frequent than the trains.

BANGKOK — AYUTTHAYA
OTT Tables 7060/7071

Service	RAIL	🚌	🚌	RAIL	RAIL	⛴	RAIL	RAIL	RAIL	RAIL	RAIL
Days of operation	Ⓐ	Daily	Daily	Daily	Daily	Daily	Daily	Daily	Daily	Daily	Daily
Special notes		A	B			D	C				
Bangkok ....d.	0420	0530	0540	0600	0700	0800	0905	1115	1430	1905	1940	2010
Bang Pa-In ....a.	0534	0700		0720			1002	1247		2010		2110
Ayutthaya ....a.	0547	0730	0710	0742	0845	D	1027	1300	1604	2034	2111	2146

Special notes:
A–Additional services about every 30 mins to 1830
B–Additional services about every 20 mins to 1920.
C–Additional services 1400, 1610Ⓐ, 1615Ⓒ, 1715Ⓐ, 2045, 2200.
D–Several operators run trips along Chao Phraya River to Ayutthaya.

HEADING NORTH

Siam's royal capital for over 400 years is close enough to Bangkok to make it a popular day excursion. Ayutthaya and Bang Pa-In are both on the main railway line from the capital to Chiang Mai so it is possible to take them in while leisurely making your way up to northern Thailand. Bang Pa-In is hardly worth a trip for its own sake, though if time allows it is easy to drop off for a quick visit before moving on to Ayutthaya.

Most Bangkok trains to Ayutthaya travel on to Chiang Mai and northern Thailand. It is possible to catch these trains from Don Muang railway station directly opposite Bangkok's international airport. You could visit Ayutthaya and move on to the north, leaving Bangkok for the last leg of your trip.

CRUISING THE CHAO PHRAYA RIVER

Bangkok's Chao Phraya Express Boat Co's **Sunday boat cruise** to Bang Pa-In stops at an arts and crafts centre at Bang Sai, and Wat Pai Lom temple and a bird sanctuary on the return journey. Departs 0800 from the Maharat pier and returns 1730. The fare is 280B (transport only). Tel: 0-2222–5330.

The Oriental Hotel organises **daily day trips to Bang Pa-In and Ayutthaya**. Trips depart 0800, travelling one way by boat and the other by coach. Cost, including lunch and a tour guide, is 1800B. Tel: 0-2236-0400.

Luxury cruises to Ayutthaya (with an overnight stay), which make the Oriental Hotel's operation seem cheap, are conducted through the Marriott Royal Garden Hotel. Tel: 0-2476-0021.

BANG PA-IN

In the middle of the 17th century, when the royal capital was at Ayutthaya, the king built a country retreat for himself a few miles downstream on the Chao Phraya River. When the royal seat of power shifted to Bangkok, the Bang Pa-In pad gracefully declined until Rama IV, quick to take advantage of the new steamboat technology, began a restoration programme. But it was his son, Rama V, who set about commissioning the eccentric mixture of architectural styles that make the **Royal Palace, $$**, open daily 0830 – 1530, such a novelty.

THAILAND

Using the free brochure that comes with your admission ticket, begin by identifying the **Warophat Phiman Hall**, a colonial-style private residence built in 1876 and containing a throne hall as well as private rooms. A covered bridge leads from here to the inner palace grounds, where the king and his retinue were left to their own devices and the only commoners allowed to enter were the ladies in his harem.

As you cross the lake it is impossible to miss the **Isawan Thipay-art Hall**, the only purely Siamese structure in the palace. Its elegant oriental curves contrast shockingly with a European-style country chalet in the inner palace painted in lurid shades of green. Behind the country house lurks a lovely Chinese creation, the **Palace of Heavenly Light**, which was brought here from China as a gift to the king from grateful merchants in the capital. The rich and lush interior is open to visitors.

The only other structure of note is the **memorial stone** to one of Rama V's wives, who accidentally drowned in the river in 1887 even though there were servants around who could have easily rescued her. An edict forbade any commoner from touching a royal, under pain of death, so she was left to drown.

From Bang Pa-In's railway station it takes about half an hour to walk to the Royal Palace, though *samlors* are readily available.

AYUTTHAYA

The city was the Siamese capital from 1350 until 1767, when it was attacked and virtually destroyed by invaders from Burma. The historic ruins, which have World Heritage status, stand as testimony to this eventful period in Asian history. Ayutthaya traded with Malacca, Java, China, Japan, India and Persia, and diplomatic ties were established with many European countries. What you see today – fading red-brick ruins dotted about a flat expanse of land – do not so much evoke a rich imperial past as capture a sense of a lost era.

A good way to start a tour is with a visit to the tourist office (see below) to collect a map. Across the road stands the **Chao Sam Phraya National Museum, $,** Rotchana Rd, open Wed–Sun 0900–1600. There are various finds from the temples and information about Buddha figures and their iconography.

It takes less than 10 mins to walk along Rotchana Road to the **Historical Study Center, $$$,** open 0900–1630. This museum recreates historical Ayutthaya using models, offering a good introduction to its subject. The admission charge includes entry to an annexe situated some distance away – ask for directions. It has well-researched material on Ayutthaya's relations with foreign states around the 16th

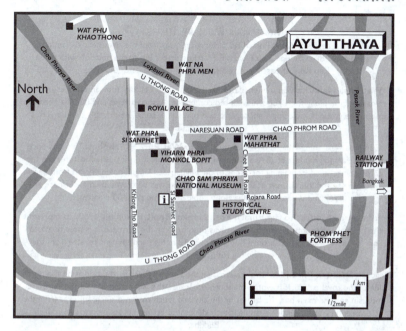

AYUTTHAYA

WAT PHU KHAO THONG

WAT NA PHRA MEN

Chao Phraya River

Lopburi River

U THONG ROAD

North

ROYAL PALACE

NARESUAN ROAD

CHAO PHROM ROAD

WAT PHRA SI SANPHET

WAT PHRA MAHATHAT

VIHARN PHRA MONKOL BOPIT

Chee Kun Road

Pasok River

RAILWAY STATION

Bangkok

CHAO SAM PHRAYA NATIONAL MUSEUM

Rojana Road

HISTORICAL STUDY CENTRE

PHOM PHET FORTRESS

Khlong Tho Road

Sri Sanphet Road

U THONG ROAD

Chao Phraya River

0   1 km

0   1/2 mile

century, when scores of nationalities were living in and around the city, and its population was bigger than London's.

The main reason for any visit to Ayutthaya is to view the ruined temples. As there are too many to take in on one day, choices have to be made. The temples covered in the box opposite start with Wat Phra Mahathat, which can be visited on foot. To reach the others it is best to avoid the hot part of the day and hire a bicycle or use a *tuk-tuk*. Between 0800 and 1830, the official opening hours, there is an admission charge ($).

i **TAT Office,** Sri Sanphet Rd, tel: 0-3524-6076. If only all TAT offices were like this one. It has a map of all the sites, up-to-date information on transport, suggested walking itineraries with maps and even a list of *tuk-tuk* fares.
The tourist office is next to the City Hall, opposite the Chao Sam Phraya National Museum.

AYUTTHAYA'S WATS: AN ITINERARY

This route begins at Chao Phrom Rd, facing west away from the river near the railway station. Walk or cycle up Chao Phrom Rd for less than 2 km to the junction with Chee Kun Rd. Just past it are two temples on either side of the road.

Wat Phra Mahathat, on the left, dates back to the 14th century. You can clamber up the remains of the *prang* for a good view of the compound. Assorted ruins and Buddha heads lie around the grounds, including a photogenic one that has become inextricably tied up with the roots of a bodhi tree.

Continue west along what is now Naresuan Rd to **Wat Phra Si Sanphet.** This was once the richest and grandest of all Ayutthaya's *wats*. Now its most distinguished features are the three central *chedi* containing the ashes of once-illustrious kings. Looking north from here you can see the foundations of the **royal palace** that was destroyed by the Burmese in 1767 and where the stables alone could accommodate 100 elephants.

Head due south instead to find **Viharn Phra Monkol Bopit**, built in the 1950s to represent the original 15th century structure that was destroyed by the Burmese. It is now home to one of the world's largest bronze Buddhas, over 12 m high and thought to date from the 16th century.

Reaching **Wat Na Phra Men** involves crossing the Lopburi River by the bridge on the north side of the royal palace. It is worth the journey because this *wat* managed to avoid Burmese vandalism and the main bot, the largest in the city and much restored since, survives from the 16th century. Inside, under a resplendently decorated ceiling, sits an imperious 6-m-high Buddha.

If you are on a bicycle it is worth travelling a couple of km north-west to **Wat Phu Khao Thong**. This monastery was constructed in 1387 and, although there is little left to appreciate now, the journey there takes you into scenic countryside and rice paddies.

ORIENTATION The ancient capital was built on an island around the meeting of three rivers and enclosed by a high wall. Accommodation and eating options tend to be clustered at the east side of the island, around Chao Phrom Road and within walking distance of the railway and bus stations.

Bicycles are the best way to visit the temples. The least expensive rates are found along the road from the railway station to the ferry jetty. *Tuk-tuks* are plentiful for short hops between ruins – or negotiate a price for a tour.

📷 **Ayothaya Hotel $$$$** Tessabarn Say Rd, tel: 0-3523-2855, fax: 0-3525-1018. Centrally located just off Chao Phrom Rd, but hardly worth the rack rate. Modern rooms and a swimming pool though, so try for a hefty discount.

Tevaraj Tanrin Hotel $$$ Rochana Rd, tel: 0-3524-3139. Turn left out of the railway station and this hotel is a few hundred metres down the road. Handy in this respect, but not for sight-seeing across the river. Large rooms with air-con and fridge, views of the river and a snooker table.

Phaesri Thong Guest House $–$$ 8/1 U Thong Rd, tel: 0-3524-6010. Attractive location by the river, dorm beds and rooms with air-con make this one of the better places for a one night stopover.

T.M.T. Guesthouse $ 14/4 Soi Tro Kkro Sor, off Naresuan Rd, tel: 0-3525-1474. Typical of the budget accommodation available in this *soi* off Naresuen Rd. Dorm beds and rooms with shared bathroom and one en-suite room.

📷 **Good Luck Café $** Soi Tro Kkro Sor, off Naresuan Rd. A pleasant street-side café with the usual array of Thai dishes, plus a vegetarian menu with dishes like tofu with lotus stems and mushrooms.

Across the road the **Moon Café $**, more of a bar than a café, opens late in the evening for light meals and beers.

Guesthouses in this area all have their own restaurants, which are worth checking out.

Krung Si River Hotel Restaurant $$–$$$ 27/2 Mu 11, Rochana Rd. One of three floating restaurants near the railway station. A large menu featuring salads, steaks, fish, curries, and Chinese and Japanese dishes.

WHERE NEXT?

It's well worth making the short hop to Lopburi (pp. 151–152) before heading north to Phitsanulok and Chiang Mai. It's a fascinating town of monkeys and palaces, elephant stables and fine restaurants. Afterwards, continue north to Phitsanulok (pp. 153–154), Sukhothai (pp. 168–170) and Chiang Mai (pp. 155–166).

AYUTTHAYA – CHIANG MAI

NOTES

Seven trains a day run between Bangkok and Chiang Mai. Four stop at Ayutthaya.

Berths to Chiang Mai from Bangkok are often sold out and reservations should be made as far in advance as possible.

Cheap buses to Chiang Mai from Bangkok's Khao San Rd may be cramped, uncomfortable and take you to an inconveniently located guesthouse.

From Lopburi, Phitsanulok, Sukhothai and Mae Sot there are possible transport links with other parts of the country. Details are given below under the towns.

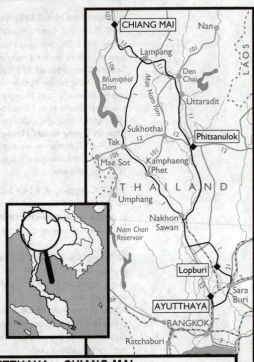

AYUTTHAYA – CHIANG MAI
OTT Tables 7060/7071/7076

Service	RAIL	BUS	RAIL	RAIL	RAIL	RAIL	RAIL	RAIL	BUS	BUS	✈
Days of operation	Daily	Daily	Daily	Daily	Daily	Daily	Daily	Daily	Daily	Daily	Daily
Special notes		A							B	C	D
Bangkok	0600	0800	0830	1430	1800	1925	1940	2200	....	0500	D	....
Ayutthaya ....d.	0742	|		1604		|	2111	2330	....	|		....
Lopburi ....d.	0858		1045	1718		2139	2217	0029	....	0710	|	....
Phitsanulok....................d.	1257	|	1355	2140	|	0058	0158	0445	2330	....	D	....
Chiang Mai....................a.	2055	1800	1945	0535	0650	0720	0855	1150	0515	....	D	....

Special notes:
A–VIP bus. Additional services: 0900, 0930, 1900, 1930, 2000, 2030, 2100, 2130, 2145 also about ½ hourly from 0630 – 2200 by standard bus.
B–Additional services 0335, 0515, 0525, 0530.
C–Additional services about every 25 minutes to 2030.
D–There are 18 flights a day to Chiang Mai and 3 to Phitsanulok. Journey time approx 1 hour.

This is a long route and many visitors cover the ground in one 12–13-hr rail journey. Travelling the route in short hops brings the advantage of being able to observe the transition, geographic and cultural, between central Thailand and the north of the country. The central plains around the valley of the River Chao Phraya are not scenically exciting but they function as the country's breadbasket in terms of rice production. By the time you reach Phitsanulok the plains have been left behind and the distinctive character of northern Thailand begins to make itself felt. The accent of the language is different, people prefer sticky rice to the ubiquitous white rice of the south and there seems to be more variety in the culture of everyday life. Chiang Mai is the capital of northern Thailand, cosmopolitan in nature yet surrounded by various hill tribes whose traditional ways of living are inexorably succumbing to the march of 'progress'. Expect a pleasant suprise if stepping off the train in Chiang Mai after a night's sleep since departing Ayutthaya.

LOPBURI

Lopburi is a very old town dating back to the 6th century. It came under Khmer influence in the 10th century, but after 300 years fell into obscurity until King Narai started rebuilding work in the second half of the 17th century. Lopburi was to be his second capital and his palace, built with the help of European architects, is the best reason for stopping off at Lopburi on your way north. A more frivolous motive would be to see playful monkeys in an urban environment; they are all over the old part of town.

THE KING'S PALACE

The palace's main entrance leads to the **outer courtyard**, now mostly composed of ruins, where the food stores, stables for elephants and horses, and a reception hall for visitors were located. The ruins of another reception hall, once lined with elegant French mirrors to impress foreign dignitaries, can be seen in the **middle courtyard**, but the main interest here now is the **museum, $,** open Wed–Sun 0830–1200 and 1300–1600 Housed in a colonial-style building built in the 1860s by King Rama IV, the museum has an impressive displayof Thai art across the centuries as well as plenty ofmonumental art from Lopburi. The **inner courtyard** was reserved for royalty, but only ruins remain of **Suttha Sawan Pavilion**, the king's private residence and where King Narai died in 1688.

HIGHLIGHTS One of the city's more minor attractions can be seen immediately after you leave the railway station – **Wat Phra Si Ratana Mahathat, $,** open daily 0830–1630. It is noted for its refined, slender Khmer *prang* made of laterite, which may date back to the 12th century. It has little in common with the nearby ruined *viharn* with its distinctly Gothic aspects, but King Narai's interest in European forms reappears in the King's Palace.

The King's Palace, **Phra Narai Ratchaniwet,** free, open daily 0730–1730, is not far away on Sorasak Rd. Built between 1577 and 1665 with the help of French and Italian architects, there are three courtyards to the palace complex.

The north entrance of the king's palace leads onto Rue de France on the other side of the main Ratchadamnern Rd. Halfway down this road, on the left, stands the white **Wat Sao Thong-Thong**, another example of Narai's penchant for mixing Thai and European architectural styles. Inside, tucked into niches along the wall where lamps were once placed, are some good examples of dragon-headed Buddhas.

ROUTE DETAIL

Rail

By taking an early train from Ayutthaya you can get a full day in Lopburi (left luggage facilities at station, 10B per item) before continuing the route.

Bus

Buses run between Lopburi and Suphanburi, from where there are regular buses to Kanchanaburi which allows you to link up with the Bangkok–Nam Tok route (see p. 106) in western Thailand. A link with the Bangkok–Nong Khai route (see p. 196) in the north-east is possible by taking one of the regular buses between Lopburi and Khorat (Nakhon Ratchasima).

i The **TAT Office** is conveniently located in the old part of town, not far from the King's Palace, on Phraya Kamjat Rd, tel: 0-3642-2768.

Asia Lopburi Hotel $–$$ Sorasak Rd, tel/fax: 0-3641-1892. A short walk from the railway station and overlooking the King's Palace, this is the obvious place to stay for one night. Avoid rooms on the noisy main road.
Nett Hotel $ 17/1-2 Soi 2, Ratchadamnern Rd, tel: 0-3641-1738. This neat little hotel offers the best budget accommodation.

White House Garden Restaurant $–$$ Phraya Kamjat Rd. The best place for a good value meal in the old part of the city, conveniently close to the palace and hotels. The Thai food has some flair and the alfresco setting is pleasing.
The main road outside the railway station, **Na Phra Karn Rd**, has a number of inexpensive Chinese-style restaurants. Worth seeking out along this road is the **Boon Bakery**, especially if you step off a morning train feeling hungry. Turn right outside the station, walk up Na Phra Karn Rd to junction with Ratchadamnern Rd and the bakery is next to the Indra Hotel.

PHITSANULOK

Journeying north, there are good reasons for considering an interruption at Phitsanulok. There is enough to see to easily justify one night's stay, and the town also serves as the beginning of an interesting route that heads due west to Sukhothai, Mae Sot and Umphang (see p. 167). Sukhothai is close enough to be taken in on a day trip from Phitsanulok, which itself has a fair range of places to stay. Especially good value in Phitsanulok are the competitively priced top-end hotels, and there are some excellent restaurants.

HIGHLIGHTS **Wat Phra Si Ratana Mahathat**, on the east bank of the Nan River and known locally as Wat Yai, is the town's most important temple and worthy of a visit to view one of the most highly revered Buddha images in the country. The 14th century haloed bronze figure is dramatically positioned with the help of interior lighting in its *viharn*. The low-ceilinged *viharn* is a work of art in itself, with mother-of-pearl doors and marble flooring. The whole temple is so highly regarded that visitors are expected to dress appropriately. This is not the place for flip-flops, tatty shorts or sleeveless shirts.

ROUTE DETAIL

Rail

All but one of the seven daily trains to Chiang Mai from Bangkok make a stop in Phitsanulok, as do six out of the seven that make the return journey.

Bus

Phitsanulok is well connected by bus with Bangkok, Chiang Mai and Chiang Rai, as well as smaller towns in between.

Phitsanulok's **Folk Museum** is at 26/43 Wisutkaset Rd, open Tues–Sun 0830–1630, admission by donation. You will not see a better ethnographic collection in Thailand, and a visit here is recommended because there are so many artefacts and items on display that are fast disappearing from Thai culture. Traditional rooms in a village home have been reconstructed and there is a wealth of clever little home-made devices that bear testimony to Thai ingenuity. The museum is within walking distance of the youth hostel, or take bus no. 8 from the town bus station.

Cross the road from the folk museum and a short distance south is a **Buddha-casting Foundry** that welcomes visitors who wish to watch the production process. The statues are made using the 'lost wax' process, which is explained with the help of photographs.

i There is a good **TAT office** on Sithamtraipidok Rd open daily 0830–1630, tel: 0-5525-2742. From the railway station walk south on Ekathosarot Rd for ½ km and turn right onto Sithamtraipidok Rd.

FLYING VEGETABLES

Phitsanulok is famous for its flying vegetable shows – culinary acrobatics involving the humble morning glory (*phak-bung*). The cook stir-fries the vegetable as normal but then hurls the *phak-bung* up and through the air to land on a plate held by a balancing waiter some distance away. The act is turning into a bit of a tourist show but is still fun to watch.

Topland Plaza Hotel $$$ 68 Ekathosarot Rd, tel: 0-5524-7800, fax: 0-5524-7815. A multi-storey hotel that deserves its name if you take a room on the higher floors. A swimming pool, restaurants, fitness centre and adjoining shopping centre combine to make this great value for money.

Amarin Nakhon Hotel $$$ 3/1 Chaophraya Rd, tel: 0-5521-9070. Reliable, run-of-the-mill establishment with a good restaurant.

Phitsanulok Youth Hostel $–$$ 38 Sanam Bin Rd, tel: 0-5524-2060. For the most pleasant budget accommodation in town take a *samlor* or *tuk-tuk* $ from town or the station, or bus no. 4, which runs past the hostel. Dorm beds, and rooms with air-con.

For budget rooms closer to the town centre, take the first turning right after leaving the train station and turn left. Saireuthai Road has a number of similarly priced $ hotels and guesthouses that are fine for a one night stay.

Phitsanulok Youth Hostel Restaurant $–$$ 38 Sanam Bin Rd. Open-air restaurant serving Thai and Western food in a very relaxed setting. There are a number of other restaurants along this stretch of road, most with air-conditioning and menus offering a good selection of Thai and Chinese meals.

Song Khwae Floating Restaurant $$–$$$ Buddhabucha Rd. Close to the post office on the east bank of the Nan River are a number of floating restaurants serving seafood and a mix of Chinese-style dishes. Not cheap, but good food and a lively atmosphere.

Follow the river to the south of these restaurants for a lively **night market** where a multitude of food stalls compete for business and where the 'flying vegetable' show is most likely to be seen.

For American fast food, head for the shopping complex at the Topland Plaza Hotel. Along Ekathosarot Rd, the road that runs past the railway station and up to the Topland Plaza, there are a number of food stalls and small restaurants.

A trip to moated Chiang Mai is a highlight of any visit to Thailand. By no means typical of Thai towns, Chiang Mai combines quaintness with modernity and has the best of everything the country has to offer, except for white sandy beaches. In terms of tourist infrastructure the place is hard to beat. It has an exemplary choice of places to stay and eat, undoubtedly the best shopping opportunities outside of the capital, and its compact size makes it a pleasure to get around. On top of this, Chiang Mai has pleasingly cooler evenings than many other parts of Thailand and is the nicest place to enrol in a course on Thai cooking, Buddhism, or a host of other learning programmes. However long your intended stay, the chances are you will consider staying longer.

The old part of the city is a neat square surrounded by moats. Moonmuang Rd, Chiang Mai's chic version of Khao San Rd in Bangkok, is a centre for inexpensive accommodation in and around Soi 9, and a good place to meet other travellers. There are plenty of good-value places to eat, tour agents, genuine massage centres, cookery schools and ice-cream parlours. There isn't a designer café there yet, but watch this space.

> **MUST SEE/DO IN CHIANG MAI**
> Visit Wat Phra Singh
> Hire a bike and go exploring in the narrow lanes of the Old City
> Visit the night bazaar
> Sign up for a course – Thai cookery, Yoga, Buddhism, Meditation . . .
> Take a picnic to the Tribal Museum
> Go on an excursion to Doi Suthep
> Check out the hill trek options
> Visit Doi Inthanon, Thailand's highest peak
> Try some *ahaan meuang*, Thailand's delicious northern cuisine

GETTING THERE AND GETTING AROUND

AIR As well as Bangkok, flights from Chiang Mai go to Chiang Rai, Mae Sot and Phuket. There are international connections with Singapore, as well as Vientiane, Mandalay, Yangon, Taipei and Kunming.

BUS The long-distance bus station is called the Arcade Bus Station, tel: 0-5324-2664, on Kaeo Nawarat Rd about 4 km out of the centre. The following list does not cover every route but gives an idea of availability: Chiang Rai 3–4 hrs ($$); Khorat 12 hrs ($$$); Mae Sot 6 hrs ($$$); Sukhothai 5–6 hrs ($$$); Udon Thani 12 hrs ($$$).

GETTING AROUND

A **BICYCLE** is ideal for temple-hopping trips. Along Moonmuang Rd there are places to rent bicycles and motorbikes such as Mr Kom just past the Shuffle restaurant at no. 131, tel: 0-5341-9114, and another operator right next door. There is also a place renting bicycles next to the tourist office on the east side of the river.

TUK-TUKS are useful when arriving and departing but always bargain for around 40B to or from the bus or train station or 50B to the airport.

SONGTHAEWS run up and down the main streets of Chiang Mai. Just flag one down and check it's going your way. The standard fare is about 10B.

CAR HIRE places are not in short supply. Always ask to see evidence of any insurance paid for, especially when dealing with smaller companies. Avis have a desk at the airport, tel: 0-5320-1574, and in town at the Royal Princess Hotel, tel: 0-5328-1033, e-mail: avisthai@loxinfo.co.th. National are also at the airport, tel: 0-5321-0118, and on Charoenmuang Rd, tel: 0-5324-5936, e-mail: smtcar@samart.co.th. Two local firms with good reputations are Queen Bee, Moonmuang Rd, tel: 0-5327-5525, and North Wheels, tel: 0-5341-8233, e-mail: sales@northwheels.com.

INFORMATION

MEDICAL SERVICES

There are lots of well-equipped hospitals with English-speaking doctors. Two that are well used to foreigners are McCormick Hospital, Kaew Nawarat Rd, tel: 0-5324-1311, and Chiang Mai Ram Hospital, Bunreuangrit Rd, tel: 0-5322-4861. You could also try the Global Doctor Clinic, Huay Kaew Rd, tel: 0-5321-7762.

i The **TAT office** is at 105/1 Chiang Mai-Lamphun Rd, open daily 0830–1630, tel: 0-5324-8607 or 0-5324-8604. Offers free town maps, general information and a list of approved tour operators. A few doors down is the **Tourist Police** office, tel: 0-5324-8130, fax: 0-5324-8974.

Chiang Mai Municipal Tourist Information Office at 135 Praisanee Rd, open Mon–Fri 0830–1630, tel: 0-5325-2557. Has a good free map of town showing all the hotels and guesthouses, and if that's all you want it is closer to the town centre than the TAT office.

Look out too for various free publications, like the monthly *Welcome to Chiang Mai & Chiang Rai* and *Chiang Mai Newsletter*, which are useful sources of information. Nancy Chandler's *Map of Chiang Mai* is worth buying if you're staying in the city for more than a couple of days.

CHIANG MAI

Scale: 0 — 1000 m / 0 — 1000 yd

N

To Tribal Museum

Chiang Mai National Museum

Phothara

Wat Chang Kham

Wat Chet Yot

Wat Ku Tao

Holiday Garden

Northern Palace

Chiang Mai Hills

Chomdoi House

Chonprathan

Nimmanhemin

Huai Kaeo

Chotana

Khlong Mae Kha

Erawan

Northern Inn

Lanna

Chiang Mai Orchid / Amity Green Hills

Swedish Consulate

Japanese Consulate

Bangkok

Maharaj

Sri Mangkhalan

National Library

Suan Dok Gate

Chiang Mai Come

Immigration Office

Terminal

Chiang Mai International Airport

International Trade Centre

Old Chiang Mai Cultural Centre

Super Highway

Thaipanet Market

Suan Prung Gate

Suan Dok

Hill Tribe Craft Shop

Suthep

Toti Payem Market

Agricultural Research Centre

Social Research Institute

Wat Suan Dok

Wat Chedi Luang

Phra Singh

Wat Phra Singh

Inthawarorot

Wiang Kaeo

Chang Phuak Gate

Wat Chiang Man

Sompet Market

Ratchaphanikai

Tha Phae

Tha Phae Gate

Wat Mahawan

Wat Bupharam

Wat Saen Fang

Chang Saen

Chiang Mai National Theatre & Fine Arts College

Suriwong

Chinese Consulate

Chang Loh Gate

Nantharam

Chiang Mai – Lamphun

Night Bazaar

Anusan Night Market

Chiang Plaza

Cinema

Empress

Charoen Prathet

River Ping Place

Chang Khlan

Klah Mosque

Lanna Palace

Mother and Child

Wat Ket Karam

Chiang Mai Plaza

Diamond

Riverview Lodge

Prince Kawila Monument

Kawila Barracks

Boxing Stadium

Samlaung

San Pa Koy Market

106

Naipol

Rat Uthit

Golf Course

Chiang Mai – Lamphun

Wat Pa Satoi

Railway Station

Rot Fai

Royal Park

Cinema

Charoen Muang

Dr. Watig

Wat Ku Kham

Telephone Exchange

Thung Hotel

Northern Crafts Centre

Super Highway

Wat Pa Khrang

Wiang Inn

Thanet Ping

Angket

Payap University

1006

Jet Liang

Wang Sing Kham

Mae Nom Ping

C. Pitakiat Bridge

Wat Chetupon

Wat Sri Khong

Nakhon Ping Bridge

Toh Lamyai Market

Worarot Market

Wiang Ping Bazaar

Nawarat Bridge

Charoen Prathet

Loikhro

Siam Paidoee

Rakang

Wat Phra Non

Bamrung Rat

Thai Tribal Crafts

British Council

McCormick

Montri

Baitong Garden Restaurant

Chinda

American Consulate

British Consulate

Muang Samfut Market

Wat Pa Pang

Ratchawong

Wat Papao

Wat Upakut

Loi Kroh

Sri Ping Muang

Ratchamanka

Chiang Mai Municipality Stadium

Pattana Chang Puak

Khuang Sing Market

Tharin Market

Wat Chang Kham

Nong Hoi

108

Sri Ping Muang

Chonprathan

Websites worth consulting are:
www.chiangmai-chiangrai.com,
www.chiangmai-online.com and
www.chiangmainews.com. As well as general information,
these sites can be used to reserve rooms at a variety of hotels
(and not just the five-star ones). Sometimes the rates are well
below the quoted rack rates.

ACCOMMODATION

Chiang Mai has a terrific range of accommodation possibilities but at peak times it
still pays to have something arranged for at least the first couple of nights. The peak
period is Dec–Feb and during the Songkhran festival in April.

Imperial Mae Ping $$$ 153 Sri Dornchai Rd, tel: 0-5327-
0160, fax: 0-5327-0181. The place to stay for comfort and
luxury. Good restaurants and a swimming pool in this well-
managed, busy hotel.

River View Lodge $$$ 25 Charoen Prathet Rd, Soi 4, tel:
0-5327-1109, fax: 0-5327-9019, website:
www.riverviewlodgch.com. In an attractive area of green by the
river with lots of shade and a small pool.

Traveller Inn $$$ 66 Loi Khraw Rd, tel: 0-5328-0977, fax:
0-5327-2078. Good, clean, value-for-money accommodation.
Mediocre restaurant but lots of cafés and restaurants along the
road. Centrally located and close to night bazaar.

Galare Guest House $$$ Soi 2, Charoen Prathet Rd, tel:
0-5381-8887, fax: 0-5327-9088. Comfortable rooms in a
pleasant setting and appealing restaurant overlooking the river.

Montri Hotel $$–$$$ 2 Rajdamnern Rd, Thapae Gate, tel:
0-5321-1069, fax: 0-5321-7416, e-mail: am-intl@cm.ksc.co.th.
One of the smarter hotels in this area, with an inviting bakery
in the lobby. Free airport transfer.

SP Hotel $$ corner of Soi 7, Moonmuang Rd, tel: 0-5321-
4522, fax: 0-5322-3042. Zero atmosphere in this large,
nondescript block but you get what you pay for.

Green Lodge $–$$ 60 Charoen Prathet Rd, tel: 0-5327-9188, fax:
0-5327-9188. Functional but perfectly adequate for a short stay.

Libra $–$$ 28 Soi 9, Moonmuang Rd, tel/fax: 0-5321-0687.
Well-established guesthouse with cooking school and trekking
options that gathers a hip crowd.

Daret's House $ 4, Chaiyaphum Rd, tel: 0-5323-5440, fax:
0-5323-2960. Centrally located with lots of cheap rooms.

FOOD AND DRINK

The Gallery $$$ 25 Charoenrat Rd, tel: 0-5324-8601. For a romantic, candle-lit dinner, reserve one of the riverside tables under lantern-lit trees. Delicious meat and vegetarian Thai food. Live music most evenings from 2000 and last orders around midnight.

Oriental Style $$$ 36 Charoenrat Rd, tel: 0-5326-2746, fax: 0-5324-5724. A stone-paved courtyard between two mid-19th century Chinese merchant houses has classical music, cocktails by candlelight, a choice of fish and imported steaks alongside many less expensive Thai dishes and a little surprise ceremony.

Piccola Roma $$$ 144 Charoen Prathat Rd, tel: 0-5382-0297. Chiang Mai is not noted for its European food but this restaurant has superb Italian food and a wine list to match. Free transport.

The Riverside $$ 9 Charoenrat Rd, tel: 0-5324-3239. The mother of all menus has Thai, European and vegetarian food, pizzas, curries, burgers, noodles, salads, sandwiches and breakfast. Live music nightly with an unfortunate bias for country and western. Open 1000–0100

Whole Earth Restaurant $$ Si Donchai Rd, tel: 0-5328-2463. Dine indoors or on the pleasantly shaded balcony from a menu which features Indian food alongside shrimp tempura and minced bean curd with chilli.

Tha Phae Gate $$ Moonmuang Rd. Tasty pizzas from a large wood-fired oven. Open 1100–0100, no air-conditioning.

Anusarn Market $–$$ Chang Khlan Rd has numerous food stalls and small restaurants at night to choose from.

Indian Restaurant $ Soi 9, 27/3 Moonmuang Rd. Small Indian place offering very inexpensive dishes and a choice of thalis. The proprietors also run cookery classes.

Vihara Liangsan $ off Chang Khlan Rd. A little tricky to find but worth the effort for the very cheap vegetarian Thai food. Walk south down Chang Khlan Rd from junction with Si Donchai Rd for about 1 km and turn left after a low-level white plaza to the restaurant less than 100 m away. Pile up your plate from ten or so dishes and take it to be weighed and priced. Rice and soup is included.

Galare Food Centre $ on Chang Khlan Rd has half a dozen outlets. Mostly Thai and some seafood and a very average Indian place. A nightly show of music and dance is a plus.

Aum Vegetarian Food $ 65 Moonmuang Rd, tel: 0-5327-8315. Low, Japanese-style and regular tables. Vegetarian Thai dishes like fried pumpkins with mushrooms and tofu. Decent coffee but disappointing desserts. Open 0830–1400 and 1700–2100, closed last Sun of month.

HIGHLIGHTS

If you are interested in the culture and art of northern Thailand it may be worth visiting the **National Museum, $,** open Wed–Sun 0900–1600, although it warrants a journey in itself because it is stuck out on Highway 11. Apart from the usual collection of Buddhas there are exhibitions on pottery and artefacts of ethnographic interest. Coming this far, it makes sense to walk west for 10 mins to **Wat Jet Yot** and its distinctive seven-spired *chedi*. The temple dates from the 15th century and its bas relief stucco work has been well preserved.

CHIANG MAI'S WATS

The old city is littered with temples but one that should be top of your list is **Wat Phra Singh** in Ratchdamnoen Rd. This delightful complex of buildings includes the photogenic **Lai Kham Viharn** which houses the much-revered Phra Singh image of the Buddha. Equally interesting are the late 18th century **murals** with all sorts of fascinating details of past life in northern Thailand.

On the way back to town along Ratchdamnoen Rd, turn right into Phra Pokklao Rd for the ruins of **Wat Chedi Luang**. Even the remains of this huge *chedi*, which once stood some 90 m high, are impressive, and when the present restoration work is completed the sight should be quite something.

A third *wat* worth seeing is **Wat Chiang Man**, off Ratchaphakhinai Rd in the old city. This is the city's oldest temple, founded in the late 13th century, with lovely gilded woodwork and fretwork that typifies northern Thai temple architecture. The *viharn* on your right, after entering the temple, contains two highly regarded Buddha images. The small one carved in stone is the Phra Sila, thought to come from India, while the really tiny crystal one from Lopburi is carried in procession through the streets during the Songkhran festival.

The most interesting museum is the **Tribal Museum**, Ratchamangkhala Park, open Mon–Fri 0900–1600, especially if you are planning a trek into the countryside. There are models of villages, exhibitions on agriculture, costumes, musical instruments, as well as useful general information on the cultures of the various tribes living in northern Thailand. A video is shown at 1000 and 1400. Food is not available at the museum but the nearby park makes a good picnic site.

THE BASTIONS OF CHIANG MAI The sleepy moats, bastions and gates which encompass old Chiang Mai are a dominant feature of this ancient city. They also make a good walking tour, though the full circuit is really only for the dedicated walker. The overall distance is just over 6 km, and though much of the walk is shaded by moat-side trees, except in the cool season it is probably better to go some of the way by bicycle, samlor or *tuk-tuk*.

A good place to start your tour is **Pratu Tha Phae**, the city's eastern entrance. About 5 m across (said to be 'the width of an elephant with one person on either side'), and protected by heavy, steel-bound wooden doors, the reconstructed gate sits on a flagstone square, dominating an area which has become the focal point for Chiang Mai's festivals and celebrations.

Turning southwards and proceeding clockwise, the first bastion reached is **Jaeng Katam**, or 'Fish Trap' Corner, where local people used to catch fish in a large pond which has long since disappeared. Continuing clockwise around the Old City, the next gate encountered is **Pratu Chiang Mai**. Dating from 1296 but rebuilt entirely 1966–69, this gateway used to lead to the old Lamphun Rd.

Further to the west **Pratu Suan Prung**, the entrance to the Old City's south-western quarter, is something of a curiosity. For centuries the citizens of Chiang Mai have used this gate to take their dead out of the city for cremation. Today Suan Prung is perhaps the quietest and most attractive of Old Chiang Mai's gates.

The next bastion reached, at the Old City's south-west corner, is **Jaeng Ku Ruang**. The bastion is in excellent condition, with well-preserved battlements offering clear views of Doi Suthep. The surrounding area, too, is pleasant, with children often to be seen swimming in the moats.

Continuing north beyond Ku Ruang corner, the ancient walls extend for some distance towards Chiang Mai's western entrance, **Pratu Suan Dok** or 'Flower Garden Gate'. In former times the gardens of King Ku Nu lay outside this gateway. It was he who, in 1371, founded Wat Suan Dok or the 'Flower Garden Temple'.

Head north for another 750 metres and you'll reach **Jaeng Hua Rin**, the city's north-western corner. This bastion, which faces Huai Kaeo Rd and offers fine views of Doi Suthep, is also well preserved.

To the east, set square in the centre of the Old City's northern wall, is the venerable **Pratu Chang Phuak**. Originally established by King Mangrai in 1296, this gate was once known as Pratu Hua Wiang, or 'Head of the City Gate', for it was the way by which rulers of the Kingdom of Lan Na entered the capital en route to their coronation. During the reign of King Saen Muang Ma (1385–1401), however, the neighbouring Chang Phuak (Albino, or 'White' Elephant) monument was erected, and the name of the northern gate was subsequently changed to Pratu Chang Phuak.

The fourth and last of the Old City bastions, **Jaeng Sri Phum** or 'Light of the Land' corner, is situated at the Old City's north-eastern corner, about 750 m due north of Tha Phae Gate.

EXCURSIONS **Hill trekking** (see p. 174 for details and tour operators) is the main activity undertaken by visitors to Chiang Mai but there are plenty of other options. One of the best is the trip to **Doi Suthep**, a mountain 16 km north-west of the city. The road to the summit leads past several attractive waterfalls, most notably – about 7 km from town – the Monthatharn Falls, a good spot for picnics. At KM14, and about two-thirds of the way up the mountain, is the beautiful and much revered **Wat Phrathat Doi Suthep**. This temple, which dominates the Chiang Mai skyline, provides wonderful views across the valley and should not be missed. Nearer the summit, the gardens of Phuping Palace can be a riot of colours depending on the season; they are open to the general public when the Royal Family is not in residence. From the top of the mountain there are breathtaking views and a delightful temple. *Songthaews* travel the paved road to the top of the mountain and leave Bangkok along Huay Kaew Road; they can be picked up outside Chiang Mai University. Most tour companies include a Doi Suthep trip in their itineraries.

BO SANG UMBRELLA VILLAGE This attractive village on Route 10076, about 10 km east of Chiang Mai, is devoted to the manufacture (and sale!) of umbrellas. Almost every household seems to be involved in the business, and craft shops abound. The whole process is readily visible to the visitor, and photography within the workshops is quite welcome. The objects manufactured, besides painted and lacquered paper umbrellas, include fans, silverware, bamboo and teak furniture, celadon and lacquerware. There's even a local Muslim family making fans decorated with verses from the Koran.

WAT PHRA THAT HARIPUNCHAI Lamphun, just half-an-hour's drive south of Chiang Mai, was founded in about AD 950 and is the oldest continually inhabited city in Thailand. Getting there is part of the attraction, as the old Chiang Mai–Lamphun road is lined with 30-m-high *yang* trees of venerable age. Lamphun is chiefly remarkable for the beautiful Wat Phra That Haripunchai, one of the very few examples of Dvaravati Mon architecture surviving anywhere in Thailand. Nearby hangs a giant gong, claimed to be the largest in the world. Opposite the temple is the excellent Lamphun National Museum.

Chiangmai Green Tours 29 Chiangmai–Lamphun Rd, tel: 0-5324-7374, fax: 0-5324-1504, e-mail: cmgreent@cmnet.co.th, have tours that are typical of those available from the better companies. Choose from **daily sightseeing tours** (Doi Suthep, elephant camp, handicraft factories, river cruise), mountain bike tours (half to two days), nature tours, elephant rides, bamboo rafting and an 'organic-agro tour'.

Tour companies can be found everywhere in Chiang Mai but Moonmuang Rd is a good hunting ground because they are all within walking distance of one another. Expect to pay around 450B for Doi Suthep and 900B for elephant riding and bamboo rafting.

Every day on the hour between 1000 and 1500 a **boat** leaves the pier at the Nawarat Bridge for a slow ride to Wat Tahlug Market and an agricultural centre. Guided **microlight flying trips** give an aerial perspective on the ancient city, tel: 0-5386-8460, e-mail: flying@cmnet.co.th.

SHOPPING

Many visitors to Chiang Mai skip the museums and only see a *wat* from the seat of a *tuk-tuk* because **shopping** takes up all their time. There is a great variety of handicrafts at prices that are generally affordable, and the whole experience of looking around shops is infinitely more enjoyable than anything Bangkok can offer.

The **night bazaar** starts mushrooming every evening on every night of the year on the pavements of Chang Khlan Rd between Loi Khraw Rd and Nawarat Bridge. This is the scene of Thailand's busiest tourist night market and a visit here should not be missed. A lot of the merchandise is the usual tourist junk consisting of counterfeit designer items and cheap handicrafts, but there is plenty to see and some of the clothes are very good value.

YOGA

Courses that could change your life abound in Chiang Mai. Take promises of metaphysical alchemy with a pinch of salt and establish exactly what is being offered, course numbers, duration and the tutor's experience.

Hatha Yoga Centre, tel/fax: 0-5327-1555, e-mail: marcelandyoga@hotmail.com. Marcel claims 20 years' experience. Weekday sessions 0800-1000 and 1700-1900.

Meditation and martial art **Tai Chi Chuan** classes start on the 1st and 16th of each month at Naisuan House, 3/7 Doi Saket Kao Rd, Soi 1, Room 201, tel: 0-5330-6048 ext. 201, www.taichithailand

Yoga Centre, 65 Arak Rd, tel: 0-5327-7850, www.infothai.com/yogacenter, e-mail: yogacntr@chmai.loxinfo.co.th.

The permanent shops on both sides of the street are also buzzing at night and have better quality goods and clothes. A few shops have a fixed price policy, which can be a welcome relief, but hard bargaining is the usual name of the game. Have a good look around to establish prices and work towards a hefty discount of anywhere between 20 per cent and 60 per cent off the first quoted price.

Export Co-Op, 9 Chang Khlan Rd, is a large store full of wonderful handicrafts, all with clearly displayed fixed prices. A shipping service is available; expect to pay around 8000B per cubic metre.

The non-market end of Chang Khlan Rd has a fair sprinkling of art and craft shops and some, like **Ishikawa Trading** at no. 185/1, have fixed prices. Ishikawa Trading has a neat collection of bags, hemp cloth sold by the metre and basketry.

Moonmuang Rd has a selection of mid-range shops like **Baan Welcome** at no. 155. It's at the north end of the road, just before the fruit market, and has fixed prices for its silk sold by the yard. Thapae Rd is similar, with shops like **City Silk** at no. 336 and its modern display of silk items.

Loi Khraw Rd, to the south, is well worth a look. **Nanthakan Chantarar** at no. 69 has a small but elegant selection of women's clothes at reasonable prices. **Earth Tone** is a similar kind of place about 100 m up the road on the other side. As well as clothes shops, this is a good area for handicrafts and souvenirs. **Chiangmai Hemp Store** at no. 15/3 is typical of the smaller stores along this road.

The **shopping plaza** opposite the Galare Food Centre on the night market street offers a quieter environment and better quality goods than the street outside. Good wood carvings, more serious art and craft shops selling 'antiques', and some talented artists can be found here.

Jewellery making: **Nova Collection** 201 Thapae Rd, tel/fax: 0-5327-3058, www.nova-collection.com, e-mail: nova@thaiways.com. Workshops in jewellery making, weekdays 1000–1530. A full five-day programme is US$100, excluding the cost of materials.

A good book makes all the difference on long journeys. The very useful **Lost Bookshop** 34/3 Ratchamanka Rd has a good selection of second-hand books and a discount if the book is returned. The best regular bookshop in town is the **Suriwong Book Centre,** 54 Si Donchai Rd.

NIGHTLIFE

Moonmuang Rd has lots of pubs, cafés and restaurants. At no. 47 **True Blue**, tel: 0-5327-8503, opposite the restored ancient wall, is open 0800–2400 for drinks, conversation, darts and pool. There is a garden area and food is served.

Kafe, next to the Shuffle restaurant at Soi 5, has a happy hour from 1600 to 1900 for beer by the pitcher.

Life Bar, on Loi Khraw Rd near Charoen Prathet Rd, is a roadside watering hole with a pool table which stays open until the last customers leave. **Joe's Place** next door is open until around 0100, dishing up hamburgers and steak and chips.

For a bit more bar space than Life Bar can manage, try around the corner on Charoen Prathet Rd where the **White Lotus Bar and Restaurant** has been serving reasonably priced cocktails for more than ten years.

The Good View, 13 Charoenrat Rd, tel: 0-5324-1866, is a well-stocked bar and restaurant with music from 2000 to 0100.

TRAVELLING AROUND THE NORTH AND NORTH-EAST OF THAILAND

Travelling around the north and north-east regions of Thailand on a budget is best achieved by hiring a motorcycle or bike, as hire and fuel costs are minimal. A motorcycle is generally B200 per day, a bike B50 per day (it never costs more than B50 to fill the fuel tank).

Also, by opting for these methods of transport, you get the chance to begin to venture out into the unexplored landscapes of the region, away from the tourist prices and into a world of many unique and fascinating cultures.

WHERE NEXT?

Before leaving Chiang Mai, consider hiring a car for a day and driving the 'Samoeng Loop' around Doi Suthep, the mountain which dominates the skyline to the west of the city. Head north-west along the Mae Sa Valley past butterfly farms, elephant camps and snake farms, then swing south past the isolated settlement of Samoeng over Krisda Doi, a winding pass leading back to Chiang Mai via the small town of Hang Dong. The entire drive takes about three hours, and en route you can visit the Queen Sirikit Botanical Gardens, currently being developed with the help of Kew Gardens in London. Another recommendation is a trip to the craft village of Ban Tawai, 15 km south on Route 108, famous throughout Thailand for its ceramics, woodcarvings and antiques.

To head further north, follow the Chiang Mai–Chiang Khong route, pp. 178–195.

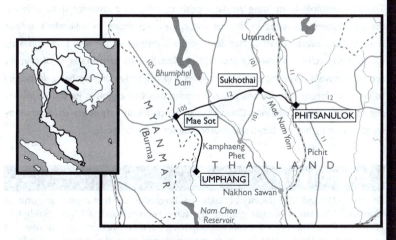

PHITSANULOK — UMPHANG
OTT Table 7076

Service	🚌	🚌	🚌	🚌	🚌	✈	✈
Days of operation	Daily	Daily	Daily	Daily	Daily	Daily	Daily
Special notes	**A**	**B**	**C**	**D**	**E**	**F**	**G**
Bangkok ....d.	0810	1040	0800	....	....	**F**	**G**	....
Phitsanulok ....d.	1340	|	|	**D**	....	**F**	|	....
Sukhothai ....a.	....	1740	|	**D**	....	....	|	....
Mae Sot ....a.	....	....	1600	**D**	**E**	....	**G**	....
Umphang ....a.	....	....	....	....	**E**	....	....	....

Special notes:
A–Additional services 1200, 1520, 2130, 2200, 2250.
B–Additional services 2200, 2240.
C–Additional services 0900, 1930, 2050, 2130, 2200, 2230.
D–Buses and *songthaews* operate throughout the day, journey time 3½ hrs.
E–Buses and *songthaews* operate throughout the day, journey time 5½ hrs.
F–5 flights a day. Journey time 40 mins.
G–1 flight a day. Journey time 30 mins.

Notes

Sukhothai can also be reached directly by bus and air from Bangkok and Chiang Mai and by bus from Khon Kaen.

There are buses to Mae Sot from Bangkok (8 hrs) and Chiang Mai (8 hrs).

The **Phitsanulok–Umphang route** appeals to different people for quite different reasons. Visitors interested in Thai art and culture are drawn to Sukhothai's ancient ruins, and the nearby town of Mae Sot and the Burmese border with their appealing mix of living cultures. Travelling south from **Mae Sot to Umphang** is of primary appeal to travellers seeking outdoor activities. Trekking and rafting are being developed to cater for foreign visitors, and this is a chance to visit a region in its tourist infancy and to escape from overdone Chiang Mai province. It's an easy route to discover by *songthaew* or by hiring a bicycle or motorcycle for a day or more.

SUKHOTHAI

Between 1238 and 1376 the city of Sukhothai reigned as the first capital of a unified Thailand. The ruins of that golden age have been restored to form Sukhothai Historical Park. This is the focus of any trip here, but there are other ancient sites and scenic spots in the vicinity. The more enterprising guesthouses organise affordable tours to the various attractions.

Sukhothai Historical Park, open daily 0600–1800, covers a large area and is divided into five zones, each of which charges a separate entrance fee ($) plus a small fee for a bicycle, motorbike or car. The central zone charges a little extra ($$).

There are so many ruins that there is a high risk of temple fatigue. It pays to select just one or two of the more interesting temples. Begin with a quick visit to the **museum, $,** open daily 0900–1600, near the entrance to the central zone. There is not a lot to see but it introduces King Ramkhamhaeng and his famous stele.

Inside the entrance to the central zone is the 13th-century moated **Wat Mahathat**, the most important site in the Park and well worth seeing. This was the kingdom's spiritual capital and the central *chedi* dominates the complex. It is the epitome of the lotus-bud style of *chedi* architecture that Sukhothai has come to represent.

A short way west is another fine example of the lotus-bud style in the *chedi* of **Wat Trapang Ngeon**. The *bot's* remains stand on a small island which you can walk to and the well-preserved stucco reliefs alone are worth a visit here.

Of the remaining four zones, all of which are spread out and best visited by bicycle, a visit to the north zone is the most fulfilling. There is a small information centre with a model of the whole site and the Khmer **Wat Phra Phai Luang**, converted into a Buddhist temple. Half a kilometre away, **Wat Sri Chum** boasts the largest Buddha in the Park, a fine example of monumental art.

GETTING TO AND AROUND SUKHOTHAI HISTORICAL PARK *Songthaews* run regularly throughout the day from New Sukhothai to the central zone. Once there, the best way to get around is to hire a bicycle from the vendors who congregate close to the museum. Be warned that during the hot months between March and October cycling around Sukhothai can be gruelling. Carry lots of water and consider turning up early in the morning. This also gives you an edge over the tour coaches and buses that start arriving after 0900. Alternatively, use the trolley bus that departs regularly from near the museum (\$) and shuffles visitors around the central zone.

A HISTORY LESSON

In the past it was the Khmer Empire, based at Angkor in what is now Cambodia, that ruled the land of what is modern Thailand. Early in the 13th century, however, two Thai generals overthrew the waning Khmer power and established the kingdom of Sukhothai.

Ramkhamhaeng, the son of one of the generals, Intradit, has a leading role in Thai nationalism because he is regarded as having established the modern Thai alphabet and encouraged the spread of Theravada Buddhism. His most famous inscription, known as the Ramkhamhaeng Stele, resides in Bangkok's National Museum. By the second half of the 14th century Sukhothai was losing out to the growing power of the Ayutthaya kingdom and the glorious childhood of Thailand was coming to an end.

Modern historians dispute this simple narrative and the whole role of King Ramkhamhaeng, and the stele may be a piece of political myth-making, but there is no doubting the significance of Sukothai and the richness of its artistic culture.

SRI SATCHANALAI HISTORICAL PARK

You can take a *songthaew* (\$) from Sukhothai to the Sri Satchanalai Historical Park, which many people consider prettier than the Sukhothai Historical Park. Do make the worthwhile detour to Wat Phra Sri Ratana Mahathat en route – this temple, housing one of Thailand's most beautiful images of the Buddha, is at Naresuan bridge, on your right heading out of Sukhothai towards Phitsanulok. Bikes can be hired to get around the park (\$), and antiques are on sale at the entrance. \$, open daily 0800–1700; tel: 0-5567-9211.

Lotus Village \$–\$\$ 170 Ratchathani Rd, tel: 0-5562-1484, fax: 0-5562-1463, e-mail: lotusvil@yahoo.com. One of the most attractive places to stay. Gardens, lotus ponds, rooms to suit different budgets and a stylish restaurant.

Number 4 Guest House $ 140/4 Soi Khlong Mae Lumpung, off Jarot Withithong Rd, tel: 0-5561-0165. Eight thatched bungalows surrounded by greenery, with private bathrooms. Thai cooking courses available. Charming setup. Although 20 mins on foot from town, it is on the road to the Historical Park.

🍴 Sukhothai has a very good **night market $** in the centre of town, where stalls serve up simple but delicious rice and noodle dishes.

Some of the hotels around the night market have decent restaurants. One of the best is the **Chinawat Hotel Restaurant $–$$** Nikhon Kasem Rd. Thai and Western dishes at very reasonable prices.

Dream Café $–$$ opposite the Bangkok Bank on Singhawat Rd, has a touch of class. It serves up good ice creams and coffees as well as a fair range of meals.

PHITSANULOK PROVINCE

A few other suggestions for Sukhothai and beyond, while you are in Phitsanulok province:

Folk Museum, housed in a traditional Thai house, at 26/43 Visutkhasat Rd, Muang District, Sukhothai 65000. Free; tel: 0-5525-8713

Thai cuisine at the night market on the town's riverside

Wat Phra Sri Ratana Mahathat at Naresuan bridge, which houses the nation's most beautiful Buddha image

Photo opportunity of the 'Indochina Intersection' stating how many kilometres to Da Nang, Rangoon and Kuala Lumpur, as Phitsanulok is the most central province of Thailand!

Homestay. Phitsanulok province offers an introduction to homestays with local villagers. Contact the **Hilltribe Welfare and Development Centre** on tel: 0-1674-8349; ask for Mr Shinji Miura for further details

Waterfalls and national parks. Consider taking a day trip to see Phitsanulok's waterfalls or Pichit's national parks (Chat Trakan, Thung Salaeng or Phu Hing Rong Kla)

MAE SOT

The town of Mae Sot is only 6 km from the Burmese border and, although there is not a great deal to do here, it is a relaxing and interesting place to break the journey from Phitsanulok or Sukhothai to Umpang. Mae Sot has a cultural mix of inhabitants – Burmese, Thais and Karen with their respective religions of Islam, Buddhism and Christianity – and there is still a perceptible sense of a border region that has only recently come in from the cold. Twenty years ago, when black-market traders almost openly carried guns, only the reckless traveller would have dreamt of spending time in this corner of the country.

Songthaews run throughout the day to the **Burmese border** at Rim Moei. The short journey is worthwhile if you have the time. The border is formed by the Moei River and, depending on the current political situation, you may well be able to take the ferry across for a day visit to Myanmar. The **border market** on the Thai side of the river is the main focus of interest, and although most of the merchandise takes the form of dried foods and domestic items there is always a smattering of Burmese goods that may take your fancy.

ARRIVAL AND DEPARTURE When travelling by bus to Mae Sot from Phitsanulok it is sometimes quicker to change buses at Tak rather than wait for a through bus.

Mae Sot is a friendly little town. When arrriving by bus, mention your guesthouse to the driver and the chances are he will drop you off close by.

The main bus station is right in the centre of town on Indharakiri Rd, although sometimes minibuses depart from around the nearby First Hotel. State your destination and you will be directed to wherever your bus leaves from.

Central Mae Sot Hill Hotel $$$ 100 Asia Rd, tel: 0-5553-2601, fax:0-5553-2600, www.centralgroup.com. A touch of luxury amidst jungle hills. Swimming pool, massage service, two tennis courts, comfortable rooms and a shuttle bus into town.
First Hotel $$ off Indharakiri Rd, tel: 0-5553-1233, fax: 0-5553-1340. Conveniently located for public transport. Non-air-con rooms are good value, although air-con rooms are also available.

Mae Sot Guest House $ Indharakiri Rd, tel: 0-5553-2745. A 10-min walk from the bus station. Very cheap but spartan rooms, some with air-con.

🍴 **Pim Hut $$** Tang Kim Chang Rd (turn left out of the bus station onto Indharakiri Rd and then right). The menu in this sociable place is a surprising blend of Asian and western cooking, with steaks and pizzas served alongside fried noodles and green curries.

Chez John $$, 656 Indharakiri Rd, tel: 0-5554-7206, offers an equally surprising combination of French and Thai dishes.

UMPHANG

The journey to Umphang from Mae Sot is a memorable one, as befits one of the most off-the-beaten-track destinations in the country. The road from Mae Sot climbs high into the mountains and follows a dizzying course up, down and through valleys until it drops into the soporific backwater of Umphang. It is more of an overgrown village than a town, where the streets have no names. Once you've had a look around you may well wonder what you are doing here. The answer should be trekking, because there is little other reason for making the journey.

The usual **trek** takes four days and three nights, and is usually a combination of rafting down the Mae Khlong River, 3- to 4-hr jungle walks, overnight camping and an elephant ride thrown in somewhere along the route. Cynics might say that this is just a copycat of the treks based around Chiang Mai, but at least you are not walking in the footsteps of many thousands of previous trekkers, which gives the whole experience a degree of novelty. Equally important, perhaps, you are less likely to encounter other groups using the same route.

Nearly every trek involves a visit to the **Thilawsu Falls**, a particularly memorable sight after the rainy season. Day trips are available through guesthouses in Umphang.

EN ROUTE

Most buses depart from both Mae Sot and Umphang in the first part of the day and the bum-numbing journey usually involves a lunch break along the way.

🛏 **Umphang Guesthouse $** tel: 0-5556-1021. On the left down the road that leads to the river. Cheap, adequate rooms with their own shower and toilet in a large wooden longhouse. This guesthouse is owned by BL Tours, one of the main trekking companies.

Phu Doi Campsite $ tel/fax: 0-5556-1279. There is a campsite, but stay in one of the wooden bungalows overlooking a pond. Clean rooms and a proprietor well versed in the trekking scene. Less than a 10-min walk from the centre.

TREKKING FROM UMPHANG

Some of the larger tour companies in Bangkok can arrange treks from Umphang, but they will probably subcontract the work to a local operator. The extra money you are paying is purely for the convenience of having the whole thing arranged in advance. Even with companies in Mae Sot you will end up paying the extra cost of private transport from there to Umphang.

So if you want to keep costs to a minimum just turn up and be prepared to spend a day or two asking around the guesthouses. At least this way you can be sure of determining exactly where you are going and the modes of transport – raft, elephant, jeep, whatever – involved.

The costs quoted here are based on trips arranged in Umphang and work out at around 3000B each for two people on a four-day/three-night trip, or 2000–3000B in a larger group of four people or more. These prices should cover transport, accommodation, meals and guide.

Umphang Hill Resort $ tel: 0-5556-1063, fax: 0-5556-1065. This is the prettiest location for accommodation. There are large expensive chalets $$$$ for groups as well as simple folksy bungalows for budget travellers. On the southern bank of the river, across from Umphang Guesthouse.

Umphang's new entry into the trekking scene is reflected in the scarcity of places to eat. Give it a few years and all will have changed but for the moment there is only one decent restaurant.

Phu Doi Restaurant $ on the main street, west of the *wat*. Thai rice, noodle and curry dishes make up the bulk of the menu but the meals are good. Without the Phu Doi life a trip to Umphang would be dismal indeed.

MYANMAR–THAILAND BORDER

In 2002–2003 there were several incidents involving Karen ethnic mountain people disappearing near the border between Myanmar and Mae Hong Son/Tak provinces; the bodies were mostly found in nearby rivers. Foreigners are at no risk – these incidents are between the Burmese and the Karen ethnics, not even the Thai natives. However, there are so many other Northern provinces that are peaceful and stable, so consider exploring these before the provinces right up against the Myanmar border.

TREKKING AND HILL TRIBES

TREKKING

Trekking in northern Thailand is not the same as trekking in Nepal, North America or most other parts of the world. The emphasis is not on day long walks through rugged landscapes, testing one's stamina and being rewarded with magnificent views of scenery or opportunities to observe wildlife. However, if it's landscape and views you're after, as opposed to the hill tribes, this can be arranged in areas such as Doi Ang Khang, Doi Chang Moob and Therd Thai villages.

The highlight in the north of Thailand is the hill tribes that inhabit the countryside. The people-spotting nature of some treks is something worth considering before setting off in the first place. Not everyone who goes on a trek enjoys playing the role of earnest Western traveller poking their nose into other people's cultures. Fortunately, the treks come in all shapes and sizes and you should be able to find one that suits your needs.

With the number of annual trekkers now approaching one hundred thousand (about one for every eight tribespeople) and the majority travelling within relatively small and defined areas, it should be obvious that the experience is not one of adventure exploration in virgin territory.

Different companies offer different types of treks. The trick is to know what you want and find a trek that can deliver. There is a multitude of companies promoting treks.

TREKKING COMPANIES

One company that offers genuine, long-distance treks operates through the **Libra Guesthouse** (see p. 158), tel: 0-5321-0687.

Companies that specialise in visits to hill tribes include **Trekking Collective**, tel: 0-5341-9079, fax: 0-5341-9080, e-mail: altreks@cm.ksc.co.th, and **Siam Adventures**, tel: 0-5384-2395, fax: 0-5384-2589.

Queen Bee Travel Service, tel: 0-5327-5525, fax: 0-5327-4349, is another reputable company that offers both long-distance treks and visits to hill tribes.

The **Population Development Association** (PDA) operates the Hilltribe Handicraft Centre and Museum in Chiang Rai city as well as supporting hill tribe villages in northern Thailand. They specialise in walking treks to the villages that they support, either daily or for two nights or more. They're open Mon–Fri 0900–2000 and Sat–Sun 1000–2000; 3rd Floor, PDA Building, 620/1 Thanalai Rd, Muang District, Chiang Rai 57000; tel: 0-5374-0088; e-mail: crpda@hotmail.com.

Track of the Tiger is based at Maekok River Lodge, Tha Ton, Chiang Mai province. They specialise in Kok river rafting treks and long tail boat journeys, especially into Chiang Rai. Tel: 0-5345-9328; fax: 0-5345-9329; www.siam.net/tiger; e-mail: tiger@loxinfo.co.th.

TREKKING AND HILL TRIBES

The tourist office in Chiang Mai has a list of those belonging to the Northern Thailand Jungle Tour Group. This group aims to maintain certain standards, use qualified guides and practise an awareness of the social impact of trekking on the tribes people and their culture.

Costs vary but expect to pay between B1500 and 2000B for a three-day/two-night trek with elephant riding and rafting. Many of the more popular treks hardly justify the name

because the actual amount of walking is minimal. Transport in four-wheel drive jeeps, elephant riding and river rafting only leave time for as little as 3 or 4 hrs' walking a day.

A good tour company will provide all the essentials, including food, water and sleeping bags, but still bring some water of your own and perhaps a sheet. Stout walking shoes are not essential in the dry months. Bring a small amount of cash but leave documents and valuables in a safe deposit box at your hotel or guesthouse. Only do this, of course, if you feel you can trust the place, and get a signature on your inventory.

You are paying for what you get but you are still a guest of the hill tribes and some rules of etiquette should be observed. While staying in a hill tribe settlement dress modestly and do not assume you can go anywhere and photograph anyone. It is not necessary to take gifts. Smoking opium appeals to some travellers but, while it undoubtedly provides something to talk about back home, it probably only encourages young villagers to take up the habit. Often the opium given to tourists is not of a quality to get anyone high. Needless to say, a drug-addicted guide hardly enriches the experience and many companies are able to guarantee a drug-free trek.

Chiang Mai remains the main centre for organising treks but Chiang Rai is rapidly developing in this respect. It is also possible to organise treks in Mae Sot and Umphang and other small towns. While some of these will usually work out to be less expensive they will also be less organised. The best time to trek is between November and February when the climate is cool, but it is possible anytime of the year.

HILL TRIBES

The word 'tribe' has all sorts of unfortunate connotations and it is not the best term to describe the ethnic minorities living in the northern highlands of Thailand. In the Thai language they are 'mountain people', and each ethnic minority has its own language and culture. None of the tribes are exclusively Thai and they can be found in various parts of South-East Asia and southern China. To find out more about them, a visit to the museums in Chiang Mai and Chiang Rai is recommended, particularly the new Hill Tribe Handicraft Centre and Museum in Chiang Rai City operated by the Population Development Association, where the volunteers speak good English and will increase your knowledge of these mountain people considerably.

KAREN (KARIANG OR YANG IN THAI) Karen people form the single largest group in Thailand, with a population of about 350,000 living west of Chiang Mai and along the border with Myanmar (Burma). They are engaged in a long-running guerrilla war against the military government in Myanmar. In Thailand they live in settled villages with their own small farms. Their homes look familiarly Thai, thatched and built on stilts, and although animism is their traditional religion the influence of Buddhism is making itself felt. Christian missionaries have also made a significant impact on their forms of worship and belief system. Unmarried females wear white, characteristically V-shaped, dresses with brighter colours reserved for those who marry.

HMONG (MEO) The Hmong are the second largest group, numbering somewhere in the region of 100,000 in Thailand. Many still live in south China, from where they originally came. Strongly associated with opium farming in the past (and today to a lesser degree), their homes are built at ground level in high altitudes. They make batik and their dress is highly distinctive with colourful embroidery and heavy silver jewellery worn by the women. On special occasions the wearing of multi-tiered neck rings, chains and rings is a striking sight.

LAHU (MUSSUR) More so than other groups, the Lahu have been converted by missionaries to Christianity and their traditional culture is steadily eroding. Their dress is colourful but varied and it is hard to recognise them by their clothes. Famous for their embroidered shoulder bags, most Lahu now wear factory-produced clothes. At around 80,000 in number, they make up the third largest ethnic minority in the country.

MIEN (YAO) The only group with its own written language, their Chinese origins are apparent in the use of Chinese characters in their writing. In addition, their traditional religion is a form of Chinese Taoism. Mien houses are built on the ground and are large enough to accommodate extended families of 20 or more members. More so than any other hill tribe, the Mien women can be instantly recognised by their customary large black turbans and striking red woollen ruffs. The embroidery work that characterises both male and female dress is wonderfully intricate and an opportunity to visit a Mien village when a ceremony like a wedding is taking place should not be missed.

AKHA (KAW, EEKAW) Originally from Tibet and in Thailand mostly living around Chiang Rai, the Akha have a lower standard of material life than most other tribes but have also preserved their traditional cultural forms more stubbornly than others. They still follow a shifting system of cultivation, and the fields that are fixed are commonly devoted to the cultivation of poppies to produce opium. Akha people smoke the opium themselves as well as using it as a cash crop. Their forms of dress are distinctive, particularly the women's headdresses made up of their finest jewellery and often including coins collected over a period of time, which makes the value of each headdress quite substantial. Their distinctive dress makes the Akha people easy to distinguish on the local *songthaews* travelling between Mae Sai border town and Chiang Rai city, stopping off at the Chiang Saen Sunday markets to sell their produce. Akha children wear colourful caps, also decorated with beads, silver coins and tassles, while the men's dress tends to be more restrained.

LISU (LISAW) Only numbering about 30,000, the Lisu inhabit high lands north-west of Chiang Mai where they used to grow opium (and where, probably, some still do). Their dress is very colourful. Tassles are a major feature, hanging from the waist or from turbaned headgear. Women wear knee-length tunics and skirts with bright reds and greens and a wide black sash around the waist.

HILLTRIBE HANDICRAFT CENTRE AND MUSEUM

Be sure to make a special detour to Chiang Rai City to visit this attraction and increase your knowledge of the mountain people's culture and way of living before trekking to their villages. The museum is managed by the Population Development Association (PDA), a worthy association that has the mountain people residing within Thailand truly at heart. One of the most interesting Akha villages currently under development is Ban Lorcha in the Doi Mae Salong mountain range.

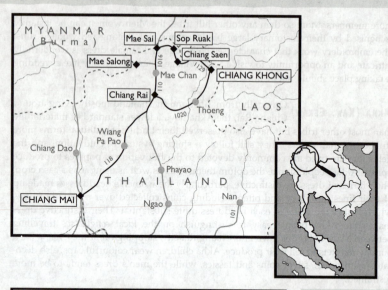

CHIANG MAI — CHIANG KHONG
OTT Tables 7076/7072

Service	🚌	🚌	🚌	🚌	🚌	🚌	🚐	✈
Days of operation	Daily	Daily	Daily	Daily	Daily	Daily	Daily	Daily
Special notes	A	B	C	D	E	F	G	H
Bangkok ....d.	0630	0730	1830	1900	....	....	....	H
Chiang Mai.............d.	|	|	|	|	....	0830	....	H
Chiang Rai ....d.	|	|	0630	|	0730	|	....	H
Mae Sai ....a.	|	1930	....	|	0845	1330	G	....
Sop Ruak ....a.	|	....	....	|	....	....	G	....
Chiang Saen ....a.	|	....	....	0930	....	....	G	....
Chiang Khong ....a.	1930	....	....	....	....	....	G	....

Special notes:
A–Additional services 1810, 1900, 1930, 1940, 2000.
B–Additional services 1805, 1900, 1940, 2030.
C–Additional services 1700, 1910, 1915, 1930.
D–Additional services 1530, 1800.
E–Additional services 0745, 0930, 1000, 1015.
F–Additional services 1000, 1045, 1400, 1445, 1615.
G–Frequent services operate between these towns.
H–There are 5 flights a day between Bangkok and Chiang Rai, journey time 1½ hrs, and 2 a day between Chiang Mai and Chiang Rai, journey time 25 mins.

Notes

Chiang Rai has useful bus connections with other parts of Thailand, besides Chiang Mai and Bangkok. There are daily buses to Khon Kaen (see p. 201), taking 11–12 hrs, and Phitsanulok (see p. 153), taking 5–6 hrs.

There are good transport links between Chiang Saen and other towns, including direct buses to and from Chiang Rai and Chiang Mai.

Route 118 connects Chiang Mai (see pp. 155–166) with Chiang Rai and takes the visitor from well-heeled cosmopolitanism to workday earthiness. Chiang Rai may be the tourist centre for trips around the self-acclaimed Golden Triangle area but it is also recognisable as a working town which looks as if it could survive a collapse in tourism less painfully than Chiang Mai. A lot of visitors spend a couple of nights in Chiang Rai before heading off on a hill tribe trek.

Another activity worth considering is hiring a car and heading further north to meander along the banks of the River Mekong. This is the Golden Triangle region, with Myanmar (Burma) and Laos on the other side of the river, luridly evoked in films about drug running. There is no danger for the traveller but it adds an enjoyable frisson and local Thais have sensed its commercial potential, retailing a whole line of T-shirts featuring opium plants and the like.

Travellers who are pressed for time and cannot complete all of this Chiang Rai–Chiang Khong route should consider skipping out Mae Sai and Sop Ruak and hop from Chiang Rai to Chiang Saen and then return by way of a direct bus to Chiang Mai.

CHIANG RAI

Not so many years ago, Chiang Rai was the ultimate northern outpost for intrepid travellers but now it is more of a centre for tourists who look down on Chiang Mai as *passé*. The generally high standard of accommodation is attracting an increasing number of visitors and Chiang Rai is steadily beginning to rival Chiang Mai as a centre for organising ethnographic treks into the countryside. A basic observation: Chiang Mai is best for shopping; Chiang Rai is best for cultural adventures.

If this is your thing, a good place to start is the **Hilltribe Museum & Education Centre**, 620 Tanalai Rd, open daily 0900–2000, tel: 0-5371-9167. A big new centre, six times the size of the old one, is currently being constructed next door to the existing museum. This will mean more of everything: handicrafts,

TRIPS TO LAOS

A typical one-day trip from Chiang Rai involves a boat crossing to Huaixai village, Bokeo province, in Laos and a shopping-oriented visit to a hilltribe village, followed by a visit to a sapphire mine or a disused airport used during the Vietnam War. A couple could expect to pay 4000B–4500B including transport, a guide, lunch and visa fee. The visa needs three days to process; consider arranging this in Bangkok or Chiang Mai.

TOURS FROM CHIANG RAI

As in Chiang Mai the tourist office has a list of approved tour companies which includes a guide to average prices for different types of tours and treks.

One of the companies, **PDA Tours** tel/fax: 0-5374-0088, e-mail: crpda@hotmail.com, is based at the Hilltribe Museum & Education Centre. Profits go directly to support community development projects amongst the hill tribe communities.

A company that caters for long-distance treks is **Golden Triangle Tours** 590 Phaholyothin Rd, tel: 0-5371-1339, fax: 0-5371-3963. It is worth comparing their deals with PDA who can also organise serious treks.

Chat House 3/2 Soi Saengkaew, Trirat Rd, tel: 0-5371-1481, has been recommended for backpackers seeking good deals. Its treks in the Chiang Rai area cover Amphoe Muang, Amphoe Mae Suai and the banks along the Mekong River.

Many tour companies also offer one-day visits into the countryside with either no trekking at all or very easy walks lasting a couple of hours at most.

Maesalong Tours 882 Phaholyothin Rd, tel: 0-5371-6505, fax: 0-5371-1011, e-mail: msltour@loxinfo.co.th, for example, organise a one-day trip using *tuk-tuk*, speedboat and elephant to visit a Mien village before a splash at a waterfall and then an Ahka village. The cost for one person is 600B.

Tour East is possibly the most helpful and professional tour company in Chiang Rai city. The office is about 5 mins from the airport; tel: 0-5370-2902. The company offers friendly guides with excellent English. Their tours include river, border, hill tribe, elephant, rafting and mountain scenic trips. You can follow one of their programmed tours or design one yourself.

jewellery, tapes of tribal music and so on. There are useful exhibits on the six major hill tribes and a slideshow in various languages, as well as very knowledgeable English-speaking volunteers.

During the day Chiang Rai takes on a desultory mood and there is little to do, but at night the place livens up a little as the shops come alive, stalls appear on the street pavements and the night bazaar gets going. The town itself is not particularly attractive and, despite its situation on the south bank of the Kok River, little is gained by the riverside setting.

There is not much to see about town but a temple that is worth a visit during daylight hours is **Wat Phra Kaeo**, on Trairat Rd within easy walking distance of the tourist office (see opposite). The story goes that a bolt of lightning in the 15th century split open the *chedi* and out popped the Emerald Buddha, the country's most revered image which is now in Bangkok (see p. 86). In the 1990s an imitation of the figure was commissioned by a local Chinese millionaire and although not an exact replica – that would break temple protocol – the differences are minor. A new shrine built for the new image stands behind the temple's *bot* by the ponds.

ARRIVAL AND DEPARTURE

Bus: There are two bus routes between Chiang Mai and Chiang Rai, designated 'old route' and 'new route'. Make sure you take the new route to avoid stopping at various towns along the way and lengthening the journey considerably. However, if you have the time, the bus on the old route passes some beautiful mountain scenery and links Tha Ton to Chiang Rai by boat along the Kok river. The bus station is a couple of blocks south of Phaholylothin Rd in the centre of town, which is fine for some of the hotels that are within walking distance but an exhausting trek in the heat to some of the guesthouses.

The free map provided at the TAT office lists bus routes, schedules and prices, but the TAT office is quite a walk from the bus station, so if you've a pack on your back splash out and catch a *tuk-tuk* **($)**.

Air: Chiang Rai's airport is 10 km north of town, off the main highway to Mae Sai. Car hire desks are at the airport, taxis run into town for a steep fee **($$)**, but sometimes if you walk to the front of the airport gates and wait a little time, there are taxis that will take you into Chiang Rai for a lesser fee **($)**, after a bit of haggling. Many of the hotels have minivans waiting for passengers.

> *i* **TAT Office** 448/16 Singhaklai Rd, tel: 0-5374-4674, open daily 0830–1630. Provides useful map of Chiang Rai, which includes little maps of Mae Sai, Chiang Khong and the Golden Triangle region as a whole. Accommodation and tour company lists and a great range of brochures on many attractions are available and the staff are cheerfully helpful.
>
> **PDA Tours** at the Hilltribe Museum and Education Centre function as a general tour agency and can provide travel information, from booking hotels and air tickets to elephant rides and treks.

🛏 **Wiang Inn $$$$** 893 Phaholyothin Rd, tel: 0-5371-1533, fax: 0-5371-1877. Set back from the main road, this is the plushest hotel in the town centre, with a swimming pool.

Kaven Guesthouse Bang Tung Phiao, 14 Moo 8, Wawi, PO Box 21, Mae Suái 57180 Chiang Rai, tel: 0-1885-7621, email: kavenguesthouse@hotmail.com. Kaven family-run guest house.

Bez $ So Soi Sanpanard Paholyothin Rd, Chiang Rai, tel: 0-1993-4404. Hot water, food and drink.

Pintamorn Guest House $–$$ 509/1 Rattanaket Rd, tel: 0-5371-5427, fax: 0-5371-3317. A good all-purpose guesthouse with a spacious restaurant area, choice of rooms with and without air-con, motorbikes for hire and the chance to meet travellers returning from treks. Close enough to the centre of town to reach on foot from the bus station.

Chat House $ 3/2 Soi Sangkaew, off Trairat Rd, tel: 0-5371-1481. Well known to veteran Thai travellers, laid-back Chat House is still going strong and continues to offer a good deal to budget travellers. Some rooms have air-con and dorm beds are also available. Bicycles and motorbikes can be hired and competitively priced trekking tours can be arranged.

🍽 **Cabbages and Condoms $$** Hill Tribe Museum, 620 Tanalai Rd. Still one of the most pleasant places in town for a Thai meal with dishes like *tao hoo song kreung* (stir-fried chicken with tofu and eggplant). Few vegetarian options.

Aye's Place $–$$ on Phaholyothin Rd near the bus station is Chiang Rai's best Western-style restaurant. Service can be slow but the menu has a cheering variety of cocktails and non-alcoholic drinks, a vegetarian selection, the usual Thai dishes and a set of 'world dishes' like goulash, wiener schnitzel, chilli con carne and lasagne. Aye's Place is a good place to meet fellow travellers and swap stories, and has good nightly live bands.

Easy Bar and Restaurant $–$$ Thanon Jet Yot Rd, opposite the Wangcome Hotel. Tastefully decorated in northern Thai handicrafts and Mekong river driftwood, this place serves Chiang Rai's biggest sandwiches as well as offering comfortable accommodation.

Lotous Bakery House $ located in the street opposite Edison department store off Paholyothin Rd, near the Thai Air Office. Thai and European cuisine including speciality ice creams.

Pintamorn Restaurant $ 509/1 Rattanaket Rd, is the dining area of the guesthouse of the same name. Very American, with Confederate flags decorating the walls and pancakes on the breakfast menu. A sociable place.

The night food market $ near the bus station has the best selection of inexpensive food in town and is well used to tourists. Tables are laid out in a central square and the food brought to you from whatever stalls you order from. Or you can sit on the balcony at **Ratanakosin Restaurant $$** and watch the hoi polloi eating in the market below. The menu is Thai and there are reasonably priced set dinners.

The two roads that run into each other, Jet Yod Rd and Suksathit Rd, parallel to Phaholyothin Rd behind the Wangcome Hotel, have half a dozen inexpensive eating places and small bars. It is worth a stroll after dark to see which ones are the most lively. **Moom-Thammachat $** 897/2 Jed Yod Rd is a quiet little place with tables tucked away in the shade of trees and plants with art work for sale on the walls. The food is good, including some spicy vegetarian dishes.

GETTING AROUND THE MEKONG AREA

Taking an organised tour (see p. 180) is one way to get around the border area along the Mekong River to places like Mae Sai, Sop Ruak, Chiang Saen and Chiang Khong. But hiring a car or motorbike gives you a lot more freedom and control over your time and itinerary. The roads are good, generally well marked and there is little traffic, making driving in this corner of northern Thailand a leisurely and enjoyable experience.

Expect to pay between 900B and 1500B for a jeep or 200B to 500B for a motorbike. A reputable company that won't pull any insurance scams is Avis, at the airport and Dusit Island Resort tel: 0-5371-5777. Other reputable companies include Budget, 590 Phaholyothin Rd, tel: 0-5374-0442 and VR Car Rent, opposite Wangcome Hotel and around corner from Edison, tel: 0-5375-2857; 0-1764-1885; B110 per day per car B700 per day per jeep. The three companies will deliver the car to your hotel and collect it for a small fee, usually around B100–200.

SHOPPING The **night bazaar,** off Phaholyothin Rd and near the bus station, can't compare with Chiang Mai's in terms of size or variety, but prices are considerably lower and there isn't as much pure tourist junk. This is probably the cheapest place in northern Thailand for handicrafts and souvenirs, spread out on stalls and the pavements by importuning but friendly tribes people. Amongst the trinkets and bric-a-brac there is enough of interest – shoulder bags, gorgeous picture frames, hand-made cushions, bags, brass – to warrant buying another piece of luggage to carry it all. You can also enjoy northern Thai classical dance shows and live folk music nightly at the bazaar.

Phaholyothin Rd has a few shops selling wood sculptures, small mobiles and other handicrafts. **Silver Birch** at no. 891 is fairly typical. **Lily's Handicrafts**, opposite the Wangcome Hotel on Pemavip Rd, is not worth visiting for its handicrafts but there is a large selection of ethnic-style clothes, mostly for women. There is a small department store along this road, Edison, which also serves as a recognisable landmark for taxi drivers.

EXCURSION TO MAE SALONG

The unique village of Mae Salong, now officially called Santikhiri, but no one calls it that, lies north-west of Chiang Rai. The origins of Mae Salong's strangeness go back to Mao Tse Tung's victory over the Chinese Kuomintang nationalists in 1949. The main body of nationalists fled to Taiwan under Chiang Kai-shek, where they still defy mainland China, but another group found refuge in northern Thailand and Burma.

As hopes of toppling the communists faded, the nationalists turned to the opium trade and became a permanent presence. After being expelled from Burma, Mae Salong became their main settlement and the isolated location – the road from the highway has only been paved in the last few years – made it difficult for the Thai military to impose their authority. Even today you are just as likely to hear Yunnanese – the Chinese dialect of the Kuomintang nationalists – being spoken as Thai, although the opium trade is now restricted to land across the border in Burma.

The Thai government has worked assiduously to deal with the situation and replace opium growing with other forms of agriculture. This has been largely successful, hence the change of name to mark Mae Salong's new identity. But the Chinese character of the village remains and a visit here is well worth considering because it is a very singular place. Although there are no particular sights or sites, it is enjoyable just to wander around and take in the obvious and not-so-obvious reminders of Chinese culture.

If you are here early in the morning, check out the **morning market** near the Shin Sane guesthouse when Akha, Mien and Lisu people display their produce. Also worth visiting is the tea factory in town (tours can be arranged through the Chiang Rai TAT office). On some of the pavement stalls and at the traditional Chinese medicine store near the Shin Sane guesthouse there are curious bottled concoctions of whisky made from local corn. Look closely and you will see some unlikely pickled ingredients, including the odd centipede. At weekends especially, Thai people flock here in groups to sightsee and buy local goods, but if you stay overnight you will have the place to yourself.

The surrounding countryside presents **trekking** opportunities. The Shin Sane guesthouse can organise day treks to nearby hill tribe villages, including donkey journeys.

GETTING THERE Take any bus from Chiang Rai heading north to Mae Sai and ask for Ban Basang (also spelt Ban Pasang), just north of Mae Chan village on the highway. This leg of the journey takes about 40 mins. From Ban Basang there are *songthaews* running the 36 km to Mae Salong. It takes about an hour to climb up to an altitude of 1200 metres. A *songthaew* should charge about B50–60.

By car, drive north from Chiang Rai on Highway 110. After Mae Chan look for the turn off left for Mae Salong on road no. 1130. After a short while this becomes the 1234 road to Mae Salong.

You could visit Mae Salong as a day trip from Chiang Rai but the last *songthaew* back to Ban Basang leaves in the late afternoon and then you have to wait on Highway 110 for a late bus travelling south from Mae Sai. Better to spend a night and set off early the next morning, because there is reasonable accommodation in the village and the hotels and guesthouses are all easy to locate. Alternatively, you could charter a *songthaew* back to Chiang Rai for B500 or to Mae Sai for B250, or even to Chiang Saen for B600.

🛏 **Asa's Guest house** tel: 0-1961-0268, fax: 0-5339-2763, www.infothai.com. Now travellers are choosing accommodation with a difference, so thy this home stay in a Lisu hill tribe village between Tha Ton and Mae Salong. The village is called Louta.

Mae Salong Villa $$–$$$ tel: 0-5376-5114, fax: 0-5376-5039. Good value bungalows with moody views of Burma just a short distance away.

Shin Sane Guest House $ tel: 0-5376-5026. The best deal for budget accommodation. Friendly, well-informed management.

🍽 The places to stay all have restaurants. The one at Mae Salong Villa has an especially attractive setting. Well worth sampling from any of the numerous food stalls in town is the tasty Yunnanese chicken noodle dish.

MAE SAI

This is the northern end of the line as far as Thailand's territory goes, and Mae Sai thrives on its proximity to Myanmar, more familiar as **Burma**, which is just across the river. The town would be a dusty backwater without its border crossing, but the constant coming and going of people and cross-border trade give it a degree of atmosphere. Travellers hang out here for days because the place feels foreign and ever so slightly illicit. Tourists do not arrive in their thousands, and because Mai Sai gets along fine without them the place has a likeable authenticity.

It is easy to cross from Mae Sai into Burma, which is another attraction of being here. Even if you stay on the Thai side of the border, there are constant reminders of Burma's closeness. Cafés and restaurants serve Burmese food, characteristically Burmese handicrafts like the shining lacquerware are displayed on pavement stalls, and every morning and evening there is a constant flow of human and vehicular traffic across the bridge.

For a good view of Mae Sai walk south from Top North Hotel down Phaholyothin Rd and turn right to **Wat Phrathat Doi Wao**. The temple itself is definitely not worth the journey but from the top of the hill there are great views of the town and the languid Sai River, with Myanmar stretching away on the other side of the water and Laos visible in the east.

ARRIVAL AND DEPARTURE

Car: Highway 110 from the south makes its way into Mae Sai and leads right up to the border bridge. If arriving by car stay alert or you'll find yourself in the queue for cross-border traffic, though just before the bridge a turning on the left leads to Sawlongchong Rd, the main drag for inexpensive accommodation and eating.

Bus: The main bus station is 4 km south of town but every 15 mins a *songthaew* leaves from opposite the Leo Hotel, outside the Mail Boxes Alliance Co. Ltd office. (This office, incidentally, is a good little setup from where you can send e-mails and faxes.) The most frequent bus connection is with Chiang Rai but buses also depart for Chiang Mai (5 hrs) and Bangkok (around 14 hrs). Air-con buses to Chiang Mai can also be picked up from the Mae Sai Plaza Guest-house at 0715 and 1400 daily. The buses from here to Chiang Rai leave every 15 mins 0600–1830.

Wang Thong Hotel $$$ 299 Phaholyothin Rd, tel: 0-5373-3388, fax: 0-5373-3399. The most ostentatious and expensive hotel in town, with a pool, bar and restaurant. Room rates are dropped when business is slack.

Kobra Joe's Guest House $ Sawlongchong Rd, tel: 0-5373-3055, e-mail: kkmaesai@chmai.loxinfo.co.th. Very popular with travellers. The owner, American Joe, arranges 'unorganised' treks and does very substantial breakfasts. Watch out for the bottled snakes though.

Mae Sai Plaza Guesthouse $ 386/3 Sawlongchong Rd, tel: 0-5373-2230. This photogenic place could win a prize for its location, with tiered shack-like bungalows hanging on to a hillside overlooking the river. The upper levels have terrific views across to Burma and there is a useful choice of rooms ranging from singles with shared bathroom to doubles with private facilities.

Northern Guest House $ Sawlongchong Rd, tel: 0-5373-1537. Right by the river, this crazily designed place has rooms with balconies, and bungalows with shared outdoor facilities.

The best place for a meal for comfort and service is the **Wang Thong Hotel Restaurant $$** (see above) but if you're unlucky a tour bus will turn up and disgorge its passengers just as your appetiser arrives. There are a few decent eating places along **Phaholyothin Rd**, in particular **Jo Jo Restaurant $**, opposite the Thai Farmers' bank. This is very popular with Thais and tourists alike and serves good vegetarian choices as well as tasty Muslim influenced foods. There are also some inexpensive restaurants in the various guesthouses along **Sawlongchong Rd. Northern Guest House Restaurant $**, for example, has a pleasant setting and a large menu featuring omelettes, salads, chips, chicken and fish.

TRIPS INTO BURMA For a day trip across the Mae Sai international bridge to Thakhilek (also spelt Tachilek), the town directly opposite Mae Sai in Burma, go to the Immigration Office 3 km south of the border on Paholyothin Rd to pay the B250 fee.

There is nothing exotic about Thakhilek, in fact it looks just like Mae Sai, and you pay for everything using baht. The handicrafts and 'antiques' for sale are indistinguishable from what's displayed back on the Thai side but the food is Burmese and there are lots of cheap places to enjoy a quick meal. Westerners can even spend a night down by the river in fairly cheap, basic bungalows.

A longer trip into Burma, for up to two weeks, means travelling past Thakhilek to the town of **Kengtung** (Chiang Tung in Thai), over 160 km away. From here, it is not a huge distance to the Chinese border but foreigners are not yet allowed to travel past Kengtung. To arrange this trip enquire at any of the guesthouses in Mae Sai.

Bear in mind, though, that Myanmar is a military dictatorship and Burmese human rights groups argue that foreigners should not visit the country until the present state of affairs shows some improvement.

EXCURSION TO DOI TUNG The journey to the 1800-m summit of Doi Tung is half the fun of the trip but when you do arrive there are spectacular views of the Chiang Rai region from **Wat Phrathat** on the summit. The border with Myanmar is very close indeed and opium poppy cultivation is going on within a few miles of where you stand. The *wat* is supposed to date back to the early 10th century and Thai pilgrims earn spiritual brownie points by ringing its row of bells. The story goes that when the *wat* was completed in 911 the local king unfurled a huge flag from the twin *chedis*.

There is a Thai **royal villa** near the summit. The idea was that royal patronage would encourage government endeavours to wean villagers off poppy growing and into alternative forms of agriculture. The project seems to have been very successful to judge from the dense woods of planted trees and cash crops.

OPIUM'S GOLDEN TRIANGLE

The northernmost province of Chiang Rai is part of the infamous poppy producing Golden Triangle formed by the converging borders of Myanmar, Laos and Thailand and southern China not far away. The amount of opium being cultivated in the Chiang Rai province today is so insignificant, mainly as a result of government policy and law enforcement, that locals resort to conjuring up suitably enticing images from its recent past to entice tourists.

Hill tribe people cultivated opium mainly because it can flourish at high altitudes, climate permitting, and it can be readily converted into cash. Attempts to dissuade farmers from growing poppies were doomed to failure until grants backed up campaigns to switch to more benign crops like tea, coffee and cabbage. Opium addiction is still a fact of life among some of the hill tribes, especially the Hmong. To find out more on the subject a visit to the small opium museum at Sop Ruak is recommended.

From Mae Sai travel south by car on Highway 110 for around 25 km to Ban Huai Klai or, from Chiang Rai, travel north on the highway for about 35 km. A paved road leads from a turn off on Highway 110 at Ban Huai Klai. From here it is only 24 km to the summit, but the route follows a torturously winding road and due care is required if driving. The journey is an exciting one as the road gropes its way through Akha and Lahu villages, passing what were once poppy plantations.

Tours to Doi Tung can be arranged in Chiang Rai or Mae Sai. Public transport is also available by asking the driver of a Mae Sai–Chiang Rai bus to drop you off at Ban

Huai Klai, from where *songthaews* travel to Doi Sai. *Songthaews* only make the run during the mornings and afternoons, mostly taking Thai pilgrims to the temple at Doi Tung, and at weekends are always more regular. It is possible to hitch a ride or consider paying the full whack, about 500B, to hire an empty *songthaew*.

SOP RUAK

Sop Ruak, where two rivers and three countries meet, has become the designated tourist centre of the Golden Triangle, especially for tour groups who are not always dissuaded from thinking fierce bands of drug-dealing bandits are lurking behind trees. A reassuring line of stalls selling T-shirts and tourist junk should help remove this misapprehension.

GETTING THERE

There is no bus service to Sop Ruak, but *songthaews* travel every 20 mins or so from Mae Sai. *Songthaews* also travel every 30–40 mins between Chiang Sae and Sop Ruak with the last service no later than 1500.

UP THE MEKONG

From the many boat piers in Sop Ruak there are longtail boat trips visiting Don Sao Island in Laos. The cost of a boat trip is B400 per boat and the driver will wait as long as you like on the island. There is an admission fee to the island of B20 per person and it is well worth the visit. This is also a great place to buy good French wines at very cheap prices as well as beautiful, natural toned Laotian textiles.

What does lend some romance to the location, apart from the fact that Thailand, Laos and Myanmar converge exactly at this spot, is the broad but sluggish sweep of the Mekong River and its confluence with the Ruak River. Sop Ruak itself is very much an invented tourist destination, by and large constituted by an excess of tourist stalls and a number of large hotels along and around the main road east of Mae Sai.

Roadside signs constantly proclaim that visitors are now in the Golden Triangle but the only evidence of this is a small museum, the **House of Opium, $,** open daily 0800–1800. The museum, clearly signposted on the road in Sop Ruak, is far more engaging than one might suspect, given the tourist hype about the subject. There are well-presented displays and many fascinating exhibits, including farming tools, decorated and crafted weights, and delicate scales and pipes. A new museum is under construction, situated in a 200-acre landscaped garden opposite the Baan Boran hotel.

Sop Ruak's drawback is the scarcity of mid-range and budget accommodation and places to eat, adding argument to the value of hiring a car or motorbike in Chiang Rai or Mae Sai and touring the region as a day trip (see p. 180). From Chiang Saen it is quite feasible to travel here by bicycle and take a picnic to enjoy on the banks of the Mekong or have lunch with the local Tai Yai tribal people at Doi Sa Ngo in the Sop Ruak village.

🛏 **Baan Boran Hotel $$$$$**, tel: 0-5378-4084, fax: 0-5378-4095, e-mail: lmbboran@loxinfo.co.th. Clearly signposted, this elegant hotel has a swimming pool and stirring views in all directions. Mountain bikes and elephant rides are available.

Maekhong Balcony $$ tel: 0-5378-4333/0-5378-4310. Bamboo hut accommodation also includes fan, bathroom, hot water and beautiful views. Local Thai restaurant $ daily 0700–2200.

S. V. $–$$ tel: 0-5378-4026, 0-1950-0994, fax: 0-5378-4027. Easy to find on the main road, just past the opium museum in the direction of Chiang Saen. Clean, large rooms with air-con and bathrooms and a small restaurant next door.

Buakam Resort $$ tel: 0-5378-4035, 0-1951-7861, fax: 0-5378-4036 follow the signs off the Golden Triangle's main road. Includes restaurant, fan and air con rooms, bathroom, TV, fridge.

Camping Ground $ 41 Moo 1, Tambon Wieng, Chiang Saen district, Chiang Rai 57150. Tel: 0-5378-4205/0-9757-6041. Ask for Mr Sangwien. Just behind the Golden Triangle, very central to the 'House of Museum'. Hot water in the bathrooms. Bungalows and a restaurant are planned for the end of 2002.

🍽 **Ban Boran-Hotels Suan Fin $$$** is the most comfortable and enjoyable place for a meal, and it has an **Opium Den** pub.

Thai Kitchen $, tel: 053-65-1112 offers local Thai cuisine $, as well as karaoke. Daily 1000–2400.

Sriwan Restaurant $, opposite the Imperial Hotel open daily 0700–2100 for great well-known Thai dishes.

PARADISE RESORT & CASINO

If you really want to be able to say you've been to all three countries, but don't have time to go any further beyond the Golden Triangle to Mae Sai for Myanmar or Chiang Khong for Laos, then cross over the Ruak river, which flows in front of the Golden Triangle village, to the Paradise Resort & Casino for B250 per person daytime and B500 per person night-time (to cover the Laos section, go further downstream from Paradise to Koh Don Sao, which is an island that belongs to Laos).

CHIANG SAEN

This small town by the side of the Mekong River has a lot more going for it than commercial Sop Ruak. As well as better accommodation the town itself has a faded

THE GIANT CATFISH

What is said to be the largest freshwater fish in the world, the giant catfish (pla beuk), is only found in the Mekong River. In Thailand at least it is fished primarily in the stretch of the river that flows past Chiang Khong. Growing in length over a period of many years, it reaches up to 3 m and can weigh as much as 300 kg.

The fishing season is very brief, from mid-April to the end of May, when the river is shallow and the fish are moving upstream to spawn. Before the fishing boats cast their first nets a ceremony is held, invoking the assistance of the appropriate goddess, and much acclaim is accorded to those who get the first catch.

Up to 60 fish are caught each season and are immediately sold at up to 500B per kilo. By the time it reaches the restaurants in Bangkok and Chiang Mai the price has increased many times. The danger of over-fishing to the point of extinction has been recognised for decades, and a system of artificially induced spawning has been perfected by the Thai Fisheries Department.

charm, having grown up haphazardly amid the crumbling ruins of a more glorious past.

The ancient kingdom of which Chiang Saen was the capital goes back a thousand years; the town itself was founded in 1328. It was conquered by Burmese forces in the 16th century and remained under foreign rule for 300 years until Rama I recaptured it. Fearing that the town might later fall back into enemy hands, the king ordered its destruction and it was only in the last century that it started coming back to life.

Chiang Saen is another one of those delightful places in Thailand where there are no compulsory sights but where the mood and character of the place prove intrinsically interesting. Old wooden shop-houses blend seamlessly with the scattered ruins and extant ramparts of the ancient city.

This is a place to wander aimlessly, seeking shade near a dusty temple and enjoying a picnic lunch. The centre of activity is where the main Sop Ruak – Chiang Khong road meets the town's main street from Chiang Rai at the river. From early morning onwards, all along this stretch of river there is a buzz of mercantile activity as boats from southern China and Laos load and unload their wares. There is a lot more to see and do here than Sop Ruak, during the day at least, and tour coaches tend to trundle past without stopping.

At the end of Phaholyothin Rd on the left, just before the end of the ramparts, there is a small **national museum, $,** open Wed–Sun 0900–1600, with a small but significant collection of Buddha images, various local finds and some ethnographic exhibits.

Of the many crumbling *wats* around town. **Wat Phrathat Chedi Luang**, opposite the museum, is one of the more noteworthy ones. Built in the early 14th century, this was once the city's main temple, and its distinguishing feature is the 60-m-high *chedi* rising from its octagonal base, which is currently being restored, but still has an austere feeling to it.

The most impressive *wat*, not least because it has benefited from restoration work, is **Wat Pa Sak**. From the museum, walk down Phaholyothin Rd beyond the ramparts and cross the road after 200 m. It is always open but 0900–1600 there is likely to be a charge, $. Again, it is the *chedi* that captures one's attention, and art historians have written monographs on the cultural influences that might account for its odd shape. The stucco work is also worth admiring. Every nook and cranny of this temple is worth admiring.

ARRIVAL AND DEPARTURE Chiang Saen's transport hub, just west of the T-junction on Phaholyothin Rd, is where *songthaews* for Sop Ruak congregate and the station for Chiang Rai and Chiang Mai buses is located. The work involved is endlessly intriguing.

By car from Mae Sai simply follow road 1290 to Sop Ruak and continue, with the Mekong River still on your left, to Chiang Saen. From Chiang Rai stay on Highway 110 for 30 km to Mae Chan, and bear right on road 1016 for about the same distance to Chiang Saen.

SLOW BOAT TO CHINA

In 1992 the first boat in a very long time made an official trip from Yunnan down the Mekong River to Chiang Saen. Following an ancient trade route, the success of the '92 trip heralded a new era in Sino-Thai trade in this corner of the world. Thai entrepreneurs looked forward to a bustling tourist trade only to be suddenly shattered by the collapse of the baht. Now that the country's economic health seems to be recovering, there are well-advanced plans for this route to be resuscitated for travellers.

Chiang Saen River Hill Hotel $$ Tambon Wiang, tel: 0-5365-0826, fax: 0-5365-0830. A block from the river, south from the main T-junction, this is easily the nicest place to stay. Attractive Thai décor, friendly service and rooms with air-con, fridge and telephone.

Gin's Place $–$$ tel: 0-5365-0847. A pleasant, laid-back establishment. Car, motorbike and bicycle rental and tours arranged. Overseas call box, Thai massage, laundry service and visas for Laos. 2 km out of Chiang Saen towards Sop Ruak. Free transport from the Eng. Cent. (English Centre) from where you can send e-mails.

Colour Section
(i) Summer Palace Temple at Bang Pa-In; gold-leaf Buddha; saffron-robed Buddhist monks
(ii) Woman working in rice paddy field; River Kwai bridge
(iii) Phuket beach – view of Phi Phi Le island
(iv) Kuala Lumpur Old Railway Station; bullock cart in Malaysia

Ban Suan House $$ near Wat Chom Killi temple on the Chiang Suen bypass, tel: 0-5360-5907 Fan/hot water, but no restaurant.

📷 **Wieng Saen Phu Restaurant $$** at the Chiang Saen River Hill Hotel wins hands down as a place to eat. Food is average, but there is air-conditioning, pleasant service and attractive décor.

Keaw Varee $ opposite the newly built police station, has a menu of familiar Thai dishes. Although the food is a bit bland, they do offer sensational ice cream sundaes.

Food stalls can be found nearby and sometimes down on the bank of the river. Set up each evening 1700–2100; known to th locals as 'The Nam', or 'River Pier' in English.

At Gin's Place **The Cowboy Restaurant $** has a Wild West theme, with breakfasts of muesli and pancakes and meals like fried garlic chicken and a good selection of curries.

Rim Khong Restaurant $ located just outside Chiang Suen on the road to Sop Ruak, caters for large coach tours usually offering delicious well-known local Thai dishes, but a little spicy if not requested otherwise! Daily 0800–2000.

CHIANG KHONG

North Thailand's most easterly town on the Mekong is the end of this route and, unless you are planning a trip across the river into Laos, it is a matter of heading back to Chiang Rai. There is not a lot to do here. Cross-border trade, which more or less accounts for the town's existence, generates a certain amount of activity. The 13th-century **Wat Luang** was restored in the late 19th century and a result of this are the fiery murals decorating the *viharn*. Near Baan Golden Triangle hotel, at the northern end of town, there is a cemetery on a hill with graves of nationalist Chinese soldiers and panoramic views.

ARRIVAL AND DEPARTURE

Car: The 1129 road from Chiang Saen brings you to a T-junction at Chiang Khong. A left turn leads to the river crossing to Laos. To the right, the town's single main street, Saiklang Rd, becomes Highway 1020 heading south to Chiang Rai.

Bus: There are a few *songthaew* services daily between Chiang Saen and Chiang Khong but the Chiang Rai bus service is a lot more frequent. Four or five buses daily

run to and from Chiang Mai (6 hrs) and three daily to and from Bangkok (13 hrs). It is also possible to take a *songthaew* to or from Chiang Saen.

Boat: Between sop Ruak Chiang Saen and Chiang Khong long tail boats leave anywhere there is a boat driver waiting for customers along the riverbank, at any time of day. It takes about 1½ hours and costs about B1200 per boat.

Baan Golden Triangle $$$ Tambon Wiang, tel: 0-5379-1350. Large air-con bungalows with bathrooms are at the bottom end of this price category. High on a hill (on the left before the T-junction on the 1129 from Chiang Saen), with atmospheric views of Laos across the sluggish Mekong.

Ruan Thai Sophaphan $–$$ Soi 1, Saiklang Rd, tel: 0-5379-1023. Agreeable accommodation close to the river.

Ban Tam Mi La $$ Soi 1, Saiklang Rd, tel/fax: 0-5379-1234. Next door to the Ruan Thai Sophaphan, a deservedly popular guesthouse. Attractive riverside setting and huts with private or shared facilities. Catch the proprietor for information on short walks in the neighbourhood.

Bamboo Riverside Guesthouse $ 70/1 Moo 1, Huaviang, Chiang Khong, Chiang Rai 57140, tel: 0-5379-1621, email: saweepatts@hotmail.com. Individual bamboo huts set in single landscape on the riverbank fuering Laos. Offers a Thai and European restaurant.

There are cheap rice and noodle stalls along Saiklang Rd but the eating places attached to the guesthouses and hotel are the best bet for a decent meal.

The riverside restaurant at **Ban Tam Mi La $** has more than just token vegetarian dishes.

The **Tippie Hippie Bar and Restaurant $** is on the High St opposite Ban Tam Mi La. It is a popular meeting place for travellers.

There is little to do in the evenings so it is worth wandering down the sois that lead to the river and checking out the small restaurants here. The road that hugs the river at the southern end of town, from Soi 5 off the main road, has a couple of places worth looking at. The **Rimkhong $** has a menu in English but if you see something good on another table just point to it.

TRAVELLING TO LAOS

Chiang Khong is one of the few places where foreign travellers can legitimately cross the border into Laos, though the crossing at Nong Khai (see p. 197) is a lot more convenient if Vientiane is your main destination. Agents who handle the paperwork for visas are easy to find along the main road, and many of the guesthouses can also do this.

One of the more well-established agents is Ann Tour 6/1 Moo 8, Saiklang Rd, tel: 0-5365-5198, fax: 0-5379-1218. The standard rate for a 15-day visa is B1200 per person. Ann Tour can obtain a visa in three days if you turn up when the office opens at 0800. So it could pay off to arrange your visa in Bangkong before heading north or better still, back in your home country.

Getting across the Mekong River is by way of one of the cargo boats that make daily crossings. A good agent should be able to arrange this and accompany you to the boat to ensure visa formalities are completed or alternatively, you could just arrive at the border if you've already obtained a visa and catch a boat over – it's no hassle to get across the river. There are plenty of officials always showing you what to do and once on the other side plenty of business-hunging *tuk-tuk* drivers willing to take you where you need to go – just ask! The Laotian town across the river is Ban Huai Sai (Huay Xai), and from here boats depart for Luang Prabang. There is also a small airport at Ban Huai Sai with flights to Luang Prabang and Vientiane on certain days of the week. Again, a good agent will be able to provide details and current timetables for onward travel in Laos. There are places to stay in Ban Huai Sai, so staying there overnight is not a problem.

WHERE NEXT?

If you've not been able to get a visa for Laos, are tired of big cities, and are still hankering for that much talked about Laotian scenery, there is an alternative without leaving Thailand that gives you the chance to venture into a completely different region – the north-east. Continue from Chiang Khong to Thoeng, which leads to Chiang Kham taking the highway route 1148 (mountains of beauty considering it's a highway!) to Nan province, which is the far eastern northern province hugging the border with Laos. Because of Nan's location on the cusp, the north-east is the next most logical destination. The mountains through Nan are dry, barren, but beautiful. Nan holds a rich cultural diversity in its hill tribes. It is a very pretty province with national parks and waterfalls, and can be linked up with another route quite easily: Phitsanulok–Umphang (see pp. 167–173), which offers completely different adventures of history/architecture/trekking/rafting.

BANGKOK — NONG KHAI

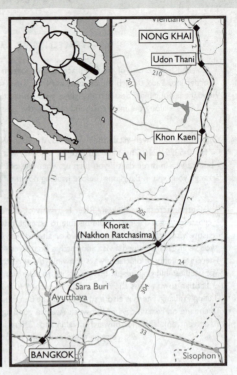

NOTES

Two of the four trains from Bangkok to
Nong Khai leave from Bang Sue station
in Bangkok. For the 12-hr Bangkok –
Nong Khai journey, consider Express 69
night train departing 2045 (Express 70
in reverse). Train 137 from Bang Sue
station, 0630, is the only day train.

DRIVING ROUTE

Highway 2 (Friendship
Highway) stretches from
the outskirts of Bangkok to
the banks of the River Mekong at
Nong Khai (615 km). Take Highway 1
from Bangkok to Saraburi. Here, take
a right turn onto Highway 2, which
goes straight to Khorat. Avis car hire
is available at Khon Kaen airport, tel:
0-4334-4313, and Udon Thani airport,
tel: 0-4224-4770.

BANGKOK — NONG KHAI
OTT Tables 7065/7079

Service	🚆	🚌	🚆	🚆	🚆	🚌	🚆	🚌	✈	✈	✈
Days of operation	Daily	Daily	Daily	Daily	Daily	Daily	Daily	Daily	Daily	Daily	Daily
Special notes	A	C	B	A	B	D	BJ		E	F	G
Bangkok..................d.	0630	0800	0820	1855	2000	2030	2045	2200	E	F	G	....
Khorat (Nakhon Ratchasima) d.		1045			0051				E			....
Khon Kaen ....d.	1432	1430	1550	0356	0320		0519			F		....
Udon Thani...............d.	1635	....	1720	0602	0540		0724	0700	....	....	G	....
Nong Khai.................a.	1725	....		0705	....	0630	0810	....	....	....	....	....

Special notes:
A–Departs from Bangkok Bang Sue station.
B–Departs from Bankok Hualampong station.
C–Additional services: 0845, 0930, 0945, 1000, 1030, 1100, 1130, 1300, 1400, 1500, 1600, 2030,
   2100, 2130, 2200, 2215, 2230, 2245, 2300, 2310, 2320, 2330, 2340, 2350.
D–Additional services 2040, 2100.
E–3 flights a day. Journey time 45 minutes.
F–4 flights a day. Journey time 1 hour.
G–3 flights a day. Journey time 1 hour.
J–This train has 1st-class sleepers and 2nd-class couchettes.

NORTH-EAST THAILAND

Every year the north-east of Thailand, known as Isaan, receives less than 2% of the total number of visitors to the country. This alone makes it one of the country's more authentic and attractive destinations. The big cities along this route – Khorat, Khon Kaen and Udon Thani – have no major visitor attractions but their busy and bustling natures capture the everyday rhythms of urban life in north-east Thailand in a way that touristy Bangkok and Chiang Mai have long lost.

At the end of the cool season (Nov/Feb), landlocked Isaan begins to bake and with temperatures of 40°C it is hard to expend energy during much of each day. The searing heat combines with the dry red infertile soil to make the north-east the poorest part of Thailand. The Thais you see in Bangkok engaged in menial jobs or backbreaking hard labour are very likely to be seasonal immigrants from Isaan.

In the decades after the end of World War II, the poverty of the north-east made many farmers sympathetic to communism, and the US-supported government poured money into the making of new roads in an attempt to defeat insurgents. During the Vietnam War, American purchasing power fuelled the development of 'massage parlours' as towns like Khorat and Udon Thani became large bases for American forces intent on bombing Thailand's eastern neighbours.

Reasons for travelling this route include the imposing Angkor ruins at Phimai, opportunities for buying silk and other cloths at relatively low prices, and the enticing vista of Laos across the River Mekong at the attractive border town of Nong Khai. It is easy to cross the river into Laos, and Vientiane is a mere 24 km away.

ROUTE SUGGESTIONS

A visit to the north-east could join with the Chiang Mai–Mae Sai Route (see p. 178) by a 9-hr bus journey from Chiang Rai to Khorat, or a 12-hr bus ride between Chiang Mai and Khorat.

The Bangkok–Pattaya Route (see p. 122) can be linked via a 6-hr bus journey from Pattaya to Khorat, or with the Pattaya–Ko Samet Route (see p. 128) by a 4-hr bus journey to Rayong. There are also buses between northern Thailand and Udon Thani.

You will need B1200 per person with your passport to pay to cross into Laos from Nong Khai (see also p. 207).

KHORAT (NAKHON RATCHASIMA)

The official new name of this large commercial city is Nakhon Ratchasima but everyone still calls it by its old name, Khorat (aka Korat). During the Vietnam War the Americans had a large airbase outside the city, although the military fatigues you'll see about town belong to members of the Thai armed forces who now have their own important base here.

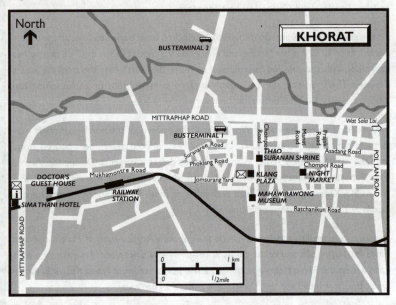

Nakhon Ratchasima, which translates literally as 'Frontier Country', is the transport gateway to the north-east, and the main reason for stopping off here is to visit the nearby Khmer ruins at Phimai or for an overnight stay after a day's travelling.

Khorat is not a compact city. The railway station and some of the better accommodation is situated in the older, western half, while shops, banks and amenities are mostly clustered in the busy eastern part of the city.

There are no must-see attractions, but the **Thao Suranari Shrine** is centrally located on the western side of the moat and if anything is happening in town it will take place here. Evening devotions often include performances of folk songs and at the end of March/early April there is a ten-day festival celebrating the Thao Suranari.

The nearby strip of grass is the town's public park, a good place to while away time and observe Thai social life. South of the shrine, just outside the moat, the **Mahawirawong Museum, $,** open daily, 0900–1600, has a modest collection of local Khmer art, mostly Buddha statues. An evening stroll from the north-east corner of the moat leads to the architecturally interesting Wat Sala Loi, built in the 1970s and representing the heavenly boat journey to nirvana.

ORIENTATION The size and scale of Khorat can be disorientating when you first arrive. It is worth a trip to the TAT office to collect their useful city map that pinpoints transport links, hotels, restaurants, temples, plus the main bus

THE BRAVE LADY
The Thao Suranari, 'brave lady', was the braveheart who led the people of Khorat against Laotian invaders from Vientiane in 1826. Her name was Khun Ying Mo and the story goes that she and other townswomen plied the enemy with alcohol and promises of sensual delight before slaughtering the gullible invaders and saving the town.

routes across town. Bus nos 1, 2 and 3 all travel between the tourist office in the west, via the railway station, to the eastern part of Khorat inside the moat. The main bus terminal is inconveniently situated in the north of the city on Highway 2, and *tuk-tuks* have a standard fare ($$). The train station is on Mukhamontre Rd.

[i] The **TAT Office** is on Mittraphap Rd at the western end of town, tel: 0-4421-3666/0-4421-3667 and ask for Mr Patai who is very helpful indeed. Tours around this diverse province include visits to the nearby Khao Yai national park. Open daily 0830–1630.

HORSE RIDING AT CHOK CHAI
You can take a day trip out to the Chok Chai farm, 30 km from Khorat by *songthaew*. This is a top quality horse stud farm (just like you'd expect to find in Texas, USA) from where you can go riding through the rugged countryside of the north-east.

[🛏] **Sima Thani Hotel $$$$$** Mittraphap Rd, tel: 0-4421-3100, fax: 0-4421-3122, e-mail: sales@simathani.co.th. Best hotel in town, with good restaurants and full-sized snooker table.

Chumsurang $$$ 2701 Mahadtthai Rd, tel: 0-4425-7088, fax: 0-4425-2897, has air-con rooms and a small pool. Easy to find on the road that goes east from Klang Plaza, near the night market.

Anachak $$ 62 Jomsurangyard Rd, tel: 0-4424-3825 is a good value hotel with air-con rooms in the centre of town. From the Klang Plaza it is just past the post office. There is a 24-hr café and a Thai restaurant next door where you can point at whatever takes your fancy. Almost as good value is the

Farthai Hotel $$ 3535 Phoklang Rd, tel: 0-4426-7390, with a choice of rooms. The café is fine for breakfast but not much more.

Thai Hotel $$ 640 Mittraphap Rd, tel: 0-4424-1613. Includes aircon.

Doctor's Guest House $ 78 Soi 4, Suebsiri Rd, tel 0-4425-5846. Leafy Soi 4 runs parallel with Mukhamontre Rd, off which Suebsiri Rd runs. A quiet, clean place which shuts up nightly at 2200; a little English spoken.

If the hustle and bustle of Khorat are too much to bear, consider spending a night at peaceful Phimai instead.

[TO] Two good places to eat are near the tourist office.

Nat Ruen $$ at the Sima Thani hotel has an excellent lunch buffet of Asian and European food.

Cabbages and Condoms $$ just past where Soi 4 meets Suebsiri Rd, near the Doctor's Guest House, is not as green as the name might suggest and vegetarians will be frustrated. A good choice is *gung phun oil* (spring rolls), followed by *kai pud 'medmamuang'* (cashew nuts with chicken and garlic). Try also the

Krua Khun Ya Restaurant 1113 Det-Udom Rd tel: 0-4427-4499. Open 0600–0200.

Around **Klang Plaza** is the usual cluster of western-style donut, chicken and burger fast-food joints and there is a Swensen's here as well as a supermarket.

Around the corner, at 698 Ratchadamnoen Rd, there is a small but adequate **vegetarian restaurant $** next to a bakery.

The **night market $** has the usual array of stalls serving good Thai food.

EXCURSION TO PHIMAI A day trip to Phimai, 60 km from Khorat, is easily managed by catching an early no. 1305 bus from Bus Terminal 2 and returning to Khorat in the late afternoon.

Thailand's best-preserved Khmer ruins are well worth the journey.

The dusky pink sandstone **Prasat Hin temple complex, $$**, open daily 0730–1800, has been well restored, and hours can be spent admiring the ancient carved Buddhist and Hindu motifs that adorn the lintels and pediments. The 12th century complex was linked by a road to Angkor Wat, though it predates the Cambodian site and may even have served as an inspiration for it. There is an **open-air museum $**, open daily 0900–1600, with more superb examples of carved stonework. Stalls sell neat little sandstone reproductions of the more graceful carvings.

Old Phimai Guesthouse $, tel 0-4447-1918, off the main street, is the backpackers' favourite haunt and a good place to meet and chat. **Phimai Hotel $$,** Haruethairome Rd, tel 0-4447-1306, is equally close to the ruins and has a restaurant, though there are plenty of places for an inexpensive lunch or dinner. If overnighting in Phimai, rent a bike from Old Phimai Guesthouse and get directions to Thailand's largest and most ancient **banyan tree**. It really is colossal.

KHON KAEN

Khon Kaen is another large commercial town but with a far more relaxing sense of space than Khorat. If you just want to rest for a day, enjoy some creature comforts and check out some quality shopping for silk and cotton fabrics, then Khon Kaen is the place to go.

The town's **Museum, $**, open Wed–Sun, 0830–1630, ½ km north of the tourist office on Lungsun Rachakhan Rd, is a branch of the National Museum and ranks as one of the best anywhere outside of Bangkok. Carved stonework, artefacts from the Ban Chiang site (see p. 203) and an ethnographic collection make up the exhibits.

i The **TAT Office** is at 15 Prachasamoson Rd, 5 mins east of the bus station, tel: 0-4324-4498, open daily 0830–1630.

A very good range of hotels is spread out along Klang Muang Rd, around the corner from the tourist office.
Kaen Inn $$$ 56 Klang Muang Rd, tel: 0-4323-7744, has decent rooms with air-con and fridge, and plenty of amenities on the premises.
Roma $–$$ 50 Klang Muang Rd, tel: 0-4323-6276, may lack a touch of style but is very good value and has a choice of rooms.
Sansumran $ 55 Klang Muang Rd, tel: 0-4323-9611, is a popular budget place but some rooms are better than others. No hot water.

🆃🅾 **Blue Parrot $–$$** Si Chan Rd, opposite Kosa Hotel.
Open 0730–2200 for popular fried breakfasts, real coffee, tasty
pizzas and other standard Western food.
Pizza and Bake $–$$ Klang Muang Rd is just as good as
Parrot, with similar food.
Krua We $$ I Klang Muang Rd has authentic Vietnamese food.
Local Isaan cuisine is best enjoyed from the **food stalls $** that
spring up at night along the top end of Klang Muang Rd around
Kaen Inn.

SHOPPING   Khon Kaen has the best shopping in the north-east. A good place to start
is the huge **Prathamakant Local Goods Centre**, 81 Ruen Rom Rd. All the
Isaan arts and crafts are represented here, including triangular-shaped pillows, *mut
mee* fabrics (see box below), jewellery, basketry and small furnishings. Klang Muang
Rd has a number of small shops specialising in silks and other textiles.

FOOD AND FABRICS SPECIALITIES

Even by Thai standards the food of Isaan is noted for its spicy pungency. One of the most popular
dishes is *som-tam*, a piquant salad of grated papaya over a mix of fish sauce, lime, peanuts, chillies
and other spices.

Mut mee is the name of the weaving method that is especially characteristic of Isaan culture. It
describes the process of tie-dying cotton thread in bundles before it is woven by hand. The dye is a
paste extracted from the indigo plant, and the depth of colour depends on how often the yarn is
dipped in the solution. The traditional pattern is a geometric one, using chevrons, lozenges and
human figures.

EXCURSION TO CHONNABOT   'Chonnabot' means 'countryside', an appropriate
name for this silk-weaving town 50 km south-west of
Khon Kaen. It can be reached by *songthaew* from the regular bus terminal in about an
hour, or by bus or train to Ban Phae and then a *songthaew* for the 10-km hop to
Chonnabot. The journey takes you through through some beautiful north-eastern
landscapes.

Visitors are welcome to stroll into the town workshops to watch the women skilful-
ly manipulating their wooden machines. Prices for silk are always negotiable, and
always lower than you would pay in Bangkok.

UDON THANI AND BAN CHIANG

The town of Udon Thani is not as cosmopolitan as Khon Kaen, even though it is over 100 km north of Khon Kaen, but it is an easy place to spend a day or two. The atmosphere is friendly and unhurried and the roundabouts are encircled by palm trees as if to emphasise the laid-back mentality of the town. While there is little to do in Udon itself, an excursion to the archaeological site of Ban Chiang, 50 km to the east, can be managed as a day trip. If you can plan your trip to Ban Chiang during October you'll catch the Ban Chiang World Heritage Fair, which is well worth a visit.

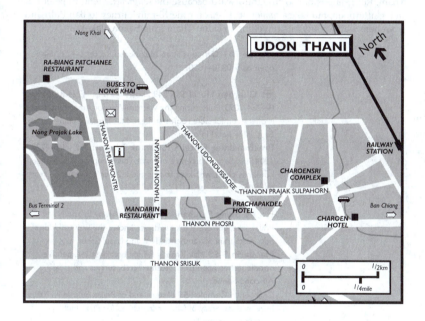

WHO STARTED THE BRONZE AGE?

Orthodoxy was overturned when bronze finds at Ban Chiang were first dated as being earlier than 3000 BC, the accepted date for the origins of the Bronze Age in ancient Mesopotamia in the Middle East. The dates have since being revised but grounds remain for questioning the orthodox view that bronze was first discovered in the Tigris and Euphrates basin. Ban Chiang has also revealed that bronze metallurgy spread from Thailand to China and not the other way around.

THAILAND

A shopping trip to the weaving village of Ban Naka, about 20 km north of town, is a chance to buy silk, *mut me* fabrics and ready-made clothes at prices that are less than half those of Bangkok. A *tuk-tuk* ride (\$\$) can also be taken to visit the Udorn Sunshine Fragrant Orchid Farm in the north-east of the town.

An area of the archaeological dig at **Ban Chiang** can be visited, but the main focus is the exemplary **museum, \$,** open daily 0900–1600, with its attractive displays of artefacts from the local site. Check opening days on tel: 0-4226-1351. Getting to Ban Chiang is easy because *songthaews* regularly make the 50-km journey from Udon Thani. Returning is not so straightforward because the *songthaews* tend to peter out in the afternoon, but take a *samlor* or *tuk-tuk* for the 10-min journey to Ban Pulu and from here wait for any bus travelling to Udon Thani from Sakon Nakhon.

i The **TAT Office** is at 16 Mukmontri Rd, tel: 0-4232-5406, open daily 0830–1630.

🛏 **Charoen Hotel \$\$\$** 549 Phosri Rd, tel: 0-4224-8115, fax: 0-4224-1093. Built during the Vietnam War for Americans, today it offers comfortable rooms and good facilities, including a pool. Best value hotel in town.
Prachapakdee Hotel \$ 156 Prajak Sulpakorn Rd, tel: 0-4222-1804, is right in the centre of town. This friendly, old-fashioned hotel has clean, well-kept rooms and a 24-hr convenience store next door.

🍽 **Ra-Biang Patchanee \$\$** is tucked away by the Nong Prajak lake, but every *tuk-tuk* driver knows the way to Udon's best restaurant for authentic Thai and Isaan dishes.
Mandarin \$–\$\$ Mak Khaeng Rd for breakfast, inexpensive noodle dishes, appetisers, steamed crab, curries and steaks. Air-conditioned.
Charoensri Complex \$\$ eastern end of Prajak Sulpakorn Rd is huge, with an array of familiar franchises for Pizza Hut, Swensen's and the like.

ENTERTAINMENT There is a string of little bars opposite the Charoensri Complex and two e-mail shops are also located here. The Charoen Hotel has the **Cellar Pub** with a Filipino band performing nightly from 2130, and a nightly disco with no cover charge.

NONG KHAI

Nong Khai is an interesting destination in itself, while offering the tantalising prospect of further travel across an international border. Thailand's main north-east railway line and its US-financed Friendship Highway terminate at the riverside town of Nong Khai, where the broad Mekong sweeps by as another reminder that this is indeed the end of the line. The best places to stay are huddled close to the river, with the land of Laos beckoning and its capital city a mere bus ride away.

Nong Khai's appeal is based on its frontier status and riverside setting, a few stylish dilapidated wooden houses that hint at the influence of French colonialism from across the river, and an almost romantic air of having arrived at a terminus. It's an easy place to hang out for a couple of days, the kind of place where you could conjure up an Asian version of Casablanca with an ex-pat Bogart type running a bar and guest house for *farangs* with dubious pasts. And, like every other north-east province, Nong Khai offers endless side trips to wildlife sanctuaries, national parks and waterfalls.

To soak up the atmosphere take the **evening boat ride** ($, excluding food or drinks) that departs around 1700 from a floating restaurant between the Mutmee and

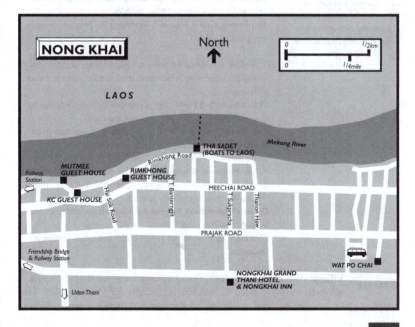

Mekong guesthouses. The boat keeps to the Thai side of the river and opens a window on riverside life in what is still a quiet backwater.

Wat Pho Chai, an exception to the mostly undistinguished *wats* dotted around town, is near the bus station. The spacious interior is remarkably glossy and ornate, with the burnished gold head of Buddha taking pride of place on the lustrous altar lit by a large chandelier. Murals decorate the *bot* and tell the story of how the Buddha image was taken from Laos and sank in the Mekong before miraculously reappearing.

Bicycles and motorbikes can be hired from guesthouses, and a 2-km trip brings you to the **Friendship Bridge,** open for foreigners wishing to visit Laos.

DEPARTURE TIPS

At the Sawasdee Guest House there is a hot shower room, metered for 10 mins at a time, that can be used before setting off on a long train or bus journey. Nobbie's on Meechai Rd sells large, tasty, takeaway sandwiches, ideal for that long journey back to Bangkok.

🖭 It is hard to beat Nong Khai for value for money accommodation.
Sawasdee Guest House $–$$ 402 Meechai Rd, tel: 0-4241-2502, fax: 0-4242-0259. Quaintly restored, well-managed townhouse. Hot water, laundry service and bikes for hire.
Mutmee Guest House $ 111 Kaew Worawut, tel/fax: 0-4246-0717, is deservedly one of the most popular budget places. Friendly, well-informed management, excellent restaurant, good travel info and bikes for hire.
Rimkhong Guest House $ Rimkhong Rd. Not on riverside, but pleasant garden.

🍴 Along Rimkhong Rd there is a good choice of small Thai eating places offering inexpensive local and Vietnamese dishes, including:
Mae Khong $–$$ with a large riverside balcony overlooking the river and wild boar with chilli on the menu.
Fish Restaurant $ offers a large menu in its wooden shack. Good views of the river and dusty wind chimes lend the place some charm.
At the **Mutmee Guesthouse** the food lives up to the promise of its superb setting among bamboo and green plants. Vegetarian choices and daily specials.
Danish Baker $–$$ Meechai Rd has hearty breakfasts, hamburgers and Thai food.
Nobbie's $$ Meechai Rd serves pizzas and other European favourites.

SHOPPING **Village Weaver Handicrafts** 1151 Chitapanya Lane, tel: 0-4241-1236, is a self-help project created to promote an income for local weavers. The weaving process can be watched in situ behind the shop and there is a good selection of *mut mee* cotton, clothes and woven bags. Prices are marked but a discount is usually available.

To find the shop, walk east from the bus station along Prajak Rd. After about ½ km, turn left down Chitapanya Lane at the Honda bike shop opposite the Esso station. The shop is on the right past the school.

Shops and stalls along Rimkhong Rd sell a miscellany of inexpensive Thai and Lao items, including filigree (silver wire) jewellery. The **Wasambe Bookshop** near the Mutmee Guesthouse has arty T-shirts and cards as well as new and second-hand books. A fax and e-mail service is also available here.

NONG KHAI WALKABOUT

This walk begins at the ferry crossing point in the centre of town by the riverside. The ferry is only for locals, but there is an observation platform where you can watch the river traffic and gaze across the expanse of the Mekong for picturesque and enticing views of Laos.

Wander westwards along Rimkhong Rd past the shops and restaurants until the road becomes a narrow lane. Enjoy a cup of Laos coffee at the Fish Restaurant, gazing upriver to the Australian-financed **Friendship Bridge** which spans the Mekong.

Walk south from the restaurant to Meechai Rd and turn right to pass the hospital and the delightful flower garden in front of the public library. Take the first turning right back towards the river and look for the lane on the right with a sign to the Mutmee Guesthouse. This lane, with the useful Wasambe Bookshop and places offering meditation courses and the like, is developing an inviting hippy atmosphere. Check out the menu and daily specials at the Mutmee before returning to Meechi Rd, and turn left to walk back towards the town centre.

Along Meechi Rd you pass the Danish Baker, banks and shops. Pass the Sawasdee Guest House and then take the sixth turning on the right, Phochai Rd, that cuts down to Prajak Rd. Cross Prajak Rd and continue to **Wat Pho Chai** (see p. 206), where the walk ends.

SONG KHRAN THAI NEW YEAR FESTIVAL

Believe it or not, even in the mountains of the north, temperatures still reach 40 degrees, in mid-April, so it's a good thing the Song Khran Thai New Year festival is celebrated during this period for three whole days … and the rest! If you really want to be able to rave on about how friendly the Thais were during your vacation, then stay around and join in with them to celebrate this festival in their villages. Song Khran, a water-throwing festival, is believed to help cleanse the soul of past sins. Whether you believe in the principal or not, it's great fun and very refreshing in the heat.

WHERE NEXT?

All you need to enter Laos via the Friendship Bridge is a US$50 note and your passport, but make sure that your Thai visa has enough days left for you to return to Thailand (or get a new one in Vientiene). The Laos visa is usually valid for 30 days, but, if not, you can apply for a 30-day visa at the Laos consulate in Khon Kaen, tel: 0-4322-3698, or Bangkok, tel: 0-2539-6667. This takes from one to three days.

By the time you read this a new twice-daily bus service should be in operation across the border, Nong Khai – Vientiane, 30 mins, fare 30B.
You'll need to have your visa sorted before boarding the bus.

Nong Khai as a railhead is literally the 'end of the line', and most visitors not entering Laos will return to Bangkok before, perhaps, heading south to the Andaman coast (pp. 222–233) or the Samui archipelago (pp. 243–254).

ROYALTY

Royalty is a feature of Thai and Malaysian life and in both countries it is treated with a very high degree of respect. In Thailand especially, saying or doing anything that might be interpreted as disrespectful towards the royal family carries a maximum jail sentence of 15 years. In 1995 a French visitor was arrested on landing at Bangkok airport, having been heard to express anti-royal sentiments on the plane (a Thai princess was on the same flight).

The present Thai king, Bhumibol Adulyadej, was born in the US and it is very much his efforts that have maintained a high profile for royalty within the country. He is a cosmopolitan individual, a fan of jazz music, a noted saxophone player and the winner of a yachting gold medal in the Asian Games. He has handled political minefields with finesse and emerged as a popular people's king. In both 1973 and 1992, when political turmoil raged in Bangkok, the king made decisive interventions that were welcomed by ordinary people. Whether this success will be maintained by his eldest son and successor remains to be seen, although his daughter has achieved noted public relations success in representing and promoting royalty.

Various semi-compulsory practices endorse the unquestioned role of the royals in Thai society and visitors will see some of these for themselves in public places. People stand for the national anthem in bus and train stations at 0800, as they do in small towns and villages across the countryside. Any visit to the cinema is incomplete with an obligatory standing to attention while the anthem is played. Visitors are often expected to join in with these observances.

In Malaysia they go one better, or rather nine times better, and enjoy the spectacle of nine different royal families. The Malaysian head of state is the *yang di-pertuan agong*, the 'king', who is elected every five years from amongst the nine sultans attached to nine of the peninsular states. All nine royal sultans are immune from the normal workings of the law and all are above public criticism, a fact that visitors should bear in mind. Their position and privileges are enshrined in the constitution and are likely to remain unchallenged for the foreseeable future. The sultans are seen as custodians of traditional Malay, Muslim culture and, given the sensitive nature of multicultural Malaysia under firm Malay political control, no public figure would take the risk of questioning the status quo.

While the Thai royals have managed to avoid the whiff of scandal and slander, their Malay peers have not been quite so successful. The most notorious cases have involved the Johor royal family and even in the mid-1980s scandalous stories about the son of the Johor sultan were still common currency. In 1976 the son was actually convicted of manslaughter before being pardoned by his father who was the sultan of the state. Less serious shenanigans have surrounded the sultan of Kelantan and his passion for expensive, European cars.

BANGKOK — CHUMPHON

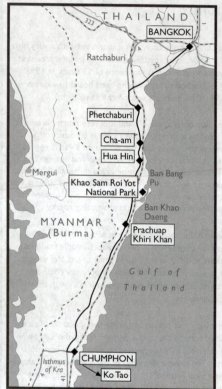

Notes

Trains All Bangkok–Phetchaburi trains from Hualamphong have sleeping cars except the 2250.

The Bangkok–Butterworth Southern Line:

This Bangkok–Chumphon route forms part of Thai Railways' main Southern Line. The ten trains that depart daily from Bangkok's Hualamphong station go through Surat Thani (see p. 240) while train 35, which departs early afternoon, goes all the way to Butterworth in Malaysia.

Buses Although buses are faster than the trains, they leave from Bangkok's Southern Bus Terminal, which takes longer to get to.

TIP

If you intend to go right through to Ko Tao island, don't leave Bangkok any earlier than the 1915 sleeper train, which arrives at Chumphon at 0408, with a couple of hours' wait for the bus. Bus/boat tickets can be bought at Bangkok railway station.

Travelling south on this route means seeing a slow shedding of many of the characteristics associated with Thailand. Buddhism starts giving way to Islam and the call of the mosque becomes more common than the sight of colourful wats. The familiar view of rice paddies from train and bus windows begins to be replaced by plantations of rubber, palm oil and coconut trees. The further south one travels, the more Malay the mood becomes, and the feeling grows that it is more than kilometres that separates the south from Bangkok and the rest of the country.

History, it seems, is to blame. Until around the 13th century the south was culturally tied to the Malay peninsula, and traded more with China than with land to the north. Even when the emerging kingdom of Sukhothai began to be more influential, the south retained considerable de facto independence. As late as the 1970s, when the rest of Thailand had a cultural and political coherence, in the south Thai communists were still making their presence felt. The remnants of the communist opposition that fought the British in 1950s Malaya and never accepted the new Malaysian government had its strongholds in the borderlands between southern Thailand and northern Malaysia. They outlasted their Thai comrades and it was 1990 before the last of the guerrillas came out of the jungle and handed in their arms.

The transition from 'mainland' Thailand to southern Thailand is not sudden or dramatic, but by the time you reach Chumphon the differences are apparent.

BANGKOK — CHUMPHON
OTT Tables 7055/7067/7078

Service	🚌	🚌	RAIL	RAIL	RAIL	RAIL	RAIL	🚌	🚌	🚌	🚌	⛴
Days of operation	Daily	Daily	Daily	Daily	Daily	Daily	Daily	Daily	Daily	Daily	Daily	
Special notes	B	C	A	A	H	H	H	D	E	F	G	
Bangkok ....d.	0500	0520	0745	1300	1330	1550	1905	D	....	....	....	....
Phetchaburi ....d.	|	0720	1017	1608	1652	1909	2149	|	E	....	....	....
Cha-am ....d.	|	....	|	|	1736	1942	2228	D	|	....	....	....
Hua Hin ....d.	|	....	1100	1640	1807	2000	2243	D	E	F	....	....
Khao Sam Roi Yot ....d.	|	....	|	|	|	|	0013	....	|	F	....	....
Prachuap Khiri Khan....d.	|	....	1202	1919	1930	2123	0013	....	|	F	G	....
Chumphon ....a.	1200	....	1415	2125	....	0038	0340	....	E	....	G	0730
Ko Tao ....a.	....	....	....	....	....	....	....	....	....	....	....	0945

Special notes:
A–Additional trips: 1420, 1515, 1705, 1735, 1820, 1915, 2250.
B–Additional trips: 0600, 2100.
C–Additional trips: 0550, 0650, 0720, 0820, 0920, 0950, 1020, 1120, 1220, 1250, 1350, 1420, 1450, 1520, 1550, 1620.
D–Frequent service. Journey time: To Cha-am 3½ hours, to Hua Hin 4 hours.
E–Frequent service. Journey time: To Hua Hin 1½ hours, to Chumphon 6 hours
F–Frequent service. Journey time: To Khao Sam Roi Yot 2 hours, to Prachuap Khiri Khan 2 hours.
G–Frequent service. Journey time 3 hours.
H–These trains depart from Bangkok Thon Buri station.

PHETCHABURI

Commonly shortened to Phetburi or Petchaburi, this ancient town has about 30 *wats* but the number worth seeking out can be counted on one hand. The best ones can be taken in on a walking tour, outlined below. It starts from the railway station where most visitors arrive. To skip the first leg of the walk take a *samlor* from the station to Wat Yai Suwannaran.

If temple fatigue takes the shine off this idea, an alternative destination is **Khao Wang**. This 95-m-high hill to the west of town is admittedly crowned with a host of *wats*, *chedis* and *prangs*, but they are architecturally insignificant and the view from the top, best enjoyed as the sun starts to go down, is the sole reason for making the ascent.

It is a stiff climb but a tram, **$$**, Mon–Fri 0800–1730, Sat–Sun 0800–1800, saves the leg-work. The hilltop **Phra Nakhon Khiri**, built by Rama IV as a summer pad, is now a museum, **$**, Wed–Sun 0900–1600, filled with a miscellany of artefacts collected by the king.

A WALKING TOUR

Coming out from the railway station, turn left and follow the road past the night market for almost ½ km until you see the bus station on your left. The road turns right here, passing Siam Commercial Bank on your left, and reaches a busy crossroads. Turn right here to the Chomrut bridge that crosses the river.

On the other side of the bridge walk straight ahead past the Chom Klao Hotel on Phongsuriya Rd until **Wat Suwannaram** looms on your right. Two points of interest here are the graphic murals decorating the *bot* and the elegant old library building in the middle of the pond. Two other *wats* a little further down the road hardly merit attention. When you reach them, turn right instead into Phokarong Rd and after a 5-min walk turn right into Phrasong Rd for **Wat Kamphaeng Laeng**.

This 12th century temple was built to honour Hindu deities. Its ancient lineage helps explain its unspectacular appearance. Continue on Phrasong Rd, passing two undistinguished *wats* on either side of the road. At the crossroads with Matayawong Rd you can either turn left for three *wats*, stretched out along the left side of the road, or walk straight across the junction, still on Phrasong Rd, back towards the river and a bridge.

Cross the bridge for the important and hard to miss **Wat Mahathat** on Damnoenkasem Rd. Extensive restoration work on the five *prangs* and the *bots* have turned this into the town's most visited temple. There is plenty to see and lots of detailed art work to admire, especially the *bot's* imaginative murals.

A short way north up Damnoenkasem Rd brings you back to the junction near Chomrut Bridge.

ARRIVAL AND DEPARTURE **Bus**: The main bus station is near Khao Wang, too far from the town centre to walk with luggage in the heat, but *samlors* are always on hand. Buses to and from Hua Hin and Chumphon, however, use another bus station more conveniently located in the centre of town (see walking tour on p. 212).

🛏 **Chom Klao $** 1–3 Phongsuriya Rd, tel: 0-3242-5398. The best of fairly dismal choices in the town. Centrally located at least, next to Chomrut Bridge, and service with a smile. Some rooms with bathrooms, some with river views.

Phetkasem Hotel $–$$ 86/1 Phetkasem Rd, tel: 0-3242-5581. Convenient for Bangkok bus station and the better rooms have air-con, hot water and bathrooms.

🍴 **Rabieng** restaurant **$** Damnoenkasem Rd, tel: 0-3242-5707, in the town centre at Chomrut Bridge. Open-fronted riverside location. English menu with a good mix of inexpensive seafood and meat dishes.

If you are staying at the Phetkasem Hotel, there are a number of inexpensive restaurants along the road which are also useful when arriving or departing by bus.

CHA-AM

The small seaside resort of Cha-am, between Phetchaburi and Hua Hin, is best avoided at weekends and during school holidays unless you thrive on crowds and noisy families. Arrive during the week, though, and the sandy beach is all yours. There is nothing to see or do, so only drop by if you want to do simply nothing but lie on a beach and work on your tan. Getting to Cha-am is a breeze, with buses and trains from Bangkok running every day.

Beach umbrellas and deckchairs are widely available for hire and there are freshwater bathing facilities for those leaving the sea.

🛏 There are lots of places to stay that are horrendously busy with families over the weekends, but during the week are so empty that generous discounts of up to 50% should be available. Unless they appeal to you, skip the condo-style apartment blocks that line the main drag by the sea, Ruamchit Rd, and pick out the beachside wooden bungalows that can be found in between them. Here are a couple to consider, but there are plenty more.

Santisuk $$–$$$ 263/3 Ruamchit Rd, tel: 0-23247-1212/4. A terrific range of accommodation, from inexpensive wooden huts to regular rooms.
Kaenchan $–$$$ 241/3 Ruamchit Rd, tel: 0-3247-1314. Another place with wooden bungalows and air-con rooms. Also a small rooftop pool.

HUA HIN

The first royal palace at Hua Hin was built in the early 1920s. Ever since Rama VII chose the site for another summer palace at the end of that decade, Hua Hin has been a premier domestic beach resort and possibly the oldest in Thailand. The king named his palace Klai Kangwon, 'Far From Worries'. Current tourist literature continues his tone: 'Long, sandy beaches, unspoilt and uncluttered'. Well, sort of. Hua Hin's beach is 5 km long and there is sand, but there are also countless deckchairs, beach umbrellas and lines of sailing boats, jet skis and vendors touting horse rides.

Most weekends see an invasion from Bangkok. On quieter days, Hua Hin is worth a short visit because it has a good tourist infrastructure, local seafood with a deservedly high reputation and a safe beach for swimming. Also, there is the wonderful renamed Railway Hotel, which is always worth nosing around. In addition, Hua Hin is conveniently close to Khao Sam Roi Yot National Park (see p. 217).

The best stretch of Hua Hin's **beach** is at the end of the main road that begins once you step out of the railway station. This explains the location of the famous old **Railway Hotel**, now unglamorously renamed the Sofitel Central. The railway line was extended to Hua Hin because of the royal palace, and when Thailand's social elite followed the king's example and started holidaying here the railway company began construction of the hotel in 1923.

By the 1980s it had failed dismally to move with the times (although it was used in the filming of *The Killing Fields* in 1983) but by the end of that decade a French company had moved in on a long lease and helped finance a major renovation project. The restoration work proceeded with loving attention to detail, and what you see today fairly accurately creates the character of the original open-fronted, colonial-style hotel.

The extensive grounds and airy lobby are a pleasure to walk around, and a visit is recommended. It does not radiate the social snobbery that afflicts the Oriental in Bangkok and it also helps to show just how hollow the restored Raffles in Singapore is by comparison.

WHAT'S IN A NAME?

Rama VII (1925–1935) may have called his palace 'Far From Worries' but it hardly lived up to its name. While he was staying here in June 1932 news reached him of a coup d'état in Bangkok. It was not a popular people's revolution (although there was general discontent at the economic consequences of the Great Depression), and there was no attempt to topple the monarchy. But it did result in a constitutional monarchy, and presumably spoiled the king's seaside summer holiday.

TRAIN Hua Hin is on the main Southern Line and all trains on this line from Bangkok stop here. Hua Hin's quaint railway station is at the west end of town and within walking distance of the centre.

Most trains from Bangkok arrive in the late evening or late at night, so it pays to have the first night's accommodation booked in advance. Trains travelling up from the south, on the other hand, arrive early in the morning.

🛈 There is a **TAT Office** at the southern end of town, open daily 0830–1630, tel: 0-3247-1005, with information on accommodation and Hua Hin. The phone never seems to answer, though, so you may have more success telephoning the TAT office in Bangkok.

🛈 The **local tourist office** is just east of the railway station, at the corner of Damnoenkasem Rd and Phetkasem Rd, open daily, 0830–1630, tel: 0-3251-1047. General information, details of hotels and restaurants, and local transport information available. The post office is on the other side of the junction, across from the tourist office.

🛏 **Chiva Som $$$$$** 73/4 Phetkasem Rd, tel: 0-3253-6536, fax: 0-3251-1154. A visit to this health resort begins with a brief consultation with the resident nurse, prior to choosing from the various forms of treatment on offer (paid for separately). Two pools, health-conscious restaurant (meals included in the room rates), gym, spa, tai-chi pavilion and a stretch of beach directly outside.

Hotel Sofitel Central $$$$$ Damnoenkasem Rd, tel: 0-3251-2021, fax: 0-3251-1014, e-mail: sofitel@sofitel.co.th. The restored Railway Hotel, complete with polished wood panelling, industrial-sized ceiling fans, large rooms and lovely grounds. Expensive but worth enquiring about discounts for mid-week.

Ban Boosarin $$$ 8/8 Poonsuk Rd, tel: 0-3251-2076. Still one of the best mid-range hotels in Hua Hin. Fridge, phone and television in rooms and no weekend surcharges.

Jed Pee Nong Hotel $$–$$$ Damnoenkasem Rd, tel: 0-3251-2381. Nondescript, functional hotel but reliable. A choice of rooms and a swimming pool.

Bird $$ 31/2 Naretdamri Rd, tel: 0-3251-1630. One of the very best guesthouses in this price range. All rooms have bathrooms and while not spacious they have outdoor space overlooking the sea.

All Nations $ 10 Dechanuchit Rd, tel: 0-3251-2747, fax: 0-3253-0474, e-mail: gary@infonews.co.th. The best of the really budget places. Shared facilities, fan, balcony, informative and helpful management.

Pattana Guest House $ 52 Naretdamri Rd, tel: 0-3251-3393, fax: 0-3253-0081. Basic rooms in two wooden traditional style houses. Tucked down a *soi*.

OTHER TOP HOTELS

Outside of Bangkok, Hua Hin has one of the best concentrations of top-notch hotels anywhere in Thailand. They are expensive of course, but the competition means healthy discounts during quiet periods, and it is worth shopping around.

Apart from the Hotel Sofitel, and the Chiva Som (which doesn't discount), other four- and five-star hotels worth checking out are:

Hilton Hua Hin, off Naretdamri Rd, tel: 0-3251-2879, fax: 0-3251-1135.

Hua Hin Marriott Resort & Spa 107/1 Phetkasem Rd, tel: 0-3251-1881, fax: 0-3251-2422.

Sirin Hotel, Damnoenkasem Rd, tel: 0-3251-1150, fax: 0-3251-3571.

Anantara Resort and Spa, Phetkasem Rd, tel: 0-3252-0250, fax: 0-3252-0259, e-mail: info@anantara.com

🔟 **Chatchai Market $$** off Dechanuchit Rd and Phetkasem Rd near the bus station. A great place for seafood in the evenings and inexpensive Thai dishes during the day. There is another night market specialising in seafood near the train station.

Naretdamri Rd, which runs north off the beach end of Damnoenkasem Rd, has a good choice of restaurants for international and European food as well as excellent seafood eateries at its northern end. Pasta, pizzas, lasagne and the like appear with a monotonous regularity on too many of the menus, but there are some honourable exceptions serving quality continental cuisine.

Le Chablis $$ 88 Naretdamri Rd. French food, but also some good Thai dishes. A restaurant that works hard to create an enjoyable and entertaining atmosphere.

SEAFOOD

Hua Hin is justly famous for its seafood and enjoying good food at moderate prices is one of the resort's main draws. All kinds of fish appear on the menus – crab, mussels, squid, cottonfish (kingfish), shrimp, garoupa, perch – and many of the seafood restaurants display their fresh catch wrapped in ice outside their premises. Methods of cooking are equally varied. You can have your fish raw (Japanese style), grilled, fried, steamed or served in a classic Thai spicy sauce.

KHAO SAM ROI YOT NATIONAL PARK

Khao Sam Roi Yot ('Three Hundred Mountain Peaks') National Park borders the Gulf of Thailand. Its 98 sq km support a variety of habitats and are rich in wildlife. There are forest walks, caves, two beaches, and well over 200 species of birds. The only drawback is the relative difficulty of getting there by public transport. The best solution is to either hire a car or motorbike in Hua Hin or take a day tour from there.

Toodtoo Tours, 69/8 Apirat Plaza Building, Hua Hin, tel: 0-3253-0553, run day trips. **Avis** have outlets at the Sofitel Central Hotel, tel: 0-3251-2021, and at the Chiva Som Resort, tel: 0-3253-6536.

From the **visitor centre**, there are two marked trails. One leads through a forest and the other winds through a mangrove environment. The kind of wildlife you are most likely to spot includes long-tailed macaques, dusky langur monkeys, barking deer, monitor lizards and perhaps dolphins cruising off the coast. To appreciate the birdlife either bring your own binoculars or rent them from the park headquarters.

Accommodation: $$–$$$ at the park is organised by the Forestry Department and either arranged at the visitor centre when you arrive or through the Bangkok office, tel: 0-2561-4292.

GETTING THERE

Bus/Train: To reach the park by public transport, take a bus from Hua Hin to Pranburi, and from there hire a *songthaew* all the way to the park headquarters.

Car: From Hua Hin travel south on Highway 4 for 25 km to Pranburi before turning left at the signposted junction. It is another 36 km to the park headquarters and visitor centre.

EN ROUTE

PRACHUAP KHIRI KHAN

This small town on the route between Hua Hin and Chumphon does not receive a lot of foreign tourists but suggests itself as a quiet destination for an overnight stay. The beach is poor and the most enjoyable activity is a climb up the 400 plus steps to Khao Chong Krajok at the north end of town. From the summit there are views of Myanmar, only a few miles away, and of the coast to the east. The authors first came here some years back to visit Ao Manao, a beach about 5 km south of town, where the Japanese landed in December 1941 as part of their co-ordinated invasion of Thailand and Malaya. The beach is actually more appealing than the main one in Prachuap, and there are a couple of places to stay.

ℹ There is a small **tourist office**, reached from the bus or train station by walking down Kong Kiat Rd and turning left into Sarachip Rd.

Buses depart regularly throughout the day from Hua Hin, as do the **trains** that nearly all stop at Prachuap Khiri on their journey south to Chumphon.

🛏 **Yuttichai Hotel $** 115 Kong Kiat Rd, tel: 0-3261-1055, is easy to find on the right side of the main road that leads from the railway station to the beach.

CHUMPHON

The town of Chumphon has little or no intrinsic appeal to the traveller, but it does mark an important junction. One route continues directly south to Surat Thani, the jumping-off point for Ko Samui, and on to the border with Malaysia. The other route heads down the west coast of southern Thailand to Ranong and Phuket.

Chumphon, in a slowly developing endeavour to be more than a mere junction, is also marketing itself as the gateway to the island of Ko Tao. There are two good tour agents in town, both close to the bus station, where bus and train information can be obtained as well as details for onward travel to Ko Tao.

Infinity Travel Service, 68/2 Tha Taphao Rd, tel: 0-7750-1937, also organise tours to local beaches and caves. Songserm Travel, tel: 0-7750-2023, is on the same road. All the guesthouses that have got their act together have information on local trips and ways to occupy a day or two in the vicinity.

🏨 **Jansom Chumphon Hotel $$–$$$** 118/138 Sala Daeng Rd, tel: 0-7750-2502, fax: 0-7750-2503. Run of the mill town hotel, but perfectly adequate for a night's stay and a modicum of comfort. The attached disco may be either a distraction or irritant at weekends.

Tha Taphao Hotel $$ 66/1 Tha Taphao Rd, tel: 0-7751-1479. If using buses, more convenient than Jansom Chumphon, though very similar.

Mayaze's Resthouse $ tel: 0-7750-4452, fax: 0-7750-2217. Down a quiet *soi* between Tha Taphao Rd and Sala Daeng Rd. Handy for the bus station and travel agents. Good reputation for friendliness and cleanliness. Shared bathrooms but the welcoming and homely atmosphere makes this a cut above other budget guesthouses and a good place to meet fellow travellers.

New Chumphon Guest House $ Soi 1, off Krom Luang Chumphon Rd. Another friendly guesthouse with lots of experience of catering for backpackers.

🍽 **Sarakrom Wine House $$** Tha Taphao Rd. Only open in the evening. Refreshing change for anyone seeking respite from rice and noodles. Thai food and a wine list. **Sala Daeng Rd**, where the Jansom Chumphon Hotel is situated, has a number of inexpensive options for an evening or lunch-time meal. **Tha Taphao Rd** is another good hunting ground.

KO TAO

The small island of Ko Tao is just over 20 sq km, with an established reputation as a centre for scuba diving and now very popular indeed with young backpackers. During the peak tourist season, Dec–March, there are more travellers arriving than the island can support, and the appeal of being here during those months is questionable. More mature divers and families might do better to book a four-day package on Ko Samui (see p. 243) to avoid the hoards of youngsters.

At other times, though, it has its charm, and for non-divers the fun of snorkelling in the clear, clean water is a reason for making the long journey from Chumphon. The drawback for non-divers, however, is that the bungalow operators aren't extracting as much money from you and have a tendency to downgrade you to second-class status.

The plus side is that Ko Tao offers a good opportunity to learn scuba diving at competitive rates. Expect to pay around 7000–8000B for a complete four-day course leading to a PADI certificate, including all costs. Courses can be booked from the Bangkok office of **Larry's Dive** (see p. 93). Beyond diving, there is not a lot to do on Ko Tao, though most restaurants show English-language films in the evening.

There are dozens of places to stay, all more or less the same in terms of facilities and most in the $–$$ price range. If arriving in the high season it's advisable to have your accommodation booked in advance through one of the travel agents in Chumphon. At other times you can wander along the beaches and check out the options. All the bungalow operations have their own restaurants and expect guests to use them at least some of the time.

Boats for Ko Tao depart daily in the morning from Pak Nam, 14 km south of Chumphon. The journey takes about 4 hrs, depending on the weather. You can also reach the island from Ko Pha Ngan; in reverse, a boat leaves Ko Tao for Ko Samui at 0930 and takes around 4 hours via Ko Pha Ngan. The minibus transfer offered on the boat costs 50B to your chosen resort.

WHERE NEXT?

From Ko Tao you could return to Chumphon by boat, or consider taking an inter-island ferry from Ko Tao to Ko Pha Ngan and then Ko Samui (pp. 243–254).

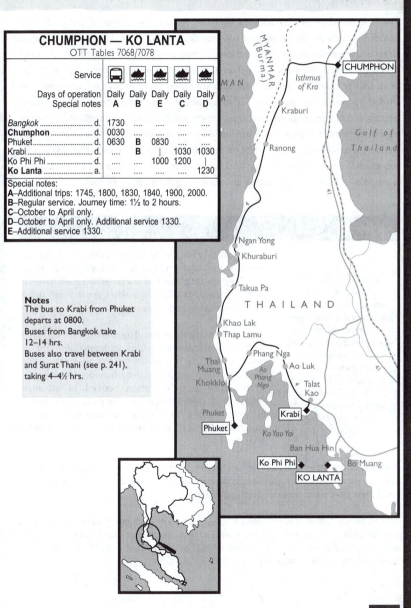

CHUMPHON — KO LANTA
OTT Tables 7068/7078

Service	🚌	⛴	⛴	⛴	⛴
Days of operation	Daily	Daily	Daily	Daily	Daily
Special notes	A	B	E	C	D
Bangkok .... d.	1730	....	....	....	....
Chumphon .... d.	0030	....	....	....	....
Phuket................................. d.	0630	B	0830	....	....
Krabi .... d.	....	B	|	1030	1030
Ko Phi Phi .... d.	....	....	1000	1200	|
Ko Lanta .... a.	....	....	....	....	1230

Special notes:
A–Additional trips: 1745, 1800, 1830, 1840, 1900, 2000.
B–Regular service. Journey time: 1½ to 2 hours.
C–October to April only.
D–October to April only. Additional service 1330.
E–Additional service 1330.

Notes
The bus to Krabi from Phuket departs at 0800.
Buses from Bangkok take 12–14 hrs.
Buses also travel between Krabi and Surat Thani (see p. 241), taking 4–4½ hrs.

THAILAND

The long Andaman Sea coastline of southern Thailand has scores of idyllic offshore islands that offer hedonism without the grossness of Phuket or the gloss of Ko Samui. Krabi is fast transforming itself into the main departure point for visits to the islands of Ko Phi Phi and Ko Lanta. The Chumphon–Ko Lanta route will attract travellers in search of an activity holiday as well as those who are content to chill out on pristine beaches shaded by gently swaying palms. Trips by inflatable sea canoe open up the hidden lagoons and mangrove forests, and scuba divers and snorkellers are spoilt for choice as regards coral reefs teeming with marine life. Local agents in Krabi also cater for rock climbers who want to try their skills on the challenging limestone cliffs. If all this sounds too much like hard work, head for Ko Lanta. It sounds like a cliché but Ko Lanta really is unspoilt and the perfect place to just do nothing for a couple of days.

KRABI

MANGROVE TOURS

A boat trip to the mangrove forest in the estuary of the Krabi River is one of the most worthwhile tours available. It offers an opportunity to view the weird architecture of mangroves close up as well as a chance to see fiddler crabs and mudskippers.

The small, tidy town of Krabi is fast developing into an important transport hub for travel in the region. Krabi is still a pleasant place, and is a possible base for excursions to nearby beaches. It is also the place to catch a boat to Ko Lanta and other islands.

The town has plenty of **travel agents**. All take bookings for boats and buses as well as accommodation on the beaches. They can be a good source of information, and during the high season it is not a bad idea to have your first night's accommodation booked in advance. Information and tickets for onward travel to Malaysia can also be obtained. Two well-established travel agents, **Jungle Book** and **Chan Phen**, are next to each other on Utarakit Rd.

The agents also offer a variety of **local tours**. Boat trips to local mangrove swamps are well worth considering, although the trips to nearby islands, hidden lagoons and coral reefs may seem more instantly appealing.

The accommodation in Krabi town is mixed, with lots of cheap guesthouses offering claustrophobic rooms that quickly exhaust their charm after one night's stay. There are a couple of exceptions, listed below. While hotels are a better bet they hardly earn their room rates for a short stay.

ⓘ The **TAT Office** on Utarakit Rd, tel: 0-7561-2740, has use-ful maps of the town and area, and up-to-date information on accommodation.

🛏 **Ban Ao Nang Resort $$$** 211 Moo 2, Ao Nang, tel: 0-7563-7071, fax: 0-7563-7070, email: info@aonangresort group.com. Very clean, good-sized pool.
City Hotel $$–$$$ 15/2–3 Sukhon Rd, tel: 0-7562-1280, fax: 0-7562-1301. Good, centrally located hotel with clean rooms and the option of air-con.
Grand Tower $–$$ 73/1 Utarakit Rd, tel: 0-7561-2456. Calls itself a hotel but is basically a guesthouse with nondescript but adequate rooms, a restaurant, a roof-top balcony and a reliable travel agent.
KR Mansion $ 52/1 Chao Fah Rd, tel: 0-7561-2761. One of the best budget places, a 10-min walk from the centre. Airy rooms, friendly management and a roof-top balcony to watch the sunset. Tours and tickets can be booked here, and there is a decent restaurant as well.

🍽 **Thammachart $–$$** Kong Ka Rd. Easy to find by the riverside and close to the piers. One of Krabi's more interesting places to eat, with an imaginative menu and delicious vegetarian food.
Baan Thai Issara $$ Maharat Soi 2. Another great place but it closes at 1600, so come for breakfast or lunch. Home-baked breads, imported cheeses, and delicious fresh pasta and Thai dishes.
Ruan Phae $$ Utarakit Rd. Like most floating restaurants in Thailand, the food plays second fiddle to the concept. Still, it's a pleasant place to relax and take in the views.
Muslim Restaurant $ Pruksa Uthit Rd. Rotis and curries – everyone's favourite for a quick but tasty and filling meal. Walk west on Utarakit Rd. Turn left into Phattana Rd just before Chan Phen Travel and right into Pruksa Uthit Rd.

KRABI'S BEACHES The beach at **Ao Nang**, 18 km west of Krabi, is reached by a 30–45-min *songthaew* journey. It is the most developed of Krabi's beaches, with a host of dive shops and a raft of tour agents offering kayak-ing expeditions, snorkelling trips, boat rides through the mangrove swamps and tours to idyllic looking islands. Between December and February the hotels are packed with Western holidaymakers, and rates are at a premium. Outside the high season discounts on rooms are hefty, but between June and October high winds makeswimming inadvisable, and the beach tends to collect wind-borne rubbish.

Laem Phra Nang is the headland south of Ao Nang, reached only by boat. This does not diminish the crowds, because the dramatic limestone cliffs, soft, white sand beach and crystal clear water make up everyone's fantasy of a tropical paradise. You can have fun just being here for a day or two, enjoying the beauty of it all, but there is plenty of scope for activities as well.

The **snorkelling** is great and **rock climbing** is beginning to develop into a major attraction because of the proximity of limestone cliffs. Tour agents and guesthouses can all handle bookings for short introductory courses. Prices range from 500B to 1000B for a half- or full-day course, and up to 3000B for a full three days. These courses are run by professionals and include insurance and all equipment.

There are two main beaches at Laem Phra Nang. The one on the west side, called variously Hat Tham Phra Nang, Princess Cave Beach, or Ao Phra Nang, is the most stunningly beautiful. Most visitors are awestruck by its picture-postcard perfection. The beach to the east, East Railae, is less attractive but a lot more developed, and only a 10-min walk to the west beach.

Boats for Laem Phra Nang depart from Krabi and Ao Nang at regular intervals throughout the day.

KO PHI-PHI

Ko Phi-Phi is the name for two islands, Phi Phi Le and Phi Phi Don, 40 km south of Krabi. Both islands are beautiful, with soft sand beaches and transparent water full of colourful fish, but they are not undiscovered. This is painfully obvious between mid-December and early March, and in July and August. Accommodation is only available on Phi Phi Don, and rooms are at a premium during the high season so it is advisable to have somewhere booked in advance.

Diving, snorkelling and **kayaking** are the most popular activities on Phi Phi Don. Dive operations in Phuket and Krabi run trips to Ko Phi-Phi, and there are also dive shops on Phi Phi Don. Most of the guesthouses and tour agents run snorkelling trips to the neighbouring coral reefs and uninhabited islands.

Boats to Phi Phi Don run daily from Krabi, taking 2 hrs, **$**, and from Phuket, which take a little longer. During the high season there are also some boats from Ao Nang and Ko Lanta. The only way to reach Phi Phi Le is by boat from its sister island; longtail boats are fun and cheap, but keep an eye on the weather and make sure the boat has life jackets – it can be a dramatic ride!

All the boats pull in at Ton Sai, where a lot of the accommodation is based as there are no roads on the islands. The places to stay listed below are the tip of a burgeoning accommodation iceberg (budget accommodation for backpackers is increasing) but it is still essential to have something reserved in advance, especially over Christmas when demand pushes room rates even higher. On departure there are two boats daily to Phuket leaving at 0900 and 1430. Tickets cost 250B.

> **Phi-Phi Hotel $$$$** Ton Sai, tel: 0-1230-3138, e-mail: phiphi@samart.co.th. Low-rise hotel set back from the main drag.
> **Phi Phi Pavilions $$$** Lo Dalam, tel: 0-7562-0633. Picturesque wooden bungalows, with the sea on your doorstep. Lo Dalam beach is a ten-minute walk from Ton Sai and a little quieter.
> **Charlie Beach Resort $–$$** Lo Dalam, tel: 0-7562-0615. Thatched bungalows similar to Phi Phi Pavilions next door. Close to the sea, with a beach bar.

> Every resort and bungalow operation has its own restaurant, and their prices tend to reflect the kind of accommodation they offer. In Ton Sai there are a number of independent restaurants with menus that have evolved to satisfy tourists. A well-established place that has maintained its high standard of cooking is **Mama Resto**. Multilingual menus feature a good range of Western favourites as well as Thai food. **Cia Bella**, next to Phi Phi Pavilions, is recommended and reasonably priced.

DICAPRIO'S BEACH

The filming of *The Beach,* based on Alex Garland's novel, began at the end of 1998 on Phi Phi Le's Maya beach, with heart-throb Leonardo DiCaprio as the big star. By the time of the film's premiere in Bangkok in early 2000, environmental activists were staging a mock ritualistic suicide. They urged the public to boycott the film, claiming that 20th Century Fox had ruined the fragile ecosystem of Maya Bay. It is true that 100 palm trees were planted on the beach and sand dunes had been bulldozed. The sad fact, now, is that Maya beach has been ruined by travellers following the elusive trail for the perfect beach.

'I think to alter a natural treasure just for the benefit of 15-year-old American movie fans is not a very good idea,' voiced a tourist at the protest event. The irony is that *The Beach* – a mediocre film that begins with a pimp's words, 'Do you want a girl?' – bombed in America and Europe, and will only make a profit from ticket sales in Thailand and other parts of Asia.

KO LANTA

Ko Lanta is the generic name for a large group of islands south of Krabi. One of the largest, 25-km-long Ko Lanta Yai, has been developed to offer inexpensive beach accommodation. Transport to the island and accommodation is easy to arrange through tour agents in Krabi, Ao Nang and Phuket.

NO ANSWER?

See p. 140 for advice on overcoming difficulties in trying to make a booking on a mobile phone number.

Ferries for Ban Sala Dan, on the northern tip of Ko Lanta, depart from the pier in Krabi and from Ko Phi-Phi, but note that regular transport is only available between October and April. At other times of the year the journey from Krabi involves travelling over 40 km south to Ban Hua Hin for a ferry over the narrow waterway to Ko Lanta Noi, and then continuing south to Ko Lanta.

Ko Lanta Yai has nice beaches on its west coast, interspersed with rocky outcrops. The further south you walk the more the Robinson Crusoe effect kicks in. Although the beaches are not as spectacularly beautiful as those on Phi Phi or Laem Phra Nang, they do not attract mass crowds and large tour groups. Ko Lanta is still an island where you can see normal life going on, unlike most of the other big resort areas in this part of Thailand. This means there is not a lot to do except sunbathe, swim and generally relax, though dive operators have set up shop at Ban Sala Dan and snorkelling trips to smaller islands are readily available.

Transport on the island is by motorbike taxi from the beaches to the pier, but service is haphazard. Motorbikes can be rented but Ko Lanta is very much an island where visitors hang out rather than feel the need to organise something active. Anything that is going to happen will start at **Ban Sala Dan**, the pier and village at the north of the island.

Bear in mind the lack of transport when choosing where to stay. Luckily, the most attractive beach, **Hat Khlong Dao**, is only half an hour's walk from Ban Sala Dan. It also has the widest choice of bungalows and places to eat. When you step off the ferry many of the guesthouses will have minivans waiting. The places listed below are only a selection, and new places are popping up all the time.

Kaw Kwang Beach Bungalows $–$$$ Hat Khlong Dao, tel: 0-1228-4106. A good range of bungalows on the best stretch of beach. Snorkelling trips can be arranged.

Golden Bay Cottages $–$$ Hat Khlong Dao, tel: 0-1229-0879. Clean, comfortable bungalows on another lovely stretch of beach.

Deer Neck Cabana $ Hat Khlong Dao, tel: 0-7561-2487. Not the best bit of beach but friendly management and inexpensive rooms.

Lanta Palm Beach $ Ao Phra-Ae, tel: 0-1723-0528. Bamboo huts and coconut trees on a lovely beach. Peaceful Ao Phra-Ae is a couple of kilometres south of Khlong Dao.

Lanta Coral Beach $ Hat Khlong Khoang, tel: 0-1228-4326. Thatched huts, some with bathrooms. This beach is further south again, not as sandy but ok for snorkelling and very quiet.

TO Every bungalow has its own restaurant, but there is no pressure to eat where you are staying. Prices and menus are fairly standard. In Sala Dan there are a few independent restaurants. One that serves quite good food is **Danny's Bar**.

WHERE NEXT?

There are numerous semi-discovered islands in the vicinity of Ko Lanta including Ko Jam (Ko Pu) and Ko Si Boya. Both are ideal for those seeking real peace and quiet away from the trappings of Patong and Pattaya – videos, go-go bars and the like. Boats to both islands leave twice daily from Ban Laem Kruat, about 30 km south of Krabi. From Krabi a logical next destination would be Phuket (pp. 228–239).

THAI KICK BOXING

The historical roots of *Muay Thai*, literally 'Thai boxing' and known in the West as 'kick boxing', go back to the late 16th century when a Thai monarch made it a compulsory part of military training. Nowadays it is big business, and making frenzied bets before a bout is all part of the drama.

It is well worth attending a live *Muay Thai* competition because the atmosphere is terrific, although the bouts that are advertised in places like Phuket are mainly for the tourist market and standards tend to be lower. In Ko Samui it is not uncommon for Westerners to seek out tuition and practice sessions and even to participate in local competitions.

Modern fights are regulated and the basic rule is that you can use any part of the body in attack, except for the head, and any part of your opponent's body is fair game when it comes to landing a blow. In the 1920s, when boxers fought to the bitter end without gloves, deaths and serious injuries became so common that the sport was banned.

The secret to winning, apparently, lies with the elbows and knees; a punch to the body is less effective than an angled stab with the elbows.

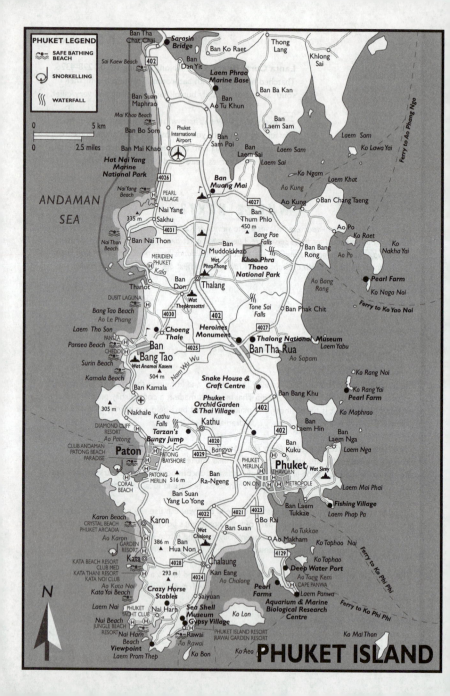

Pronounced 'Pooket', the island is Thailand's largest and every year more than three million overseas visitors arrive here. Tourism has made a huge impact on the island and its culture, and anyone arriving here for their first trip to Thailand will receive a rather distorted view of the country and what it can offer.

Phuket is the most un-Thai place in the country, and it is not too much of an exaggeration to say that some Thai restaurants in London offer a more authentic glimpse of the country's culture than parts of Phuket's west coast. On the plus side, the island offers wonderful beaches, a wealth of watersports and years of experience in catering to the needs and whims of holiday-makers.

MUST SEE/DO IN PHUKET

Try out watersports, horse riding or bamboo rafting

Take an elephant ride or an eco tour

Phuket FantaSea

See the glamorous transvestites at the Simon Cabaret

Join a Thai cookery class

Buy some good-quality locally made clothes

Hire a moped and tour the surrounding villages

The capital of the island is **Phuket town** on the south-east coast, and, because it is not close to the airport, 32 km away, many people never visit it. The town is well worth seeing and can make a welcome break from the beaches. Travellers counting their bahts, or anyone who wants to see Phuket without being holed up in a resort, could consider staying in town and making day trips to the beaches. The differences between the various beaches are not as pronounced as on Ko Samui, although **Ao Patong** is definitely the most developed and **Ao Kata** the quietest.

No matter where you are in Phuket, the price of just about everything is significantly higher than anywhere else in the country. Many of the lobster-red holidaymakers, having flown in from abroad with no plans to travel anywhere else in Thailand, have no idea of this and happily accept the inflated prices.

ARRIVAL AND DEPARTURE

AIR Thai Airways operate numerous daily flights between Bangkok and Phuket, taking just under 1½ hrs. There are also flights to Chiang Mai, Hat Yai and Surat Thani. The office is at 78/1 Ranong Rd, tel: 0-7621-1195 and 0-7622-3016.

Bangkok Airways flies daily between Phuket and Ko Samui. The office is at 158/2-3 Yaowarat Rd, tel: 0-7622-5033.

International routes connect Phuket with Kuala Lumpur, Langkawi, Penang and Singapore. There are also flights to other Asian and European cities. Malaysia Airlines (MAS) have an office in Thungkha Rd, tel: 0-7621-6675. Singapore Airlines and Silk Air have their offices in Thungkha Rd as well.

Phuket international airport, tel: 0-7632-7230/5, has money exchange facilities and a tourist office.

A minibus service runs between **the airport** and all the main beaches. Tickets are bought at a central counter, and the bus driver will usually drop passengers off at their hotel or guesthouse. Taxis, more expensive, are also readily available.

Transport to your hotel can be booked through most of the hotels. There is also a less expensive airport service run by Tour Royal Enterprises, tel: 0-7623-5268. The buses depart 0700–1800 from a station on Wichit Songkhram Rd, the continuation of Ranong Rd in Phuket, and within walking distance of the town centre.

BUS Air-con buses and minibuses link Phuket with Bangkok, taking 14 hrs and departing from the Southern Bus Terminal in Bangkok. Other destinations include Hat Yai (7 hrs), Krabi (3 hrs), Nakhon Si Thammarat (8 hrs) and Surat Thani (5 hrs by minibus). See OTT table 7078.

The bus station is at the eastern end of Phang Nga Road in Phuket town, within walking distance of the road where *songthaews* depart for the beaches. The tourist office has a useful brochure listing all routes, journey times and fares.

INFORMATION

[i] The **TAT Office** is at 73 Phuket Rd, Phuket town, open daily 0830–1630, tel: 0-7621-1036. This very well-run office supplies a useful map of the town and the island, information on local transport, and schedules and fares for long-distance buses. From the fountain roundabout near where the *songthaews* from the beaches congregate, walk along Ratsada Rd to a junction near the river and turn right into Phuket Rd.

A few doors down from the tourist office there is a good **bookshop** with a small **internet café**. E-mails can be sent and collected from a number of places around town, but this is one of the more comfortable and competitively priced places.

MAPS AND MAGS

The free *A-O-A Phuket Map* has good inset maps of Patong, Karon, Kata and Phuket town, showing accommodation and places to eat. It's useful for drivers because it shows petrol stations.

There is a lot of other free literature on Phuket which can be picked up in hotel foyers, most of it containing maps. Look for the advertising-fuelled monthly pocket-size guide to food, shops and entertainment and the monthly *Phuket Guide*. The 20B fortnightly *Phuket Gazette* is worth dipping into for local current affairs and a round-up of the music and pub scene.

USEFUL TELEPHONE NUMBERS

Tourist Police: 1699

Phuket International Hospital: 0-7621-0935 (emergency), 0-7624-9400 (switchboard)

Bangkok Phuket Hospital: 0-7625-4421

Lost Credit Cards: American Express, 0-2273-0022. MasterCard (001) 80011-887-0663 (toll-free), Visa (001) 80044-13485 (toll free)

Overseas Phone Service: 100

GETTING AROUND

There are good roads around the island, and *tuk-tuks* make their way from one beach to the next for what is by Thai standards an extortionate amount. Expect to pay *at least* 100B for a *tuk-tuk* between Patong and Karon, 120B between Patong and Kata. The best deal on public transport is by *songthaew* from Phuket town to the main beaches for around 30B.

Motorbikes and mopeds are available for hire everywhere, and provide the best means of getting around. Cars and jeeps can be hired at the airport and from countless agents in the beach areas. Avis have a desk at the airport, tel: 0-7635-1243, and at Le Meridien Hotel, tel: 0-7634-0480. Budget, tel: 0-7620-5396, www.budget.co.th have competitive rates. One-way rentals to Ko Samui and other parts of Thailand are possible.

ACTIVITIES

Watersports, diving, fishing, speedboat excursions to the Phi Phi islands (see p. 224), bamboo rafting, horseback riding, Thai boxing, target shooting, jungle and elephant treks, 'eco' tours, bungy jumps, golf, canoeing and anything else an entrepreneur can come up with are available on Phuket.

A few of the more well-established companies, most with websites that you can check out before you arrive, are listed here, but pick up any of the free literature in your hotel and their advertisements fill the pages.

Sea Canoe, tel: 0-7621-2252, www.seacanoe.com. Sea-caving in kayaks is their speciality.

Khao Lak Safari, tel: 0-7622-5522, www.phuketunion.com. All sorts of day trips in and around Phuket.

Siam Safari, tel: 0-7628-0116. Jungle safaris and elephant treks.

Andaman Divers, tel: 0-7634-1126, www.andamandivers.com.

Coral Seekers, tel: 0-7635-4074, www.coralseekers.com.

West Coast Divers, tel: 0-7634-1673, www.westcoastdivers.com.

Bungy Jump, tel: 0-7632-1351, www.phuket.com/bungy.

Elephant Treks, tel: 0-7629-0056, website: www.phuketdir.com/kalimtrek.

Big Game Fishing, tel: 0-7621-4713, e-mail: wahoo@phket.loxinfo.co.th.

PHUKET TOWN

Only in Phuket town is there any sense of a community not dependent on tourism for its livelihood. It also boasts some lovely examples of Chinese urban buildings of a lost era – Hokkien merchants' houses in pastel colours with shutters, small balconies and fading sculpted woodwork. Wandering around Talang Rd, Yaowarat Rd, Ranong Rd and Damrong Rd you will come across some unexpected **architectural treasures**. If you have been to Georgetown in Penang or Ipoh the buildings will come as no surprise, but they are still classics and only now are some of them being restored.

For a glimpse into Phuket's 20th-century history, stroll around the lobby and bar of the **Thavorn Hotel** on Ratsada Rd. This veritable museum is packed with old photographs and artefacts from the past, and the bar has some great photos of 1940s Phuket.

SHOPPING IN PHUKET TOWN There is no shortage of shops lining the beach roads in the west of the island, but the merchandise tends to be the usual assemblage of tacky 'handicrafts' and poor quality fabrics that look good on display but won't last many spins in the washing machine. A day trip to Phuket town at least offers a chance to look at some more interesting shops and Yaowarat Rd is a good place to start.

Just up from the fountain roundabout, **Ayoraya** at no. 27 has an assortment of fabrics and home furnishings. At no. 51, **Ban Boran Textiles** has a small but select range of quality cotton clothes for women. At no. 43, **China House** has clothes for both sexes and assorted *objets d'art* but nothing very special.

The Loft, 36 Talang Rd, displays artefacts and antiques from South-East Asia on two floors of a converted Hokkien merchant's house. It is a pleasantly stylish shop with some lovely Burmese and Thai antiques, as well as carpets and items of furniture. A shipping service is available, but the cost of transporting some of the larger items exceeds their shop price. **Touch Wood**, 12 Ratsada Rd, next to The Circle café, also sells furniture, fine arts and ornaments.

Phuket Reminder, 85 Ratsada Rd, tel: 0-7621-3765, retails raw silk by the yard and a collection of cutlery and crockery made from coconut shells. This shop also conducts **Thai cooking classes,** and recipe sheets are sold in the shop. Across the road from the tourist office, **Phuket Unique Home** has a varied display of items for the home, such as ceramics, glassware, crockery and wood carvings.

🛏 **Imperial Hotel $$$** 51 Phuket Rd, tel: 0-7621-2311, fax: 0-7621-3155. A few doors down from the tourist office, this is a neat, modern hotel with hot water and air-con.

Thavorn Hotel $–$$$ 74 Ratsada Rd, tel: 0-7621-1333. Large rooms with fan and bathrooms or more modern rooms with air-con. The lobby certainly has character.

On On Hotel $ 9 Phang-Nga Rd, tel: 0-7621-1154. Terrific period piece of a building, dating back to the late 1920s. Some air-con rooms.

🍴 **Sawadee $$$–$$$$** 8/5 Maeluan Rd. Colonial-style restaurant with wooden floors and live music. European (including steaks and fondue) and Thai food.

The Circle $$ at the fountain roundabout. This delightful café has a European touch. Good coffee and tea, a breakfast menu that includes strawberries and cornflakes, with meals like beef stew, tuna pie and beans on toast. Britain's *The Guardian* is among the newspapers and magazines for patrons to peruse.

On On Hotel Café $ on Phang-Nga Rd, open 0730–2000, has a full menu of fish and meat dishes. Next door is an ice-cream parlour and a few doors down an inexpensive Thai place.

Ooh-Khao $ Opposite Thavorn Hotel on Ratsada Rd, this little Thai restaurant makes elegant use of newspaper for tablecloths. Open 0930–2130 Mon–Thur only.

For **vegetarian food $** walk past the line of *songthaews* on Ranong Rd and the caged bird shop until you see two restaurants on the left with yellow signs. The second one is the best, with both white and brown rice and a good selection of dishes. Just point and enjoy.

ENTERTAINMENT The town does not try to compete with the beaches in terms of big bands and rowdy pubs, but the **Bepob Rock Pub and Restaurant**, Takuapa Rd, does its best. Open at 1800, the music gets going after 2200 and finishes around 0300.

AO PATONG

Fifteen kilometres west of Phuket town, Ao Patong is the heart of Phuket's beachland. Its 3 km of sandy beach filled with deckchairs and bodies barbecuing on the sand can be a surreal sight, until it starts to pass for normal. Ao Patong is packed with hotels, restaurants, and an increasing number of bars with hostesses that suggests the direction this resort area might be heading in – if it hasn't already arrived.

At night the beach road turns into one long market of stalls selling cheap clothes, cheap music, cheap batik from Indonesia, and junk knick-knacks. Bargain hard.

What Patong has going for it is a sociable nightlife, a beach that is safe for swimming and suitable for children, a centre for diving operators who every year introduce the sport to complete novices, and a complete holiday environment. All it lacks is a sense of being in Thailand.

🛏 **Phuket Cabana Resort $$$$$** 41 Patong Beach Rd, tel: 0-7634-0138, fax: 0-7634-0178. Centrally located and artfully designed set of bungalows very close to the beach.

Neptuna $$$$ Rat Uthit Rd, tel: 0-7634-0824, fax: 0-7634-0627. Good location, a little tight on space but good value.

Patong Palace $$$ 39 Rat Uthit Rd, tel/fax: 0-7634-1998, e-mail: patongpalace@phuketinternet.co.th. Ten-min walk from centre. Very clean, nice pool and gardens.

Safari Beach $$$ 83/12 Patong Beach Rd, tel: 0-7634-0230, fax: 0-7634-0231. Small pool, restaurant, good value given its location in Patong's centre and close to the beach.

Shamrock Park Inn $$–$$$ Rat Uthit Rd, tel: 0-7634-0991, fax: 0-7634-0990. Adequate rooms with own showers. Roof garden.

PS 2 Bungalows $$–$$$ tel: 0-7634-2207, fax: 0-7629-0034. Ten minutes from the beach and a choice of rooms. Good value, traveller-friendly.

🍽 **Baan Rim Pa $$$$** 100/7 Kalim Beach Rd, tel: 0-7634-0789. Popular open-fronted Thai restaurant on a hill at north end of beach. Reservations usually necessary.

Karlsson's Steak House $$$–$$$$ Soi Patong Tower, tel: 0-7634-5035. Imported steaks and seafood, Swedish chef.

Navrang Mahal $$–$$$ 58/3 Soi Bangla, Patong Beach, tel: 0-7629-2280. Vegetarian and non-vegetarian Indian food. Telephone for a free pickup.

ExPat Hotel $$$ Soi Sunset, tel: 0-7634-2143. Open 24 hrs for hamburgers, hot dogs and Thai dishes. In-house videos.
Ghadafi $$$ 178 Phratharamee Rd, tel: 0-7634-0639. Thai Muslim and Arabic food, lovely roasted chicken. Open 24 hrs.
Kwality Indian Cuisine $$$ Soi Kepsab, tel: 0-7629-4082. Tables outside or air-con inside, set menus at under 500B for two people and including two beers.

ENTERTAINMENT The **Banana Pub** beneath the Banana Disco on Beach Rd, tel: 0-7634-0301, open 1900–0200. Expats and tourists turn up to display their musical talents, and anyone is welcome to give a musical twirl. There are three Irish theme pubs in Phuket at the last count, and flavour of the month at the moment is **Molly Malones**, on the beach road. Draught Guinness and Kilkenny beer, open from 1100 for food, live music at night.

Most of the big hotels have bands performing live in their bars; the *Phuket Gazette* carries the latest details. The **Novotel Phuket Resort**, tel: 0-7634-2777, usually has music every night except Sunday in its Hourglass Lounge. The **Holiday Inn Resort**, tel: 0-7634-0608, goes in for safe theme nights three times a week 2200–2400.

The **Simon Cabaret**, tel: 0-7634-2114, has nightly transvestite shows at 1900 and 2100 for which reservations can be made. Like the Pattaya shows, the emphasis is on colour and choreography rather than anything naughty. The **Pakarang Restaurant**, at the Meridien Hotel, has a nightly dinner theatre show with a Filipino troupe; dinner at 2000 and a show at 2100.

Banana Disco, Beach Rd, tel: 0-7634-0301. Phuket's oldest disco and still going strong, open until 0200. **The Tin Mine 21** is a disco in the Royal Paradise Hotel, tel: 0-7634-0666, with a DJ; open until 0400. For hi-tech, eardrum-bursting noise **The Titanic**, Soi Sunset, gets going around 2300. A new disco is **The Shark Club**, at the corner of Soi Bangla and Rat Uthit Rd, tel: 0-7634-0525.

PHUKET FANTASEA

A nightly dinner buffet with a show that claims to blend Thai culture with Las Vegas-style flair. One of the advertised highlights is a disappearing act involving elephants. This is Phuket-style entertainment and some people find it fun. A ticket for the dinner and show is 1500B (1100B for children). Tel: 0-7627-1222, www.phuket-fantasea.com.

AO KARON

Ao Karon is only a couple of miles south of Ao Patong, but not so crowded and far better in terms of mid-range accommodation. The least expensive places to stay tend to be set back off the road, but this also gives them some privacy. Patak Rd encircles the beach area, and a *songthaew* can be flagged down anywhere along here for a short hop along beach road or into Phuket town. The beach and its talcum powder sand are lovely.

The top end of Karon, sometimes called Karon Noi or Relax Bay, is dominated by the plush Le Meridien hotel but they cannot claim the beach as their own.

Thavorn Palm Beach Resort $$$$$ tel: 0-7639-6090, fax: 0-7639-6555, e-mail: info@thavornpalmbeach.com Plush, large and filled with palm trees, one of the better top-end resorts. A pool and a relatively empty beach across the road.
South Sea Resort $$$$$ Moo 1, Patak Rd, tel: 0-7639-6611, fax: 0-7639-6618. So-so rooms but with balconies. Has a pool.
Phuket Ocean Resort $$$ 9/1 Patak Rd, Karon Beach, tel: 0-7639-6599, fax: 0-7639-6470, e-mail: info@phuket-ocean.com. Far north end of the beach, pleasant rooms with sea views and balconies, pool. Fair value.
My Friend $–$$ Katong Beach, tel: 0-7639-6344. Huts on a terrace, pleasant enough for the price, and a small restaurant.
Lume & Yai Bungalows $–$$ Katong Beach, tel: 0-7639-6383, fax: 0-7639-6096. Sea views, friendly management. Well worth considering.

The Old Siam $$$–$$$$ Thavorn Palm Beach Resort, tel: 0-7639-6090. Thai food in a very scenic setting if you reserve a terrace table.
The Little Mermaid $$$ 36/10 Patak Rd, tel: 0-7639-6628. A menu in 13 languages. Popular with Scandinavians. Steaks, free salad bar and open 24 hrs.
Il Pirata $$$ Thavorn Palm Beach Resort, tel: 0-7639-6090. Wood-fired pizza, live music in the evening.
Al Dente $$$ 35/7 Patak Rd, tel: 0-7639-6569. Pasta, pizza and home-made ice cream.

ENTERTAINMENT **The Phuket Arcadia Hotel**, tel: 0-7639-6038, has live music nightly from 1800 until after 2400. A table can be reserved in the Lobby Bar. At **Marina Phuket** at the south end of the beach, English-language movies are shown on a large screen, tel: 0-7633-0625.

KATA YAI AND KATA NOI

Kata Yai lies to the south of Ao Karon, separated by a headland but linked by road. Another headland divides it from Kata Noi further south. The *songthaew* station is outside Kata Beach Resort. There is a little island, Ko Pu, that makes an achievable target for swimmers, and the snorkelling is not too bad here.

Kata Yai, where the water remains shallow for over 20 m from the shore, is dominated by Club Med, but there are no private beaches in Thailand so use the beach by all means. More peaceful Kata Noi has three top-end resorts who again think the public beach is all theirs, although they do help to keep it clean.

🛏 **Kata Thani Resort $$$$$** Kata Noi, tel: 0-7633-0124, fax: 0-7633-0127, e-mail: katathani@phuket.com. A vast resort that almost takes over the beach. Well-organised and great for families too. A bit of a walk to the main spread of restaurants, as *songthaews* outside the resort like to overcharge.
Chor Tapkaew Bungalow $$$ tel: 0-7633-0433, fax: 0-7633-0435. Currently the best mid-range accommodation close to the beach.
Pop Cottage $$$ Kata Yai, tel: 0-7633-0181, fax: 0-7633-0794, e-mail: popcott@loxinfo.co.th. Between Kata Yai and Kata Noi, not as attractive as Chor Tapkaew Bungalow but the next best.

🍴 The place for a splurge is **The Boathouse $$$$$** Kata Beach, tel: 0-7633-0015. Pricey wine list, Thai, European and seafood, and soft live jazz on Saturday nights from 2100. Samba and bossanova Latin music on Wednesday nights from 2100.
Gung Café $$$ next to The Boathouse, tel: 0-7633-0015, serves less expensive Thai food. Lobster is the house speciality.

The main road has a run of small restaurants **$$–$$$** that look their best at night when lit up. One of them, the **Flamingo**, has a good range of pizzas and always seems to attract a steady number of diners. The cul-de-sac opposite the *songthaew* station has a few inexpensive places to eat and a couple of bars like **Club 44** with free use of the pool table.

CAPE PANWA

South of Phuket town, Cape Panwa is easily reached by regular *songthaews* from Ranong Rd in about 15 mins. There is no beach to speak of, and the only place of interest is the **Phuket Aquarium, $,** open daily 1000–1600. It is worth a visit with children, and the multicoloured fish might stimulate a newcomer to try snorkelling.

🛏 **Cape Panwa Hotel $$$$$** tel: 0-7639-1123, fax: 0-7639-1117, e-mail: cape@phuket.com. Stay here and you might have the same room that Leonardo DiCaprio or Pierce Brosnan used when filming *The Beach* and *Tomorrow Never Dies* respectively. Watersports, tennis court, gym, and a tram to trundle lazy guests down to what is effectively a private beach.

🍴 There are a couple of tourist restaurants **$$$** in the small complex of buildings facing the sea. The friendly **Cat Bar Garden $** at the bottom of the road to Cape Panwa Hotel is a shack with a kitchen inside, but the tables are outside facing the sea.

There are a couple more affordable places **$$** on the road towards the aquarium but nowhere worth singling out.

WHERE NEXT?

Several companies based in Phuket offer canoe tours of Phang-nga Bay and the Sea of Phuket. The inflatable kayaks used are able to enter semi-submerged caves inaccessible by larger boats. It's possible to explore in a number of ways: there are organised tours aboard large boats, or individually chartered 'long tail' boats that are fast but noisy; nothing beats kayaking, though. Kayaks can enter narrow crevices, sometimes passing beneath overhangs so low that the canoeist has to lie flat to enter. Once you are in one of the many sea caves or hidden bowls that are scattered throughout the bay, you are in a different world.

From Phuket, unless you are tired of tropical island paradises, head east across the isthmus to Surat Thani and join up with the Chumphon–Ko Samui route (pp. 240–254).

CHUMPHON — KO SAMUI

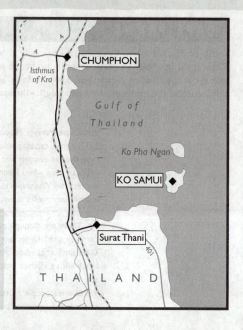

Notes

From Bangkok to Surat Thani the 1820
(rapid) and 1915 (express) trains have
sleeping carriages.

From Surat Thani there are also buses
to Krabi (see p. 222), and Phuket (see
p. 228).

CHUMPHON — KO SAMUI
OTT Tables 7055/7067/7078

Service	RAIL	RAIL	RAIL	RAIL	RAIL	RAIL	RAIL	RAIL	🚌	✈	⛴	✈
Days of operation	Daily	Daily	Daily	Daily	Daily	Daily	Daily	Daily	Daily	Daily	Daily	Daily
Special notes		A	B	B	A	A	A		C	D	E	F
Bangkok ....d.	0745	1300	1420	1515	1705	1820	1915	2250	C	D	....	F
Chumphon ....d.	1415	2125	2242	2320	0157	0310	0408	0557	|	D	....	|
Surat Thani ....d.	1620	0100	0134	0215	0500	0610	0650	0800	C	D	0800	|
Ko Samui ....a.	....	....	....	....	....	....	....	....	....	....	0930	F

Special notes:
A–This train has 2nd-class couchettes available. All journeys should be reserved in advance.
B–This train has 1st-class sleepers available. All journeys should be reserved in advance.
C–Frequent service. Journey time: 10 hours.
D–2 trips daily. Journey time: 70 minutes.
E–Additional trips: 1000, 1400, 1430, 1700.
F–Regular service. Journey time: 80 minutes.

From Chumphon, Route 41 skirts the coast and follows the railway line as it heads south for Surat Thani, the access town for travel to Ko Samui in the Gulf of Thailand. Ko Samui has never looked back since it was first discovered by backpackers in the early 1970s, and most travellers in Surat Thani are either heading to or back from the island. This makes Surat Thani a good place to garner information, pick up news and organise your next few days. Ko Samui is perhaps Thailand's most sophisticated beach resort, and yet it is still able to welcome and accommodate people on shoe-string budgets. Accommodation can be at a premium on the island at peak times, and it is very advisable to have something booked in advance for the first couple of nights at least.

SURAT THANI

Most visitors in Surat Thani are on their way to or from Ko Samui. There is little other reason for being here other than as a base for a day trip to Chaiya, 60 km north. Surat Thani itself is a busy and prospering commercial town but ideally your travel plans will not delay you here. But you may well find yourself having to spend a night in town, especially if you have not booked a train ticket in advance. If you miss the day boats to Ko Samui there is a useful slow night boat that departs at 2300 (see p. 245).

ORIENTATION Talat Mai Rd is the main artery through town, and the two bus stations are helpfully close to it. The departure point for the night boat to Ko Samui is centrally located by the river.

$\boxed{i}$ The **TAT Office** is at 5 Talat Mai Rd, tel: 0-7728-8818, open daily 0830–1630. Maps of the town and area and general information on the region, including meditation retreats at Chaiya (but not Ko Samui).

Phantip Travel 293/6-8 Talat Mai Rd, in front of the bus station, is more usefully situated for transport and Ko Samui information.

Train: The train station, tel: 0-7731-1213, is at Phun Phin, 13 km to the west. Buses to and from town run regularly throughout the day until around 1900, and shared taxis are always waiting during daylight hours to do the same run. Advance train tickets can be booked in town at Phantip Travel, and on Ko Samui Songserm Travel can make reservations.

Air: Thai Airways, 3/27 Karunarat Rd, flies twice a day to Surat Thani, tel: 0-7727-2610. Ask here about the minibus to and from the airport, 27 km south of town.

EN ROUTE

PHUN PHIN

If you are in Phun Phin, the chances are you are waiting for a train connection. If you are heading for Bangkok, the 2155 sleeper train arrives at a convenient hour, 0930. The station has a left-luggage office, and there are a couple of places for a meal nearby. Buses from the ferry drop passengers off outside the **Queen Hotel $–$$,** tel: 0-7731-1003, within sight of the railway station. It is easily the best place to stay and where most people eat, although it is not the only option.

Across the road is a 7–11 store, and the road to the railway station takes you past a side street filled with tables. An English menu **$** has standard rice, noodle and chicken dishes. With time to waste, wander around the night market behind the block with the 7–11 store where there are food stalls but no tables.

Wang Tai $$$ | Talat Mai Rd, tel: 0-7728-3020, fax: 0-7728-1007. Best value for money hotel at the top end. Stuck out of town but there's little to do there anyway. Clean, comfortable rooms, swimming pool and restaurant.

Tapi Hotel $$ 100 Chonkasem Rd, tel: 0-7727-2575. Another very good value hotel with some less expensive rooms. Within walking distance of the bus stations.

Ban Don Hotel $ Na Meuang Rd, tel: 0-7727-2167. Functional but clean rooms and an inexpensive Chinese restaurant.

Eating: The best place for a quick meal is one of the stalls in the **food market** near the long-distance bus station. For more comfortable surroundings, take a *samlor* out to the Wang Tai hotel's restaurant. Closer to the town centre, the Chinese restaurant at Ban Don Hotel is fine for a meal.

MEDITATION RETREATS

The ancient town of Chaiya enjoyed its heyday 1000 years ago when it was the capital of southern Thailand, but there is little to evoke its past glory today. The reason to come here is the temple of **Wat Suan Mokh**, 6 km south of town, and its meditation retreats.

The retreats take place at the **International Dhamma Hermitage**, 1 km from the temple, during the first ten days of each month. Bookings are made in advance at the temple, tel: 0-7743-1552. Expect to pay around 1000B to cover accommodation and food for the ten days. The courses are conducted in English but are not a soft option, and participants are expected to help out with chores.

Chaiya is 3 km off Highway 41, the main road between Chumphon and Surat Thani, and any bus travelling this route (an hour from Surat Thani) will drop passengers off at the junction. Motorbike taxis are usually waiting during the day for the short hop into town, and walking is always an option.

In Chaiya buses and *songthaews* run past the temple. *Songthaews* and shared taxis run to the temple from outside the local bus station in Surat Thani. You can also take a north bound train from Phun Phin to Chaiya and then a *songthaew* from the station.

KO SAMUI

Palm-fringed, white tropical beaches first attracted enterprising backpackers in the late 1960s and early '70s, and Ko Samui hasn't looked back since. Thailand's third largest island after Phuket and Ko Chang is now the country's most sophisticated beach resort but can still offer budget accommodation and quiet beaches.

You need to know what kind of a holiday you want on Ko Samui to choose the appropriate beach because different areas offer quite different environments. All in all, it beats Phuket by a mile and although it does become very busy during high season Ko Samui still manages to cope with a smile.

Travel inland and there are literally millions of coconut trees. Many visitors never leave their beach strip, but hiring a vehicle and exploring the less touristy parts is recommended. The south-west is the least visited part of the island where there are some remote and quiet bungalow operations. They are easily reached with your own vehicle but troublesome if relying on *songthaews*. There are also some impressive waterfalls after periods of rain and the well-visited Temple of the Big Buddha.

Accommodation caters for all budgets throughout the year. Costs drop during June and early July, and between October and 20 December. Many top-end places accept internet bookings. Advance reservations are advisable over the busy months.

KO SAMUI'S BEACHES: THE ESSENTIALS

Chaweng: The longest beach strip and social centre of the island (i.e. raucous and loud).

Lamai: Labelled seedy and loose by some. Lots of bars, strong on nightlife.

Maenam: Relatively undeveloped but some good places to stay.

Choeng Mon: Quiet and subdued, no discos but a choice of accommodation.

WATERFALLS Within walking distance of Nathon, the popularity of **Hin Lat Falls** sometimes affects the enjoyment of a visit. The falls are 3 km south of Nathon and signposted off the 4169.

The **Na Muang Falls** are in the centre of the island, signposted off the 4169 south of Nathon. At weekends and holidays, the number of other visitors may be off-putting, but there are different levels and it is over a mile to reach the upper one. *Songthaews* travel to Na Muang Falls from Nathon, Chaweng and Lamai.

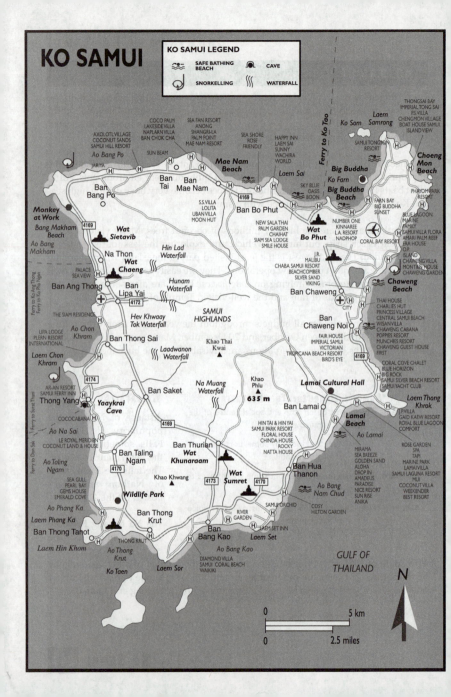

TEMPLE OF THE BIG BUDDHA

The temple is on a small island reached by a short causeway at **Bophut**. The Buddha figure, erected in 1972, is colourful and conspicuous but not especially remarkable. Over the last couple of years the area around the temple has developed to cater for the constant stream of tourists. There are stalls selling clothes and trinkets, and one quite pleasant place to eat.

ORIENTATION Ko Samui is 25 km long and 21 km wide, and most people arrive by ferry at Nathon on the west coast. A ring road, the 4169, encircles the island, heading north from Nathon and around to the main beaches of Chaweng and Lamai before striking inland and cutting off the south-west corner of the island. The 4170 road loops off the 4169 to take in this south-west corner before rejoining the 4169 south of Nathon.

i The **TAT Office** is at the northern end of Nathon, Chonwithi Rd, tel: 0-7742-0504, open daily 0830–1630. Excellent glossy maps of the island are freely available everywhere. There is also a free accommodation, food, shopping and entertainment guide, updated monthly, which carries maps of the beaches. Ko Samui's newspaper is available online at www.samuiwelcome.com.
Websites that are very useful for general information on Ko Samui and for booking accommodation include www.go-siam.com and sawadee.com.

GETTING THERE Flights from Bangkok tend to fill up quickly during the high season, and while flying to Surat Thani from Bangkok on Thai Airways might seem a viable alternative there is still the time and hassle of getting from there to the island. Then again, Bangkok Airways has the monopoly on flights from Bangkok and the cost might outweigh the convenience.

Night Boat: The cheapest route is by the night ferry from Ban Don pier in Surat Thani, arriving in Nathon the next morning before 0600. The return from Nathon arrives inconveniently at 0300, but passengers can stay on board until 0700 or later. Pillows and mattresses are provided for the journey and it's worth paying the little extra for the upper deck.

Day Boat: These are run by Songserm Travel, and their buses wait at the bus and train station in Surat Thani and Phun Phin for free transfer to the pier for these departures. Tickets include a bus from Tha Thong to the train station at Phun Phin or Surat Thani town.

Train: From Bangkok to Ko Samui it is worth considering the purchase of a combination train/bus/boat ticket from the State Railway at Hualamphong station. It doesn't save money but it does avoid having to arrange the boat connection on arrival at Surat Thani.

Bus: Bus/boat combination tickets are available from the Northern Bus Terminal in Bangkok, and although private companies advertise cheaper deals in Bangkok's Khao San Rd they are generally less comfortable and more prone to delays and irregularities.

Vehicle and Passenger Boat: The car ferry runs between Don Sak, 70 km east of Surat Thani, and Thong Yang, 8 km south of Nathon. These ferries leave every couple of hours during the day for most of the year, and take passengers without vehicles. Travellers buying a combination bus/boat ticket in Hat Yai (see p. 260) are likely to find themselves on this car ferry, and the price includes a bus ride into Nathon.

On leaving Ko Samui it's possible to buy a combination boat/bus ticket from Ko Samui to Surat Thani and on to Krabi. Travel agents in Nathon can arrange this for you for as little as 350B.

GETTING AROUND   *Songthaews* wait on the waterfront in Nathon, to your right after disembarking, and depart at regular intervals in clockwise and anti-clockwise directions around the island. Their routes are indicated on the front or side of the vehicle, but always double-check with the driver.

Fares are fixed (currently 40B to Chaweng and 30B for a shorter run, like Chaweng to Lamai). The *songthaews* can be hailed down anywhere along their route, but after dusk they are infrequent and tend to charge more. Once you know the fare for a particular journey, or can judge what it should be, just hail down the vehicle and step on without checking the cost. Being asked the fare (always paid at the end of the journey) is an irresistible temptation to some drivers to overcharge.

Jeeps and motorbikes can be hired from scores of places, especially on Chaweng. Most have the annoying habit of trying to retain your passport. This should be strenuously resisted not only on principle but also because you will be in an extremely vulnerable position should there be any problem. Leaving your driving licence should be acceptable, and if it isn't go elsewhere.

Insurance is not usually available for motorbikes but it is best not to hire a car without comprehensive cover; check the small print. Budget, tel: 0-7742-7188, have a desk at the airport and one-way rentals to Phuket are an option. **P.K. Tours**, Chaweng, tel: 0-7723-0950, almost opposite the Central Samui Beach Resort, asks for a passport but will accept your licence.

ACTIVITIES A trip to the **Ang Thong National Marine Park**, a packed group of over 40 islands some 30 km to the west of Ko Samui, provides the most enjoyable alternative to lying on a beach for a day. The only way to access the Park is on a tour that departs from Nathon pier at around 0830 and returns at 1800.

There are white sand beaches, coral reefs and an opportunity for snorkelling (gear can be hired but bring your own if you have it). The standard tour also includes a chance to walk up the hill on Ko Wua. This is the largest of the small islands, and from the 430-m summit there are fine views, especially if you can be there around sunset.

Any of the tour agents in Nathon or Chaweng will take a booking for the tour, which costs around 350B. This includes lunch but bring some snacks of your own and plenty of water. The Park authorities manage bungalows for rent and sometimes there are tours that include an overnight stop.

Island Safari, Bophut tel: 0-7723-0709, run daily **'eco-safari tours'** at 0800 and 1400. The programme covers a baby elephant show, elephant 'trek', ox-cart ride, rubber-tapping demo, coconut-picking monkey show and a meal at the end. Phone to check on transport to and from your accommodation or beach.

The **Samui Snake Farm**, off road 4170, tel: 0-7742-3247, has shows with snakes and scorpions at 1100 and 1400, and there is a restaurant attached.

DIVING There are lots of dive companies on Ko Samui and most of them have their offices at Chaweng. They conduct courses for complete novices, leading to a recognised PADI (Professional Association of Diving Instructors) certificate that is accepted around the world as proof of basic proficiency. An introductory course costs around 2500B, but many people think it makes more sense to shell out about three times that amount for a basic four-day certification course.

One of the better established companies is **Easy Divers**, tel: 0-7723-1190, fax: 0-7723-0486, with offices at Chaweng and Lamai. They do everything from a one-day 'discover scuba diving' programme with a supervised fun dive to certificated courses lasting from four days to six weeks.

Other established companies include:
Mui Divers Padi Resort tel: 0-7723-3201, e-mail: info@muidivers.com, www.muidivers.com.
Pro Divers tel: 0-7723-3399, e-mail: prodivers@bigfoot.com.
Samui International Diving School tel: 0-7742-2386, e-mail: info@planet-scuba.net

NATHON Many travellers pass through the island's capital and hardly notice it. The layout of Nathon is straightforward, with the pier abutting Chonwithi Rd and two roads running parallel with it. The third of these roads, Thawiratpakdee Rd, is full of shops and some places to eat. Should the need arise, there are a few places to stay and, indeed, if beach fatigue kicks in, a night in town might seem a good idea.

Songserm Travel, tel: 0-7742-1316, its main office on Chonwithi Rd opposite the pier where has its boats arrive and depart from. Also along this road to the south are **banks**, while at the north end near the TAT Office is the **post office**. There are private clinics and hospitals in Chaweng but the perfectly adequate government **hospital**, tel: 0-7742-1230, is just outside Nathon. The immigration office, tel: 0-7742-1069, is not far away on the 4169 road.

🏨 **Palace Hotel $$** 152 Chonwithi Rd, tel: 0-7742-1079. Large rooms, with and without air-con, close to town centre. **Seaview Guest House $–$$** 67/15 Thawiratpakdee Rd, tel: 0-7742-0052. No sea views but easy to reach, close to town, and obliging management.

🍴 **Mumthong Food Corner $** on the corner of Thawiratpakdee and Na Amphoe Rd is a popular open-fronted restaurant. Good breakfasts, salads, sandwiches, lots of Thai and Chinese dishes, and beer that is not overpriced. If you've just disembarked, cross the road to Songserm Travel and walk left around the first corner.
A few other places are scattered along **Chonwithi Rd** facing the sea and **Thawiratpakdee Rd**. Worth seeking out on this road is **RT Bakery** for its meals and above average breads for taking on the boat.

MAENAM Maenam, 13 km from Nathon, along with Hat Choeng Mon, is one of the quieter beaches on the island. It also has a good supply of budget accommodation. At night there is not a lot of activity on the beach, but on the main road is **Jazzer**, tel: 0-7742-7010. The bar has live music, but call to check what is on because without the music there is zero atmosphere.

🏨 **Paradise Beach Resort $$$$$** 18/8 Maenam Beach, tel: 0-7724-7227, fax: 0-7742-5290, www.kohsamui.net/paradise, e-mail: paradise@loxinfo.co.th. Villas and bungalows by the beach in a tropical garden setting.

Pools, restaurants, and well-equipped rooms in this upmarket resort.

Cleopatra's Palace $ east end of Maenam Beach, tel: 0-7742-5486. Basic bungalows with fans and a decent restaurant.

Friendly $ east end of Maenam Beach, tel: 0-7742-5484. Clean bungalows with own bathrooms right on the beach.

Home Bay $ west end of Maenam Beach, tel: 0-7724-7214. The very cheap huts are nothing special, but the bungalows with bathrooms are worth considering.

Eddy's $$ Main Rd, tel: 0-7724-5127. Definitely the best place for an evening meal. Despite its location on the main road (1 km east of turn-off to Paradise Beach Resort) traffic noise is not a problem. The burger meals are great and the jazzy atmosphere of the restaurant makes a welcome change from Ko Samui's usual style.

BOPHUT Bophut is a quiet beach like Maenam with a modest but adequate infrastructure that includes a money exchange facility, tour agents, watersports, supermarket, shops and restaurants. Budget accommodation is in short supply, but there are quite a few mid-range guesthouses. From the Bophut pier a boat leaves daily for the neighbouring island of Koh Pha Ngan.

Samui Palm Beach Resort $$$$$ tel: 0-7742-5494, fax: 0-7742-5358. The best of the top-end places, with a beach-front setting, pool and restaurants.

Ziggy Stardust $$$ west end of Bophut, tel: 0-7742-5173. Typical of the better quality mid-range bungalow operations on the beach. Wooden chalets with welcoming décor and a good restaurant.

Smile House $$–$$$ west end of Bophut, tel: 0-7742-5361, fax: 0-7742-5239. A well-maintained operation – not on the beach side of the road but with a fair-sized swimming pool. Rooms to suit different budgets.

Phrayo Restaurant $–$$ Big Buddha, Bophut. The most pleasant place for a meal on a visit to the Big Buddha. Tables overlooking the sea with orchids and other plants growing up the walls. The menu is a mix of good Thai, Western-style and vegetarian dishes.

Ziggy Stardust $$ has a great location by the beach and a menu of Thai dishes and seafood.

CHOENG MON   There is no central village to draw in crowds, and a generally peaceful and subdued atmosphere prevails. The crescent-shaped, white sand beach is beautiful. The shallow sea makes it attractive for families, although they don't overrun the place. At night the guesthouse restaurants that back onto the beach are lit with fairy lights and oil lamps. Bar staff arrange deckchairs on the sand and a controlled bonfire invitingly encircled by empty slingchairs is about as active as things become. Choeng Mon is our favourite beach, an unhurried place to relax and unwind.

🛏 **The Tongsai Bay $$$$$** 84 Moo 5, Bophut, tel: 0-7742 5015, fax: 0-7742-5462, e-mail: info@tongsaibay.co.th, www.tongsaibay.co.th. The ultimate luxury accommodation on the island. Private beach, 25 acres of gardens, beach front, and cottage suites and villas. Bathtubs on the balcony and superb restaurants.

The White House $$$$$ tel: 0-7724-5315, fax: 0-7724-5318, e-mail: info@samuidreamholiday.com; www.samuidreamholiday.com. Smart, Bali-esque décor with two restaurants, a beachside pool, library and a delightful sitting room.

P.S. Villa $$ tel: 0-7742-5160, fax: 0-7742-5403. Bungalows with fans or air-con in this modest and friendly establishment right on the beach.

🍽 It is very much a matter of just checking out the restaurants attached to the various guesthouses and those along the main road, and picking one that takes your fancy. The differences in the food and prices are less important than the setting and the style.

The beachside **P S Villa Restaurant $** usually has barracuda and shark on the menu, and is often less busy than some of the bigger restaurants.

Lotus Restaurant $$ at the Chaweng end serves reasonably priced Chinese food.

Kontiki $$, away from the beach, has spaghetti, salads, steaks and curries as well as Thai and Chinese food. A tin-roof but it's pretty enough inside.

Chef Chom's $$$$$ The Tongsai Bay Hotel, tel: 0-7742-5015, is the place to go for a special night. Excellent Thai cuisine prepared by the chef who was Keith Floyd's collaborator for the Thai section of his *Far Flung Floyd* TV series.

CHAWENG Ko Samui's most popular and lively beach, 7 km in length, is still stunningly beautiful despite the rampant tourist developments that threaten to turn Chaweng into Thailand's equivalent of Bali's Kuta. Watersports galore are available on the beach, and although this is easily the busiest beach on the island there is still room to breathe and fling down a towel on the hot sand for some serious sunbathing.

Chaweng has endless bungalows, hotels, bars, restaurants and shops. The accommodation ranges from international-style luxury hotels to thatched huts at under 200B a night. The effect of this is a refreshing mix of people, and eating options to suit all budgets.

After sunset the main street turns into a night bazaar with pavements lined with stalls selling the usual merchandise, including inexpensive pirated CDs. Entrepreneurs have only just sensed the untapped shopping market. The small number of permanent boutiques presently in existence is likely to multiply over the next twelve months.

Central Samui Beach Resort $$$$$ 38/2 Moo 3 Borpud, Central Chaweng, tel: 0-7723-0500, fax: 0-7742-2385, e-mail: whenne@asiatravel.com; ww.centralhotelsresorts.com/samuibeach. Some 200 rooms, all overlooking the beach, in-house movies, 24-hr room service, good restaurants, tennis courts, pool, fitness centre and spa. A place to spoil yourself.

Tradewinds $$$$–$$$$$ 17/14 Moo 3 Borpud, Central Chaweng, tel: 0-7723-0602, fax: 0-7723-1247, e-mail: info@tradewinds-samui.com Twenty comfortable bungalows in a garden setting by the beach, pleasantly quiet and well run. The best accommodation of its kind on Chaweng.

The Island $$$–$$$$ North Chaweng, tel: 0-7723-0942. Combines attractive accommodation with an excellent restaurant and a 'cool' ambience.

Chaweng Villa Beach Resort $$$ 157 Moo 2, buphud, Chaweng Beach, tel: 0-7723-1123, fax: 0-7723-1124, email: info@chawengvilla.com. Nice bungalows, pool, loungers on beach, good restaurant.

Long Beach Lodge $$ North Chaweng, tel: 0-7742-2162. Good value bungalows in a reasonably attractive setting surrounded by coconut trees.

Charlie's Huts $–$$ Central Chaweng, tel: 0-7742-2343. Popular, hip accommodation. Straw-roofed huts spread across a lawn that leads down to the beach.

⌖ Poppies $$$$$ South Chaweng Beach, tel: 0-7742-2419. Reserve a table by the sea under the pandan trees for a romantic setting in this busy restaurant. Salads, pasta, pizza, seafood and meat dishes. A bit pricey.

Betelnut Restaurant $$$–$$$$ Central Chaweng, tel: 0-7741-3370. Chic, Californian-style cuisine.

Hagi $$$ Central Samui Beach Resort, tel: 0-7723-0500. Japanese food at affordable prices. Sitting at the counter can be too hot because there is no air-conditioning.

Chez Andy Restaurant $$$ Central Chaweng, tel: 0-7742-2593. Steaks imported from Australia, wine list, open-air dining room.

Oriental Gallery $$$ Central Chaweng, tel: 0-7742-2200. The real draw here is not so much the food – Thai, Italian, steaks, salads and seafood – as the stylish interior.

Ali Baba $$ Central Chaweng, tel: 0-7723-0253. Vegetarian and non-vegetarian Indian delights. Open for American breakfast at 0900.

Piccola Italia $$ Central Chaweng, tel: 0-7723-0026. Opposite the Central Samui Hotel. Large menu of pasta and pizza options, with decent coffee.

Ninja Crepes $ opposite Charlie's Huts on main road. Decent budget-traveller-friendly café serving salads, vegetarian food, crepes and lots of cheap rice and noodle dishes. Open for breakfast.

The Deck $$ situated close to the Green Mango has a wide choice of Western food and is a great place to relax.

LAMAI Very quiet during the day, Lamai comes into its own at night when the bars light up and the hostesses materialise. Some travellers find Lamai a bit tacky but the 5-km-long beach is lovely, and other visitors find its slightly dishevelled character is more fun than Chaweng. There is a good range of places to stay, but the food scene is a definite drawback compared to the other beaches.

ENTERTAINMENT

Chaweng has the widest range of bars and discos, and attracts a good mix of people. **The Green Mango** is the place to be, though at 300B to get in, neighbouring venues are just as fun. The **Reggae Bar** pub is still a firm favourite and always worth a visit after 2300. A visiting ten-piece band is not unusual, there is no cover charge and the place is fun. **Santa Fe**, opposite Poppies on the main road, gets going around 0300. The **Blues Brothers** pub never seems to be busy and has a poor reputation, but that could change. Lamai has dozens of bars, some of which are clearly pick-up joints.

⌂ **Aloha Resort $$$$$** 128 Lamai Beach, tel:
0-7742-4014, fax: 0-7742-4419, www.sawadee.com/samui/aloha,
e-mail: aloha@sawadee.com. Bungalows and rooms, pool, beach
bar, tour agent and restaurant. Friendly.

Weekender Resort $$$–$$$$ tel: 0-7742-4429. Three types
of accommodation in this well-organised resort that caters for
tour groups as well as individual travellers.

Spa Resort $–$$ tel: 0-7723-0855, fax: 0-7742-4126,
www.spasamui.com, e-mail: thespa@spasamui.com. Eighteen
bungalows, all with fan and bathroom, at low prices. A range of
rejuvenating health programmes for the body and mind. Classes
in shiatsu, reiki, Thai massage and yoga for residents only.

White Sand $ southern end of Lamai, tel: 0-7742-4298. A
favourite with old Thai hands on a shoestring, beginning to
show its age but still a good place to meet other travellers.

🍴 There are plenty of places to eat along the road, but
nowhere is worth singling out. **Mira Mare $$** has tables
fronting the beach and is pleasant enough.

Spa Resort $–$$ has an authentic vegetarian restaurant open
0700–2200. Features dishes like garlic and cashew pesto with
spinach fettuccini, salads and special fruit drinks.

SOUTH AND WEST COAST The lack of long stretches of sandy beaches has ham-
pered the development that characterises the rest of the
island, but this of course is what makes the south and west coast so appealing. It
helps enormously to have your own wheels, at least for some of the time.

⌂ **Laem Set Inn $$$$$** 110 Mu 2, Hua Thanon, tel: 0-7742-
4393, fax: 0-7742-4394, www.laemset.com, e-mail: inn@laem-
set.com. Compared to a Gauguin painting in one magazine, this
stylish and ecologically aware resort remains fairly exclusive
due to its prices.

Coconut Villa $$–$$$ Phang Ka, tel/fax: 0-7742-3151. Tucked
away in the south-west corner with a choice of reasonably
priced bungalows. A pool, restaurant and motorbikes for hire.
A terrific little place.

Wiesenthal $–$$$ Ao Taling Ngam, tel/fax: 0-7723-5165.
Bungalows with a bit of space around them and an excellent
restaurant are two good reasons to stay here.

FULL-MOON PARTIES

Ko Pha-Ngan is the island and Hat Rin the location for monthly full-moon raves that attract anywhere from between five and ten thousand party people. Unless you arrive at least a day or two before the party the chances of finding somewhere to stay are fairly remote, but that doesn't deter day trippers from Ko Samui. The parties can be a lot of fun but it is advisable not to bring valuables with you. Drugs are available, but there are plenty of plain-clothes policemen and, in addition to fines, the police can *and do* put offenders in prison.

TO **Big John Seafood $$** Tang Yang Beach, tel: 0-7742-3025. A Thai and European-style seafood restaurant run by an ex-policeman, with good sunset views. A great place, unless the occasional tour group turns up. Taxi service.

SHOPPING The **Oriental Gallery**, between the Central Hotel and Charlie's Huts on the main road at Chaweng, open 1200–2300, has a range of handicrafts, souvenirs and furniture. This is one of the better outlets in a cluster of shops on this block. Next door **Golden Antiques** plays very loosely with the definition of an antique, but it's worth a look.

WHERE NEXT?

Some 20 km from the north coast of Ko Samui, only ½ hr by boat, the neighbouring Ko Pha-Ngan is developing with the overspill from Samui. There are now over 150 bungalow operators so the island is hardly a remote tropical paradise but compared to Samui it is still a low-key destination and less expensive as well. Hat Rin, in the south-west of the island, is famous for its raves and full-moon parties.

The main port for boats from Ko Samui is Thung Sala, and on arrival the usual armada of touts are waiting to whisk you off to their selected bungalows.

Songserm Travel *tel: 0-7737-7046, runs boats every day from Nathon to Ko Pha-Ngan, and boats also reach the island from the pier at Bophut. There is a night ferry from Surat Thani at 2300 which takes about 7 hrs. Around the time of the monthly full-moon party there is a dramatic increase in the number of boats departing from Bophut.*

For more information on Ko Pha-Ngan, check out the website, www.kohphangan.com.

THE BUDDHA AND HIS POSES

Buddha (563?–483? BC) was a Hindu prince named Siddhartha Gautama, born in present-day Nepal. He achieved fame for his holy love of all living creatures and for his meditation upon the meaning of life, suffering and death. Sitting one day in solitude under a bo tree, he experienced a deep spiritual awakening and became known as the Buddha, a term meaning 'the enlightened one'. He began preaching and teaching over the next 40 years of his life and after his death temples began to appear in his honour. Although his beliefs became a religion, Buddha did not see himself as divine or as in special communication with a divine spirit. He prayed to no higher being and Buddhism remains unique among religions as a belief system without a God, without a Creation and without a Heaven.

There is an entire iconography surrounding Buddha images that goes back to the early centuries of the last millennium. The easiest way for a visitor to appreciate this is by focusing on the pose of the Buddha statue and the position of the hands and feet. The posture of the Buddha is not something that can be freely rendered by the artist; it must be recognizable within the Thai tradition. He is often shown placed on an open lotus flower, itself full of significance because the lotus germinates in lowly mud but blossoms into a thing of beauty in the light and air. The reclining Buddha is a classic pose, signifying the moment of passing into *nirvana*, a state of being beyond desire and the individual consciousness. Another classic pose shows the Buddha with his hands together in reverence, resembling the Western gesture of prayer.

Bhumisparcamudra shows the right hand of the seated figure resting on the right knee while the tips of the fingers make contact with the ground. The story goes that while the Buddha was meditating, the king of malignant demons, Mara, tried to scupper his concentration by presenting him with various distractions. The Buddha conquered his foe by touching the earth with his fingers, a gesture of calling upon the earth goddess for support.

Abhayamudra is a common pose that signifies the granting of protection and the expulsion of fear. The Buddha is in a standing position, occasionally even a walking position, with at least the palm of the right hand, sometimes both, raised outwards.

The **Buddha calling for rain** also shows a standing Buddha but with both hands held down by the side and the fingers pointing downwards. This pose is most likely to be seen in northern Thailand.

Vitarkamudra sometimes seems to express an oddly modern gesture, that of the thumb and index finger of the right hand touching to form a circle. It signifies the teachings of the Buddha.

Dhyanamudra depicts a state of meditation. Both hands rest open in the lap of a seated figure. The palms point upwards, with the right hand always over the left.

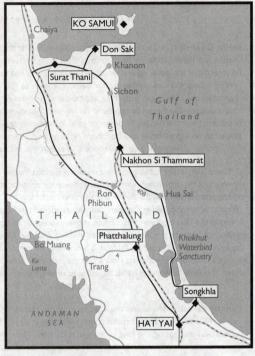

Note
There are seven boats daily between Ko Samui and Surat Thani, journey time 1½ hrs. OTT Table 7067.

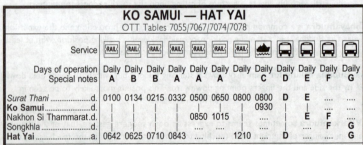

KO SAMUI — HAT YAI
OTT Tables 7055/7067/7074/7078

Service	RAIL	RAIL	RAIL	RAIL	RAIL	RAIL	RAIL	⛴	🚌	🚌	🚌	🚌
Days of operation	Daily	Daily	Daily	Daily	Daily	Daily	Daily	Daily	Daily	Daily	Daily	Daily
Special notes	A	B	B	A	A	A		C	D	E	F	G
Surat Thani ....d.	0100	0134	0215	0332	0500	0650	0800	0800	D	E	....	....
Ko Samui ....d.								0930			....	....
Nakhon Si Thammarat.d.					0850	1015		....		E	F	....
Songkhla ....d.					....	....		....		....	F	G
Hat Yai ....a.	0642	0625	0710	0843	....	....	1210	....	D	....	....	G

Special notes:
A–These trains have 2nd-class couchettes available. All journeys should be reserved in advance.
B–These trains have 1st-class sleepers available. All journeys should be reserved in advance.
C–Additional daily trips: 1000, 1200, 1400, 1430, 1700.
D–2 trips daily. Journey time: 5 hours.
E–Every 30 minutes. Journey time: 3 hours.
F–Frequent service. Journey time: 3 hours.
G–Frequent service. Journey time: 30 minutes.

The Ko Samui–Hat Yai route suffers from being regarded as a functional journey that just takes you to somewhere else more desirable. Intrinsic attractions are hard to discover in Hat Yai, a dynamic city with a reputation for prostitution that attracts Malaysian and Singaporean males, who arrive on a daily basis. They are easy to recognise, self-consciously noisy in their small packs, and many of the hotels would go bankrupt without them. Places worth a stopover in their own right are Nakhon Si Thammarat and Songkhla. Situated on a mere spit of land, Songkhla's charms are underplayed, and the ethnic mix of the population – Thais rub shoulders with Malays and Chinese – is one of its attractions.

NAKHON SI THAMMARAT

Travellers always seem to have another pressing destination, either Ko Samui to the north or Malaysia to the south, that takes them through or past Nakhon Si Thammarat. This is both a pity and a blessing. The attractive town deserves more recognition but of course its charm is partly dependent on the fact that it remains unspoilt by mass tourism.

HIGHLIGHTS **Wat Mahathat** is the town's claim to fame, and a visit here is sufficient justification for stopping off in Nakhon Si Thammarat (if you like temples, that is). At the southern end of the main Ratchdamnoen Rd, any of the numerous *songthaews* on this street will stop nearby. Everything about this *wat* is big, with the main *chedi* almost 80 m in height and the golden spire a distinctive sight. The cloisters have their share of Buddha images and a quirky little museum.

The town's **national museum, $,** open Wed–Sun, daily 0900–1200 and 1300–1630, is not spectacular but mildly diverting with its collection of prehistoric artefacts, Hindu and Buddhist images, and regional ethnographic exhibits. To reach the museum continue south along Ratchdamnoen Rd for about ½ km.

A **shadow puppet workshop** is also at this end of town, a block east of Wat Mahathat at 110/18 Soi 3 off Si Thammasok Rd. Visitors can see the puppets being made and buy them at reasonable prices, knowing the money is going straight to the producer.

Nakhon Si Thammarat is good for shopping for **handicrafts**. There are shops near the tourist office selling silverware and basket work better than anything found in the tourist shops elsewhere in southern Thailand.

THAILAND

ARRIVAL AND DEPARTURE

Train: The station is centrally located on Yommarat Rd but most of the north–south trains stop at Thung Song, 40 km west of Nakhon Si Thammarat, which means a bus or taxi ride into town. There are, however, two trains from Bangkok that pull into the town station: the Rapid 173 from Hualamphong at 1735 and the Express 85 that leaves at 1915. Trains travelling up from Butterworth only stop at Thung Song.

Bus: The station is outside of town but buses can be picked up at various points, in addition to the private minibuses that cover most of the popular routes. The tourist office has the latest information on pick-up points, fares and schedules, and you can also enquire at your accommodation.

Shared Taxis: These are a good way to travel. There is a large gathering point for the taxis on Yommarat Rd, and as soon as a vehicle is full it chugs off to Krabi, Hat Yai or Phattalung. Shared taxis for Surat Thani and Chumphon use a separate terminus at the north end, past the railway station, of Ratchdamnoen Rd.

i The **TAT Office** Sanam Na Muang, off Ratchdamnoen Rd, tel: 0-7534-6515, open daily 0830–1630. From the railway station, walk onto Yommarat Rd and turn right. Continue past the junction with Phaniat Rd that crosses the river to the end of the road near the park and police station.

🛏 **Grand Park Hotel $$$** 1204/79 Pak Nakhon Rd, tel: 0-7531-7666, fax: 0-7531-7674. The best hotel in town, modern and within walking distance of train station.
Montien Hotel $–$$ 1509/40 Yommarat Rd, tel/fax: 0-7534-1908. Conveniently close to train station. Looks dreadful but rooms are a lot better than you might think.
Thai Lee Hotel $ 1375 Ratchdamnoen Rd, tel: 0-7535-6948. Singles and doubles with fan and bathroom. Fine for one night.

🍴 Nakhon Si Thammarat is full of excellent, affordable places to eat. The restaurant at the Grand Park is worthy but bland compared to the street food and small restaurants along Yommarat Rd and neighbouring side streets.

Bovorn Bazaar off Ratchdamnoen Rd, not too far from the train station. Food stalls set up here at dusk. Banana rotis and chicken or vegetable pancakes are good, but there are lots of choices and some open-air restaurants as well.

SONGKHLA

The town of Songkhla has an interesting location, perched on a very narrow peninsula between the Gulf of Thailand and a lagoon. Compared with neighbouring Hat Yai it can fairly claim to be sophisticated. If travelling by train through southern Thailand the town is bypassed completely, but it is so close to Hat Yai, with buses running between the two every 10 mins, that it makes for a good day out. Apart from the few sights, there are decent hotels and good restaurants, and just strolling around the waterfront and admiring the Sino-Thai architecture can be enjoyable.

HIGHLIGHTS The main attractions are clustered in the centre of town, and the **National Museum ($)** is a good place to start. It is on Jana Rd, open Wed–Sun 0900–1600, and even when closed the building itself is a minor work of art. Built originally as the private mansion of a local bigwig in the 1870s, it has been successfully restored. Inside there is an oddball collection of artefacts, furniture, weapons, farm tools and religious art. One of our favourite museums in Thailand, there is bound to be something on display that will catch your interest.

A little south of the museum, on Saiburi Rd, is the photogenic **Wat Matchimawat**. Over 400 years old, the temple is most interesting as an example of Sino-Thai architecture and for its colourful murals. To see more of this hybrid architecture, albeit of the domestic kind, just wander around the small streets near the waterfront. During the second half of the 19th century there was an influx of Chinese immigrants into southern Thailand, hoping to find work as miners, and many settled in Songkhla.

ARRIVAL AND DEPARTURE Songkhla has good transport connections using buses and shared taxis. Government and private buses run to and from Bangkok, taking 13 hours, but you are more likely to find yourself hopping on or off one of the buses running to and from Hat Yai. They all run down Wichianchom Rd and Saiburi Rd, or just ask your hotel or guesthouse where the most convenient point is to hail one down.

Pavilion Hotel $$$ 17 Platha Rd, tel: 0-7444-1850, fax: 0-7432-3716. Large rooms, good facilities and fine views from the rooms on the higher floors.
Royal Crown Hotel $$$ 38 Sai Ngam Rd, tel: 0-7431-2174, fax: 0-7432-1027. Rooms with air-con and fridge at the bottom end of this price category make them very good value.
Amsterdam Guest House $ 15/3 Rong Meuang Rd, tel: 0-7431-4890. Deservedly popular budget place. Friendly atmosphere.

EXCURSION TO KO YO

Ko Yo is a small island west of Songkhla that is worth a day trip for shopping and its Folklore Museum. **Ban Nok**, the main settlement, has turned into a permanent marketplace, with opportunities to purchase top-quality cotton fabrics from the island's weaving villages.

The **Folklore Museum, $$,** open daily 0830–1700, is at the north end of the island near the bridge, in a park area with terrific views over to Songkhla. Displays and exhibits cover handicrafts, shadow puppets, religious art, domestic and military items and, the pièce de résistance, a set of coconut graters that will surprise you with their imaginative and risqué design.

Transport to Ko Yo is by way of chunky wooden *songthaews* that depart from near Jana Rd's clock tower in Songkhla. On their way to the terminus in Ko Yo they pass the folk museum first and then the cloth market, so passengers can hop off at the museum and then walk the 2 km to the marketplace in Ban Nok.

🍴 There are lots of restaurants in the centre of town, with some pricier seafood places near the beach. **The Skillet** Saket Rd, is a pub and restaurant serving pizzas and the like, with other western style places close by.
Jazz Pub, opposite the Pavilion Hotel, has an air-con restaurant serving European and Thai food.

HAT YAI

Because of its major transport links with other parts of the country as well as with Malaysia, only 50 km away, many travellers find themselves here. There is no reason to spend any time in this busy, commercial city. Arriving in Hat Yai from Malaysia on a first trip to Thailand can give an unfortunate first impression, but it serves as a good introduction to the intricacies of the country's public transport systems.

ℹ️ The **TAT Office** is at 1/1 Soi 2, off Niphat Uthit 3, open daily 0830–1630, tel: 0-7424-3747. If you have just arrived by train, walk out of the station and go up Thamnoonvithi Rd straight ahead for four blocks. Turn right into Niphat Uthit 3 and keep walking for 600 m to Soi 2.

The **immigration office** is on Phetkasem Rd, tel: 0-7424-3019.

ARRIVAL AND DEPARTURE

Train: Hat Yai is on the main southern line of Thai Railways, and there are five trains daily travelling to and from Bangkok's Hualamphong station.

Hat Yai has excellent bus connections with other parts of Thailand. Some of the more important routes are:

Bangkok	– 14 hrs
Ko Samui	– 7 hrs
Krabi	– 4 hrs
Nakhon Si Thammarat	– 2 hrs
Phuket	– 6 hrs
Songkhla	– 30 mins
Sungai Kolok	– 4 hrs
Surat Thani	– 6 hrs

Bus: The bus station is inconveniently located outside of town, and using an agent makes a lot of sense. A useful agent for booking long-distance buses is **Pak Dee Tours** tel: 0-7423-4535, at the Cathay Guest House. There are plenty more travel agents scattered along Niphat Uthit 2 and Niphat Uthit 3 Rds.

Green-coloured buses for Songkhla depart regularly from near the clock tower on Phetkasem Rd.

Air: The airport is 12 km from town. Thai Airways run a shuttle bus service between the airport and their office at 190/6 Niphat Uthit 2, tel: 0-7423-4238.

As well as Thai Airways flights to Bangkok and Singapore, Malaysian Airlines (MAS) fly between Hat Yai and Kuala Lumpur and Johor Bahru. MAS have an office in the Lee Gardens Hotel, tel: 0-7424-5443.

🛏 **Central Sukhontha Hotel $$$$$** 3 Sanehanuson Rd, tel: 0-7435-2222, fax: 0-7435-2223. Comfortable, relaxed centrally located hotel with 24-hr café, pool and Chinese restaurant. From the station, walk up Thamnoonvithi Rd for five blocks and left into Sanehanuson Rd
Regency $$$$ 23 Prachathipat Rd, tel: 0-7435-3333. Huge lobby and swimming pool, comfortable and well run, though often very busy.
King's Hotel $$–$$$ 126 Niphat Uthit Rd, tel: 0-7423-4140, fax: 0-7423-6103. Straightforward hotel with air-con and hot water; fine for an overnight stay.
Indra Hotel $$ 94 Thamnoonvithi Rd, tel: 0-7424-5886, fax:

0-7423-2464. Showing its age a little but still good value. Chinese restaurant and coffee shop.

Cathay Guest House $ 93 Niphat Uthit 2 Rd, tel: 0-7424-3815, fax: 0-7535-4104. Popular because of its cheap rooms, central location and travel service. Range of rooms and dorms. Laundry service, videos in the small lounge where beers can be purchased and inexpensive breakfast. Easy to reach from the train station.

🍽 Thai, Chinese, Muslim and Western food is all available in Hat Yai.

Nai Yaw $$ corner of Thamnoonvithi Rd and Niphat Uthit 3 Rd, is a popular and often busy restaurant serving very good Chinese and Thai food.

Pee Lek 59 $$ 185/4 Niphat Uthit 3 Rd, on the corner with Niyomrat Rd, is a first-rate open-air seafood restaurant. Western fast-food outlets from all the brand names are on Thamnoonvithi Rd and along Prachathipat Rd near the Regency Hotel. Opposite the Regency there is a **Sizzlers $$** steak house and an ice-cream parlour.

Muslim-O $ 117 Niphat Uthit 1 Rd, near the King's Hotel, is a clean and friendly little restaurant turning out curries and rotis. There are more Muslim cafés in the area, including the modest but friendly **Sulieman Restaurant $** on Niphat Uthit 2 Rd, almost opposite the Cathay Guest House.

WHERE NEXT?

The logical next destination from Hat Yai – at least if you're travelling south – is Malaysia. This can either be approached via the quiet Islamic east-coast port of Kota Bharu (pp. 338–344), or down the west-coast road or railway line to Penang (pp. 316–329). Either way, it's worth stopping off for a quiet day or two in one of Thailand's quiet southernmost Muslim towns – the most attractive is Narathiwat, right on the Malaysian frontier.

1926 Thomas Cook brochure cover

THAILAND — MALAYSIA

TRAINS BETWEEN THAILAND AND MALAYSIA There is one train a day that travels each way between Thailand and Malaysia. A sleeping berth is necessary unless you want to stay in a seat all night. The station at Padang Besar becomes the border crossing for immigration, where the train waits while passengers disembark with their luggage and clear immigration and customs before getting back on the train. Don't be confused by apparently conflicting times given in Thai and Malaysian timetables – each country shows its own time zone timings (see p. 67).

THAILAND — MALAYSIA
OTT Tables 7013/7055

Service	RAIL	RAIL	RAIL	RAIL
Days of operation	Daily	Daily	Daily	Daily
Special notes	C	C	D	C
Bangkok...................d.	1300	1420	1515	....
Hat Yai...................d.	0602	0724	0654	1550
Sungai Kolok A.........d.	1020		1040		
Padang Besar B.........d.	....	1000	....	1730
Butterworth.............a.	....	1255	....	2055
Kuala Lumpur...........a.	....	....	....	0645

Special notes:
A–From Sungai Kolok it is 1km to the border at Golok Bridge, and from there it is a further 1km to Rantau Panjang. Trishaws are available on both sides of the border. From Rantau, there are bus and taxi services to Kota Bahru and several other destinations.
B–The station at Padang Besar is used as the border crossing point. Passengers leave the train, taking all their luggage with them, and rejoin the waiting train once they have cleared customs.
C–This train has 2nd-class sleepers available. All journeys should be reserved in advance.
D–This train has 1st-class sleepers and 2nd-class couchettes available. All journeys should be reserved in advance.

MALAYSIA — THAILAND
OTT Tables 7013/7055

Service	RAIL	RAIL	RAIL	RAIL
Days of operation	Daily	Daily	Daily	Daily
Special notes	C	C	C	D
Kuala Lumpur...........d.	2010	....	....	....
Butterworth.............d.	0610	....	....	1410
Padang Besar B.........d.	0932	....	....	1800
Sungai Kolok A.........d.			1150	1405		
Hat Yai...................d.	1115	1525	1740	1820
Bangkok.................a.	....	0755	0935	0955

Special notes:
A–From Rantau Panjang it is 1km to the border at Golok Bridge, and from there it is a further 1km to Sungai Kolok. Trishaws are available on both sides of the border. There are bus and taxi services from Kota Bahru to Rantau Panjang.
B–The station at Padang Besar is used as the border crossing point. Passengers leave the train, taking all their luggage with them, and rejoin the waiting train once they have cleared customs.
C–This train has 2nd-class sleepers available. All journeys should be reserved in advance.
D–This train has 1st-class sleepers and 2nd-class couchettes available. All journeys should be reserved in advance.

BUSES BETWEEN THAILAND AND MALAYSIA

Between Hat Yai in Thailand and Malaysia and Singapore there are a number of important bus routes, using modern buses with air-conditioning: Pak Dee Tours, tel: (074) 234-535, at the Cathay Guest House (see p. 262) in Hat Yai, is the most convenient way of booking seats on these buses.

Journey times from Hat-Yai: Kuala Lumpur – 12 hrs

Penang – 4 hrs

Singapore – 15 hrs

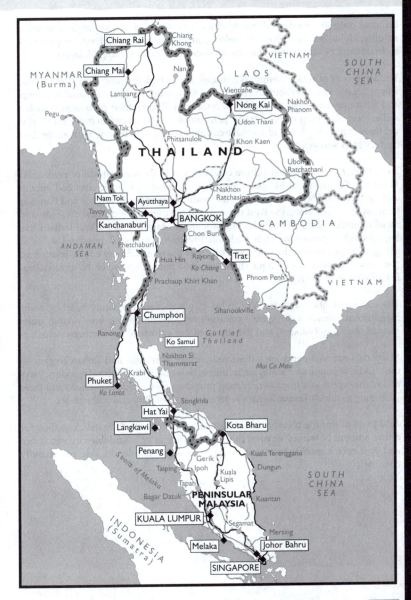

PENINSULAR MALAYSIA

Cultural diversity, modern dynamic cities, vast tracts of virgin jungle, accessible wildlife, idyllic beaches, affordable resorts, an amazing variety of food, sleepy towns and laid-back beach communities are all good reasons for visiting Malaysia.

The capital city of Kuala Lumpur is a strange mix of high tech and third world chaos, where great concrete behemoths rise up beside quaint neogothic colonial buildings and where internet cafés sit beside *roti canai* men flipping their pastries at roadside stalls. From shopping malls to traffic jams this is a modern city in every sense, and yet there is a strong sense of an older culture existing side by side with all the 21st century steel and glass.

Part of this more traditional culture can be found in the western half of peninsular Malaysia. The towns of Melaka, Penang and Ipoh offer historic sites and superb architecture, while close at hand are the beautiful islands of Pangkor and Pangkor Laut. In the towns along the west coast and in the capital the cultural diversity and racial tolerance of this country become apparent. Malays, Chinese and Indians live together while preserving their traditional religions, forms of dress and styles of eating. Georgetown on the island of Penang is the most Chinese city in South-East Asia, and the town has a unique character while remaining one of the most visitor-friendly cities in the region.

The east coast offers hundreds of miles of white, deserted sandy beaches, some magnificent islands with great opportunities for snorkelling and diving, quiet seaside *kampungs* (villages) and the strong Malay culture of the northern states.

Malaysia's national parks are a deservedly major attraction, and Taman Negara, in the middle of peninsular Malaysia, is one of the world's great natural wonders. Days and nights spent in a tropical rainforest provide a memorable experience and there is nothing to match Taman Negara in terms of accessibility and authenticity.

Add to all of this the pleasure of sitting at a roadside stall eating delicious food for a tiny amount of money or even dining in luxury at an affordable city restaurant and you have a multitude of good reasons to visit this tolerant, safe and friendly country.

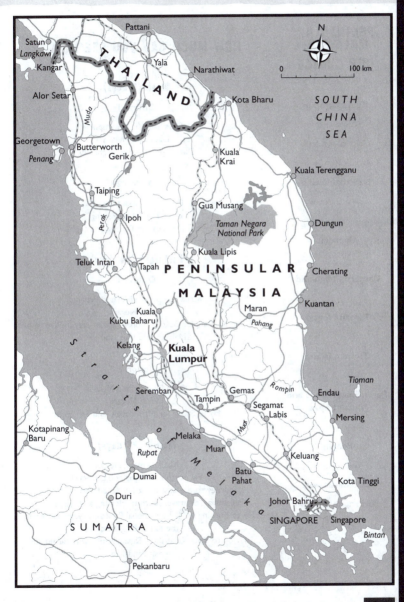

PENINSULAR MALAYSIA: OUR CHOICE

Kuala Lumpur

Chinatown

Colonial-era walk

Petronas Twin Towers

National Museum

Lake Gardens

Melaka

Cameron Highlands

Taman Negara

Tioman Island

Perenthian Islands and Pulau Kapas

Penang

Georgetown

Colonial-era walk

Boat trip to Langkawi

HOW MUCH CAN YOU SEE IN A ...

Week (7 days)

Option 1

Days 1–2: Kuala Lumpur
Days 3–4: Melaka
Days 5–7: Cameron Highlands

Option 2

Days 1–2: Kuala Lumpur
Days 3–4: Fly to Penang
Days 5–7: Boat from Penang to Langkawi

Fortnight (14 days)

Option 1

Kuala Lumpur, Melaka and Penang
Taman Negara
Fly to Kuching for Bako National Park or stay in Peninsular Malaysia and visit Tioman

Option 2

Kuala Lumpur and Melaka
Taman Negara
Fly to Sabah for Mt Kinabalu and Sandakan

Month (28 days)

Kuala Lumpur, Melaka
Fly north to Penang and Langkawi
Journey to the east coast for Kota Bahru and Pulau Perenthian, or travel south to Mersing and visit Tioman
Fly to Kuching for Bako National Park and fly on to Miri for the Kelabit Highlands
Fly on to Kota Kinabalu in Sabah, climb Mt Kinabalu and visit Sandakan

Kuala Lumpur is the capital of Malaysia and its biggest city. Until a decade ago it slumbered peacefully, unaware that the 20th century was drawing to a close and leaving it behind. Now it has the second-highest towers in the world and buildings of steel, glass and concrete are springing up all the time. Sometimes it seems that all this has happened too fast. Old cultural institutions are disappearing, pedestrians are discounted, road systems and overhead rail systems are multiplying, and the city risks losing its unique identity.

Although things may seem bad in rush hour on a hot afternoon, in 30 mins you can get out of the city and into the surrounding forest and plantations. Side by side with the steel and glass, amazing old colonial hotels still serve steak and kidney pudding on the same marble-topped tables that the colonial planters ate at. Curious old shop-houses sell equipment used in Malaysian households for generations, and hawkers cook amazing delicacies on street corners on gas cylinders just as their grandfathers did.

KL, as it is normally called, unlike its neighbouring capital Singapore, has kept much of its lively street life while adding sophisticated shopping malls and architectural wonders. About five days is enough time to get the feel of this city, familiarise yourself with its rail and bus systems, visit the best of its sights and sample some of its excellent and very inexpensive cuisine.

> **MUST SEE/DO IN KUALA LUMPUR**
>
> The Skybridge of the Petronas Twin Towers
>
> The night market in Chinatown
>
> Arts and crafts in the Central Market
>
> Retail therapy in the KLCC or Sungei Wang shopping centre
>
> Murtabak and lime juice at Restoran Ramzaan

ARRIVAL AND DEPARTURE

AIR Kuala Lumpur's KLIA (Kuala Lumpur International Airport), tel: (03) 8777-8888 or, (03) 8776 2000 is some 50 km south of the city centre at Sepang, and an airport coach or taxi will take you into town.

TRANSPORT TO AND FROM KLIA

TAXI

Taxis come in two classes – luxury and regular. Tickets can be bought at the counters inside the arrivals hall at the airport. The fare for regular taxis to central KL should be about RM70. Luxury limousines are around RM100. With four passengers a regular taxi is cheaper than the bus. The journey time is about 45 mins.

AIRPORT COACH

There are several bus and minibus/LRT (light railway) options. The easiest and most expensive is the KLIA – Hentian Duta – Hotel air-conditioned coach. It takes you to the outskirts of the city for transfer to a minibus which drops people off at their hotels. It takes about 1½ hours. Buses depart every 30 mins. Price is RM45 return for adults, RM25 for children.

Another coach goes to Chan Sow Lin LRT station, from where you take the LRT to your destination. Buses run every hour and take 1 hr. Price is RM10 for adults, RM6 for children, one way, plus your LRT fare – about RM2.

TRAIN

The KLIA Ekspress rail link between the airport and KL Sentral railway station departs every 15 mins and takes about 30 mins. The fare is RM35.

FACILITIES AT THE AIRPORT Malaysians are very proud of their new airport, which boasts a post-modernist design with exposed structures and great glass walls. Aesthetically, the airport is very pleasing but look behind the hi-tech decor and everything is not always so wonderful. The 'duty free' shopping is nothing of the sort, and the currency exchange facilities are inadequate.

EATING Inside the departures area the food is terrible, but the food court on the way to the bus station is reasonable and includes an Indian outlet serving *murtabaks* and chicken curries. Alternatively there are Burger King, Delifrance and a few other fast food joints in the Arrivals Hall, as well as a second food court above it.

In the adjoining Pan Pacific Hotel there are three good eating places: the Pasta and Mee Restaurant where a buffet is usually available, the more expensive Pacific Market restaurant and the hotel bar, which also serves food.

i A **tourist office** in the Arrivals Hall is open 0900–2100. Next door, a traveller's service centre will book transport and hotels for you.

Left luggage in arrivals hall. Open 24 hrs.

Post office Level 5 open 0830–1700 Mon–Sat.

Money exchange There is a bank in the arrivals hall near to the left-luggage office. Outside of banking hours a booth outside will change cash but not travellers'cheques. In the Departures Hall there is an exchange facility and in the bus station area the exchange facility stays open until 2100.

AIRLINES

Aeroflot, tel: (03) 2161-0231, Wisma Tong Ah, 1 Jalan Perak 50450

Air India, tel: (03) 2142-0166, Agksa Raya Building, Jalan Ampang

Air Lanka, tel: (03) 2072-3633, MUI Plaza, Jalan P Ramlee

British Airways/Qantas, tel: (03) 2167-6188, Rohas Perkasa, Jalan P Ramlee

Canadian Airlines International, tel: (03) 248-8596, Lot 25 Bang Angkasaraya, Jalan Ampang 50450

Cathay Pacific, tel: (03) 2078-3377, UBN Tower, 10 Jalan P Ramlee

China Airlines, tel: (03) 2142-7344, Amoda Building, 22 Jalan Imbi

Egypt Air, tel: (03) 2145-6867, Plaza Berjaya, Lot 3-25, 12 Jalan Imbi, 55100

Japan Airlines, tel: (03) 2161-1722, 20th floor, Menara Lion, Jalan Ampang

Lufthansa, tel: (03) 2161-4666, 3rd Floor, Pernas International Building, Jalan Sultan Ismail

Malaysia Airlines (MAS), tel: (03) 7846-3000, Ground Floor, Bangunan MAS, Jalan Sultan Ismail

Pakistan International, tel: (03) 2142-5444, Angkasa Raya, Jalan Ampang

Singapore International Airlines (SIA), tel: (03) 2692-3122, Wisma SIA, 2, Jalan Dang Wangi

TRAIN Kuala Lumpur's new railway station is at KL Sentral on the PUTRA light railway system, tel: (03) 2273-8000/2267-1200. There are trains to and from Thailand and Singapore as well as national destinations. Facilities include left luggage and an information office (open daily 0630–2200). Tickets can and should be booked 30 days in advance. Taxis from the railway station are booked using a coupon system from a clearly marked taxi desk. There is a money-exchange facility on the second level of KL Sentral, just by the café.

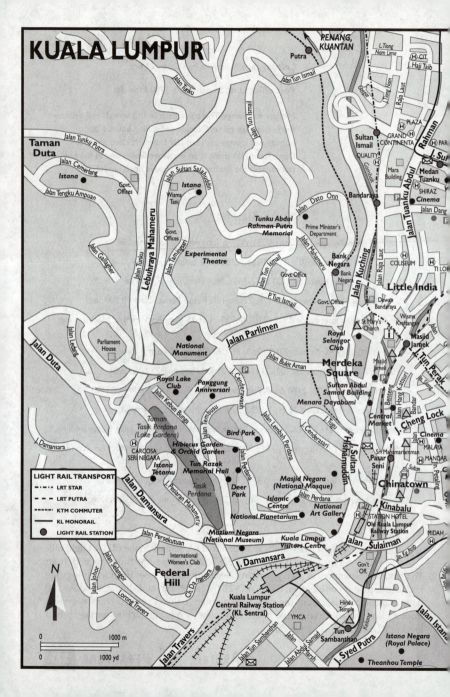

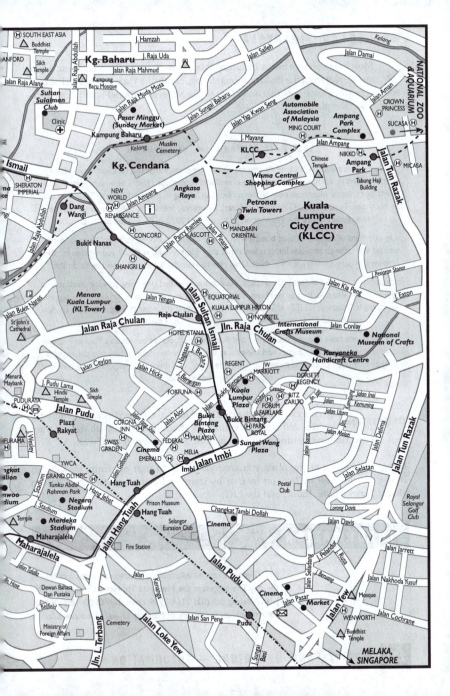

PENINSULAR MALAYSIA

BUS Most long-distance buses, including those from Singapore and Thailand, arrive and depart from the Puduraya bus station, beside the Plaza Rakyat LRT station – see box below. Please note that according to the Malaysian tourist board this relocation is still in the planning stage.

LAST DAYS OF PANIC IN THE PUDURAYA

Puduraya bus station is completely chaotic, and an experience that will pass into travel history. At some point in the future it is due to be closed and redeveloped into a new commercial centre. It will be replaced with three new terminals: Lembah Subang in the north, Bandar Tasik Selatan in the south and Taman Melati, Gombak, in the east. Before you join in the general mayhem of the old bus station, notice the information point, tel: (03) 2070-0145, and the police post.

Up one flight of stairs are ticket booths with people clustered around shouting. Men wandering around will offer to help you buy a ticket. What they actually want is to sell you a ticket for their own company, or more likely a shared taxi ride to your destination. They will lie to do this.

Each booth is an independent bus company. Walk around and find one going to your destination at the time you want. As long as you book a day in advance you will have no problem. The biggest company is Transnational (03) 4256-1055 and their booth is the most chaotic, but there are any number of other companies competing with them at similar or lower prices.

Long-distance taxis depart from the second floor of the Puduraya bus station. Taxis collect four passengers before they depart and the cost is shared between them. When one passenger is dropped off another may be picked up along the route. Get there early, expect a long wait and negotiate a fare beforehand.

ORIENTATION KL is a city without a centre. Instead, there are clusters of shopping centres and hotels in various locations in the city. With the city train lines up and running, getting around is no longer the misery it once was.

Taking Chinatown as the place you are most likely to start out from, the Golden Triangle is due east by taxi, on foot, or by train, and a stroll north brings you to Masjid Jamek, 'Little India', and the LRT.

INFORMATION

i There are tourist information centres scattered around the city. The biggest is the **Malaysia Tourism Center** at 109 Jalan Ampang, tel: (03) 2164-3929, open daily 0900–1800. It has information on the whole of Malaysia as well as counters for the various National Park headquarters and booths for booking long-distance buses.

At The PUTRA World Trade Centre is the **Tourism Malaysia Office**, tel: (03) 2693-5188, open six days 0900–1800. There are also tourist information offices in the underground shopping plaza by Merdeka Square, and at the train station and airport.

INTERNET There are internet shops in Sungei Wang Plaza, the Central Market and in several other shops in Jalan Cheng Lock. There is also one opposite Planet Hollywood in the row of shops before the Regent Hotel. Budget guesthouses and hostels usually have computer access for guests.

EXCHANGE Banks are open Mon–Fri 1000–1600 and Sat 1000–1230. Most banks have an exchange section but you will get a better rate if you shop around for moneychangers, who often do not charge a commission on traveller's cheques and give better rates than the banks. There are moneychangers in KLCC, Sungei Wang Plaza, The Mall and most smaller shopping centres.

HOSPITALS There are 24-hr Accident and Emergency departments at Assunta Hospital, Petaling Jaya, tel: (03) 7782-3433, City Medical Centre, 415-27 Jalan Pudu, tel: (03) 2121-1255.

IMMIGRATION The immigration office at Block 1, Pusat Bandar Damansara, can supply visa extensions; tel: (03) 255-5077.

EMERGENCIES

Dial 999 for the police or ambulance service and 994 for the fire service. The tourist police hotline is (03) 249-6590.

EMBASSIES AND CONSULATES

Australia, tel: (03) 2146-5555, 6 Jalan Yap Kwan Sweng

Brunei, tel: (03) 2161-2800, Wisma Sin Heap Lee, Jalan Tun Razak

Canada, tel: (03) 2718-3333, Menara Tan & Tan, 207 Jalan Tun Razak

China, tel: (03) 2142–8495, 299 Jalan Ampang

France, tel: (03) 2148-4122, 196 Jalan Ampang

Germany, tel: (03) 2142-9666, 3 Jalan U Thant

Singapore, tel: (03) 2161-6277, 209 Jalan Tun Razak

UK, tel: (03) 2148-2122, 185 Jalan Ampang

USA, tel: (03) 2168-5000, 376 Jalan Tun Razak

POSTAL SERVICES GPO, Dayabumi Complex, Jalan Sultan Hishamuddin. Poste restante counter, tel: (03) 2274-1122. Most shopping malls have a post office.

KL'S MAIN AREAS

Chinatown borders the Central Market to the west and the Puduraya bus station/new commercial centre on its eastern side. Several budget hotels are in this area, as well as shopping centres and some tourist sights.

The Golden Triangle, the area around the junction of Jalan Bukit Bintang and Jalan Sultan Ismail, is home to several of the big hotels, lots of good value budget hotels, an infinity of malls and the amazing Bintang Walk, where caffeine levels must be the highest in the world. Running behind this road is Jalan Alor, an incredible strip of hawker stalls at night.

Little India is the area north of Masjid Jamek where there are lots of good, inexpensive Indian restaurants, street markets, some discount stores and historic Merdeka Square nearby.

KLCC and Jalan Ampang is another area of interest to tourists, with a vast shopping complex and old colonial style bungalows and hotels along Ampang Road.

To the west of the Central Market are the **Lake Gardens**, bird park, orchid garden and several other places of interest worth an afternoon's wandering.

GETTING AROUND

Once upon a time KL was a nightmare of slow buses, taxi drivers with unmetered taxis, crazy traffic and lunatic *trishaw* drivers. The LRT and the introduction of taxi metres have got rid of the worst excesses of the system, although the city still snarls up during rush hour.

Drivers will very quickly realise that there is very little lane discipline in KL and driving is defensive to say the least. There are few pedestrian-friendly areas of the city, crossing some of the major junctions means taking your life into your hands and pavements are often only parking spaces for mopeds.

LIGHT RAILWAY (LRT) There are two LRT systems, chiefly running along elevated lines. The **STAR** system runs from Sentul Timur in the north of the city, through Little India, and divides into an eastern line going towards the suburb of Ampang and a southern line going towards the suburbs of the south. The section of most use to tourists is the northern end, which accesses several good hotels, the World Trade Centre, the Mall and south as far as Plaza Rakyat.

LIGHT RAILWAY (LRT) The **PUTRA** system, using driverless trains, runs roughly east–west and meets the STAR system at Masjid Jamek (you have to leave one station and cross the road to reach the other). Trains travel eastwards to KLCC and Ampang Park and continue to the south-western suburbs. The closest stop to the Central Market is Pasar Seni, a 5-minute walk away.

MONORAIL (PRT) The PRT is a useful line that connects KL Sentral with the Golden Triangle area, interconnecting with the STAR system at Hang Tuah.

BUS Fares are around RM1.20. Make sure you have the right money as no change is given. Destinations are clearly displayed on the outside of buses but ask the staff in your hotel or guesthouse for information on how to get somewhere by bus.

TAXI These are plentiful and metered. If a driver suggests a fare in advance find another cab and make sure the driver switches the meter on. Fares start at RM2 and go up 10 sen per 200 m. Drivers can charge another ringgit for the use of the boot and for going to a hotel. There are taxi stands all over the city and you should not try to flag down a cab on the street.

Several hotels and especially KLCC have cabs lurking about outside. Drivers here want an airport trip or a minimum RM10 fare and aren't interested in short journeys. Also avoid the large maxicabs which park outside the big hotels. Their flag charge is RM4 and they have a higher rate per meter.

Don't be alarmed if your cab takes off in the opposite direction to your destination – it's often quicker to get outside the city and go back in than to shuffle through blocked city streets. A regular cab fare to the airport should be around RM60. Long-distance taxis are not metered so agree a fare beforehand.

ACCOMMODATION

Kuala Lumpur is awash with grand hotels whose rates compare favourably with much more modest accommodation in Europe. The five- and even six-star hotels often have discounted rack rates and special offers. You may get a better deal through an agent in your home country or from an agent in KL than from the hotels directly. The mid-range hotels, chiefly in the Golden Triangle area and Chinatown, compete with each other for special offers, so shop around. Real budget places are a bit thinner on the ground. The price brackets below are for room rates before any discount.

Chinatown Area	**Mid-range**	**Cheng Traveller Lodge** $ 46–48 Jalan Utara, tel: (03) 2143-3960. Dorms and choice of rooms. Garden, barbecue area, laundry, shared bathroom.
		Impiana Hotel $$$ Jalan Tun Tan Cheng tel: (03) 2026-6060 www.impiana.net. Best-value hotel in this category, close to Puduraya bus station and Plaza Rakyat Station. May be changing its name to Ancasa. Breakfast included. Recommended.
		Hotel Malaya $$$ 16, Jalan Hang Lekir, tel: (03) 2072-7722, www.hotelmalaya.com.my. Good sized, clean rooms, breakfast included, fridge and kettle in rooms.
		Swiss Inn $$$ 62, Jalan Sultan, 50000, tel: (03) 2072-3333. Warren-like corridors and small, spartan, but clean, rooms. Good coffee shop in heart of Petaling St night market but with expensive beer. Very busy hotel so few discounts.
	Budget	**Backpackers Travellers Lodge** $–$$ 158 Jalan Tun H S Lee, tel: (03) 2031-0889, e-mail: btl@tm.net.my. Opposite the Malaya Hotel, on the corner; air-con rooms, fan rooms and dorm beds. Not wonderful but conveniently located in the heart of Chinatown.
		Excel Inn $ 89, Jalan Petaling, tel: (03) 2031-8621. Clean but windowless en suite rooms.
		Hotel City Inn $$ 11, Jalan Sultan, tel: (03) 2078-9190. Quiet hotel, small comfortable rooms, a little above budget rates but worth it.
		Pudu Hostel $ 3rd floor, Wisma Lai Choon, 10 Jalan Pudu, tel: (03) 2078-9600, www.puduhostel.com. Opposite Puduraya bus station (Plaza Rakyat on the STAR line), dorms, singles, doubles and triples and all the facilities of a top hotel. Recommended.
The Golden Triangle	**Mid-range**	**Bintang Warisan Hotel** $$$ 68, Jalan Bukit Bintang, 55100, tel (03) 2148-8111, fax: (03) 2148-2333, www.bintangwarisan.com. All the facilities of a good hotel, breakfast included.
		Sungei Wang Hotel $$$ 74–76 Jalan Bukit Bintang, tel: (03) 2148-5255, fax: (03) 2142-4576. Look for special offers which put this well into the economy range. All mod cons and good location. Ask for breakfast to be included.

BUDGET

Cardogan Hotel $$ 64, Jalan Bukit Bintang, tel: (03) 2144-4883, fax: (03) 2144-4865, e-mail: cardogan@po.jaring.my. One of several busy good value hotels with lots of special offers along this road. Check them all out first for the best rates. The higher rooms are less noisy and more expensive. Good value coffee shop/restaurant.

Hotel Imperial $$ 76–80 Cangkat Bukit Bintang, 50200, tel: (03) 2148-1422, fax: (03) 2142-9048. All the basics, central location. Nice Chinese fast-food place downstairs.

Hotel Seasons View $$ 59–61 Jalan Alor, tel: (03) 2145-7577, fax: (03) 2143-3532. Good value rate includes breakfast. Right in centre of Jalan Alor food stalls, so a lot of coming and going.

Hotel Nova $$ 16–22 Jalan Alor, 50200. tel: (03) 2143-1818, fax: (03) 2142-9985. New, stylish place near Jalan Alor food stalls. Very good value.

Park Hotel $$ 80 Jalan Bukit Bintang, tel: (03) 2142-7284. Choice of small and large rooms, all with air-con but no TV in rooms.

JALAN TAR

There are lots of hotels in this area, some sleazier than others, but one or two whose history makes them worth staying at.

Central Hotel $ 510 Jalan TAR, tel: (03) 4042-2981. Doubles with air-con and en suite bathroom.

Coliseum Hotel $ 100 Jalan TAR, tel: (03) 2692-6270. Large spacious rooms and original bar, restaurant and menu from 1921.

Rex Hotel $ 132 Jalan TAR, tel: (03) 2698-3895. Fan and shared bathroom but lots of 1920s atmosphere.

Dynasty $$$$ 218 Jalan Ipoh, 51200, tel: (03) 4043-7777, fax: (03) 4043-6688, e-mail: resvn@dynasty.com.my. Big rooms, close to LRT and the Mall. Lots of five-star facilities but not as pricey as one might expect.

AIRPORT

Pan Pacific Hotel $$$$$ KLIA, tel: (03) 8787-3333, fax: (03) 8787-5555. If your flight is seriously delayed then hope the airline puts you up here. Bars, restaurants, outdoor pool, indoor tennis court, 24-hr fitness centre, and some rooms looking out on the main runway.

FOOD AND DRINK

Ten years ago you'd have been hard pressed to spend a week eating out in KL, but now places to eat are tripping over each other in their rush to make their mark on an affluent and discerning public. If you want quick, cheap tasty meals try one of the indoor food courts or hawker centres, or if you want to flash your diamonds check out the restaurants in the five-star hotels. In between are thousands of small independent bistros, fast food joints and cafés, with every type of cuisine you care to mention. The list below is a fraction of what is available at amazingly reasonable prices.

CHINATOWN AREA

Amata $$ 2 Jalan Panggung, tel: (03) 2026-9077. Delicious mock meat vegetarian food where the small portions, averaging RM8, are sufficient for two to share. Try the coffee chicken, lightly marinated in Nescafé, or *bak hup* (lily buds). Open daily 1100–2200.

Naili's Place $–$$ Central Market Annexe, Jalan Hang Kasturi. A colourful place with tables on the quiet side by the river. Western and local dishes, from 0800 until 2300 daily.

Restoran Hameed $ Jalan Hang Kastri, next to Pasar Seni train station. Malay and Indian dishes in a clean and colourful restaurant that is more relaxing than similar places around Central Market, like Restoran Yusoof by the entrance to the Market.

Wan Fo Yuan $$ 8 Jalan Panggung, tel: (03) 2078-0952. Just up from Amata, similar vegetarian dishes in more modern premises with air-con but without the character.

THE GOLDEN TRIANGLE

Estana Curry House $–$$ Jalan Sultan Ismail. Located between Finnegans Irish Pub and the corner with the Istana Hotel. A range of vegetarian and meat dishes, open 24 hours.

Oggi $$–$$$ Regent Hotel, Jalan Bukit Bintang, tel: (03) 2141-8000. The place to go for that special meal, taking in the colour-changing cocktail lounge and stylish dining area. Lunch is good value and the Italian food is superb.

L'Opera $$$ Bintang Walk, tel: (03) 2144-7805. Pizza and pasta in this trendy joint, next to Planet Hollywood, with outdoor tables and Italian opera ringing in your ears.

Restoran Ramzaan $ Jalan Bukit Bintang. Old-style Malay-Indian restaurant of the kind that is fast disappearing (like Irish theme pubs, mock versions have started appearing in hotels). Rotis, murtabaks, six types of *nasi goreng* and vegetable naans. Useful for a cheap bite in-between shopping, and the *nasi lemak* with egg is ok for breakfast as well.

Sentidos Tapas $$ Star Hill Centre, Jalan Bukit Bintang, tel: (03) 2145-3385. A stylish but not outrageously expensive setting for a pleasant meal after a heavy bout of shopping.

Shook! $$–$$$ Star Hill Centre, Jalan Bukit Bintang, tel: (03) 2716-8535. Terrific restaurant with four kitchens serving up Chinese, Japanese, Italian and Western grill. Raw fish and a Caesar salad works surprisingly well and there are dishes and wines to suit most budgets.

ELSEWHERE

Bangles $$$ 270 Jalan Ampang, tel: (03) 4252-4100. An old favourite, of 35 years' standing, For North Indian food: the butter chicken and the mutton biryani are recommended.

Coliseum Café $ Jalan TAR, tel: (03) 292 6270 Mostly English menu, including sizzling steaks and baked crab, barely changed since planters took lunch here in the 1930s. You might sit in a chair once used by Somerset Maugham.

Marché $$$$ Renaissance Hotel, Jalan Sultan Ismail, tel: (03) 2162-2233. Mediterranean food and some extraordinary desserts from a talented new chef.

Pacifica Grill $$$$ Mandarin Oriental, KLCC, tel: (03) 2380-8888. Trans-ethnic cuisine from an open kitchen, chic interior for the enjoyment of dishes like turbot with curried artichokes or lamb with Thai couscous.

HAWKER STALLS The best, most atmospheric place to eat on the street in KL is in Jalan Alor, in the Golden Triangle. Mostly Chinese hawker stalls cook wonderful things for very little, and all you have to do is wander along, take your pick and find an empty table. Behind the stalls are cafés and more restaurants so you really could eat here every night.

BANGSAR

If you are seriously into the KL food experience, then head for Bangsar by taxi, feeder bus from Bangsar LRT station or on a town bus from outside Pasir Seni train station. A small area of Bangsar is packed with Chinese, Indian, Western and fusion restaurants. Current favourites are **The Chamber**, Telawi Tiga, tel: (03) 2283-1898, a strange blend of Japanese and Thai; **Telawi Street Bistro**, Jalan Telawi 3, tel: (03) 2284-3168, very cool and informal; and **Al Sabeel**, Telawi 5, tel: (03) 2283-2822, Arabic cuisine but no alcohol. All the Bangsar restaurants fall into the $$$ category.

PENINSULAR MALAYSIA

At **Jalan Hang Lekir**, near Petaling St, night market stalls spread out from the cafés, cooking satay and barbecued fish, but the prices and atmosphere are much more touristy than Jalan Alor. On the street you have to side-step waiters who thrust menus under you nose and almost drag you to a seat.

Near Jalan TAR is the **Chow Kit market,** where in rather seedy surroundings you can choose from the myriad of options at the *nasi campur* stalls. On Sunday mornings in the Golden Triangle there are *roti canai* stalls in the street behind Jalan Sultan Ismail.

At **BB Park** shopping mall in Jalan Bukit Bintang is an upmarket open-air hawker centre. It has prices to match the jazzy style, traditional dance performances on some evenings and souvenir stalls. The Chinese, seafood, Indian tandoori and Western food stalls are popular with locals.

FOOD HALLS Under cover and usually with the comfort of air-conditioning, there are several food halls that provide excellent value for money. In the Golden Triangle area the best option is the non-air-con but covered-roof area of **Sungei Wang**. It has a Buddhist vegetarian place, several *roti canai* and chicken rice stalls, and lots of Chinese buffet places where you collect what you want and the owner eyes it up and names a price. There is a particularly good Indian vegetarian restaurant to the left of the lift from KFC on the ground floor. On the same floor is an air-con place with a few lacklustre food stalls, nothing so lively as those outside. In the basement of **Lot 10** there is another air-con and fast food place with plenty of great options from Japanese sushi to chicken rice, *nasi campur*, fish and chips and lots more. Upstairs in the **Central Market** are several good places, especially Kampung Padang, an Indian Muslim restaurant piled high with seafood options.

On the top floor of KLCC there is a modern food hall with outlets serving Hainanese chicken rice, *nasi padang*, *tom yam*, Penang cuisine and Indian and Malay food.

ENTERTAINMENT

In this drug-free society it sometimes seems that the biggest buzz you're likely to get is from a Starbuck's iced cappuccino, but when KLites decide to go out there are places to see and to be seen in.

Finnegan's, 51 Jalan Sultan Ismail, tel: (03) 2145-1930, www.finneganspubs.com, is a cheerful pub that is popular with visitors. It has outdoor tables and familiar nosh.

BINTANG WALK

The latest craze to hit KL is the open-air designer coffee bar. Not so long ago locals wouldn't have been seen dead in the open air when there was air-con available, but now hanging out on the sidewalk is the thing to do. Some places even have machines blasting cold air onto the seating areas.

Bintang Walk – the stretch of pavement between Lot 10 and the JW Marriott hotel – must have the densest concentration of caffeine in Asia. Every imaginable combination of coffee and other ingredients, are available along this stretch of pavement. Linger long enough and you may find yourself an unwitting extra in a Malay soap, or see a wannabe pop star with entourage slinking past. Some of the coffee is pretty good too.

Donington, 230 Jalan Sultan Ismail, tel: (03) 2143-4100. A venue with a huge menu of international dishes and DJ music; closes around 0200.

Liquid, Central Market, tel: (03) 2078 5909. The coolest place to be at night in Chinatown; there's a gay disco with the same name upstairs.

SHOPPING

Some people say the best thing to do in KL is shop. The prices are dramatically lower than Singapore which is why so many Singaporeans are here. Clothes and shoes are cheaper than at home by a long way, except of course British imports like M&S, and there are some tempting computer software bargains to be had. Computers are cheaper than in Europe and electronics are cheaper than in Singapore if you shop wisely, but a good duty-free shop at Changi on the way home is probably cheaper.

Fake items are everywhere but they are cheaper and more readily available in Thailand or even Penang. Although it sounds obvious, bear in mind that fakes aren't as good quality as the originals. KL is a centre for crafts but they are cheaper in the areas where they are made – batik in Terrengganu or Khota Bharu, kites in Khota Bharu, basketware in Sabah and Sarawak, silver in the north, 'antiques' in

Melaka. The following is a list of the malls and streets with suggestions for what to look for.

KLCC AND JALAN AMPANG Floors and floors of upmarket shops, especially clothes. Lots of chain stores, an excellent food hall, supermarkets, restaurants, moneychangers, and an Isetan department store. KLCC is designed for spend-happy locals rather than tourists, but it's still a place to wonder at; look up at the Twin Towers from the fourth floor.

THE GOLDEN TRIANGLE The Sungei Wang shopping mall on Jalan Sultan Ismail (www.sungeiwang.com) links up with the BB Plaza, which is almost as big. Those of a nervous disposition should get a floor plan before venturing inside. Its once spacious atrium and halls are now crowded with stalls selling belts, jewellery and mobile phones and it can get very noisy. There is a cheap and cheerful Parkson Grand Department store and an IT centre on the third floor, including a noisy internet café. Scattered throughout are some good restaurants, a multiplex cinema two flights up from the main entrance, an excellent and cheap hawker centre and good moneychangers. BB Plaza links up with Sungei Wang and has Metrojaya as its anchor department store. **Lot 10** has more expensive brand-name stores, as does **Star Hill Plaza**.

MARKETS

Jalan Petaling is held nightly but is totally tourist-oriented (see p. 287); to get there, take a STAR train to Plaza Rakyat, or the PUTRA line to Pasar Seni and walk along Jalan Tun Tan Cheng Lock until you see the bridge over the road at Jalan Petaling. **Bangsar** is more for locals and usually takes place at Jalan Telawi on Sundays. An excellent non-touristy night market is on Saturday at **Jalan TAR**. On Sunday mornings the backstreets around Jalan TAR see an unusual array of herbal and animal remedies, along with some gory before and after pictures.

Imbi Plaza, closer to Imbi station on the monorail line, sells computer software and hardware, and if you know what you want and its price at home you should save some money here.

CRAFTS The **Central Market** is a good place to browse and buy if you are good at bargaining. A fixed price alternative is the **Craft Complex** in Jalan Conlay open 0845–1800 daily. It is a huge park where you may be able to watch people making batik or throwing pots or weaving or painting. The real reason to go there is to visit the two huge craft shops which have goods from all over Malaysia. There are no bargains but just about everything you are likely to see in the rest of the country is here. It might be an idea to inquire about guided tours, tel: (03) 2162-7459, since the place seems to fall asleep between tour bus visits.

HIGHLIGHTS

Kuala Lumpur is not really a city dedicated to tourists. Its attraction lies in its fascinating contrasts of old Malaya and hi-tech, high-rise steel and plate glass. There are a number of museums, the Lake Gardens, the photogenic old railway station, Menara Kuala Lumpur (or KL Tower), the Petronas Twin Towers, and the local markets. At night KL comes alive with street vendors, trendy coffee shops and cafés, and restaurants sprawl out across the streets.

KL TOWER This 421-m telecommunications tower is the fourth highest in the world, and it provides stunning views of the city and its surrounding hills for RM15. Kuala Lumpur is only 150 years old, a fact that is visually brought home when you see the entire city spread out before you from the observation platform. High-rise tower blocks are popping up everywhere, many of them ugly and badly designed and with little thought for their surroundings. The distant hills are shrouded in smog from the city, and you can see thunderstorms looming towards you. Open 0900–2200 daily, the tower is best approached by taxi since it is on a steep hill. Taxis wait around at the top to carry visitors down, and consequently charge a RM3 waiting surcharge.

PETRONAS TWIN TOWERS The 88 storeys, soaring to 452 m, make these the world's second tallest free-standing towers. They were designed by the Argentine-born US architect Cesar Pelli and completed in 1996. Much of the office space in the two towers is occupied by Petronas, the national petroleum corporation, and associate companies. There are good views of this famous KL landmark from the park down below, and from the higher levels of the KLCC shopping mall, and the Skybridge, connecting the two towers, is open to visitors, Tues–Sun 1000–1245 (1215 on Fri) and 1500–1645. Arrive early for the limited free tickets, available at the Petronas reception area from 0915 and 1430. The Twin Towers are built on the site of the old Selangor Turf club where once the popular sport of horse racing took place.

COLONIAL KL **Merdeka Square** is at the heart of colonial Kuala Lumpur. It was once a swamp, then a police training ground and later the Padang, the field where colonial types played cricket, sipped their gin and tonics and gossiped with their friends. During World War II bananas and tapioca were grown on what is now a neatly manicured green. Independence was celebrated here on 31 August 1957. The Tudor style building is the **Royal Selangor Club**, still as exclusive as it was in colonial times. The square is used for state occasions, most notably the annual celebration of independence. Below the square is Plaza PUTRA, an underground shopping centre with a tourist information office, theatre, shops and restaurants.

Around the square are several of KL's famous Moorish buildings. Mostly built by the British architect A C Norman, they are a fascinating mix of fantasy Middle Eastern architecture and Victorian Gothic. To the east across the road is the **Sultan Abdul Samad** building, looking like a Christmas tree at night and like a magnificent sultan's palace during the day. New Year is celebrated here as its 40-m-high clock strikes midnight.

North of Merdeka Square is another late-19th-century creation of A C Norman, **St Mary's Cathedral**, built in 1894 for the British community. It still contains the original pipe organ made by the famous organ maker Henry Willis.

On the south side of the square at 29, Jalan Rajah, tel: (03)-2694-4590, is another colonial building, now the **National History Museum**. Open daily 0900–1800, free, it's worth a look inside for an overview of the country's history. Next door is another Norman building, the old City Hall, now a **textile museum,** admission RM1, with displays of batik, songket and pua, open daily 0930–1800.

Further south looms the **Dayabumi building**, all soaring concrete and Islamic arches. Another little masterpiece in Gothic Moorish fantasy is the **Old Railway Station**, designed by British architect A B Hubbock and built in 1910.

Opposite the former station on Jalan Sultan Hishamuddin are the **KTM Offices**, another Hubbock fairytale extravaganza. Beside it is the **National Art Gallery**, once the Majestic Hotel, open daily 1000–1800.

To the north-east of Merdeka Square at the confluence of the Kelang and Gombok rivers is **Masjid Jamek**. It marks the spot where the first Chinese tin prospectors set foot on what was to be the capital city. The mosque is a pretty, quiet spot in the middle of a raging traffic jam. It is all pink and white stripes and domed minarets, again designed by Hubbock, with a walled courtyard complete with palm trees and views of the river. For an overhead view of the mosque you can climb the stairs to the STAR LRT, or the main entrance is in Jalan Tun Perak.

CHINATOWN   This area is best visited during the evening when the quiet daytime streets come alive with market traders, restaurants and coffee shops. The centre of activity is **Jalan Petaling**, a hive of bargaining with streams of tourists wandering between the copy watch, T-shirt and odds and ends stalls. Pasir Seni or Plaza Rakyat are the two closest stations.

In **Jalan Hang Lekir** live seafood is displayed on barrows so you can choose your evening meal as it wriggles about. Beware starting negotiations if you don't intend to buy. Bear in mind also that most things are cheaper in Penang.

In Jalan Tun H S Lee, south of **Jalan Hang Lekir**, is the **Sri Mahamariammam Temple**, originally built in 1873 by Tamil contract labourers and funded by wealthy Chettiar traders. The building you see is much more recent, dating from 1985, and positively glows with gold leaf, precious stones and elaborate tiles. The temple is the starting point for the Thaipusam festival when the silver chariot dedicated to Lord Murugan is taken in procession to the Batu Caves.

To the west of Chinatown is the refurbished **Central Market**, now a dedicated arts and crafts and 'antiques' venue where serious bargaining needs to be done if you want to buy anything. Most things are going to be cheaper in the provinces than here. Upstairs in the Central Market are some good inexpensive restaurants.

LAKE GARDENS   A popular place with Malaysians at weekends, the **Lake Gardens** are a man-made, 91.6 hectares of jogging tracks, lakes, bird and butterfly collections and statuary. At the south end is the **National Museum, $**, tel: (03) 2282-6255, open daily 0900–1800. Well worth a visit, the museum includes exhibits on the country's history, culture, natural history and much more.

Moving northwards into the park you can enjoy the lakes with pedal boats for hire, a hibiscus garden, an orchid garden and a deer park. At the north end is the **National Monument**, designed by Felix de Weldon, creator of the famous Iwo Jima statue in Washington, to represent Malaysia's recovery from the threat of Communism. An attempt was made in 1975 to blow it up.

Beside it is the **ASEAN Sculpture Garden**. The Lake Gardens contain a huge enclosed **bird park** with many local and foreign birds, **$**, open daily 0900–1700, and a **butterfly park, $$**, where butterflies are bred on site and released into the rainforest setting, open daily 0900–1800.

DAY TRIPS

A few kilometres outside the city are two major places of interest: **Batu Caves** and **Templer Park**. The park is about 10 km beyond the turn-off from Highway 1 for the caves, so both places could fit into a day trip.

Situated in a vast limestone outcrop 13 km north of KL, **Batu Caves** were discovered in 1881 and quickly became a Hindu shrine dedicated to Lord Subramanian. For most of the year the rather shabby shrines and soot-caked walls are silent and empty. But during the Thaipusam Festival in February thousands of people come here, and visitors can watch penitents wearing vast metal *kavadis* with their bodies pierced with metal spikes.

The main cave is 272 steps up into the limestone outcrop, where fairy lights illuminate the various cave formations. Below is a museum dedicated to Hindu mythology. During the war the Japanese used the caves as munitions factories, and the cement floors and machinery bases can still be seen. Take bus no. 11 from Central Market.

Templer Park ($) is 21 km north of the city with 1200 hectares of forest, the 3000-m-high Kanching waterfall and several limestone outcrops. Very busy at weekends, the park is quiet during the week and there are lots of walks and picnic spots. Take bus

En Route

On the way to Templer Park, about 8 km before it, is **Kampung Kuantan**, a small village where millions of fireflies can be seen, attracted to the berembang trees that hang over the river. The best time to make the brief river trip is just after dark, around 1930. The females flash their lights and the males synchronise their flashing.

Local people run river trips from the village, or you can have the entire trip organised by one of the KL tour agencies. The Nature Park can also arrange the Kampung Kuantan trip and has chalet accommodation $, tel: (03) 3289-2294.

The Orang Asli Museum

This little museum 25 km north of KL is dedicated to the culture and life of the original inhabitants of Malaysia, the Orang Asli (see p. 300). There are about 60,000 Orang Asli living in 18 tribes in remote areas of the mainland.

The museum displays artefacts still in use, such as blowpipes, traps and fishing equipment. Open Sat–Thur 0900–1730, free, tel: (03) 6189-2122. Take bus no. 174 from Lebuh Ampang.

For more information on the Orang Asli, contact the Centre for Orang Asli, 86B Jalan SS24/2, 47301 Petaling Jaya, Malaysia.

Colour Section

nos 66, 78, 83 or 81 from Puduraya bus station (NB this will change when the Puduraya bus station closes; see box on p. 274).

Kuala Selangor Nature Park, 250 hectares of mud flats and river estuary, as well as forest reserve, is 65 km north west of KL, entrance RM2, tel: (03) 3289-2294. Several trails run out from the entrance, some a considerable walk and others a brief stroll. All lead to hides where typical estuary and wading birds of the region can be seen, as well as migratory birds making their way from Siberia, China and Russia to Australia. The park keeps captive birds too. Milky storks, extinct now in Cambodia and Thailand, are being bred here in captivity in an effort to save the species.

WHERE NEXT?

If you've been staying in the bustling Malaysian capital, consider heading north for just over 100 km to the tiny, old-world hill resort of Bukit Fraser. Here you can hike various trails and revel in the abundant wildlife and flora before returning to KL and pushing on to Malaysia's Taman Negara National Park (pp. 292–300).

MALAYA'S KL

In between the vast soaring steel and glass monoliths that now dominate the city, lots of more elderly buildings have survived. The outrageous fantasy buildings at Merdeka Square are the most outlandish of these, but there are many other simpler buildings whose design reflects the necessities of living in the tropics as well as the fashions of the day.

Around the Central Market there are several examples of colonial architecture. The shops opposite the market demonstrate the traditional shop-house design brought into Malaya by Chinese merchants and adapted by the city's architects at the end of the 19th century. They are typically two-storey buildings, with the business premises downstairs and the merchant's living quarters upstairs. The upper storey extends over the lower, creating the 'five foot way' where goods could be displayed and customers could shelter from the heat of the day (or the tropical rains). The buildings opposite the market, in Jalan Hang Kasturi, are neo-classical in design, built around the early 1900s, and display Greek pediments, Roman columns and decorated window frames. Here the typical Chinese shop-house has come under Western architectural influence.

The Central Market building itself is much later, dating from 1936, and is clearly art deco in style with strong horizontal features and abstract geometric designs. Further up Jalan Hang Kasturi is the OCBC building (1938), also art deco in design but this time more curved and less angular in appearance.

Directly opposite the OCBC building is another block of neo-classical shop-houses, again with elaborate façades, each one slightly different from the others. The block was originally red brick and was known as the Red House.

Back on the other side of the junction is the Old Federal Stores Building, erected around the turn of the 19th century. It is very much out of line with other turn-of-the-century shop-houses, with an elaborate Chinese roofline and garlic finials and no five foot way. For many years the building was home to the Cycle and Carriage Company, which imported the first of Malaya's cars. The area of which these buildings form the southern corner is called Pasar Malam or Old Market Square. This was the area which preceded the present Central Market as Kuala Lumpur's main wholesale wetmarket. In the late 19th century it was a series of attap huts holding traders as well as gambling dens. They were swept away in a grand clearance in 1907 and replaced with the present row of neo-classical shop-houses, three storeys high and with ornate rooftops, window decorations and some beautiful plasterwork. In the centre of the block is the clocktower, erected in 1937 to commemorate the coronation of George VI. At its base is a typical art deco design – a stylised sunburst.

How to See

SINGAPORE

The Malay Peninsula and Penang

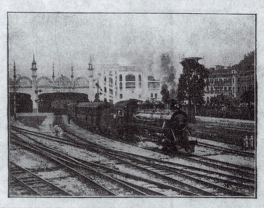

Express Train Leaving Kuala Lumpur Station.

Programme of

Sightseeing Arrangements

Under the Management of

THOS. COOK & SON, LTD.,

General Foreign Passenger Agents, Pennsylvania Railroad,

18, BATTERY ROAD, SINGAPORE.

Tel. Nos: 3016 & 3017. Cable Address: "COUPON"

1928 Thomas Cook brochure cover

KUALA LUMPUR — TAMAN NEGARA

Notes

The easiest way to reach Taman Negara from KL is by way of NKS; their desk is at Hotel Malaya in Petaling St, Chinatown, tel: (03) 2072-0336, (09) 266-4499, www.taman-negara.com. Their packages vary to suit all budgets. Also, see www.mutiarahotels.com for their trips from KL.

DRIVING ROUTE

It takes around 3 hrs to drive to Kuala Tembeling (170 km). Take the Kuala Lumpur–Karak highway east to Mentakab and 3 km after Mentakab take the turning for Kuala Krau, which leads to Jerantut. There is a car park at the jetty that costs RM5 a day.

The buses to Jerantut necessitate another bus or cab ride to Kuala Tembeling in time to catch one of the two boats into the park. There is now a road all the way into the park, and Jerantut hotels organise bus rides for about RM25 per person, but this cuts out one of the best aspects of the visit to the park – the boat journey upriver into the rainforest.

Gua Musang

TAMAN NEGARA NATIONAL PARK

Kampung Cenih

Kuala Lipis

Kuala Tahan

Kuala Tembeling

Jerantut

PENINSULAR MALAYSIA

Maran

Pahang

Mentakab Temerluh

KUALA LUMPUR

KUALA LUMPUR — TAMAN NEGARA
OTT Table 7006

Service	🚌	⛴	🚆	🚆	🚌	🚌
Days of operation	Daily	Daily	Daily	⑤⑥	Daily	Daily
Special notes		A	B	B	C	D
Kuala Lumpur................d.	0800	....	1955	2240	C	....	....	....
Jerantut................d.	|	....	0219	0527	C	....	....	....
Kuala Tembeling ....d.	1200	A	....	....	....	D	....	....
Taman Negara Park HQ.a.	....	A	....	....	....	....	....	....

Special notes:
A–2 trips daily. Journey time: 2 to 3 hours.
B–This train has 2nd-class sleepers available, and all journeys should be reserved in advance.
C–Hourly service. Journey time: 3 hours.
D–4 trips daily. Journey time: 45 minutes. Minibuses are also available.

KUALA LUMPUR – TAMAN NEGARA

The medium is the message, and the recommended way to reach Taman Negara is by means of an eight-plus-seater *perahu*, a timber boat with an outboard motor. It takes nearly 3 hrs to travel up the Tembeling river (Sungai Tembeling) from the jetty at Kuala Tembeling, but it's a memorable experience and puts you in the right frame of mind to enjoy the national park. Kampong life unfolds on the banks of the river with children, women and water buffalo all taking advantage of the water to wash clothes, take a dip or just enjoy nature. A sudden flash of blue as a kingfisher darts across the river, or a 2-m, lazy monitor-lizard (*Varanus salvator*) sliding off a mudbank, is a sign of the glorious wildlife yet to come. In the summer months, keep an eye open for the majestic blue-throated bee-eater.

TAMAN NEGARA

If you only make one journey in peninsular Malaysia, make the trip to Taman Negara. The forest here is probably the oldest in the world. The area was never affected by assorted ice ages by volcanic eruptions so besides man there has been little interference with the 4343 sq km of virgin jungle in the last 130 million years.

Taman Negara means 'National Park'. Designated a national park in 1938, this place is home to Malaysia's 300 or so tigers, elephants, civet cats, tapir, wild ox, sambar deer and lots more. Unfortunately the most dangerous creature in the park is *Homo sapiens*. They poach, hunt (the indigenous Orang Asli people are allowed to hunt in the forests), wear out forest trails and generally encroach on the lives of the animals, which subsequently become less accessible each year. Nonetheless, leave the resort and its paths behind and even if you don't see a tiger you'll see and hear the forest and its creatures.

ECOPOLITICS

Taman Negara was a well-kept secret for many years, visited by hardy souls who didn't mind roughing it a bit. Then someone saw the tourist dollars to be made and it was privatised in 1991. Expensive accommodation was built and prices for boat hire and guides shot up.

Although the thousands more people who visit the park every year bring in much needed revenue, they also cause erosion and damage. In addition, the huge expansion of towns and villages around the perimeter is reducing the space available to animals which once roamed beyond the park boundaries.

Now a road has been built all the way into the park, access is no longer dependent on river water levels. The park, once closed for the rainy season, is now open all year. It is just a matter of time before there is more development of tourist accommodation and the Orang Asli and the animals are driven even deeper into the forest.

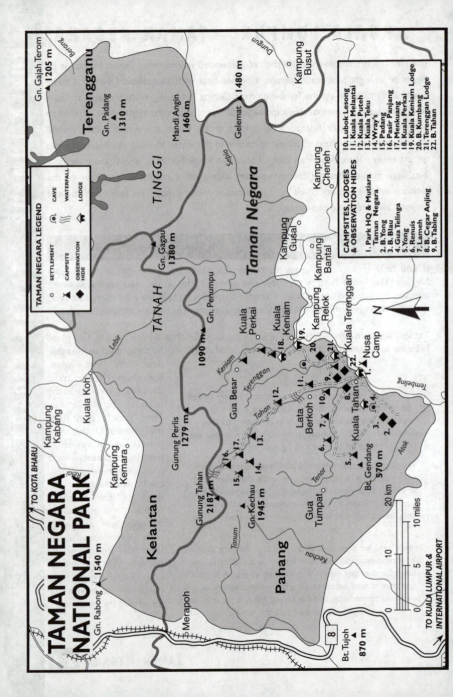

JERANTUT

There is little reason to visit this town except as a stopping point on the way to Taman Negara. It is possible to book your trip into the park from here, and it is a good stocking-up point if you plan to do your own catering there.

GETTING THERE **Buses** from KL to Jerantut leave from the Pekeliling bus station in Jalan Tun Razak in the north of the city, tel: (03) 4043-0648. There are several buses a day, but you should enquire about times and book in advance. There is also a train from the railway station at KL Sentral, tel: (03) 2273-8000/2274-94222.

Buses for Kuala Tembeling from Jerantut bus station are designed to catch the boat to the national park, although with delays they do not always do so. The boats leave at 0900 and 1400 daily except Friday, when there is only one boat at 1445. Private buses to the jetty or even all the way to the national park headquarters are organised by several of the hotels in town. See p. 300 for package trips from KL.

ENTRY PERMITS
Taman Negara is a protected national park and all who enter must have permits (photographers also need a permit to use their camera). These can be purchased for a nominal sum at the jetty at Kuala Tembeling. Bookings and reservations to stay in the park must be made in advance or upon arrival at the reservations office in Kuala Tahan; tel: (03) 263-4434.

SRI EMAS HOTEL
This hotel, the centre for trips to Taman Negara, has thought of everything for the budget traveller and offers a range of package deals through sister company NKS Hotel and Travel (see p. 292).

Share taxis for Jerantut leave from the Puduraya bus station in Kuala Lumpur and cost RM30 per person (note that the Puduraya is due to close; see p. 274). Taxis from Jerantut to Kuala Tembeling should cost about RM18, and are a much more reliable way of getting the boat than a local bus.

Boats to Taman Negara park headquarters are operated by the Mutiara hotel and Nusa Camp in the park.

i **A travel agent close** to the railway station takes bookings and has information about the Mutiara hotel.
At the bus station is a booking office for the Nusa Camp, tel: (09) 266-2369.
Several of the town's guesthouses also offer information to guests and will book transport into the park for them.

🛏 **Sri Emas Hotel $** Jalan Besar, tel: (09) 266-4499. fax: (09) 266-4801. Dorm beds, rooms with fan or air-con, left-luggage facility.

🍴 Coffee shops in Jalan Besar, food stalls between the market and the railway station and Chinese restaurants in Jalan Besar. Also, KFC near the bus station.

KUALA TAHAN

Kuala Tahan, where the Tahan river joins the Tembeling, is the site of both the national park HQ and a small village which has built up budget accommodation and places to eat to serve the thousands of travellers who want to enjoy the park but can no longer afford the prices at the main Mutiara hotel (Mutiara Taman Negara) alongside the park HQ. Wherever you stay, there is a good week or more of enjoyment to be had.

BOAT The Mutiara/HQ leaflets warn that only people with reservations at the Mutiara can book seats in their boats from Kuala Tembeling. Their fares are RM19 one way. They also operate a speedboat (twice daily) which takes only 45 mins, but loses much of the joy of getting there.

The Nusa Camp runs boats (twice daily) from Kuala Tembeling to the park HQ and then on to their camp for RM38 return. Nusa also offers a regular riverbus service to many of the locations in the park, at much lower prices than chartering a boat at park HQ. This includes a service every 2 hrs to and from the park HQ to Nusa Camp and a twice-daily service to the canopy, to some of the caves and to some distant campsites.

BUS SPKG Tours operates a shuttle bus service between KL and Kuala Tembeling that can be booked through the Nusa Camp offices in KL and Kuala Tembeling. The resort also arranges a daily shuttle bus to meet the Kuala Tembeling ferry. Enquire about prices and pickup point at the KL office.

HIGHLIGHTS Hardier visitors can spend a week **trekking** to the farthest reaches and back or even trek all the way out of the park to Merapoh on the border of Pahang and Kuantan. Get a copy of David Bowden's *Taman Negara Visitor's Guide* before you go if planning some substantial trekking. There are also lots of hides and salt licks close to HQ or within a short boat journey. Be prepared for walking in high temperatures and high humidity, and for carrying heavy backpacks and roughing it.

Very close to the HQ is **Bumbun Tahan**, which overlooks a clearing and waterhole. Deer, macaques and various birds are quite regular visitors. The best time to look is in the evening. Further away from the HQ and a morning's walk or an excellent river-boat ride away are several more hides. **Bumbun Blau** and **Yong** are south of the HQ and about a 2-hr walk or a boat journey. They are close to **Gua Telinga**, a cave system with a river running through it where bats and snakes are often spotted.

Bumbun Tabing and **Bumbun Cegar Anjing** are both accessible by river-boat or by a hot hour or so's walk, and look out on salt licks in clearings. **Tabing** has a toilet and washing facilities, and clean water nearby. **Bumbun Kumbang**, 11 km from the HQ and a 45-min boat ride followed by a 45-min walk, is where lucky visitors have spotted elephants.

WALKING Those who come to Taman Negara in the hope of seeing a tiger or elephant may well go away disappointed. Others will realise that the true beauty of the place isn't the exotic creatures but the amazing jungle itself. Walking around it is like being inside a great, heaving living creature. At every step there is some outrageous life form teeming away inches away from you. Walking in the rainforest is both safe and exhilarating, and you should spend every day on one of the walks.

> ## WHAT TO BRING
>
> The hides are very basic with earth toilets. If you stay overnight you must take all provisions and a sleeping sheet with you. The jungle never really cools down so a sheet and mosquito net are a better choice than a sleeping bag. Basic first aid in terms of iodine and sticking plasters and something to clean up minor wounds is important.
>
> Long-sleeved clothes and long trousers made of thin cotton keep off the insects, and a good pair of canvas jungle boots are protection against leeches. Mosquito repellent and insect repellent for the leeches are vital, as is a torch. You should also bring a string bag to hang up your food. Rats invade the shelters at night and will carry away anything they can get their paws on. Water-purifying tablets or a gas stove to boil water are also important.

The 3-hr **Bukit Indah Trail** is the best introductory walk. It follows the course of the Tembeling river to the canopy walkway, which has an entrance fee. From there, follow the signs to Bukit Terasek where there are fine views.

Alternatively you can follow the signs to Lubok Simpon from the walkway and spend some time in a swimming area before returning to the park HQ. Or from the canopy follow the Bukit Indah trail for more fine views over the forest canopy.

> ## OTHER SHORT WALKS
>
> **Kuala Trenggan**, about 5 hrs, 9 km along the river bank. You can stay at the lodge (book 2 days in advance at the park HQ) or get the river boat back to Kuala Tahan.
>
> **Gua Telinga**, about 2 hrs from the HQ. Then you can crawl through the cave system itself; about half an hour following a rope guide. Take a torch.
>
> **Latah Berkoh**: about 4 hrs, 8 km north of the HQ, on the Gunung Tahan trail. Latah Berkoh is a series of cascades on the river which are good for paddling and picnics. There is a very basic lodge nearby, which can be booked for the night. You must bring supplies. There is also a camp site en route at Kemah Lameh to stay overnight, or you can book a ride back on one of the boats to the waterfall.

LONGER TREKS For all longer treks a guide must be hired, which increases the cost. Trips can be planned around the vari-

THE CANOPY WALKWAY

Walking along the forest floor means you miss out on much of the rainforest activity taking place high above you in the canopy of huge trees which form the top layer of the forest. The canopy walkway leads you along 400 m of rope bridge suspended from the biggest of the trees at a height of about 25 m from the ground. Probably the noise of all the other walkers has driven anything interesting away, but it's a good experience and gives a different view of the forest. Entrance to the walkway is RM5 and it is open daily 1100–1445, except Fri, 0900–1145.

ous lodges and camping grounds in the park so that you have accommodation for the night, but it is best to try to join a group rather than take on the cost of boat rides and guides on your own. The park HQ organises and has details of longer treks which include:

Gunung Tahan: Nine days. Fifty-five kilometres to the summit of Gunung Tahan and the same distance back. A guide and supplies are essential for the full 9 days. Not to be undertaken lightly. Camp sites en route have water and firewood.

Rentis Tenor trail: Three–four days, depending on your route. Only 15 km from park HQ. A guide may not be necessary as all the trails are marked. Crossing the Tahan river, the trail goes to Kemah Yong on the banks of the Sungai Yong and makes a brief, 570-m ascent up Bukit Guling Gendang. Nights are spent at the Yong campsite. The third day is a day-long trek to Kemah Lameh beside the Sungai Tenor. The last day is spent retracing your steps to Kuala Tahan.

INHABITANTS OF THE FOREST

You won't see tigers peering out of the jungle at you or rampaging herds of elephants. But you may catch sight of the laughably ungracious hornbills who honk their way around the jungle. Or the primeval monitor lizards, looking like great logs rolling down the river until they open an eye to give you a stare. Or the pink coral snake, which is deadly poisonous except that its jaws are only wide enough to bite the bit of skin between your fingers.

Then there's the teeming insect life. Great trails of ants carrying huge butterflies that they've killed back to their nests. Flocks of exotic butterflies attracted to the sweat on your boots. Even the leeches have a certain comic dignity as they slip out of your boots, three times the size they went in and drunk on your blood. Especially rewarding are those unsought moments. You glance up to see a flying fox, an orchid is growing on the path beside your foot, or an entire colony of bats surges out of the hillside at dusk. You can see tigers at the zoo. Taman Negara is special.

ORGANISED ADVENTURES Long gone are the pioneering, make-your-own adventure days of Taman Negara. The Mutiara hotel and park HQ organise trips into the jungle at night, into the caves, up the rivers and into the Orang Asli settlements. You can ride the rapids in an inflatable raft, fish in the rivers and even hold a conference or banquet here. All of it costs, especially boat and guide hire, which unfortunately prevents some people doing some of the more exciting activities.

🛏 **Mutiara Taman Negara $$$–$$$$** tel: (09) 266-3500, Kuala Tahan. KL sales office Lot G 01A, Ground Floor, Kompleks Antarabangsar, Jalan Sultan Ismail, tel: (03) 2142-1601, fax: 2142-9822, www.mutiarahotels.com. This 3-star hotel also has the national park office for booking boat trips and overnight stays in the jungle.

On the other side of the river, opposite the Mutiara hotel and Park HQ, a village offers cheaper accommodation and places to eat.
Rainforest Resort $$$ tel: (09) 266-7888 or (03) 4256-7707, e-mail: resvns@rainforest-tamannegara.com, comes closest to the Mutiara in terms of creature comforts and prices can be good value if a discount is offered, e.g. RM100 for a deluxe room with breakfast.
Tahan Guest House $$ tel/fax: (09) 266-7752, www.tahanguesthouse.tk. Colourful and more cheerful than most of the competition. RM65 for a double room with bathroom.
Nusa Camp, tel: (09) 266-3043, is 15 minutes upriver from Kuala Tahan and offers a more authentic jungle experience. Various packages and types of budget accommodation bookable in Jerantut, tel: (09) 2662-369, e-mail: 5pkg@tm.net.my; KL, tel: (03) 4042-8369; or Kuala Tembeling, tel: (09) 266-3043.

🍽 The Mutiara hotel/HQ has two restaurants with set meals or an *à la carte* menu, from **$$$–$$$$**. There is also a restaurant at Nusa Camp, with a more restricted menu and lower prices. In Kampung Kuala Tahan are lots of restaurants in boats and barges along the bank of the river. Any one of them will ferry you over to the village. The Mutiara/HQ has an expensive supermarket so if you want to save money, bring as much food in as you can.

When to Visit

Taman Negara is at its driest between February and September, which is the best time for walking. But if the rivers get too dry much of the fun of the place is lost. During school holidays the place gets very crowded and winter brings Europeans escaping their climate. In July is the Taman Negara Festival, with traditional dance shows and handicrafts made by the Orang Asli and Batek.

THE ORANG ASLI

These people, with their distinctive appearance, dark skin, short stature and curly hair, are the true sons of the soil in this part of the world. They are thought by anthropologists to be the original inhabitants of the Malay peninsula, and cave paintings discovered in the Gua Batu Luas caves in Taman Negara are believed to be those of their ancestors. This suggests that they were once cave dwellers rather than nomadic hunters.

As other, younger cultures have penetrated deeper into the jungles of Malaysia, the Orang Asli have either developed settled lives or retreated ever further into the jungle. They are traditionally nomadic forest dwellers, creating temporary settlements out of native materials, which last for a few months while they gather fruits and vegetables and hunt in the locality. They always move on before an area is exhausted, leaving it to regenerate. Their tools are chiefly gathered from the forest itself. You will see them punting along the river in makeshift canoes and rafts as they fish or travel about. They build blowpipes out of cane and gather the poison for their darts from the ipoh tree. Home is a raised wooden platform strung above the forest floor with rattan cords to protect them from floods or animals.

In modern times the Orang Asli, or Batek, as they call themselves, trade with settled communities for cooking pots, T-shirts, fast food and snacks. In return they sell woven rattan goods, food covers, bags and sleeping mats. Like the Malays, the Orang Asli are considered *bumiputra*, or 'sons of the soil', and are entitled to the same economic advantages as the Malays, although few of them exploit these advantages. They are largely poor, little educated and have a much shorter life expectancy than settled people.

PACKAGE TRIPS

There should be no problem finding a hotel or tour agency in Jerantut. Hotel Sri Emas, Jalan Besar, tel: (09) 266-4499, fax: (09) 266-4801, e-mail: tamannegara@hotmail.com, www.taman-negara.com, has a three-day/two-night package that starts at RM100 per person, with hostel accommodation, breakfast and transport, and goes up to RM185 per person for chalets with air-con. In KL, ALIF Travel & Tours, tel: (03) 4256-7707, fax: (03) 4256-1677, e-mail: alifattrvl@po.jaring.my, does a three-day/two-night package with air-con room, meals and transport from RM250 per person.

KUALA LUMPUR — PENANG
OTT Tables 7005/7030/7035/7036

Service	RAIL	🚌	✈	🚌	🚌	🚌	🚌	🚌	🚌	⛴	🚌	🚌
Days of operation	Daily	Daily	Daily	Daily	Daily	Daily	Daily	Daily	Daily	Daily	Daily	Daily
Special notes	A	B	C	D	E	F		G	D	H	D	J
Kuala Lumpur............d.	2010	B	C	D	....	0730	0830	....	....	....	....	....
Tapah.............................d.	2343	|	|	D	E	|	|	G	....	....	....	....
Cameron Highlands .....d.	|	|	|	....	E	|	1400	|	....	....	....	....
Ipoh................................d.	0113	|	|	....	....	1130	....	G	D	....	....	....
Lumut.............................d.	|	|	|	....	....	....	....	....	D	H	D	....
Pangkor.........................d.	|	|	|	....	....	....	....	....	....	H	|	....
Kuala Kangsar ....d.	0233	|	|	....	....	....	....	....	....	....	D	J
Taiping...........................d.	0320	|	|	....	....	....	....	....	....	....	....	J
Butterworth ....a.	0545	B	C	....	....	....	....	....	....	....	....	J

For crossings to Georgetown (Penang) see timetable for Penang – Langkawi – Alor Setar – Penang route.

Special notes:
A–This train has 1st and 2nd class sleepers available, and all journeys should be reserved in advance.
B–Several services daily. Journey time: 8 hours.
C–Frequent service. Journey time: 2 hours.
D–Hourly service. Journey time: 2 hours.
E–Hourly service. Journey time: 1 hour.
F–Hourly from 0730 to 2230.
G–Hourly service. Journey time: 1½ hours.
H–Every 30 minutes. Journey time: 30 minutes.
J–Hourly service. Journey times: Ipoh – Kuala Kangsar 1 hour; Kuala Kangsar – Taiping 1 hour; Taiping – Butterworth 2 hours.

DRIVING ROUTE

The north–south expressway, a toll road, takes you to Tanjung Malim on the Selangor/Perak border and then on to Tapah. From Tapah route 59 leads to the Cameron Highlands. From Tapah to Ipoh the route again follows the north–south highway. From Ipoh to Lumut, take route 5. Ipoh to Kuala Kangsar is back on the north–south highway, as are Taiping and Penang.

The Scenic Route

The north–south highway is an easy road to drive but it could be anywhere in the world with its multiple carriageways, toll booths and rest stops. If you would rather see a little more of the country on your trip it is possible to get off the highway at Tanjung Malim and take old highway 1.

This passes Slim River where the British fought a battle against the encroaching Japanese forces, Teluk Intan with its pagoda-style leaning clock tower and Kampung Pasir Salak where the first British Resident of the state was assassinated in 1875. The town is also home to some traditional style houses given over to museums of history and culture.

PENINSULAR MALAYSIA

EN ROUTE
TAPAH

Of little interest except as a staging post on the journey to the Cameron Highlands, Tapah is an example of small-town Malaysia. It has rail links with Thailand in the north and Singapore in the south, a few small hotels, and coffee shops, but generally a sense that life goes on without it. You may spend an hour or so here on the journey to the Cameron Highlands, in which case you could hang out for a while at the coffee shop in the Hotel Timuran. An overnight stop can be made at Bunga Raya Hotel, Jalan Besar.

The train station is 9 km west of town with links to Penang and Kuala Lumpur, and there is a half-hourly bus service to and from town.

Long-distance buses leave from outside the Caspian restaurant in Main Rd or from the bus station. Buses for the Cameron Highlands leave from the bus station in Jalan Raja. Close to the bus station is the taxi station where you can get a share taxi to Ringlet, the first village in the Cameron Highlands. Buses up to the Cameron Highlands can sometimes be a little scary, so taking a taxi is a good option.

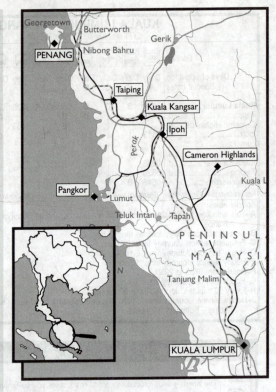

PERAK

The great north–south highway has made a trip to Penang from KL a brief morning's drive through the state of Perak rather than a major undertaking. It has also opened up the 21,000 sq km of the state once dedicated to tin mining and rubber plantations to visitors, with Ipoh as the major attraction. The Cameron Highlands are a gentle reminder of the old days of colonial life. Pulau Pangkor, with its burgeoning beach resorts, shows the new side of the state, while historic Kuala Kangsar has its famous black ceramic pottery and mosques.

TRAVEL SICKNESS
Travelling by bus or even by car along the winding mountain road to the highlands can cause travel sickness. Sufferers should take motion sickness pills beforehand and try to sit at the front of the bus.

Part of the attraction of the Cameron Highlands is the cool climate. When evening comes holidaymakers in the old government bungalows light unnecessary log fires just to remember what it feels like. In between tea plantations you can visit strawberry farms and in gardens see roses, honeysuckle and lupins side by side with bougainvillea and hibiscus.

THE CAMERON HIGHLANDS

Sixty kilometres off the main north–south highway, 1300–1800 m above sea level, miles of tea plantations, vegetable and flower farms and a golf course and tourist resorts make up the Cameron Highlands. Unlike the heady 30°C or more in the rest of Malaysia, this place rarely tops 24°C.

The area was unknown to the world until 1885 when a surveyor, Cameron, discovered it. Its potential as a hill resort was spotted straightaway, and clearance of the wooded slopes began. For a hundred years or more it has remained fairly inaccessible except by a slow grind up winding hills.

WALKING IN THE HIGHLANDS

Walkers should be aware that it is very easy to get lost in the hills here. Every year search parties end up looking for lost walkers. Tell someone which trail you are going on and when you intend to be back. Carry a whistle and lots of water as well as matches, wet-weather gear, food and warm clothing. For missing walkers contact the District Office, tel: (05) 491-1222.

An unsolved mystery surrounds the disappearance of Jim Thompson, the American Thai Silk King. On Easter Sunday 26 March 1967, at the age of 60, he went for a walk in the Highlands and was never seen again.
(See also pp. 87–88)

ORIENTATION The narrow mountain road leads through Ringlet, a working Malay town. It passes the man-made and nearly choked up lake beside the Lakehouse Hotel before reaching Tanah Rata, where most of the tourist interest is centred. The road continues to the golf course and upmarket hotels, and on to Brinchang, a more Chinese town. Beyond that the road goes to tea estates and another small road winds its way up Gunung Brinchang.

TEA AND THE CAMERON HIGHLANDS

Tea comes from the evergreen shrub *Camellia sinensis*, and is suited to hill slopes in the tropics where regular rainfall on acid soil can be expected. It has been cultivated for thousands of years in India, South-East Asia and the Far East and today the main producers are India, Sri Lanka and China. *Camellia sinensis* means 'Chinese camellia' and, as the Chinese writer of the 8th century observed, there are 'a thousand and ten thousand teas'. In terms of world production Malaysia's contribution is infinitesimal but Boh tea, the product of the Cameron Highlands, has its own followers and is widely regarded as a very respectable tea.

The Highlands owe their name to William Cameron, a British surveyor who mapped the region in the late 19th century – though the actual Highlands were first mapped by a Malay, Kulop Riau. In the 1920s the British began building bungalows for colonials who could afford this means of escaping the heat and humidity. At 1524 m above sea level, the Highlands were ideal for tea plantations and in 1926 the first tea was planted.

Techniques of tea-gathering, as you will discover if you visit one of the working plantations, have not changed much since the days of the British in India. Modern technology comes in the form of electric clippers but the shoots are still collected in large baskets which are adroitly carried on the head. A few of the tea workers, mostly Tamils, may be descendants of those who were first brought over from Ceylon (Sri Lanka) in the 1920s.

Five kilograms of leaves are needed to make 1 kg of tea. The first stage is a mechanical drying process that reduces the moisture in the leaves by simply blowing hot air underneath the now soft and pliable leaves.

The next step is a vigorous shaking of the leaves in a special rolling machine that was developed in India in the 1880s. The fermenting juices are released when the cell structure of the leaf is fractured by the rolling machine and it is these juices that give tea its flavour. When the leaves have fermented there is another drying stage to remove moisture and it is at this stage that they take on their characteristic black colour. It is basically a process of oxidation that produces this colour. Unfermented tea is green tea while the semi-fermented variety is oolong tea. The last stage at the Cameron Highlands plantations is a selection procedure that grades the tea according to its quality. The criteria for this is explained during the tour and tea of differing qualities can be purchased at the plantation.

There is a lot to do in the highlands and the mild climate encourages activity. There are many clearly marked walking trails, details of which can be found at the tourist office. Two easy and popular trails are no. 4 to the **Parit Falls** and no. 9 to the **Robinson Falls**. Much more strenuous but worth the effort is trail no. 10, climbing up **Gunung Jasar**, which takes about 3 hrs.

A brief walk off the main road near Brinchang brings you to the huge **Sam Poh Temple**, dedicated to the Lord Buddha with a giant golden Buddha inside. Beyond Brinchang there are lots of fruit farms and apiaries. Visits can be organised by local tour companies in Brinchang. Titiwangsa, tel: (05) 491-1200, or CS Travel, tel: (05) 491-1200.

Look out for **Uncle Sam's**, which grows kaffir lilies, strawberries, apples and cacti. Beyond that is **Kea Farm**, which grows tomatoes, cauliflowers and other vegetables more common in moderate climates. Continuing along the main road past the turn-off to the Kea Farm are two **butterfly parks** competing with one another. They sell dead butterflies and insects, but in the gardens, as well as exotic butterflies, there are some classic European plants.

There are two rose gardens along this stretch of road. One, **Rose Valley**, entrance RM3, has hundreds of roses, including a green and a black rose and a thornless rose. Not to be missed are the **tea plantations**. The best one to visit is the Boh factory and estate, signposted from the main road north of Ringlet. It has a visitor's centre, regular tours of the factory and estate and tea for sale.

Arrival and Departure

Bus: An hourly bus leaves Brinchang via Tanah Rata for Tapah where there are connections to KL and Penang.

Car: 158 km north of Kuala Lumpur turn off the north–south highway at Tapah. The 59 km to Tanah Rata take an hour at least.

ⓘ A small **tourist office and museum** are at the western end of Tanah Rata, open Mon–Thur 0800–1615, Fri 0800–1216 and 1445–1615, and Sat 0800–1245.
www.cameronhighlands.com.

🛏 The Cameron Highlands are very popular with both Malaysians and Singaporeans. During school holidays in May, Sept and December accommodation gets very booked up and very expensive, with prices sometimes doubling.
The Old Smokehouse $$$$ Tanah Rata, tel: (05) 491-1215, www.thesmokehouse.co.my. Deliciously olde worlde

ex-colonialist mock Tudor residence. Each room beautifully individually furnished. Lovely gardens, bric-à-brac everywhere and a natural genteel feel to the place. Centrally located with views over the golf course.

Cool Point Hotel $$–$$$ 891, Pesiaran Dayang Endah, tel: (05) 491-4914, e-mail: hotelcph@tm.net.my. Good value out of high season. Lots of facilities.

Jurina Hill Lodge $$–$$$ Tanah Rata, tel: (05) 491-5522. Good value rooms, use of kitchen and sitting room.

Hill Garden Lodge $$ 15–16 Jalan Besar, Brinchang, tel: (05) 491-2988, fax: (05) 491-2226. The main street can get noisy, but good rooms with en suite bathroom and TV. Low season discounts.

Father's Guest House $–$$ Tanah Rata, tel: (05) 491-2484, www.fathersplace.cjb.net. Easily the best value-for-money place to stay, with dorm beds and a choice of doubles with own bathrooms or sharing. Tours and information, restaurant and internet. Recommended.

Cameronian Holiday Inn $ 16, Jalan Mentingi, tel: (05) 491-1327. Nicely furnished rooms in a quiet side street. Hot showers, garden, restaurant. Dorm beds available.

🍴 There are foodstalls at Tanah Rata serving good inexpensive Malay and Chinese food. Brinchang has a night market with stalls serving mostly Malay food, as well as a permanent food centre at the southern end of the street.

Smokehouse $$$$ traditional English dishes, speciality beef Wellington, cucumber sandwiches, cream teas.

Lakehouse $$$$ same as above, slightly different setting.

Bala's $$ outside Tanah Rata on road to Brinchang. Vegetarian options, cream teas, good breakfasts.

Thanum $ 25 Jalan Besar. Indian food as well as Hainanese chicken rice. Seating outside.

Kwan Kee $$ Brinchang. Steamboat at very reasonable prices.

IPOH

The capital of Perak state and Malaysia's third largest city (also known as Bougainvillea City) sits in the Kinta valley between two mountain ranges, the Keledang Mountains and the Main Range. Ipoh made its fortune in the 19th and early 20th centuries from tin mining, and many of the mansions of the Chinese tin miners still stand to tell the tale. Many of the town's old features still survive.

The oldest part of town, and the one most worth visiting, is to the west near the railway line. The **train station** and **Majestic Hotel** were built as a piece in 1917. They have the same Moorish domes and minarets combined with Victorian Gothic that characterise the colonial architecture of KL. The hotel in particular is magnificent in its recall of the old days of punkah wallahs, with its huge marble balconies and planter's chairs and tables ready to hold the mandatory colonial gin and tonic. From the balcony you can see neoclassical **Edwardian Town Hall**, white as a Christmas cake.

Along Jalan Dato Maharaja Lela is the ornate **Hong Kong and Shanghai Bank** with its Corinthian pillars and tower. Opposite it is the **Birch Memorial Clock**, built in memory of the state's first president, assassinated in 1875 at Pasir Salak.

The town has two museums. The **Darul Ridzuan Museum** open daily 0930–1700, free, on Gantang Wahab is a converted tin millionaire's house full of old photographs of the town and the history of tin mining and logging. The **Geological Museum** open Mon–Fri 0800–1600, free, is a little out of town to the east on Jalan Harimu, and is full of minerals and precious stones.

Good places to visit in a half day's taxi hire or with your own transport include **The Perak Tong Temple**, open daily 0900–1700, free, but make a donation. A cave temple 6.5 km north of Ipoh, this is on several levels with huge statues of the Buddha and walls painted by various pilgrims over the years. At certain points openings in the limestone rock reveal views of the surrounding countryside. Bus nos 3, 41 or 141 to Kuala Kangsar.

The **Sam Poh Tong Temple,** open daily 0730–1530, free, but make a donation. This is another converted limestone cave with one large cave and several smaller ones. It has a vegetarian restaurant and a turtle pool where thousands of the creatures thrash about hoping to gain a little more space in the sickly green water. In front of the temple are pretty Chinese gardens. No. 66 or no. 73 bus.

Three kilometres north of town on the Taiping road is a **Thai Buddhist temple** where you can see the difference between Thai and Chinese Buddhism in the figure of the highly elaborate reclining Buddha.

Kek Lok Tong Temple at Gunung Rapat is another one worth visiting. It is affiliated to the famous Kek Lok Si Temple in Penang.

Hot Springs at the foot of the limestone hills provide bath/sauna facilties (1500–midnight).

> ℹ️ The **tourist office** is at Jalan Sambathan, tel: (05) 241-2957, open Mon–Fri, 0800–1245, 1400–1615.

Arrival and Departure

Train: Train timetables change every six months so inquire at the station about times, tel: (05) 254-7987.

Bus: The long-distance bus station is in Jalan Tun Abdul Razak in the south-west of the city. Opposite it is the Perak Roadway bus depot for buses to Lumut. From the bus station buses depart regularly for all areas of Malaysia.

Air: Malaysia Airlines has four flights a day into Ipoh from KL. The airport is 15 km south of town. A taxi should cost around RM12.

🛏️ **Casuarina Parkroyal $$$$** 18, Jalan Gopeng, tel: (05) 255-5555, fax: 255-8177. Big rooms, spacious gardens, swimming pool, a little way out of town.

Syuen Hotel $$$$ 88, Jalan Sultan Abdul, tel: (05) 253-8889, fax: 253-3335. Big modern concrete and glass edifice. Close to town, small, rooftop pool.

Hotel Seri Malaysia $$$ Lot 10406, Jalan Sturrock, tel: (05) 241-2936, fax: 241-2946, e-mail: smiph@pc.jaring.my. At the bottom end of this price range. One of a chain of inexpensive, basic hotels with big rooms and very good value family rooms.

Ritz Kowloon $$ 92–96 Jalan Yang Kalson, tel: (05) 254-7778, fax: 253-3800. Good basic hotel. Ask about discounts.

Majestic Station Hotel $$ Bangunan Stesen Keratapi, tel: (05) 255-5605, fax: 255-3393. Beautiful old hotel, recently renovated. Basic, big rooms are good value, and rates include breakfast on the balcony. Ask about discounts.

New Hollywood Hotel $–$$ 72 Jalan Yussuff, tel: (05) 241 5404. Bottom of this price range, air-con, clean, restaurant.

Golden Inn $ 17, Jalan Che Tak, tel: (05) 253-0866. Clean, well organised, air-con rooms with bathrooms.

🆃🅾 Ipoh is known for its *hor fun* noodles and steamed chicken with bean sprouts, readily available at the Wooley Food Centre, Ipoh Garden.

LUMUT

This is the departure point for **Pangkor Island** and has little to interest tourists. It is a major navy base and has a naval museum, and a good beach. Teluk Batik, 7 km south of town and another at Teluk Rubiah. It is also the venue for the August sea carnival each year.

The tourist office is in Jalan Titi Panjang, open irregular hours, near the jetty.

Car: Lumut is accessible from Ipoh, 101 km to the north-east. There is a long-term car park at the Shell petrol station. RM6 per day.

Bus: Lumut has a bus station from where there are direct buses to Ipoh and Butterworth.

Boat: In the high season ferries leave from the Lumut jetty for Pulau Pangkor every 20 mins from 0645–2100, RM3. At other times ferries are less frequent. The ferry for the two northern resorts leaves every 2 hrs. A separate ferry leaves for Pangkor Laut every 2 hrs or so but this is for residents only.

PANGKOR ISLAND

Small and pretty with several white sandy beaches, Pangkor Island is a major Malaysian holiday destination. At peak times, especially the Malaysian and Singaporean school holidays in May, September and December, it is probably well worth avoiding unless you head for one of the more exclusive beach resorts. Off peak it's a nice little island with places to visit, cycle rides and some good food.

ORIENTATION Most people in Pangkor live on the east side of the island, which is basically a single inhabited strip of land fronting the beach, occupied by fishermen and boatbuilders.

Motorbikes can be hired for about RM20–30 a day in Pangkor village from several places, including Soon Seng Motor, 12 Main Rd, near the jetty, tel: (05) 685-1269. There are also hire places at Pantai Pasir Bogak. Many of the hotels rent **bicycles** at around RM10 a day.

From Pangkor a bus service goes to the first of the tourist areas on the west coast, Pasir Bogak, the most developed, crowded and often dirty beach. The more northerly beach, Teluk Nippy, where most of the budget accommodation is, is accessible by taxi only.

The ferry from Lumut lands at two places along this strip, Sungei Pinang Kecil and Pangkor Village. At the north end of the island are two quite exclusive resort hotels, which are served by a separate ferry that lands at Tele Dalam.

Highlights The size of the island and shortage of reasonably priced taxis make cycling a good option. Many of the resorts hire bikes to their guests. From **Pasir Bogak** there are lots of little bays and empty beaches along the western side of the island, with hotels where you can stop for lunch.

Passing the Pan Pacific Resort and the northern headland of the island, head downhill and south to the village strip where there are lots of little shop-houses, boat-building yards, coffee shops and temples. At the south end of the island there are the remains of a Dutch fort, dating back to the 16th century.

Other activities include hiring a boat to go around the island or for a day trip to smaller uninhabited islands, or even for a quick visit to Pulau Pangkor Laut where for a large fee you can enjoy the very exclusive resort's facilities. The clear waters are good for snorkelling and the resorts have sailboats and other water sports.

Prices at all these places can double at peak times, which include the school holiday months in Malaysia (May, September and December) and weekends. During term time, weekdays are quiet and cheap but you must ask for a discount.

Pan Pacific Resort $$$$$ Teluk Balanga, tel: (05) 685-1399, fax: (05) 685-2390. Very exclusive, beautiful resort with all facilities and a glorious beach watched over by great hornbills.

Sea View $$$ tel: (05) 685-1605, seafront location.

Teluk Dalam Resort $$$$ Teluk Dalam, tel: (05) 685-5000, fax: (05) 685-4000. All the facilities of the other hotels but not such a good location.

Nipah Bay Villa $$$ Teluk Nipah, tel: (05) 685-2198. Air-con chalets, price includes meals.

Seagull Beach Resort $–$$$ Teluk Nipah, tel: (05) 685-2878, fax: (05) 685-1050. Simple huts with a fan to air-con chalets. Water sports equipment available.

Sri Bayu Beach Resort $$$$$ Pantai Pasir Bogak, tel: (05) 685-1929, fax: (05) 685-1050, e-mail: sbbr@po.jaring.my. Pool, sports, several restaurants, but right in the middle of all the beach accommodation.

Khoo's Holiday Resort $–$$ Pantai Pasir Bogak, tel/fax: (05) 685-1164. Chalets with fan or air-con set on hillside. Good value.

Pangkor Village Beach Resort $–$$$ from basic huts to air-con bungalows right on the beach. Prices include meals.

🍴 Most people tend to eat in their hotels as part of a package or, in the case of the resorts, out of necessity. There are food stalls on the beach at Teluk Nipah, as well as the hotel restaurants and one or two cheap places. In Pangkor village there are lots of seafood places and roti shops where for very little you can enjoy good fresh food.

Bayview Café $–$$ Teluk Nipah, tables outside, good food, pleasant atmosphere.

The Hornbill Hotel Restaurant $$$ Teluk Nipah. Western food, wine list.

No. 1 Seafood Restaurant $$$ Teluk Bogak. Chinese seafood, children's menu.

Sea View Hotel $$ Pantai Pasir Bogak. Nice setting with a garden overlooking the sea.

KUALA KANGSAR

Now a small sleepy little backwater halfway between Ipoh and Taiping Kuala, Kangsar was once the capital city of Perak and home to the state's sultans for over 500 years. It lies on the Kangsar River beside whose banks the sultan's palace sits. Kuala Kangsar is Malaysia's site of the **first rubber tree**, beside the District Office, surrounded by a protective fence and a little plaque.

Kuala Kangsar's other sights are all slightly out of town along the river and then up Bukit Chandan. The **Ubudiah Mosque** was completed in 1917 and really stands out from the many other mosques in the country with its glimmering gold onion dome and elegant minarets. It is surrounded by the graves of the Perak royal family, the living members of which live in the Istana on the top of the hill. This was built in 1930 and is a glorious mix of Art Deco and Islam. This palace is not open to the public but the old one next door is.

RUBBER

In the early 19th century most people were getting around on steel-rimmed wooden carts and carriages, blissfully unaware that deep in the forests of South America were trees, *Hevea brasiliensis*, that would change the world. Once the Brazilian government discovered the uses of latex from the trees, they banned their export and kept the source of their amazing new product a secret.

But, like all good capitalists, the British stole some of the seeds and germinated them at Kew Gardens. From there seeds went to Singapore and an industry was born. Mad Rubber Ridley, the Director of the Botanic Gardens in Singapore, persuaded Hugh Low, the then Resident of Perak, to try some out in Kuala Kangsar. And so the first tree was planted in 1871. This apparently survived out of nine seeds brought to Perak via Kuala Kangsar.

By the time pneumatic tyres were in demand in the West around 1905 a rubber plantation was producing latex in Perak, and within ten years there were plantations in every state. Today, with Indonesia, it produces half of the world's rubber, all from some seeds stolen from Brazil.

It is a **museum** open Sat–Thur 0930–1900, free, dedicated to the history and insignia of the state and the royal family. More interesting is the exterior of the building, which is wooden and built entirely without architectural plans or nails. Close to the Padang with its pavilion from which the sultan once watched the cricket matches is the **Malay College**, still a prestigious school with beautiful architecture. Anthony Burgess, author of *A Clockwork Orange*, taught here.

THE JAPANESE LEGACY

There are two signs of the Japanese years of occupation in this area. In Taiping the town's prison was built by the Japanese on the site of an earlier one of 1885, and the road up to Maxwell Hill was built by Japanese prisoners of war.

🛏 **Rumah Rehat, Kuala Kangsar $$** Bukit Chandan, tel: (05) 777-3705. Big airy rooms with air-con with great river views. Good Malay restaurant.
Mei Lai $ 7 Jalan Raja Chulan, tel: (05) 776-1729.

🍴 There are food stalls and cafés close to the bus station. Two Indian Muslim cafés serve roti in Jalan Kangsar: **Restoran Muslim** and **Restoran Rahmaniah**. The rest house has a good Malay place.

TAIPING

At one time visitors to Taiping, or Larut as it was known in the 19th century, would have come across a Chinese Wild West, full of tin miners working in a harsh and lawless land and rival groups of Chinese clans breaking out into open warfare. The British put a stop to that, confidently renaming the place 'Everlasting Peace', probably the oldest town in Peninsular Malaysia.

Economic booms and swings quietly made Taiping a backwater, but like Kuala Kangsar it has retained lots of Malay and colonial architecture, and is a quiet place for a day's visit or a night's stay, especially if you want to take a look at the hill station of Maxwell Hill.

HIGHLIGHTS Centred around the 62-hectare **Lake Gardens** are several places to visit. The gardens themselves were once the site of an opencast tin mine. Beside them is an **allied war cemetery**, full of the graves of men who fell under the Japanese onslaught of December 1941. On the north side of the Lake Gardens is the **Museum**, built in 1883 and the oldest in Malaysia. Its architecture, like many of the country's museums, is more interesting than its displays. Nearby is the Anglican **All Saints church**, built in 1889.

In town are the **Ling Nam Temple** and the colourfully painted **Hindu temple**, both worth a look around.

🛏 **Seri Malaysia $$** 4, Jalan Sultan Mansor, tel: (05) 806-9502, fax: (05) 806-9495. Good value, big, family-sized rooms, coffee shop.
Panorama Hotel $$ 61–79 Jalan Kota, tel: (05) 808-4111, fax: (05) 808-4129. Big rooms, all mod cons, coffee shop, good value.
Town Rest House $$–$$$ 101 Jalan Stesyen. The old governor's residence, its colonial style buildings recently renovated.
Rumah Rehat Bahru $–$$ Taman Tasik, tel: (05) 807-2044. Set in the Lake Gardens with lovely views and huge fan-cooled or air-con rooms.

🍽 The best places for food in Taiping are in the town centre near the Standard Chartered Bank, both Chinese and Malay. *Nasi Kandar* and banana leaf rice found in Market Road, opposite the post office and along main Kamunting Rd.

MAXWELL HILL

Maxwell Hill, or Bukit Larut, is the wettest, oldest and smallest of Malaysia's hill stations. It makes an excellent day trip, especially since there is very little in the way of accommodation except bungalows, and these are always booked up especially during the school holidays.

It has very little in common with the other hill stations – no golf, casinos, smoke houses, or even much in the way of eating places (only the Surau Kanteen, near the Land Rover office or some of the guesthouses, if you book in advance). One way up the road, with its 70 or so hairpin bends, is by government Land Rover (bookable on tel: (05) 807-7243/7241), or a 4-hr walk, or by your own car.

At the top there are gardens and some trails into the jungle, but for long walks you need a guide. You will almost certainly see macaques, amazing butterflies and leeches. Land Rovers depart hourly from the bottom of the hill near the Taiping Lake Gardens for a RM2 fare. Remember to book your return journey as soon as you get to the top or be prepared for a pleasant but long walk down.

ARRIVAL AND DEPARTURE

Bus: Buses on the Penang–Kuala Lumpur highway stop at Kamunting, 7 km outside Taiping. Buses are frequent to KL, Ipoh and Butterworth. From Kamunting there are regular buses into Taiping. From Taiping it is possible to get buses directly to Ipoh, Lumut and Kuala Kangsar, but for Butterworth you need to take the no. 8 bus back to Kamunting.

WHERE NEXT?

Few people en route from Kuala Lumpur to Penang will stop to break their journey in the industrial town of Butterworth, yet nearby is the Taman Burung Pinang or Penang Bird Park, just 7 km east of the ferry terminal to Penang. This beautifully landscaped park has more than 300 species of birds including parrots and hornbills. It's open daily 0900–1900, tel: (04) 399-1899, and the no. 515 bus from Butterworth will take you there.

TRADITIONAL MALAY CULTURE

Traditional Malay cultural forms like top spinning and shadow puppets are an endangered species, despite their vigorous promotion in states like Kelantan and Terengganu in Malaysia. Indeed, the chances of seeing a performance outside of this region is diminishing all the time so if you want to see a show then head for the east coast of peninsular Malaysia. On the plus side, these performances are not tourist-fuelled and what you see will be a genuine show that finds meaning purely within the culture of the local community.

Top spinning, *gasing*, may not be an Olympic sport but it is very popular in parts of peninsular Malaysia. There are two areas of competition, the 'spinning' contest and the 'striking game'. With spinning, the object is simply to keep the top spinning for as long as possible and the current record is around 2 hrs. The 'striking game' is a little more aggressive because competitors use their tops to try and unbalance their opponent's efforts. It may all sound a bit silly but it requires expertise to launch a powerful spin using a long rope wound around the top and secured to a nearby tree. Once the top is furiously spinning, the player has to scoop it off the ground and position it on a post so that an exact timing is achieved when the spinning stops.

Shadow puppets, *wayang kulit*, are made from buffalo hide and set up on rattan sticks. The puppeteer is supported by a small orchestra that plays a musical accompaniment to the enactment of traditional takes from venerated sources like the *Ramayana*. The link with India can be traced back to the 14th century when the Javanese are thought to have introduced the Hindu epics to the Malay peninsula.

Kite flying, *wau ubi*, is most likely to be seen in the state of Kelantan and in the logo of the national airline, MAS. As with top spinning, the rules are fairly simple and the objective is to keep the kite as high in the air as possible and for as long as possible. The activity of kite flying has an honourable place in Malay history and there are accounts of it as a pastime with the royal nobility in the 15th century. Modern competitions can be tense affairs, with marks being awarded for skill in manoeuvring (i.e. avoiding attempts by opponents to knock your kite off course) as well as height and duration.

Drumming, as in Africa, has its origin as a means of communication. It is now a highly colourful spectacle that creates a great deal of noise. The wooden drums, *rebana*, are about 60 cm in diameter and covered in animal hide before being painted in as dramatic a design as possible. There is also the *kertok* drum, made from extra-large coconuts with a special string obtained from the sago plant stretched across its mouth to form the sounding board.

PENANG

PENANG

Penang is an island, a state and a town. The entire state includes a strip of mainland once known as Province Wellesley after Lord Wellington (Arthur Wellesley), more commonly known as Sebarang Prai. Penang also refers to Pulau Pinang, the 300-sq-mile island and the centre of interest for visitors. The main town on the island is Georgetown, and people often have the urban centre in mind when referring to Penang.

WHAT'S IN A NAME?

The name Penang comes from the Malay words for the areca nut, *pokok pinang*, used by the Portuguese when they arrived in the 16th century. When the British settled here in 1786 they renamed it Prince of Wales Island, but somehow it didn't stick. Georgetown, after the same Prince of Wales, became the principal settlement, and the name has stayed attached to the town even after Malaysian independence.

As you wander around the island you will notice that there is also some confusion about street names. Many of them have been changed from the old colonial ones honouring assorted British dignitaries to lengthy titles involving sultans, datos, maharanis and Malaysian figures. The trouble is that people still use the old names, so that while the street signs say one thing locals say another.

Modern Georgetown is a vibrant, predominantly Chinese city with its share of office blocks and apartment buildings, but much of its past has survived. This is partly because of the efforts of Penang's conservation societies and clan groups, but mainly because of a system of rent control that kept Georgetown's rents so low that owners lacked an incentive to renovate or rebuild.

The rent control system has now been scrapped and it will be interesting to see what happens to the many old buildings that give Georgetown such character. The Chinese vernacular architecture is so impressive that both the federal and state governments hope to turn Georgetown into a World Heritage Site.

The rest of the island also has lots to offer the visitor, especially Batu Ferringhi, where there are resort hotels, beach sports, good food and a street market that comes alive each evening.

MUST SEE/DO IN PENANG

Street market at Ferringhi

Temples and clan houses of Georgetown

The Botanic Gardens

The Snake Temple and its pit vipers

The museum and art gallery

Funicular railway to the top of Penang hill

Nattukotai Hindu temple

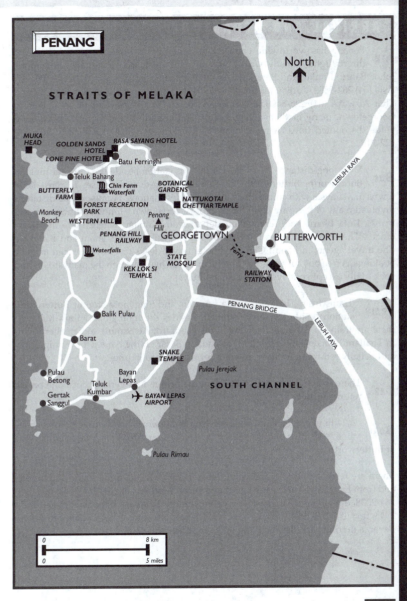

ARRIVAL AND DEPARTURE

Air Penang has worldwide connections, usually via Kuala Lumpur. There are direct flights, mostly with Malaysia Airlines, to KL, Langkawi, Singapore, Johor Bahru, Phuket and Bangkok. As well as Malaysia Airlines, (04) 262-0011, Air Asia (04) 262-9882, Cathay Pacific (04) 226-0411, Singapore Airlines (04) 226-3201 and Thai Airways (04) 226-6000 also operate out of Penang. Several travel agents in Georgetown, many of them along Lebuh Chulia and around Komtar, have good value discounted fares. A reliable one is MSL Travel, tel: (04) 227-2655, fax: (04) 227-2102.

Bus Most long-distance buses stop at the bus station beside the ferry terminal in Butterworth. Butterworth has frequent, long-distance buses to most large towns in Malaysia with connections to smaller destinations. Because of the distances involved many of these are night buses. From Georgetown a limited number of buses to KL, Kota Bharu and Terengganu depart from Komtar, where there are ticket offices. There are also buses for Hat Yai, Krabi, Phuket, Surat Thani and Bangkok. The travel agents in Lebuh Chulia or hotel travel desks or receptions can arrange bookings. A free bus shuttle goes from Jalan Weld Quay through the main streets and back (daily except sundays and public holidays).

Train Trains from Thailand, Kuala Lumpur and Singapore stop at Butterworth station beside the ferry terminal. Besides the train stops within Malaysia there are trains to Bangkok, Hat Yai, Surat Thani (for Ko Samui) and smaller towns in Thailand. This means getting off at Padang Besar on the border for immigration, and usually returning to the same train for the onward journey.

Car There is a one-way toll of RM7 on the bridge into Penang but none on the return journey.

Boat A 24-hour car ferry operates between Butterworth and Georgetown. Journey time is 15 mins and the 60-sen foot passenger fare is paid when embarking at Butterworth.

There are ferry services to and from Penang from Medan, Sumatra, in Indonesia, and from Langkawi, run by the **Langkawi Ferry Services**, tel: (04) 264-3088, fax: (04) 264-2008, e-mail: info@langkawi-ferry.com, and by **Ekspress Bahagia**, tel: (04) 263-1943, fax: (04) 263-1994. Langkawi Ferry Services also runs a daily service to Pulau Payar, a marine park. The booking office is at 8 Lebuh King.

GETTING AROUND

Bayan Lepas, Penang International Airport, is on Penang Island, 18 km south of Georgetown. Taxis are operated on a coupon system and a journey into Georgetown is RM20. Journey time is 45 mins. Bus no. 83 operates to and from the airport at hourly intervals, RM1.40. Journey time is an hour.

Most taxis in Penang do not use meters. You must determine a price before you get in.

BUS It is worth taking the trouble to use the buses in Penang since its various sights are spread out around the island. Most start at Pengkalan Weld beside the ferry terminal. Many of them can also be picked up in the bus station at Komtar, which has an information desk for assistance.

Bus nos 93 and 202 go to Batu Ferringhi and Teluk Bahang from the Komtar station, no. 7 to the Botanic Gardens, no. 78 or minibus no. 32 to the snake temple. Bus nos 136, 93 and 94 go to Gurney Drive. Bus nos 1 and 91 and minibus no. 21 go from Pengkalan Weld to Air Itam, from where it is a 5-min walk to the funicular railway up Penang Hill. Bus no. 321 is a handy service for zipping between Lebuh Chulia and Komtar. Most of these are red and white Transitlink buses.

CAR Hiring a car is a good way to explore the island, and there are several places offering inexpensive car hire. All the main companies are represented but there are better prices at some of the smaller places. For a very inexpensive sightseeing tour, or just a good taxi service try **Thomas Chin**, mobile, tel: (017) 477-8895.

INFORMATION

i **Malaysian Tourist Promotion Board** in Jalan Tun Syed Sheh Barakbah, open Mon–Fri 0800–1700, Sat 0800–1300, tel: (04) 261-9067.

More useful is **Penang Tourist Guides Association** at level 3 in the Komtar building, open daily 1000–1800, tel: (04) 261-4461. They have little literature to hand out, but useful and accurate information from volunteer tour guides.

Another useful place is the **Penang Tourist Centre** in Pesara King Edward, open Mon–Fri 0830–1300, 1400–1630, Sat 0830–1300, tel: (04) 261-6663.

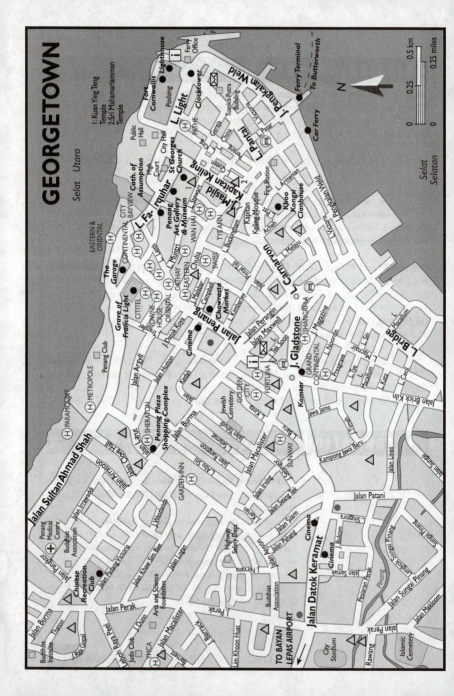

MONEY   There are moneychangers along Lebuh Chulia, Beach St, at the airport and in various locations around town. They are open longer hours and have better rates than the banks. Shop around before you change money and ask what the fee is for traveller's cheques if you have them.

POST AND PHONES   There is a small post office at street level in Komtar and another branch in Lebuh Buckingham. The main post office in Lebuh Downing has a telecentre from where you can make international calls and there is a Telecom Centre in Jalan Burma, which opens 24 hrs. E-mail is available all over town with several places at Komtar and lots of internet cafés in Lebuh Chulia. The cheapest but least salubrious are those at Komtar. Phone cards are widely available at a minimum price of RM5.

ACCOMMODATION

GEORGETOWN

Eastern and Oriental Hotel $$$$ 10 Farquhar St, tel: (04) 261-8333, fax: (04) 261-6333.

Hong Kong Hotel $$ Jalan Tokong, tel: (04) 890-8515, fax: (04) 890-8623. A boat 4 km from city centre, near the Super Tanjong shopping mall.

**Hotel Equatorial $$$$$** Jalan Batu Ferringhi, tel: (04) 881-2641, fax: (04) 881-2660, e-mail: wresort@hotmail.com. Close to the beach, RM$ 130 for a 2-bedroomed apartment.

Hotel 1926 $$$ 227 Jalan Burmah, tel: (04) 228-1926, fax: (04) 227-7926. Recently renovated old government quarters, all wooden floors and shady balconies. Malay cuisine and set close to a recently restored set of shop-houses.

The Oriental $$–$$$ 105 Jalan Penang, tel: (04) 263-211, fax: (04) 263-5395. Centrally located near to Lebuh Chulia, big rooms, coffee shop, restaurant. Good value.

Cathay Hotel $$ 15 Lebuh Leith, tel: (04) 262-6271, fax: (04) 263-9300. Old colonial building, big rooms, often fully booked.

Waldorf $$ 13 Lebuh Leith, tel: (04) 262-6140, fax: (04) 263-7906. Anonymous building but good value en suite and air-con rooms.

Honpin Hotel $$ 273B Lebuh Chulia, tel: (04) 262-5234. Centrally located, popular café, basic air-con and en suite rooms.

Trang City Lodge $–$$ 18–26 Jalan Trang, tel: (04) 604-2260001, fax: (04) 604-2299657, e-mail: trangcl@po.jaring.my.

THE E AND O

Brothers Martin and Tignan Sarkie built the Eastern Hotel on the seafront in Penang in 1884. When they built another, the Oriental next door, it wasn't long before the two combined to become Penang's biggest and classiest hotel. In 1903 they added a ballroom and after 1918 a Victory wing, and the hotel quickly gained a reputation as the finest in the East.

Writers Somerset Maugham, Noël Coward and Herman Hesse and film stars Douglas Fairbanks and Mary Pickford all stayed here. The hotel was in the grand style with a huge copper dome, gardens running down to the seafront and one of the earliest lifts to be installed in a hotel. The Planter's Bar served stengahs to colonial types discussing the price of rubber, and powdered European ladies dressed up for the grand balls that were held here.

The Sarkies went out of business in the 20th century and, like its sister hotels Raffles in Singapore and the Strand in Rangoon, the place gradually slipped into a state of crumbling grandeur. It now has a 21st-century new look, having been nearly gutted and rebuilt according to the old design, preserving the huge copper dome and other architectural features. What has emerged is a modern version of what the hotel was like in its heyday.

Air-con lodge with reasonable facilities and good security. Within walking distance of Komtar.

Broadway Hostel $ 35F Jalan Masjid Kapitan Keling, tel: (04) 262-8550, fax: (04) 264-5622. Family size and cheaper fan-cooled rooms as well as dorm beds. The hostel organises buses to Hat Yai, Ko Samui and Bangkok.

FERRINGHI BEACH

There is little in the way of budget accommodation at Ferringhi Beach. Most of them are small, old tin-roofed houses close to the food stalls on the beach.

Bayu Emas Apartments $$$ Jalan Batu Ferringhi, tel: (04) 881-2641, fax: (04) 881-2660, e-mail: wresort@hotmail.com. Close to the beach, RM$130 for a two-bedroomed apartment.

Penang Parkroyal Resort $$$$$ tel: (04) 881-1133, fax: (04) 881-2233, e-mail: inqppr@sphc.com.my. Pleasant family resort hotel, with big rooms overlooking the beach, free use of non-motorised water sports and good Japanese restaurant.

Shalini's Guesthome $$ Jalan Batu Ferringhi, tel: (04) 881-1859. By the seafront, close to the Penang Parkroyal Resort, with air-conditioned rooms for RM$60.

Holiday Inn Resort $$$$$ 72 Batu Ferringhi, tel: (04) 881-1601, fax: (04) 881-1389, e-mail: hirp@holidayinnpenang.com. Excellent facilities include swimming pool and tennis courts.

Casuarina Beach Resort $$$$$ tel: (04) 881-1711, fax: (04) 881-2788. Smaller, older hotel, pleasant gardens, all rooms with balconies, beach sports.

Lone Pine Hotel $$$$ tel: (04) 881-1511, fax: (04) 881-1282, e-mail: lonepine@penang-hotels.com. Very different from the other places at Ferringhi Beach. Small, quiet, almost Bali-esque. Some rooms have private gardens, and hotel gardens include hammocks, pool and an animal farm.

Popular Ferringhi Motel $$ tel: (04) 881-3333, fax: (04) 881-3494. Small rooms but with most things you need. Off the beach, central for night market, restaurants etc.

Ali's $ tel: (04) 881-1316, fax: (04) 881-2703. A few small rooms with fans, some with bathrooms. Nice garden.

Ah Beng Guesthouse $ tel: (04) 881-1036. Rooms with balconies and good sea views.

FOOD AND DRINK

GEORGETOWN

For excellent noodles, try Chap Seng Campbell St.

Kashmir $$ Penang Rd. Excellent northern Indian cuisine.

Dragon King $–$$$ Lebuh Bishop. 23 years old, specialising in Penang version of nyonya cuisine: hot and sour rather than sweet with coconut. 16 tables only, very basic décor.

Hot Wok $$ Tanjung Tokong. Well out of Georgetown on the road to Ferringhi Beach, another good nyonya place occupying two shop-houses and crammed with Peranakan antiques. Try *otak otak* (fish in coconut cream paste), curry Kapitan or Assam prawns. Hot Wok is also at Gurney Plaza.

Subahan's $$ Junction of Burmah Rd and Tavoy Rd. Double storey shop-house serving vast range of curries and roti. Open till 0400.

Yasmeen Restaurant $ 177 Jalan Penang. Tiled floor and walls and industrial-size fans. Biriyani, roti, murtabaks and fresh juice drinks.

Line Clear $ Junction of Penang Rd and Chulia St. Excellent 24-hr *nasi kandar* and roti stall.

Roti Canai Stall $ Argyll Rd. On the street in the shade of a tree. Excellent roti with choice of curries, mornings only.

HAWKER FOOD

The best places to get good, authentic food in Georgetown are the hawker stalls and coffee shops. Gurney Drive, 1 km of stalls along the promenade, is the best-known and the most expensive. Stalls and coffee shops start to open around 1730, and by about 2100 it is impossible to find a seat. Chinese, Malay and Indian stalls all do a roaring trade.

The Esplanade, near the Padang and right on the seafront, has Malay and a few Chinese stalls. Around Chulia St and are lots of stalls along the five-foot ways. In Tamil St is a series of *nasi kandar* and roti stalls which are very popular. Convenient places are the Food Courts in Komtar. There are some good Indian Muslim stalls in all three courts. Try also one-stop Midlands and the new Gurney Plaza.

FERRINGHI BEACH

Ferringhi also has its share of hawker places. There is an unnamed collection of stalls on the beach close to the cheaper accommodation, and all along the beach strip are open-air cafés $$–$$$ doing Western, seafood and Indian dishes. There are also some restaurants that combine good food and service with a comfortable and pleasant setting.

Sigi's by the Sea $$$–$$$$ Golden Sands Resort, tel: (04) 881-1911. Bistro which spills out onto hotel pool side. Familiar menu of Californian style dishes with some east–west fusion.

Il Ritrovo $$$$ Casuarina Beach Resort, tel: (04) 881-1711. Dark, very Italian place with extensive classic Italian dishes. Live guitar combo serenades you as you eat.

Gion $$$$ Penang Parkroyal Resort, tel: (04) 881-1133. In the Parkroyal hotel. Sit at the teppanyaki bar to watch the chefs at work. Reasonably priced, good Japanese food.

Lat Café $$ Jalan Batu Ferringhi. Malay food served for lunch and dinner. There are also two Chinese restaurants near the jetty at Teluk Bahang that serve good evening meals.

Popular Ferringi Motel $$$–$$$$ Just past The Ship, a road-side restaurant serving seafood, steaks and Chinese meals in a sociable setting.

The Ship $$$ Jalan Batu Ferringhi. A great steak house with good buffet and salads. Also serves some Chinese dishes.

HIGHLIGHTS

A COLONIAL ERA WALK This walk begins in the heart of colonial Georgetown, where the town's white rulers paraded their wealth on Sunday afternoons. It ends where they ended, in the city's Protestant graveyard.

The 60-ft-high **Victoria Clock Tower** was built to commemorate the queen's Diamond Jubilee (1837–97), with each foot of height representing a year of her reign. Strangely, it wasn't erected by loyal colonialists, but by a Chinese tin millionaire, Cheah Chin Gok. Beside the clock tower are the remains of **Fort Cornwallis** (1808). Little is left but the remains of the Christian chapel and the storeroom. The ramparts of the fort are home to a series of cannons.

West of the fort is the **Padang**, where the city's elite played bowls and cricket and walked in the cool of the evening. **The Esplanade** was, and is, used for parades and festivals. On the night of the full moon during Chinese New Year young Peranakan girls would throw oranges into the sea in the hope of getting a good husband. Really it was an opportunity for them to be paraded in front of the young men in their community.

West again are the **City Hall** (1903) and the **Town Hall** (1880), both emblems of the grandiose Victorian confidence of the time. The Town Hall was an all-white social club with a ballroom and stage for theatrical productions.

Walk south away from the Town Hall along Lebuh Pitt (Jalan Masjid Kapitan Keling), past the **Court Buildings** (1905), another example of the grand colonial style, to **St George's Church** (1818), Malaysia's oldest Anglican church. In the grounds is a **memorial** to Francis Light, the man who arranged for the East India Company to take control of Penang, then a deserted jungle. The church can only be viewed on Sundays when the shutters are opened. Nowadays the congregation is mixed, rather than just the white people for whom it was built.

Next door to the church is the **Penang Museum and Art Gallery, $,** open Mon–Sun 0900–1700, closed 1215–1445, tel: (04) 261-3144. Formerly a school and recently renovated, it has good displays about the history of Penang's appealing multiculturalism. There are also exhibits about the East India Company and the Japanese occupation, although no mention of the ignoble evacuation by the British that they kept secret from the rest of the island's population.

Next door again is the **Cathedral of the Assumption**, named after the day that the first Eurasians arrived in Penang. The Eurasian community who once lived in bungalows here built the church in 1860. Opposite the cathedral is the **Convent of**

the Holy Infant Jesus, a former convent and still a girls' school. In its grounds is the 1790 bungalow that Francis Light built for himself. Stamford Raffles is said to have worked in the bungalow after it became the offices of the East India Company.

Pass the grand old **E and O** hotel to the **Protestant cemetery** in Jalan Sultan Ahmad Shah. It is well worth a wander around to see the names of the early European pioneers. One of the graves marks the burial place of Thomas Leonowens, husband of Anna, who later became the inspiration for the movie *The King and I*. Oddly, its remake, *Anna and the King*, was filmed just a few streets away. The grave of Francis Light, the British founder of Georgetown, is also here.

A Georgetown Walk Lebuh Pasar, Penang, Queen and Chulia make up the area known as **Little India**. It is a vibrant, thriving area full of tiny shops, banana leaf restaurants and mamak stalls selling *roti canai* and *teh tarik*.

Start in Jalan Masjid Kapitan Keling (also known as Lebuh Pitt). This road was designated by Francis Light specifically for places of worship, and was to be known as the **Street of Harmony**. On the corner of Lebuh Farquhar is **St George's Church**.

Streets in Georgetown

When Francis Light first had the streets of Georgetown laid out, he designated certain areas for different ethnic groups. Chulia St was for the Indian community, Bishop St for the church of the Eurasian community, Lebuh China for the Chinese and Lebuh Pasar for the market. Lebuh Light was reserved for the officers and their families.

But by 1908 the British had moved to the suburbs, and these streets were given over to the 'natives'. Because of this the streets of Georgetown are probably the most intact and diverse record of 19th-century colonial architecture in the world. They incorporate not only the British Raj at its most arrogant, but a corresponding history of the Chinese clans, Indian temple architecture and the styles of the other ethnic groups that settled in Penang.

A little further south at the junction with Lrg Stewart/Lebuh China is the **Kuan Ying Teng temple** (1801), dedicated to the Goddess of Mercy and built by the Cantonese and the Hokkien. Its huge courtyard is always full of visitors, hawkers and beggars. During festivals, puppet shows and dances are held here. Opposite the temple is a news-paper office which was once a government storage depot for opium. The British made much of their revenue from the trade of this drug.

Further south is the **Sri Mahamariamman temple** (1833), with its modern entrance on Queen St. Outside in the street is usually a painted *kolam*. The *gopuram*, or entrance sculpture, consists of 38 statues of gods and goddesses and four swans.

Inside, a statue of Lord Subramaniam is encrusted with precious stones and gold and silver leaf. It is paraded through the town during the Thaipusam festival.

Parallel with Lebuh Queen is **Lebuh King**. A diversion down here will reveal amazing street architecture where almost every building is a clan house or temple of some sort, each with its own distinctive roof design.

Further south again on the corner of Lebuh Buckingham and Lebuh Pitt is the **Kapitan Keling mosque**, serving the Indian Muslim community. The current building retains part of the 1905 Moghul structure but is largely a construct of the 1930s.

Off Lebuh Pitt, at Lebuh Cannon, is the alleyway entrance to **Cannon Square**, and the Khoo Kongsi clan house and temple. Founded in 1851 by immigrants from Xiamen in Fujian, China, the square also contains houses let by the Khoo clan to its members. At the time they were built there were great wars going on between the various clans, hence the very few, narrow entrances.

At the road junction of Lebuh Aceh is the **Acheen St Mosque**, built by a wealthy Arab merchant to serve the Achinese community, which settled here in 1808. Its minaret is Arab in style rather than Moghul, and the story goes that the round window halfway up was actually made by a cannonball during the Penang Riots of 1867.

Turning right into Lebuh Armenian brings you first to the former home of Dr Sun Yat Sen at no. 120 and then to the **Syed Atlas Mansion** ($) once the home of a wealthy pepper trader and now open to the public Mon–Sat 0900–1700. The street is also a centre for stoneworkers who you can see carving inside some of the shop-houses.

THE FIVE CLANS

During the 19th century, Georgetown's Chinese community was dominated by the five great clans – the Khoo, Cheah, Yeoh, Lim and Tan – all Hokkien-speaking groups from various villages in the Fujian province of China. Each clan formed its own kongsi or guild dedicated to the betterment of its own members. Each built their own clan house and temple in the area around Medan Cannon.

During the inter-clan wars of the 19th century the clans became embroiled in street fighting and the buildings that they erected reflected this unstable life with narrow courtyard entrances that could easily defend clan housing.

Returning to respectability in the 20th century, the clan houses have become less important to the clans and the Khoo Kongsi is now little more than a tourist attraction and venue for corporate nights out.

OTHER HIGHLIGHTS **The Cheong Fatt Tze Mansion** ($) in Leith St was built by a 19th-century Richard Branson called Cheong Fatt Tze. He left China a penniless young man and ended up as economic advisor to the Empress of

China. Involved in shipping, banking and railways, he decided in the 1880s to build a mansion that would befit his status in life. The result is this house with 38 rooms, seven staircases and five courtyards in an amalgam of classic Chinese design, art nouveau and Victorian cast iron. The house crumbled for a few decades but is now open to the public Mon, Wed, Fri and Sat.

There are great views from the observation level on the 58th floor of the Komtar Tower, but it costs RM5. Instead, take the lift to the 60th floor (not the same lift that accesses the 58th floor). Buy an ice cream or a drink at the restaurant serving Malay and western food and keep the receipt. Walk down two floors to the viewing level and flash your receipt for free admission.

Wat Chayamangkalaram in Jalan Burma on the Ferringhi Beach road is a Thai temple, open early morning until 1730, dedicated to the reclining Buddha. In the complex is also a nine-storey pagoda. Opposite it is the **Dhammikarama Burmese Buddhist temple**, with an upright Buddha and a pagoda built in 1905. In the same street a third Buddhist temple, the **Penang Buddhist Association temple**, is very different from the first two, with lots of Italian marble and chandeliers.

A walk through Burmah Square leads to heritage houses at Jalan Chow Tye, off Burmah Rd. The houses sell antiques, souvenirs and there is a variety of small restaurants.

SHORT EXCURSIONS

The **Nattukotai Chettiar temple** on Waterfall Rd is the biggest Hindu temple on the island, with two other temples nearby. One stop further along on bus no. 7 are the **Botanic Gardens**, open daily during daylight hours, an excellent afternoon's entertainment, especially if the macaques are in fighting mood.

A short bus ride west of Georgetown brings you to **Air Itam** and the **Kek Lok Si temple**, supposedly the largest Buddhist temple in Malaysia. Twenty years in the building, it has gardens, a turtle pond, lots of tourists as well as followers of the Lord Buddha and a pagoda with 10,000 Buddhas.

Nearby is the 1923 **Penang Hill** funicular railway, open daily 0630–2115, 830 m high and much cooler than the city. The railway is good fun and the hill has lots of food-stalls, walks and a Sarkies hotel, now a government building.

Not to be missed is the **Snake Temple**, dedicated to Chor Soo Kong, on the road to the airport. The temple itself is nothing special but the snakes inside it are. They are mostly harmless green tree snakes, but there are also Wagler's pit vipers, which you wouldn't want to step on accidentally. In the entrance are stalls selling 'I touched a pit viper' T-shirts and other objects.

Penang has many other attractions, including **fruit farms**, a **butterfly park** and **cultural centre** at Teluk Bahang, lots of beaches to explore if you have transport, and walks through the **Pantai Acheh Forest Reserve**. Teluk Bahang itself is home to the fabulous **Mutiara Beach Resort**, lots of cafés and several cheap home-stay places.

SHOPPING

In Georgetown, **Komtar** has all the big names as well as local department stores. The top floor has a few internet places. One of them, Lot B2, 4.02, has a better choice of computer software than the operators on the bottom floor. Just behind the Komtar building is **Prangin Mall**, a big new shopping centre. **Chulia St**, where little open-fronted shops sell clothes and some bric-à-brac, is worth a bit of window-shopping. There is a good second-hand **bookshop** on this street next to the Swiss Hotel.

Ferringhi is always worth a stroll at night when stalls line either side of the road and diplay their fake designer gear. Music CDs, watches, T-shirts, sunglasses, belts and jeans sit alongside items from Thailand, beautiful batik and dresses from India.

FESTIVALS

Penang celebrates most of Malaysia's big festivals. **Thaipusam** is a Hindu festival usually held in February when penitents pierce themselves and carry huge metal frames embedded into their skin. **Chinese New Year** is big in Penang, with lion dances and cultural shows all over the island, plus displays by the *kongsis*. June sees the international **Dragon Boat Festival**. There is a **Lantern Festival** in September and in November is **Deepavali**, the Hindu festival of light. In October is the **Nine Emperor Gods Festival**, when you can see Chinese opera performances along Burmah Rd.

NIGHTLIFE

In Georgetown, Chulia St has a nice collection of bars and cafés which come alive at night. Opposite Cheong Fatt Tze Mansion is the renovated row of shop-houses called **Leith St**, which is very fashionable at the moment. At Ferringhi beach there is the **Reggae Club**, open till 0300 nightly, with an emphasis on Bob Marley hits and a nice atmosphere. Several of the big hotels have good happy hour rates until late.

PENANG – LANGKAWI – ALOR SETAR – PENANG

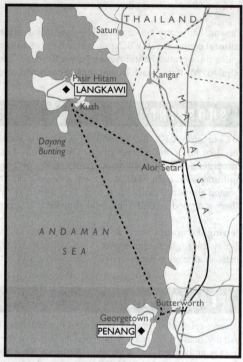

PENANG — LANGKAWI — ALOR SETAR
OTT Tables 7013/7016/7017/7021

Service	🛳	🛳	🛳	🚌	RAIL	RAIL	🛳	
Days of operation Special notes	Daily	Daily	**A**	**B**	Daily	Daily		
Penang...............d.	0830	0845	....	....	....	....	....	....
Langkawi...............d.	1130	1145	**A**	....	....	....	....	....
Alor Setar.............d.	....	....	**A**	**B**	1108	1851	....	....
Butterworth..........d.	....	....	....	**B**	1255	2055	**C**	....
Georgetown (Penang) ..a.	....	....	....	....	....	....	**C**	....

Special notes:
A–9 trips daily. Journey time: 2 hours.
B–Frequent service. Journey time: 2 hours.
C–Every 30 minutes, 24 hours a day. Journey time: 15 minutes.

PENANG – LANGKAWI – ALOR SETAR – PENANG

The two destinations in this route, the island of Langkawi and the town of Alor Setar, are what take visitors to the north-west state of Kedah. It is one of the most Malay and the most rural states in the country. Alor Setar has a distinctly Thai flavour, reflecting the fact that this corner of Malaya was under Siam sovereignty for most of the 19th century. British colonialism hardly got its nose in and traditional Malay culture was left undisturbed. Langkawi island produces different responses in visitors because some people enjoy its lazy appeal and low-octane atmosphere, while others grow bored with the package-holiday syndrome that tends to characterise the place. It is a good place to relax but not a destination for those seeking activities and variety.

LANGKAWI

In theory, Langkawi is the perfect place for a beach holiday, with resorts, restaurants, places to visit and blue skies. But it has undergone such massive tourist development in the last decade that there really aren't many more sites for resorts, and the existing ones are either bursting at the seams or going under. Many of the people who run the tours, and particularly the Mafiosi cab drivers, seem intent only on getting hold of as many tourist dollars as possible.

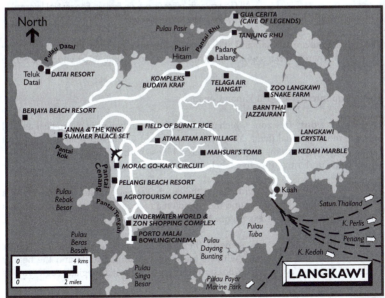

PENINSULAR MALAYSIA

ARRIVAL AND DEPARTURE

Boat: Boats to Langkawi travel to and from Kuala Kedah west of Alor Setar at least nine times daily, mostly between 0800 and 1800. An alternative route into Langkawi is via Kuala Perlis, further north on the mainland where there are more frequent boats. A ferry connects with Penang four times daily and there is a connection with Satun in Thailand. The ferry offices are all located at the ferry terminal. **Langkawi Ferry Services** tel: (04) 966-9439, operate the Penang, Perlis and Kuala Kedah trips.

Air: Langkawi International Airport is 20 km from Kuah, about RM20 by taxi. There are daily connections with KL, Singapore, JB and Penang.

Car: Most beach resorts have cars for hire or they can be hired from one of the loud touts at Kuah. Rates should be around RM85 a day. There are places all over the island to hire mopeds or bicycles. The rate is around RM25 per day for a moped, RM12 for a bike. A taxi costs around RM50 for a couple of hours, which is all you need to 'do' all the sights.

> *i* The **tourist office** tel: (04) 966-7789, open daily
> 0900–1300, 1400–1700, is in Kuah, near the Al Hama mosque.
> All Government offices close on Fridays. For general information: www.langkawitravelnet.com

The only **banks** are at Kuah and at the beaches the only places to change money are the resorts where the rates will not be the best. Try to change what you need before you arrive.

There is an **internet** shop at Pantai Cenang.

Langkawi is a **duty free zone** which means that you can buy very cheap beer as well as some more unusual items. You will see groups of Chinese people hauling giant cardboard boxes on to the ferries. These are Chinese herbal remedies and medicines, which come under the duty free label.

HIGHLIGHTS Go to Langkawi to lie on the beach, eat reasonable food and spend a day whipping round the island on a moped. Don't go to find out what life in Langkawi is like or experience Malaysia, because you won't.

The island has a few sights, some of them spectacular in ways that were never intended. The first is the jetty with its hysterical screaming touts and the nearby landscaped theme park, which boasts the biggest, ugliest fibreglass eagle you've ever seen.

Pantai Cenang is the most pleasantly relaxed part of the island, full of little cafés, shops, budget accommodation and obligatory big resorts. The white sand beach is huge and mostly underused, as most people sit around their hotel pools. But between November and January you can walk out to the island of Pulau Rebak Kecil from a sandbar which appears at low tide. Along the main drag at Pantai Cenang is **Underwater World**, a series of fish tanks and some gardens. Open daily 1000–1800, RM15.

At Kuala Muda, north of Pantai Cenang is **Aquabeat**, a swimming complex with wave machine. North again is **Pantai Kok**, a lovely white strip of beach dominated by resorts but with a few food stalls. **Telaga Tujuh**, a huge waterfall inland from Pantai Kok, is definitely worth hiring a moped for. At Padang Lalang a major road junction in the north of the island is Compleks Budaya Craf, a very big **craft centre** and shop selling Malaysian crafts. No bargains though. There is a **cultural village** nearby at Air Hangat where there are nightly cultural shows with **hot springs** close by.

MAHSURI

A few kilometres west of Kuah, the main town, is Mahsuri's tomb, the final resting place of a Malay princess unjustly accused by her mother-in-law of adultery. She was put to death by being buried up to her waist in sand and a kris knife shoved through her shoulder blades. White blood poured from her wound and in her dying breath she cursed the island so that it wouldn't prosper for the next seven generations. Some say this is why the island paradise has never been quite as profitable as the government hopes. The mausoleum has the regulation genuine Malay house on stilts beside it flogging artefacts.

DAY TRIPS **Pulau Payar Marine Park** makes an excellent day's outing. It consists of several small islands, all with crystal clear waters and vast numbers of very tame, colourful fish. Lots of tour groups organise trips to the marine park. **Langkawi Coral** tel: (04) 966-7318, fax: (04) 966-7308, e-mail: lgkcoral@pd.jaring.my, RM220, has a good tour to a platform anchored off the main island from where you can snorkel to the shore, take a trip in a glass-bottomed boat, view the fish from an underwater viewing platform, or take scuba diving lessons. The platform has a bar and lunch is included in the price. The main island has pleasant sandy beaches from where you can venture into the interior. Also try Scuba East Marine Holidays, tel: (04) 226 3032.

OTHER ACTIVITIES

The island is dotted with caves, many of which can be visited on a tour. There is also a mangrove swamp trip, which takes a boat out in the evening as the bats begin to emerge for the night. Other trips include an island tour and island hopping to the many smaller islands of Langkawi. Your hotel will gladly arrange any of these activities for you, or you can try a company like SALA Travel and Tours, tel: (04) 966-7521, fax: (04) 966-8521, e-mail: sala@tm.net.my.

Tanjung Rhu Resort $$$$$ Mukim Ayer Hangat, tel: (04) 959-1033, fax: (04) 959-1899, e-mail: resort@tanjung rhu.com.my. If you can afford it, this place is everything you ever wanted in a beach resort and it's well away from the tourist traps. All-day beach café, Mediterranean restaurant and miles and miles of countryside.

Pelangi Beach Resort $$$$$ Pantai Cenang, tel: (04) 955-1001, fax: (04) 955-1122, e-mail: pelangi.pbl@meritus-hotels.com. A huge spread of pretty wooden, two-storey chalets with golf cart transport.

Berjaya Langkawi Beach and Spa Resort $$$$ Pantai Kok, tel: (04) 959-1888, fax: (04) 959-1886, e-mail: resum@b-langkawi.com.my. Wooden chalets. Very busy, nice beach and a health spa.

Langkawi Holiday Villa Beach Resort $$$$ Pantai Tengah, tel: (04) 955-1701, www.holidayvillagelangkawi.com. Moderately priced, yet all the necessities of a resort. Bring your own tea and coffee. Accommodation in rooms, not chalets, but all overlook the sea.

Grand Beach Hotel $–$$$ Pantai Cenang, tel: (04) 955-1457. Beach front rooms with fan and bathroom are good value. Also more luxurious air-con rooms.

Since the vast majority of people on holiday here come as part of a package they tend to eat in their hotels. Most of the resorts have good but pricey restaurants.

Pelangi Beach Resort has a particularly good buffet dinner, but if they are busy you should make a reservation (see accommodation listing above).

Pantai Cenang is the best source of good, inexpensive food.
Fat Mum's at the Pantai Tengah end of the built up strip of beach comes highly recommended.
Eagle's Nest in Pantai Cenang has tables in a sheltered garden. It serves basic Western-style food with nice desserts.
Bon Ton is a new restaurant with good food north of Pantai Cenang, set up by the people who opened the famous Bon Ton in Kuala Lumpur.
Barn Thai, 9 km north-west of Kuah, serves good Thai cuisine to the sounds of live jazz.

Along Pantai Cenang are small grocery stores where you can stock up on things for lunch or fresh fruit for breakfast. Kuah has several places to eat if you can bear the shouting. In the terminal itself is McDonald's and KFC as well as a very nice Indian Muslim place, which serves roti until about 1100.

ALOR SETAR

There's no real reason to visit Alor Setar. It's a sleepy little town with a few interesting places. But it's pure northern Malaysia, utterly unused to tourists or even non-Malays, and it makes a change for locals to be rubbernecking at you rather than the other way round.

The town has several Thai temples and a padang, where there are some interesting buildings including the Muzium de Raja, once the **royal palace**. Open daily 1000–1800, it is full of regalia and photos of the sultan with important people. Also here is the **Balai Seni Negara**, in another old colonial building. It contains some interesting local painters' work and is open during the same hours. Also on the square is the **state mosque**, all domes and spires and epic outlooks.

Two kilometres north of the town centre is the **National Museum**, which contains the royal barges used in ceremonial occasions, plus lots of archaeological material found around Alor Setar. There is also a museum dedicated to Dr Mahathir (Malaysia's prime minister), in his one-time family home at 18 Lorong Kilang.

ARRIVAL AND DEPARTURE
Bus: From the bus station in Jalan Langgar buses leave half hourly to local destinations including Kuala Kedah and to Butterworth.

For towns to the north and the Thai border buses leave from a different bus station on Jalan Sultan Badlishah.

Long-distance internal buses leave from a third bus station in Jalan Mergong, north of the town centre. From here there are buses to Melaka, KL, Johor Bahru and the east coast.

Train: More fun and less fuss is the KTM line from Singapore to Thailand (change at Kuala Lumpur) with stops at Butterworth, Padang Besar (for Thai immigration), Hat Yai, Surat Thani (for Ko Samui) and Bangkok. Train timetables tend to change so collect a current timetable in KL. For information tel: (04) 733-1798.

Hotel Grand Continental $$$ 134, Jalan Sultan Bandishah, tel: (04) 733-5917, fax: (04) 733-5161, is very central.

Hotel Grand Crystal $$$ 40 Jalan Kampung Perak, tel: (04) 731-3333, fax: (04) 731-6368, has a pool.

Hotel Seri Malaysia $$$ Lot 005127, Mukim Alor Malai, Jalan Stadium, tel: (04) 730-8737, fax: 730-7594, e-mail: asetar@serimalaysia.com.my, is a little out of town. Big rooms with a public pool next door and a coffee shop with a very Malay buffet breakfast.

There is a KFC opposite Hotel Seri Malaysia and several sleepy but functioning Indian Muslim places in Jalan Tunku Ibrahim and Jalan Badlishah. Beyond the Thai temple is an outdoor nameless café and some food stalls which are usually crowded. Hai Choo on Jalan Tunku Yaakub must be doing something right, as it's been around for over 100 years.

WHERE NEXT?

The tiny state of Perlis is Malaysia's smallest, and draws few visitors. The state capital, Kangar, is just 45 km north-west of Alor Setar, and is the gateway to Taman Negara Perlis, a state park covering about 5000 hectares along the border with neighbouring Thailand. Rich in wildlife, this remote region is the last remaining home in Malaysia for the stump-tailed macaque. White-handed gibbons also thrive here.

DRIVING ROUTE

Highway 3 runs the entire route from Kota Bharu to Johor Bahru (689 km). For the most part it is a single carriageway road with no overtaking lane, passing through each town rather than bypassing them. In the north it is scenic as it closely follows the coast, offering lots of opportunities for stops.

This route along the east coast of peninsular Malaysia is a fine introduction to the country's attractions. There are magnificent beaches and delightful fishing villages where the pace of life has slowed down to an imperceptible crawl. This is not a route to travel in a hurry and only by adjusting to the local tempo will some of the magic begin to rub off. Four states share the coastline – Kelantan, Terengganu, Pahang and Johor – and our favourite is Kuala Terengganu. Historically, it was cut off from the rest of the peninsula because Europeans found little of economic value there, and so never built roads into the state. Ethnically, it is overwhelmingly Malay in tone and character. Some of the best beaches in South-East Asia are to be found here, especially a short way offshore on the Perhentian islands, where white-sand beaches and snorkelling possibilities draw in a constant stream of discerning travellers.

KOTA BHARU — JOHOR BAHRU
OTT Table 7024

Service	🚌	🚌	⛴	🚌	🚌	🚌	🚌	⛴	🚌
Days of operation	Daily	Daily	Daily	Daily	Daily	Daily	Daily	Daily	Daily
Special notes	A	B	C	D	E	F	G	H	J
Kota Bharu ....d.	A	....	....	....	....	....	....	....	....
Kuala Terengganu ....d.	A	B	....	....	....	....	....	....	....
Marang.........................d.	....	B	C	D	....	....	....	....	....
Pulau Kapas ....d.	....	....	C	|	....	....	....	....	....
Rantau Abang ....d.	....	....	....	D	E	....	....	....	....
Cherating ....d.	....	....	....	....	E	F	....	....	....
Kuantan ....d.	....	....	....	....	....	F	G	....	....
Mersing........................d.	....	....	....	....	....	....	G	H	....
Tioman.........................d.	....	....	....	....	....	....	....	H	J
Johor Bahru ....a.	....	....	....	....	....	....	....	....	J

Special notes:
A–7 trips daily. Journey time: 3 hours.
B–4 trips daily. Journey time: 30 minutes.
C–2 trips daily. Journey time: 30 minutes.
D–Hourly service. Journey time: 1 hour.
E–Hourly service. Journey time: 1 hour. Change of bus required at Dungun.
F–Every 30 minutes. Journey time: 1 hour.
G–3 trips daily. Journey time: 3 hours.
H–1 to 3 trips daily. Journey time: 1½ to 3½ hours.
J–7 trips daily. Journey time: 2½ hours.

KOTA BHARU

Probably the most foreign place you will visit in Malaysia, KB has a distinctly different atmosphere from the south of the country. Part Wild West frontier town and part electronic superhighway, KB is still sleeping under a durian tree yet at the same time charged with excitement about the future.

The town sits in the valley of the Kelantan River and is still relatively undeveloped. It is dominated by its rural surroundings, with rice its biggest export. Although the women are all covered, they wear shockingly gaudy clothes in fine silks, often with long slits in the skirts and bright makeup. If the sexes have to keep apart for fear of an unholy thought entering men's heads there is enough flirting going on to keep the air seriously charged. Islam and Malay culture are a strange mix, and they are at their strangest in this interesting little town.

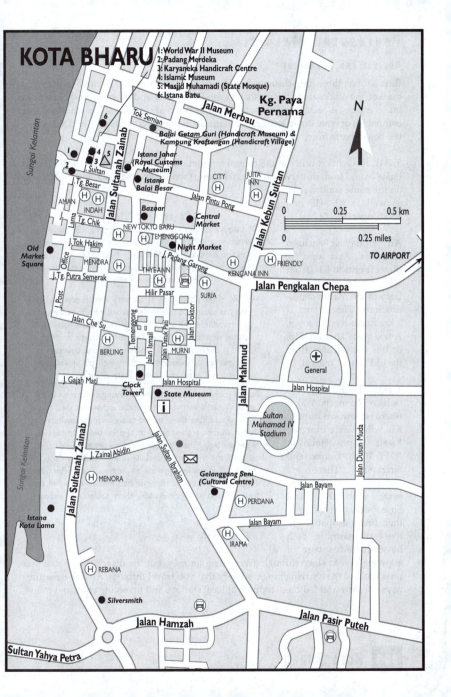

PENINSULAR MALAYSIA

ARRIVAL AND DEPARTURE

Bus: KB has three long-distance bus stations: the most central is close to the night market, the others are to the south, on Jalan Pasir Puteh and Jalan Hamzah. The main bus company is SKMK and most of its routes begin at the central bus station. Other companies operate out of Langgar or Hamzah. Buy tickets in advance and ask where the bus departs from.

SKMK has a ticket office at the central bus station and is easier to deal with. It runs buses to and from Butterworth (8 hrs), Penang (about 8 hrs), Melaka, and most towns on the route southwards, as well as KL, (10 hrs) and Singapore (12 hrs).

Air: Malaysia Airlines and Air Asia operate direct flights to KL, from where there are connections to international destinations. The airport is 8 km north-west of town. A taxi costs about RM15, or bus no. 9 leaves from the old central market.

Train: The KTM jungle railway connects Wakaf Bharu, a few km outside KB, with Kuala Lumpur, Kuala Lipis, Jerantut (OTT 7006), Gemas and Singapore. There are evening trains that connect with KL and Singapore, arriving at their final destinations in the early morning. Both have the advantage of allowing you to sleep through a very long journey, but the disadvantage that you miss most of the amazing jungle scenery that you travel through. All day-time journeys are slow and tedious, stopping at local stations and involving changing trains.

AN ISLAMIC STATE

Like its southern neighbour, Terengganu, KB's state government is strongly influenced by the Islamic Party, which seeks to introduce the Shariah or Islamic law. Penalties include dismemberment for 'crimes' such as extramarital sexual intercourse and theft.

As 10% of the population, at the very least, is non-Muslim this has caused considerable discord with the federal government, which seeks to practise a liberal, tolerant Islamic regime. In terms of the effect it might have on visitors it doesn't add up to much – separate counters at supermarket for men and women which are universally ignored, a ban on alcohol in state-run hotels.

Rather more serious is the belief among some men in KB that all Western women are available, otherwise their menfolk would have them stored safely away somewhere. Muslim women are expected to, and for the most part do, wear the *baju kurung* traditional Malay dress, as well as a headscarf, and the state is seeking to enforce the wearing of a headscarf for all female state employees. During Ramadan things get a bit stickier. Party officials go into cafés and any Muslims found eating or drinking there are publicly shamed.

HIGHLIGHTS The Padang Merdeka was once the town's marketplace, where in 1915 the British government displayed the body of Tok Janggut, a local elder who had led a failed rebellion against British land taxes. Around the outskirts of the padang are several museums, all worth a quick glance.

The **World War II Museum ($)** is housed in the town's oldest brick building, the former Mercantile Bank. During the Japanese occupation it became their headquarters and today houses old photos, weapons and a bicycle that may have been used in the so-called bicycle invasion. Open Sat–Thur 0830–1645.

Next door is the **Muzium Islam**, showing a collection of Islamic art and its influence on everyday life in the state. Open Sat–Thur 0830–1645, free. The **Istana Jahar** or Royal Customs Museum was once Kelantan's first Islamic School. Its exterior is almost as beautiful as the royal artefacts inside. Open Sat–Thur 0830–1645, free.

Next is the bright blue **Istana Batu**, another, later royal palace, this time containing royal possessions, clothes, replicas of the crown jewels, furniture and old photos. Open Sat–Thur 0830–1645, free. Behind is the **Balai Getam Guri**, or handicraft museum, and the associated **Kampung Kraftangan**, handicraft village, where you can watch craftsmen at work. The museum is beautifully built, showing that the skills used to build the two previous palaces are still alive in Kelantan. Open daily except Fri, 0830–1645,

---

HANDICRAFTS

Because of its cultural associations with Thailand, Kelantan has some craft skills more naturally associated with that country. There is a tradition of woodcarving, which can be seen in the two *istanas* and in the new handicraft village. Wooden buildings are highly decorated with fretwork, and craft items such as wooden frames and furniture find their way into tourist shops all over the country.

Silver work is another skill inherited from the north. Fine filigree jewellery is common and more cumbersome epoussé items abound. Silver workshops can be visited in Jalan Sultan Zainab or at Kampung Badang on the way to PCB Beach. Along the same road are *songket* weaving work-shops, where silver and gold thread is worked into ceremonial cloth, and many batik factories, often in someone's backyard, where you can watch the entire process of mass producing intricate patterns using wax. There are bigger factories at Kampung Puteh and Kubor Kuda.

DRUMMING

While you are in KB you may see an exhibition of the giant drums, which are a traditional form of communication between *kampungs* isolated by dense jungle and rivers. Nowadays it is quite a spectacle. The drums, called *rebana*, are made from hollowed out logs, 60 cm in diameter and covered in a taut buffalo hide. In July there is a drum festival when teams of drummers compete. There is one of these drums in the lobby of the Perdana hotel.

WATS

Wat Phothivihan at Kampung Berak, 12 km east of KB, is a relatively new (1973) Buddhist temple with a huge reclining Buddha statue, 40m long, the largest in South-East Asia. **Wat Kok Seraya** and **Wat Phikulthong** are north of KB at Chabang Empat. To get to the temples, you can take a taxi or bus nos 27 and 19 to Chabang Empat. Get out at the crossroads. Wat Phothivihan is 3 1/2 km from the junction to the left, and Wat Kok Seraya and Wat Phikulthong are 1 km from the police station to the right. All are interesting for the simple fact that such temples even exist in this Muslim dominated state.

$. Unless you visit the handicraft village on a busy day, you may be disappointed, though – it is sometimes deserted.

The **Cultural Centre** in Jalan Mahmud, opposite the Perdana Hotel, has displays of drumming, top spinning, cultural dances and shadow puppetry on most days. It opens three times a week (Mon, Wed and Sat) from March to October every year.

Pantai Cahaya Bulan, or Pantai Cinta Berahi as it was known in pre-Islamic times, is the most easily accessible and popular of KB's beaches. The original name meant the beach of passionate love, which is why the government wanted to change it. En route are any number of silversmiths and batik factories.

The beach itself is a fine, vast sandy strip with Malay fishing villages dotted along it and lots of places to eat including the Perdana Resort with a very reasonable café. **Pantai Irama** is 25 km south of KB but is reputed to be the most beautiful beach in the state. It is backed by landscaped gardens; bus 2A or 2B. **Pantai Seri Tujuh**, 7 km north of KB, is the site of the annual kite-flying festival, normally held in May.

TOURS AND TRIPS Lots of people stay much longer in KB than they intended because there are so many activities to be organised from here. Several tour companies offer homestay packages where you live with a local family in a *kampung* and watch handicrafts being made. There are good trips up the Sungai Kelantan to the rainforest and to Dabong village upstream, as well as trips to the many waterfalls that grace the mountains close to KB.

Sampugita Holidays Lot 1 Perdana Hotel, tel: (09) 748-2178, fax: (09) 748-5000, organises tours of the countryside around Tumpat to the *wats* and batik factories, river trips and visits to boatmaking and woodcarving centres. Both Ideal Travellers' House and Johnty's Guesthouse, tel: (09) 747-8677, organise packages to the temples and Jelawang jungle.

i The **tourist information office** is in Jalan Sultan Ibrahim, beside the State Museum, tel: (09) 748-5534, open Sun–Thur 0800–1245 and 1400–1630.

E-mail is available in McDonald's and at KB Backpackers' Lodge, 2 Jalan Padang Garong.

🖃 **Perdana Hotel $$$$** Jalan Mahmud, tel: (09) 748-5000, fax: (09) 744-7621, e-mail: perdana@tm.net.my. Quiet, pleasant place with well-equipped rooms, good coffee shop, restaurant, swimming pool, but alcohol free.

Perdana Beach Resort $$$$ Jalan Kuala Pa'amat, PCB, tel: (09) 774-4000, fax: (09) 774-4980. A pleasant alternative to staying in town, this place has a pool, fishing pond, horses and lots of other activities. Accommodation in spacious chalets. Fills up at weekends and school holidays but ask for a discount midweek.

Safar Inn $$$ Jalan Hilir Kota, tel: (09) 747-8000, fax: (09) 747-9000. Close to the padang, a small quiet place with good value rooms.

Kencana $$ Jalan Doktor, tel: (09) 744-0944 Jalan Padang Garong, tel: (09) 744-7944, Jalan Sri Cemerlang, tel: (09) 747-7222. Three branches of the same hotel. Basic but good value, TV, en suite bathrooms, air-con and breakfast included.

KB Backpackers' Lodge $ 2981F Tkt 2 Jalan Padang Garong, tel: (09) 743-2125. Dorms and private rooms, kitchen, rooftop garden, and internet access. Also organises tours and bus tickets.

Ideal Travellers' House $, 3954 FXG Jalan Kebun Sultan, tel: (09) 744-2246, e-mail: idealtrahouse@hotmail.com. Dorms and private rooms provides detailed information on tickets and tours.

🍴 The most exciting place to eat is the night market where there are lots of Malay foodstalls selling *nasi kerabu* (rice with coconut sauce) and *ayam percik* (barbequed chicken marinated in coconut milk and spices). There are also some roti stalls here, and several curry places. The whole thing closes down for evening prayers 1900–1945.

Meena Curry House $ in Jalan Gaja Mati serves *daun pisang* meals in a dilapidated setting.

Razak and Hamid's are two *daun pisang* and roti places close to the market. Razak's is the more organised of the two.

At the west end of the padang by the river is a series of attractive places selling Malay food, some with pleasant seating beside the river. There are foodstalls in the old market and beside the stadium in Jalan Mahmud. There are plenty of Chinese Restaurants and coffee shops in Jalan Padang Garong and Jalan Kebun Sultan.

ISLAND TRIPS

Off the coast between KB and Kuala Terengganu are three popular islands with resorts, opportunities for snorkelling and golden beaches. All of them are more easily accessed from Kuala Terengganu because of bus services and because the infrastructure for packages is better there. It is possible, however, to get tour companies in KB to organise the trips. (See p. 342.)

KUALA TERENGGANU

Sitting on a little promontory jutting out into the South China Sea and bordered to the west by the Sungei, Kuala Terengganu has grown in the last decade from sleepy fishing village into a city. It has fewer sights than KB and fewer ethnic minorities to balance out the strong Islamic tendencies of the north, but it is friendlier, the old part of town is less frenetic and it too has good nightmarkets and some excellent places to shop for local crafts.

HIGHLIGHTS The **central market** is the liveliest place, especially in the early morning when fishing boats deliver their catches at the jetties just behind the market. Downstairs the market sells fresh food while upstairs is a good source of craft items.

South of the market is **Chinatown**, full of little shops selling strange things, and a very brightly coloured **Chinese temple**. Near to the central market is **Bukit Puteri**, a hill with fine views of the city and some ancient remains.

From the jetty opposite the tourist office you can get a boat to **Pulau Duyung**, where you can still see boatbuilders making the traditionally-shaped local fishing boats. The ferry **($)** goes whenever it has enough passengers. On the way out of town is **Pantai Batu Buruk**, the city's beach, dominated by the Park Royal Hotel but with a good promenade and excellent foodstalls nearby.

The **State Museum ($)** is a few kilometres south-west of the city at Losong, accessible by minibus no. 6 from the central bus station. The museum is housed in the old sultan's palace and has displays of local craftwork, kris knives and a boat museum. Open daily 1000–1800, closed on Fridays.

Seven kilometres south of town at Chendering is **Pusat Kraftangan Malaysia**, a craft centre with beautiful crafts on display and for sale. Open Sat–Thur 0830–1700, free. Next door is **Nor Arfa** batik factory where you can watch batik being made and buy some as well. Also nearby is **Sutera Semai** silk factory where you can watch the entire process of silk production.

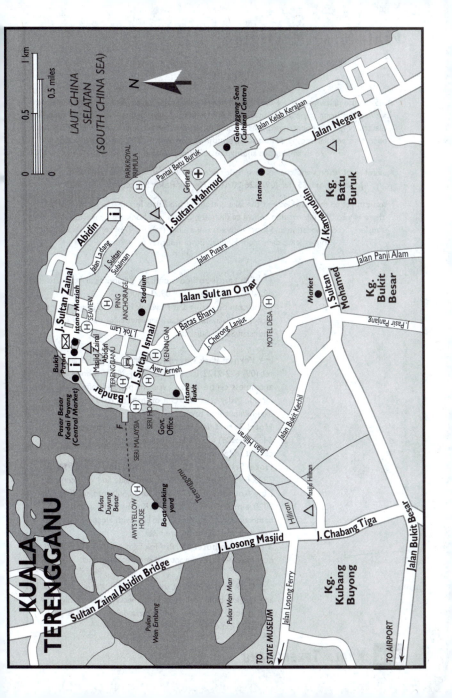

KENYIR LAKE

A 45-minute drive from Kuala Terengganu, Kenyir Lake is the largest man-made lake in South-East Asia, featuring some 340 islands and 14 waterfalls. It plays an important role in supplying electricity for the country, provides a home for freshwater fish and exotic wildlife and has become a popular escape destination from the city crowds. Fishing, trekking, kayaking and camping are among the activities available here.

A number of resorts and chalets have built since the 1980s, all with basic facilities. Try **Uncle John Resort $$,** tel: (09) 626-2020, or **Remis Rakit $$,** tel: (09) 681-2125.

You can get to the Gawi jetty at the lake entrance from Kuala Terengganu by taxi (RM60); there is a tourist information centre at the jetty. Or you can book a package, inclusive of transfers, accommodation and food, with a travel agency (see p. 347). From Kuala Lumpur, buses leave daily from Hentian Putra (journey time 9 hrs).

i The **tourist office** is on Jalan Sultan Zainal Abidin, tel: (09) 622-1553, open Sat–Thur 0900–1600.
Money can be changed at Maybank Money Changer near the Hotel Sri Malaysia. There are internet cafés on Jalan Tok Lam and Jalan Sultan Sulaiman.

Permai Park International $$$$ Jalan Sultan Mahmud, tel: (09) 622-2122, fax: (09) 622-2121. Modern hotel with pool and fitness centre and an excellent, popular coffee shop. Rates include Malay breakfast. Out of town on road to Marang, but free minibus into town.
Hotel Seri Malaysia $$$ Lot 1640, Jalan Hiliran, tel: (09) 623-6454, fax: (09) 623-8344, e-mail: smtgg@po.jaring.my. Very central and with good value rooms.
Hotel Sri Hoover $$ 49, Jalan Sultan Ismail, tel: (09) 623-3833, fax: (09) 622-5975. Very good value and very central.
Ping Anchorage $ 77A Jalan Sultan Sulaiman, tel: (09) 626-2020, e-mail: patrvl@tm.net.my. Rooms with fan and bathrooms, rooftop restaurant, bar (with alcohol), café and excellent tour agent on premises.
YTMidtown hotel $$ Jalan Tok Lam, tel: (09) 623-5288. Brand new hotel with restaurant and good value rooms.

Café in the Park at the Permai Park Inn International has an excellent buffet dinner of local specialities every night, as well as good lunch offers and a pizza delivery service: tel: (09) 622-2122 ext 611.

Along the beach front at **Pantai Batu Buruk** are lots of foodstalls that open in the evening, as well as fast food places. In **Jalan Air Jernih** are two or three reasonable *daun pisang* places. **Restoran Kari Asha** is particularly good and very popular. Along **Jalan Sultan Ismail** are more foodstalls in quite pleasant surroundings.

The **Traveller Café** at Jalan Sultan Sulaiman serves good and inexpensive food. Chinese food can be found in Chinatown at Jalan Bandar.

SHOPPING The central market is a good source of crafts, as are the places at Chendering. In Jalan Sultan Ismail is a good state run craft shop with fixed prices. **Teratai** in Jalan Bandar is an excellent little craft shop selling lots of unusual things, not all of them from Malaysia, but worth a look. The Batik Gallery at Jalan Sultan Sulaiman sells innovative marine batiks and other souvenirs.

TOURS Several agencies organise trips into the interior and to the offshore islands. **Ping Anchorage** (see p. 346) has the largest range of trips, and at very competitive prices, including jungle trekking, the islands, river trips, turtle watching and more. Most tour agencies will know which island resorts have vacancies and can get better prices than the walk-in rates. In addition, transport and food, which can be difficult for an independent traveller, will be part of the tour.

THE PERHENTIANS The easiest way to make a trip to the Perhentians is with one of the tour agencies. There are resort offices in Jalan Bandar in Kuala Terengganu but each one deals only with its own resort. The resorts are pretty much fully booked weeks in advance between February and October, particularly at weekends, and are closed the rest of the year due to the monsoon season. Any vacancies are held by the agencies, particularly Ping Anchorage.

Both islands are still the

PULAU REDANG

Redang is part of a marine park consisting of nine islands with white sandy beaches and wonderful opportunities for snorkeling and diving. It is easier to go there with a tour company than on your own since most places are fully booked and it is cheaper to buy a package than to book the room and boat ticket separately. An agency will also get you a better rate and be able to find available rooms.

In most places a twin air-con room with meals, return transfer to the island and snorkelling trips is about RM280 per person. Boats leave from Merang and there are daily buses from Kuala Terengganu. Taxis cost about RM10. Close by is Pulau Lang Tengah, which has two resorts, both quite expensive, and again a package is far easier and possibly cheaper than just turning up.

cleanest, most beautiful and most unspoilt in Malaysia, and the effort of making the trip is well worth it. The larger island, **Perhentian Besar**, has accommodation of around 16 resorts and collections of chalets on the west side. The biggest and most luxurious is the **Perhentian Resort $$$**, tel: (09) 691-0946, www.perhentianresort.com, for the resort office in Kuala Besut. Surprisingly, they serve beer at the café. An internet shop can be found here near the resort. The **Coral View Island Resort $$$,** tel: (09) 691-0946, neighbouring with Perhentian Resort, offers fan or air-conditioned chalets and rooms, with a sea or garden view, while the cheaper places have beach chalets for around RM25 for a chalet with a fan and shared bathroom. Most places have their own restaurants and there are a few foodstalls and cafés. Camping is possible on the beaches.

The smaller island, **Kecil**, has much more basic accommodation, chalets with primitive bathrooms and mosquito nets. It is advisable to book before departure. Ferries run to the two main beaches and it is possible to walk between them. There are some cafés and a shop, and you can rent snorkelling equipment and boats to explore the coastline.

Impiana Beach Resort $$$, on the south coast (no phone), has air-con chalets. Both speedboats and slower boats depart regularly from Kuala Besut for various destinations on both islands. If you have booked a chalet you must make sure you are being taken to the right place. From Kota Bharu buses go to Jerteh on the main road, from where you can get another bus or taxi to Kuala Besut.

MARANG

Once a laid-back little backpackers' haven, Marang is now a suburb of the city. It succumbed badly to developers who knocked down the old wooden houses and built a concrete precinct, but it still has some advantages as an alternative to Kuala Terengganu. It has some good beaches and in the evenings fishing boats bring in their catches. It is also the stepping-off point for Pulau Kapas, a pretty island well worth a day trip or a few nights' stay.

Arrival and Departure Long-distance buses stop on the main road at several different places, so you must ask where you should wait at your hotel or when you buy your ticket. For Rantau Abang take the Dungun bus.

> **Hotel Seri Malaysia $$** Lot 3964, Kampung Paya, tel: (09) 618-2889, fax: (09) 618-1285. Outside the main village and facing the sea, this place has excellent value rooms and frequent special offers.
>
> **Marang Guesthouse $–$$** tel: (09) 618-1976. Well organised with a good restaurant with Western and Malay food. Sea views and island and river trips offered.

Anggulia Beach House Resort $$ Km 20, Kampong Rhu Muda, tel: (09) 618-1322. Right on the beach with a good if expensive restaurant.

PULAU KAPAS

Only 6 km offshore, this is still a pretty unspoiled island with fine sandy beaches. It is good for a day trip as long as you avoid the school holidays and weekends, and there is accommodation on the island at **The Light House** $, tel: (019) 215-3558. Dorms and rooms, bar, trips, snorkelling. Boat transfer from Marang Tourist Jetty, tel: (019) 983-9454. Other budget options are also available and **Zaki** has a popular restaurant.

TO This place is popular with Singaporean weekenders, so there is a whole series of seafood places up on the main road. There are also some foodstalls along the waterfront near the jetty.

LEATHERBACK TURTLES

Dermochelys coriacea, the giant leatherback turtle, lays its eggs in five known places in the world, and one of them is the beach at Rantau Abang. The turtles are 3-m-long, 350-kg monsters that live deep in the Pacific Ocean all their lives except when the females struggle their way ashore to lay their eggs. The males' only contact with land is when they hatch out of their eggs. Female leatherbacks can weigh up to 750 kg and can grow to over 3m in length.

Although these turtles have a family tree dating back 150 million years, there are now thought to be only about 60,000 females left in the world, and the Rantau Abang sightings are about 5% of what they were 30 years ago. They live on a diet of jellyfish and spend most of their day seeking out their own bodyweight of them. The females probably come ashore to the place where they hatched, and are thought to navigate their way around the oceans by means of magnetite in their brain.

A female lays about 150 eggs each time she comes ashore and lays about nine batches each season. Of those, about two-thirds hatch out and face the challenge of the rush down to the sea and the shallows where they can be picked off by gulls or other predators. Their worst enemy is man who dumps plastic and rubbish into the sea or traps them in nets. Their shells are used for decoration and their flesh is a delicacy in many cultures.

The villagers believe that the giant turtles are attracted to Rantau Abang because of a large black stone there, resembling a turtle. This legendary stone lies on a hill in the village. Take the junction beside the Petronas fuel station, opposite Awang's, then walk into the village. There are signs for the stone along the road.

PENINSULAR MALAYSIA

RANTAU ABANG This is in the centre of a long strip of sandy beaches, good for a stop at any time but especially popular May-August, the turtle egg-laying season. There is little to do here – a trip into busy, noisy Dungun is about the most exciting things get – but the water is clear and the beach is clean. The **Turtle Information Centre**, 13th mile, Jalan Dungun, tel: (09) 844 4169, is right on the beach and full of information about the four types of turtle that lay their eggs here. A documentary film on turtles is shown six times a day. The centre opens every day except Friday, and public holidays.

🛏 **Awang's $–$$** tel: (09) 844-3500. Beside the Turtle Information Centre. Guides here will wake you up to take you to where a turtle has been spotted. You can enjoy making your first piece of batik here.

Ismail Beach Resort $–$$ tel: (019) 983-6202. Next door and similar in style to Awang's.

Dahimah's $–$$$ tel: (09) 845-2843. 1 km south of the centre, signposted from the road. Restaurant.

Merantau Inn $–$$ tel: (09) 844-1131. 3.5 km north of the turtle centre, restaurant, big rooms, close to village of Kuala Abang.

TO Most of the accommodation has restaurants and there are stalls near to the bus stop and in Plaza R&R.

SOME SMALLER ISLANDS

While most tourists head for the well-known Perhentians and Pulau Redang, a few smaller islands in the area have been developed on a more modest scale and may be more attractive for those seeking somewhere quieter.

Lang Tengah, between the Perhentians and Redang, is accessible from Marang. As there are only two resorts on the island, Lang Tengah is less crowded than the better-known islands. **Blue Coral Island Resort $$$$**, tel: (03) 705 2577, has air-conditioned chalets, swimming pool and restaurant. **Square Point Redang Resort $$$**, tel: (09) 623-5333, has rooms in a double-storey wooden building.

Bidong, a quiet and unspoilt island, was once the site of a Vietnamese refugee camp, abandoned in the 1980s. There are no resorts on the island, but a day trip can be arranged by travel agencies (see p. 347) to see the Vietnamese houses and temples or to hear stories of the island.

Tenggol is an hour from Dungun, a fishing port 20 km from Rantau Abang. This small and rugged island is a paradise for divers. **Tenggol Aqua Resort $$$**, tel: (09) 848-4862, is the only resort on the island, with timber chalets and fully equipped for diving trips. As for the other islands, it is cheaper to book your stay through a local travel agency or buy a package.

CHERATING

Another of the east coast's sleepy villages, Cherating is tolerant and laid-back. It has also given way to developers, but if the big resorts have moved in and fenced off their land there are still quiet places to hang out, practise batik making and just enjoy the beach. There are two good travel agents in the village and you can make lots of the inland trips from here as easily as from Kuantan. Alcohol flows freely and there are fewer stares for bare-shouldered foreign women than in the north. The really big resorts are a couple of km south of the old village and don't really have much connection with the village atmosphere, but they are good places to stay.

ARRIVAL AND DEPARTURE Local buses stop along the main road at designated bus stops and basically wherever someone hails them. Buses run every ½ hr between Kemaman north of Cherating and Kuantan to the south. They are not air-conditioned and the journey is a slow one, stopping every few minutes. Long-distance buses can be booked at the two travel agents in the village, and you must arrange when and where they will stop for you on the main road because there is no designated stop at Cherating. They can arrange direct buses to the Thai border, Kota Bharu, Jerteh, Terengganu, Marang and Rantau Abang.

HIGHLIGHTS **Activities** include batik printing classes, exhibitions of martial arts, top spinning, kite flying and trips up the **Cherating River**. You can also watch trained monkeys collecting coconuts and small turtles coming ashore to lay their eggs. The **Cherating Cultural Village** puts on shows in the restaurant with traditional musicians and dancers.

> *i* Two travel agents in the village will book onward journeys, local and more distant trips and change cash and traveller's cheques, but at a poor rate.
> **Badger Lines**, tel: (09) 581-9552, is in the centre of the village and **Travel Post**, tel: (09) 581-9825 is opposite the Rhana Pippin. Both offer **tourist information**, **internet** service, car rental, international calls, poste restante and more, including trips to local night markets, Pulau Ular, upriver, Lake Chini, and the Charas Caves.

> 🛏 **The Legend Resort $$$$** Lot 1290, Mukim Sg, Karang, tel: (09) 581-9818, fax: (09) 581-9400, e-mail: legend@po.jaring.my. Big sprawling resort, two pools, right on the beach, two good restaurants, lovely big rooms with sea views, some chalets on the beach. A public bus runs half-hourly to the village or a cab is RM20.
> **Residence Inn Cherating $$$$** Lot 826–Mukim Sg Karang, tel: (09) 581-9333, www.ric.com. Big resort on village outskirts,

restaurant and café, architecturally interesting, special offers, but away from the beach. Rates go up at weekends.

Duyung Beach Resort $$ tel: (09) 581-9335. Wooden chalets with a restaurant that serves Chinese food.

Cherating Cottage $–$$ tel: (09) 581-9273, opposite Matahari's. Wooden chalets on a well-maintained site, nice café, rooms with bathroom, TV and hot water.

Green Leaves Inn $ tel: (09) 337-8242, beside river in quiet location, very basic accommodation in mangroves.

Matahari Chalets $ tel: (09) 581-9126/9835 On road in from the highway, close to the river. Pleasant garden setting, nicely spaced chalets and a longhouse, kitchen and TV room.

🍴 There are lots of places to eat in Cherating, all offering variations of Chinese seafood and some Western dishes.

Blue Lagoon $$ is a typical neon-lit roadside place with a long menu that includes quail, squid and stingray.

The Dragon Seafood Restaurant $$–$$$$ is another simple roadside place at the crossroads in the village, with a vast seafood menu.

Mimi's $$ close to the Rhana Pippin does good inexpensive Indian food.

The **Driftwood Restaurant** on the beach front offers good meals and beer.

NIGHTLIFE Unusually in this part of the world, Cherating has a good, active nightlife.

La Blues Bar is very popular, situated right on the beach and gets going at about midnight.

Pop Inn is close to La Blues Bar, so if you get bored of one place you can try the other.

The Moon at the chalet resort of the same name close to the main road is also good.

TOP SPINNING

Gasing, or top spinning, is a sport practised seriously by adults in Malaysia. There are two kinds of games. In one, the person who can make a top spin the longest is the winner. The wooden tops, made from *merbau* wood, can weigh up to 5 kg, be spun by a 5-m rope and spin for as long as 2 hours. The other game is a little like conkers where one person sets a top spinning and the other tries to knock it over.

KUANTAN

The end of the huge 300-km-long beach strip, Kuantan and its suburb Chempedak, are good places to stop for a day or two after days of beach and island. Kuantan is a busy Malaysian town with a population of about 100,000, relatively liberal, with predominantly Chinese and Indian communities.

ARRIVAL AND DEPARTURE

Bus: The long-distance bus station is in Jalan Stadium. Buses leave from here for most larger towns in Malaysia. The ticket offices are all two floors above street level where you can wander around choosing the best time and price for you. KL is 5 hrs and buses leave hourly, Mersing is 3 hrs and buses leave twice a day, JB is 5 hrs and Singapore 7 hrs.

The local bus station for buses to Cherating is at Jalan Haji, not far from the New Capitol Hotel. Look on the front of the bus for its destination and pay once on board. Buses to Teluk Chempedak, Jalan Besar, the Mosque and the long-distance bus station. Look for buses 39A and 39B.

Air: Sultan Ahmen Shah Airport is 20 km south of Kuantan. Malaysian Airways flies direct to KL and Singapore. The MAS office is in Wisma Bolasepak Pahang, Jalan Gambut, tel: (09) 515-7055.

HIGHLIGHTS   The river in town is a good place for a stroll and the **mosque**, in the centre of town near the padang, is quite a sight – modern, airy and marbled. The main tourist focus is **Teluk Chempedak Beach** where there is a good sandy beach, rocks to clamber over, lots of good foodstalls and a Vietnamese refugee boat made into a beach bar.

EXCURSIONS   **Tasik Chini** is a series of freshwater lakes in the heart of the rainforest. The area is inhabited by Orang Asli people called Jakun who live in simple *kampungs* and believe, or so they say, that a serpent inhabits the lakes. The area is good for fishing, walks in the jungle and wildlife spotting. The lakes are covered in lotus flowers between June and September. They can be reached by boat from Belimbing or by road from Pekan. The alternative is to take a bus from Kuantan to Felda Chini. Mara bus no. 121 leaves Kuantan five times a day and the journey takes 2 hrs. Get off at Felda Chini, from where it is another 11 km to the resort. You can hire a motorbike to get you there, or walk. **Lake Chini Resort $$**, tel: (09) 456-7897, has good cabins with bathrooms; the restaurant offers simple food.

Gua Charas (Charas caves, $) is 26 km north of Kuantan at Panching, a limestone outcrop sitting in a palm plantation. Inside is a reclining Buddha carved out of the cave wall, as well as lots of shrines and other statues. The cave system goes on beyond the main lit caves and you can explore if you have a torch. Again a tour is the easiest option but it is possible to get there by bus no. 48 to Sg. Lembing from the main bus station in Kuantan and get off at Panching, from there it is a 4-km walk or hitchhike to the caves.

i The **tourist office** is in Jalan Mahkota, opposite the Kompleks Terantum, tel: (09) 513-3026.

A good place to change **money** and traveller's cheques is Hamid Bros, 71 Jalan Mahkota, marked on some maps as Jalan Abdul Aziz. The **post office** is further east along the same street.

There is an **internet** shop, Network 21, two floors up from street level in the Berjaya Megamall in Jalan Tun Ismail.

🚮 **Hyatt Regency \$\$\$\$** Teluk Chempedak, tel: (09) 566-1234, fax: (09) 567-7577, e-mail: hyatt_kuantan@hrktn.com.my. Two pools, beach bar made from an old Vietnamese refugee boat, water sports, fine rooms with garden or sea view, tennis, health centre, popular coffee shop on beach which fills up for Sunday buffet lunch, Chinese restaurant.

Hotel Grand Continental \$\$\$\$ Jalan Gambut, tel: (09) 515-8888, fax: (09) 515-9999. A good, newish city hotel close to the Megamall with pool, Chinese restaurant and coffee shop.

Shazan \$\$–\$\$\$ 240 Jalan Bukit Ubi, tel: (09) 513-6688, fax: (09) 513-5588. Another new hotel close to the mosque, overlooking the padang, all mod cons, coffee shop.

Megaview \$\$ Lot 567, Jalan Besar, tel: (09) 555-1888, fax: (09) 555-3999. Very new, right beside the river with excellent views, nice rooms, coffee shop. Rate includes breakfast.

Hotel Classic \$\$ 7, Bangunan LKNP, Jalan Besar, tel: (09) 555-4599, fax: (09) 513-4141. Big rooms with TV and fridge, rate includes breakfast, coffee shop.

🍴 In the **Berjaya Megamall** there are lots of fast food places, plus a good food court dominated by a Chinese steamboat restaurant with one of those signs warning that people who leave food on their plates will be fined.

Near the local bus station and beside the river is a whole strip of **Malay stalls** well worth checking out if only because you can watch the river while you eat. There are banana leaf places along Jalan Bukit Ubi and an excellent roti place, **Restoran Mubarak**, next door to the long-distance bus station.

TELUK CHEMPEDAK

Four kilometres east of Kuantan, this is really a much nicer place to spend your time than the city. The foreshore is paved and there are lots of hawker stalls in the area behind. There is a cliff walk around to the next beach, **Bukit Pelindung**, as well as longer walks into the **Teluk Chempedak Forest**.

In the row of shop-houses leading down to the beach are several good restaurants and a shop selling handicrafts and batik. Accommodation is either the Hyatt (see p. 354) or the **Kuantan Hotel $$** opposite, tel: (09) 513-0026. In the row of shop-houses leading down to the beach are the **Country Ranch**, an Indian place, and the **Checkers Pub**, also serving Indian food.

MERSING

A wacky little place, Mersing is really only a stepping-off point for Tioman and some other smaller islands lite Besar, Sibu and Aur but it has a scruffy beach of its own and that Wild West atmosphere that is so attractive in some Malaysian towns. There are lots of places to stay and most of the cheaper places are used to independent travellers passing through on their way to find a perfect beach.

The government rest-house is a little wonder and has the beach behind it with a long walk possible around the shore. Nine kilometres north of town is **Air Papan**, a good beach, and 6 km south is **Sri Pantai**, less well known but almost as good.

ARRIVAL AND DEPARTURE
Bus: Most buses depart from the R&R Plaza bus station. Ticket booths are at the back of the plaza. There are departures for KL, three times a day; Kuantan, twice a day; Terengganu, Rantau Abang and Cherating, three times a day; and Melaka once a day. In addition, the north- and south-bound buses sometimes stop outside the **Restoran Malaysia** on the main road. The restaurant sells bus tickets and will provide information.

Boat: There are ferries from Mersing for Tioman, Pulau Rawa and Pulau Sibu. There are no hard-and-fast sailing times for any of the ferries, which depend on the tides, the number of bookings and the weather. For Tioman the big boats usually depart twice a day at high tide and the faster boats, which are not dependent on the tide, depart several times a day, depending on bookings. At the bus stop beside the Malaysia restaurant is **Island Connection Travel and Tours**, which will be able to give you sailing times and book accommodation for you. Mersing jetty is just a 5-minute walk from the city centre.

ℹ️ The **tourist office** is in Jalan Abu Baker on the way to the jetty. It is open daily and closes at 1630.

Several of the offices for the resorts are at the R&R Plaza beside the jetty. Travel agents and bus and ferry **booking offices** are also here.

There are two **banks** in Jalan Ismail where you can change traveller's cheques.

Cyber World **internet** shop is at 36, Jalan Abu Bakar.

🛏️ **Government Rest House $–$$** 490 Jalan Ismail, tel: (07) 799-2102. Huge, shabby rooms, great restaurant, pretty gardens overlooking the beach, big common balcony with views.

Hotel Timotel $$$ 839 Jalan Endau, tel: (07) 799-5888, fax: (07) 799-5333. Special offers bring the cost right down. Newly built, all essentials, coffee shop popular with locals, bar with alcohol, on main road opposite bus stop.

Hotel Embassy $ 2 Jalan Ismail, tel: (07) 799-3545, fax: (07) 799-5279. Very basic air-con rooms with simple bathroom and hot water. Good coffee shop.

Mersing Hotel $ Jalan Ismail, tel: (07) 796-1004. Same standard and rates as the Embassy.

🍴 There are good seafood restaurants in town, notably the **Mersing Seafood Restaurant** in Jalan Ismail, which is air-conditioned.

The **Golden Dragon** is the café below the Embassy Hotel and is popular with locals. There are several good Indian Muslim places doing roti in the mornings and evenings.

Try **Zam Zam**, near **Omar's backpacker's Hostel**.

At the jetty are lots of **nasi kandar stalls** selling reasonable curries.

There is also a **KFC** in Jalan Abu Bakar for fast air-con eating.

PULAU TIOMAN

Once a magical, innocent, beautiful island hideaway, Tioman has succumbed to the developers but still has lots to offer visitors. One of its biggest attractions is its accessibility – it is easy to bus it to Mersing, jump on a boat, get out there and find a good place to stay. The island is excellent for diving and snorkelling, particularly the beaches on the west side and Pulau Rengis, the little rock just offshore from the Berjaya Resort. Check out the website www.tioman.cc.

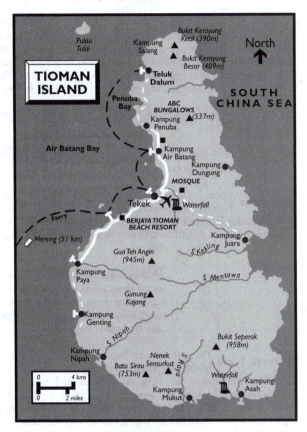

TIOMAN ISLAND

Pulau Tulai

Kampung Salang

Bukit Kerayung Kecil (390m)

Bukit Kerayung Besar (409m)

North

Teluk Dalum

SOUTH CHINA SEA

Penuba Bay

ABC BUNGALOWS

Kampung Penuba

(537m)

Air Batang Bay

Kampung Air Batang

Kampung Dungung

MOSQUE

Tekek

Waterfall

BERJAYA TIOMAN BEACH RESORT

Ferry

Mersing (51 km)

Kampung Juara

S. Kesling

Gua Teh Angin (945m)

S. Mentawa

Kampung Paya

Gunung Kajang

Kampung Genting

S. Nipah

Bukit Seperok (958m)

Kampung Nipah

Nenek Semurkut

Batu Sirau (753m)

S. Raya

Waterfall

Kampung Asah

Kampung Mukut

| 0 | 4 kms |
| 0 | 2 miles |

ARRIVAL AND DEPARTURE

Boat: High-speed boats leave Mersing at around 0730, 1030 and 1400 while the Seagull Ferry, which is a slower boat, leaves around 1130, depending on the tide. More boats run according to demand and all of these times vary from day to day. The slower ferries charge RM45 return while the faster boats charge RM30 one way.

Boats call first at Kampung, Genting, then in the following order: Paya, Berjaya Resort, Tekek, Air Batang and Salang. A round-island ferry leaves Tekek at 1630,

SANDFLIES

These evil little creatures can ruin a holiday if you are at all sensitive to their bites. Go to Tioman equipped with mosquito coils and insect repellents because on a bad day you can be badly bitten by them.

stops at Air Batang and Salang, and goes on to Juara. It costs RM420 for a chartered boat, which takes a little over an hour for the full journey and returns from Juara at 1500. The Sea Bus allows you to travel between the beaches of the west coast of the island and Juara. A round-island trip and Pulau Tulai (Coral Island) trip is also possible. The round-island trip will stop at most of the beaches. The Coral Island trip drops you off in the morning and picks you up in the afternoon.

A daily boat leaves Singapore for Tioman at 0830, journey time 4½ hours, and leaves for Singapore at 1430.

Air: There is an airport on the island. For Air Berjaya, tel: (07) 419–1303, with daily flights to KL and Singapore.

HIGHLIGHTS There are good walks around the coast from Berjaya to Paya and Genting, and southwards from Salang to Tekek, into the hills and across the island to Juara (2–3 hrs) through virgin rainforest. The Sea Bus takes you to Salang, Air Batang and Tekek. In season turtles lay their eggs around Nipah Beach and there is lots of other wildlife to see.

> 🖥 The number of expensive resorts has multiplied but there are still simple fan-cooled beach chalets to be found. From late August to the monsoon season in November you are in a buyer's market and should visit each office getting the best rates. The beaches are as follows:

KAMPUNG TEKEK This is the main village on the island, with shops and some places to eat. The best place to stay here is **Swiss Cottage $–$$**, tel: (07) 224-2829, with small chalets close to the beach and its own restaurant. Packages include board and transport. Round the headland from Tekek beach is the **Berjaya Resort $$$$$**, tel: (03) 2142-9611, e-mail: bhr@hr.berjaya.com.my, with all mod cons, sea sports, a pool, tennis, horse riding and an excellent beach. Between November and February, when there are few visitors, you can get big discounts.

AIR BATANG This is the major traveller's place to stay and has mostly fan-cooled chalets. There is a small information office at the jetty where you can buy boat tickets. The better places are **Mawar's $**, with its own restaurant, tel: (09) 419-1153, **Bamboo Hill Chalets $$**, tel: (09) 419-1339, very small and often

> ### FINDING ACCOMMODATION
> There are many offices in town selling accommodation and packages at the various resorts. Check these out before you go over to the island or book a trip with Seagull, Island Connection or one of the other tour agencies. Do not be persuaded at the jetty by touts that the cheaper places are full; this rarely happens.

full, and **Nazri's Beach Cabins $$,** tel: (011) 333-486, with big bungalows and its own restaurant. **Johan's House $$,** has chalets dotted around a lawn on the hill.

KAMPUNG PENUBA North of Air Batang, the best place here is **Penuba Inn Resort $-$$$,** tel: (011) 952-963, with air-con chalets for RM58. The resort sits on a hill overlooking the sea and is often booked up so phone ahead.

SALANG North again is Salang with a pretty beach with restaurants but lots of resorts. The **Salang Indah $$,** tel: (09) 413-1406, with fan-cooled and air-con chalets, its own restaurant, a bar and shop. **Salang Beach Resort $$$,** tel: (07) 799-3607, has a restaurant with reasonable prices and offers packages, including transport and food, which work out cheaper.

PAYA South of the resort is Paya beach, where there are some expensive resorts. **Tioman Paya Resort $$$$** has its own restaurant, coffee shop, bar and karaoke lounge. Packages include full board and transport and work out cheaper. Inquire at **Sea-Gull Express**, 26 Jalan Sulamein, tel: (07) 799-4297.

GENTING This beach is less accessible than the others and has fewer eating options outside its resorts. Try **Genting Damai Resort $$,** tel: (07) 799-1200, which has a restaurant and minimarket. It too offers packages with full board and trips. **Yacht Resort $$$** can be booked through Seagull and has air-con rooms.

NIPAH Very isolated with a glorious beach great for snorkelling. The only place to stay here is **Nipah Beach Resort $$$,** tel: (07) 799-1012. Only boats to and from Mersing stop here by arrangement. With only one restaurant, food and drinks are more expensive than elsewhere on the island.

RAWA, BESAR, SIBU, TENGAH

Other islands are also accessible from Mersing. Rawa and Sibu both have resort hotels where packages can be arranged.

Rawa is surrounded by a coral reef. The island is dominated by the **Rawa Safaris Island Resort $$$** which has fan-cooled and air-con rooms. Outside food is not allowed on the island but there is a restaurant. The only way to the island is via its own boat, RM40 per person, which can be booked on tel: (07) 799-1204 at Plaza R&R.

Besar has several resorts, is close to the mainland and is accessible by a regular ferry service. It is possible to go to the island without accommodation and find somewhere to stay there. Sibu is also easily accessed and much less crowded than Tioman. There is a good range of accommodation from simple beach huts to the **Sibu Island Cabanas $$$.** tel: (07) 331-7216, and **Rimba Resort; $$$,** tel: (010) 714-7495, (012) 710-6855, email: rimba@pd.jering.my. Close to Besar, Tengah was once a Vietnamese refugee camp. Leatherbacks come to lay their eggs in July every year. **Sibu Island Resort $$$,** tel: (07) 799-5555, e-mail: sirsb@tm.net.my.

JOHOR BAHRU

Capital of the state of Johor, JB suffers a little from being placed so close to the wonders of Singapore. Just over the causeway is everything you could ever ask for in terms of food, shopping, tourist attractions, public transport, hotels and more. JB, on the other hand, is chaotic, unregulated and dirty.

Most travellers arriving here from Singapore stop long enough to sort out immigration and move on. But JB is worth more than a glance out of a bus or train window. In a way its chaos is a welcome antidote to 'Fine City', as Singapore has come to be called, and as the last stop on the east coast trip it can seem a little oasis of shopping malls, seafood restaurants, and fast food delights.

Singaporeans come to JB when the regulations over the causeway get them down. Many of them live here: housing, petrol, clothes, food, beer and entertainment are all cheaper. Lots of tour groups even arrange their clients' stay in JB and bus them over the causeway each day to save on accommodation and eating costs.

Getting There

Air: There are direct flights between JB and KL, Kota Kinabalu, Kuching, Penang, and Surabaya in Indonesia. The Malaysian Airways office is in the Menara Pelangi building on Jalan Kuning. **Sultan Ismail** airport is 32 km north of the city at Senai. An SPS coach service leaves from the **Pan Pacific Hotel** and is timed to meet incoming and outgoing flights, or local bus no. 207 will take you to the airport, but departures are infrequent. A taxi should cost about RM25. Most taxis are metered.

Bus: There are buses between JB's **Larkin bus terminal**, 5 km north of the city and Queen St bus terminal in Singapore leaving at 15-min intervals. It is also possible to get the SBS service 170 or the air-conditioned Singapore-Johor Bahru Express at Larkin or at the causeway where you can buy tickets on the bus. Coming from Singapore buses go to Larkin or you can disembark at immigration and walk into the city.

At Larkin buses depart to all major cities on Malaysia. None of them needs to be booked in advance, although it might be advisable in holiday seasons. You can get tickets from booths in Larkin or the bus booking office on the second floor of Merlin Tower facing the railway station and wait here for the transit buses to take you to Larkin. An extra charge will be made for this.

Train: There are direct links with KL and the west coast. Change at Gemas for the jungle railway to Kota Bharu. The railway station is on Jalan Abdul Razak in the city centre. The booking office is open 0900–1800 and it is best to book in advance for longer journeys.

Boat: East of JB is a ferry terminal at the Stulang Duty Free Trade Zone from where there are connections to Singapore and Sumatra. From Tanjung Belungkor, near Desaru, a car ferry goes to Singapore.

GETTING AROUND Taxis have meters for the most part but make sure that the driver switches it on or gives you a price before the journey begins. Most of the big car-hire companies have offices in JB.

i There are two **tourist offices** in the JOTIC building, on Jalan Air Molek west of the causeway. The state tourist office is more useful for information about the state of Johor, while the Tourism Malaysia office on the fifth floor deals with the city. Both are open Mon–Sat 0900–1700. They don't officially close for the lunch hour but everyone disappears then.

Moneychangers litter the street in the roads around the causeway. All have competitive rates but don't change small Singaporean bills when the rates are poor.

The **post office** is in Jalan Ibrahim.

There are **internet** shops in JB City Centre and Plaza Kotaraya.

HOURLY ROOM RATES

The seedier side of JB nightlife means that quite a lot of the less classy hotels rent rooms by the hour. The five-star hotels offer all the facilities expected at prices to match, so the cheaper hotels offer good value accommodation despite all the coming and going. Those listed here are the more respectable ones. Rates in the cheaper hotels go up at weekends when the Singaporeans hit town.

🛏 **Hyatt Regency $$$$$** Jalan Sungei Chat, tel: (07) 222-1234, fax: (07) 223-2718. Two km west of town on a hill overlooking the Straits of Johor and Singapore. Pool, sculptured gardens, good restaurants, excellent buffet breakfast. Large rooms with luxurious bathrooms.

Crowne Plaza $$$$ Jalan Dato Sulamein, tel: (07) 332-3800, fax: (07) 331-8884, e-mail: cpjb@tm.net.my. Pool, coffee shop, Italian and Szechuan restaurants, free local calls, free shuttle service, some excellent full-board packages. In northern outskirts of the city centre, close to the Holiday Inn Plaza.

Mercure Ace $$$18, Jalan Wong Ah Fook, tel: (07) 221-3000, fax: (07) 221-4000, e-mail: mercure@po.jaring.my. Right in the centre of things, this modern hotel has stylish rooms, a wholefood café and attentive service.

Gateway Hotel $$ 61, Jalan Meldrum, tel: (07) 223-5048, fax: (07) 223-5248. All the basics, at a reasonable rate.

Top Hotel $$ 12, Jalan Meldrum, tel: (07) 224-4755. All the basics, next to a good coffee shop, right in centre of town.

🍴 There are two restaurants among the many in the five-star hotels that are worth a look.

Selasih $$ in the **Pan Pacific** serves a Malay buffet along with some traditional music and dancing. You can try lots of local specialities here and have things explained as you eat.

Meisan $$$$ is at the Crowne Plaza and serves Szechuan food.

Foodstalls are good and popular, especially with Singaporeans who flock here at weekends to eat the seafood. Right beside the drain and outside the Hindu temple is the very popular **night market $** where you can try Malay Chinese and Indian food.

Along the waterfront running west of the Causeway are lots of Chinese seafood places. Close to the hospital is the **Tepian Tebrau hawker centre** where all the stalls have similar seafood menus.

For a more expensive Chinese seafood meal you could try **Eden Park Seafood Garden** in Jalan Gelam, noticeable for its huge sign on the hillside. It is open 1730–0100 daily.

JB City Centre, a huge new shopping complex, has an excellent food court on its top floor with Thai, Japanese, Western, and *nasi padang* stalls and a good *laksa* stall serving heavily coconut-flavoured *laksa johor*. There is also a fairly rare *yong tau fu* stall where you select the all-vegetarian food items for the stallholder to dunk in gravy to cook for a few minutes. In City Square and Holiday Plaza are branches of the excellent and very popular **Restoran Hameed's**, serving Indian Muslim food, roti and dose.

HIGHLIGHTS The main attraction is the **Royal Abu Bakar Museum $$$**, open daily 0900–1800. It is well worth the high price and is a good afternoon's visit. The building is the old royal palace (built 1864–1866), which is no longer used by the sultan, except on state occasions. The architect was British and much of the furniture on show is European.

The place is an amazing mixture of everyday items and great wealth. The treasury contains all the gifts given to the sultans including silver kris. Special women's *kris* were kept on their persons in case of attack when they could commit suicide rather than be violated. Also on display are execution swords with which murderous or adulterous criminals were stabbed through the back. Other gory relics include various dismembered animals made into ashtrays and doorstops.

Sultan Abu Bakar Mosque (built 1892–1900) is one of those curious mixtures of Islamic and English Victorian architectural styles common in KL. The minarets have a distinctly colonial feel and would not be out of place on, say, Manchester City Hall.

The **Sultan Ibrahim** building on Bukit Timbalan overlooking the city centre is another very distinctive style and dominates the JB skyline. Built in the 1940s, it looks almost medieval.

The **Istana Bukit Serene** is not open to the public but it too has an imposing appearance with beautiful gardens and a private zoo. Its 1930s tower was used in November 1941 by General Yamishita, the commander of the 25th Army, to watch the invasion of Singapore. When his troops signalled that they had established a bridgehead on Singapore soil, the general wept from the window here. This Art Deco influenced building can be viewed on Jalan Skudai.

ENTERTAINMENT JB has a distinctly sleazy element to its nightlife, but this is easily avoided. There are lots of karaoke places and late-opening nightclubs and discos. Just wander around and the person at the door will lure you in.

Qudos in Plaza DNP, Jalan Datuk Abdulah Tahir, is a new and very trendy place. It plays some interesting music, has a dance floor and pool table, lots of happy hour offers and is open late. A similar place is the **Blues Café,** 55 Jalan Kuning, open till 0200.

For something a little different you can join the **Amusement World Cruise** package, tel: (07) 222-9898. It is an all-night boat party with karaoke, cinema, disco and live bands – all for RM50 including a room and three meals.

SHOPPING The other thing that Singaporeans flock here for is the shopping. Many of the plazas cater almost entirely for Singaporean tastes and only really come alive at weekends. JB is probably a little more expensive than other places because of this.

The best of the malls is **JB City Centre**, newly opened and bursting with expensive shops. **Holiday Inn Plaza** is cheaper and has more small places and bargains.

JASON'S BAY

Also known as Teluk Mahkota, this is an isolated and rather muddy beach. Apart from some wandering cattle it is utterly deserted. The foreshore is lined with palms and casuarina trees and macaques swing boldly over the approach road to stare at passing cars. Apart from **Jason's Bay Beach Resort** tel: (07) 881-8077 there is little else. Come for a picnic to an unusual black beach but don't stay here. There is no public bus service and you really need your own transport.

EXCURSIONS **Desaru,** 88 km from JB, is full at weekends with Singaporeans heading for the first bit of sand they can find. The beach is good but the waves are very strong, and the entire place has one resort after another. **Desaru Impian Resort $$$$,** tel: (07) 838 9911, has rooms with TV and in-room safe. There are water and land recreational facilities. Prices match the high demand and the only places to eat are the resorts. Take a bus to Kota Tinggi and then another to the beach. Taxis cost about RM100 from JB per taxi.

EN ROUTE

Thirty km south of Mersing and still fairly inaccessible is **Tanjung Leman**, a promontory a few km off the Kota Tinggi–Mersing road. It has pretty white sandy beaches but very little in the way of accommodation. It is, however, the only way to get to several rather pretty offshore islands, all of which were once accessed via Mersing. Conspiracy theorists might think that it is all a plot to make tourists dependent on tour agencies.

A good place to visit is **Gunung Ledang**, or Mount Ophir, 38 km north-east of the town of Muar. There are waterfalls at the foot of the mountain and trails going up it. At the base is accommodation in the form of chalets, campsites and longhouses, all very basic, including the **Gunung Ledang Resort**, tel: (06) 977-2888. Take the bus to Segamat and ask to be dropped off at Sagil, from where it is a 1-km walk through rubber plantations to the falls.

Seafood and Singaporean food lovers must make the trip to **Kukup**, 40 km south west of JB on the Straits of Melaka. It is a Chinese *kampung* which has gained a huge reputation for its seafood dishes, especially chilli crab and chilli prawns. The restaurants are mostly stilt buildings leaning out over the water at the shoreline. A boat trip to Kelong (fishing trap built on stilts) is included in some packages. They tend to cater for Singaporean coach parties, which come in droves at the weekends. Take the bus to Pontian Kecil, then change for Kukup.

Kota Tinggi, 42 km north-east of JB, is a stop on the route to Mersing, but it also has the Lumbong Falls set in a pretty country park with some chalet accommodation. The falls start on Gunung Muntahak and descend via a series of pools. They are good for dips and there are nice walks in the area, but the place is to be avoided at all costs at the weekend when it heaves with people. Entrance fee to the falls is RM2 per adult. Take bus no. 41 or 227 from Larkin to Kota Tinggi, one of several express buses, or bus no. 43 from the town.

Pulau Tinggi, an extinct volcano and a marine park, has miles of sandy white beaches, great diving and snorkelling and a few resorts. **Nadia's Inn Island Resort $$,** tel: (07) 799-5582, has air-con rooms, while **Tinggi Island Resort $$$,** tel: (07) 799-4451, has chalets and fishing, boating and windsurfing facilities. There are no regular ferries to Tinggi since most people book the whole package at one of the resorts, which is probably the easiest and cheapest option. The boat journey to the island is 2 hrs.

Pulau Sibu is much more accessible, although still only from Tanjung Leman which has its own access problems. There are good beaches and coral banks as well as jungle walks. Again the easiest option is to book the whole trip through an agent, but it is possible to turn up at the island and find accommodation (see p. 358).

Pulau Pemanggil and **Pulau Aur** are also accessed via Tanjung Leman. Both are big resorts catering for large diving parties. Packages tend to run from Friday evening to Sunday afternoon, with little going on during the week. Try **Pemanggil Holiday Heaven $$$**, tel: (07) 799-5582, or **Green Chalet $$**, tel: (07) 799-4360. There are two jetties to access islands in Johor, at Mersing and Tanjung Leman. Islands like Besar, Rawa, Pemanggil and Tinggi are accessible via Mersing Jetty whereas Sibu, Tengah and Tinggi are from Tanjung Leman. To get to Mersing, you can get a bus from Larkin; the journey takes 3 hours. To get to Tanjung Leman from JB take the Mersing bus and ask to be dropped off at Tenggaroh Junction. From here taxis wait (but only before a boat is due to leave) to make the journey to the jetty.

WHERE NEXT?

The Seribuat archipelago, off Mersing, is chiefly characterised by Pulau Tioman (pp. 356–359) and a number of smaller islands including Rawa, Besar, Sibu and Tengah (see box p. 359). Further away from the mainland and enduringly popular with scuba divers are the less-visited islands of Pulau Pemanggil and Pulau Aur. Famed for their crystal-clear waters, these havens can be reached through Dive Atlantis in Singapore, tel: (02) 295-0377.

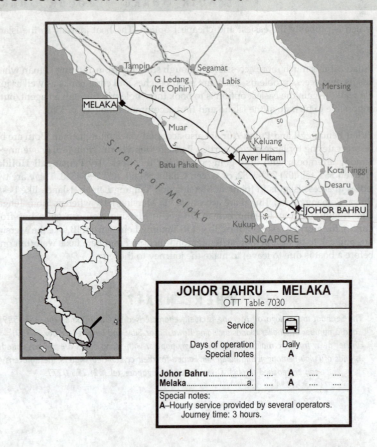

JOHOR BAHRU — MELAKA
OTT Table 7030

Service	🚌			
Days of operation	Daily			
Special notes	**A**			
Johor Bahru............d.	....	**A**	....	....
Melaka........................a.	....	**A**	....	....

Special notes:
A–Hourly service provided by several operators.
Journey time: 3 hours.

Notes

Several bus companies operate this route and there is little need to book ahead.

This route offers a contrast of two very different Malaysian towns, and along the way you will see dramatic evidence of what fuels the country's economy. Thousands of acres of land, clearly visible from the roadside or the air, are devoted to huge estates of rubber, pineapple and palm oil. They seem to go for ever and account for the relative prosperity of the Johor state. There was a time, half a millennium ago, when the small state of Melaka was a big player on the international economic stage. Its status as the trading port of South-East Asia was unchallenged, and successive waves of Europeans washed up on its shores. It is their cultural legacy that makes Melaka the favourite destination of historically minded travellers. Under the British, Melaka was one of the Straits Settlements along with Penang and Singapore.

MELAKA

Melaka spent many years as a sleepy town and is now in the middle of a massive development project, which has seen the beachfront give way to land reclamation, and new man-made islands appear off the coast. Fortunately, all this development is on reclaimed land and the amazing winding old streets and ancient shophouses have been beautifully restored.

BATU PAHAT
If you are driving through, this place is good for Chinese food and has some interesting architecture.

EN ROUTE
Muar, on the west coast, was once a busy centre and is very Malay in character. The mosque is another Victorian Moghul mixture and there are some old colonial buildings. The rest of the coastal road between here and Melaka has lots of *kampung* villages with traditional Melaka-style houses, built on blocks with elaborate tiled fronts and a space underneath the house.

Six hundred years ago traders spotted the economic value of this small town in the Straits of Melaka, halfway between China and India, and sheltered from the monsoons by the island of Sumatra. It became a natural refuelling and resting stop for great trading ships where ships from China would later bring goods to trade with vessels from India.

AYER HITAM
This little town at a major road junction is worth the stop for its many roadside pottery stalls. Much of the work here is made in potteries along the road, which is not available in other craft shops in Malaysia. Pottery animals, jugs, bowls and much larger pieces can be bought here at very reasonable prices.

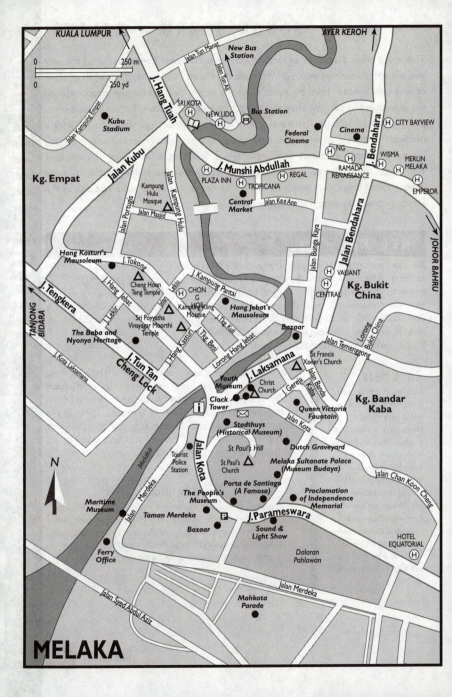

Eventually someone realised that whoever controlled Melaka governed all the trade of the East and people began to fight over it. Melaka was first ruled by the Sumatran Prince and his descendants from the 14th to 16th centuries, during which time Melaka enjoyed good relations with China and received protection from the emperors of the Ming Dynasty. News of the prosperity of Melaka attracted first the Portuguese in the 16th century, and then, in the 17th century, the Dutch and finally the British. In 1824 Melaka became part of the British Empire. But then irony struck – the port silted up, Singapore and Penang took off as trading centres and Melaka sank into obscurity and remained a little dinosaur until the tiger economy of the 1980s took hold.

ARRIVAL AND DEPARTURE

Bus: Long-distance buses travel between Melaka and most of the major towns in peninsular Malaysia as well as Singapore. By the time you read this, the bus station will have moved north of its present location; see **Getting Around** below. There are booking offices around the bus station.

Boat: Four ferry companies run regular trips to Dumai in Sumatra: Astoria, tel: (06) 282-9888; Indomai Express, tel: (06) 281-6107; Tunas Rapat, Utama tel: (06) 283-2506; and Madai Shipping, tel: (06) 284-0671. Ferries travel to Pulau Besar from Umbai jetty, tel: (06) 261-0492, and to Pulau Upeh from the TIC jetty.

GETTING AROUND

Melaka is small enough to walk around. Local taxis are rare but there are plenty of *trishaws*. They charge a minimum of RM15 and RM30 an hour for tours. Negotiate a price before beginning a journey. Bus no. 17 connects the town centre and the new bus station. Bicycles are also available for renting at most of the guesthouses.

> i The **tourist office**, tel: (06) 281-4803, www.melaka.net and www.tourism-melaka.com, is in Jalan Kota at the roundabout opposite Christ Church. Open 0845–1700 daily, closed Fri 1215–1445. It should have a map of the town. Many of the hotels have similar maps.
> The post office is at Stadthuys.

> 🛏 **Hotel Equatorial $$$$** Bandar Hilir, tel: (06) 282-8333, www.equatorial.com. The best hotel in this range, terrific restaurants and facilities.
> **Aldy Hotel $$** Jalan Kota, tel: (06) 283-3232, www.aldyhotel.com.my. New hotel, minutes from the main attractions, good café (see p. 370).

Robin's Nest $ 205B Taman Melaka Raga, tel: (06) 282-9142.
Near the Mahkota Parade shopping mall. Dorms and private
rooms with fans and air-con. Good value.

Sama-Sama $ 26 Jalan Tukang Besi, tel: 012-305-1980. A place
with character, rooms with mosquito nets, use of kitchen and
laundry, bikes for hire. Good address for chilling out.

Travellers' Lodge $ 214B Jalan Melaka Raya, tel: (06) 226-
5709. The best budget accommodation in town. Laundry,
lounge, restaurant and friendly staff. Bus 17, stop after Mahkota
shopping mall.

FOOD   Melaka is most famous for its Baba Nyonya style of cooking, a mix of
Malay slow cooking with coconut and lemon grass and Chinese fast frying. Most famous and widely available is *laksa*, not the hot, red spicy sour stuff from
Penang but a mellow thick creamy soup, full of coconut and mildly spiced. It is sold
in most hawker centres and food courts.

Another influence on cooking in this area is the legacy of the Portuguese who settled
here and intermarried. Try the spicy, seafood-based dishes like 'devil curry' at the
restaurants at Medan Portugis. For a cheap and good meal, visit the permanent stalls
along Jalan Merdeka (or 'Bandar Hills' by the locals), which used to be the waterfront.

PERANAKAN   **Seri Nyonya $$$** Equatorial Hotel, tel: (06) 282-8333. Superb
food in Peranakan-style restaurant.

Heeren House $ 1, Jalan Tun Cheng Lock, tel: (06) 281-4241.
Coffee shop in Peranakan-style guesthouse. Peranakan and
Portuguese dishes. Good breakfast, closed Mondays.

PORTUGUESE   **Restoran de Lisbon $$** Medan Portugis. Good seafood and
devil curry. Bands most night and cultural dances in the square.

San Pedro $$ 4, Jalan D'Aranjo. Portuguese seafood dishes
served in an intimate atmosphere.

INDIAN   **Selvan $** on main junction of Jalan Bandaraya and Jalan
Bandahara. Very busy banana leaf restaurant serving vegetarian
and meat curries, dosa and roti.

Restoran Vazhai $ 40 A, Jalan Munshi Abdullah. Small, elderly
banana leaf restaurant. Good dosa for a light breakfast.

OTHER   **Bamboo Hut $–$$** Jalan Kota, part of the Aldy Hotel. Breezy,
laid-back joint with local and Western food.

Geographer's Café $–$$ Jalan Hang Jebat. Good choice of
local dishes and pizzas and a satisfying intrepid-explorer kind of
character to this popular haunt.

HIGHLIGHTS In the old city is the beautiful **Stadhuys**, which houses a number of museums today. It was built between 1641 and 1660 by the Dutch in a very different style from much later British colonial buildings. It is the only Dutch building in the East that is painted red and is also believed to be the oldest, open Sat–Thur 0900–1800, closed 1245–1445. The ethnography section is the most interesting, with its displays on the ceremonies and customs of Melaka's ethnic groups from the Babas and Nyonyas, the Chittys and the Portuguese, to the dominant culture of the Malays.

SIR STAMFORD RAFFLES

By the early 19th century Melaka was past its prime as a trading post and the governor, Mr Farquar, decided it would be a good idea to abandon Melaka and to blow up the walls rather than have a rival empire make use of them. The walls were 4.5 m thick and 18 m high, so this was no easy task. He was halfway through the job, sending huge pieces of masonry sky high, when Sir Stamford Raffles, then a minor secretary in Penang, intervened. He persuaded his government not to abandon Melaka and the explosions stopped, but much of the damage had been done.

Close by and just as red is **Christ Church**, made from real Dutch pink bricks and not just painted. Built as a Dutch reformed church to commemorate 100 years of Dutch rule, it was made Anglican by the British. The bell tower, porch and vestry are later English additions. The 15-m-long ceiling beams were each cut from a single tree. Open Sun–Fri 0900–1700.

The **People's Museum ($)** on Jalan Kota has exhibits on local economic development and a more interesting section about international ideas of beauty. This includes mutilations practised for vanity, such as foot binding, piercing, neck rings and scarification as well as cosmetic surgery. A strange display but worth a look. Open Sat–Thur 0900–1800; closed 1245–1445.

THE MALACCA CLUB

The early 20th century saw the opening of a fine new club for the white rulers of the settlement and their wives and daughters. Carriages, and later automobiles, pulled up in front of the padang where games of bowls and cricket regularly took place. Planters fresh from upstation would drop in to pick up the gossip and do a bit of trade while they sipped their stengahs. Later still, famous world travellers would call in and gather ideas for their next novel, like Somerset Maugham who set his short story 'Footprints in the Jungle' partly in the building.

The stone archway of **Porta de Santiago** is all that remains of extensive Portuguese fortifications. Once, a four-walled fort here running along the bank of the river protected the Portuguese settlement. There was a four-storey-high keep, 120 big guns protecting the walls, and inside were palaces,

THE LEGEND OF HANG TUAH

According to the Malay poem *Hikayat Hang Tuah*, Hang Tuah and his three companions were martial arts experts who in the 17th century saved the life of the prime minister. They were awarded positions in the Malay court and pledged themselves to the service of the sultan. Hang Tuah became very influential and as a court official was awarded his own special *kris* (knife) which was said to have magical powers.

Like all closed communities jealousy set in and rumours began that Hang Tuah had seduced one of the sultan's wives. The Bendahara whose life he had saved hid Hang Tuah away and put it about that Hang Tuah had been executed. When Hang Tuah's friend, Hang Jebat, heard of his death he ran amok, killing people and could not be stopped. When the sultan's life was threatened Hang Tuah came out of hiding and a terrible battle raged between the two friends, ending in Hang Jebat's death.

Hang Jebat's mausoleum is in Jalan Kampung kull, while Hang Tuah's soul is in a well on the road to Muar. He is said to appear from time to time in the form of a white crocodile which only the holy can see.

schools, hospitals, and churches including St Paul's – the remains of which can be seen on the hill. The walls were never impregnated. The Portuguese gave the fort up to the Dutch, who extended it. When the British arrived in the 19th century they blew it up rather than maintain an expensive colony here. Through the gateway and up the steps is what remains of **St Paul's Church**. The first church on this site was built by the Portuguese in 1521 on the site of a sultan's palace. St Francis Xavier preached in this Catholic church before the Dutch made it Protestant and named it St Paul's. The British built their own churches and made the old building into a weapons store. Today you can walk among the ruins and admire the headstones. The empty tomb in the church once held the body of St Francis Xavier.

The **Malacca Sultanate Palace ($)** is more attractive from the outside. This wooden replica palace was built according to the description in the *Malay Amnals (Sejarah Melayn)* of palaces in the 15th century. Inside are dioramas and information about the structure of the sultan's court. One interesting display tells the story of Hang Tuah and his group of Malay musketeers who went around doing good deeds and serving the sultan. Open Sat–Thur 0900–1800, closed 1245–1445.

Close to the Sultanate Palace is the **Memorial of the Proclamation of Independence, $,** open Sat–Thur 0900–1800. Closed 1245–1445. This very British-looking building was once the exclusive Malacca Club and

THE FLORA DEL MAR

This Portuguese ship sank off Melaka loaded with tons of gold in the early 16th century. It has never been found, or at least no one has ever claimed to have found it. Its cargo is estimated to be worth about US$9 billion.

it is fitting that it should hold exhibits on the Malaysians' struggle for independence. The 'M' on all four sides stands for 'Merdeka' or 'Independence' in the Malay Language. Outside is a 1957 Chevrolet used in the elections of that year.

The **Maritime Museum** in Jalan Laksamana next to the river is a reconstruction of a Portuguese ship the *Flora Del Mar*. Inside are displays of spices that the ship carried and models of other ships, as well as bits and pieces salvaged over the years. Across the street is **The Royal Malaysian Navy Museum**, which has salvaged items from the *Diana*, which sank in the shallow waters of Melaka in 1817. The ship was salvaged in 1993 and huge quantities of pottery were recovered.

The streets of **Chinatown**, the roads around Jalan Tun Cheng Lock, Jalan Hang Jebat, Jalan Tengkera and the roads between are a living museum to the history of the people who lived here. Jalan Tun Cheng Lock is full of the life of the Babas and Nyonyas, who built these shop-houses and lived in them. The houses along Jalan Tengkera were designed with the fronts narrower than the backs because housing taxes were paid according to the width of the front door.

The **Baba and Nyonya Heritage Museum ($$)** at nos 48 and 50 is a faithfully reconstructed Peranakan home. Built in 1896 in the Chinese Palladian style, it has Roman pillars, Chinese roof tiles and ornate Malay-style carved shutters. Inside are furniture, clothes, porcelain and old photographs of the family that lived here. Inside is an internal courtyard open to the sky where water was collected in a little pool. Open daily 1000–1230, 1400–1600. Admission includes a very informative tour of the house.

Still in Chinatown, the **Cheng Hoon Teng Temple** in Jalan Tokong is probably the oldest in Malaysia. Its name means the Evergreen Cloud Temple and it is dedicated to Kuan Yin, one of the acolytes of the Lord Buddha who subsequently entered the pantheon of Taoist deities. Originally built in 1646, all the materials used in its construction were imported from China.

Inside, beside Kuan Yin is Tin Hau, the Goddess of Seafarers. In front of the two deities worshippers tip out little pots of *chim* (bamboo sticks) to see what their future holds; the way the sticks fall indicates the future. In the courtyard, huge incinerators burn offerings to ancestors, usually 'hell money' sent to them so that they pay their way in heaven.

Opposite this temple is another – a more modern temple dedicated to the Lord Buddha. In the shops around here you can see paper products that people burn to send to their ancestors. The paper windmills are blessed by the priests and are taken home. As the wind turns them the house is blessed.

In the same street is the **Masjid Kampung Kling**, built in 1748 in the Sumatran style, with a tiered roof rather than the typical onion dome. Both the roof tiles and the minaret are reminiscent of Chinese architecture, and the tiles around the water baths are European. An English chandelier hangs in the prayer hall. You may not enter the prayer hall itself but it is possible to stand in the courtyard if your shoulders are covered.

Another mosque nearby in Jalan Kampung Pantai is the **Masjid Kampung Hulu**, the oldest mosque in Malaysia, built in 1728. It too has a pagoda style minaret.

St Peter's Church in Jalan Tun Sri Lanang was built in 1710 during the Dutch occupation, but by Portuguese settlers. Their original church, Christ Church, was then Protestant and until this time all Catholic worship had been banned. It is a quiet place, unused except at Easter when the Portuguese community celebrate Good Friday.

MELAKA'S PORTUGUESE CUISINE

Very much Malay in style, the cooking of the Portuguese relies on the typical Malaysian flavourings of lemon grass and chilli as well as candlenuts and coconut milk. Vinegar, onions, ginger and star anise give the food its distinctive flavour. The famous devil curry gets its peculiar taste from the ground, fried spices in which the meat is slowly cooked. Another type of Portuguese curry, *curry seku*, is drier with the meat baked in the sauce.

In the new roads beside Mahkota Parade is the **Jade Museum**, a private collection of about 200 pieces of jade. Some of them are over 2000 years old and include carved mythical creatures, drinking vessels and even a large phallic symbol drinking cup used by newlyweds. The collection is changed regularly from a larger collection of thousands of pieces. You need to be deeply interested in old jade to visit as the entrance fee is a steep RM20.

Medan Portugis, 3 km east of town, was created in 1933 for the descendants of the first European settlers in Melaka. Unlike the Dutch, the Portuguese intermarried with the local Malay people and a cross-cultural community evolved just as the Peranakan had. The Portuguese in Melaka have their own language, their own cooking style and traditional dances, which owe much to the culture of Portugal.

Today, there are only about 500 people of Portuguese descent living in the medan. The modern square only dates back only to 1985 and survives because of its attraction to tourists. There are regular dance performances in the square and several restaurants serving Portuguese/Malay food. Bus nos 17 and 25 go to the square.

SHOPPING   Melaka is famous for its **antique shops** along Jalan Hang Jebat (Jonkers Street) and the adjacent streets. There are some genuine antiques here but most of them are huge old pieces of furniture badly in need of restoration. The smaller 'antique' shops sell craft items from Malaysia, Thailand and Indonesia at quite high prices, but you can haggle if there is something you really like.

Along the streets here are art galleries such as **Malaqa House**, 70 Jalan Tun Cheng Lock, decorated like a Peranakan home and selling some beautiful but expensive things. **Orangutan**, 59 Lorong Hang Jelat (www.charlescham.com), has original T-shirts and paintings and is definitely worth a look. **Mahkota Parade** is the town's modern shopping mall, with a large department store.

NIGHTLIFE   The **Sound and Light Show** near the Porta de Santiago is held nightly at 2030. It is quite a powerful event, illuminating the ruins and telling the story of the history of Melaka. The show lasts 1 hr and costs RM10. There is live music and free pick-up for the **Rock and Roll Grill**, Jalan Taman Melaka, tel: (06) 284-9652.

TOURS   There are daily river trips through the city, which depart from behind the tourist office. They go past old warehouses to kampung Morten, a Malay-style area with old houses. The tours last 45 mins and depart at 1100, 1200 and 1300, but only leaves kampung if there are at least six passengers.

PENINSULAR MALAYSIA

EXCURSIONS **Ayer Keroh**, 12 km north of town, is a tourist development aimed at locals. The **zoo ($)** is popular with children and has some rare Asian creatures such as Malayan sun bears and rhinos from Sumatra. Nearby is a **crocodile farm ($)**, the largest in the country according to the tourist literature. The collection includes albinos and hunchbacks, although you have to wonder if the hunches are due to cramped conditions rather than genetics.

PULAU BESAR

Five kilometres off the coast of Melaka, Pulau Besar is a pretty island with pleasant beaches and wooded hills, which can be explored. The island has a few historic graves and reminders of the Japanese occupation. It has resort hotels and a golf course, and like Malaysia's other islands is most easily accessed by booking a trip with one of the resorts. It is accessed from Umbai, 10 km south-east of Melaka. (See p. 369 for details of the ferry.)

More worthwhile is the **Orang Asli Museum ($)** containing artefacts and displays on the culture of the indigenous people. The **Air Keroh Recreational Forest** is the best reason to go to Ayer Keroh and has well signposted trails going off into the secondary forest. Cabins can be rented for an overnight stay and there is a campsite.

Taman Mini Malaysia and **Mini Asean ($)** has reconstructions of the various styles of houses common in Malaysia and its ASEAN neighbours. Like the forest park it is worth the trip.

Last but by no means least is the **Butterfly Farm ($$)** with 200 local species of butterfly, including the Rajah Brooke, a huge creature, and the birdwing butterfly, another king-sized lepidoptera. The farm also has a collection of snakes, stick insects, spiders and other creatures that children love.

TANJUNG BIDARA Twenty-five kilometres north-west of Melaka on the road to Port Dickson is this pleasant and as yet unspoiled beach, a little dirty from the passing tankers but with lots of hawker stalls along the shore. A large part of the beach is taken up by the Tanjung Bidara Beach Resort but there is still plenty of room for everyone. Bus nos 51, 42 and 18.

Tanjung Bidara Beach Resort $$$$, tel: (06) 384-2990, swimming pool, tennis courts and restaurant. **Bidara Beach Lodge $$,** 78 Lorong Haji Abdullah, tel: (06) 384-3340.

WHERE NEXT?

Pulau Besar, a small island about 5 km south-east of Melaka, is a popular getaway spot for those seeking powder-white sands and fringing palm trees. Easily reached by boat from the jetty on Jalan Kota in Melaka, the island makes a pleasant day trip – though it's also possible to stay overnight at the well-equipped Pandanusa Resort (tel: 281-8007).

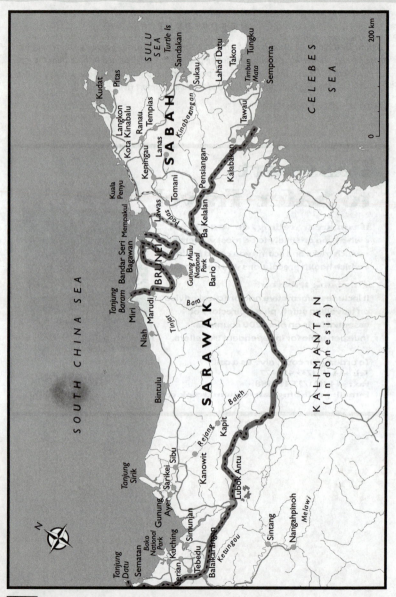

SARAWAK AND SABAH, EAST MALAYSIA

The two east Malaysian states of Sarawak and Sabah, occupying a small part of the island of Borneo, up in the north, are separated from mainland Malaysia by hundreds of miles of sea. The distance between east and peninsular Malaysia, though, is far more than one of nautical miles. They are also divided by history, culture and geography. The result is an almost unique destination and one of the world's best-kept secrets in terms of natural wildlife habitats.

Sarawak served as the personal fiefdom of the Brooke family from the 1840s until the outbreak of World War II in 1939. Sabah also had a separate identity because it was owned lock, stock and barrel by the British North Borneo Chartered Company from 1880 until the war. Both states have a rich variety of ethnic groups. Malays are just one of many minorities that include Ibans, Bidayuhs, Chinese, Kadazans, Bajaus, Filipinos and a host of smaller tribes, like the forest-dwelling nomads called the Penans.

The unique lifestyle of the Penans has been virtually destroyed by a combination of logging and government inducements to abandon the forest, but other cultural groups have been more successful in preserving aspects of their traditional way of life. Visiting an ethnic tribe and spending a night or two in their longhouses is one of the highlights of a visit to Sarawak.

Underlying the separate history and culture of Borneo is a distinctive geography characterised by mighty rivers, jungle and forest, which offer unique travel opportunities for the intrepid tourist. A visit to Sarawak and Sabah requires a bit more organisation and advance planning than peninsular Malaysia, Thailand or Singapore, but the rewards are more than compensation for anyone with an interest in activity holidays, nature and wildlife. Transport costs are not high, and while the cost of tours needs budgeting for there are still great places, like Mount Kinabalu and Bako National Park, that can be visited independently and without great expense.

EAST MALAYSIA: OUR CHOICE

Sarawak
Kuching
Kuching town
Bako National Park
Sarawak Museum

Kelabit Highlands
Trekking from Bario

Mulu National Park

Sabah
Climbing Mt Kinabalu

Kota Kinabalu
Tunku Abdul Rahman
National Park

Sandakan
Sepilok Orang-Utan Centre
Turtle Island
Kinabatangan River

HOW MUCH YOU CAN SEE IN A ...

Sarawak
WEEK (7 DAYS)
Days 1–2: Kuching
Days 3–4: Bako National Park
Days 5–7: Santubong peninsula

FORTNIGHT (14 DAYS)
Days 1–7: As above, for one week
Second week: Miri, fly to Mulu National Park and on to Bario for a jungle trek

MONTH (28 DAYS)
Days 1–14: As above, for a fortnight
Weeks 3–4: Travel on to Sabah, via Brunei

HOW MUCH YOU CAN SEE IN A ...

Sabah
WEEK (7 DAYS)
Days 1–2: Kota Kinabalu
Days 3–5: Climb Mt Kinabalu
Days 6–7: Santubong peninsula

FORTNIGHT (14 DAYS)
Days 1–7: As above, for one week
Second week: fly on to Miri, visit Mulu National Park before continuing on to Bario and a trek in the Kelabit Highlands

MONTH (28 DAYS)
Days 1–14: As above, for a fortnight
Weeks 3–4: Travel on to Sarawak, via Brunei

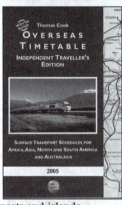

SARAWAK

Malaysia's largest state can seem like another country. On arrival you need to fill out a separate immigration form and have your passport stamped. This act of officialdom reflects the cultural independence of Sarawak. Islam is a minority religion here and the state has a distinct geographical identity as a part of Borneo. Historical sights and sandy beaches are secondary to Sarawak's wildlife and national parks, while the state's indigenous cultural groups are a major reason for leaving peninsular Malaysia and flying to the state capital of Kuching. More than 30 per cent of the population are **Ibans**, the famed headhunters of a bygone era and now a remarkably laid-back and friendly people who live throughout the state. Most still live in longhouses and earn a living as farmers. The **Malays** make up 20 per cent of the population, and along with the **Melanau** (6 per cent), mostly live along the coastal area, as opposed to the **Bidayuh** people (8 per cent) who are found inland. Around 30 per cent are **Chinese** people, found in all major towns. The various other indigenous tribes, including the endangered **Penan**, who were once all nomadic forest dwellers, are referred to generally as the **Orang Ulus**.

AN UNLIKELY HISTORY

From the 14th century Sarawak was part of the powerful kingdom of Brunei, but by the 18th century there were signs of discontent from the Malay population. Malays had first moved north from Kalimantan (the main land mass of Borneo, now part of Indonesia) into Sarawak around 200 years earlier and now, as Brunei's power started to wane, they flexed their muscle. In 1836 the Sultan of Brunei sent his uncle to quell disorder and protect the valuable trade in *serawak*, the Malay word for antimony.

James Brooke sailed into this volatile situation in 1839. Brooke was an English adventurer keen to emulate Raffles' achievement in Singapore. When the sultan's uncle offered him the title of Raja (ruler) of Sarawak in return for crushing the Malay rebels he jumped at the chance, and an astonishing offshoot of Britain's colonial conquests began. Brooke gradually acquired more and more territory by slaughtering the native Ibans so that by the time he died in 1867 he owned more than half of what is now Sarawak.

His nephew, Charles Brooke, took over the title in 1863 and before he died in 1916 he passed the throne to his son, Charles Vyner Brooke, who held power until the Japanese rudely interrupted this imperial idyll in 1941. Britain took over after the war, in acrimonious circumstances, and remained in charge even after Malaya's independence in 1957. It was 1963 before the state became part of the federation of Malaysia.

Transport within Sarawak is different from peninsular Malaysia. Malaysian Airlines internal flights and submarine-like river boats are the main forms of long distance travel. Over-land routes are possible but very time consuming; internal flights are affordable. Travellers also usually find themselves using tour operators as they offer the best way of getting to some of the most interesting places.

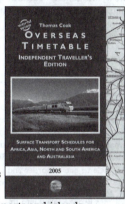

SARAWAK

Malaysia's largest state can seem like another country. On arrival you need to fill out a separate immigration form and have your passport stamped. This act of official-dom reflects the cultural independence of Sarawak. Islam is a minority religion here and the state has a distinct geographical identity as a part of Borneo. Historical sights and sandy beaches are secondary to Sarawak's wildlife and national parks, while the state's indigenous cultural groups are a major reason for leaving peninsular Malaysia and flying to the state capital of Kuching. More than 30 per cent of the population are **Ibans**, the famed headhunters of a bygone era and now a remarkably laid-back and friendly people who live throughout the state. Most still live in longhouses and earn a living as farmers. The **Malays** make up 20 per cent of the population, and along with the **Melanau** (6 per cent), mostly live along the coastal area, as opposed to the **Bidayuh** people (8 per cent) who are found inland. Around 30 per cent are **Chinese** people, found in all major towns. The various other indigenous tribes, including the endangered **Penan,** who were once all nomadic forest dwellers, are referred to generally as the **Orang Ulus**.

AN UNLIKELY HISTORY

From the 14th century Sarawak was part of the powerful kingdom of Brunei, but by the 18th century there were signs of discontent from the Malay population. Malays had first moved north from Kalimantan (the main land mass of Borneo, now part of Indonesia) into Sarawak around 200 years earlier and now, as Brunei's power started to wane, they flexed their muscle. In 1836 the Sultan of Brunei sent his uncle to quell disorder and protect the valuable trade in *serawak,* the Malay word for antimony.

James Brooke sailed into this volatile situation in 1839. Brooke was an English adventurer keen to emulate Raffles' achievement in Singapore. When the sultan's uncle offered him the title of Raja (ruler) of Sarawak in return for crush-ing the Malay rebels he jumped at the chance, and an astonishing offshoot of Britain's colonial conquests began. Brooke gradually acquired more and more territory by slaughtering the native Ibans so that by the time he died in 1867 he owned more than half of what is now Sarawak.

His nephew, Charles Brooke, took over the title in 1863 and before he died in 1916 he passed the throne to his son, Charles Vyner Brooke, who held power until the Japanese rudely interrupted this imperial idyll in 1941. Britain took over after the war, in acrimonious circumstances, and remained in charge even after Malaya's independence in 1957. It was 1963 before the state became part of the federation of Malaysia.

Transport within Sarawak is different from peninsular Malaysia. Malaysian Airlines internal flights and submarine-like river boats are the main forms of long distance travel. Over-land routes are possible but very time consuming; internal flights are affordable. Travellers also usually find themselves using tour operators as they offer the best way of getting to some of the most interesting places.

Despite rampant economic development over the last 10 years, Kuching retains a tangible sense of history that makes it the most unique town anywhere in Sarawak or Sabah. The town still has some quaint touches that date back to the era of the Brookes, and its multi-ethnic identity may come as a blessing if you're just arriving from the monocultural east coast of peninsular Malaysia.

Outside of Penang and Ipoh, the west side of Kuching has the best pre-war vernacular Chinese architecture in Malaysia, and there are good examples of colonial architecture as well. Kuching's many museums are nearly all worth a visit and most are free. Another good reason for lingering in Kuching is the excellent food scene, easily the best in Sarawak.

ARRIVAL AND DEPARTURE

AIR The most common route is on a Malaysian Airlines (MAS) or AirAsia flight from KL but there are also direct flights from Singapore using Singapore Airlines. The least expensive way of reaching Kuching from Singapore or the south of peninsular Malaysia is on a MAS flight from Johor Bahru. MAS in Singapore encourages this by running a direct bus from the Novotel Orchid Hotel to the Malaysian airport.

MAS have their office at Lot 215, Jalan Song Thian Cheok, tel: (082) 246-622.

Air Asia, tel: (082) 283-222, www.airasia.com, operates a daily flight between KL and Kuching. Some restrictions apply. Air Asia flights operate from the old KL Subang airport, not the new KL International.

TRANSPORT TO AND FROM THE AIRPORT Kuching International Airport, tel: (082) 454-242 or 457-373, is 11 km from town. Bus no. 8A, blue and white in colour, runs between town and the airport 0600–1935 at roughly hourly intervals. The green and cream bus no. 12A does the same run 0630–1915 on a similar schedule. These buses can be picked up near the tourist office on Main Bazaar or around the corner, outside the main post office.

East Malaysia

A coupon system operates at the airport for taxis into town. See Getting Around on p. 385 for taxis to the airport from town.

Domestic Flights MAS flies to Sibu, Miri and Bintulu in Sarawak, and Kota Kinabalu in Sabah.

Bus Long-distance buses leave from the Regional Express Bus Terminal on Penrissen Rd, 5 km south of town, reachable by local bus no. 3. There are many long-distance bus companies and the local newspaper carries the schedules, as well as the tourist office. Leaving Kuching, it is quicker to get a boat to Sibu and then a bus from there.

Borneo Highway Express, tel: (082) 461-277, and Biaramas Express, tel: (082) 452-139, run daily services from Kuching to Miri at 0630, 0900, 1300 and 1700, journey time 13 hrs.

Boat It's about 4 hrs on a high-speed boat from Kuching to Sibu, and tickets should be bought in advance at the jetty. The main company, Ekspres Bahagia, tel: (082) 410-076, has a daily departure at 0830 and the fare is RM35. Bus nos 17 and 19 from the market on Main Bazaar and no. 1C travel to the jetty at Pending, 6 km out of town.

Orientation Kuching is mostly spread out along the south side of the Sarawak River in a schizophrenic manner. The west side of town has all the history, the main museum, and bus stations, while the east side has modern hotels and shopping centres. A riverside road, with a promenade for part of the way, connects the two halves of the city and the distance is easily walkable.

The north side of the river is not very developed but it does house Fort Margherita (currently closed due to renovation work) and the **Cat Museum**.

MAPS

There is one excellent, free colour map available from the Visitors' Information Centre, entitled *Sarawak & Kuching*, that is well worth getting hold of. As well as providing a good overall map of Sarawak and a detailed street map of Kuching, it also contains inset maps of the Kuching area, Damai, Sibu, Kapit, Miri and Bintulu.

Colour Section

(i) Climbing Mount Kinabalu, Sabah; Mount Kinabalu in its forest setting

(ii) Danum Valley canopy walkway; orang-utan; traditional Malay house

(iii) Singapore skyline at dusk

(iv) Traditional Chinese actor, Singapore

INFORMATION

RAINFOREST MUSIC FESTIVAL

Kuching is particularly famous for its Rainforest World Music Festival, held every year in July or August. Featuring musicians from all over the world, it's also an ideal place to hear local musicians holding forth. It's held at the Sarawak Cultural Village (p. 396) where it's also possible to visit a number of different styles of long-houses. Check out the website for details: www.rainforestmusic-borneo.com.

i If only all tourist offices in Malaysia were like those in Sarawak and Sabah. Kuching has two exemplary **tourist offices**, both centrally located and full of useful information. The **Visitors' Information Centre**, tel: (082) 410-944, Padang Merdeka, opposite the Merdeka Palace Hotel, is open Mon–Fri 0800–1800, Sat 0800–1600 and Sun 0900–1500. www.sarawaktourism.com.

The **National Parks and Wildlife office**, tel: (082) 248-088, fax: (082) 256-301, for booking accommodation at Bako, is in the same building.

The **Sarawak Tourist Association** (STA) Main Bazaar, tel: (082) 240-620, is open Mon–Thur 0800–1245 and 1400–1615, Fri 0800–1130 and 1430–1615 and Sat 0800–1245. There is also a small Visitors' Information Centre, at the airport, tel: (082)-450-944.

Tourism Malaysia has an office on Jalan Song Thian Cheok, tel: (082) 246-575, only worth a visit if you need information on Sabah or peninsular Malaysia.

From the tourist offices and hotels look for a free copy of *The Official Kuching Guide*, packed with useful and reasonably accurate information on accommodation, places to eat and local tours. Daily video shows are run at the Information Centre at 1000 and 1500.

The **immigration office**, tel: (082) 245-661, is part of the government offices on Jalan Simpang Tiga, 4 km south of town on the road to the airport, which can be reached by bus nos 8, 8A, 8B, 11, 14, 14A, 14B or by taxi.

GETTING AROUND

Most places of interest in Kuching can be visited on foot, and those that can't can be reached by public bus. There are five bus companies, each with differently coloured buses. The Visitors' Information Centre dispenses a useful map of the town with all the relevant destinations reachable by bus and their colours, fares and schedules listed on the back. There is no central bus terminal.

Kuching has taxis but hailing them down on the street is not common because they are only empty when returning from somewhere. Instead, taxis gather at the open-air market at the end of Gambier Rd, the long-distance bus station and the big hotels at the east end of town.

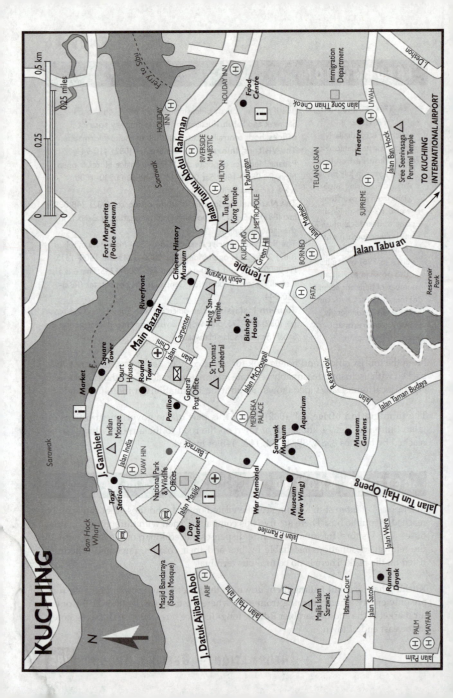

Car rental is available through various companies, including Pronto, tel: (082) 236-889, fax: (082) 236-889, Mayflower, tel: (082) 410-110, fax: (082) 410-115, and Wah Tung, tel: (082) 248-888, fax: (082) 646-900. Some have desks at the airport. Expect to pay around RM120 to RM140 per day.

A TOWN WALK This walk takes in many of Kuching's places of interest and begins outside the Sarawak Tourist Association office on Main Bazaar. Take the cross-river **sampan ($)** from the jetty along the waterfront. The fare is payable on leaving. From where the boat pulls in on the other side of the river, it is a short walk to **Fort Margherita**, built by Charles Brooke in 1879 on the site of an original fort built by his father, which was burnt down by Chinese miners. The fort is an interesting police museum with assorted memorabilia and well worth a visit. Open Mon–Fri, 0800–1230, 1400–1630.

From outside the tourist office, pause to look at the splendid examples of **Chinese shop-house architecture** across the road. Resist the temptation to cross because this walk will bring you to them later. Instead, with your back to the tourist office, turn right and walk along Jalan Gambier with its historic buildings from the 1920s and '30s and the town's fish market. The sacks of dried fish, spices and rice and flour spilling out onto the pavement hark back to the time when merchants set up shop here to be close to the river where boats unloaded their cargoes.

On reaching the busy junction and taxi station, turn left and first left again into pedestrianised **Jalan India**. Despite the name, this street is unmistakably Chinese and there is often a Chinese medicine 'stall' spread across the pavement. Notice how prominent the Chinese characters on the shop signs are; in peninsular Malaysia they are not allowed to be written large. Notice, too, the Muslim restaurants and money-changer on the left.

At the end of Jalan India, walk across Jalan Barrack and through the **Courthouse**, first built by Charles Brooke as his lawcourt and still fulfilling that judicial function today. It is an elegant structure that uses its space to create maximum shade, with a memorial to Brooke outside that was added in 1924. The bronze panels at the bottom are in recognition of the state's four main ethnic groups: Ibans, Chinese, Malays and Orang Ulu.

From the other side of the Courthouse from where you entered the impressive **General Post Office** on Jalan Haji Openg is clearly visible. Built in 1931, its neo-classical and imperious style was presumably chosen by the last rajah, Vyner Brooke, to express the power of the white man. The building opposite, the **Pavilion**, has been undergoing renovation for years. It was originally a hospital and then the education department before being used by the occupying Japanese as an 'information bureau'.

Cross the road and head down **Jalan Carpenter** with its unmistakably Chinese gold-smiths and pawnshops and a colourful Chinese temple on the right. Some of the shops are worth nosing into, particularly the one on the left selling old coins from the Brooke era and banknotes from the Japanese occupation. At the junction with Jalan Chini, with the temple-like facade of the Kuching Hainese Association across the road, turn left and walk up Jalan Chini to the craft shops on Main Bazaar. If you turn right at the top into Main Bazaar, the shops are in the order they appear below.

SHOPPING

SHOPPING ON MAIN BAZAAR **Galleri M**, 26 Main Bazaar (and in the lobby of the Hilton hotel), has the sort of tribal artefacts that will be seen in every shop on Main Bazaar, plus paintings and prints. Next door, **Bong Gallery** has some Chinese work in amongst the chiefly Iban craftwork. There are some great wooden frames and a shipping service can be arranged. Next door is a more regular souvenir shop with colourful T-shirts, batik and Penan-style basketry.

Kelvin's Gallery, at no. 32, is perhaps a little pricier but bargaining might iron out the differences. **Arts of Dyaks** at no. 34 is a friendly little shop with reasonable prices. Further along, at the corner with Jalan Bishopgate, a shop retails jars of Sarawak peppers, sago biscuits and laksa mixes. At no. 57, **Sin Ching Loong** has a good selection of inexpensive batik from Indonesia as well as fabrics from Malaysia.

By the time all these shops have been checked out, it will be a time for a drink and a gourmet sandwich in the old Chinese coffee shop now converted into **Denis' Place**.

All of these shops are closed on Sunday.

CAT MUSEUM

Petra Jaya, north of the river, free, open daily 0900–1700, tel: (082) 446-688. Kuching has a thing about cats, as this museum shows. A motley and modern set of exhibits looking at cats from all angles. There are stuffed cats, cats in music, cats in ancient Egypt, cats in theatre posters, cats in medieval society... Bus nos 6 and 2B will take you there.

HIGHLIGHTS

The **Sarawak Museum,** which claims to be the best museum in South-East Asia, is spread out in two buildings on Jalan Tun Abang Haji Openg. Admission is free, open daily 0900–1800. For up-to-date information on current exhibitions, tel: (6082) 244 232, check the website, www.museum.sarawak.gov.my/main.htm, or e-mail webmaster@museum.sarawak.gov.my.

The museum was inspired by the socialist scientist Alfred Russell Wallace (1823–1913) whose travels in this part of the world led him to develop the theory of evolution by natural selection. It was his letter to Darwin announcing his theory that scared the more famous scientist into finally publishing his own views.

The **old wing** is the original museum, with the floor on street level devoted to stuffed animals and birds and the floor above largely given over to a re-created longhouse (complete with authentic shrunken skulls) and a room packed with ethnographic artefacts. Look for the Melanau *blum* images and the description that explains their purpose, though the pagan totem-like ceremonial poles are the most dramatic exhibits.

The **new wing**, or Dewan Tun Abdul Razak (Tun Abdul Razak Hall), formerly used as the State Legislative Assembly and as a banqueting hall, became part of the museum in 1982. After renovation work, the new wing reopened in 2003 and now houses temporary exhibitions and the Museum Shop and Café.

The **Islamic Museum**, Jalan P Ramlee, is accessible from the new wing of the Sarawak Museum, free, open Sat–Thur 0900–1800. Seven galleries, each with a separate theme, set about a central courtyard. More interesting than anything comparable in peninsular Malaysia and well worth a visit.

Chinese History Museum, on the waterfront, free, open Sat–Thur 0900–1800, tel: (082) 231-520. Built in 1912 as a courtroom for the Chinese (spot the scales of justice over the entrance), this is another great little museum covering all the immigrant groups: Cantonese, Chao Ann, Foochew Hainan, Hokkien, Luichew and Teochew.

ACCOMMODATION

Borneo Hotel $$–$$$ 30 C-F Jalan Tabuan, tel: (082) 244-122, fax: (082) 254-848. Large rooms with air-con, TV and telephone.

Telang Usan Hotel $$–$$$ Ban Hock Rd, tel: (082) 415-588, fax: (082) 425-316, e-mail: tusan@po.jaring.my. Famously friendly hotel with laundry service, safety deposit boxes, café and Chinese restaurant.

Fata Hotel $$ Jalan McDougall, tel: (082) 248-111, fax: (082) 428-987. Air-con, TV, telephone and laundry service available.

Orchid Inn $$ 2 Jalan Green Hill, tel: (082) 411-417, fax: (082) 241-635. Situated at the east end of town and close to some good places to eat.

B&B Inn $ 30–1 Jalan Tabuan, tel: (082) 237-366, fax: (082) 239-189, e-mail: gohyp@po.jaring.my. Dorms and rooms with fan or air-con. Central, well run and helpful to travellers.

Tai Pan $ Jalan Ban Hock, tel: (082) 417-363. A small but comfortable set-up with good-value rooms, including air-con.

FOOD AND DRINK

Ristorante Beccari $$$$ Merdeka Palace Hotel, Jalan Tun Haji Openg, tel: (082) 258-000. Elegant restaurant, excellent Italian food.

Steak House $$$$ at the Hilton Hotel has top quality European food. The hotel also has Kuching's best pastry outlet.

Denis' Place $–$$$ 80 Main Bazaar. Sandwiches, salads and steaks. Good coffees, happy hour for beer 1600–1800.

Benson Seafood $$ east of the Holiday Inn. Great place for an al fresco seafood meal. All the fish are on the display. Prawns are a speciality but also try the 'bamboo snails'.

Cat City $$ Taman Sri Sarawak Mall, tel: (082) 243-699. Live music every night, pool tables, happy hour from 1700 until the music starts at 2200.

The Royalist $$ Taman Sri Sarawak Mall, opposite the car park of the Hilton hotel. An English-style pub, named after the ship that brought James Brook (and beer) to Borneo, with a jolly atmosphere and a happy hour that starts daily at 1700 and lasts until 0100 (later at weekends).

Hornbill's Corner Café $–$$ Jalan Ban Hock, tel: (082) 252-670. The steamboat barbecue is an eat-all-you-can affair, soccer by satellite, and a good atmosphere in the open-air bar. Open daily from 1700 till after midnight.

National Islamic Café $ Jalan Carpenter. Been here for as long as I can remember and still serving excellent vegetable biryani and idli, as well as chicken and murtabak dishes. Airy and clean.

Briyani Café $ opposite the tourist office on Main Bazaar, serves similar Muslim food.

Malaya Restaurant, Jubilee and **Abdul Rashid $** are a cluster of restaurants on Jalan India that are always reliable for an inexpensive meal.

FOOD CENTRES

For sheer value for money and freshly cooked food, it is hard to beat Kuching's food centres.

Open Air Market $ Jalan Market. Not open-air, good selection of Malay and Chinese food.

Top Spot Food Centre $ Jalan Bukit Mata Kuching. Open-air, on top floor of a car park, with a wide range of Malay and Chinese food.

Taman Sri Food Centre $ behind Parkson Department store at Crowne Plaza Riverside hotel. Block of Malay and Chinese foodstalls popular with office workers during the day. At night the little cafés and bars around here come alive (see above).

ORGANISED TOURS

Joining a tour at some stage is fairly inevitable in Sarawak, because a visit to a long-house and to some of the parks (although not Bako) is a lot more practicable this way. Eco-tourism is a familiar oxymoron that pops up in some of the brochures but the good news is that many of the tour companies are sophisticated and reliable operations, and one or two are clued up about the ecological and cultural implications of mass tourism.

The downside is what tends to be an inverse relationship between the quality of the experience and the cost of the tour. The least expensive ones involve short visits to commercialised longhouses that are hardly worth it; the time would be better spent looking at the ethnographic exhibits in the Sarawak Museum. Expect to pay around RM50 for a city tour, around RM150 for day trip to a local longhouse, and a minimum of RM300 for a two-day/one-night trip involving a stay in a longhouse. A more interesting visit to less touristy longhouses will cost more. (See p. 404 for more on visits to longhouses.)

Singai Travel Service, Lot 257 Jalan Chan Chin Ann, tel: (082) 420-918, fax: (082) 258-320, www.singai.com. This is probably the most responsible tour company in Sarawak. While they offer standard city tours and local excursions they also organise programmes covering traditional Chinese medicine, therapy massage, *feng shui*, acupuncture, and Malay and Indian cooking. Their longhouse tours last from half a day to four or five days, and they also run safari-type treks on foot or by car, river safaris and trips to Mulu Caves, Sibu, Miri and Sabah.

Borneo Adventure, 55 Main Bazaar, tel: (082) 245-175, fax: (082) 422-626, www.borneoadventure.com. This well-established company has gained a reputation for some of its longhouse trips.

WHERE NEXT?

Across the Sarawak River to the north-west of town there are numerous Malay villages or kampong, often on stilts, best reached by boat from Jalan Gambier. It's a different and very typically Malay world of small shops, fishing vessels, mosques and houses all linked by wooden walkways, and makes a fascinating excursion.

AROUND KUCHING

Service	🚌	🚌	⛴	🚌
Days of operation	Daily	Daily	Daily	Daily
Special notes	A	B	C	D
Kuching.................d.	A	B	C	D
Santubong ....a.	A			
Damai.....................a.	A			
Bako National Park......a.	....	B	C	
Serian ....a.	....	....	....	D

Special notes:
A–Regular service. Journey time 40 minutes.
B–Regular service. Journey time 45 minutes.
C–Regular service. Journey time 30 minutes.
D–Regular service. Journey time 1 hour.

Kuching is an excellent base for experiencing what Sarawak has to offer and this route offers a choice of different kinds of trips. Bako National Park, one of the best destinations for nature lovers anywhere in South-East Asia, is very easy to visit from Kuching. Santubong and Damai make up a different kind of attraction, constituting as they do a relatively expensive tourist area of the package-holiday type. The Sarawak Cultural Village is worth a visit by anyone new to the cultural and ethnic diversity of east Malaysia, but staying at the plush hotels without your own transport does tend to keep you confined to the peninsula. All the tour agents in town handle trips to longhouses in the vicinity and this is another highlight of any extended stay in Kuching.

GETTING THERE

BAKO NATIONAL PARK

The first leg of the journey to Bako National Park is by bus no. 6 from near the market in Jalan Gambier to Bako Bazaar, a small fishing village. The first bus departs at 0640 and the last one back is 1700. From Bako Bazaar a boat is chartered to the national park and the cost is RM30, which will have to be paid in full if no one else is on the boat. Try to avoid weekends and public holidays when the park is full of visitors and all the accommodation likely to be booked up. A bus schedule is available from the tourist office.

SANTUBONG AND DAMAI

Bus no. 2B goes from near the market in Jalan Gambier to Santubong, the first departure is at 0640 and the last one back is at 1900. Each day six of the 2B buses continue on to Damai and the Sarawak Cultural Village – at 0720, 0840, 1000, 1320, 1640 and 1750. These buses depart from Damai at 0820, 0940, 1100, 1420, 1740 and 1900. A bus schedule is available from the tourist office.

CAR HIRE

Hiring a car (see p. 387) for a day would allow you to explore the Santubong peninsula and make for easy transport to the two fishing villages of Santubong and Buntal and their seafood restauraunts.

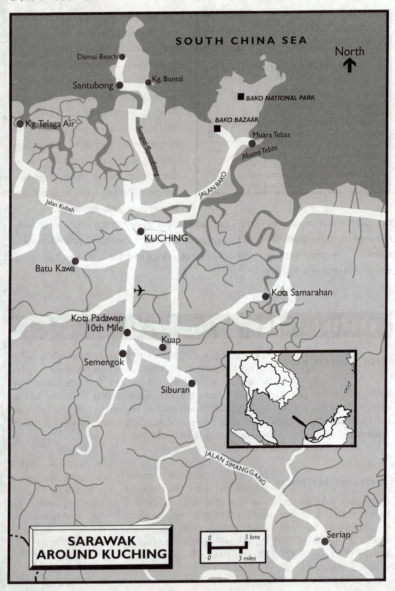

SOUTH CHINA SEA

North

Damai Beach

Kg. Buntal

Santubong

BAKO NATIONAL PARK

Kg. Telaga Air

BAKO BAZAAR

Sungai Santubong

Muara Tebas

Muara Tebas

Jalan Kubah

JALAN BAKO

KUCHING

Batu Kawa

Kota Samarahan

Kota Padawan
10th Mile

Kuap

Semengok

Siburan

JALAN SIMANGGANG

SARAWAK
AROUND KUCHING

0   5 kms

0   3 miles

Serian

All the tour companies run organised trips to Bako and Sarawak Cultural Village and there is a shuttle bus from the Holiday Inn in Kuching to the sister hotel at Damai that can be booked by non-residents.

BAKO NATIONAL PARK

A visit to Sarawak's most interesting and most accessible park is highly recommended. Day trips are possible but an overnight stay would be more rewarding. Bako contains almost every type of vegetation found in the state, including beach, mangrove, dipterocarp forest, grassland, and swamp forest.

Jungle trails access the different eco-systems and there are opportunities to see five species of **pitcher plants** as well as a variety of **wildlife**. Around the park headquarters wild bearded pigs and macaque monkeys scavenge for food, while deeper into the park look out for otters, monitor lizards and some of the 150 species of birds. The star attraction is the proboscis monkey, most likely to be seen early in the morning or at dusk. Stay overnight and you might see mouse deer, flying lemurs, bats and fireflies.

All the **walking trails** are colour-coded and easy to follow without a guide, as long as you plan to get back to park headquarters before dusk at around 1830. The **Lintang trail** is a good one to start with because it passes through all of Bako's vegetation types and pitcher plants will certainly be seen after a climb up to a barren plateau where the plants lie among the shrubs. You should be able to find *Nepenthes gracilis* hanging from trees, the pot-shaped *Nepenthes ampullaria* and the distinctive *Nepenthes rafflesiana* with red and white stripes around its bowl.

The **Telok Delima** and **Telok Pako trails** are the best places to see proboscis monkeys. A walk to the **Tajor waterfall** includes a detour to **sandy beaches**, a rare sight in Borneo and far more inviting than those at Damai.

ORIENTATION   The park headquarters, **Telok Assam**, has the park accommodation and a central office where all visitors sign in and pay a small entry fee. Free maps showing the walking trails are available and there is an information centre with displays covering the park's ecology. A slide show on Bako's wildlife is shown in the evening.

ACCOMMODATION   Park accommodation consists of Forest Lodges with two rooms with three single beds each, at RM150 or RM100 per room, sharing a bathroom. Other lodges have two single beds at RM75 or RM50 per room. Hostel rooms with four beds are RM40 or RM15 per person.

Accommodation must be booked in advance through the National Parks and Wildlife office, Padang Merdeka, Kuching, tel: (082) 248-088, fax: (082) 256-301, in the same building as the Visitors' Information Centre. Reservations may be made in advance by telephone or fax but payment must be made before the first night's stay.

FOOD There is a park café, open 0800–2100, serving adequate but dull rice and noodle dishes. Definitely consider bringing some food with you to make it a more enjoyable experience. Packed meals are necessary for lunch when out walking. Bring lots and lots of water, as well as snacks and goodies for breaks along the way.

SANTUBONG AND DAMAI

The Santubong peninsula, at the mouth of the Sarawak River, is dominated at its northern end by Mt Santubong (810 m). It has a beach at Damai which has been turned into an upmarket beach resort dominated by two Holiday Inn hotels.

The main attraction out on the peninsula is the **Sarawak Cultural Village, $$$,** open daily 0900–1730, tel: (082) 846-411, www.sarawakculturalvillage.com. It can be reached by public transport or there is a package offered by the Village for RM75, which includes transport from your hotel, entrance fee and lunch. Given that the entrance fee alone is RM45 this is quite reasonable.

The Village is a living museum, consisting of examples of Iban, Bidayuh and Melanau longhouses and other traditional habitations, with tribespeople demonstrating aspects of their lifestyle. The Penan dwelling, for example, has an animal trap, and elsewhere are displays of weaving, sago processing and basketry.

Visitors are invited to try their luck using a blow pipe, and there are scheduled performances of traditional dance with an element of audience participation, which is either good fun or plain embarrassing, depending on your point of view. Unavoidably touristy, but managed with a degree of authenticity, a visit may well whet your appetite for a trip into the interior and a night at a genuine longhouse.

Jungle treks are possible on the peninsula. There is also a marked walking trail that begins near the Holiday Inn Resort Damai Beach and takes little over ½ hr to complete. An ascent of Mount Santubong is a stiffer proposition and takes a whole day. A guide is recommended for this – enquire at the tourist office in Kuching.

🏨 **Holiday Inn Resort Damai Beach $$$** Santubong, tel: (082) 846-999, and **Holiday Inn Resort Damai Lagoon $$$** Santubong, tel: (082) 846-900. Both resorts, www.holidayinn-sarawak.com, are worth considering when promotional rates make them more affordable than you might expect.

Nanga Damai $$ Jalan Sultan Tengah, Santubong, tel: (019) 887 1017, www. nangadamai.com. Facilities such as air-con, telephone, TV and fridge available. Multi gym, pool for guests. Not suitable for small children. Twenty-minute walk from/to Damai area. Room rates include breakfast.

🍴 The **Sarawak Cultural Village restaurant $–$$** has a menu service but most visitors have the buffet at lunch time. The restaurant closes around 1700 after the last dance show. There are various restaurants at the three hotels and the one at the Holiday Inn Resort Damai Beach has been recommended. The circular **Peninsula Terrace $$$–$$$$** at the Damai Lagoon hotel overlooks the sea and there are tables outside, but only about half the seating area gives a view of the sunset.

The best food is from the seafood restaurants at Buntai, but as there is no public transport in the evenings you need a car to get home unless you are staying at one of the hotels. Typical of these restaurants is **Beach Sea Food Restaurant $$$** tel: (082) 846-701, on stilts over the water and offering a car service from the hotels. Prawn, crab, lobster and plenty of other fish feature on the menu, as well as beef, chicken and deer.

SERIAN

Although this town south-east of Kuching can be visited as a day trip from Kuching, most visitors are likely to make a stop here as part of an organised tour to a long-house on one of the tributaries of the Lupar River. Along the way, look out for the rich agricultural produce that is most of the inhabitants' livelihood. Cocoa plants are common and small pepper plantations are readily identifiable because of the way they are grown up 1.2-m sticks planted in rows close to the road.

Serian, one of the first inland settlements populated by Chinese immigrants, is full of roadside restaurants and small shops. The main point of interest, and usually included in longhouse trips taking this route, is the **food market** behind the main street.

ACCOMMODATION Accommodation usually takes the form of a night in an Iban longhouse (see p. 404) on the Lemanak or Skrang rivers, but there is one notable exception.

Hilton Batang Ai Longhouse Resort $$$$, tel: (083) 584-388, www.hilton.com. A traditional longhouse with Hilton-style amenities. There is a small pool, a slide show at night, and activities such as fishing and trips to a local longhouse. It is a 4-hr drive from Kuching, followed by a 15-min boat ride, so a one-night stay is hardly worth the trouble. Reservations and transport are arranged through the Hilton in Kuching, tel: (082) 248-200.

EATING Typical of the eating places in Serian is the **Shin Fug Café $,** opposite the Shell garage on the main street. Chicken, vegetables, rice and noodles make up the standard menu, along with some interesting drinks like peppermint tea and sweetish, green wheat-grass juice.

SARAWAK MARKETS

A visit to a market in Sarawak can prove a fascinating experience, and both Kuching and Serian have interesting ones. At **Kuching's Sunday market** on Satok Rd villagers start arriving on Saturday afternoon, so everything is up and running by sunrise the next morning. **Serian's market** is busy every day of the week.

Some of what you see at a market will be familiar enough – dried fish, pumpkin, bananas, mangoes – but there will also be lots of strange exotic fruits and vegetables. Round aubergines, spinach-like ferns, bags of *gula apong* (a brown sugar) and *mengkuang*, the essential ingredient in *rojak* salads, are nearly always available. Occasionally there will be some illicit produce for sale, like the bud of the rafflesia plant (see p. 426) in its pre-flowering stage, which is credited with medicinal properties for women after childbirth.

The benefit of visiting a market as part of a tour is the opportunity to quiz your guide about what you can see. But even on your own it should be possible to identify and purchase *salak*, a brown palm-tree fruit with a scaly skin that needs to be peeled before its sweet taste can be enjoyed. Another common fruit is *keranji*, which comes in two flavours: honey and sour.

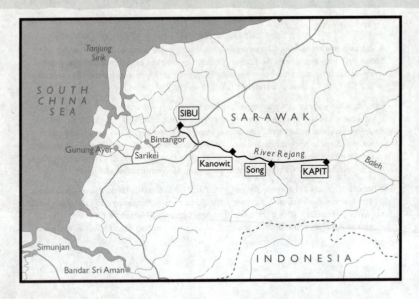

SIBU — KAPIT
OTT Table 7019

Service	🛥️	🚌	✈️	🛥️
Days of operation	Daily	Daily	Daily	Daily
Special notes	**A**	**B**	**C**	**D**
Kuching...................d.	**A**	**B**	**C**	....
Sibu......................d.	**A**	**B**	**C**	**D**
Kapit......................a.	....	....	....	**D**

Special notes:
A–Regular service. Journey time: 4 hours.
B–Regular service. Journey time: 7 hours.
C–Regular service. Journey time: 35 minutes.
D–Regular service. Journey time: 2½ hours.

This route introduces the traveller to the characteristic mode of transport in Sarawak, very fast steel-bottomed, submarine-like boats that jet through the water at more than 30 km an hour. If your attempt at conversation is not drowned out by the sound of the engine then it will certainly be extinguished by the non-stop videos that play at maximum volume on all the trips up river. The journey to Kapit takes you past down Kanowit, a settlement on the River Rejang where Charles Brooke built a fort to assert his authority and enforce his ban on headhunting. The fort is still there but hardly worth stopping off to see. Boats also stop at Song, where during World War II Ibans were allowed to renew their headhunting pastime, as long as it was against the Japanese. By the time Kapit is reached, you should feel like an intrepid adventurer ready to enjoy a night or two in a longhouse.

SIBU

Sibu is the second largest city in Sarawak and is situated on the mighty 563-km-long Rejang River, the longest river in Malaysia. A busy commercial centre, Sibu is not a city that invites lingering. Travellers find themselves here because it is the jumping-off point for travel on the Rejang and for tours to **Iban longhouses** along its tributaries.

There is not a lot to see in Sibu, but worth a visit while waiting for transport is the Taoist **Tua Pek Kong Temple**, often marked on maps as the Chinese Pagoda or the Seven Storey Pagoda. Situated close to the jetty, the site dates back to before 1871. A stone-built temple appeared in 1897 but was destroyed by Japanese aerial bombing in 1942. The present structure was built in 1957; renovation work in 1987 added the seven-storey pagoda. When the caretaker is around, which he is most of the day and early evening, you can climb to the top of the pagoda for Conradian views of the river.

ORIENTATION Sibu lies on the north bank of the Rejang, 60 km from the sea. The centre of all the action is down by the waterfront where boats for Kuching and Kapit congregate at their jetties and issue piercing whistles to announce an imminent departure. Hotels and places to eat are all within walking distance of the waterfront.

BOAT There are two jetties on Sibu's waterfront, one handling boats to and from Kuching, via Sarikei, and one for trips up the Rejang to Kapit. Destinations and departure times are all clearly marked, and passengers can buy their ticket and leave their luggage on board for up to an hour or more before departure. **Ekspres Bahagia's** boats, tel: (084) 319-228, depart for Kuching at 1100, and boats to Kapit depart roughly every 2 hrs between 0600 and 1500. Most of these boats stop at Kanowit and Song along the way.

A CHINESE CITY

Sibu's unmistakable Chinese character goes back to the early 20th century, when Wong Nai Siong from China's Fukien province came to an agreement with Charles Brooke to develop land along the Rejang basin. He quickly brought 70 immigrant families from China and more followed. Many changed from rice farming to rubber farming, and the settlement developed into a thriving town.

The city was largely destroyed by fire in 1928 and occupied by the Japanese in 1942, forcing thousands of Chinese into slave labour. The timber trade took off in the 1950s. Logging convoys on the Rejang are constant reminders that this remains the mainstay of Sibu's economy.

AIR Malaysia Airlines flights connect Sibu with Kuching, Bintulu, Miri in Sarawak, Kota Kinabalu in Sabah and Kuala Lumpur. Malaysia Airlines have their office at 61 Jalan Tunku Osman, tel: (084) 326-166. Sibu airport, tel: (084) 307-799, is 25 km from town and best reached by taxi.

BUS The local bus station is by the waterfront, a short distance west of the jetties, but the long-distance station is west of town at Sungai Antu, easily reached in 15 mins by bus no. 7 from the local station. There are various bus companies at the long-distance bus station and their ticket offices display their routes and prices. The 418-km journey to Miri takes about 8 hrs, and while there are also buses to Kuching the journey by boat takes half the time but costs more or less the same.

i The **Visitors' Information Centre** is at 32 Jalan Cross, open Mon–Fri 0800–1700, Sat 0800–1250 (closed first and third Sat of every month) tel: (084) 340-980, e-mail: stbsibu@tm.net.my. Here you can obtain detailed information on travel within Sarawak and a useful colour map of the town that also lists all local and long-distance bus routes, their schedules and fares. The **tourist office** is just over ½ km from the waterfront, in the centre of town.

ORGANISED TRIPS UP THE REJANG There is nothing to stop you boating up the Rejang and enquiring in Kapit about a local longhouse that will accept you for a night's stay. In practice, though, it can be less fun than going in a group through a tour company and having all the transport arrangements organised for you with an interpreter on hand.

As with any tour, it pays to ask all the questions about the package before

you commit yourself. Some tours using the Rejang spend a day and night in Sibu and use the Regency Pelagus Resort as the accommodation base with only a day trip to a local Iban longhouse. Another typical three-night trip uses a hotel in Kapit for the first night and continues on to Belaga for the second day, spending the night at a Kejaman or Kenyah longhouse, with the last night in a hotel back in Belaga.

All the tour companies in Kuching (see pp. 391–392) offer trips like these. **Sazhong Trading & Travel Service**, 4 Central Rd, Sibu, tel: (084) 336-017, fax: (084) 338-301, www.geocities.com/sazhong, is a company based in Sibu.

Tanahmas Hotel $$$$ Jalan Kampung Nyabor, tel: (084) 333-188, fax: (084) 333-288, e-mail.tanamas@po.jaring.my. Within walking distance of the waterfront, with a pool and some rooms facing the river.
Sarawak Hotel $$ 34 Jalan Cross, tel: (084) 333-455, fax: (084) 320-536. In the centre of town near the tourist office. Large, clean rooms and good value for money.
Hoover House $ Jalan Pulau, tel: (084) 332-973. The best budget place, but telephone in advance to check availability.

The **Premier Hotel Restaurant $$$** Jalan Kampung Nyabor, tel: (084) 323-222, two blocks north of the Tanahmas Hotel, is the place for a comfortable and enjoyable meal.
The **New Capital Restaurant $$–$$$** is a good Chinese restaurant with air-con, across from the Premier Hotel.
There is a **food centre** at the end of Jalan Market, one block north of the Tanahmas Hotel.

OVERNIGHT IN AN IBAN LONGHOUSE On arrival at a longhouse, guests are normally introduced to the families and the chief. A tour of a guesthouse and its surroundings is as stimulating as you make it by asking the sort of questions that interest you. Looking around the vegetable gardens can be educational, as sugar cane, tapioca, papaya, pepper and aubergines are grown in a small space.

In the evening, guests are served with a meal, which can be surprisingly good. The women then display their handicrafts for sale, but there is no obligation to buy. Rice wine, *tuak*, is normally served before a gong announces the performance of a traditional dance in ceremonial dress. More *tuak* follows, usually with an element of audience participation, so that the residents have a chance to gawk at you for a change.

Depending on the arrangements made by your tour company, your bed will either be outside on the *ruai* or in a separate room. Some longhouses have guesthouses built next to the longhouse for tour groups. If you don't expect hot-water showers in a tiled cubicle and enter into the spirit of things, you will have a very enjoyable time.

THE IBAN LONGHOUSE

The Iban longhouse is traditionally made of wood, built close to the banks of a river and raised off the ground by stilts. On entering you see a long vacant gallery between the bedrooms and the balcony, traditionally called the *ruai*. This is the social centre for the various families, typically about 15, who have their own private bedrooms but share the *ruai*. This is where the men and women do their work, making mats, baskets and farming apparatus, and where children play when not outside. At night, this is usually the sleeping area for young men and visiting male guests.

The *ruai* and the balcony command a view of the river and function as the front of the house, harking back to the days when anything that happened, such as hunting trips or enemy raids, took place on the river. Headhunting is a thing of the past but the river is still the lifeblood of any longhouse settlement.

The lifestyle here is communal. Any gifts brought will be divided equally by the chief between families, although property isn't shared. Each family has its own land and living space and is responsible for the area outside their apartment.

KAPIT

Kapit was an obscure outpost on the Rejang until the blistering pace of Malaysia's economic boom made it into a thriving little town. But arriving here after more than 2 hrs travelling upriver, there is still a satisfying sense of a frontier settlement. Kapit might have the trappings of a town but the roads don't lead anywhere because the jungle surrounds it and the river is the only way in or out. Redmond O'Hanlon's book *Into the Heart of Borneo* describes his trip up one of the tributaries of the Rejang, the Batang Balleh, reached from Kapit.

To your left, stepping onto the jetty, is **Fort Sylvia.** It was built in 1880 to deter the Ibans and named after Vyner Brooke's wife in 1925. The tabulated high-water marks on the outside give some idea of how much the river can rise during heavy rain. A plaque records the signing of a big peace treaty here in 1924 between the Ibans, the Kayans, Kenyahs and Kajongs, supervised by the white rajah himself. The fort is well preserved as it is built of belian (ironwood), but is not open to the public.

A small **museum**, free, open Sat–Thur 0900–1200 and 1400–1600, in the civic centre on Jalan Hospital is not especially interesting, though it does have some old photographs.

RAFT SAFARI

*If you're in Kapit for the last weekend in April, it's well worth seeing the **Baleh-Kapit Raft Safari**. This is a testing two-day race by raft celebrating the riverine lifestyles of the local Iban and Orang Ulu people. Participants stay overnight in Iban longhouses en route from Baleh to Kapit. For further details contact the Visitors' Information Centre in Kuching (p. 385).*

🛏 **Greenland Inn $$** Jalan Teo Chow Beng, tel: (084) 796-388, fax: (084) 797-989. A smart, modern hotel with a range of rooms with air-con. Best value in town.

New Rejang Inn $$ Jalan Teo Chow Beng, tel/fax: (084) 796-600. A little less expensive than the Greenland Inn. Decent rooms with fridge, phone and bathroom.

Dung Fang $–$$ Jalan Temenggong Jugah, tel/fax: (084) 797-779. Not as bad as it sounds. Rooms with fan or air-con, adequate for a night's stay.

🍴 **The Orchard Inn $$** 64 Jalan Airport, tel: 084-796-325, Fax: 084-798-633 (Kapit used to have an airstrip, hence the street name.) An air-conditioned, comfortable restaurant with good food.

Kah Ping Restoran $$ Jalan Teo Chow Beng at the town square. Standard Chinese-style meals at reasonable prices.

LOGGING THE RAINFOREST

It would be difficult for visitors to Sarawak not to notice the evidence of logging that goes on in this part of the world – boats haul huge numbers of trees along the rivers, lorries block up the roads, the view from the aeroplane is of bare mountainsides, sad groups of Penan people sit listlessly in plywood huts built for them when their forests were taken over… Very little virgin rainforest remains in Sarawak, although there is still claimed to be 60% forest cover. The government of Malaysia responded to the environmentalists' criticisms in the 1980s and '90s by establishing annual timber quotas, banning the export of whole logs and practising 'environmentally-friendly' means of logging. It also practises 'sustainable forestry' – replanting areas with cash crop trees, leaving a proportion of standing trees in each area logged so that the ground can regenerate itself, and using helicopters to log the trees to avoid the damage caused by big logging machinery.

Environmentalists continue to protest, spotlighting the damage this 'sustainable forestry' does – the destruction of thousands of species of plants and animals, the destruction of the way of life of the nomadic forest dwellers, the disease brought by the loggers (lorry tracks fill with rainwater, mosquitoes breed in the water, malaria and dengue increase), the damage to delicate soil systems and the filling of rivers with eroded soil, which makes them unnavigable, kills off the fish and makes the water unsafe to drink.

The forests of Sarawak supported communities of both nomadic forest dwellers and slash-and-burn communities for thousands of years. These people gathered what they needed, cleared tiny areas of land by hand and then moved on, leaving the forest to regenerate. The forest provided building materials, food, medicine and clothes. Its rivers formed highways for the people who lived there. Set against this were the needs of the Third World country that ruled the forests – the need to become a modern state with well-educated citizens, good healthcare, and a welcoming infrastructure to encourage foreign investment. To the government of Malaysia, logging provided a lot of income, a means of making inroads into the interior and converting its 'backward' citizens to modern life. To the logging companies, many of whom were actually owned by members of this same government, logging meant getting very rich very quick and be damned to the consequences.

In the 1980s and '90s, when environmentalists raged, the Swiss Bruno Manser became a spokesperson for the indigenous people who set up road blocks, threatened loggers with their blowpipes and took the loggers to court. In the 21st century it's really all over, bar the shouting. The big machines have been shipped off to Papua New Guinea where there are more forests to log and no 'sustainable forestry' rules, the government is off the international hook because of its reformed image. Manser, once the bane of the Sarawak loggers, is missing, possibly dead, somewhere in Sarawak's mountains, and the Penan have resigned themselves to the destruction of their lifestyle.

The Malaysian government has one telling riposte: is it any worse than what the developed world did to its own virgin forests in their past?

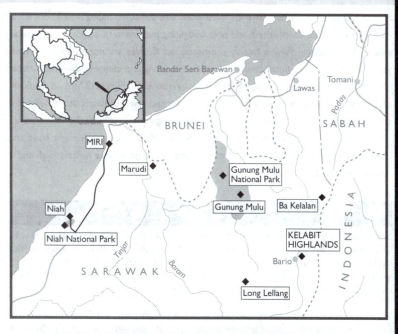

AROUND MIRI & THE KELABIT HIGHLANDS
OTT Table 7019

Service	🚌	✈	🚌	✈	⛴	✈	🚌	✈
Days of operation	Daily	Daily	Daily	Daily	Daily	Daily	Daily	ex⑦
Special notes	**A**	**B**	**C**	**D**	**E**	**F**	**G**	**H**
Kuching..................d.	A	B	....	....	....	....	....	....
Sibu..........................d.	|	|	C	D	....	....	....	....
Miri...........................d.	A	B	C	D	E	F	G	H
Mulu Caves.................a.	....	....	....	....	E	F	....	|
Kelabit Highlands........a.	....	....	....	....	....	....	G	|
Niah National Park......a.	....	....	....	....	....	....	....	H

Special notes:
A–Regular service. Journey: 15 hours.
B–Regular service. Journey: 35 minutes.
C–Regular service. Journey: 8 hours.
D–Regular service. Journey: 35 minutes.
E–Regular service. Journey: Unknown.
F–3 services daily. Journey: 35 minutes.
G–Regular service. Journey: 2 hours.
H–Journey: 50 minutes.

East Malaysia

Miri, like Kuching, is an ideal base for excursions into the surrounding area. There are a number of possible destinations, and time budgeting may mean that choices have to be made. Mulu National Park is heavily promoted but if caves are not to your fancy, or you're not the type to undertake some serious trekking and climbing, then the Kelabit Highlands suggest themselves as an enjoyable alternative. Set high (1127 m) on the floor of a valley in the highest inhabited region of Borneo, the Highlands are a delightful suprise for visitors who welcome fresh air and invigorating walks in the countryside. The Niah Caves are best visited as a day trip from Miri, although overnight stays are possible. If time is pressing, our recommendation is to go for the Kelabit Highlands, simply because it is a unique place.

MIRI

With a population of over 200,000, Miri emerged from obscurity in 1910 when oil was discovered in the region. The city is still on an economic roll with hundreds of wells, on land and offshore, pumping out some 80 million barrels of oil a year. Plans are well under way to transform the city into a major resort centre, evidence of which can be seen on the ride from the airport into town.

There is not a lot in the town itself to detain the traveller but the developing tourist infrastructure and the ease of getting about makes it a pleasant base for trips to **Niah National Park**, the **Mulu Caves**, and the **Kelabit Highlands**.

Miri has a beach to the south, **Hawaii Beach**, easily reached on bus no. 13 from the local bus station in less than 15 mins. Popular at weekends, during the week it suggests itself as a place to enjoy a picnic because there are barbecues and picnic tables to rent, as well as accommodation in beach chalets.

Getting There

Air: Malaysia Airlines has non-stop flights between Miri and Sibu, Kuching, Kuala Lumpur and Kota Kinabalu. The MAS office is at Lot 239, Halaman Kabor off Jalan

Yu Seng Salatan, tel: (085) 414-144, open Mon–Fri 0830–1600 and Sat 0830–1600. The airport, tel: (085) 615-205, is 9 km from town, from where a coupon system ($$) operates for taxis into town.

Bus: The long-distance bus station, tel: (085) 434-053, is about 5 km north of town on Jalan Miri Pujut. The local bus station is in the centre of town across from the tourist office and a regular bus service operates between the two.

DIVING NEAR MIRI

Miri is best known for its proximity to the riverine access to the island's interior, but it's also perhaps the best place for diving in Sarawak. A short boat journey out to sea (about 45 minutes) leads to a series of small shoals, while there's a larger coral reef 2 hours offshore. A Japanese World War II wreck, the *Atago-maru*, can also be dived – it's just a short distance off the jetty south of town.

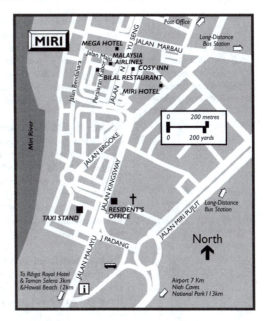

To Brunei Brunei, www.tourismbrunei.com, is reachable by bus from Miri though it involves a number of changes: first at Kuala Belait, then a river crossing and immigration, then a Brunei bus to Sangai Belait, then Seria and on to Bandar Seri Begawan, the capital city, familiarly known as BSB.

To Kuching and Sibu **Borneo Highway Express**, tel: (082) 427-035, runs buses from Miri to Kuching via Sibu at 0630, 0730, 1330 and 2100 (OTT 7019). **Biaramas Express**, tel: (082) 452-189, does the same route at 0630 and 1330. So too does **Lanang Rd Bus Company**, tel: (084) 335-973 at 0630, 0830 and 1130, and they also run buses just between Miri and Sibu. **Borneo Amalgamated Transport**, tel: (084) 654-308, runs a night bus from Miri to Kuching via Sibu at 2100.

To Niah National Park **Syarikat Bas Suria** runs buses to Batu Niah from 0630 and then roughly every hour until 1600. These yellow and light blue buses depart from behind the Park Hotel, close to the local bus station.

i The **Visitors' Information Centre** is centrally located on Jalan Melayu, tel: (085) 434-181, e-mail: stb@po.jaring.my, open Mon–Fri 0800-1700, Sat 0800-1250. It is worth calling in for their free colour map of the town, showing places to stay, restaurants, bus schedules, and other useful information. The Visitors' Information Centre is also where permits and accommodation for Niah National Park and the Mulu Caves are arranged, tel: (085) 434-184.

Bintang Plaza, north of the tourist office, has an **internet** café as well as a Parkson department store.

Cosy Inn $$ Jalan Yu Seng Selatan, tel: (085) 415-522. One of a few mid-range hotels down this road and more or less living up to its name. Small but clean rooms.

Kingwood Inn $$ 826 Jalan North Yu Seng Utara, tel: (085) 415-888. Well run, good rooms.

Thai Foh Lodging House $ 19 China St, tel: (085) 418-395, e-mail: thaifoh@hotmail.com. Near the local bus station, rooms with and without air-con, bathroom and free internet use for the first 30 mins.

Bilal Restaurant $–$$ Jalan Persiaran Kabor. Excellent, long-standing establishment at the corner of a pedestrianised street in centre of town. Tandoori chicken, curries, rotis and murtabaks served against a background of Indian videos.

Insaf Restaurant $–$$ is a similar restaurant across the road.

Chatterbox Coffee House $$–$$$ in the Mega Hotel can be relied on for its local and western food. The hotel also has a Chinese restaurant, **Lotus Court $$$** and a lounge bar with live music in the evening.

Taman Selera Food Centre $–$$ out at the beach has a good variety of stalls selling Malay and Chinese dishes and seafood at night.

NIAH NATIONAL PARK

The Niah National Park, situated near the coast between Miri and Bintulu, is most famous for the **Niah Caves**. They may be geologically insignificant compared to the Mulu Caves but more than make up for this by their human interest. Tom Harrison (see p. 418), the curator of the Sarawak Museum in 1957, led an archaeological dig at the mouth of the largest cave and the following year a human skull estimated to be 40,000 years old was unearthed. Rock paintings confirmed that early man had lived in the caves.

But the human interest that draws visitors to the caves today has more to do with bats and swiftlets than prehistoric man. Hundreds of thousands of bats (naked bats and Cantor's roundleaf bats) and swiftlets live in the caves and drop about one tonne of guano (dung) on a daily basis.

The guano forms a living carpet on the ground of the caves, supporting a colony of cockroaches and scorpions, and approaching the caves along the walkway you may well encounter men carrying away sacks of it for sale as fertiliser. The caves' swiftlets (*Collocalia fuciphaga*) – white-bellied and black-nest birds – provide a more dramatic means of livelihood for local workers.

The 3-km-long walkway to the caves takes you through primary forest. Towards the end of the walk bear right to reach the main cave. If you don't have your own torch, it is worth hiring one at the park headquarters. When you arrive at the **park head-quarters** at Pangkalan Lubang there is an entrance fee ($) to pay before heading down to a small river, the Sungai Niah, where a boatman waits to ferry you across in a sampan for a small fee. The wooden walkway begins on the other side of the river and it takes about ½ hr to reach the main cave.

Tour Operators for Niah, Mulu and the Kelabit Highlands

Virtually all the established tour companies in Sarawak handle trips and package deals for Niah, Mulu and the Kelabit Highlands, and if they don't they will sub-contract the work to a company that does.

Kuching-based tour companies have already been mentioned (see pp. 391–392) and there are some more good companies based in Miri. They all offer the same type of standard trips to Niah and Mulu and they should also be able to tailor-make an itinerary to suit particular interests.

Seridan Mulu has an office at the RIHGA Royal Hotel, tel: (085) 414-300, fax: (085) 416-066, e-mail: gracie@pc.jaring.my. As well as day trips to Niah and two/three/four/five-day packages to the Mulu Caves, the Pinnacles and Mount Mulu, they also have some interesting treks in the Kelabit Highlands.

A 3-day/2-night trip covers a flight to Bario from Miri, a local longhouse visit and a 3-hr, 10-km trek to Pa' Lungan for lunch with a trek back to Bario for the night. This costs RM600 per person for a minimum of two people. A five-day trip with three days trekking over the border into Indonesia and back costs RM1000 per person in a group of two. A more demanding ten-day trek up and down hills and crossing rivers over a total distance of around 50 km is also possible.

Getting There People spend good money on a day tour to the Park from Miri but it is not difficult to make the journey using public transport. Syarikat Bas Suria runs nine buses ($$), from the local bus station in Miri, tel: (085) 424-311, to Batu Niah at 0630, 0900, 1000, 1200, 1500 and 1600 and then on the hour until the last bus leaves at 1600. The return buses from the Batu Niah bus station, tel: (085) 737-179, depart at 0700, 0900, 1300 and 1530.

From Batu Niah boats ($) wait to ferry passengers to the park headquarters and taxis ($$) are also waiting by the bus station for the short journey. You could also walk to the park in less than an hour by following the track by the side of the river.

Deadly Work

The swiftlets glue their nests onto the walls of the caves using an edible saliva and their nests are highly sought after by the Chinese for their medicinal properties. The nest-collecting season lasts from August to December (before eggs are laid, thus forcing the birds to rebuild) and from January to March (when the young have flown away and the nests are empty).

At these times if you crane your neck you can see the acrobatic, death-defying skills of the collectors as they scale fragile bamboo poles to scrape away the nests using 10-m poles with torch lights attached. Even if you reach the caves outside the collecting season, some of their climbing equipment can still be seen. Safety nets have not been removed because they are never used, and serious accidents and fatalities do occur.

🛏 **National Park Chalets and Hostel $–$$$$** Pangkalan Lubang, reservations made either at the Visitors' Information Centre in Miri, tel: (085) 434-184, fax: (085) 434-179, or at National Park headquarters, tel: (085) 737-450, fax: (085) 737-918. Online booking at: http://ebooking.com.my; website: www.forestry.sarawak.gov.my. Forest lodges ($$$$), rooms ($$) and hostel beds ($) available.

Niah Cave Inn $$ Batu Niah, tel: (085) 737-333. Rooms with a fridge as well as air-con and telephone.

Park View Hotel $$ Batu Niah, tel: (085) 737-021. Probably the best value for money, comfortable rooms with air-con and bathroom.

Niah Caves Hotel $ Batu Niah, tel: (085) 737-726. Close to the river for access to the Park; plain rooms with air-con and a small restaurant attached.

🍴 **National Park Canteen $** serves rice and noodle dishes.

There is also a kitchen for the use of guests in the chalets and hostel with crockery, cutlery and cooking equipment provided. Some provisions in cans can be bought on the premises but it is better to bring your own food from Miri or use the supermarket in Batu Niah.

The restaurant at the **Niah Caves Hotel $** is always an option, and the small restaurants/food stalls **$** along the road leading to the river are OK for rice, noodles and chicken.

GUNUNG MULU NATIONAL PARK

Sarawak's largest national park has been open to the public since 1985 and the Mulu Caves, their main attraction, are so effectively advertised that they receive a constant stream of visitors from around the world. The spectacular cave system, the largest limestone **cave system** in the world, was first explored and mapped in the late 1970s and only four caves, the so-called Show Caves, are always open to the public.

Lang Cave, open afternoons daily, has a visually exciting variety of stalactites, stalagmites, helicites (branched stalactites) and rock formations, and an ever so tiny cave worm that you need a torch to see. A visit to **Deer Cave**, open daily in the afternoon, begins inauspiciously with a 1-m-deep carpet of guano covered with wriggling cockroaches at the entrance (don't worry, the walkway protects visitors).

After a short distance inside the cave look back to see the Lincoln profile at the cave's entrance. Try also to spot the centipedes on the ground that give off a luminous green glow when touched. Every evening between 1700 and 1830 a million bats fly out of the cave in sinuous waves, and there is a viewing platform outside where people gather to view the spectacle. Look out, too, for the hawks that turn up to pick off an easy meal of batmeat.

Wind Cave, open mornings daily, is probably the least interesting of the Show Caves. Halfway along the walkway there is a viewing platform with steps down to the entrance to a 7-km-long tunnel that links up with Clearwater Cave. It takes 4–5 hrs to work your way along this linking passage, and a guide for this caving trip costs around RM100 for a group of one to five cavers.

From the entrance to Wind Cave a boardwalk hugs the rock as it follows the course of the river to **Clearwater Cave**, open mornings daily, where there is a lovely pool safe for **swimming**. Many of the tour groups organise a picnic lunch at this spot.

The crystal-clear water of Clearwater Cave certainly earns the cave its name and brings home the impact of logging in Sarawak when compared to the murky and muddy brown colour of the Rejang. Some 200 steps lead up to Clearwater Cave and at the top, near the entrance on the left, look out for the *Monophylaea glauca*, the one-leafed plant that is shown in a photograph in the display room at Park headquarters.

The **walking trail** that leads to the Wind and Clearwater Caves from the Park headquarters takes about ½ hr and can often reveal fascinating glimpses into the micro-wildlife of the jungle. Raja Brooke's birdwing butterfly can often be seen fluttering about (scarlet head and green margins on the wing), and you may spot a feathery innocuous-looking caterpillar on the handrail. It shouldn't be touched as it produces a terrible itchy skin rash.

About three-quarters of the way along, coming from the Park headquarters, there is a fine specimen of the *Antiaria toxicaria* tree on the right, clearly labelled. Also called the Ipoh tree, it once provided the Penans with poison for their blow darts.

There are three main options for **trekking** in the Park. In order of difficulty these are the **Headhunters' Trail**, a climb of the **Pinnacles** (see p. 416) and an ascent of **Mt Mulu**. All take a minimum of three days, with overnight stays in longhouses and hostel-type camps, and can be expensive for just one or two people. Guides are compulsory, and necessary, for these treks. Full details are available at the Park headquarters.

Getting There

Air: Malaysia Airlines flies to a small airstrip close to the Park headquarters, and if the weather permits the pilot will often fly in low over the Pinnacles for a breathtaking view of the Park's natural beauty. From the airstrip it is a 2-km walk to the Park headquarters, though guests at the Royal Mulu Resort will have a minibus waiting.

Bus and Boat: Not much money is saved and a lot of time is spent making it to Mulu by bus and boat. The first leg of the journey is the 0600 bus from Miri to Kuala Baram and then a 3-hr boat journey to Marudi. From Marudi another boat goes to Long Terawan, sometimes involving a change of boat if the water level is not high enough, and then a third boat to the Park. The moral of the story is book ahead and get a seat on the plane.

Useful Gear for the Mulu Caves

A torchlight is useful, and essential if there is no guide waiting at the entrance to Deer Cave, plus swimming gear and a towel for a dip in the pool at Clearwater Cave. Binoculars are helpful when observing the mass exodus of bats from Deer Cave. Lots of water is essential (and far cheaper if purchased in Miri than in the Park). When walking through the Deer Cave, resist holding onto the railings because they tend to be covered in slimy bats' droppings. If you are keen to try some caving it is advisable to bring your own helmet and torches because hiring them at the Park is very expensive.

GUIDES AND FEES There is a small entry fee to the Park ($) and visiting the caves entails a compulsory RM18 charge for Deer and Lang caves and another RM18 for Wind and Clearwater. Guides are supposed to be waiting at the cave entrances but sometimes demand outstrips supply and you are left to go around on your own (your guide fee will not be reimbursed).

All the caves can be reached on foot from Park headquarters but it takes about an hour to reach Wind and Clearwater caves, and a boat there and back costs RM20 per person if five or more people want to go. Otherwise it is RM85 to charter the whole boat.

The charges for a guide on a trek depend on the destination, becoming affordable if a group of up to five shares the cost of RM600 for the Pinnacles and over RM1000 for the three-night trip to the Mulu summit.

All charges for guides, boats and accommodation are set out on schedules available at the Park headquarters.

Royal Mulu Resort $$$$ Sungai Melinau, tel: (085) 790-100, fax: (085) 790-101, www.rihgamulu.com. This much-touted luxury accommodation, with an admirable design that blends in with the environment, might be worth considering as a package but is hardly worth the money when most of your time is going to be spent out and about. The restaurant serves mediocre meals and drinks are outrageously priced.

National Park Accommodation $–$$$$$. The Chalets **$$$$$** are not worth the extra money when compared to the perfectly adequate longhouses **$$$$** and rainforest cabins **$$**. There are also beds in the hostel **$** with lockable storage space.

Booking Park accommodation should be done at the Visitors' Information Centre in Miri. It is advisable to get some proof of room reservation just in case the booking is not relayed.

THE PINNACLES TRIP

The Headhunter's Trail is a manageable trek for anyone who is reasonably fit. The Pinnacles trip is a little more demanding but no special skills are required, just stamina. It takes three days and two nights, and could be organised as an independent trip by just paying for a guide and the various fees for the boat trip and camp fees.

However, by the time you throw in the cost and trouble of buying your own food, cooking utensils and fuel it is very tempting to have a guide organise the food. The cost per person is RM600 (RM800 if you book through the resort hotel), and you need to come prepared with walking boots, wet gear, sufficient water and a sleeping bag.

🍴 The food at the resort's restaurant is disappointing and most guests sooner or later discover the **canteen** just across the bridge at the entrance. The meals are inexpensive $–$$ and the drinks almost a third of the resort's prices.

At the Park headquarters the **canteen $$** does adequate set lunches and set dinners. Usual hours are 0800–2300 but ask about early openings. Across the road is a canteen, the **Buyuu Sipan** (literally 'salt lick') $–$$, serving beer, rice and noodle dishes and a set lunch.

KELABIT HIGHLANDS

The Kelabit Highlands (www.kelabit.net), the highest inhabited area of Borneo, are refreshingly cool and highly recommended for anyone interested in trekking. The only way to get here is by plane from Miri to Bario, a tiny settlement adjoining the airstrip.

Although tour companies all run **trekking** expeditions it is not difficult to organise something for yourself when you are there. Shorter half-day and whole-day treks are possible without a guide and it only takes 2 hrs to reach a longhouse at Pa Umor, from where a path continues over a small bridge to a salt spring.

For a real adventure it is well worth organising a longer trip and spending a couple of nights in jungle huts and longhouses. Expect to pay around RM80 a day for the services of a local guide. The most enjoyable trek the authors ever experienced in Malaysia was a four-day return walk to Pa Tik. Although this is no longer possible as a direct trek from Bario, due to the encroachment of logging operations, it is still possible to take a more roundabout route. One of the longer treks is to Long Lellang from where MAS runs a rural airstrip with flights back to Miri on Thursdays and Saturdays.

Another possibility for an adventurous trek through the jungle is a walk to Ba Kelalan, with a night's stay at Pa Lungan in a longhouse. From Ba Kelalan MAS runs a daily rural air service to Lawas, and from there MAS has flights to Miri and Kota Kinabalu. The journey from Bario to Ba Kelalan takes four or five days and leads through a landscape of lush paddy fields, and up and down steep hills in the jungle. There is only one place to stay in Bario. The proprietor can put travellers in contact with local guides and offer suggestions and advice on the trekking possibilities. A journal records some of the treks undertaken by guests in the past which provide lots of ideas for walking trips. If you organise a trip with a local guide this will include food provisions, but it makes sense to bring your own food too. A small store in Bario sells tinned and dried food but Miri offers a far wider range.

Officially, permits are required to visit Bario and although no one seems to bother about inspecting them it is a mere formality to obtain one from the Resident's Office on Jalan Kingsway in Miri. The tourist office in Miri should also be able to offer some help planning a trek from Bario. The best time for highland trekking is before and after the rains, between September and November, and between March and May.

Getting There Malaysia Airlines flies between Miri and Bario, via Marudi, every day of the week except Saturday, departing between 1020 and 1220. The Bario airstrip is tiny and there are delays in the service caused by bad weather, something that is most likely in the rainy months between October and March. The service at Bario is managed through the Co-operative Society, no telephone.

Accommodation and Food Tarawe's $ is the nearest, a short walk from the airstrip, no telephone.

Bariew Lodge and Café $ is 10 minutes away; e-mail: galihparan@kelabit.net. **De Plateau Lodge $** is 3 km away; e-mail: munneybala@kelabit.net, and **Gem's Lodge $** is 6 km away; e-mail: gemslodge@kelabit.net. The last two offer free transport from the airstrip and all can organise treks and provide helpful information.

The World Within

Tom Harrison, an English anthropologist, was parachuted down to the Kelabit Highlands with a small group of men towards the end of World War II. His mission was to organise local resistance to the Japanese, who had not reached the Highlands. His sojourn in Bario gave him a unique opportunity to study the people and their lifestyle.

His book, *The World Within*, is an account of the Kelabit culture. It is a fascinating read because it records the culture before Christian missionaries arrived in the 1950s and effectively destroyed many of the traditional beliefs and customs. A few senior citizens in Bario still remember Tom Harrison and in one of the longhouses outside the village you might spot an old black and white photograph of him, probably next to a colour picture of the Blessed Virgin.

SABAH

The north-east corner of the large island of Borneo was known as British North Borneo until it became part of Malaysia in 1963. Now the state of Sabah, the land has tremendous opportunities for lovers of wildlife and the natural environment. The highlight has to be Mount Kinabalu, the highest mountain in South-East Asia at 4095 m, and waiting to be climbed by any reasonably fit person. The other main natural attractions of Sabah are mostly in the south near the town of Sandakan. Here there is an orang-utan sanctuary and offshore, close to the Philippines, a tiny island where turtles come to nest. To the south of Sandakan, along the Kinabatangan River, the rare proboscis monkey can be seen. This are is now a Wildlife Sanctuary and all the flora and fauna of this incredibly rich ecosystem will soon by protected by the state government.

The capital, Kota Kinabalu, is where most visitors to the state arrive. All of Sabah's tour companies have offices here and many visitors use them, or are passed on to them via tours originally booked in Kuching. However, independent travel is more feasible around Sabah than Sarawak, and many places of interest can be visited on your own.

BOOKS ON SABAH'S WILDLIFE

If you are travelling to Sabah to see some of the wildlife, there are some good books that can be bought in Kota Kinabalu that are difficult to find in bookshops elsewhere. They are published by Natural History Publications and can be purchased in Borneo Books on the ground floor of Wisma Merdeka. All but one of the following are paperbacks and affordable. (For bird books see p. 435.)

Mount Kinabalu, K M Wong and C L Chan. The natural history of the mountain, and its plant and animal life.

The Natural History of Orang-Utan, Elizabeth Bennet. Lots of colour illustrations and sound text.

Proboscis Monkeys of Borneo, Elizabeth Bennet and Francis Gombek.

A Walk through the Lowland Rainforest of Sabah, Elaine Campbell.

National Parks of Sarawak, Hazebroek & Morshidi. Hardback and lavishly illustrated, RM150.

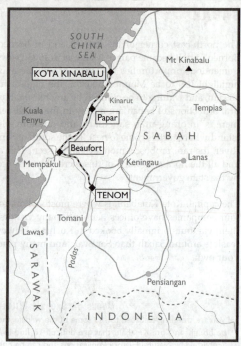

KOTA KINABALU — TENOM
OTT Table 7012

Service	RAIL	RAIL	RAIL	RAIL	RAIL	🚌		
Days of operation	ex⑦	⑦	ex⑦	ex⑦	⑦	Daily		
Special notes						A		
Kota Kinabalu............d.	0745	0745	0950	1340	1350	A	....	....
Papar.........................d.	0845	0845	1105	1446	1459	A	....	....
Beaufort.....................d.	1000	1005	1330	1555	1620	A	....	....
Tenom........................a.	1145	1155	1540	1745	1810	A	....	....

Special notes:
A–Regular service. Journey time: 3 hours.

Kota Kinabalu's urban feel can soon become tiring and an excursion suggests itself. The Rafflesia Forest Reserve is one possibility, and the islands of Tunku Abdul Rahman Park are conveniently reached by a short boat trip from the centre of town. A journey by rail seems unlikely in east Malaysia but it makes for a far more relaxing experience than that provided by the cacophony on the river boats. The line runs through dense jungle, following the course of the Padas River. At Beaufort it turns inland across the Crocker mountain range, and views from the windows make this most definitely the highlight of the route. The local people are the Murut, easy-going and friendly, and while there is not a lot to do in Tenom there is the interesting new Sabah Agricultural Park to visit.

KOTA KINABALU

Completely razed during World War II, the tourist office, formerly the post office, is one of less than a handful of pre-war buildings remaining from the days when Kota Kinabalu was known as Jesselton.

The place to find some history is the **State Museum**, $, open Mon–Thur 0900–1700, Sat and Sun 0900–1800, Jalan Tunku. A bit too far to reach on foot from the town centre, catch any bus heading south along Jalan Tunku Abdul Rahman and ask to be let off the stop before the mosque. Built in the style of a longhouse, there are interesting archaeology, history and ethnography sections. An adjoining **Art Gallery**, with the same opening hours, has some appealing folksy paintings. There is a restaurant and pleasant garden grounds that are worth a stroll.

NORTH BORNEO STEAM TRAIN

Colonial-style carriages pulled by a mid-20th-century steam engine chugs and puffs its way from Kota Kinabalu to Papar (with plans to extend the service to Beaufort) and back, on Wed and Sat at 1000, returning by 1400. The fare is RM160 and includes a tiffin-style lunch and soft drinks on board. Popular with British tourists and train buffs. Tickets and departures from Tanjung Aru railway station, tel: (088) 263-933.

It doesn't take long to tire of Kota Kinabalu's town centre but **Tunku Abdul Rahman Park** is the perfect diversion, consisting of five islands a few kilometres off the coast, with lovely sandy beaches and transparent coral water suitable for snorkelling. Best avoided at weekends and public holidays, **Pulau Manukan** has especially good coral, accessible to snorkellers with gear that can be hired from the island's small shop. There is also a restaurant ($$) here that stays open until late in the evening.

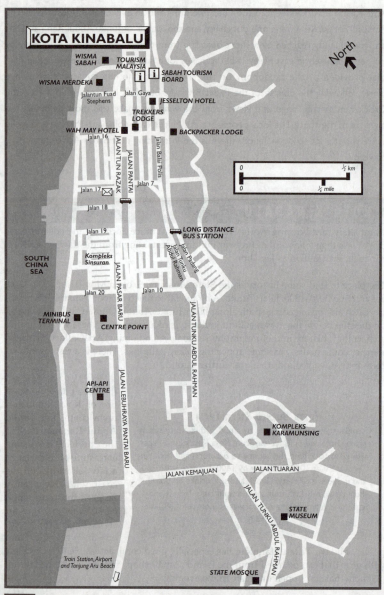

KOTA KINABALU

WISMA SABAH
TOURISM MALAYSIA
SABAH TOURISM BOARD
WISMA MERDEKA
Jalantun Fuad Stephens
Jalan Gaya
JESSELTON HOTEL
TREKKERS LODGE
WAH MAY HOTEL
BACKPACKER LODGE
Jalan 16
JALAN TUN RAZAK
Jalan Pantai
Jalan Balai Polis
Jalan 17
Jalan 18
Jalan 7
Jalan 19
LONG DISTANCE BUS STATION
Jalan Padang
SOUTH CHINA SEA
Kompleks Sinsuran
Jalan Tunku Abdul Rahman
JALAN PASAR BARU
Jalan 20
Jalan 10
MINIBUS TERMINAL
CENTRE POINT
JALAN TUNKU ABDUL RAHMAN
API-API CENTRE
JALAN LEBUHRAYA PANTAI BARU
KOMPLEKS KARAMUNSING
JALAN KEMAJUAN
JALAN TUARAN
STATE MUSEUM
JALAN TUNKU ABDUL RAHMAN
Train Station, Airport and Tanjung Aru Beach
STATE MOSQUE

North

0 ⅕ km
0 ¼ mile

Boats depart for Pulau Manukan from in front of the Port View-restaurant at the Sabah Port Jetty. They leave on demand, subject to a minimum of six passengers, and chalets on the island can be booked through Sutera Sanctuary Lodges (see below); RM 200 per chalet. Beach Bums, tel: (088) 222-210, e-mail: tattsb@tm.net.my, run daily connections from their jetty next to the Shangri-La Tanjung Aru Beach Resort. They also offer a range of watersports, island cruises and BBQs.

ARRIVAL AND DEPARTURE   **Air:** The airport, tel: (088) 238-555, is 7 km outside of town and a coupon system operates for taxi transport into town, $$. From the bus station behind Centre Point, minibuses run past the airport. Malaysia Airlines have their office in the Kompleks Karamunsing, tel: (088) 213-555, which is south of the town centre and a bit too far to reach on foot. To and from Kota Kinabalu, there are direct flight connections with Johor Bahru, Kuala Lumpur, Kuching, Lahad Datu, Miri, Sandakan and Singapore. Some of these flights sometimes involve a stop at Kuching.

Bus: Long-distance, air-con buses for Kinabalu Park, Sandakan and Lahad Datu use Jalan Pandang, parallel to Jalan Tunku Abdul Rahman. It is a matter of turning up and taking a seat until there are enough passengers, and the best time for a quick get-away is from 0700 to 0900. Minibuses travel to towns like Beaufort and Tenom, and the station is the empty ground behind Centre Point. They are usually over-crowded, and the train is preferable.

Train: The train station, tel: (088) 254-611, is 5 km south of town at Tanjung Aru, and the line runs to Beaufort and Tenom. Trains depart Mon–Sat at 0745, 0950 and 1340 and Sun at 0745 and 1350. The economy fare to Tenom is RM7.50 and there is a first-class service between Beaufort and Tenom for RM8.35.

i The **Sabah Tourism Board** is at 51 Jalan Gaya, tel: (088) 212-121, fax: (088) 212-075, www.sabahtourism.com, e-mail: info@sabahtourism.com. Open Mon–Fri 0800–1700, Sat 0800–1400. A town map in colour should be freely available. An adjoining shop retails some craft items. For enquires regarding other parts of Malaysia, cross the road to **Tourism Malaysia** on the floor at street level of the Eon-Cmg Life building, 1 Jalan Sagunting, tel: (088) 211-732. Open Mon–Fri 0800–1245 and 1400–1615, Sat 0800–1245.

Bookings for accommodation in Mt Kinabalu and on Pulau Manukan are made through **Sutera Sanctuary Lodges**, tel: (088) 255-634, 245-742, fax: (088) 259-552, www.suterasanctuary lodges.com. The company is at present located at Wisma Sabah. Information on Sabah's parks at www.sabahparks.org.my and Lot 3, Block K in the Sinsuran Complex.

Car rental, which makes more sense in Sabah than Sarawak, will cost around RM200 a day from companies like Aband-D, tel: (088) 722-300, fax: (088) 721-959.

EAST MALAYSIA

The best deal for the **internet** is K K Internet opposite the Merdeka Plaza, but the Jesselton Cyber Café in Gaya Street, near the Rasa Nyonya restaurant, offers more privacy and quietness.

SHOPPING **Wisma Merdeka** is the most convenient place for general shopping. There are moneychangers on the floor at street level, as well as Borneo Books, which has a good selection of material on Sabah wildlife, arts and ecology, as well as guidebooks to the region. Next door, **Rafflesia Gift Centre** sells souvenirs and gift items, and there are a few shops like this in the centre. Also worth seeking out is **Borneo Page**, Lot BG 58 B, a tiny shop selling *pareos*, a general-purpose type of sarong.

Centre Point has a department store and floors of shops selling shoes and clothes. There are moneychangers and a food centre.

The Jesselton $$$$ 69 Jalan Gaya, tel: (088) 223-333, fax: (088) 240-401. A lovely place, with a colonial accent that befits the oldest hotel in the city. Modern, cosy rooms.

Gayana Island Eco Resort $$$$ Pulau Gaya, tel: (088) 301-132, www.gayana-ecoresort.com. One of the Tunku Abdul Rahman Park islands, with lovely thatched chalets on stilts over the water; seafood restaurant, PADI scuba-diving courses.

Hotel Wah May $$$ 36 Jalan Haji Saman, tel: (088) 266-118, fax: (088) 266-122. Rooms with air-con and bathrooms. Laundry service and safety deposit boxes.

Trekkers Lodge $–$$ Sinsuran Complex, 2nd floor, Block L, tel: (088) 244-096, fax: (088) 258-263, e-mail: trekkerslodge@hotmail.com. Another Trekkers Lodge is at 46 Jalan Pantai (entrance at rear of building), tel: (088) 231-888, fax: (088) 258-263. These two centrally located places have dorm beds $ and double rooms $$ with fan or air-con. Breakfast is included, and there is internet connection, safety deposit boxes, and a laundry service as well as a booking service for all the regular Sabah tours.

Backpackers Lodge $ Australia Place, tel: (088) 261-495, www.welcome.to/backpackerkk, e-mail: backpackerkk@yahoo.com. Dorm beds for RM18, laundry facilities and plenty of travel information.

Spice Islands $$$$$ Magellan Sutera Hotel, tel: (088) 312-222. Asian fusion is one of the more imaginative menus in the many restaurants at the two Sutera hotels. Starters like minced prawns on sugarcane sticks and main courses of garoupa with tempura lobster and spiced sirloin with yam cakes. Far quieter, too, than the more popular Italian-style Ferdinand's $$$$$.

Gardenia Restaurant $$$$ The Jesselton Hotel, 69 Jalan Gaya, tel: (088) 223-333. Elegant, candlelit tables and fine food that includes snails from Spain, oysters from Australia and steaks from the US and Scotland.

Tam Nak Thai Restaurant $$–$$$ Street level, Api-Api Centre, tel: (088) 257-328. Pleasant and popular place, serving Thai favourites like green curry, papaya salad, *tom yang goong*, and lots of seafood.

Rasa Nyonya $$–$$$ 50 Jalan Gaya, tel: (088) 218-092. A short walk from the tourist office, a café-style place doing dishes like stir-fried beef with celery, chicken with ginger, steamed fish, lamb

FOOD CENTRES

Kota Kinabalu has plenty of food centres, usually located in the shopping centres, which are convenient for inexpensive food. The **SEDCO Complex $–$$** in the town centre is particularly good for seafood but only opens at night.

The street level of Kompleks Sinsuran is not especially appealing but the **Restoran New Arafat $** is OK for curries and murtabaks and **Restoran Anuar $** opposite has a good choice of Malay dishes set out cafeteria style. The **Wisma Merdeka Food Centre $** has a self-service food court with a choice of meats, vegetables and rice.

curry, plus a Western menu with steaks from New Zealand.

Jesselton Hotel $$–$$$ has a café-style restaurant popular with locals who come here for dishes like beancurd and seafood in a claypot and curry *laksa*.

Jothy's Curry $ Api-Api Centre, is reached from the main road outside the Centre. A limited menu of masala, chicken tandoori and fish-head curry.

TOUR COMPANIES

The standard tours offered by all the companies include city tours of Kota Kinabalu (RM60) and a day trip to Kinabalu Park (RM135). Sabah Sightseeing also arrange white-water rafting trips (RM150–180) and mountain biking (RM150–200). A trip to the Rafflesia Centre is around RM180; it costs a lot less to visit an orchid centre.

Borneo Adventure, tel: (088) 238-731, www.borneoadventure.com.

Nature Heritage Travel and Tours, Ground Floor, Wisma Sabah Bld, Jalan Tun Razak, tel: (088) 318-747, www.nature-heritage.com.

Sabah Sightseeing, tel: (088) 235-302, e-mail: sabahsightseeing@hotmail.com.

EXCURSION TO RAFFLESIA FOREST RESERVE

This is where visitors have a chance to see the world's largest flower, the rafflesia. The plant does not flower to order and it is worth telephoning the reserve, tel: (087) 774-691, to ask if one is in bloom.

The reserve, 60 km south-east of Kota Kinabalu, can be reached by taking any minibus to Tambunan or Keningau from the station behind Centre Point, and asking to be dropped off on the main road outside the reserve. Getting back to Kota Kinabalu means waiting on the main road for a minibus, though it may be worth hitching while waiting.

From the reserve's information desk it takes between 30 and 60 mins to reach a flower site, and you can ask the staff to draw a rough sketch showing the nearest location. Bring plenty of food and perhaps a picnic lunch because there are places to rest along the paths.

RAFFLESIA

There are 14 species of the flower, three of which are found in Sabah. The most common is *Rafflesia pricei*, which grows to a maximum of 30 cm in width. (*Rafflesia arnoldii*, in Sumatra, grows to over 1 m in diameter.)

The rafflesia is a leafless parasite that grows and feeds off a vine. After a growing spell of up to 18 months, the buds emerge from inside the vine's roots and the flower opens during the night. Within a couple of days the flower has faded, producing a rancid smell that attracts carrion flies who carry the pollen from male to female plants. The rafflesia's fruit holds the seeds, which are distributed by the rodents that eat the fruit.

TENOM

This is the end of the passenger railway line from Kota Kinabalu, which is the main reason for being here. The really interesting part of the railway line is the 50 km between Beaufort and Tenom, best enjoyed from a seat on the right side of the carriage. The train follows the Padas River and trundles across wooden bridges and through thick jungle. It is a terrific journey, one of the best rail trips in Malaysia and comparable to the train ride from Bangkok to Kanchanaburi (see p. 106).

Taking the first train from Tanjung Aru and arriving in Tenom around midday would allow 3 hrs (½ hr less on Sunday) to look around town and have lunch before returning on the afternoon train. Minibuses are faster but far less fun. The best reason for staying overnight in Tenom would be to take in a visit to the new Sabah Agricultural Park, tel: (087) 737-952, fax: (087) 737-571, www.sabah.ne.my/agripark. The Park is open Tues–Sun and there are guided Tours ($$) of the various projects and gardens, including an Orchid Centre. There is a cafeteria, and hostel accomodation is available.

The railway station, tel: (087) 735-514, is right in town and places to stay and eat are all within easy walking distance. Departure times for the return trip to Tanjung Aru are Mon–Sat 0800, 1015 and 1450, and Sun 0800 and 1430.

Hotel Sri Jaya $$ Jalan Padas, tel: (087) 735-669. A standard mid-range hotel with rooms with bathroom and TV. From the railway station, walk to Jalan Padas and turn left.
Sabah Hotel $ Jalan Padas, tel: (087) 735-534. Less expensive than the Sri Jaya but the clean rooms have either fan or air-con.

📷 **The Bismillah Restaurant $** at the Sabah Hotel can be relied on for tasty, fresh rotis and murtabaks, and is a good place for lunch, although it is also open in the evening.

If staying overnight, a **night market** sets up in the car park further down the main road.

WHERE NEXT?

Sabah Agricultural Park, a large research and development facility aimed at tourists and visitors, lies just 15 km south-east of Tenom. More than 600 hectares of parkland are given over to orchid gardens, forest walking trails, exhibitions of cash crops such as coffee and tea, plus some fine examples of rainforest trees. To get there take a minivan from Tenom. Tel: (087) 737-952, open 0900–1730 every day except Monday.

KOTA KINABALU — SANDAKAN

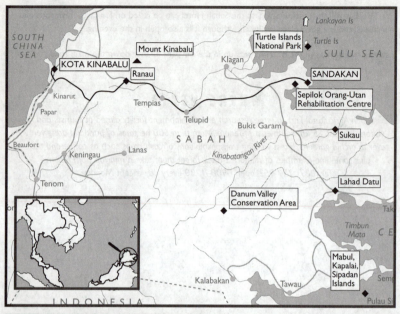

KOTA KINABALU — SANDAKAN
OTT Table 7039

Service	🚌	✈
Days of operation	Daily	Daily
Special notes	**A**	**B**
Kota Kinabalu..............d.	A	B ....
Sandakan......................a.	A	B ....

Special notes:
A–Frequent service. Journey time: 2½ hours.
B–Frequent service. Journey time: 40 minutes.

There is little point in travelling to Sabah without undertaking at least one leg of this route. Climbing Mount Kinabalu, the first stop along the way, is a manageable challenge for anyone who is reasonably fit, and the ascent may well turn out to be one of your most memorable experiences in South-East Asia (see p. 429). The town of Sandakan has little intrinsic appeal but it is the jumping-off point for trips to the well-known Turtle Islands, the even better-known orang-utan sanctuary, and the unknown Lankayan Island, the latter being one of Sabah's best-kept secrets. Sandakan is also the starting point for more nature-loving journeys, this time across land to the south. The state's longest river, the Kinabatangan, provides the focus of an environment that supports a rich diversity of wildlife, including the proboscis monkey. Unlike the exclusively priced Danum Valley Conversation Area, the Kinabatangan region caters for all budgets.

CLIMBING MOUNT KINABALU

Climbing Mount Kinabalu, half the height of Everest, is one of the highlights of a visit to Sabah and afterwards, when the muscle aches have subsided, you will undoubtedly regard it as *the* highlight. Anyone who is reasonably fit can make it to the top and children aged ten and people in their sixties have proudly collected their certificates after a successful climb. However, large reserves of mental and physical stamina are needed, because it is a steep climb and there will probably be times when you wish you had never started. Take plenty of rests, start off slowly and develop a steady pace to suit your constitution.

It takes two days to reach the summit and your rucksack should include some warm clothing for the early morning start on day 2. No special equipment is needed, even climbing boots are not essential, but bring plenty of water, some food for snacks, extra socks and wet weather gear. Suntan lotion is essential and a torch is needed for the early morning start on the second day. It is a good idea to put spare clothes into ziplock bags in case it rains.

The ascent starts with a minibus ride from the Park headquarters to the power station at 1830 m, where the 8-km walk begins. The first bus leaves around 0700, and it pays to make an early start because that gives a whole day to reach Laban Rata at 3300 m. The thought of accommodation, hot showers and a restaurant at **Laban Rata** should keep you going as the first day's climb draws to an exhausting end. Getting to sleep early should not be a problem.

Day 2 begins around 0400, to allow for the ascent before clouds set in. The first hour is spent crossing and climbing bare rock in the dark, with the help of ropes and hand rails. This is the most exciting part of the climb, making everyone feel like a professional mountaineer, but when it is over it takes at least another 2 hrs to get to the top. If you can reach the top by 0615 you can watch the sun rise.

This is when you may need to draw on your emergency supply of stamina, but all is worth it when you finally reach the tiny perch that constitutes the summit. It is a forlorn spot and few climbers linger here for long; the view down into

KINABALU'S FLORA

The first day's walk up the mountain can be, and should be, regularly interrupted by opportunities to look at pitcher plants along the way. Most common is *Nepenthes villosa*, found at the base of trees or on the ground, identified by its peristome that points down inside its cup. Also look for *Nepenthes tentaculata*, which can be seen along the sides of the trail between the power station and an hour before Laban Rata. Bring a guidebook (see p. 419) with colour photographs to identify other pitcher plants that you might spot.

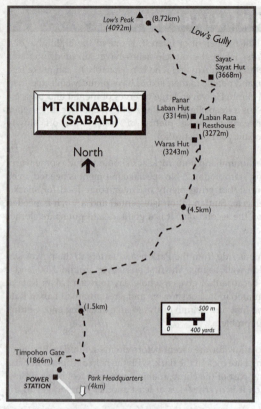

Low's Peak (4092m) (8.72km)

Low's Gully

Sayat-Sayat Hut (3668m)

MT KINABALU (SABAH)

Panar Laban Hut (3314m)
Laban Rata Resthouse (3272m)

Waras Hut (3243m)

North ↑

(4.5km)

(1.5km)

0   500 m
0   400 yards

Timpohon Gate (1866m)

POWER STATION

Park Headquarters (4km)

the black depths of **Low's Gully** can be quite frightening.

It takes between 3 and 6 hrs to make your way down, depending on your fitness, and there is no bus waiting at the power station so it is a long haul. This is when your leg muscles really get stretched, although it will be the next morning before you begin to feel the effect.

ACCOMMODATION

AT PARK HEADQUARTERS

All accommodation at the park headquarters should be booked as far as in advance as possible, by contacting Sutera Sanctuary Lodges in Kota Kinabalu (see p. 423). It is more expensive at weekends, the eve and day of public holidays and school holidays.

MENGGILAN AND MEDANG HOSTELS

Dorm beds $ with cooking facilities and a dining area with a fireplace. **Twin bed cabins** come with attached bathrooms and hot-water showers, costing RM92. The **annexe room** costs RM184, and sleeps up to four with a shared bathroom. **Duplex cabins**, a **single storey cabin** and a **double storey cabin**, all **$$$$**, sleep up to six, five and seven people respectively. **Nepenthes Villa**, **Kinabalu Lodge** and **Rajah Lodge**, all **$$$$$**, sleep up to four, eight and ten people.

ON THE MOUNTAIN Laban Rata Resthouse $ shared bathroom facilities and a bed in a four-bedroom heated room costs RM34. There is one two-person room with attached bathroom for RM115 and a four-person room for RM230. **Panar Laban Hut $** and **Waras Hut $** are huts near Laban Rata and, while they only cost RM17, there is no heating. Accommodation is also available at **Sayat-Sayat $**, an hour's climb from Laban Rata, but there is no electricity and it is very basic.

NEAR PARK HEADQUARTERS If the Park accommodation is fully booked, there are a number of private hotels with rooms for most budgets situated on the main road close to the Park entrance. **Haleluyah Retreat Centre $–$$$**, tel: (088) 423-933, e-mail: kandiu@tm.net.my, has hostel beds, double rooms (RM40) and chalets with hot water and a kitchen (RM150).

There are two restaurants at Park headquarters. **Kinabalu Balsam $–$$**, with a variety of Chinese, Malay and Western dishes at fair prices, receives the bulk of business. The **Mt Kinabalu Restaurant $$–$$$** is a little more expensive but has a wider choice of food. There is also a shop selling drinks, canned food and provisions.

The **Laban Rata Restaurant $** serves simple rice and noodle dishes (you are halfway up a mountain) and after you collapse into a seat here after the first day's climb the food will taste wonderful. There is also a shop selling drinks and snacks; consider calling in here on the way down for one of the walking sticks.

ARRIVAL AND DEPARTURE An air-con bus departs from Kota Kinabalu (see p. 423) for the Park every morning around 0700 and until 0900 you can also catch a bus for Sandakan and ask to be dropped off outside the Park on the main road, from where it is a short walk. Coming from Sandakan, any bus going to Kota Kinabalu will drop you off at the turn-off.

To return to Kota Kinabalu or to travel on to Sandakan, wait on the main road and hail down a minibus. This is no problem until noon, but the service becomes infrequent as the afternoon goes on. Hitching is not uncommon.

SANDAKAN

Sandakan town, completely destroyed during World War II, is a drab and non-descript place but it has a number of nearby places of interest so you are quite likely to spend at least one night here. All the tour companies offer a city tour but really there is little to see apart from the market down by the riverside, and this is easy to visit on your own. You can save money by visiting the orang-utan centre on public transport, but for Turtle Islands you have to go through the private company that runs the park (see pp. 433–434). Visits to the Kinabatangan River need to be organised through a tour company.

Organised Tours All the tour companies, in Kuching (p. 391) and Kota Kinabalu (p. 425) as well as Sandakan, offer city tours, trips to Sepilok, Turtle Islands, and the Kinabatangan River and various combinations of some or all of them.

SI Tours, tel: (089) 673-503. Reliable and experienced company, with an office at Sandakan airport.

Uncle Tan (see p. 434), tel: (089) 531-639, www.uncletan.com. Offers the least expensive tours to the Kinabatangan River and includes free transport to Sepilok (see below).

Wildlife Expeditions, tel: (089) 219-616. An office in town at Wisma Khoo Siak Chiew and at the Sandakan Renaissance Hotel, tel: (089) 273-093.

A major attraction is the **Sepilok Orang-Utan Rehabilitation Centre, $$$,** tel: (089) 215-330, open daily 0910–1100 and 1410–1530, easily reached in 40 minutes by bus from Central Market. Barbara Harrison, the wife of Tom Harrison (see p. 418), suggested the idea of a rehabilitation centre for orang-utans raised in captivity. A year after the 1963 law that made it illegal to keep the animals, the centre was established to help released orang-utans learn how to adapt or re-adapt to jungle life. Now most of the animals are there as the result of jungle logging.

Feeding time is 1000 and 1500, but try to turn up as early as possible to secure your place. Sepilok is very popular and large, video-camera-toting groups are often impossible to avoid, but seeing the animals is so much fun that it is worth putting up with it. There is a restaurant ($) serving basic meals and snacks from 0700 until mid-afternoon.

Coming from Kota Kinabalu, you can ask the driver to drop you off at the turn-off to the Centre. From Sandakan, take the bus showing Sepilok as its destination from the local bus station or one of the minibuses, and check with them the return times to Sandakan. The budget guesthouses will advise on the easiest and cheapest way to reach the centre.

ARRIVAL AND DEPARTURE

Air: The airport, tel: (089) 660-525, is 13 km from the city, and there is an airport bus into the city as well as taxis, **$$$**. The Malaysia Airlines office is on the corner of Jalan Pelabuhan, just south of the town roundabout, tel: (089) 273-966. AirAsia, www.airasia.com, fly direct to and from KL.

Bus: The long-distance bus station is along Jalan Leila, west of the town roundabout and within walking distance of the town centre. Local buses, to Sepilok, use the bus station near Central Market on the waterfront.

SANDAKAN MEMORIAL PARK

The Sandakan Memorial Park occupies the site of the Prisoner of War camp where 2700 Australian and British prisoners were held by the Japanese. Early in 1945 they were forced to march 260 km to Ranau: some 500 prisoners died on the three forced marches, and the remainder mostly died at Ranau or the camp itself. By the end of August only six men were still alive: two escaped on one of the marches and four escaped from Ranau.

The exhibition room at the Park, open daily with free admission, tells the story of the POW camp and the Death Marches through a moving set of photographs and survivors' memories. In the Park itself there is rusting machinery that the prisoners sabotaged, and the whole place is disturbingly empty of visitors.

To get there, take any bus going to Sepilok on the main road to Ranau and ask to be dropped off. Look for an Esso garage on the right, after the airport roundabout, on the corner of the road that leads up to the park. The Sri Rimbawan restaurant is across the road on the other corner. A large residential block is being built nearby which will probably affect the peaceful atmosphere that presently prevails.

TURTLE ISLANDS NATIONAL PARK The Park comprises three islands around 40 km north of Sandakan and very close to Philippine waters, but only one of them, Pulau Selingan, is open to visitors. Day trips are not possible and visitors stay the night to watch the turtles nesting and hatching. The green turtle is the most common. The female leaves her mate out at sea while she comes ashore and digs a metre-deep hole in the sand to bury her eggs. A hatchery on the island allows visitors to see the baby turtles emerge from their eggs, and it is not only children who delight in watching them being released on the sand and scurrying bravely into the sea to face a very uncertain future – only 1 per cent will survive marine predators.

All trips to the island are organised through Crystal Quest, tel: (089) 212-711, e-mail: cquest@tm.net.my, in Wisma Khoo Siak Chiew in Sandakan. The cost, nearly RM400 for two people, includes transport, accommodation for one night in a chalet and meals.

🛏 **Hotel Sandakan $$$** Wisma Sandakan, tel: (089) 221-122, e-mail: tengis@tm.net.my. Good value, with large rooms and a restaurant.

Sanbay Hotel $$–$$$ Jalan Leila, tel: (089) 275-000, e-mail: sanbay@po.jaring.my. Decent hotel, out of town centre.

Hotel London $$ Lebuh Empat, tel: (089) 216-371. From the bus station, walk up Jalan Tiga to Lebuh Empat and turn right. Decent mid-range place, though one traveller told me he could hear rats in the ceiling of the top floor.

Hotel New Sabah $$ Jalan Singapura, tel: (089) 218-711. Just west of the town roundabout, clean rooms with air-con and bathroom.

Uncle Tan $ Mile 16, Gum Gum, tel: (089) 531-639, www.uncletan.com. Popular with backpackers because of the budget-priced packages on the Kinabatangan river. Situated 9 miles from the airport, a taxi costs RM25; if coming by bus from Kota Kinabalu, ask the driver to let you off at Mile 16, Gum Gum.

🍽 There are lots of cheap places to eat around the waterfront but more salubrious establishments are not so common. The Renaissance hotel has the **Ming Restaurant $$–$$$** serving Cantonese and Szechuan food. For western food try the **XO Steak House $$–$$$** opposite the Hsiang Garden Hotel on Jalan Leila. Along Jalan Tiga, the road that runs up from the market place has a few affordable restaurants with a degree of comfort: try the **Fairwood Restaurant $$** or **The Boss 2 $–$$**.

Kinabatangan River

Wildlife lovers should not miss a trip to the lower reaches of the Kinabatangan River, 80 km south-west of Sandakan, and its tributary, the Menanggul. The most unusual animal to see is the bizarre proboscis monkey, and the chances of not seeing one are virtually nil. There are also long-tailed and pig-tailed macaques, silver langur, red and silver leaf monkeys, the occasional wild orang-utan and dozens of species of birds, including the beautiful hornbill.

LANKAYAN ISLAND

The most famous diving resort in Sabah is at **Pulau Sipadan**, 36 km off the south-east coast. A little known alternative is Lankayan Island, the only dive resort in the Sulu Sea, managed by Pulau Sipadan Resort and Tours. They are also one of the companies operating on Pulau Sipadan but they have Lankayan Island all to themselves.

This idyllic little island is too small to accommodate more than one setup, and the result is a near perfect diving resort. Unless a large group of macho divers turns up, which is unlikely, the island is a haven of tranquillity and, unlike Pulau Sipadan, a non-diver could enjoy a couple of nights here just snorkelling, sunbathing and taking in a Robinson Crusoe experience (albeit with creature comforts). For details of inclusive package deals contact Pulau Sipadan Resort and Tours, tel: (089) 228-081, 765-200, fax: (089) 763-575, 271-777, www.lankayan-island.com.

BIRD-WATCHING IN BORNEO

Bird-watching is one of the real delights of any visit to Borneo. A good guidebook makes all the difference. The affordable *Pocket Guide to the Birds of Borneo*, by Charles Francis, is readily available in Kota Kinabalu (published by the Sabah Society, sbs-online.com/sabahsociety). The *Field Guide to Birds of Borneo, Sumatra, Java & Bali*, published by Oxford University Press, has far better colour prints and may be worth the extra cost.

If you want to spoil yourself fork out RM270 and buy B E Smythies' great classic *Birds of Borneo*, published by Natural History Publications, 9th Floor Wisma Merdeka. In the UK it can be ordered through Natural History Book Services, Devon (e-mail: iaustin@nhbs.co.uk), and in the USA through The Borneo Company, Cincinatti (www.theborneocompany.com, e-mail: rs888@aol.com). The fourth edition is an astonishing achievement and should remain the definitive guide.

For bird-watching, the Oxbow lake is a prime area. Ask your guide to point out any birds and if you are lucky you should see the rhinoceros hornbill (*Buceros rhinoceros*), the largest and most flamboyant of the species. The pied hornbill and bushy-crested hornbill are also common, as are flocks of oriental darters (*Anhinga melanogaster*), the Chinese egret, Jerdon's Baza, the broad-billed roller, white-chested babbler, stork-billed kingfisher and the black-naped monarch.

Although travel and accommodation have to be booked in advance through a tour company, there are packages to suit most budgets. All the tour companies in Sandakan handle trips and most of them have their own lodges on the river. Uncle Tan charges RM240 per person for a 3-day and 2-night package that includes transport from Sandakan, accommodation and meals. At one of the more up-market lodges, the rooms have a fan and attached bathrooms: expect to pay up to twice that much for a similar deal. All the packages include boat rides on the river and a guide.

ORANG-UTANS

The Malay word for 'man of the jungle' is orang-utan. It is their very human behaviour that fascinates the crowds of visitors that flock every day to the rehabilitation centre at Sepilok. Perhaps, too, Borneo's orang-utans played a part in the development of Alfred Russell Wallace's theory of evolution quite independently of Darwin.

I still cherish the memory of walking through the Park at Sepilok when a young orang-utan strolled out of the bush and casually took my hand to escort me down the pathway. The power of the juvenile's grip was tremendous; an adult has the strength of half a dozen men. But orang-utans are not aggressive animals. They are solitary creatures, sleeping alone in the branch of a tree, sharing an area of around 2 sq km during the day with others, and only coming together when sharing food or mating. At around the age of five the young orang-utan leaves the mother and wanders off alone into the jungle.

DANUM VALLEY

Danum Valley is privately owned by the Sabah Foundation, the innocuous name for a large logging company. A part of their concession has been turned into a conservation area of primary rainforest. It is unique to Sabah because every other corner of forest has been logged, which is what makes a visit here so memorable. The big drawback is the prohibitively expensive rates charged for visitors.

But, apart from Taman Negara in peninsular Malaysia, Danum Valley is the best opportunity to experience the wildlife of the rainforest firsthand. The Borneo Rainforest Lodge is in the heart of the forest, where around 1800 each evening the imperial cicada (aka the 6 o'clock cicada) responds to the change in the light. It emits its alarming ruckus by vibrating a membrane across a cavity in the side of its body which acts as a sound box.

The guided tours conducted from the Lodge include a night ride in the open back of a truck when visitors can hope to see a flying squirrel gliding up to 100 m across the night sky. Wild elephants are often seen between May and July when the hot weather encourages them to come out of the jungle to seek more open, cool space and eat the plants by the side of the road. There are good opportunities to observe wildlife very close to the Lodge itself, including bands of acrobatic gibbons, orang-utans, bearded pigs and samba deer.

GETTING THERE The nearest town is **Lahad Datu** and it takes well over an hour's drive from there to reach the Danum Valley Conservation Area where the only accommodation is located. Malaysia Airlines flies direct between Kota Kinabalu and Lahad Datu, and buses from Sandakan take 3 hrs to reach Lahad Datu.

🛏 **Borneo Rainforest Lodge $$$$$** Danum Coordinator, Rakyat Berjaya Sdn Bhd, Block 3, Ground Floor, Fajar Centre, Lahad Datu, tel: (089) 881-092, e-mail: danum@care2.com. Over 20 bungalows with their own balconies and bathrooms. Rates of RM350 per person for a standard room include meals and guided jungle activities. It is another RM230 per person for transport from Lahad Datu and entry permit.

The Executive Hotel $$$–$$$$ Lahad Datu, tel: (089) 881-333, e-mail: tehotel@tm.net.com. The best place to stay and the most comfortable place to eat in town.

Hotel Ocean $$ Lahad Datu, tel: (089) 881-700. Just past the KFC between the two roundabouts, this modest hotel has clean rooms with attached bathrooms.

🍴 The Executive Hotel's **Plantation Coffee House $$–$$$$** has a good menu of salads, grills, steaks, chicken satay, burgers, seafood and Chinese dishes.

The **Azura Restaurant $–$$** Jalan Bunga, opposite the minibus station, serves tasty Malay-Indian Muslim food like murtabaks, rotis and chicken.

If you arrive by air and are going to Danum Valley, the chances are you will be taken across the road from the airport to Borneo Nature Tours who handle transport to the Borneo Rainforest Lodge. A few doors down from their office, **Restoran Tarhamiza $–$$** does Muslim food of the chicken murtabak kind.

Further down, **Serai Wangi $** has a menu in Malay, but it is easy to see what is available.

WHERE NEXT?

Sandakan is pretty much the end of the road in Sabah, but before returning to Kota Kinabalu or Kuala Lumpur you should certainly visit Sandakan's most unexpected destination. The English Tea House and Restaurant, 2002 Jalan Istana, on the hill top above town with fine views over the bay, is a restored colonial delight with period music, rattan chairs set on a well-kept lawn, and everything from cream teas to roast beef and Yorkshire pudding. A real delight.

SINGAPORE

SINGAPORE: OUR CHOICE

Asian Civilizations Museum

Bukit Timah Nature Reserve

Botanic Gardens

Chinatown

Indian food in and around Serangoon Road

HOW MUCH YOU CAN SEE IN ...

ONE DAY (24 HOURS)

Morning: Bukit Timah Nature Reserve

Afternoon: Asian Civilizations Museum or shopping on Orchard Road

Night: Quick visit to Raffles Hotel on the way to a meal in Serangoon Road or a food centre in the city centre

TWO DAYS (48 HOURS)

Day 1: as above for one day

Day 2: Sentosa and more time for culinary adventures

'THE HANDIEST CITY I EVER SAW'

'Singapore is certainly the handiest city I ever saw, as well planned and carefully executed as though built entirely by one man. It is like a big desk, full of drawers and pigeon-holes, where everything has its place, and can always be found in it.'

W Hornaday, 1885

SINGAPORE

Singapore, an island state off the southern tip of Peninsular Malaysia, arouses strong reactions from people. Unnervingly clean, organised and high tech, it sometimes seems as if there isn't a square inch that isn't regulated, sorted, tidied up and smoothed over, like a Sim City project done by a headmaster. But there is much more to the place than this.

The city has anything a tourist could ask for, from excellent food to enough sights to keep you for much longer than you intended to stay. There are beautifully renovated colonial buildings, thousands of good places to eat from hawker stalls to five-star restaurants, museums, boat rides, offshore islands and acre upon acre of shops. A tolerant, truly multicultural society with distinct areas dedicated to different ethnic groups and a multiplicity of cuisines, this tiny city-state's few square miles are packed with places of interest.

Best of all, considering its size and population, it has some wonderful green areas consisting of wetlands, primary rainforest, manicured parks with plants from all over the world and even uninhabited sandy islands. Coming from the relative chaos of Johor Bahru, the order and regulation of Singapore can be very welcome, even if you know that after a while it will wear thin and you will long for a bit of litter and a wily cab driver.

MUST SEE/DO IN SINGAPORE

Eat out in Singapore style in the Maxwell Rd hawker centre

Bukit Timah Nature Reserve

Boat Quay at night

Serangoon Rd and Sri Veeramakaliamman Temple

A day at Sentosa

GETTING THERE

AIR Singapore is a major transit point and connected by direct flights to many of the world's capitals. **Singapore** and **Malaysia Airlines** do a joint walk-on service between Changi Airport in Singapore and Kuala Lumpur's KLIA airport. Flights leave roughly every half-hour 0630–2130.

SINGAPORE

Singapore is also connected by direct flight with **Malaysia Airlines** to Kota Kinabalu (1 daily), Kuantan (2 daily), Kuching (2 daily), Langkawi (5 daily) and Penang (2 daily).
Bangkok Air has a direct flight between Singapore and Ko Samui (daily). Thai Airlines has direct flights between Singapore and Bangkok (7 daily).

Silk Air, the domestic arm of Singapore Airlines, flies to Chiang Mai, Hat Yai, Phuket and Langkawi.

The least expensive form of travel between the airport terminal and the city is by the MRT (see p. 444) – the journey takes half an hour. Taxis from the airport are metered with a S$3 supplement. A trip into town should cost about S$15. There are shuttle buses, tel: 6542-1721, into town leaving at half-hourly intervals 0700–2300 which deliver passengers to their individual hotels. Tickets cost S$7 and can be bought at the shuttle kiosks in either terminal.

FACILITIES AT CHANGI AIRPORT
You could almost spend a pleasant holiday in Singapore without ever leaving the airport. Terminal 1 handles most international flights and terminal 2 Malaysia Airlines, Ansett Australia, Air New Zealand, Philippine Airlines, Royal Brunei Airlines, Silk Air and Singapore Airlines, Air France, Finnair and Lufthansa.

ACCOMMODATION
Each terminal has its own transit hotel, on level 3 of the transit lounges. There are also recliner chairs along the windows of the departure transit lounges.

FOOD
Both terminals have fast food places as well as regular restaurants, from sushi bars to Chinese seafood places, with a similar range of places to eat. In addition there is a 24-hr minimarket on level 3 of terminal 2. In the rooftop of the car park outside terminal 2 is a good hawker centre and there is another in the basement of terminal 1. Both are much less expensive than the outlets inside the terminals.

ENTERTAINMENT
There is a cinema on level 3 of terminal 2 as well as a video games room on the same level. There are rooms for watching sport (level 2 terminal 2) and the news (level 2 terminal 1) on TV, a fitness centre, showers and swimming pool (level 3 terminal 1).

POST, PHONES AND INTERNET
There are Singapore Telecom outlets in the transit and public areas of level 2 in both terminals. They have postal services. Internet facilities are on level 3 of terminal 1 and level 2 of terminal 2. Both are in the transit areas.

TOURIST INFORMATION

There are information desks located throughout both terminals. It is easy to book a hotel at the airport, whatever your budget; a S$10 deposit is required. Moneychangers are in the transit areas of level 2 of both terminals and in both arrivals halls. There are 24 automatic left-luggage lockers throughout both buildings.

TOURS

There is a free tour of Singapore available for transit passengers with 5 hrs or more to spare, 1000–1900. It is also possible to book trips to various locations in Singapore but these are not free.

TRAIN Singapore is connected by KTM, the Malaysian rail service, to JB, Kuala Lumpur and stations along the west coast. There is a train service into Thailand (change at Kuala Lumpur, see p. 23). There is also a route via Gemas to Jerantut for Taman Negara and Kota Bharu in the north-east. The train station is in Keppel Rd, tel: 6222-5156.

AIR TICKET PRICES

Bear in mind if buying air tickets to Malaysian destinations from Singapore that it is often much cheaper to fly from Johor Bahru airport. JB also has more direct flights to Malaysian destinations than Singapore.

BUS Air-conditioned express buses leave for Johor Bahru from the Queen St bus station every 15 mins. Price is S$2.40. There is also a local bus SBS 170 that can be picked up along the route, and costs S$1.70. At the Singapore immigration point passengers disembark, retaining their ticket, and go through immigration.

The Express bus usually waits for passengers to reboard but if it has gone, you can get on the next one. The 170 doesn't wait but keep this ticket and get the next one. Passengers disembark a second time at Malaysian immigration and from there you can either get back on the bus and go to the bus station at Larkin, 6 km north of town, or walk out of immigration into the city.

For destinations beyond JB there are direct buses to Melaka and the east coast of Malaysia from **Lavender St bus station**. For Kuala Lumpur there is a choice between Lavender St and Queen St. For other destinations north of Melaka and Kuala Lumpur buses leave from the **Golden Mile Complex** in Beach Rd. Tickets for all routes can be bought at the bus stations concerned or from travel agents. For Thailand, buses leave from the Golden Mile Complex. Most departures are in the afternoon and travel overnight. Tickets can be bought at the bus station.

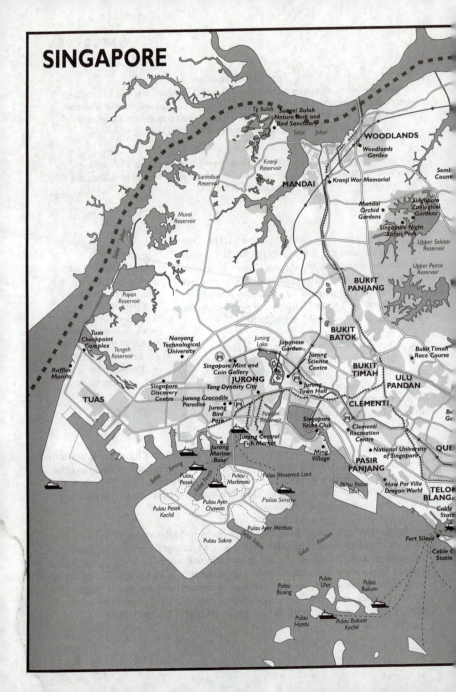

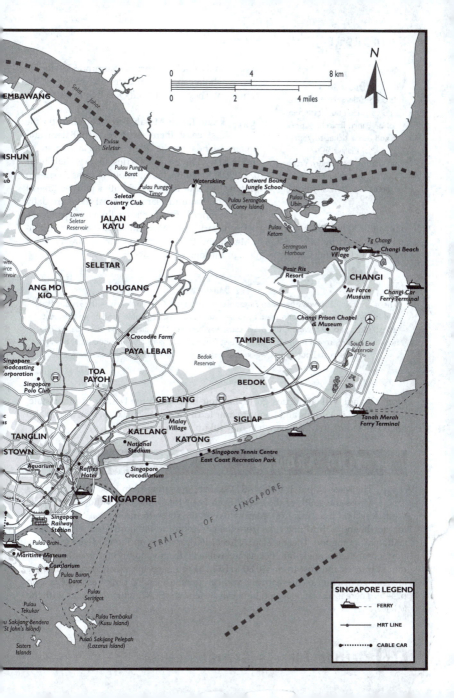

TAXI Taxis to Johor Bahru cost around S$30 for the whole cab, more if there are queues at the causeway. They depart from Queen St bus station.

BOAT From **Tanah Merah Ferry Terminal** on the east coast there are ferries to Batam and Bintan islands in the Riau Archipelago, part of Indonesia. There are ferries every half-hour 0730–2000 to Batam, taking about 45 mins. Ferries to Bintan cross four times a day with a journey time of about 1 hr. From the same terminal there are daily ferries to Johor Bahru. Ferries to Pulau Tioman leave daily at 0830 outside of the rainy season (early Nov–Mar). Tanah Merah ferry terminal is accessed by MRT to Tanah Merah and then bus no. 35. Tickets are available from the ticket offices at the terminal or through a travel agent.

THE CAUSEWAYS

There are two causeways between Singapore and Malaysia. One links Tuas with Geylang Patah in Malaysia and is really only used by long-distance lorries, or people heading up the west coast. Most people travel on the older causeway between Woodlands and Johor Bahru. The new link has improved things but there are still huge traffic jams and long queues at immigration at rush hour and at weekends. It is possible to walk over the causeway.

From **Changi Village** ferries go to Tanjung Belungkor, for Desaru in Johor state. Journey time is 45 mins and there are four ferries a day. Small, 12-person ferries also go to Pengerang in Malaysia when they fill up with passengers.

GETTING AROUND

TRAIN The Mass Rapid Transit (MRT) system, operating from 0530 to 0030, travels across the south of the island from Pasir Ris in the east to Boon Lay in the west. A second line runs from Marina Bay in the south to Jurong via Woodlands in the north, and a third line runs from the city centre to the north-east with a useful station at Serangoon. There is also a direct MRT service from Tanah Merah to the airport, cost S$1.20. Single-fare tickets are available from vending machines at the station entrances and cost from S$0.80 to S$1.20. You need the exact change but there are change machines. Alternatively, you can purchase an EZ Link Card (see box on p. 445). There is also an elevated light rail system, the SLRT, which connects with the MRT.

Bus Singapore has a vast network of buses, which travel all over the island. Fares range from S$0.70 (non-air con) to S$1.50 and you need the exact fare or your EZ Link card.

The Singapore Trolley, which you see scooting about town, costs S$14.90 (S$9.90 for children) per day. That's the equivalent of eight trips across the island on a regular bus, but it has the advantage of a route that covers most tourist attractions, and you can hop on and off as you like.

Taxis All taxis in Singapore are metered, air-conditioned and very clean. Fares start at S$2.40 and go up S$0.10 for every 240 m after the first 1 km. There are surcharges for a call out, for journeys beginning in the Central Business District (CBD) and a 50% surcharge after midnight. Some taxis accept credit cards.

Car Traffic drives on the left in Singapore. The speed limit is 50 km per hour, 80–90 km on expressways (signs state the limit). Parking is by a coupon that you can buy in shops. Car hire is much more expensive in Singapore than JB and it is even more expensive if you plan to take the car over the causeway. It is cheaper to bus over to JB and hire one. There are tolls on both causeways, and petrol tanks must be three-quarters full on leaving Singapore.

INFORMATION

i The main tourist office is the **STB Tourist Information Centre** at Tourism Court, 1 Orchard Spring Lane, tel: 1-800-736-2000 (toll-free), Mon–Fri 0830–1700, Sat 0830–1300. Smaller offices include the **Singapore Visitors Centre** at Liang Court Shopping Centre, 177 River Valley Road, Level 1, tel: 6336-2888, open daily 1030–2130; **Singapore Visitors Centre** at Suntec City Mall, 3 Temasek Boulevard, tel: 1-800-332-5066 (toll-free), open daily 0800–1800; **Travel Café Tourist Information Centre** at Prinsep Place, 44 Prinsep Street, tel: 6336-3660, Sun–Thur 1100–2300, Fri and Sat 1100–1400; and **Chijmes Service Centre**, 30 Victoria Street, tel: 6338-2529, Mon–Sat 1000–1800.

E-MAIL AND INTERNET There are internet cafés in the Funan Centre, Tanjong Pagar Rd, Boat Quay and many other shopping centres. There are also two at Changi airport.

EMERGENCIES For police, phone 999, for ambulance and fire 995. Lost property tel: 6733-0000 (Tanglin Police Station). Lost and stolen credit cards: American express tel: 1-800 732-2244, Diners tel: 1-800 294-4222, Mastercard tel: 1-800 110-0113, Visa tel: 1-800 345-1345.

EMBASSIES AND CONSULATES

Australia, tel: 6836-4100, 25 Napier Rd
Brunei, tel: 6733-9055, 325 Tanglin Rd
Canada, tel: 6325-3240, 15th floor IBM Tower, 80 Anson Rd
China, tel: 6734-1025, 70-76 Dalvey Rd
France, tel: 6880-7800, 101 Clung Park Rd
Germany, tel: 6737-1355, 14th Floor, 545 Orchard Rd
Indonesia, tel: 6737-7422, 7 Chatsworth Rd
Malaysia, tel: 6235-0111, 268 Orchard Rd
Philippines, tel: 6737-3977, 20 Nassim Rd
Thailand, tel: 6737-2644, 370 Orchard Rd
UK, tel: 6424-4200, 100 Tanglin Rd
USA, tel: 6476-9100, 27, Napier Rd

EXCHANGE There are licensed moneychangers in all of the big shopping centres. They are open longer hours than banks and do not charge a fee for changing traveller's cheques. Banking hours are 0930–1500 Mon–Fri, 0930–1130 Sat. Singaporean ATMs (auto teller machines) accept a range of credit cards.

HOSPITALS **Singapore General Hospital**, tel: 6222-3322, in Outram Rd has an Accident and Emergency department.

POSTAL SERVICES The main **post office** is in Eunos Rd 8 but there are many smaller branches in the shopping centres. Most post offices are open 0830–1700 Mon–Fri, 0830–1300 Sat. Eunos Rd 8 has a post restante service.

ACCOMMODATION

Singapore has a good range of accommodation, from five-star designer hotels to dorm beds in flats in Geylang. Prices are higher than over the causeway, and one way of offsetting the cost of your stay in Singapore is to stay in JB and bus over. But the expensive Singapore hotels have much to offer in terms of design and luxury, and the more moderate ones are very central and well regulated. Hotels add 14% to their bills in taxes and service charges, and where the room rate has a series of pluses after it you can add the 14% on the bill. Cheaper places include that in the room rate.

EXPENSIVE **Damenlou Hotel $$$$** 12 Ann Siang Rd, tel: 6221-1900, fax: 6225-8500. Nicely renovated Chinese shop-houses. All facilities in room, coffee shop downstairs.

MODERATE **Backpacker Cozy Corner Hotel $$** 5 Teck Lim Rd, tel: 6225-4812, fax: 6225-4813. Good location in Chinatown, cash only, under 10 minutes to Outram Park MRT station.

Broadway Hotel $$$ 196 Serangoon Rd, tel: 6292-4661, fax: 6293-6414, e-mail:broadway@pacific.net.sg. Well-maintained older hotel with all requirements in air-con rooms at much lower rate than others in this category. Downstairs is a very good Indian restaurant.

Dickson Court Hotel $$$ 3 Dickson Rd. tel: 6297-7811, www.dicksoncourthotel.com.sg. Close to heart of Serangoon Rd, this renovated building has good rooms and an open-air coffee shop.

Hotel Hamilton $$ 40 Hamilton Rd, tel: 6296 2296, fax: 6296 2996, www.hotelhamilton.com.sg. Over 40 rooms, good location, 7 minutes away from Lavender MRT station.

Madras Hotel $$ tel: 6392 7889, fax: 6392 6188, www.madrassingapore.com. Centrally located for shops and restaurants; nearest MRT station is Bugis, 12 minutes on foot.

The Metropolitan $$ 60 Stevens Rd, tel: 6737 7755, fax: 6235 5258, www.mymca.org.sg. Nearly 100 beds, accepts credit cards and centrally located. The nearest MRT is Orchard.

Perak Lodge $$$ 12 Perak Rd, tel: 6299-7733, fax: 6392-0919, www.peraklodge.net. Restored shop-house close to Serangoon Rd. Good security, price includes breakfast, bar and coffee shop.

RELC, International House, $$$ 30, Orange Grove Rd, tel: 6885-7888, fax: 6733-9976, www.hotel-web.com. Ugly building, a little out of the way but huge rooms with all the basic requirements, launderette, kitchen.

South East Asia Hotel $$$ 190 Waterloo St, tel: 6338-2394, fax: 6338-3480, www.seahotel.com.sg. Very clean, basic place in the newly pedestrianised Waterloo St. Café, vegetarian restaurant, all mod cons in room. Excellent value for two people sharing. Payment in cash, daily.

Strand Hotel $$$ 25 Bencoolen St, tel: 6338 1866, www.strandhotel.com.sg. A very good base in Singapore, within walking distance of the Marina, Raffles and Orchard Rd.

Tai Hoe Hotel $$ 163 Kitchener Rd, tel: 6293 9122, fax: 6298 4600, www.taihoehotel.com. Over 70 rooms and excellent location in Little India area. Lavender MRT station is an 8-minute walk away. Budget eateries in the vicinity.

Victoria Hotel $$ 87 Victoria St, tel: 6338 2381, fax: 6334 4853. Some 50 rooms, accepts credit cards, fairly central – 10-minute walk to Bugis MRT station.

BUDGET

Alana Hotel $$ 9 Lorong 10, Geylang, tel: 6745-9909, fax: 6743-9033, e-mail: alanahotel@pacific.net.sg. TV, attached bathrooms, air-con, tea and coffee making facilities, 15 mins from MRT.

Backpacker Hotel $$ 11-A Mosque St, tel/fax: 6224 6859. Only 11 rooms, no advance bookings. Ten-minute walk to Outram Park MRT station.

Chinatown Guesthouse $ 325c New Bridge Rd, 4th Floor (opposite Pearls Centre), close to Outram MRT, tel: 6226-1139, e-mail: patrick@nycmail.co. Dorms and rooms.

Deluxe Hotel $ 37 Lorong 8 Geylang, tel: 6743 1163, fax: 6748 2975, e-mail: mode4694@mbox4.singnet.com.sg. Nearly 30 rooms, cash only. Less than 10 minutes away from Kallang MRT station.

Inn Crowd $ 35 Campbell Lane, tel: 6296-9169. Excellent guesthouse in Little India.

MacKenzie Hostel $ 114A MacKenzie Rd, tel: 6837-2887, fax: 6334-3277. Open 24 hrs, walkable from Little India MRT. Dorms, single and double rooms, good facilities.

Yew Lian Hotel $ 549A 2nd Floor Geylang Rd (off Lorong 29), tel: 6744 8509. Ten minutes from Aljunied MRT station.

FOOD AND DRINK

One could write a two-volume tome on places to eat in Singapore. It is a constant topic of conversation among Singaporeans, and when food reviews in the newspapers mention a place its customers quadruple overnight for about a week until the next issue. The following list scrapes the surface and you would need a couple of years of eating out several times a week to do the place justice.

Singapore has fewer of the chaotic-looking hawker places that still survive in Malaysia but there are a few. Most people eat cheaply in air-conditioned food halls in the big shopping malls. Food here is about twice the price of food in Malaysia, taking the exchange rate into account.

Indian roti and banana leaf places flourish, and the east coast is famous for its Chinese seafood. At a much higher price bracket the big hotels make a large portion of their income from their food and beverage outlets. There are hundreds of little bistro-type places coming and going as areas go in and out of fashion. This year it's Boat Quay, last year it was Clarke Quay, before that Holland Village and there was a brief spell when Chijmes was the place to eat. The next place will be the next hyped up multimillion-dollar conservation project.

HAWKER FOOD Hawker stalls are alive and well and situated in the many wet-fish markets all around Singapore. The centres have a series of stalls cooking their own versions of fast food with communal tables and chairs. You can order dishes from several different stalls and eat it all together. The plates are colour coded and everyone seems to get their own utensils back without too much fuss.

An exception to this is the thoroughly nasty Newton Circus, a tourist trap, where if you try to sit at a table claimed by one of the hawkers, he'll chase you off. Two of the older ones that survived the big clean-up of the last 20 years are great places to eat.

The **Adam Road** hawker centre, at the junction of Adam Rd and Duneam Rd, is a small centre with good Malay and Chinese food. The *roti john*, *mee goreng* and fish-ball noodles are all worth savouring; the dessert stall serves a refreshing *cheng tng*, a sweet soup of fruit, nuts and sugar.

The **Maxwell Rd Food Centre** has been given a facelift and many people claim it has some of the best food in Singapore. It is very Chinese, and one of the stalls sells herbal and pig's brain soup. Another stall sells quite a rarity nowadays – *yew tao*, a kind of Chinese deep-fried croissant.

A real suburban hawker centre to visit is **Tiong Bahru** wet fish market, which has lots of foodstalls downstairs, including a very popular pau stall selling Chinese sweet buns.

ROTI PLACES These are in tiny shops scattered all over the island. Two or three of them are in North Bridge Rd near the Sultan mosque.

The Islamic Restaurant $ at no. 791 was established in 1921. It serves roti, murtabak, biryani chicken and mutton and fish-head curry in a pleasantly unreconstructed shop-house.

Zam Zam $ at no. 699 and **Victory $** at no. 701, are similar in style and slightly shabbier.

FOOD COURTS

Most of the fun of hawker centres has been lost in these clean, sanitised, muzaked places, but the food is good and if you can keep from going mad from the constant noise you can enjoy cheap food in air-conditioned surroundings.

In Orchard Rd the best places are in the basement of **Lucky Plaza**, where there are Indian Muslim and *yong tau fu* stalls, and **Scott's Food Court**, which has a *nyonya*, a *laksa* and a north Indian stall, amongst others.

Over in the colonial part of town the **Funan Centre** has a good food centre on the 7th floor. In Telok Ayer St and aimed at lunchtime office workers is **China Square,** which has two floors of stalls selling everything imaginable at slightly higher than usual prices.

Opposite, in Far East Square, **Food Opera** has collected several very famous producers of good street dishes – Liang Seah St prawn noodles, Stamford fish-head noodles, Hock Lam Beef noodles and Nam Seng Wanton noodles – all named after the original shop-houses that sold the dishes before they were relocated here.

A **24-hr Indian Muslim place $** in Bencoolen St beside the San Wah hotel serves very good roti and biryani.

Holland Village has an excellent roti and biryani place in Lorong Mambong, behind the main road.

Shahee $ at 63 Tiong Bahru Rd, close to the birdsong area, is is a good suburban version of the Indian Muslim place, with tables on the street and very good roti.

A selection of restaurants is provided below.

CHINESE	**Thien Kee Hainanese Steamboat $$** B1-20 Golden Mile Tower, Beach Rd, tel: 6298-5891. A buffet-style eatery for those with a huge appetite; walkable from Bugis MRT station.
	Crystal Jade Group $ found all over Singapore, offering excellent value meals.
	Lei Garden $$$$$ Chijmes, Victoria St, tel: 6339-3822, Rub shoulders with the rich and famous and enjoy some very high-class Cantonese-style food.
	Liang Seah Eating Place $–$$ No. 2, Liang Seah St, tel: 6334-0950. Good-value tasty noodles and other mostly Chinese dishes. Within walking distance of Bugis MRT station.
	The Mushroom Pot $$–$$$ 01–02 Singapore Indoor Stadium, 2 Stadium Walk, tel: 6342-3320. Away from the tourists, near Aljunied or Kallang MRT.
	Teochew City Seafood Restaurant $$–$$$ Centrepoint Shopping Centre, tel: 6733-3338, Reasonable prices, braised meats and seafood. Air-conditioned and oriental setting.
	Ya Kun Kaya Toast $ 39 Robinson Rd. A self-service, air-conditioned Chinese coffee shop. Good for breakfasts.
INDIAN	**Annalakshmi $$–$$$** 02–10 Excelsior Shopping Centre. Vegetarian restaurant. Nightly changing menus. Lovely atmosphere, nice but expensive food. Closes at 2130.
	Muthu's Curry House $–$$ 78 Race Course Rd. The speciality is fish-head curry. Don't believe the stories about the eye being the best bit – it's the cheek. Lots of other curries too.
	Banana Leaf Apolo $–$$ 56 Race Course Rd. Very famous banana leaf restaurant frequented by Singapore's movers and shakers as well as ordinary folk. Fish-head curry, massive prawns, lots of vegetables.

Delhi Restaurant $–$$ Broadway Hotel, 195 Serangoon Rd. Sit out on the porch and watch Serangoon Rd activity. Banana leaf, roti, naan, tandoori dishes. Inexpensive and good food.

Taj $$ 214 South Bridge Rd. Air-conditioned Indian Muslim place right beside the Jamai Mosque.

Komala Vilas $ 12–14 Buffalo Rd and 76–8 Serangoon Rd. A banana leaf vegetarian place – lovely *dosa* and south Indian style *thalis*, on steel trays, not banana leaves.

Woodlands $ 14 Upper Dickson Rd. Vegetarian restaurant with enormous range of breads and set *thalis*. There is an upmarket air-con branch of this place **$$** at B1-01 Tanglin Shopping Centre.

Komala's Restaurant $ 3–9 Upper Dickson Rd, 111 North Bridge Rd, B1-07E Peninsula Plaza, 6 Scott's Rd, #B1-05 Scott's Shopping Centre. It had to happen. This is the Indian equivalent of McDonald's, only the food is freshly cooked and tasty. Tell the cashier what you want, pay for it, give your receipt to the girls by the kitchen and out pops a sumptuous banana leaf meal only on a plastic tray. Lovely breads.

THAI

Thanying $$$ Amara Hotel, 165 Tanjong Pagar Rd, tel: 6222-4688. Royal Thai cuisine cooked by women who trained at the royal palace in Bangkok. Reservations essential. There is a second branch at Clarke Quay.

Sukhothai $$$ Lorong Mambong, Holland Village, tel: 6467-4222.

MALAY AND INDONESIAN

There are very few Malay restaurants in the city but around **Geylang Serai** market several small coffee shops serve *nasi padang*, the Malay style buffet, as well as the hawker centre in the market.

Sanur $$–$$$ Ngee Ann City, Suntec City, Centrepoint. A mixture of Malay and Indonesian cooking. *Tahu telor*, fish-head curry, very spicy grilled chicken and fish. Geared to shoppers rather than romantic evening dining.

House of Sundanese $$ 55 Boat Quay. Cuisine from west Java. No air-con. Barbecued fish, curries, even the salad is spicy. Another branch is at Suntec City.

PERANAKAN

Ivins $$ 19–21 Binjai Park (off Bukir Timah Rd), tel: 6468- 3060. Tucked away in a quiet housing estate, this is non-tourist Singapore. Good prices for excellent food.

Blue Ginger $$$$ 97 Tanjong Pagar Rd, tel: 6222-3928. Good *nyonya* food in a relaxed atmosphere.

Harbour Grill $$$$$ Hilton Hotel, 581 Orchard Rd, tel: 6730-3393, Classy international restaurant whose speciality is oysters and caviar. Lovely nouvelle cuisine menu, pleasant atmosphere. Vegetarian options. Try the ice-cold oyster shooters – served with a shot of vodka.

Mezze 9 $$$$$ Hyatt Regency, 10–12 Scott's Rd, tel: 6730-7112. Nine dining experiences to choose from – Western to Japanese – and show kitchens to entertain. Reservations recommended.

Morton's $$$$$ The Oriental, 5 Raffles Ave, tel: 6339-3740, The latest place to eat steak in style. Very American menu, from Cajun ribeye steak to hash browns and baked Idaho potatoes and New York cheesecake. Reservations always necessary.

El Filipe's Cantina $$$$ Lorong Mambong, Holland Village, 02-09 International Building, 360 Orchard Rd. Innovative, long-established Tex-Mex place serving good Mexican food and deadly margaritas.

Pasta Fresca $$$ 30 Boat Quay, Shaw House, 350 Orchard Rd. Good value, tasty Italian food. A Boat Quay branch is open 24 hrs.

HIGHLIGHTS

A COLONIAL WALK Lots of old Singapore bit the dust before the government realised the buildings were marketable, but around the old colonial core of the city lots of the old imperial-era buildings remained and have been beautified in the last few years. Some have even survived the beautification.

This walk starts, as it should, outside that bastion of colonial social life, the **Raffles Hotel**, 1 Beach Rd. Once a small beachfront bungalow owned by a merchant from the Middle East, the Sarkie brothers, who also owned the Strand in Rangoon and the E and O in Penang, bought it in 1886. When the Sarkies went out of business in the early years of the 20th century the hotel, like its sisters, grew dilapidated, until in the 1970s real riff-raff like backpackers could afford to stay here for weeks on end. Its renovation wasn't so much a facelift as major reconstructive surgery, and what emerged was the gleaming edifice you see before you. The hotel has a museum that you can visit 1000–1900, free.

St Andrew's Cathedral

The gleaming white walls of the cathedral are the result of some inventive plaster work made from crushed eggshell, egg white, lime, sugar, coconut husks and water. The original church bells were donated by Maria Revere Balastier, daughter of Paul Revere and the wife of Singapore's first American consul. In the days of bombardment leading up to the surrender to the Japanese in 1942 the cathedral became a makeshift hospital, the pews serving as beds and the vestry an operating theatre.

Two left turns into North Bridge Rd and then Coleman St bring you to **St Andrew's Cathedral** on the left, built in the 1850s in the Victorian Gothic style by convict labour to a design by Colonel Ronald Macpherson.

Ahead of you is the **Padang** and to the right is the **City Hall**, both steeped in history. The Padang was once a seafront playing field where in the early days of empire British troops were quartered, and in more peaceful times the ruling classes gossipped and strolled and watched cricket matches. At one end of the Padang is the Singapore Recreation Club, where the Eurasians fraternised, and at the other is the Singapore Cricket Club, for whites – both still as exclusive as they were a hundred years ago. In 1942 the Japanese lined up the British on the Padang, men on one side and women and children on the other, and marched them off to Changi prison.

Over to the left you can see the **War Memorial Park**, which remembers the hundreds of civilians who died during this time. On the steps of the City Hall, Lord Mountbatten accepted the Japanese surrender in September 1945. Fourteen years later Lee Kwan Yew stood on the same steps to declare Singapore independent. Next door to the City Hall is the **Supreme Court Building**, built in 1939 and one of the last of the great colonial buildings. In the lobby is a display area with information on the history of the building.

Crossing the Padang towards the sea you come to the **cenotaph**, which remembers the war dead of the two world wars. To the left is the **Tan Kim Seng fountain**, erected in 1882 with money donated by the eponymous benefactor. To the right is the **Indian National Army Monument** remembering the many Indian soldiers who died in the war. Another memorial is the **pagoda** in the Esplanade Park dedicated to Lim Bo Seng, one of the leaders of the resistance movement between 1942 and 1944.

Following the curve of the Padang you can see ahead the **Victoria Theatre and Concert Hall**, originally the town hall and only converted in 1905. Nearby, in Empress Place, is the main **Asian Civilisations Museum**, **$**, open Mon 1300–1900, Tues–Thur 0900–1900, Fri 0900–2100 (free admission from 1900), Sat–Sun 0900–1900; www.museum.org.sg/ACM/acm.shtml. The only museum of its kind in Asia, it is stuffed with art and artefacts from the Middle to Far East. The other part of the museum is on Armenian St (see pp. 456 and 458).

Walking upriver away from Cavanagh Bridge and along North Boat Quay brings you to the place where it all started – **Raffles' Landing Site**. Follow the river along to Hill St and turn right.

The Belly of the Carp and Bad Chi

The six-storey building on the corner of Hill St was the Hill St Police Station, built in 1934 and believed by most of the residents of Boat Quay to have very bad chi (energy). The curved river area was known to the Chinese as the belly of the carp, its shape bringing great good luck to the merchants who operated in the area. When the building was erected people believed that it loomed full of policemen over the river and blocked the healthy flow of chi into the belly of the carp and brought about the area's economic decline.

Sir Stamford Raffles

Born at sea in 1781, Stamford Raffles joined the East India Company at the age of 14. When Britain gained some colonies in the East, he was sent first to Java and then to Penang. Raffles saw the importance of the west coast of Malaya as a means of controlling the sea trade, and in 1819 he was allowed to seek out a site for a new base of operations.

He sailed up the Singapore River and landed in what was to be Singapore that year. The island was largely marsh, ruled by the sultan of Johor but effectively controlled by pirates. The island's ownership was in dispute between two warring sultans so Raffles went to one, Hussein Mohammed Shah, and offered him support in his war with the other sultan and a huge sum in rent for sole trading rights on the island.

The Dutch also wanted to control Singapore and things grew very nasty between the two colonial powers until a deal was struck in 1824. Raffles got Singapore and in exchange ceded Bencoolen on the west coast of Sumatra. Melaka was thrown in as part of the deal.

Singapore became part of the Straits settlements, with Penang in the north, Melaka in the middle and Singapore in the south. Raffles oversaw the development of the colony, laid out the areas in which each ethnic group were to live and built himself a bungalow on Fort Canning Hill from where he could keep a weather eye on the sea.

Singapore quickly boomed, immigrants flooded in from India and China to work in plantations and the docks, and in 1867 the island became a crown colony. Steamships followed and the opening of the Suez Canal led to even more trade links.

Further along Hill St is the **Armenian Church of Gregory the Illuminator**, designed by George Coleman and built by public subscription in 1835. It is Singapore's oldest church and its design is based on St Martin-in-the-Fields church in London. Turning up Loke Yew St brings you to another part of the **Asian Civilisations Museum**, once the Tao Nan Secondary school, built in 1910. Nowadays this beautiful old colonial-style building is home to a collection of artefacts telling the story of the development of Asian civilisations (see p. 457).

THE ASIAN CIVILISATIONS MUSEUM

39 Armenian St $, tel: 6332-3015, Mon 1300–1900, Tues–Thur 0900–1900, Fri 0900–2100 (free admission from 1900), Sat–Sun 0900–1900. This wing of the museum includes a selection of ancient jade pieces which signified kindness and warmth to the ancient Chinese. Pale green jade is from China and is the oldest of the collection. Most of the jade in modern jewellery shops is bright green, much newer jade from Myanmar.

In one of the showcases are carved jade cicadas which were put into the mouths of the newly deceased to keep the spirit of the deceased alive in the next world. Other pieces are *ruyi* shaped – an endless knot – worn by children for protection and longevity. In Gallery 4 there are displays about the religions of the Chinese – Confucianism, Taoism and Buddhism. Figures of the Buddha show the various Buddhist traditions, the ornately dressed Buddhas with elaborate hairstyles being Thai Buddhist figures and the plainer ones Chinese.
The main museum is described on p. 454–455.

From the Asian Civilisations Museum turn up Canning Rise to Fort Canning Park, once known as Bukit Larangan, the sacred burial ground of the Malay kings. The path goes past an old colonial graveyard, now the spice garden, to the **Battle Box** (see p. 458), the recently opened Fort Canning HQ from where General Percival oversaw the fall of Singapore.

Heading down from the hill towards Stamford Rd brings you to the **Singapore History Museum, $**, open Tues–Sun 0900–2100, for which we have Sir Stamford Raffles to thank. Formerly the National Museum, it now shares its exhibits with the Asian Civilisation Museum and the Singapore Art Museum. Exhibitions include the early history of the colony, life in a Peranakan home, a biographical display about William Farquar, the first British Resident of Singapore, the history of Chinese secret societies and an amazing collection of jade. On Wednesday nights there is a fun tour of the museum that includes dramatic representations of events and a chance to climb a spiral staircase to the roof.

THE DECISION TO SURRENDER

One of the main reasons the British surrendered to Japan was the acute water shortage caused by the breach in the supply pipe from Johor and the Japanese taking some of the northern reservoirs. It is ironic then that General Percival was sitting several metres underneath a large reservoir which would certainly have drowned him if it had received a direct hit.

THE BATTLE BOX

The underground fort was only three years old when it became the focus of British efforts to keep Singapore out of Japanese hands. Most of the chambers are 9 m underground and accessed by a steep staircase at the entrance and an escape tunnel at the far end of the complex. An air compressor maintained air flow through the tunnels in the event that the bunker had to be closed. Each room and its soldiers were kept locked up, and there was rarely any movement between them. Communication was through a series of pneumatic tubes. A telephone exchange maintained contact with the outside.

Very few local people ever saw the inside of the bunker and those that did found it claustrophobic, noisy and overpoweringly hot. In 1942 the British surrendered, having destroyed as much as they could and it became the Japanese communications HQ. After the war the British took it back and after independence it became the Singapore Military Forces HQ.

No one knows when the bunker was finally abandoned but it was empty by 1976 when the Singapore Armed Forces moved out of Fort Canning Hill. It was opened again in the 1990s and a massive reconstruction programme began. Today it houses a reconstruction of 15 February 1942 with an animatronic Percival and taped conversations. The bunkers have been faithfully recreated and even graffiti on the walls left by Japanese soldiers have been preserved. Open Tues–Sun 1000–1800, $$.

Walk down Waterloo St to another ancient Singaporean institution, what was St Joseph's Institution. Built in the 19th century as a mission school, in the 1980s it was one of Singapore's most prestigious schools. Beautifully renovated as **Singapore Art Museum, $,** open Tues–Thur, Sat and Sun 0900–1800, Fri 0900–2100, it has no permanent exhibition but houses travelling exhibitions.

The next stop on this tour of the colonial buildings of Singapore is the **Cathedral of the Good Shepherd** in Bras Basah Rd between Queen St and Victoria St. In 1832 the Catholic faith was established in Singapore in a house which stood opposite where the church is now. The present building was begun in 1843. It is a quiet place full of 1950s floor tiles imposed on Victorian flamboyance. Close to it in Victoria St is another part of the Catholic complex, the erstwhile Convent of the Holy Jesus, which is now a leisure complex. Originally an orphanage and school for girls, it became the place for unwanted babies to be abandoned.

A SERANGOON WALK At the top of Serangoon Rd is the tourist-oriented **Little India Arcade**. In between the tourist souvenir shops are real local shopkeepers selling Indian flower decorations, saris, bolts of cloth and even traditional Indian Ayurvedic medicine. Indian grocers sell economy-sized packets of spices, stone pestles and mortars and obscure cooking ingredients, while confectionery shops sell those excessively sweet Indian desserts.

The arcade has a section aimed at tourists, which includes an audiovisual presentation about local customs and some old pictures of the area. On the other side of Serangoon Rd is the relatively unreconstructed **Tekka Centre** with a wet-fish market underneath and clothes and haberdashery shops above. There are still a few shops up there selling real junk which are good to poke around in.

Continuing down Serangoon Rd you will see that Campbell Lane, another renovated set of shop-houses, sells more traditional goods like Indian musical instruments, furniture and brassware.

On the right you will find spice-grinding shops, fortune tellers, lots of vegetarian restaurants including Komala Vilas (p. 452) and jewellers selling great swathes of gold necklaces, earrings and bangles. When a Hindu woman marries, her wealth is displayed by the amount of gold she is wearing. Some of these places will hire out jewellery just for the wedding.

In Dunlop St turn right to see the **Abdul Gaffoor Mosque**, originally built in wood in 1859 and rebuilt in its current form in 1910. Its cupola is made of glass. Indian Muslims living in the area use this mosque. Return to Serangoon Rd via Upper Dickson Rd, the most truly unreconstructed street in Singapore. At one end are a series of scrap merchants. Stuff lies all over the road in the process of being broken up, while saleable objects are lined up beside the fence. At night a little shrine lights up the scrap here and on Sundays this place could truly be a street in India.

Back towards Serangoon Rd along Upper Dickson St a kind of normality returns. Fast food shops, the glorious Woodlands restaurant (p. 452) and shops selling tapes of Indian music and saris line the street. Outside Woodlands there is usually a pan wallah, a man making little arrangements of nuts and leaves which local men chew,

SERANGOON AT NIGHT

This walk is best done at night when the really strange atmosphere of the street emerges, particularly on Sunday night when the migrant Tamil workers come out on the streets to talk to their friends. Include dinner in your walk and it will take about 3 hrs.

THE WET-FISH MARKET

Singapore can feel like London or New York, only hot and clean. Visit the wet-fish market during the day to see what lurks beneath the sanitised walkways and air-conditioning. There are vegetables you may never have seen before, pieces of animal you wouldn't want to eat, and in the deepest corners shelled creatures waiting to have their shells ripped off while they are still alive.

leaving a bright red stain in the mouth. It is meant to be mildly narcotic so you might want to try it. In Cuff Rd is a spice grinder shop, where you can see the ancient machinery which produces freshly ground spices for the restaurants around here.

Back on Serangoon Rd is the **Sri Veeramakaliamman Temple**, dedicated to the Goddess Kali, the consort of Shiva. The temple has lots of statues of the goddess in her various incarnations, and beside her are her two sons, Murugan and Ganesh. Murugan is the god to whom the Thaipusam festival is dedicated. Tuesdays and Fridays are the temple's busy days when there may be music playing inside the temple and the priests take offerings from worshippers, but the temple is lively most evenings. The *gopuram* is the tower over the entrance of the temple which is covered in figures of gods and mythical creatures. Worshippers who can't make it all the way to the temple can see the *gopuram* and make their prayers from where they are.

Further down Serangoon Rd are two more temples. The **Sri Srinivasa Perumal Temple** is dedicated to Lord Vishnu and his consorts. Its wide courtyard area is used during the Thaipusam festival when devotees prepare themselves here for the walk through Singapore to the Chettiar Hindu Temple. Another colourful *gopuram* dominates the temple, built in 1966.

TEMPLE MANNERS

While local people are very tolerant and don't mind tourists gawping at their religious rites there are some rules to be followed. Shoes must be removed before entering the temple, make sure that your dress doesn't cause offence and avoid walking into the inner areas of worship, usually fenced off in some way. Walk around the temple in a clockwise direction. Menstruating women should not enter the temple.

Behind this temple, in Race Course Rd is the very beautiful Taoist **Leong San See Temple**, which translates as Dragon Mountain temple. Dedicated to the goddess Kuan Yin, there are also statues dedicated to Buddha and Confucius, and at the back are ancestral tables bearing the name and burial place of the ancestors of the people who worship here.

Further along Race Course Rd is the **Sakaya Muni Buddha Gaya Temple**, more commonly known as the temple of a thousand lights, home to a 50-ft-high Buddha statue. This Thai-influenced temple is typically garish, with two great stone lions guarding the door. To get the lights switched on make a donation to the temple. You can also get your fortune told daily 0800-1645, free. If you continue walking back towards town along Race Course Rd there are any number of good north Indian and banana leaf restaurants to choose from to round off your walk.

OFFERINGS AT THE TEMPLE

People wishing for something from Kali or her sons usually bring some offering. Those with physical ailments may bring a silver representation of the limb or body part to the temple and offer it to the god. Some bring garlands of flowers that are sold in the street while others offer clothes to the goddess. The priests sell the offerings to go towards the cost of maintaining the temple. By the doorway is a collection of broken coconuts. People break these in a gesture symbolic of giving up their personal needs and dedicating themselves to the god.

ARAB ST A few years ago Arab St also underwent renovations and lots of the residents were moved out to the suburbs. Restored shop-houses are at a premium and as in Chinatown prices are too high for the old community to return. But there is still a sense of the Malay community that once lived in these streets in the businesses that have survived in the unrenovated places, the mosque and the coffee shops.

The **Sultan Mosque** in North Bridge Rd is the biggest in Singapore and is the focus for most Muslim people in the country. The original mosque on this site was built with a grant from the East India Company in 1825, but it was rebuilt entirely in 1925. Open daily 0500–2030, free.

The **Istana Kampung Glam** is not open to the public at the moment but may be by the time you read this. It was built around 1840 as the residence of the Malay Sultan of Singapore who gave up control of the island to Sir Stamford Raffles. In recent

THAIPUSAM

In Indian legend a man called Iduban decided to show his love for the god Murugan by climbing a mountain carrying offerings of milk and honey. Murugan tested Iduban by putting many obstacles in his way. When he reached the top Iduban was offered a place in heaven beside the god. The devotees who take part in the Thaipusam festival are following Iduban's example. They walk in procession from the Sri Srinivasa Perumal temple to the Thandayuthapani temple in Tank Rd, about 5 km.

The participants are chiefly men but some women take part. They wear a heavy steel cage whose bars are embedded into their flesh. They often also pierce their bodies with steel rods and hang fruits from hooks piercing their flesh. Along the road they are given milk and honey and showered in water dyed yellow with turmeric. Most devotees carry out the ritual twice but some choose to do it every year. The devotion is not a penance – the person may be seeking help from the god with their education or health.

years the big old house became very run-down but is about to become a visitor centre for information about Malay kampung life.

On the corner of Jalan Sultan and Victoria St is the **Kampung Glam cemetery** where the Malay royal family are buried. The area is full of craft, batik and basketry shops and the narrow pavements along Arab St are full of gaudy things to buy.

CHINATOWN Another area turned into bijou offices and trendy craft shops. Chinatown really has lost all its sense of an ethnic identity. Some of the old herbal remedy shops and paper burial-goods shops are still here, but it is largely given over to upmarket restaurants and 'antiques', batik and other tourist collectibles.

Fortunately, the past can be revived at the excellent **Chinatown Heritage Centre, $$**, 48 Pagoda St, tel: 6325-2878, www.chinatownheritage.com. Open daily, 1000–1900, the museum opens a window on what life was like for the desperately poor Chinese immigrants in the early 1990s. There is a great deal to see, from a model junk to a prostitute's bedroom (brothels were legal until 1930).

WELD RD FLEA MARKET
At the junction of Weld Rd and Jalan Besar are two narrow unlit lanes where people sit on the ground with little piles of junk in front of them for sale. Some of it comes from the scrap merchants in Upper Dickson Rd and some from people's attics. Walking up here from one of the clean regulated streets, it is a shock that there should be people so poor in Singapore.

The **Sri Mariamman Temple**, another of Singapore's national monuments, is in South Bridge Rd. This is Singapore's oldest Hindu temple, built in 1827 and rebuilt in 1843. The temple was founded by an Indian who accompanied Raffles on his second trip to Singapore in 1819. From outside the temple the figures of Krishna and Rama can be seen at the bottom left and right under umbrellas. The small gold figure at the bottom of the frieze is Mariamman, the goddess of healing to whom the temple is dedicated. In October the Thimithi festival is celebrated here when penitents walk across a bed of red hot embers. Open daily 0600–1230, 1600–2130, free.

In Telok Ayer St is the **Thian Hock Keng Temple**, the temple of heavenly happiness. It is the oldest Taoist temple in Singapore, dedicated to Kuan Yin or Ma Cho Po, in her incarnation of protectress of those who travel at sea. Once situated on the waterfront it would have been the first place that thousands of Chinese immigrants came to after their dangerous sea voyage from China. The present building dates back to 1839 and incorporates Delft tiles, granite pillars from China and cast-iron railings from Glasgow.

A block north of this temple is another – the **Fuk Tak Chi**, now a museum incorporated into the trendy new Far East Square. It has been beautifully restored and retains its door guardians and other details, and contains some brief information about the life of the area in early times and the way that the temple was built.

WATERLOO ST If you enjoy temples than another must-see is the pedestrianised Waterloo St where two temples attract worshippers from all walks of life. The Taoist/Buddhist **Kuan Im Thong Temple** is enormously popular – so much so that you'll have to fight your way inside. The temple is dedicated to Kuan Yin, and was completely rebuilt in the 1980s. This is a working temple where busy people shake bamboo sticks out of pots to discover their future and wave joss sticks around in supplication to the goddess.

The same people call in at another temple just next door, only this time the temple is a Hindu one – the **Sri Krishnan Temple**.

Jurong Bird Park, $$, open daily 0900–1800, is an excellent afternoon's visit. It sits in 20 hectares of landscaped gardens with a massive walk through aviaries containing hundreds of species of birds. There are cages of birds as well as several hornbills, which fly free around the park and occasionally take off to the suburbs where they are an amazing sight among the high-rise flats.

There is an air-conditioned penguin house and a night birds house where you can see owls and kiwis. In the South-East Asian aviary there is a daily thunderstorm. There is a panorail system around the park and daily bird shows which are very good, particularly the birds of prey show. Additional charges for the panorail and breakfast with the birds. MRT to Boon Lay, then bus no. 194 or 251 to the park.

Jurong Reptile Park, next door to the bird park, is a poor second in interest value. Beside the sad crocs lurking about the muddy ponds there are reptile houses where you can see the tokay gecko and some truly gruesome snakes. Other compounds hold snake-necked turtles and iguanas, but no komodo dragons – see them at the zoo. Open daily 0900–1800, **$$$**. MRT to Boon Lay, then bus no. 194 or 251 to the park.

Singapore Science Centre ($) also in Jurong, is aimed at Singaporean schoolchildren but is still good fun. It is a very hands-on place, with animatronics bursting out all over and lots of things to try your hand at, including computer-generated plastic surgery on your own face. Darwin is here, as is a talking gorilla, and you can fly a flight simulator or watch the Omnimax show. Open Tues–Sun 1000–1800. Omnimax or Planetarium show, **$$$**.

SINGAPORE

Close by at 510 Upper Jurong Rd is the **Singapore Discovery Centre, $$$**, along very similar lines with an interactive robot looking frighteningly like Robin Williams in *Bicentennial Man*, virtual reality games and lots of other hi-tech fun. Open Tues–Fri 0900–1900, weekends 0900–2000. Additional charges for motion simulator and shooting gallery. Boon Lay MRT then bus no. 192 or 193.

Ming Village at 32 Pandan Rd is a factory making pottery (also in Jurong). On weekdays you can wander about and watch the craftsmen and women at work making moulds, hand-throwing pots and painting the delicate blue and white porcelain. A lot of the work is for sale and a good tour explains the whole process. Inside is a perfunctory display about pewter making and some Selangor pewter for sale. Open daily 0900–1730, free. Free shuttle bus from Orchard Rd hotels at 0920 and 1045. MRT to Clementi then bus no. 78.

EAST OF TOWN Geylang is a huge complex of high-rise government housing. A lot of Malay people have gravitated to this area as the old kampungs were gradually cleared and their residents rehoused. At the heart of it is **Geylang Serai** and the **Malay Village**, which was built as a focus for the Malay community and as a tourist attraction.

It is a series of Malay-style buildings housing craft shops, restaurants and a bird market. It includes the **Kampung Days Museum** with a steep entrance charge which includes a storytelling show. Close by is the Geylang Serai **wet market**, by far the best one to visit in Singapore, particularly during Ramadan when it comes alive each evening after dusk.

Changi Village is another aspect of Singapore which you won't find in the city centre. It is very much like a small village with a central market and lots of small shops. There are no major attractions except the **Changi Chapel and Museum** and the beach – scruffy and dominated by low-flying aircraft.

From Changi you can get a ferry to **Pulau Ubin**, a thoroughly unreconstructed part of Singapore where kampung houses fester quietly with chickens running about and taro plants growing beside bananas and coconuts. It is a very pleasant afternoon trip, especially if you hire a bicycle and cycle the one or two roads across the island. There are a couple of temples and several very popular seafood restaurants. Ferries leave from the jetty in Changi whenever they get enough passengers.

GREEN SINGAPORE For a small densely populated island Singapore has a remarkable number of places which are forested or form some other natural habitat like marshland or mangrove swamp. Each patch of natural habitat is tiny but together they make up several green belts running across the island. These belts form a sort of wildlife highway, ensuring that species can survive and do not

LIFE IN SUNGEI BULOH

The plants are the most rewarding since they can't fly off or hide. Look out for the common bright-yellow sea hibiscus or the sea morning glory – like the Western garden flower but doing an important job in these wetlands stabilising beaches and providing a firm base for other plants to colonise.

Another fascinating tree, which is marked along the trails, is the sea poison tree, the leaves of which fishermen used to kill fish. The tree provides food for the enormous Atlas moth caterpillar which is common here. The mangroves can be seen with their aerial roots sticking out of the swamp. The mud is low in oxygen and the aerial roots take in oxygen from the air. Shellfish anchor to the roots of the mangroves and provide food for the many migrant birds which pass through here.

become isolated. Taman Negara they may not be, but Singapore's green patches, manicured as many of them are, are great places to visit.

Bukit Timah Nature Reserve, free, is the best place in Singapore. It is a tiny, 71-hectare patch of primary rainforest bounded by secondary forest on the lower slopes, which were once given over to gutta-percha plantations. There is a tarmac road to a grassy patch at the top, usually inhabited by some very cheeky macaques, but there are lots of footpaths and it is worth venturing into the trees to spot some of the things lurking beneath the vegetation.

If you are lucky you will spot a tiny, deadly poisonous coral snake or a Wagler's pit viper, or a cobra – all are fairly common. You will definitely see gutta-percha trees, betel nut trees, rattan palms, any number of different orchids, sea eagles, racket-tailed drongos and great caravans of ants. At the bottom of the hill is an interpretive centre which gives you some clues about what to look for, but the best thing is just to get out there. Bus no. 171 or 182 from Scott's Rd.

Sungei Buloh Nature Reserve ($) is a mixture of natural mangrove swamp and reconstructed fishing ponds. Its 87 hectares are not as much fun as Bukit Timah but if you have no plans to visit wetlands in Malaysia it's an easy journey to see a very different ecosystem to the one at Bukit Timah.

A good interpretive centre, café and a quick video introduce you to the nature reserve but you have to take off over the lake and into the wetlands to see much of any interest. Open Mon–Fri 0730–1900, weekends 0700–1900. Guided walks are free. MRT to Kranji then bus no. 925 to Kranji Dam carpark, a 15-min walk to the park. On Sundays and bank holidays bus no. 925 goes all the way to the park entrance.

The Botanic Gardens are 52 hectares of prime real estate which have never been built on. When it was set aside in 1860 to be the Botanic Gardens most of it was nutmeg plantations with a large area of primary rainforest. The original gardens were both a pleasure ground and an experimental agricultural station, and famously Malaysia's first rubber trees came from some planted here.

Nowadays the gardens have a new lease of life, a new area of land, and a new purpose – besides recreation and research – education. They are a great place to wander round and admire the profusion of plant life. See the beautiful jade vine which looks like a brilliant green wisteria, cannon-ball trees with their giant seed cases emerging straight from the trunks, and monkey-pot trees with seed cases that produce a perfect pot with a lid.

The **Orchid Garden ($)** is truly magnificent, apart from the sycophantic naming of new hybrids after visiting dignitaries. The poor plants can't get named these days until some big shot visits the country. Look out for Margaret Thatcher, Benazir Bhuto and a few other people who were once important. Visit late in the evening and wander round the jungle in the dark – great fun. Open daily 0830-1800 free. Junction of Cluny Rd and Holland Rd.

The Night Safari is a 40-hectare site of secondary forest, turned into a kind of wildlife park except that the animals are not really roaming free but contained within large areas where the tour guides can find them. As its name suggests the place is only open at night, and visitors can wander through the park safe in the knowledge that things may seem like they can leap out and eat them but actually are safely caged up.

There is also a trolley ride around the park where guides stop the trolley when they see some interesting creatures and light them up for a few minutes. The animals are largely Asian in origin so there isn't the diversity of the zoo, but it's the atmosphere of the place where visitors can freely wander in the dark that attracts. To walk all the trails will take an hour or so. Don't be put off by the extremely tacky entrance with its gift shop and things to amuse children. This is worth the money. Open nightly 1930–2400, **$$$**. MRT to Ang Mo Kio and then bus no. 138.

Singapore Zoological Gardens ($$$) have very little about them that is natural but the zoo ranks among the world's best. Two thousand animals live in 90 hectares of gardens with many of them in large enclosures separated from visitors by moats rather than fences. There are animal shows, jungle breakfast and a wild tea party, elephant rides, baby orang-utan hugging sessions, a pets corner farm and photo opportunities with pythons. Visit the zoo if only to see the komodo dragons, a relic of the age of the dinosaurs. Open daily 0830–1800. Extra charges for breakfast and tea with the animals and tram ride. MRT to Ang Mo Kio then bus no. 138.

SENTOSA If you were blindfolded and taken on a mystery ride to anywhere in the world and then allowed to open your eyes on Sentosa you'd know it was part of Singapore. This mixture of exquisite tackiness, anally retentive cleanliness and nitpicking attention to detail could only be Singaporean. Having said that, you mustn't miss a bit of it. It's what Singapore is all about. There are several days' worth of activity on the island, especially if you have children. Singaporeans pour over to the island at weekends – they actually enjoy the place more if it's crowded.

Starting at the most westerly part of the island, **Fort Siloso ($)** is the remains of a military base, now turned into a visitor centre where visitors are treated as new recruits and shouted at by taped sergeant majors triggered off when you pass sensors. The recreation of life at the fort isn't too naff, you can try an assault course, there are weapons training games and the section on the Fall of Singapore is quite instructive. Open daily 0900–1900. Station 3 on the monorail.

The best place to visit on Sentosa has to be **Underwater World ($$$)**, an aquarium with a difference. Besides the many pools and tanks of sea creatures, including some beautiful sea dragons, there is the 'travelator' (a Singaporean word if ever there was one). You stand on a moving walkway and travel underneath a huge acrylic tank with some evil-looking denizens of the deep thrashing about. Open daily 0900–2100.

At Cable Car Plaza, the **Images of Singapore** exhibition ($$) is a waxworks focusing on the early days of Singapore and the festivals and cultures of its ethnic groups. Attached is the recreation in wax of the surrender by the Japanese to the British in 1945. Open daily 0900–2100. Stop 4 on the monorail.

VolcanoLand ($$$) is a silly singing and dancing trip through a Mayan civilisation and its concrete volcano which explodes from time to time, open 1100–1900. At **Cinemania** you can spend lots of money on video games, and at the **Butterfly Park ($$)** you can walk through an enclosed garden containing lots of butterflies and then visit some dead ones in the exhibition rooms. Open daily 1000–1900.

There is a good **nature walk** on the island, unfortunately added to by some plastic dragons, but there are macaques roaming around and you can see pitcher plants. There are a **campsite and two hotels** if you want to carry on having fun, and a food centre as well as all the fast food places. There is also a **night market** and in the evening a dancing fountain show which is quite impressive. You can hire **bikes** and cycle round the island or roller skate at the **skating rink**. You can even play golf on one of two **golf** courses. Access to the island is by ferry from the World Trade Center or by the more exciting cable car from Mount Faber.

OTHER ISLANDS   **St John's Island** is a fairly undeveloped place with a few beaches that are good for swimming and that have basic facilities. Ferries to St John's leave from the World Trade Center twice daily during the week but more frequently at weekends ($$). Closer to Singapore is **Kusu Island** where there is a Chinese temple and a Malay shrine. The ferry service to St John's calls at Kusu first. Both islands get overcrowded at weekends. **Sisters Island** has no ferry service but you can hire a bumboat at Clifford Pier. It is a tiny, concreted island with some shelters and barbecue pits, and coral reefs for snorkellers.

SHOPPING

Singapore is by no means cheap, but clothes, shoes and electronic goods cost less than in the UK and the US. Having said that, shopping till you drop is a traditional Singaporean activity.

Orchard Rd must have more retail space than any other major shopping street in the world. Starting from the top, **Tanglin Shopping Mall** has lots of good restaurants and fast food places as well as arts and crafts, antique shops and furnishings. **Palais Renaissance** opposite the Hilton Hotel heaves with big names like DKNY, Prada, Vera Wang and Versace.

In Scott's Rd **Pacific Plaza** has a Helmut Lang boutique, a Prada store and some modern furnishing shops. Opposite it, **Scott's Shopping Centre** has mostly small clothes shops. Downstairs is the Picnic Food Court.

Further up Scott's Rd is **Far East Plaza** with the excellent local department store, Metro, and lots of odd places for body piercing and punky clothes shops. Back on Orchard Rd **Wisma Atria** is getting a little elderly now but has an Isetan department store and lots of small designer boutiques. Opposite it **Tangs Department Store** has a long pedigree and quite high prices.

Next door, **Lucky Plaza** has a slightly off-the-wall tone. Don't engage one of the shopowners here unless you want to buy. Check prices elsewhere first and make sure you're getting what you think you are, including batteries (are they good ones or cheap imitations), battery charger, adaptors with the right voltage, etc. Watch your purchase being packed. There are lots of camera and electronics shops here as well as stores selling watches, sports clothes, and Chinese silks and craft items, plus a great food hall.

Ngee Ann City, the vast purple building, has **Takashimaya Shopping Centre** inside it. Besides the department store of the same name there are lots of upmarket restaurants and small designer stores. The basement has a good Japanese supermarket. Back on the other side of Orchard Rd are **Paragon** and **The Promenade**, another collection of designer names, while in the Paragon there is an outlet of the New York Metropolitan Museum of Art. Next door, the Heeren has shops catering to a younger crowd. The **Specialists' Shopping Centre** has John Little Department store, a very basic and inexpensive shop, while **Centrepoint** has Robinson's. Both these department stores often have good sales and are very popular with locals.

Outside Orchard Rd **Raffles City** is another huge mall with a Sogo department store and lots of jewellery shops. **Citilink Mall**, a subterranean mall, links Raffles City with **Suntec City**, Singapore's largest shopping centre. **Marina Square** is very tourist-oriented with prices to match but if you go in with a better price from somewhere else shops will bring their prices down. **Sim Lim Square** at Bencoblen St junction with Waterloo St near Chinatown is known for computers and electronics but like Lucky Plaza it has a bit of a wide boy reputation. The **Funan Centre** is a bit more respectable and has a good food centre.

In Chinatown there are **Chinatown Point**, full of beautiful craft shops where you must bargain, and **The People's Park Complex** and centre, both good for electronics and bargaining. In Eu Tong Sen St is an excellent shop, **Yue Hwa**, which sells Chinese arts and crafts, as well as Chinese medicines and more everyday items.

In the streets around South Bridge Rd there are lots of small arts and crafts shops. A good shop to look in is the **Yong Gallery** owned and run by Yong Cheong Thye, an expert in calligraphy. The shop opposite is the **Eu Yan Seng Medical Hall,** established in 1910 and still operating.

Out at **Holland Village** where lots of expatriates live are good fixed price and not so fixed price antique and arts and crafts shops, such as Lim's, and many more. This area is full of small restaurants as well as a Body Shop, a Cold Storage supermarket, a Metro factory outlet with some cheap if wacky clothes and inside the shopping plaza lots of dressmakers that will copy any dress that you bring them. The wet-fish market sells strange spices, and there are smaller shops on the streets worth poking around in for their beautiful Chinese pots and other unusual items.

ENTERTAINMENT

Singapore's nightlife is sedate by Bangkok standards. There are hundreds of small, well-designed independently owned bars, with live music some nights. Besides these there are the expensive discos and clubs of Orchard Rd and the big hotels with good Filipino cover bands. There are several good jazz venues and imported ballet, classical music and theatre.

In Orchard Rd **Anywhere,** 04–09 Tanglin Shopping Centre, tel: 6734-8233, has to be the oldest bar in town with the oldest resident band – Tania.

It's worth phoning **Ice Cold Beer**, 9 Emerald Hill Rd, tel: 6735-9929, to check on happy hours and any current happenings.

The beer at **The Sportsman**, 02-01 Far East Shopping Centre, Orchard Rd, is reasonably priced and top soccer games are always available to view via satellite.

Why? at 04-06, Far East Plaza, 14 Scotts Rd, is a small but popular pub because the drinks are keenly priced. Open daily until midnight.

Lot, Stock and Barrel, 29 Seah St, is a lively pub with rock music belting out from the juke box (no live music) and a happy hour from 1600 to 2000.

Outside the centre, in Holland Village in Lorong Mambong, **Wala Wala**, tel: 6462-4288, is worth the journey for the happy hours between 1600 and 2100.

In Chinatown, **Carnegie's**, 01-01 Far East Sq., 45 Perkin St, tel: 6534-0850, is well worth a visit for the nightly happy hour (1800–1900) and the boisterous (by Singaporean standards) atmosphere at weekends. **Bar Sa Vanh**, 49 Club St, tel: 6323-0145, is one of the most aesthetically pleasing drinking establishments on the island, but can prove expensive outside of the happy hour sessions from 1700 to 2000.

In **Boat Quay** and **Clarke Quay** are lots of place open till 0100 on weekdays and a little later at weekends. **Mohamed Sultan Road** is the place to go clubbing, with more than 20 outlets along a very short stretch.

Harry's Bar in Boat Quay has been there for years and attracts middle-aged expats but is a comfortable place for a drink, while **Jazz@Southbridge**, 82 Boat Quay, is one of the best joints for live jazz sessions.

BOAT QUAY AND NICK LEESON

Harry's Bar in Boat Quay was a favourite watering hole for the young Nick Leeson before his dramatic disappearance in 1995 following the collapse of Barings, the merchant bank he worked for. Injudicious trading and a panic-driven attempt to recoup losses led to the loss of nearly a billion pounds sterling. Leeson fled to Sabah and was arrested in Germany, trying to make it back to the UK. He was sentenced in a Singapore court to over six years in prison but was released after three and a half years.

Around the City Hall area is **CHIJMES** in Victoria St, where the many trendy cafés are supplemented by even more trendy bars such as **Liberte,** tel: 6338-8481.

Cinemas are all over town and the suburbs, and present most Hollywood productions as well as Bollywood offerings and Cantonese movies. Mainstream offerings

SINGLISH

Singaporeans don't know if they're proud of Singlish or ashamed of it. The language of the streets of Singapore is barely recognisable to Western visitors and the words that are clear sound like baby talk – no tenses, no subject/verb agreement, lots of slang words and lots of strange aaah noises. But after a while the ears attune, and far from being a sort of pidgin language, Singlish has a logic and vibrancy that fit the Singaporean.

Expressions like Kiasu from the Hokkien Chinese dialect play an important part, standing in where words are missing in standard English. Malay words have also entered the language so that Singaporeans talk about *makananing* – the Malay word for eat added to the English ending 'ing'. Singlish expressions come and go. You will hear *also can?* It means 'can I do this too?' or 'would you like this too?' or 'is this also the right bus for the zoo?'

Or what adds a question to a statement. Some fairly new Singlish expressions are *you see me no up* meaning 'you look down on me' and *this place got toilet or not?* meaning 'does this place have a toilet?' Also fascinating are the tags that get used instead of questions or for emphasis. *Lah* is a long drawn out noise which means 'I really think so', as in *No, lah no toilet, aah,* the aah adding even more emphasis. *Wah* is an expression of being impressed, perhaps at the size of something.

In 2000 a TV series remonstrated with Singaporeans for using Singlish, saying that they should be able to communicate with foreigners in standard English, so perhaps it has run its course. Whatever happens, it is a lively language full of self-deprecating humour and to be spoken to in it by a Singaporean means you have really become one of them and they trust you. Either that or they can't speak proper English.

are at the **Shaw Leisure Centre** in Beach Rd, **United Artists** at Bugis Junction, the **Orchard Cineplex** in Grange Rd and **Yangtse** in the Pearl Centre in Eu Tong Sen Rd in Chinatown.

For local theatre productions check out **Substation** at 45 Armenian St, tel: 6337-7800, or the **Victoria Theatre** in Empress Place, tel: 6334-6120. The Singapore Arts Festival takes place every year in June, when local production and imports from the West End are put on. Wander round the streets of Chinatown or the suburbs and you will find makeshift stages and performances of Chinese opera. The *Straits Times* will have listings.

SINGAPORE FLYER

The world's largest ferris wheel is being built in Singapore, due to be completed by the end of 2005, located at Marina Bay. The height will be 170 m (561 ft) with a diameter of 150 m (494 ft). The 32 capsules will accommodate up to 25 people each. On a clear day, you will be able to see Johor, Batam and Bintan, 45 km away. The ride will take a good half hour and will be *the* next thing to do in Singapore.

The latest addition to the Singapore arts scene, and to the island's architecture, is the **Esplanade** on Marina Bay (www.esplanade.com). Boasting a 2000-seat theatre and a 1800-seat concert hall, the Esplanade is Singapore's attempt to decisively rebut the constant criticism that the island is a cultural desert. That remains to be seen, but the Esplanade complex itself has been the subject of controversy from architects and cultural commentators on the grounds that it is little more than a monument to kitsch.

The two spiky shells that constitute the shape of the complex have been compared to insects' eyes, twin microphones, jewelled turtles, giant golf balls, copulating aardvarks, and durian fruits. Judge for yourself while wandering around the bars and restaurants and taking in the grand views across the bay. Details of current shows, and guided tours of the complex, are available from the information counter, tel: 6828-8377.

TOURS

From Clarke Quay, Boat Quay, Raffles Landing site and Clifford Pier there are **river tours** in bumboats passing old godowns (quayside warehouses) and some historic sites on the riverside. The same companies also organise longer dinner and high tea cruises out to the harbour on ancient-looking junks. **Other tours** take visitors to Jurong, to the colonial district and on evening trishaw rides around the city. Several tours focus on **Singapore during World War II**, covering Changi prison, Sentosa and Fort Canning. Details of all the tours are available from the tourist office and from companies like Singapore Explorer, tel: 6339-6833, and Singapore River Cruises, tel: 6336-6111. The tourist board conduct their own Original Singapore Walks focusing on lesser known facts about areas such as Chinatown.

CONVERSION TABLES

DISTANCES (approximate conversions)
1 kilometre (km) = 1000 metres (m)   1 metre = 100 centimetres (cm)

Metric	Imperial/US	Metric	Imperial/US	Metric	Imperial/US
1 cm	3/8 in.	10 m	33 ft (11 yd)	3 km	2 miles
50 cm	20 in.	20 m	66 ft (22 yd)	4 km	2½ miles
1 m	3 ft 3 in.	50 m	164 ft (54 yd)	5 km	3 miles
2 m	6 ft 6 in.	100 m	330 ft (110 yd)	10 km	6 miles
3 m	10 ft	200 m	660 ft (220 yd)	20 km	12½ miles
4 m	13 ft	250 m	820 ft (275 yd)	25 km	15½ miles
5 m	16 ft 6 in.	300 m	984 ft (330 yd)	30 km	18½ miles
6 m	19 ft 6 in.	500 m	1640 ft (550 yd)	40 km	25 miles
7 m	23 ft	750 m	½ mile	50 km	31 miles
8 m	26 ft	1 km	⅝ mile	75 km	46 miles
9 m	29 ft (10 yd)	2 km	1½ miles	100 km	62 miles

24-HOUR CLOCK
(examples)

0000 = Midnight	1300 = 1 pm
0600 = 6 am	1415 = 2.15 pm
0715 = 7.15 am	2000 = 8 pm
1200 = Noon	2345 = 11.45 pm

TEMPERATURE
Conversion formula: (°C x 9) ÷ 5 + 32 = °F

°C	°F	°C	°F	°C	°F	°C	°F
-20	-4	-5	23	10	50	25	77
-15	5	0	32	15	59	30	86
-10	14	5	41	20	68	35	95

WEIGHT
1 kg = 1000 g   100 g = 3 oz

kg	lb	kg	lb	kg	lb
1	2¼	5	11	25	55
2	4½	10	22	50	110
3	6½	15	33	75	165
4	9	20	45	100	220

FLUID MEASURES
1 ltr (l) = 0.88 Imp quarts = 1.06 US quarts

ltr	Imp gal	US gal	ltr	Imp gal	US gal
5	1.1	1.3	30	6.6	7.8
10	2.2	2.6	35	7.7	9.1
15	3.3	3.9	40	8.8	10.4
20	4.4	5.2	45	9.9	11.7
25	5.5	6.5	50	11.0	13.0

MEN'S SHIRTS

NZ/UK	Eur	US
14	36	14
15	38	15
15½	39	15½
16	41	16
16½	42	16½
17	43	17

MEN'S SHOES

UK	Europe	US
6	40	7
7	41	8
8	42	9
9	43	10
10	44	11
11	45	12

MEN'S CLOTHES

NZ/UK	Eur	US
36	46	36
38	48	38
40	50	40
42	52	42
44	54	44
46	56	46

LADIES' SHOES

UK	Europe	US
3	36	4½
4	37	5½
5	38	6½
6	39	7½
7	40	8½
8	41	9½

LADIES' CLOTHES

NZ UK	France	Italy	Rest of Europe	US
10	36	38	34	8
12	38	40	36	10
14	40	42	38	12
16	42	44	40	14
18	44	46	42	16
20	46	48	44	18

AREAS

1 hectare = 2.471 acres

1 hectare = 10,000 sq m

1 acre = 0.4 hectares

INDEX

Thomas Cook Publishing
PO Box 227
The Thomas Cook Business Park
15-16 Coningsby Road
Peterborough PE3 8SB
United Kingdom

Please help us improve future editions by taking part in our reader survey. Complete and return this card to the address on the reverse or e-mail your feedback to books@thomascook.com or visit www.thomascookpublishing.com. Any suggestions which are used for updating will be acknowledged in future editions.

1. Which *Independent Travellers* title did you purchase?

....

2. Is this the first *Independent Travellers* guidebook you have bought?

☐ YES   ☐ NO

3. Why is this your preferred choice of budget travel guide?

....

....

4. In your opinion, how could future editions of this book be improved?

....

....

....

5. What other titles would you like to see in this series?

....

Full Name ....

Age ☐ under 21   ☐ 21-30   ☐ 31-40   ☐ 41-50   ☐ over 50

Address ....

.... Postcode ....

Daytime telephone number ....

E-mail address ....

☐ Please tick here if you do not wish to receive details of products and services from Thomas Cook Publishing.

For my wife

While researching this book we drove
from one end of Canada to the other,
and down through parts of the USA,
with only two speeding tickets and not
many more cross words. Thank you.

Author's Note

Several actual regiments and sub-units of regiments are mentioned in this book. For example, Princess Patricia's Canadian Light Infantry and B Troop, 4 Commando. The officers, NCOs and men, however, are creations of my imagination. For that matter, with the exception of obvious historical personages, everyone written about is fictitious.

Acknowledgements

The author would like to thank the following individuals and organizations for their courteous help during the research for this book.

In Canada
George and Phyllis Lyon, of Ottawa; Mr Barry Agnew, Mr Peter Fuller and Mrs M Strachan, of the Military History Department, Glenbow Museum, Calgary; Catherine Myhr, (Maps) Glenbow Museum; Staff of the Regimental Museum, Princess Patricia's Canadian Light Infantry, Currie Barracks, Calgary; Staff of the Canadian War Museum, Ottawa; Staff of the National and Public Archives, Ottawa; Mr Mac Johnston, Editor of *Legion Magazine*, and F Hannington, Secretary-Treasurer, Ottawa; Mr Robert J Franks, formerly of 14 Commando, British Columbia; Members of the Canadian Legion, too numerous to mention individually, in the provinces of Quebec, Ontario, Manitoba, Saskatchewan, Alberta and British Columbia; last but by no means least, Colin and Linda Sumner, for their tremendous hospitality in Calgary.

In England
Mr Henry Brown and Mr R Youngman, of the Commando Association; Major A D C Smith, formerly of 14 Commando; Staff of the Canadian High Commission, London.

In the USA
Mr Bob Carfield, Minnesota; Mr Dick Walker, Wisconsin; Mr Al Bryant, Illinois.

In Germany
Herr (formerly Oberleutnant) Karl Denk, of Munich; Herr Erwin Borchers, of Frankfurt.

Everywhere
Fran Winward.

Prologue

December 1943

The American Pfc, Ryan, checked the door leading to the compound. Before he used a length of hooked wire to slip the latch, his buddy, a second Pfc named Webb, doused the hut lights.

It was snowing heavily outside, and bloody cold. The perimeter searchlights made little impression on the blizzard. Visibility was under fifty feet. If anyone was going to escape, now was the time. Except a fugitive would be dead, frozen stiff, long before morning. In any case, no one was trying to escape. The purpose of the gathering was an execution.

In the distance a dog howled. Its cries were taken up by another, and then a third. Ryan hoped they weren't loose. Sometimes they were, sometimes not. The guards liked to keep the POWs on their toes. Or in their huts, more accurately. If a guy wanted to visit another hut or attempt a blitz on the perimeter fence, he took his chances. The guards knew about the trick with the hooked wire. It didn't bother them. Half a dozen underfed Alsatians were a better deterrent than any lock or key ever devised.

Still, Ryan wasn't worried. There were others outside, watching. Guys who had stood guard, stooged, who had not been part of the tribunal but who supported the verdict. Canadians mostly, like Lambert.

They had all agreed, the leading members of the drumhead court martial, to accompany Lambert across to the main latrines and help tie the knot in the rope. Or put a hand on the rope, a gesture of shared culpability, if too many people helping to fashion the noose became impracticable. Thus they were all responsible, as they had all been responsible for bringing in a guilty verdict and deciding Lambert's fate. Guilty of treachery, collaboration. The Germans could not then single out any one man and punish him, as they might try. Especially as they had lost, or were about to lose, one of their leading informants.

Fortunately the camp was still being run by the Wehrmacht, not the SS. There were not many things to be grateful for, but that was one of them.

A second was the suggestion from Sergeant Ross, another Canadian, that Lambert's death should not obviously be an execution.

'Everyone who matters will know what happened, but why let the Jerries in on it? Make it look like suicide.'

Which was why they were going to hang Lambert and not stick his head down a latrine until he drowned. Or kick him to death or cut his throat. Whenever a man couldn't take the Stalag any longer, he usually hanged himself with a strip of blanket or whatever was handy. It wasn't always a clean death; some of the victims strangled slowly. But at least those guys could choose the way they went. Thanks to Lambert, some of the other guys had exited dangling from a few feet of piano wire in a Gestapo cellar, or at the business end of a firing squad. 'Shot while trying to escape.' There was nothing the POWs could do to prove otherwise, or pin down the culprit responsible for giving escape information to the Germans. Not until Lambert slipped up by getting too greedy, by having more cigarettes than he could account for, and several eggs that could only have come from the authorities, who did not give anything away for nothing.

He had been under suspicion for some time, little things which, by themselves, added up to zero; but the eggs and the cigarettes were the final proof. Lambert couldn't account for them; they had, he protested, been 'planted'. He couldn't explain why anyone, least of all the Germans, would want to do that.

'How's the compound?' asked a British infantry sergeant, Granger.

'Hard to tell with all this friggin' snow,' answered Ryan, 'but I'd say it was clear.'

'Dogs?'

'They sound as if they're penned up. And there won't be too many Krauts in the compound on a night like this, not if they've got any sense. We'll be okay if we stick close to the huts, searchlights or not.'

'Check Lambert's gag,' ordered Granger.

The nearest man did so, avoiding Lambert's eyes. What was in them, hatred, fear or acceptance? Or innocence? No, not innocence. He was a collaborator, Lambert, that much the kangaroo court had proved. God knows how many deaths he'd been responsible for, how many foiled escape attempts. Still, this was murder. If the Germans

2

established that, the firing squads would be set up thick and fast. For that matter, if the Canadian Government ever found out there'd be a few other necks stretched. There were rules about collaboration, the major one being that an accused had the right to defend himself, after the war, in a properly constituted court.

'Gag's fine.'

'Untie his feet,' said Granger, 'but leave his hands bound. If he tries to run for it, deck him. Let's go.'

Keeping in the shadows and freezing if a searchlight swung too close, the group surrounding Lambert hustled him the two hundred yards to the main latrines, inside of which several bright lamps burned – not for the benefit of the inmates, but to enable a patrolling guard to check that all was well. Several escapes had started from the latrines, some of them at night.

They bundled Lambert inside, praying that the blizzard was hiding their movements, curtaining the lights that shone from within the second the door was opened.

'Watch the door,' warned Granger.

Webb took up his position.

Now that they had come to it, Granger was momentarily at a loss regarding what to do next. By any decent standards a condemned man was permitted a few last words, even a bastard like Jack Lambert. But they couldn't risk removing the gag.

Still, Granger felt that something should be said.

A second British sergeant, McCann, beat him to the punch, sensing Granger's discomfort and the reason for it.

'There's nothing to say. Let's get it over with before a wandering ferret stumbles in out of the snow.'

Granger nodded, and uncoiled the rope from his shoulder. He threw one end over a crossbeam while McCann, aided by Ryan, rebound Lambert's feet. Lambert struggled and tried to shout from behind the gag. Only a few muffled sounds emerged.

Ross fetched a bench while Granger looped the noose around Lambert's neck. Lambert would not keep still on the bench until Ross and another Canadian, Jem Turner, held his feet. The bench had to be there, knocked over, to demonstrate that Lambert had killed himself.

Granger beckoned Webb across from the door. As had been agreed, everyone had either to hang on to the rope or touch it as a symbol.

There were eleven men in the execution team. As well as the two

British, Granger and McCann, the Americans Ryan and Webb, there were five other Canadians apart from Ross and Turner: Greyfoot and Tucker, McKenzie, Lucas and Kovacs.

Granger gave the signal. Turner kicked over the bench leaving Lambert dangling two feet from the floor, his limbs twitching for what seemed an eternity before he was still. No one looked at him until they were sure he was dead. Lambert, once, had been their friend. They had been through much together, some of them at Dieppe.

When they were certain life was extinct, they secured the rope to the crossbeam and cut the cords on his hands and feet. No one wanted to remove the gag; that was too intimate a gesture. But finally the American Ryan did so.

Then they all made their way back to their huts, the stooges on lookout also. No one slept well that night.

ONE

The letter arrived two weeks after the wedding. The writing on the
envelope was spidery, the words clumsily formed, written, it seemed,
by an elderly person or a sick one.

A newspaper clipping from the *Calgary Herald* fell out of the
envelope, as well as a folded sheet of cheap notepaper. Ben Lambert
recognized the clipping even before he bent to pick it up. He knew the
caption by heart, and the photograph it accompanied, as well as he
knew his own face in the shaving mirror.

Miss Margaret Anne Lambert, only daughter of the late Mr and
Mrs James Lambert, married Jonathan Margolis on Saturday last.
Mr Margolis, eldest son of Byron and the late Mrs Penny Margolis, was born and raised in Red Deer but now lives in Edmonton
from where he runs a thriving import and export business,
mostly war surplus, with home bases in Edmonton, Toronto,
Montreal and Vancouver. The former Miss Lambert's brother,
Jack, a war hero, died in a German POW camp in 1943. The
bride was given away by her surviving brother, Ben. After
honeymooning at an undisclosed destination, Mr and Mrs Margolis will reside in Edmonton.

Ben studied the caption. The words 'war hero' had been savagely
erased in red ink. In their place 'traitor to his friends' had been inserted,
also in red.

The address on the letter was given as Calgary General Hospital on
McDougall Road. In the same spidery handwriting as on the envelope,
the text made little attempt to disguise that this was blackmail.

Your brother died before he got what was deservedly coming to
him. You might find it to your advantage to talk to the un-
dersigned. Your sister would. Her new husband would. Mr

Margolis might not like being related to a collaborator's family. Think about it.

It took Ben a while to make out the signature. Finally he deciphered it as Duncan McCann.

The letter was dated two weeks earlier and the postmark on the envelope confirmed that it had been mailed the same day it was written, addressed to Ben c/o the *Calgary Herald* and marked 'Please forward'. It had taken the newspaper two weeks to comply, the envelope presumably having been buried in somebody's in-tray.

Ben read the letter again. It would not be unknown, if he were any judge, for hustlers to scrutinize the marriage announcements and then, if one of the parties was rich, which Maggie wasn't but Jon certainly was, to try to put the squeeze on by inventing some phoney story. But wouldn't a real confidence trickster have established Jon and Maggie's Edmonton address, waited until they were back from honeymoon, and put the bite directly on them, not on a far from wealthy brother? Of course, perhaps McCann had done precisely that, but was covering his bets by having two horses in the race.

There didn't seem much doubt that McCann was a veteran, perhaps even from Jack's old regiment, though that didn't necessarily apply since the period in question obviously referred to the Stalag and men from many regiments, and of different nationalities, were incarcerated in every POW camp. Nor could it be that McCann was other than broke. A man who was doing well for himself did not go in for blackmail. Then again, quite a number of Canadian veterans were feeling the pinch, but few of them turned to crime. The government had not treated them well, the returning troops. 'Thanks very much, boys, but now can we please get on with business.' $7.50 for each month of home service and $15 for each month overseas. A bit more for returning POWs, but never more than a modest year's wages. A hundred dollars for civilian clothes too, and the guarantee, if you were an employee, of your old job back. At former pay, of course. About $15 or $20 a week for a clerk or skilled tradesman at 1939 rates. Some offer!

Ben recalled his own repatriation on the troopship to Halifax, Nova Scotia, a port still reeling from the rebellion caused by the provincial liquor control board's decision, on VE Day, to ban the sale of hard liquor and close all beer parlours. The home-based naval ratings and

RCN personnel on leave hadn't taken kindly to the proclamations and had set fire to streetcars and looted liquor stores. Signs of the revolt were still in evidence when Ben disembarked.

He was tempted to ignore the letter, to treat it as dirt, but the address intrigued him. A hospital? Who the hell ever sent blackmail demands from a hospital bed, because he would lay a lot of money, based on the shaky handwriting, that McCann was a patient and not a staff member. And, ill or not, he deserved a damned good kicking before being handed over to the RCMP.

But there was another reason why he wanted to see McCann. He, Ben, had been in England, navigating Lancaster bombers with 514 Squadron out of Waterbeach, Cambridgeshire, when the telegram from the Department of National Defence, informing his parents of Jack's death, had arrived in Calgary. The news had killed his mother within weeks and his father within a year.

That was the only communication ever received. 'It is with deep regret that we must inform you . . .' Pneumonia, they had said, the information coming from the International Red Cross, but no letter, even after the war, and no personal visits from any of his friends, from within the Stalag or without. Perhaps that was understandable. Repats had their own lives to rebuild, but he had wondered at the lack of contact, even so. Jack in some German grave was an uncomfortable thought. McCann, despite his motives, his obvious lies, was the first person Ben had ever heard of who claimed to have known Jack in the camp.

Calgary General stood in north-east Calgary, just north of the Bow River. Ben took bus and streetcar, and was there in less than an hour. He did not bother checking in at reception. McCann had written his ward number as part of his address.

A staff nurse asked if she could help. He explained that he had come to see Duncan McCann. He realized he was outside normal visiting hours, but he had only just learned that McCann was ill and in which hospital. 'We aren't related, but I knew him in England.'

The nurse asked him to take a seat. She went into an office, where, through the glass panel, he saw her consult a typewritten list before crossing to a filing cabinet and extracting a folder. Then she frowned.

'I'm sorry to have to tell you that Mr McCann died a week ago,' said the nurse, rejoining him, 'and was buried three days ago.'

'I see,' said Ben. 'What was the cause?'

'In layman's terms, cancer. I'm sorry. It's always worse when they're young.'

Ben judged the staff nurse to be in her middle thirties, which meant, by implication, that McCann was her junior. Somehow he had expected him to be much older, though, when he thought about it, Jack would still not yet be thirty, had he lived. Blackmailers, however, should be greybeards. It was an old man's racket.

'Did he know he was dying?'

'He wasn't told directly by anyone here, if that's what you mean, but it's possible he knew. He'd been here for some months,' she added severely, referring to the file, 'and according to the doctor's notes received no visitors. I can appreciate why his next-of-kin couldn't visit, but I would have thought his friends might have made an effort.'

'As I told you, I only recently learned that he was ill and where he was. What do you mean about his next-of-kin?' asked Ben, puzzled.

'They *are* rather a long way off, his mother and father. Edinburgh, Scotland, is hardly a streetcar ride away. They have been notified, of course, and his personal effects sent on. In accordance with his own wishes, however, he was interred here. You seem confused.'

'I'd just forgotten he was Scottish,' bluffed Ben. 'No, not forgotten, not with a name like McCann, but forgotten he hadn't lived in Canada for several generations.'

'He was granted landed immigrant status in 1946. You met him during the war, presumably.'

'Yes. You say all his personal effects were sent on to his parents?'

'To the best of my knowledge. That's the usual procedure. Did he have something belonging to you?'

'No.'

'Well, if there's nothing more,' said the nurse, anxious to be about her business.

'There isn't. You've been very helpful.'

'That's quite all right, Mr . . .?'

'Lambert,' said Ben.

On the hospital steps Ben was lamenting the wasted journey when he heard his name called. A man in his forties, dressed in the uniform of a hospital orderly, came up to him. He was underweight and probably underfed, judging by his pinched features. He sported a pencil-thin moustache and the whites of his eyes were pink due to lack

8

of sleep or too much cheap liquor. Ben, who towered above him, thought he looked like a rat and took an instant dislike to him.

'You *are* Mr Lambert?'

The voice was an ingratiating whine. Ben had heard similar tones many times in wartime England. *If you'd like to buy some nylons, guv* . . .

'I'm Lambert. Who are you?'

'My name wouldn't mean anything to you, Mr Lambert, but I've been expecting you. I was a friend of Sergeant McCann.'

'*Sergeant* McCann?'

'He didn't tell you in his letter he was a sergeant? Perhaps I should say former sergeant.'

'How do you know about the letter?'

'I posted it for him. I was the only one he trusted, his only friend. We talked a lot. I'd run errands for him, get his newspapers and magazines.'

'You're a true Christian.'

'There's no need to adopt that attitude, Mr Lambert. Now that Sergeant McCann's dead I'm maybe the only friend *you've* got.'

'Meaning what?'

'Meaning that I overheard your conversation with the staff nurse. She wasn't quite accurate when she said Sergeant McCann's possessions were returned to Scotland. They weren't, not all of them. There was a list, a list of names that Sergeant McCann gave me for safe keeping. He seemed to think it was quite important and didn't want it lost.'

Ben could believe that, as he could believe that the list, whatever it represented, was somehow tied in with McCann's letter. What he did not believe was that McCann had handed it over to the orderly, for safe keeping or for any other reason. The orderly had steamed open McCann's letter before mailing it and made the connection between the contents and this list. When McCann turned up his toes, the orderly had purloined the list, making sure it wasn't sent to Scotland along with whatever else McCann owned.

'I don't know anything about a list.'

'Sergeant McCann told me he'd be coming into money shortly. From what I understood he expected to sell the list. To you, Mr Lambert.'

'Why should I want to buy something I know nothing about?'

'I did a lot for Sergeant McCann while he was alive, frequently using my own money because he had hardly any,' said the orderly, not

9

answering Ben's question directly. 'He made it clear that I'd share in anything he made.'

Ben was tempted to thump the little creep, deck him with a roundhouse right to the chops, or turn him over to the RCMP. Except he wasn't committing any crime. McCann had tried obvious blackmail; this little rodent was merely trying to sell a document. Not his to sell to be strictly accurate, true, but make a fuss and it might 'accidentally' get destroyed or wind up as a prosecution exhibit in a theft charge. Ben couldn't say, even later, why some instinct warned him that Jack's posthumous reputation was at stake, but he knew then and there that it would be unwise to push the rat into a corner. Provided it wasn't going to cost an arm and a leg, he would like to see what was on any list that had made McCann believe it was worth money. If the asking price was prohibitive, maybe threatening the orderly with the Mounties was the only alternative.

'I'd have to see it before I know whether I want to buy it.'

'That won't be possible. It's quite short. You'd be able to remember what was on it and then, to me, it would be valueless. You'll have to buy it sight unseen. I'd prefer not to offer it to Mr Margolis, but . . .'

So, thought Ben, the little bastard *had* opened McCann's letter.

'What sort of figure did you have in mind?' he asked.

'One thousand dollars.' The reply came back without hesitation.

'You're crazy. Where do you think I'm going to lay my hands on a thousand dollars?'

'That's your business. That's also the price.'

'I'll give you fifty.'

'Now *you're* being crazy. Fifty dollars wouldn't keep me for a week in any sort of comfort.'

'You'll get board and lodging free if I report this conversation to the police. You're trying to sell stolen property.'

'McCann gave it to me.'

'For safe keeping you said. I have my doubts about that but, fine, I'll go along with it. But McCann's dead. By rights the list now belongs to his parents.'

'It would be your word against mine if you told the police. I'd deny this entire conversation. They'd never find any list.'

'Which means you'll have to destroy it or hide it. If you destroy it it's worth nothing to anyone any more, and what's the point in hiding it? If you try to sell it to Mr Margolis later that'll prove you had it in the first place. And while the RCMP might not take my word against yours, they'd take Mr Margolis's.'

The orderly thought about it, recognizing a *fait accompli* now it was staring him in the face. Eventually he said, 'Five hundred dollars.'

'Seventy-five,' said Ben. 'Fifty now, which is yours whatever happens. Another twenty-five if, after I've seen the document, I consider it's worth buying.'

The venal glitter went out of the rodent's eyes, thoughts of a few months on easy street gone. Finally he held out his hand. Ben counted out five tens. 'Wait here,' said the orderly.

He was back in a couple of minutes. He passed over a sheet of paper, the same cheap notepaper McCann had written his letter on. And there was no doubt that the shaky handwriting was McCann's.

The first lines shocked Ben, hit him like a physical blow. He whitened visibly and had to read them again to make sure he had not made a mistake.

He read the whole document twice, a procedure that took only a few seconds. Then he put the sheet in an inside pocket and gave the orderly an extra twenty-five.

'Don't let me see you again,' he said, barely recognizing the croak that was his own voice, 'or hear from you again. Or hear that you've spoken to anyone else about this. Otherwise it won't be the RCMP you'll have to answer to. It'll be me.'

He returned home the way he had come, by bus and streetcar, to the small hotel in South Calgary he and Margaret had inherited jointly from their parents when they died. It wasn't the Palliser, having only twelve bedrooms, and he wasn't at all sure that Maggie had done him a favour when, on getting married and receiving a secure settlement from Jonathan, she had bequeathed her fifty per cent to him exclusively and in perpetuity. He didn't think he was cut out to be an innkeeper. It had been fine when he came home from the war, uncertain, after years of excitement and terror in equal proportions, what he wanted to do with the rest of his life. Unlike many other veterans he'd had a cushion, a ready-made income and haven. But that was a two-edged gift, one that had lasted almost two years. He was, he knew, well and truly in a rut. His small staff virtually ran the place, and his accountant took care of wages and made sure no one tried to rob him blind.

He said hello to the day clerk and went directly upstairs to his own quarters. There he poured himself a stiff whisky before taking out

McCann's sheet and placing it face upwards on the table. He forced himself to read each word one by one, to be absolutely certain.

The undermentioned will confirm, if asked, that Jack Lambert died by his own hand after his fellow POWs discovered that he had been collaborating with the enemy.

There followed a list of names.

Sergeant Tom Ross; Sergeant Harry Granger; Corporal David Greyfoot; Corporal Jem Turner; Corporal Bob Tucker, Pfc Zeke Ryan; Pfc Jim Webb . . . McKenzie . . . Lucas . . .

It couldn't be true. It just couldn't be. Not only was McCann accusing Jack of treachery, he was saying that Jack had committed suicide rather than face his accusers. And he had quoted names to back up his charge.

But, hell, anyone could invent a few names if the object was blackmail. The work of a moment for someone who had served in the military. There were no addresses, no nationalities, though Ryan and Webb were evidently American.

Besides, there was the telegram from the Department of National Defence. It is with deep regret that we must inform you . . . Pneumonia . . . International Red Cross . . . That was an official communication, from Ottawa. The Red Cross must have known the precise circumstances of Jack's death. The Germans would have made sure it did, not wanting to be held responsible. Would Ottawa conspire with the Red Cross to hide the truth, if McCann wasn't lying?

It would, Ben concluded. *If* McCann wasn't lying, and that was still a mighty big if, Ottawa would go along with the fiction for at least two good reasons. The first, practical politics. It was 1943 when Jack died. D-Day was six months off and the war was far from won. Ottawa would not wish it made public that a Canadian citizen with a hitherto unblemished war record had colluded with the enemy and killed himself when found out. That would do nothing for the troops' morale. The second reason was humanitarian. The Mackenzie King wartime administration had its critics, and the Prime Minister himself wasn't exactly a favourite among fighting men, but no government, surely, would want to distress a deceased's parents by accusing their dead son of the dual evils of treachery and suicide.

Ben shook his head vigorously and angrily. The insidious worm of doubt was creeping in, tempting him, on the weakest of circumstantial evidence, into giving McCann's story even a semblance of credibility.

He poured himself a second glass of whisky and carried it into the room he used as a private office. Maggie had too, when she'd lived there.

In a chest in a corner were his parents' papers, together with, as he knew because he'd read every last page when he arrived home in 1945, Jack's letters to his mother and father and sister, and one or two to his brother, before Ben had enlisted. There were even several from the Stalag, though these were so heavily censored that they said virtually nothing. Still, Ben started with them, not at all sure what he was looking for. Some indication, perhaps, that the elder brother he had revered had changed because of the war.

He found no evidence in the letters from the POW camp or elsewhere to support that. What he did find were a few names duplicating some of those in McCann's document. Ross. Greyfoot. Turner. Tucker. Kovacs. And a village in England called Chipping Saxonby, whose mention had somehow slipped past the military blue pencil.

Several female names were mentioned, without more than the vaguest comment. Whether Jack had had affairs with any or all of them, or whether they were just friends, wasn't clear.

It began to grow dark. He rang down for sandwiches and a bottle of beer. Both arrived as the sun was setting.

The hotel occupied a corner site and directly opposite was a vacant lot. Beyond that, across the prairie, seventy miles away, were the Rockies. As the crow flies from the window where he sat, though on the other side of the mountains and in British Columbia, was Radium Hot Springs, where the natural spa water could reach over 100 degrees Fahrenheit and where Jack had driven them both, in a borrowed and battered Chevy, on one of his leaves in 1939. Up to the south-west turn-off sixteen miles north of Banff, the road was fine, paved. The last sixty-odd miles to Radium were gravelled, and the Chevy gave up the ghost thirty miles short of their destination. There were not many cars on the roads in those days and they had almost hiked back to the main highway before they got a ride.

Ben recalled his brother's darkly handsome face, almost gypsyish, laughingly encouraging him to take just a few more strides before quitting, and breaking into double time every so often to show him that there was nothing to it. There were four years in age between them, but in 1939, when Jack was twenty-one and Ben only seventeen, the gap had seemed much wider. 'There'll be a truck along shortly, you mark my words. If there isn't, screw it. We'll hike it all the way home. Hell, we can hike it across Alberta, Saskatchewan and Manitoba if it comes to that. We're Lamberts, don't forget. We beat the Depression and can we beat this.'

To Ben's certain knowledge there was no Irish blood in the Lambert lineage, but, that day, with the sun on his face as he turned to gee-up his brother, Ben thought Jack looked like the archetypal Irish king, like a picture he had once seen in a children's history book.

Jack had a mickey of rye tucked down his boot, the concave half-pint bottle shaped to fit snugly against a man's calf. It was where the cowboys kept their liquor, the rodeo riders, the wild men who punched cows for most of the year and raised hell during the Calgary Stampede.

Once in a while they'd take a snort in spite of the heat. No drinker in those far off days, Ben was half-canned before his guardian angel in the truck appeared in a cloud of dust.

On another occasion, on an earlier leave, they had driven, this time in a more reliable vehicle, from Calgary to Golden, stopping en route for an afternoon's fishing on the beautiful Lake Louise. Later, atop Kicking Horse Pass, they'd paused to eat the last of their sandwiches, being immediately pounced on by hordes of whisky jacks, which, greedy brutes though they were, seemed only to want Jack's crusts, alighting on his hands to peck at them. His brother could, without even trying, literally charm the birds off the trees.

On the same trip they found a blacksmith working away in his forge in a tiny hamlet miles away from anywhere. Jack asked if he could try his hand at farriering, and within an hour had mastered the art of making a horseshoe. They drank a lot of beer that evening, that lovely late summer evening, and afterwards slept outside the tent in just their bedrolls, with the Rockies as a backdrop and the stars as a canopy.

They had climbed Mount Edith Cavell together, he and Jack, and scrambled across the Columbia icefield; they had skied up near Jasper and hunted bear, never so much as seeing one, along the banks of the Athabasca River. They had rafted down swollen torrents together,

14

ridden thirty miles a day every day for a week together, and shot skeets fired from a homemade trap.

That man couldn't be a traitor, much less a suicide.

Before he turned in Ben resolved to put the whole incident from his mind – McCann, the orderly, the list of names. The accusations. Forget it. McCann had been a dying crook looking to make a fast buck to ease his last weeks. That was all there was to it. All that had happened was that he was out seventy-five dollars.

A week later he was forced to think again.

Back from her honeymoon Maggie called him from Edmonton, her voice full of anger and distress.

The telephone line was crackling with static, but he heard enough to understand what she was saying. She was quoting from a letter and a newspaper clipping. McCann had taken out insurance by sending an identical communication to her, care of Jonathan's Edmonton office, whose address, thanks to the *Herald* article, it would have taken him no more than a few minutes to ascertain. Or the orderly – the bastard – to ascertain. Naturally enough, the undersized rodent had said nothing about a second letter.

When he could get a word in edgeways he told her that he knew what she was talking about, that he too had heard from McCann, who had died since writing. He would explain everything the following day, travelling up to Edmonton by the first available train.

'Don't ask me anything more now.'

He thought long and hard about how much he should reveal, if anything, of the contents of McCann's document. He concluded he would have to show it to her, tell her everything that had passed between him and the orderly. Hers was letter number two. God alone knew if there were any others, written to major Alberta newspapers or given to a lawyer to be made public in the event of McCann's death. He would hate her to hear about Jack's 'treachery' and 'suicide' from another source.

They met at the house Jonathan had bought for his new wife. By mutual agreement Jonathan was also present.

Margaret Margolis was the first-born of the Lamberts, two years before Jack and six ahead of Ben, though she looked more like her younger brother than her elder. She was a dark-haired, blue-eyed woman, tall for her sex, who just missed being pretty. Her attractivness came from the manner in which she carried herself, a bubbly laugh when she was happy, and a determined set to her jaw. She had shown no interest in marriage until Jonathan Margolis started paying court. That was just before Christmas 1946. They were engaged by February and married two months later.

At forty-five Margolis was thirteen years her senior, a tall, heavily built man who topped Ben by several inches and around sixty pounds. He had missed the war not only because of his age but because of a mild heart murmur. The latter had not stopped him, between the years 1939 and 1945, expanding a group of already thriving companies, though in those days profits were limited by legislation and the entire import-export business dependent upon how efficient the U-boats were being that month. But postwar his enterprises boomed. He was a millionaire several times over.

Omitting nothing, Ben told his sister and brother-in-law what had happened since his copy of the letter arrived. At the end, he handed over the McCann document. Maggie read it quickly. 'Oh, the bastard,' she swore finally, the invective almost inaudible. She blinked back a few tears of rage. 'How could he. How dare he!'

She passed the document to Jonathan.

'He was a dying man on the make, Mags,' said Ben. 'There's no truth in it, of course, and I'm sorry you had to read it. I wasn't going to say anything to you at all. I wouldn't have done if McCann hadn't written to you.'

'But why would anyone want to write such terrible things?' she wanted to know. 'Even for money. It's foul. And these other people – Ross, Greyfoot, Kovacs. The others. Why does he mention them? You'd only have to contact one of them to establish that McCann was lying.'

'They probably don't exist,' said Jonathan.

'Oh, they exist, all right,' Ben corrected him. 'At least, some of them do. I went through Jack's old letters while you were away. He mentions Ross, Greyfoot, Kovacs. Turner as well, I think. Maybe a couple more, I can't remember.' He saw Maggie and Jonathan staring at him. 'Well, hell,' he added, 'what chance would I have of tracing them two years after the war? McCann would know I couldn't, or that it would take me months. He didn't have months and almost certainly knew it. He'd have to get me to cough up right away or the money would be no use to him. Besides, they might not even have survived the war.'

'You mean they're real people,' said Maggie uncomfortably.

'Apparently.'

'There's one way of finding out,' suggested Jonathan. 'Whether or not they survived, I mean. Actually, there are two ways. The Canadian Legion, which might take time even if any of them bothered to join, or Ottawa. Thanks to the business I'm in, I have a few connections in Ottawa.'

'You mean they're all in on it?' said Maggie.

'That doesn't seem likely,' said Ben.

'No, it doesn't,' agreed Jonathan. 'For McCann to have six or eight accomplices to substantiate a lie would mean he, they, were looking for a hell of a lot more money than anyone would be likely to pay to keep this out of the newspapers. Thousands, not just a few dollars. Okay, I've got thousands, but I'm a brand-new member of the family, one that neither McCann nor anyone else involved could have known about before Maggie and I got married. Ben's probably right in suggesting that McCann, aware that he was dying and looking for a quick pay-off, jotted down the first half-dozen names he could think of from the war, to give his fiction some sort of credibility.'

'Yes, that has to be it,' said Maggie, but there was a quiver of uncertainty in her voice. 'Doesn't it?'

'Oh, come on, Mags,' protested Ben. 'Jack a collaborator, a suicide? What the hell can you be thinking?'

'I know, I know, but . . . But how was McCann to know that you couldn't trace Ross or Greyfoot or whoever overnight? He was taking a chance. He would have been wiser to invent a few corroborators. Oh, Christ, it's all so confusing. I'm not thinking straight.'

'There's a sure-fire way of finding out the truth,' said Jonathan, who had not made several million dollars by deferring decisions, by permitting tomorrow to take care of itself. 'Let me call Ottawa, talk to some military people I'm acquainted with there. They might not be in a position to discover the whereabouts of Kovacs and the others in a whole hell of a hurry, but I'm prepared to make a small wager I can get someone to dig out Jack's wartime records and establish precisely what the Red Cross said in its report. What do you say?'

'Maggie?' queried Ben.

'I'm not sure. It's as if we're doubting Jack already.'

'If it makes you feel any better,' said Ben, 'I experienced something similar. I soon realized it was crazy, of course, but it was there.'

'I never met Jack, naturally,' said Jonathan, 'but I do know from general observation that war changes people. You only have to look at the careers of senior SS officers to understand that. Family men who loved their children on the one hand, butchers on the other.'

He was playing devil's advocate deliberately. He did not believe, either, that Jack Lambert, from what he'd heard of her brother from his wife, was guilty as charged. But he knew Maggie. She would worry herself ragged until she knew the truth. He didn't want his marriage starting off on that sour note.

'Do it,' said Maggie, after a moment. 'Call Ottawa.'

'Do it,' agreed Ben.

'It may take some time. Can you stay?' Jonathan asked Ben.

'I'll stay as long as it takes.'

Margolis was on the phone for most of the afternoon. He reappeared every so often to pour himself a beer and give his wife and brother-in-law a progress report. Nothing much was happening, as yet.

Early on he asked if Ben knew Jack's service number. Lambert was hardly an uncommon name and several hundred had served in the military. The number was necessary to narrow down the search.

As was customary in the armed forces, a correspondent wrote his number before his name and rank on all letters, but Jack's letters were back in the Calgary hotel, locked in the chest. Ben thought he could remember the first four digits, however.

'That should be enough,' said Jonathan.

While he was away Ben and Maggie tried playing gin rummy, but neither could concentrate and eventually they gave it up. All three skipped lunch.

At four thirty Jonathan came back. He had a sheet of company notepaper in his hand and his expression was far from reassuring.

'Let's have it,' said Ben grimly

'There's nothing to have.' Jonathan flopped wearily into an arm-chair. 'They've found Jack's records, I think – though they won't even confirm that – but, and I quote: "We can't give any information out over the telephone." It's contrary to an Act of Parliament paragraph this, sub-section that, or some such. I threatened to go right to the top and I got close to it. But the man I spoke to confirmed what his minion said. Nothing doing. I'm on first-name terms with this character, but he wouldn't budge. Although it's strictly against regulations he'll allow me to see the file when I'm in Ottawa, but that's all.'

'Where does that leave us?' asked Maggie.

'It leaves me going to Ottawa, though I can't set out before midweek. I suppose you'll have to get back to Calgary, Ben?'

'I must.'

'I'll drive you to the station. Can you leave the McCann document with me?'

'Of course.'

In the car Jonathan said, 'I didn't want to mention this in front of your sister, but it doesn't look good. I've spent a large part of my business life reading between lines, and what I'm reading here isn't encouraging. It strikes me that if there was nothing peculiar about Jack's papers, my contact would have said as much. Simple statement.'

'Let's not second guess it.'

'No.'

It was five days before Ben heard from Jonathan, and on this occasion the lines between Edmonton and Calgary were clear. All too clear. Jonathan broke the news as gently as he could, but there was no way of softening the sickening blow. The Red Cross report confirmed what McCann had written. Jack had committed suicide while interned in a POW camp. There was also evidence to suggest that he had been collaborating with the camp authorities and that several would-be escapers had been shot dead thanks to information furnished by him. A memorandum attached to the file, written by a civil servant in the National Defence Department in 1944, stated that no action would be taken. Sergeant Lambert would be reported as having died of pneumonia.

Ben was stunned. 'How did he actually . . . die?' he managed finally.

'You don't want to hear this, Ben.'

'I do, damn it!'

'He hanged himself.'

Ben felt ill. His senses reeled. It took a superhuman effort to stop the hand holding the phone from shaking.

'How's Maggie taking it?'

'Badly. I had to call the doctor. She's in bed, under sedation. Look, do you feel fit enough to carry on talking for a while?'

'Yes. There's no possibility of a mistake, is there?'

'None. I saw the documents with my own eyes. As a matter of fact, I saw several other dossiers, which is what I want to talk to you about.'

'Go on.'

'You left me the list of names written out by McCann if you recall.' Ben said he did. 'Okay, so while I was in Ottawa I decided to do a little personal sleuthing, look up some of *their* service records, present whereabouts if known, and so on. I had to call in a few favours to pull that off. It wasn't easy without their service numbers, but with a lot of cross-checking we managed it. They would all have been POWs in the same Stalag as Jack, naturally, or McCann wouldn't have listed them, so that helped. Ryan and Webb are Americans, of course. Their ranks told us that much, so there was nothing on them. And of the remainder, we could only find dossiers on Ross, Greyfoot and Turner. No, wait a minute, that's not quite true. We found a dossier on Kovacs, but there was nothing to tell us where he is now. We obtained addresses on the other three by liaising with the Legion, who were reluctant to give out personal information until my contact pulled rank. He's a major general. All three are members. Perhaps I should say *were* members. Ross and Turner are current, but Greyfoot didn't pay his subscription in 1946. However, I have his last known address.'

'Is there a point to all this, Jon?' asked Ben. Suddenly he felt unutterably weary. He wanted nothing more than to go to bed. No, he wanted to get fire-eating drunk and then go to bed.

'Be patient, laddie. I promise you I'm not wasting your time.'

'I know. Sorry.'

'That's okay. Anyway, Turner, it transpired, lives in Ottawa. I went to see him.'

Ben became alert. 'Go on.'

'I didn't find out what his business is, though I can do so if necessary. Whatever it is, he's making plenty. Fancy house, nice-looking wife. He wanted me off the premises pretty damned sharp when I explained what I was doing there, but I managed to persuade him to talk to me.' Ben could imagine Jonathan's methods of persuasion. They would be more subtle, but they would not be dissimilar to McCann's. 'He confirmed, eventually, what Jack's dossier said. That Jack was a collaborator who took his own life when he was found out. Except — except I felt there was more to it than I was being told. I don't know what. I don't have the gift of second sight, unfortunately. But there was something there that didn't ring true. I would have expected him to curse Jack, even after all these years, say something to the effect that he deserved all he got, as McCann did in his original letter. But there was nothing like that. When I mentioned McCann, which I did without going into too many details – nothing about blackmail, for example – because he wanted to know how I'd found him, he seemed more angry with McCann than with Jack. And I swear he heaved a sigh of relief when he learned McCann was dead. I left his house not feeling too happy.'

'What about Ross and Greyfoot?'

'I hit pay dirt there – as far as ex-Sergeant Tom Ross is concerned, anyway. He lives not a stone's throw from you, right there in Calgary. Mount Royal.'

'Money,' said Ben.

'I didn't catch that.'

'There's a lot of money in Mount Royal. If he lives there he's not short of a dollar, unless he's working as a chauffeur or something for a wealthy family.'

'Well, he's close enough to visit, whatever. David Greyfoot isn't. He's a bit further afield, last known address a small town in the middle of Saskatchewan called Foam Lake. It's east of Big Quill Lake roughly midway between Saskatoon and Yorkton. He's originally from Manitoba, Greyfoot. He's part Cree Indian, part white. Anyway, it's a long way to travel on the offchance that he might still be there. Ross is a much sounder bet.'

'You want me to see him?'

'He's worth a trip, Ben. He was in the Stalag with Jack. Maybe I misread Turner. Maybe all he's up to is something shady that has nothing to do with Jack and the war. You can only find that out by having a word with Ross. Maybe we can settle this business once and for all.'

'That seems to suggest you don't think Jack was a traitor who took his own life.'

'I thought you didn't, either.'

'Until ten minutes ago I wouldn't have given the idea house room. You've just told me otherwise, that it's there in black and white, the Red Cross report and the civil servant's recommendation. You also said a few days ago that wars change people. Well, you're right in that respect. I saw men in my own squadron crack up when they'd just had enough, made one sortie too many. Guys you'd have thought were as hard as teak crying into their beer one night in the mess. I was never a POW, thank God. If I had been I don't know how much I could have taken. Short rations, long periods of solitary confinement if you break the rules. Thousands of miles from home and family. Who knows where any man's breaking point is?'

'Which is why I'd like you to see Ross, for Maggie's sake as well as yours. If you come away believing Jack to be guilty as indicted, okay, maybe we should forget it, put it down to the war, as you say. Perhaps even Maggie could accept that in time. But Turner professed not to remember too much about the autumn and winter of 1943. He wasn't only vague, he was amnesic. I'd see Ross myself, but you're on the doorstep.'

'Okay,' said Ben finally, not entirely convinced that Jonathan wasn't merely giving him something practical to do, to take his mind off the bombshell revealed in Jack's dossier. But he owed it to Maggie to be sure. Even more, he owed it to Jack. 'Give me those addresses, both of them.'

Ross refused to see him when Ben gave his name and explained his business over the telephone. He didn't even want to know how Ben had traced him.

'I have nothing against you personally, Mr Lambert, but you have to appreciate that your brother is a different matter entirely. I saw the report of your sister's wedding, and the reference to her "war hero" brother, in the *Herald*, and I was half-inclined to write to the editor and set the record straight. However, I decided to let sleeping dogs lie. I'd advise you to do the same.'

Ben tried a shot in the dark.

'McCann and Turner don't see it like that. Nor does David Greyfoot.' There was a very long silence at the other end of the line – before: 'You've spoken to McCann, Turner and Greyfoot?'

'Perhaps we should discuss it in person.'

'Very well. Tomorrow at six thirty, this address.' The phone was slammed down. Now *there's* a volte-face, thought Ben.

He drove over the following evening even though, from the hotel, Montcalm Crescent was within walking distance.

He had forgotten just how large the houses were in Mount Royal. For Calgary, anyway. To live here would take considerable capital or income unless Ross was a hired hand. And nothing in his attitude had suggested that. Ross was an owner. He was also not at home.

Ben was shown into a huge drawing-room by the maid. A brunette in her early thirties rose to greet him. She was quite small and slim, very pretty in a way that reminded him more of Englishwomen than Canadians, and perfectly groomed from her stylishly coiffured hair to her elegantly shod feet. The dress and jewellery she wore would have kept the average Albertan family in food and fuel for a year, and there was something about her manner that was aristocratic, haughty even. This was m'lady addressing an outsider.

'Hello,' she said, extending her hand, 'I'm Ruth Ross. I apologize for my husband's absence, but I'm afraid he was called away quite suddenly on business. It's likely he'll be gone for several weeks. He wanted to telephone you, but you didn't leave your number.'

Ben stayed ten minutes, accepting a whisky in order to have an excuse for remaining. He had no doubt that Ross's 'quite sudden business' was a diplomatic lie, but whether that was because he had something to hide or because he genuinely could not face Jack Lambert's brother was uncertain.

Ruth Ross might not have heard of Jack Lambert or of the events in the Stalag judging by her conversation. Again, she had that peculiar ability Ben had found among wealthy Englishwomen, though plainly she was not English, of talking about nothing and making it sound like the Sermon on the Mount. He was quite sure, too, she could make the Sermon on the Mount sound like a grocery list. She kept herself well hidden, did Mrs Ross, and if he had to make a guess he would estimate that a lot of the opulence around was hers. The surroundings fitted her like a cloak. This was someone who had been born to money, possibly power.

When he left he said he would telephone in a fortnight, in the hope that Mr Ross was back by then. He was determined not to let Ross off the hook. If all he did was confirm what Turner had said and the Red Cross official had written, well, that was something. But it was strange that he had been antipathetic towards a meeting until the names McCann, Turner and Greyfoot were mentioned. It was equally strange that he had evidently changed his mind after due reflection.

Ruth Ross tried hard to hide her distaste for someone who had the persistence, and manners, of a door-to-door salesman, but the mask slipped slightly.

'You must do what you think appropriate, Mr Lambert,' she said frostily.

Driving home, Ben made up his mind to see David Greyfoot, if Greyfoot was still in Foam Lake. Travelling by way of Medicine Hat,

Moose Jaw and Regina on the Trans-Canada, and then heading north and later east on Highway 16, would put him in Foam Lake after about six hundred miles. Not all the Trans-Canada was paved east of Calgary to the best of his recollection, but he could do it in ten hours' driving with a bit of luck. Start out at dawn and he'd be there by late afternoon. On the return journey he would stay with Highway 16 all the way to Edmonton, call in and see how Maggie was and discuss anything he had learned with Jonathan.

Foam Lake turned out to be maybe a three-horse town with very little chance of being upgraded. The railroad ran through, true, but the railroad ran through all these prairie communities. More accurately the prairie communities with their grain silos had sprung up next to the railroad. The farmers delivered their crop to the siding, made their deal with the grain agent, and left their harvests to be freighted either west to Vancouver or east to Montreal or Halifax.

The landscape was as flat as a board for as far as the eye could see. The Cypress Hills in the south-west were hidden behind the heat haze. It would be murder here in the winter, thought Ben, with the wind howling down from the north and nothing to stop or deflect the snow that came with it. Temperatures of minus thirty degrees Fahrenheit would not be uncommon, and it would never rise above freezing. They were tough bastards, these prairie farmers. They had to be.

The first person Ben spoke to, a thickset youngster lounging by a delapidated truck, knew of Greyfoot.

'Lives in a cabin down by the lake. You won't get your automobile through, though. You'll have to hike it.'

Ben listened carefully to the directions.

'You a friend of his?' asked the youngster.

'Not exactly. Friend of a friend, let's say.'

'Because if you're not you'd better get ready to duck. He's a mite crazy. Most of us around here keep clear. He doesn't bother us and we don't bother him. Some of the boys tried it once, but he chased them off. Liable to take a shot at you as soon as spit.'

'Has he been here long?'

'A year, year and a half. Came across from Manitoba so they say, after the war.'

It was a mile on foot to the cabin after Ben left his car. He could see it in the distance, set back from the lake, long before he got close. He had the uncanny feeling, also, that the occupant was watching him, a premonition that proved to be accurate when he was fifty yards away. David Greyfoot stepped out of the cabin, a hunting rifle cradled in his arms.

'That's far enough.'

Ben took the bull by the horns.

'I'm Ben Lambert, Jack's brother.'

Greyfoot didn't even blink.

'I don't care who you are, you're not welcome here.'

Ben continued to advance, slowly. He did not believe Greyfoot would shoot him, whatever his reputation locally. That sort of thing didn't happen, even in Saskatchewan, in 1947. He was less sure of his hypothesis a moment later when he heard a round click into the breech.

'I was talking to Tom Ross's wife yesterday,' he said, trying but not entirely succeeding in keeping his voice steady. 'I heard from Duncan McCann earlier in the month. A friend of mine saw Turner in Ottawa last week. We're still trying to find Kovacs and the others.'

The bullet went several yards wide of his head, but he felt the slipstream as it whistled past and the detonation almost deafened him. Involuntarily he dropped into a crouch, pale and angry.

'You crazy bastard . . .!'

'I told you, you're not welcome.'

Now that he was closer Ben could see that Greyfoot was drunk, flushed beneath his sallow skin. His hair hung down to his shoulders and was almost jet-black, and his cheekbones were high and pronounced. Other than that, however, he did not resemble any prairie Indian Ben had ever seen. The European, white, part of his heritage was clearly evident. He could have passed for an Italian or a Spaniard.

He could also have used a general clean-up, for even at thirty yards it was apparent he held no brief for personal hygiene. His faded dungarees were filthy, as was the battered straw hat he wore, and his bare feet hadn't seen water for some time. Ben found this odd. Greyfoot had held the rank of corporal, and a man didn't get two hooks unless he was not only an efficient soldier but a spotless one.

'I just want a few words,' he said, standing upright cautiously. 'I've come all the way from Calgary just to talk to you.'

Greyfoot squinted at him. 'Yes, you're like your brother. I can see the likeness now. He was never one to take no for an answer, either. But you've had a wasted journey.'

'You won't even given me five minutes?'

'I wouldn't give Jack Lambert's brother even one. He was a traitor. We proved that before we . . .'

Ben waited, but Greyfoot did not finish his sentence.

'Before what?' Ben prompted.

'Before we found him dead.'

'The telegram said it was pneumonia.'

'Then that's what it was.'

'But McCann said he killed himself, hanged himself.'

'Then that might be true also.'

'You can't have it both ways.'

Greyfoot grinned mirthlessly.

'I'm the guy with the rifle. I can have it any way I like.' He made an aggressive gesture with the weapon.

Ben turned on his heel. He would get no further here.

'He was my friend, you know,' he heard Greyfoot say. 'He was the best friend I ever had, or ever will have, the bastard.'

Ben glanced over his shoulder. If he hadn't known better, he could have sworn Greyfoot was crying.

'He started to say something,' Ben told Margolis. 'He said immediately afterwards that it was "before we found him dead", but I don't believe that's what he meant in the first place.'

'What was?'

'I'll come to that, but, for now, none of it makes any sense. Greyfoot also told me that Jack was the best friend he ever had. Ross skipped out rather than talk to me. According to you, Turner was very evasive. Not one of them reacted in the way you'd expect if remembering a genuine traitor.'

'Ross did.'

'He came closest, that's all.'

'Fair enough, McCann did, then. Or the Red Cross and Ottawa.'

'And that's another item – McCann's list. How many people were on it, ten – twelve?'

'Ten.'

'Eleven, if we include McCann himself. And God knows how many others in the camp knew that Jack, if we believe them, committed suicide. Let's be conservative and call it fifty or sixty. You just can't keep an item like that a secret. Nor was it intended to be one, because the Red Cross knew and so, eventually, did Ottawa. But no one, not one of those fifty or sixty, has said a word since the war ended. Christ, you'd expect someone to talk, tell his wife or parents, or a newspaper. Forget this pneumonia malarkey. Jack Lambert hanged himself because he was a collaborator who'd been rumbled. It should have made headlines.'

'Tell me what you're driving at.'

Ben took a moment to marshall his argument.

'I've had time to think about this, don't forget, since seeing Greyfoot. Driving up here from Foam Lake I turned it all over in my mind. I can't deny that the evidence points to Jack being guilty of collaboration, though I still find that hard to accept. But whatever the truth of that, I don't believe he killed himself. I believe Greyfoot, Ross, Kovacs, McCann, Turner and the rest found out, or thought they'd found out, what Jack was up to – and executed him. Wait – hear me out,' Ben hurried on when Margolis shook his head in disbelief. 'It's my opinion that that's what Greyfoot was going to tell me before he changed his mind. He was going to say: "We proved that before we murdered him."'

'There's not a shred of proof to substantiate that,' protested Margolis.

'I know, I know.' Ben nodded. 'I know. But it would explain why everyone is being so mysterious. All right, almost everyone. They're not cursing Jack for one reason only – they want the whole episode buried. They haven't mentioned it to anyone – wife, mother, father, newspaper – because they can't. They court-martialled him and executed him, making it look like suicide. They sold that to the Red Cross and Ottawa and, for all I know, the Germans running the Stalag.

'We agreed right from the beginning that Jack was an unlikely suicide. In my book, and Maggie's book, he was an unlikely traitor too, but that's another part of the story. If he collaborated he did if for a reason. Whichever, he would never have killed himself.'

'Not even if war alters people?'

'Not even then. Not Jack!'

Ben hammered the table they were sitting at with his fist. Hard. Margolis placed a restraining hand on his arm.

'Careful, laddie. Remember Maggie.'

Ben had arrived in Edmonton late evening. It was now almost

midnight. Not expecting her brother, Maggie had retired early. She was no longer taking more than a mild form of sedative, but she was still far from well. Her husband did not want her disturbed, not with a crazy notion like this. Ben was clutching at straws; Margolis was reluctant to let his wife reach for the same life-raft.

'Let's say you're right,' he said, keeping his voice down. 'Where does that leave us? You'll never prove anything. If Turner and the others on McCann's list formed a kangaroo court and condemned Jack, they're not going to admit it. Hell, that's a rope round their own necks. You haven't an iota of evidence with which to go to the authorities. They'd tell you to take a hike. Even if they didn't, if you went public, you'd also be admitting that Jack was a suspected traitor. You're better off as you are.'

'Not if I go further than just accusing Turner and the others of murder,' said Ben, 'if I went after the whole truth. You forget, I've got all Jack's letters, those written to our parents, to Maggie and to me. I also have an advantage that the war's now over, no more secrecy. I can find out where his regiment was, and later his commando, between the time he left Canada and the time he was made a prisoner-of-war. I've got the names of people he knew in England, not just military people, and at least one village. I can trace his whole career, find out when he changed, *if* he changed. I can talk to people who remember him. There must be someone who'll support my side of the argument.'

'And leave your hotel to run itself.'

'This is my brother we're talking about, damn it, not just some run-of-the-mill bum. I'll sell the bloody hotel.'

Margolis was silent. He could see that his brother-in-law was deadly serious. Moreover, he partly agreed with the outlined strategy. Somewhere along the line it might solve the problem, perhaps once and for all. One thing was for sure, it was going to be hard to live a normal life with this hanging over their heads.

But sell the hotel? Maggie would never forgive him if he allowed Ben to do that, get rid of his only asset, one that their parents had struggled to make viable. Nor should she. He had money. It had taken him many years to accumulate his wealth, but money was there to be used. Besides, he loved his wife. It had taken as many years to find her.

'There's no need to sell the hotel,' he said. 'If you're determined to go through with this, I'll back you. I'll also put a manager in while you're away.'

28

'Thanks, Jon, but this is my problem.'

'It's a family problem, and I'm family. Besides, Maggie has her own money now and if I don't foot the bill, she will. It amounts to the same in the end. So hear me out.

'I own some Lancaster bomber trainers that have to be returned to England. They're due to fly out of St John's in a couple of weeks, bouncing off Greenland, Iceland, Shannon in Ireland, and finally landing at Prestwick. It's cheaper for me to hire pilots to fly them across the Pond than crate them up and send them by sea. Don't ask me why I can get a better price in Europe than I can in Canada. That's my business and you wouldn't understand it anyway. Let's just say that the British Government is anxious to buy them. All I have to do is get them there. Fly in one of them as a passenger if you want, or, if your navigation isn't too rusty, earn your passage over.

'Go to England. Go wherever your nose leads you. Find out what happened. Set your mind at rest, and Maggie's. Mine too.'

'It's a generous offer,' said Ben thoughtfully.

'Its a selfish offer,' grunted Margolis. 'It'll get you out of my hair. Let's say it's also conscience money. While you guys, you and Jack, were fighting my war for me, I was making big bucks. I'm just trying to even the score. I'll write it all off as a deductible expense, anyway. Deal?'

'Deal,' said Ben.

TWO

December 1939

The troop train was packed to bursting, not only with officers and men of Princess Patricia's Canadian Light Infantry. Here and there Jack saw regimental insignia of the Loyal Edmonton Regiment and the Seaforth Highlanders, elements, like the Patricias, of the 2nd Canadian Infantry Brigade. And stragglers from the 48th Highlanders and the Hastings and Prince Edward Regiment, part of the 1st Infantry Brigade. In handfuls only, the latter, guys who had missed their own trains for one reason or another and were hitching a ride to Halifax, Nova Scotia. All were easily outnumbered by the Patricias, though they tried loyally to sing their own regimental songs. These were drowned out, however, by the Patricias roaring the words to 'Has Anyone seen the Colonel' and 'So Clear The Way', and the troops' favourite, 'The Ric-A-Dam-Doo', PPCLI slang for the regimental colours.

The train was two and a half days out of Winnipeg, a few hours from the port of embarkation, Halifax. There was a rumour going around that the regiment would sail for Scotland aboard the luxury liner *Orama*, but Jack Lambert and his fellow NCOs reckoned they'd believe that when they saw it. In any case, it wouldn't be a luxury liner for long, crammed to the gunnels, as it would be, with feisty Canadians on their way to war. Not that Sergeant Lambert would have known a luxury liner if he fell over one. He had only seen the ocean half a dozen times, the Pacific from Vancouver Island. He had never seen the Atlantic, and he knew for a fact that few of the men in the regiment, those who had joined up only when war was declared, had been further from home than the farms many of them were raised on.

He was glad to be kissing Winnipeg goodbye, not that he had anything against the city that was home to the Patricias. But the good bureaucrats of that place, before the regiment left, were already discussing blackout arrangements. Blackout, for the love of God, with Winnipeg just about as close to the middle of Canada as it was possible to get, roughly equidistant from both seaboards. Germany was approximately seven thousand miles east, Japan a couple of thousand miles further west. There wasn't a bomber in the world that could fly a fraction of that distance, nor one that could make the return trip if launched from a Jap aircraft carrier standing off Cape Scott. The east coast didn't matter as far as carriers were concerned; the Germans didn't have any. Nevertheless, Winnipeg's city fathers were beating their brains out trying to decide whether they should order the lights doused after dark and get every household to put up blackout curtains. Crazy bastards. Who the hell were they defending the city against? The last anyone heard, the Martians hadn't joined the Axis.

Jack caught the eye of one of his company lance-jacks, Alphabet Soup, and winked, receiving a weary half-grin in return. Alphabet was a Polack from somewhere in southern Manitoba, Altona or some such place, just across the border from North Dakota. He had so many consecutive consonants in his name, a lot of them Zs and Ws, that no one could pronounce it without bloody near choking, let alone spell it. Hence his nickname.

Jack was one of the few people who knew that Alphabet had served time in Headingly, a prison near Winnipeg, and had been released only because he agreed to join up and fight abroad, something that no Canadian could be forced to do, serve overseas, other than as a volunteer. He'd been given the choice of regiments – he claimed and Jack doubted – but had enlisted in the Patricias at the Portage Avenue recruiting station solely because a regiment that had so many non-vowels in its shortened title couldn't be all bad. But he'd proved to be a good soldier and had made lance-corporal within two months, unusual but not that much so in view of the chronic shortage of NCOs when war was declared on September 10, seven days after Britain, and the Permanent Force, as Canada's peacetime army was known, was suddenly bulging with raw recruits who didn't know a hand grenade from a coconut and couldn't march in step to save their lives. For the same reason Jack Lambert, though he had the advantage of being a peacetime soldier, now wore three stripes at the ripe old age of twenty-one.

Jack got along fine with Alphabet. He was a stand-up guy who could take his share of ribbing. Most Canadians of Polish or Ukrainian origin had to.

The train hammered on through New Brunswick. It was as cold as a witch's tit inside, bloody near as cold as it must be out there on the snow-covered landscape. Body heat be damned, condensation had formed icicles on the windows, and there'd be no more stops now, not for hot drinks or anything else. A man would have to survive on what he'd had the foresight to fill his canteen with. Anyway, hot drinks went straight through the plumbing system and there was a permanent queue for the train's lavatories. A few troops slept where they could, standing or crouching or, for the lucky ones, curled up in a corner which they defended against all-comers the way a lioness protects her cubs. Most troops didn't sleep, hadn't, to the best of their recollection, since they'd left Kenora or Toronto or Montreal, or wherever the hell it was they'd last stretched their legs a thousand years ago. These men smoked or played poker or told each other improbable stories about the conquests they'd made in downtown Winnipeg or in Esquimalt, British Columbia, where some of them had joined B Company.

There were men from the Manitoban and Saskatchewan prairies, rangy farm boys who hadn't been aboard a train or owned a decent pair of boots before enlisting; city slickers from Victoria and Vancouver and Regina who always seemed to have an extra deck of cards in their pockets or a spare supply of cigarettes when everyone else had run out – for sale at a price. There were some who read, quietly, turning their paperbacks or comic books to get the best of the light. Superman was a favourite, as was Flash Gordon and Captain Marvel. Before long Canadians would have their own illustrated heroes and heroines such as Johnny Canuck, the Invisible Commando, Dixon of the Mounted, and Trixie Rogers. But, for the moment, escapism and tales of derring-do were courtesy of the United States, hardly surprising when ninety-five per cent of Canada's population lived within three hundred miles of the American border.

A few read Bibles, not exactly surreptitiously but not making a big deal of it, either. Jack wondered why such apparent 'believers' had volunteered for overseas service and, inevitably, combat, when they could just as easily have stayed at home – before dismissing such thoughts. It wasn't impossible he'd grab a Bible himself one day, if the going got tough and he felt the need. He wasn't a religious man, not as far as it went, but he remembered his father telling him: 'There are no atheists in the trenches.' Just because a guy read the scriptures didn't mean to say he was a religious nut or whatever. They'd probably enlisted, anyway, because they were victims of the Depression, glad to get a roof over their heads at long last and three square a day without standing in line at the soup kitchens; glad to be away from hopping freight cars from city to city, province to province, hunting work, wages. He doubted he'd be on this particular train himself had it not been for the Depression. He certainly wouldn't be sporting three stripes.

The farmers claimed the Depression hit them worst of all. On top of crop failures, throughout the 1930s they could not sell the wheat they produced and banks foreclosed when loans were not repaid on time. Families that had worked on the land for several generations, hundreds of them, moved on or went on relief. A few went into crime.

Jack Lambert left Calgary in 1937, a few days before his nineteenth birthday. He told no one he was going, but wrote a long letter to his parents and a shorter one to his brother and sister. In both he expressed the same sentiments. The family hotel couldn't support five people now that hardly anyone ever used it, and his father's savings weren't endless. Maggie was needed to help run the place and cater for the few guests who occasionally booked in, and Ben had his studies to complete. He'd be in touch from time to time, but there was no need to worry. The Depression couldn't last for ever. He'd make out.

He very nearly didn't.

He hitched rides on the road when he could and joined others on freight trains when he could not. Sometimes he stole to stay alive – money, food, clothing when his own wore out. Sometimes he fought other men, men twice his age, for half a day's work. Sometimes he found a woman who wasn't fussy that he hadn't bathed in weeks, and joined her in a loveless coupling behind a railroad car or against a wall.

He travelled as far west as Vancouver and as far east as Toronto during the next twelve months, and the spring of 1938 found him in Winnipeg, heading west again, wondering if he should make a detour through Calgary en route. He decided against. There could be no question of him going home for good, not until things improved, and until he was ready to quit the road for ever, he'd stick with it.

He made his way to CNR's Union Station, following the signs, a station being his customary first stop whenever he hit a new city. People who travelled by rail had money and they rarely wanted to carry their own baggage. Some loose change could be picked up if a guy was fast, and fast he had to be. The competition was fierce from regular porters as well as other unemployed bums. He usually did well with ladies in their thirties, or even older, whether they were with their husbands or not; ladies who could see beyond the ingrained dirt and the weary eyes and wonder what this dark-haired six-footer would look like bathed and scrubbed.

The fight started before he knew what was happening. A train arrived and the passengers got off. There was a full load, and the regular porters had more than enough custom. The bums – there were ten or more of them – scanned the rest, hunting the heaviest potential tipper. A woman in her forties, slightly overweight, descended from a carriage, a tiny dog in her arms. Around her shoulders was a fox fur. There was no man behind her, no husband or 'companion'. There had to be luggage. Her searching expression told the waiting bums that much. The fox fur and the lap-dog also told them that there might be a couple of dollars in it.

Jack was two paces ahead of the rest of the pack, running. Then he was tripped and fell headlong. Instinctively he reached out and grabbed the nearest pair of legs, as it happened those belonging to the guy who'd felled him. The woman with the fox fur was forgotten. The two men on the platform were, in any case, too late. Others had got to her first.

Jack's adversary was quickest to his feet. His teeth were the colour of straw and he had eyes like wet grapes. He was more than several inches above six feet and also built like something that could carry off Fay Wray in the palm of his hand. He didn't look too hungry, either.

Jack took all this in at the same time as receiving a hefty kick in the ribs. A crowd began to gather. There might be a chance of a free show before the station bulls broke it up and carted the participants off to jail.

Jack staggered backwards from the first kick, but didn't fall again and avoided the follow-up more by good luck than good judgement. His lips parted in a vicious snarl, part pain, part rage at being tripped, part despair at being robbed of a tip that could have fed him that day. He had few doubts that the fox-fur woman would have given him the job of ferrying her bags to her car or to whoever was meeting her.

His adversary swung a punch, a roundhouse right that started somewhere in Ontario and would have sent his head into orbit had it connected. It didn't. Jack swayed out of reach. He was half-starved, ten or more pounds below his optimum weight, and hadn't eaten properly for several days, or at all for twenty-four hours. But what he'd lost in bulk over twelve months was made up for by a meanness he had not possessed a year earlier. He had been strong at nineteen but now, at twenty, he had something more than mere strength: a tremendous will to survive combined with a bitterness against the whole unfair system that had forced him into the gutter, characteristics that made him, if confronted by injustice, a dangerous opponent to tackle. Nor had he much time for rules devised by the Marquis of Queensberry. In the freight cars, back streets and railheads that were now his home, there was only one code: win.

He stepped inside the next right hand, blocking it easily with his own left forearm. Then he tattooed three quick rights of his own to his assailant's solar plexus, and snapped a sharp left, as the man's head came down, to the jaw.

The man reeled back, shocked as much as hurt. Jack followed up with a left-right combination to the head, and finished the argument with a scything kick to mid-calf, which swept the man's legs from under him and sent him crashing to the concourse.

Then whistles were blowing and Jack felt himself being bundled away from the remnants of the brawl by a couple of powerful arms which were encased in a uniform – and not a police uniform at that.

'Take it easy, son,' said the owner of the uniform, as Jack instinctively struggled to free himself. 'We're on your side.'

Jack saw that there were two of them, both army sergeants, both wearing red and white shoulder flashes with the initials PPCLI embroidered on. He allowed himself to be hustled away, suddenly too tired to resist.

Twenty minutes later, in a nearby cafe, he was into his third cup of coffee and wolfishly devouring the remains of his first hot meat dish for as long as he could remember. He didn't ask himself, or them – and they hadn't offered an explanation – what his benefactors wanted of him, fearful that the meat and potatoes and gravy in front of him would be whipped away if he gave the wrong answers. Nourishment first, that was the rule of the road; everything else came a poor second.

Finally he finished and wiped his mouth. He tapped his threadbare pockets, hunting for cigarettes he knew were not there. One of the sergeants offered him a packet and lit up for him. He introduced himself as Tasker. The other NCO was Payton. Jack gave his own name.

'Keep the pack,' said Tasker.

Jack left it on the table, deliberately using it as a miniature barrier between himself and the soldiers. Replete now, he was not about to be press-ganged, or soft-soaped, into joining the army. These two NCOs had 'recruiting officer' stamped all over them. He'd seen their sort in other cities, hunting for likely candidates, the more so in recent months now that a European war was unlikely to be avoided. Before that, according to the newspapers, Canada's peacetime army, the Permanent Force, numbered fewer than four thousand men. And even that figure was too many for the anti-militarists.

Tasker, Jack noted, was in his late twenties, Payton a year or two younger. Neither NCO took offence at Jack leaving the cigarettes in the middle of the table.

'Been on the road long?' asked Tasker.

There was no point in lying about his status. His clothes told their own story, as did his presence on Union Station, scrapping for an unofficial baggage-carrying job. Bumming, in other words. Besides, he wasn't alone in being a bum, far from it. Nor was it his fault. And he owed the NCOs something for the meal and for getting him away from what could have been real trouble. In spite of the fact that everyone from Ottawa down to the Provincial Parliaments knew that the unemployed were not that way through choice, vagrants were regarded with suspicion.

'A year,' answered Jack.

'Where did you learn to fight like that? By rights, that big bastard should have eaten you.'

'Maybe he wasn't as hungry as I was. On the road,' added Jack, answering the original question. 'You learn a lot on the road, mostly that there's no such thing as a free lunch.'

'This one is.'

'I wonder.'

'Don't. Ever heard of a guy named Prudhomme?'

'He won the Olympic middleweight title at the Antwerp games.'

'Correct,' nodded Payton. 'He was also a Patricia.' Payton pointed to his cap badge, a solid copper circle surrounding a crown and surmounted by the Tudor crown. The name of the regiment was spelt out around the circle. 'Princess Patrica's Canadian Light Infantry. You reminded us of Prudhomme, the way you got stuck in.'

'I'm not joining the army,' said Jack, placing his cards firmly on the table. 'I appreciate the meal and the coffee, but I'm a civilian born and bred.'

'We all were, once,' said Sergeant Tasker. 'But there are worse lives than the army providing you join a crack regiment, and they don't come any better than the Patricias. You get food and board, and there's a war coming . . .'

Jack knew it. Just because Europe was half a world away and he was on the bum didn't mean he couldn't, or didn't, read the newspapers, albeit that they were sometimes filched or used as blankets. Hitler already had the Rhineland and Austria, and Czechoslovakia seemed to be next on his shopping list. Still . . .

'. . . Besides, we're not recruiting,' went on Tasker, 'not just anyone, anyway. On the other hand, enlist before the horse pucky hits the fan and you could be wearing stripes before you know it, especially if you get into the ring and use those fists of yours. There's one sure way to get on in the army, and that's to be good at some kind of sport. Everyone'll be in before another year's out, anyway. It's worthwhile using your head. If you don't like it you can always go AWOL. Canada's a big country, but you'll know that better than we do. What kind of chance do we stand of finding you if you go over the wall?'

'That doesn't sound like recruiting talk to me,' said Jack, suspiciously, at the same time reflecting that it was an interestingly downbeat approach.

'Like I said, we're not recruiting. If you change your mind,' said Tasker, 'look us up at Fort Osborne. Anyone will give you directions if you don't know Winnipeg. Keep the cigarettes, anyway. And good luck.'

Tasker and Payton got up to leave. Jack let them get as far as the door before following – reluctantly in view of the mouth-watering aromas coming from the counter. They had left the cigarettes, true, which he appreciated, but no money for a piece of pie or anything else.

In the street, he saw them disappear round one corner at the same time as the bruiser he'd whipped in Union Station appeared round another, flanked by two constables, obviously under arrest. The shout the big man let forth would have wakened Rip Van Winkle long before twenty years were up. If he was going to jail, it seemed to say – and the pointing, accusatory finger echoed the sentiment – he wasn't going alone.

Jack was momentarily stunned into immobility. And then something happened he would not have thought possible outside a Keystone Kops comedy. The two constables both let go of the bruiser and ran at Jack. The big man couldn't believe his luck. While the policemen grabbed Jack, his ex-opponent took off and vanished as if all the devils in hell were pursuing. And that was the last anyone saw of him.

It would have been jail for sure had not Tasker and Payton, overhearing the commotion, reappeared. While one constable kept a firm grip on his newest captive, the other, at Tasker's request, went into a huddle with the two Patricia NCOs.

Jack did not know a great deal about the relationship between army non-coms and the police, but he would have laid a lot of money, if he'd had any, that the two sergeants could square his brawling misdemeanour with the civilian authorities if he played ball and enlisted. Two birds with one stone. The army gained a recruit and the police had a vagrant off the streets. It was either a cell, for he certainly could not pay any fine, or the Patricias.

It didn't take long to examine the relative merits of his two options. What the hell had he got to lose by joining up? He would have meals where before he'd had few. He would have accommodation where, previously, he'd had to take it where he found it, and pretty bloody grim some of it had been. He would belong somewhere, to something; and, perhaps, for once in his recent life, be a couple of points ahead of the game, if war came and he would be called up anyway. And, as they'd said, he could go AWOL if it all went sour.

Tasker, Payton and the cop emerged from their huddle, and approached him. Tasker was grinning, but there was no malice in it.

'You seem to have a choice here, son,' he said.

'Don't tell me,' answered Jack. 'Where do I sign?'

Jack never felt inclined, right from the beginning, to go AWOL. He took to the army like a glutton to a feast. After months of sleeping rough, basic training was a piece of cake, though he quickly perceived – and what he didn't perceive was pointed out to him by senior NCOs and officers – that Canada was poorly prepared for war, whenever, or if, it happened. Small-arms were of Great War vintage, and there were few enough of them. Available field guns were outranged by six thousand yards by more modern weapons, and some of the coastal defence guns could not fire more than a dozen rounds without danger. Until 1938 the country had not possessed a single tank. Then two arrived from England. And that brace was Canada's armour until 1939, when it actually received a whole fourteen more. It was to be hoped, some of the NCOs joked, that Hitler was aware of the situation. With any luck he'd laugh himself into a coma.

Like most good jokes it wasn't a joke at all.

No one spoke openly against Mackenzie King, though privately many soldiers thought him an appeaser cast from the Chamberlain mould.

The Patricias were one of only three infantry battalions that formed the Permanent Force, each battalion being allocated a 'home territory'. For PPCLI it was the whole of Western Canada, which was why one, and occasionally two, companies were stationed at Esquimalt, British Columbia, whereas the main base was Winnipeg.

The regimental establishment for the Patricias in 1938 called for 773 of all ranks, yet there was only money available for 353, of which Jack was an increasingly prominent member, serving with A Company at Fort Osborne.

He swiftly took pride in learning and memorizing regimental history. How it was founded by Major (later Brigadier and Honorary Colonel) Andrew Gault, an Englishman. How it got its name from Princess Victoria Patricia, daughter of the Duke of Connaught, Queen Victoria's third son. He became familiar with the photographed faces of the regiment's VCs – Lieutenant Hugh McKenzie, killed at Passchendaele; Sergeant Robert Spall, killed at Parvillers; and Sergeant George Mullin. When he wasn't boxing, he learned how to play the crazy regimental game of Broom-i-loo, part hockey, part soccer – at least there was a soccer ball on the field – part unarmed combat. He learned to respect the Ric-A-Dam-Doo, the regimental colours made and presented by Princess Patricia. And he was taught very quickly not to call the regiment the PPs or Pip Pips, or, most offensive of all, Princess Pat's or merely the Pats. The Duke of Connaught's daughter was not a 'Pat'. She was a Patricia. So was the regiment.

The backbone of the regiment, in his view, was the private soldier. NCOs, until he became one, were parentless sadists, and officers could go forth and multiply, preferably up their own backsides. One of the regimental songs said it all. 'Has Anyone Seen the Colonel' – descending through sergeants, corporals and privates, the poor bloody clowns who did all the work and took all the blame. The sergeant's lines were:

> Has anyone seen the sergeant?
> He's lying on the canteen floor . . .

For the corporal:

> Has anyone seen the corporal?
> He's hanging on the old barbed wire . . .

But for the private:

> Has anyone seen the private?
> He's holding the whole damned line . . .

Jack considered this just about summed it all up, until he got his first stripe. And then his second, neither of them due to his boxing ability. He was recognized by his superiors as being an exceptional soldier. He was an excellent shot. He could outhike and outrun most of the men in A Company. On manoeuvres he could be dropped off twenty miles from base and be the first back, frequently carrying someone else's pack. He also inspired others by example, without inviting resentment in any but the more envious, because of his natural abilities. All the boxing championships in the world would not have earned him promotion if he had not been able to lead men, in spite of his youth.

He wasn't a Goody Two Shoes, however. He could drink with the best of them and, until his stripes made it inadvisable, throw a punch and wipe the floor with anyone who offended him.

In the company commander's report recommending him for three hooks if, in the event of general mobilization, more senior NCOs were needed, it was noted that he had a quality revered above all others in crack infantry battalions: sustained aggression. Although the company commander did not put it in so many words, he meant that when the chips were down do not pick up the chips. Pick up the chip-pan and throw it. Straight in the other guy's face, if that's what it takes.

Jack had regained his former weight in a matter of weeks. Then he put on another ten pounds, none of it fat. When he was well settled in and confident he had made the right decision by enlisting, he wrote to Calgary, promising to visit his family shortly, on his first leave. His parents and, separately, Ben and Maggie, replied by return, all over-joyed that he was fit and well. Only Maggie queried his decision to join up. 'Are you a natural soldier?' Jack wrote back. 'It's the best thing I ever did.'

In the autumn of 1938 he and Ben went on a camping vacation. In the spring of '39 they had another, with not a cent of it, although the costs were minimal, paid for by Jack. The hotel business was picking up. The Lamberts had weathered the storm.

In the middle months of '39 it was obvious to all but the totally inept or myopic, which the troops thought, as all troops do, meant the government, that war could not be far off. Even so, the Patricias were still understrength, and recruiting, because of restricted finances, difficult. To the frustration of all senior officers, in other regiments as well as the Patricias, it seemed that it was going to be a case of waiting until the balloon went up and then grabbing the best of what became available.

Training continued, to keep up morale, but everyone knew that it was virtually a waste of energy mounting company attacks with only half companies.

In July and August Jack was seconded to the Small Arms School at Calgary, which gave him an opportunity to see his family and look up one or two old girlfriends. He improved his scores, both on the range and in the back of Fords.

Shortly after the Molotov–von Ribbentrop Pact was signed on August 21, the Canadian Cabinet authorized the formation of two active service divisions and dispatched a mobilization order to all Permanent Force units, decreeing recruitment to war strength immediately. Seven days after Chamberlain's historic Sunday morning speech declaring war, the Canadian Government followed suit. The following day, September 11, the Patricias began recruiting in Winnipeg and Vancouver in earnest.

Jack and another corporal, Kovacs, were deputed to help out at the Portage Avenue depot, under the command of a junior officer. Some of the volunteers – and now that war had been declared there was no shortage – had to be seen to be believed. One man claimed to be under forty, well under forty, even though several of the campaign ribbons pinned to his civilian jacket were of 2nd Boer War vintage. He had dyed his hair with boot polish, so anxious was he to enlist. At the other end of the scale a brawny youngster, protesting to be nineteen, was dragged away by his outraged mother. He turned out to be fifteen.

But there were some good recruits, among them David Greyfoot, who hung around outside the depot for over an hour after the queues had dispersed before Jack, observing him for the fifth or sixth time, left the building to see if there was any good reason for the Indian's reluctance to enter it. Or part Indian, as it should be, Jack spotted a few seconds later. The man had European blood too.

Greyfoot was about Jack's age, maybe a year younger, taller by several inches, but much, much thinner. Jack knew the signs; the guy was starving. Getting work, even on a temporary basis, had been a lot harder in the Depression for men who were half-Indian, even though Canada, on the whole, treated its Indian population much better than did its huge neighbour to the south. Still, half-breeds had it tougher than full-blooded Indians. They faced the same problems in white society, but were made to feel unwelcome on the reservations.

'Anything I can do, Chief?' asked Jack pleasantly.

'I want to join up.'

'Then why don't you come in and do just that? Fill in the form, take the medical.'

Greyfoot hesitated, hunching his thin shoulders. 'I don't read or write too good.'

'Not at all?' Illiterates were not automatically turned down, though it was harder for them to enlist now that the supply of volunteers seemed unending. Besides, there were firearms manuals to study and a host of other things.

'Some, but not good.'

'Wait here.'

Jack re-entered the depot and picked up an enlistment form. Kovacs, a hard-nosed bastard, a former professional hunter from around Duck Mountain, guessed what he was up to.

'We're not hiring half-breeds today.'

Kovacs was all right if he was kept in his place. He was of Hungarian or Czech origin, one of those ethnic minorities, and inclined to be sensitive about it.

'They hired you, didn't they? Just watch my end of the store until I get back.'

Jack took Greyfoot for a cup of coffee. The Indian was reluctant to enter the cafe at first.

'They usually won't serve me in places like this.'

'They'll serve you today.'

And they did, without any trouble, no questions asked. Jack wondered if his companion was over-sensitive about his mixed parentage. Or maybe he'd had trouble in the past not because of that, but

42

because, in his threadbare work clothes and with his jet-black hair reaching almost to his shoulders, he looked as if he didn't have two cents to rub together. From his days on the road, Jack knew that feeling well.

'Write your name at the top and then we'll take each question as it comes.'

Greyfoot was better than he thought, stumbling over only a few words. His reading ability was slightly inferior to his writing, but neither proclaimed him to be illiterate, or even close.

'You'll do, Chief.'

By the end of the third cup of coffee he felt confident he could walk into the depot and complete a form without any assistance. Jack's only concern was that Greyfoot's underfed rangy frame would somehow count against him. His fears proved groundless. The MO pronounced him fit as a flea.

Much later Greyfoot asked Jack why he had bothered.

'Let's say I thought you could use a good meal and a free haircut. Besides, you don't know I've done you a favour yet. You may be taking a scalping knife to me before the year's out.'

By the end of October the Patricias were almost up to strength, but there was still a severe shortage of equipment and, just as important, accommodation, with four hundred men sleeping head to toe in the Fort Osborne drill hall. In the middle of November B and D Companies left Esquimalt and entrained for Winnipeg. The last day of November saw the final Trooping of the Colour, and thereafter the Ric-A-Dam-Doo was placed for safety in All Saints Church, where it would stay until the regiment returned from abroad.

In the middle of December the Patricias' movement order came through. The same day Jack was called before the company commander and informed that he was being promoted to sergeant, effective immediately. In peacetime he would have had to complete a senior NCOs' course, but these days such niceties were disregarded. Men received extra chevrons based solely on their ability to do the job.

One of the first to congratulate Jack was David Greyfoot, to whom, secretly, Jack had given the occasional reading lesson and pointed him in the direction of books that would help him improve. It wasn't much of a secret, though. The company commander knew about it, as did the CO. It was one of the reasons Jack got his third hook. Any junior

NCO who went that far, out of hours, to help a fellow soldier, just had to be, in spite of his youth, worth taking a chance on.

Jack gazed in wonderment at the insignia denoting his new rank the first time he put on his battledress after the promotion. Though he said so himself, he had come a hell of a long way in eighteen months. If he ever again met up with the big bruiser who'd tripped him on Union Station, he'd thank him, not thump him.

In Halifax the rumour about the luxury liner *Orama* proved to be accurate, and the Patricias embarked on December 21, amid a snowstorm. It would be Christmas away this year, in the middle of the Atlantic if the U-boats didn't have other ideas. Most of the men had never been out of Canada before, except to the United States. A few of the more thoughtful ones wondered how many Christmases it would be before they saw their country again, or if they ever would.

As well as the *Orama* the fleet comprised the *Reino del Pacifico*, the *Almanzora*, the *Andes*, and many other former passenger liners. The escort included HMS *Revenge*, the French battlewagon *Dunkerque* and cruiser *Gloire* and numerous British and Canadian destroyers, all sounding their sirens as the convoy moved out to sea.

The troops were on deck, cheering, singing, waving goodbye to wellwishers and familiar soil. It wasn't until the snow whited-out the mainland that the singing stopped and, as one, the soldiers fell silent. As of now the war, for them, was a reality.

THREE

January–June 1940

After disembarking at Greenock, in Scotland, the Patricias entrained for Farnborough, their eventual destination being Morval Barracks, two miles north of the Hampshire town. There they arrived on New Year's Eve, 1939, to be greeted by frozen pipes and precious little heating apart from paraffin stoves. They shivered their way into the second year of the war. The British winter of 1940 was one of the coldest on record, bone-chilling even to the Canadians, who were no strangers to double-figure minuses.

Any of the troops who expected to be in combat, after a few weeks' acclimatization, were doomed to disappointment. Their major adversary in the opening months of the year was influenza, though scuttlebutt from the Orderly Room whispered that 1st Canadian Division should be ready to take the field by March 1 at the latest. Whether that meant France or elsewhere, no one knew. In any case, it was only a rumour, and before then it was to be training, training, and more training – on the firing ranges, on the assault course, and on route marches, by dark as well as day. Alphabet Soup remarked to Jack, one bitter night during a twenty-mile hike across Hampshire, that when he was in Headingly and given the option between serving the rest of his sentence and joining up, he'd asked his interrogators what he had to gain by enlisting. '"Do you like travel?" they wanted to know. "Sure," I said. "And sex?" "Damn right." "Then you'll get both in the army." Now I know what they meant, the bastards. Sex and travel? Fucking marching.'

On the firing ranges and elsewhere, Jack kept his eyes open for potential junior NCOs. There was talk that platoons were about to be strengthened by ten per section, and the company commander wanted the names of anyone deemed worthy of a stripe. In this, platoon sergeants worked closely with platoon commanders, and Jack was particularly keen to see if Greyfoot could hack it. It seemed possible, now that he would have no trouble with any written test.

Occasionally they drank together in one of the local pubs, Jack and Greyfoot, sometimes with Alphabet, Kovacs, a few others. In the Patricias the senior NCOs did not consider it beneath their dignity to imbibe with the junior NCOs, nor any NCO with an ordinary private. Nor few civilians with any Canadian soldier. Outside it might be freezing, but inside the pubs there was usually only warmth once the natives realized that the newcomers did not have two heads. And once the Canadians had become accustomed to the monetary system and figured out that thirty of the big brown coins made one of the big silver ones known as two-and-six; that two-and-six did not make eight but was shorthand for two shillings and sixpence, otherwise known as half-a-crown; and that, even more confusingly, while there were half-crowns, there were no whole crowns. Then, a shilling was a bob and two and a half bobs made half-a-crown; half a bob was a tanner, and half a tanner was a threepenny joey.

Working out the cost of something was a nightmare.

After a while, the Canadians simply thrust a whole handful of different coins on the bar and trusted the pub landlord, whom they insisted on calling an innkeeper until they learnt otherwise, to make the right change. Few cheated. The British are not much good at saying thanks, but they appreciated that these youngsters had travelled thousands of miles to help in the fight against Hitler.

If the landlord was busy – and many of the Canadians tried to make sure he was – then, for ordering another round, the barmaid would be called upon, some of them pretty, some less so, but all of them female. Whenever there was trouble between troops and civilians, or between troops of one regiment and another, or one nationality and another, at the bottom of it generally lay a woman.

Youthful civilians who were not in the British armed forces either because they were awaiting their call-up, or in reserved occupations, or because they were considered unfit, frequently resented the Canadian troops paying court to their girls, or just to any old girl in a village or town. The resentment wasn't as intense as it would be in a couple of years when the Americans arrived, but it was there, nevertheless. A Canuck would make the right noises at a good-looking girl, and then it was time to get in a little extra-curricular battle training.

Some of the girls were prick-teasers, professional virgins, erotic only in their fantasies, out for nothing more than a good time – all take and no put; some were more than available for whatever their escorts fancied. It was as well to be careful with the second group, however, for, the manner in which some of them spread it around, you could find yourself sharing favours with half the regiment – half the frigging brigade, in some instances. This had only one thing to be said for it. If the girl got pregnant, she would have to have the memory of an elephant to name the father. It was no use the CO holding an identity parade, asking the mother-to-be to point out the culprit. It would be a case of, 'Him, or maybe him . . . him possibly . . . and all that rank there . . . or those two . . . And by the way, Colonel, haven't I seen you somewhere before . . .?'

Most of the girls, however, in any village or town, in any pub, were just ordinary, wanting nothing more than to be seen on the arm of a foreign serviceman playing Olivia de Havilland to Errol Flynn. Just going to London, twenty miles away, was a big adventure. Their ambitions stretched no further than a husband, children, a house, and, as a preamble to it all, dancing at the local hop, as far as blackout and fire-regulations permitted, with young men who hailed from places with exotic names such as Medicine Hat and Moose Jaw. They may be off to fight soon, these boys with the strange accents, but they'd need someone to write to while they were away, or to come back to if they returned.

To his own astonishment, it was Greyfoot who attracted the attention of many of the local ladies, wherever the locality. Now that his hair was cut and he'd put on weight and muscle, he was striking enough, admittedly, but that wasn't what seemed to appeal to the opposite sex. That he was part Indian did. The saucy ones wanted to see his 'tomahawk'. Others wanted to know if he had a squaw back home, and whether he'd taken many scalps.

The trouble was, he was shy with women. Or maybe just wary. In March a full-blooded Blackfoot from the Reserve south of Calgary, serving with the Edmontons, was hanged for killing an English girl. She had slept with him a few times, then moved on when she got bored. He hadn't understood her reasons, so she died. Then he did.

Greyfoot was a model soldier in every respect save one; Jack would have preferred to see more aggression. He was combative enough during bayonet practice, but when it came down to hand-to-hand mock battles, he would usually back off from his opponent and was frequently dumped on his tail as a result. He would never get his stripe that way, and Jack was beginning to think that there was something sadly lacking in the Chief's make-up when, one evening in late March, he was proved wrong. The catalyst was the Blackfoot's recent execution.

Greyfoot was perceptive enough to realize he was no drinker. He would hand over his copper coins in the pub, take his pint of mild, and join any of the platoon who happened to be around. He would usually stay with one drink, never more than two, for the entire evening. He'd speak if spoken to, but generally he was content to listen.

The Royal Navy men who came into the pub that night were on leave and, if not exactly looking for trouble, not too worried if they found it.

Greyfoot was at the bar, having just walked in. Jack, Alphabet, Kovacs, several others, were there already, discussing the relative abilities of Joe Perpich, Bud Marquardt and the legendary Fritzy Hanson, the Golden Ghost. The matelot who was ordering for his two companions was in a hurry. This place was a dump. They should have stayed in Pompey or trained up to the Smoke. One drink apiece and they'd be off, to somewhere with a bit more life.

'Gangway for the Fleet,' said the sailor, waving a fistful of shore-leave money. 'Shake a leg, darling.'

'I've only got one pair of hands,' sniffed the barmaid, 'and he was here first.'

The sailor, a three-badge stoker whose features revealed that he had been in a fight or two in his life, noticed the Chief for the first time; noticed, too, his racial origins. He grinned at his mates.

'Another candidate for the rope before the year's out.'

Greyfoot chose to ignore the obvious reference to the recent hanging. He paid for his beer and started to walk away. The matelot wouldn't let it go. He placed himself in front of Greyfoot, blocking his route.

'Maybe you didn't hear what I said, War Eagle. Don't they teach you any manners back in the wigwam? Jesus, it's bad enough having to put up with bunches of white Canadians, but it's a bit much when the old country has to play host to savages as well.'

He was making no attempt to keep his voice down, and most of the small saloon bar heard what was said.

'Oh, dear,' said Kovacs, heavily ironic, getting up from the table. 'The navy needs teaching some manners.'

Jack told him not to interfere.

'Let's see how the Chief handles it.'

'There are three of them and you know what he's like.'

'Give him a minute.'

'You're in my way,' said Greyfoot, softly.

'Christ, it talks.' The stoker pantomimed with his hands. 'White man say Redman heap of buffalo dung. White man say Redman not drink at White man's water-hole.'

He jogged Greyfoot's elbow, spilling much of the beer. Greyfoot placed his glass on the bar and, a continuation of the same movement, hit the stoker in the gut. The sailor let out a noise like a giant owl, and clutched his belly. Then his two mates piled in. The landlord yelled, 'Outside, outside,' but it was too late for that.

'Now we can join in,' said Jack.

As fights went it didn't amount to much in either style or length. Four out of ten and a B for effort. There were too many Patricias for the navy, and they weren't fussy about that not being cricket. The stoker's two shipmates were thumped a few times before being frog-marched into the street. When the Patricias returned the stoker was slowly sinking to the floor like a felled chimney, though Greyfoot himself was doing a rain dance, having swung a right-handed haymaker that missed its target and clobbered a wall. He was jumping up and down, alternately shaking his damaged fist and holding it between his knees. The stoker went the way of his shipmates, being unceremoniously dumped in the street by Alphabet and a couple of others.

'Any more of that and you're all barred,' bellowed the landlord, though he was relieved that it was all over so fast and that nothing was broken – except maybe a few naval teeth.

'There won't be any more,' promised Jack. 'Let's refill your glass.' He put an arm around Greyfoot's shoulders. 'When did you become Primo Carnera?'

'I don't like being backed into a corner.' The Chief was breathing heavily, not through exertion, and there was a certain madness in his eyes. But he got over it quickly enough, and grinned. 'It brings out the Cree in me.'

'I can see that, but this afternoon you were thrown on your back a dozen times by half the platoon.'

'I've got no quarrel with the platoon. When I fight I see red. I wouldn't want a pal to be on the end of that. If I hadn't smacked my

49

fist against that fucking wall, I might have killed that sailor. Like he said, another candidate for the rope, maybe.'

'Welcome to the human race, anyway,' said Jack. And then, only half-joking: 'When you meet your first German, just pretend he's that stoker.'

But the Patricias were destined not to meet their first Germans for some time, though in April they came close.

By the 10th of that month the principal Norwegian ports were in German hands. To prevent a lightning strike becoming a rout, two British brigade groups were landed north and south of Trondheim, to oust the Wehrmacht from that port and deny Hitler Narvik. As well as the north and south contingent, a frontal attack on the forts that guarded Trondheim harbour was planned and the 1st Canadian Division asked to provide troops. The commanding general, McNaughton, nominated the Patricias and the Edmonton Regiment.

On the evening of April 18 PPCLI entrained at Farnborough and arrived in Dunfermline the following afternoon. Everyone was in high spirits. After a five-mile march to a temporary encampment they were issued with Arctic gear. Two nights later they received a rum ration, proof, it seemed, that Operation Hammer had the green light. Greyfoot sold his ration to the highest bidder. He had grown a lot more canny and confident since getting his first hook. Besides, he neither wanted nor needed hard liquor.

Then two mishaps occurred which delayed the Canadians' departure and also their usefulness, since speed was essential. The officer appointed to command the expedition died of a stroke in a London street and his replacement was badly injured in an aircraft crash while flying to Scotland. On April 21 the Patricias were stood down, and on April 24 the regiment returned to Morval Barracks, disappointed to a man not to have seen action.

By May it appeared as if they, along with the remainder of the United Kingdom, would be getting more action than even the most aggressive might think desirable.

On May 10, the same day that Winston Churchill became Prime Minister, Hitler's armour under Guderian smashed through the West's defences and seemed likely to annihilate the French and drive the BEF into the sea or captivity. The only chance of escape for the BEF was a fighting withdrawal to the Channel ports, Dunkirk especially, and the 1st Canadian Division would be responsible for the lines of communication between the British positions north of the Somme and the Channel. When General McNaughton returned from an exploratory crossing to France, however, he reported that the Allied front could not hold, and the Canadians didn't sail.

Instead, McNaughton formed Canadian Force, mobile striking units that had the status and equipment of flying columns, capable of intervening wherever there was a threat. The Patricias wound up at Kettering in Northamptonshire on the same day as the Royal Navy and hundreds of small craft were evacuating nearly 340,000 men from the Dunkirk beaches. Most of the Patricias were pissed off. What the hell were they doing in what the British called the Midlands when any likely invasion beach was a hundred miles to the south? Didn't Churchill trust them anywhere near what was likely to be a front line?

After Kettering they moved to one of the Duke of Buccleuch's estates, where they bivouacked. The weather was magnificent, a far cry from the fierce winter a few months earlier. But what was magnificent for men in the field was also ideal for an invasion force. There was a war going on down south and the Patricias had not crossed the Atlantic to sunbathe. Nor was that the intention. Almost before they had time to draw breath, the Patricias were on their way back to Morval Barracks, and from there, to help establish a new front in Brittany, to Falmouth, to embark on June 16.

War, however, is not like a game of chess, where the moves, banal or brilliant, are confined to sixty-four squares within a limited framework. On June 15, with the Wehrmacht advancing more rapidly than anyone on the Allied side would have believed possible, the movement order to Falmouth was cancelled. The Patricias, like all Canadians, like all defending the United Kingdom, would no longer have to go out looking for a fight. The fight was coming to them.

FOUR

Parts of the village of Chipping Saxonby had been there for over a thousand years, although the church was Norman. Chipping was a corruption of *ceping*, which was Old English for market-place. Thus Chipping Saxonby, in the original, meant The Market-Place Near the Saxon Encampment.

Apart from the church, a sub-post office which doubled as the village shop, where most goods required a ration book but where some, courtesy of freebooting farmers, could be bought under the counter, Chipping Saxonby contained almost three hundred people and two public houses, The Flying Fox and The Wheatsheaf, rural Englishmen and women having their priorities between the spiritual and the sensual well defined. The nearest bank was six miles away, as was the nearest butcher, and newspapers were delivered, to order only, to the village shop on the local bus – twice daily, mornings and evenings, the Luftwaffe permitting.

The High Street, still cobbled outside the ivy-covered Wheatsheaf, was two hundred yards in length; after that there was only countryside in either direction. The not-so-wealthy lived in cottages in the High Street and in tiny cul-de-sacs. The gentry occupied extensive properties outside the village, though within easy walking or bicycling distance from it, useful now that petrol was hard to come by. The solitary policeman and his wife inhabited a house-cum-police station two doors down from The Wheatsheaf, convenient, the gossips tattled, for the bobby's fondness of beer, even the weak wartime variety, was well known.

Not much had changed in Chipping Saxonby in a thousand years until the autumn of 1940. Then barrage balloons appeared overhead and a satellite fighter airfield was established, some distance from the village but near enough for the villagers to see Spitfires limping home from dogfights or doing victory rolls if the sortie had been successful.

Home Guard detachments were established, ARP wardens appointed, and fire-fighting watches implemented. Weird bits of scrap-iron known as Anderson shelters were imbedded, supplied free to anyone whose income was under £250 per annum, costing ten pounds to anyone who earned more. Members of the Women's Land Army rolled up to help with the harvest, brash young girls who smoked and swore and who were, as far as the locals were concerned, totally immoral. The landlord of The Fox swore he'd heard one answer, when asked by an impudent soldier whether she ever smoked after intercourse – 'I don't know, I've never looked.' Much to the delight of the troops and the lustier village youths, the WLA's unofficial motto of 'backs to the land' was taken literally by many of the girls.

Late in August a handful of young evacuees from London's East End arrived in army trucks; ashen-faced, undernourished children who yelled a lot and who had never seen the countryside before. Some had never seen farm animals, even in books, and one was heard to describe a pig as 'a fat black dog wearing a gas mask'. The evacuees did not remain long. Although to the inhabitants Chipping Saxonby was rural England, as bucolic as remote Devon and Cornwall, it was still too close to London and on one of the flight paths the Luftwaffe Dorniers and Heinkels regularly flew.

Jack's platoon, under the command of Second Lieutenant Brewerton, a lanky twenty-two-year-old from Portage la Prairie, Manitoba, was tasked with defending the village against a parachute drop or, if a German landing on the coast without paratroops was successful, the approach roads leading to the satellite airfield. To this end pillboxes were hastily thrown up and camouflaged.

The platoon's secondary function was anti-aircraft duties, though for this they had only Bren-guns and medium machine guns, useless against anything except an ME 109 that was low enough, and travelling slow enough, to reach out and grab anyway. The airfield itself was guarded by the RAF, and in spinneys and copses regulation AA batteries were in place.

Other detachments of Patricias had similar tasks in neighbouring villages and hamlets, and the regiment's HQ was now based at Godstone. Orderly Room bulletins announced that, in time, it was hoped to billet all ranks in village houses, but, for the moment, the platoon was under canvas. Few minded. The weather was glorious, the days hot, the nights warm. When the Luftwaffe left them alone, which wasn't often, admittedly, it was like being on a camping vacation. And as a bonus their tents were pitched in a field belonging to a nearby farm; the Land Girls slept in barns and makeshift dormitories on the farm.

Jack steered well clear of the Land Girls. One, it was hard to keep score about who had been bedded, or palliassed, by whom, and he reckoned he could catch half the diseases known to man, and a few that weren't, if he wasn't careful. Two, he already had a convenient arrangement with a young lady from the village, one unconnected with the WLA. And three, he had seen the woman he was determined to have before the battalion moved on or the Germans landed and spoiled everyone's fun. Then again, so had everyone else in the platoon, from Brewerton down, marked her as number one on his hit list, though the chances of landing such a catch were remote. Still, one thing the Patricias had taught him was never say die.

Her actual name was Caroline Manners, though she was known to the platoon as Snow White because she resembled a grown-up version of the Disney cartoon character. Very grown-up. The Snow White in the film was a pious little psalm-singing creep who didn't look as if she'd reached puberty. Mrs Manners had, and then some. If Dopey, Grumpy, Doc and the other dwarfs had lived under the same roof as this lady, they'd have chucked diamond mining and stayed home, stunted their growth by a few more inches.

She was twenty-five, Jack's unimpeachable source of gossip, the landlord's wife at The Wheatsheaf, told him, the widow of an RAF flight lieutenant who'd bought it in his Blenheim the second day of the war while attacking German shipping in the Heligoland Bight. Her hair was jet-black, as black as Greyfoot's, her eyes hazel, her face oval. She was about five-nine, full-bosomed but otherwise slim, and lived with her widower father in a huge house called Five Oaks, on the outskirts of Chipping Saxonby. Second Lieutenant Brewerton, the bastard, was a regular visitor and an occasional dinner guest, pleading duty whenever Jack pulled his leg about it. Not that a commissioned officer, even a lowly one-pipper, had to excuse his conduct to an NCO, but Brewerton and Jack, partly because they were near enough the same age, had a good working relationship. 'She's a wheel in the WVS locally, you know that. Winter's coming and I want to make sure the platoon's not short of off-duty activities when the cold weather arrives. You remember what it was like in January. Table tennis, dances, socials. We need her good will.' My flaming foot, thought Jack.

The company commander and RAF officers from the satellite field also dined with her frequently, one of the perks of holding the King's Commission. NCOs and below need not apply. Tea and buns for them in the kitchen. Well, they'd see.

Jack first met her when he was bringing the platoon back from an overnight exercise, a battalion manoeuvre but with all companies and platoons returning to their separate lines when it was over. Five Oaks was several miles from the farm where the platoon had its tents, and the Luftwaffe was early that morning, going for the satellite field. A dozen Heinkels at five thousand feet dropped their bombs and scored what appeared, to the onlookers, to be several direct hits, while the scrambled Spitfires tried to beat off the escorting 109s to get at the bombers.

Most dogfights took place at such high altitudes that it was impossible to follow the action, even if there was time. All the ground troops ever usually saw were the con-trails and, frequently, an aircraft plummet from the sky. On this morning, however, a 109, in desperate trouble, smoke pouring from it, was chased down to treetop level by the Spitfire that had made the kill. The RAF pilot was determined to deck the Luftwaffe plane.

One of the problems with low-altitude dogfights was the terrifying suddenness with which the combatants appeared. One moment the sky was empty, everything quiet. The next all hell was being let loose.

This 109 might have been crippled, but the pilot was far from dead. Maybe he was injured, maybe he was trapped in his cockpit and couldn't get out. Maybe he couldn't gain sufficient altitude to use his parachute. But he still had ammunition, and the target the platoon presented, marching along the road into Chipping Saxonby, must have proved irresistible.

Brewerton had loped off ahead, for a company commander's O-group, leaving Jack in command. Hearing the roar of aircraft engines and not knowing whether they were Merlins or Daimler Benz, he yelled, 'Hit the dirt!'

The 109 sprayed the road with what remained of its 20mm cannon shells, the pilot intent on taking something with him if his number was up. Some of the shells found targets. Even at speed, at a hundred feet he couldn't miss. Then the Spitfire found a few extra mph, and pounced, punching home the coup de grace. The Messerschmitt soared up like a kite in a crosswind and flipped over on to its back. A silence that seemed endless but which probably occupied only a few seconds descended, before a distant explosion told the ground troops that there would be one less at that Geschwader's table.

The Spit climbed rapidly, peeling left, and went into a victory roll – before disappearing to gain height and look for more action, further victims. On the ground there were no celebrations. When Jack raised his head, realizing it was all over, he called for a casrep. He'd lost two men dead. A third, Private Kominsky from the Chief's section, had taken wounds in the chest.

Jack bellowed for order. When he didn't get it right away he walked over to the nearest man – man meaning someone who was about nineteen – and clipped him on the chin. Then he picked him up. 'Grow up, for Chrissake.'

Some had, in under thirty seconds. Some were pale and shaking. These were the platoon's first casualties. The dead had been torn apart. One no longer had a head. Jack couldn't recognize him from the bits and pieces that were left, but he sensed he had panic on his hands. The Patricia closest to the decapitee was spewing, mostly over his battle-dress. Jack felt like throwing up himself. Then his training took over – that plus whatever made him what he was in the first place. There was nothing he could do for the guys who hadn't survived. That was the luck of the draw. But Kominsky had a chance, if he was seen to quickly.

He didn't have to give the Chief instructions. Greyfoot was already applying field dressings to the gaping chest wounds. Gas capes and saplings would make a stretcher. Jack got the nearest four men to build it. They could also act as bearers. The big house, the one with the telephone wires leading from it, was only a few hundred yards away. If they could get the injured man that far . . .

'Let's move it,' urged Jack. 'We'll phone the airfield. They'll have an MO there.'

He noted with approval that the platoon's wireless operator was trying to raise A Company. The platoon did not have a direct link with the battalion. He heard the signalman request medical help. Okay, the more the merrier.

Only he and four stretcher bearers set off at the double. He left the Chief to organize the platoon, cover the dead.

But Kominsky also died. The satellite 'drome had taken a pasting from the Heinkels, and the MO and the other medics were busy. No, they couldn't do anything for maybe two hours, not even send a field ambulance. The village doctor was out too, again at the airfield, to which he had driven as soon as he had identified the bombers' target. Mrs Manners's father, Colonel Charlton – although Jack did not find out either of their names until much later in the day – had a car and a petrol allowance in his capacity as civil defence organizer for the district. His daughter, however, who possessed some nursing experience, felt it would be dangerous to move Kominsky. It would be better to wait until the civilian doctor returned to his practice or someone could be spared from the RAF base. Mercifully, Kominsky was unconscious.

So the poor bastard died, gone within thirty minutes of being laid out on a camp bed and covered with blankets in the Five Oaks kitchen.

When Jack had a chance to reflect rationally, he recognized that nothing could have been done that wasn't done. But when it first sunk home that Kominsky was the third fatality of the morning, he wasn't feeling rational. It seemed to him that a private in an infantry battalion, and a foreigner at that, did not rate as highly as the ground crews on the airfield. His resentment even extended to the woman and her father. They just seemed, Christ, so clean and fresh, so distanced from a grubby little Polack. 'The bastards,' he said bitterly, and he was not only referring to the Luftwaffe.

'You look as if you need a whisky, Sergeant,' said the colonel.

Jack hadn't tasted whisky more than half a dozen times since arriving in England, and he could have used one, a big one, right there and then. But the stretcher bearers had retreated to the kitchen garden and were evidently not included in the invitation.

'I'll pass – sir.'

The 'sir' was a begrudged afterthought, but the man was a senior officer and wore medal ribbons from the Great War on the breast of his tunic. He was also missing his left arm, Jack was startled to find he'd only just noticed, which was presumably why he wasn't on active service. Though his age, because he could not be younger than his late fifties, would probably have ruled him out, war or no war.

'As you wish.'

As you wish. It was all so bloody polite, and there was Kominsky lying dead.

Jack decided he would rather be outside the house with the men from his platoon, and outside he stayed, no one saying very much, until a field ambulance drove up. Brewerton was riding shotgun.

'Jesus Christ, Jack, what the hell's happened?'

Then he saw the colonel and his daughter in the kitchen doorway and went inside the house, pausing only to throw a snappy salute. After a moment he reappeared and beckoned the ambulance crew. They returned with Kominsky's body, his face covered, on a regulation stretcher.

'They said there were some others, Sarge.'

Jack gave them directions.

'Tell Corporal Greyfoot to make his own way back.'

'We can give him a ride.'

'There's a whole platoon up there.'

'Well, some of them.'

'No, I'd prefer them to stick together.'

When Brewerton came out only Mrs Manners was with him. She came over to Jack.

'I'm very sorry about what happened.'

He could see that she was. Her deep-set eyes were full of genuine compassion. But something about her attitude made him un-characteristically churlish. There was a remoteness about her. She seemed so untouchably British, and it made him uneasy. He felt like a sweaty peasant being condescended to by the lady of the manor, like he'd sometimes felt when on the bum back in Canada, begging coppers from the well-heeled. He didn't recognize immediately that he wanted her to regard him as an equal, the way she probably regarded Brewerton with his shiny officer's pip. He'd have accepted the whisky, the bastard, no doubt had, and it would have been offered as a social gesture by the colonel, not as medicine.

'Why?' he asked. 'You didn't know Kominsky.'

'That was bloody rude, Sergeant Lambert,' said Brewerton, getting formal, as they hiked back.

Jesus, even Brew was picking up the lingo. Back at Fort Osborne he would have said, 'Don't be so fucking insolent, Lambert.'

'So what?'

That was insubordination and Brewerton wasn't having it.

'Now look here, Sergeant . . .'

Jack halted in mid-stride and faced his platoon commander.

'No, you look here. You can put me on a charge, bust me down to private, or piss off. Right now I couldn't care less. You can tell me what to do when we're on manoeuvres or in barracks, or even in the canteen. But you can't make me bow and scrape to civilians, even if she's got a friggin' colonel for a father. So stick it, Brew.'

Brewerton put it down to delayed shock. Lambert was tough, but anyone witnessing his first casualties, and wondering if he'd slipped up, whether there was anything he could have done to prevent them, was entitled to be antsy. Lambert was too good an NCO to risk him being demoted. It wouldn't look too healthy on his own records, either, and might make the company commander think he was being petty. Plus, with the Germans on the doorstep, as it were . . .

He resolved to forget all about it, and changed tack.

'If it was me,' he said conversationally as they continued back to camp, 'I'd be apologizing right, left and centre. Hell, she's some looker. I reckon I'd crawl naked over half a mile of broken bottles just to collect her nail-clippings.'

Jack suddenly tumbled part of the reason for his ill-humour. She was some looker, true, and a bit more than that, but he'd seen as good, or even better. What she was, for him, was out of his league. Unattainable. Brew would be able to wangle invitations to drinks and dinner, whereas poor old bloody Jack Lambert would be lucky to get a glass of water at the kitchen door, or be allowed to hold her horse's head while she dismounted. And Jack Lambert resented it. Still . . .

'Maybe you're right. About shooting off at the mouth, I mean. I'll call in and eat crow next time I'm over that way.'

The Luftwaffe saw to it that he didn't get the chance in the immediate future. The regiment scarcely had time to bury its dead before Goering was stepping up the pace prior to invasion, raiding all the airfields in the south-east with remorseless ferocity. The bombers with fighter escorts came over every day, mostly more than once if the weather held. And every mission had an element in it whose target was the satellite field outside Chipping Saxonby.

The troops in their slit trenches could do little more than watch, and duck when a wayward bomb came too close. This was a private battle between opposing air forces, aided, on the British side, by the AA batteries and balloon barrages. If the RAF and the anti-aircraft guns failed, well, then the infantry would have its opportunity. For the moment, no one was getting much sleep.

When the infantry was given time off, it either flopped down exhausted or, if the pubs were open and permission had been granted, repaired there for a welcome pint and a chance of normality. Those who had girlfriends among the WLA or in the village saw them as often as they could. Kominsky, a few recalled, hadn't had a girl. He hadn't died friendless because he'd had the platoon, but he'd died without someone special to mourn him. Of course, maybe that was better.

Clare Chappell was, for Jack, an oasis of sanity in a world gone mad. She was blonde, twenty years of age, and waiting to join the Wrens. Making love to her was like plunging into a warm pool.

Jack was frequently concerned about her, from the vantage point of being two years her senior. If the Germans came, she wouldn't survive a week. And a bloody unpleasant week it would be. Mind you, it wasn't going to be Christmas for anyone.

'They won't come,' she was fond of telling him.

'You're talking to Berlin on the phone? That's an offence.'

'They just won't.'

If Clare was whistling in the dark, she was performing solo. No one else was that confident. At the end of August there had been eighteen landing barges at Ostend. By September 6 there were over two hundred. They weren't there for pleasure cruising.

Also on September 6 Invasion Alert Two was flashed to battalion HQs. Invasion Alert Two meant that an attack was probable within three days. On September 7 Invasion Alert One went out: Invasion imminent, and probable within twelve hours. Only divisional commanders and above were to receive CROMWELL – Invasion Has Begun. They would pass it down to brigade and battalion level, and the churches would ring their bells.

Between September 7 and September 15, apart from two days of poor visibility, the Luftwaffe pounded London virtually round the clock, as well as making diversionary raids on the aerodromes of Fighter Command. Inevitably many bomb-loads fell short – creep-back as it was termed – or were jettisoned by panic-stricken crews in crippled aircraft. From a damaged JU 88 during the night of September 15, an entire salvo straddled Chipping Saxonby. Much of the jettison hit the church, and some were incendiaries.

The nearest fire-engines were at Godstone and Lingfield, and at the satellite field. None could be spared on this fearful night to help save the Norman church; nor could any of the would-be fire-fighters know whether the bombing was accidental, or whether there was more to come.

Brewerton wirelessed company HQ. The Germans wouldn't make a night parachute drop, not while there was an air-raid in progress anyway, and the platoon was doing nothing more than watch the fairy lights in the distance. He was given permission to release one section to help out in Chipping Saxonby, and gave the job to Jack. Jack selected the Chief's outfit. None of the other section NCOs objected. Chipping Saxonby was alight. They were safer in the slit trenches. Let some other bugger play Captain Marvel.

They were without transport, but made it to the village in twenty minutes. Overhead, the air sounded as if it were full of giant, angry bees.

Part of The Wheatsheaf had also been hit, and was blazing. The fire-fighters seemed to have it under control, however, using stirrup-pumps and garden hoses and buckets of sand. The landlord, wearing his ARP helmet, shouted that a unit of AFS, the Auxiliary Fire Service, was hoping to get through. Clare Chappell, Jack saw, was in the fire-bucket chain.

He strode over to her.

'For Chrissake, Clare, you should be in a shelter.'

She too was wearing a tin helmet, a bit too large, and in the firelight her eyes were unnaturally bright. He leant backwards when she attempted to kiss him on the cheek. Okay, so most of the platoon knew about him and Clare, but this was no time for demonstrations of affection. He wondered if she had been drinking, decided not.

'To hell with the shelter. This is where it's happening. Have you come to help us?'

'Well, the church, actually.'

On his way he came across Colonel Charlton who, with only one arm, could do little more than direct operations.

'Save the church, Sergeant,' he said pleasantly, when Jack reported to him. 'The whisky's only five years old.'

Jack couldn't help asking. 'Mrs Manners, sir?'

'She's also up by the church. And Sergeant,' he added, as Jack turned to race off, 'look after her if you see her. If you can, that is.'

'Will do, sir. Let's go, Chief.'

The fire had a firm grip. High-explosive bombs had crashed through the roof above the transept, detonated, and opened up the interior of the church to incendiaries. The onlookers prayed that there had been only one aircraft involved and that it jettisoned while hopelessly off course due to being hit by flak or fighters. Otherwise the flames would now act as markers for the following waves. Even in a war such as this the Luftwaffe probably would not think it worthwhile flattening a village containing just a few hundred souls when there was an airfield a few minutes' flying time away – if it, the Luftwaffe, knew what it was doing. Everything would look very different from the air. At altitude a bombardier might see the blaze and aim for the centre of it, feeding the inferno and encouraging the rest of the Geschwader to join in.

For the moment, though, that did not appear to be happening. Judging by the searchlights and the ack-ack flashes, the main battle was much further north, with poor old London getting it in the neck once again. The biggest dangers on the ground were from falling masonry and UXBs, either malfunctions or delayed-action fuses.

There were two hoses playing on the transept; two because the church had only two hydrants within reach. Water pressure was pathetic; the jets were barely reaching the flames until the fire-fighting teams moved closer, to be more effective. The nearer they drew, the greater the danger from a collapsing wall.

The village bobby was the leader of one team, the landlord of The Flying Fox the other. Directly behind them a handful of stalwarts kept the hoses from snaking out of control.

The vicar was in charge of the fire-bucket brigade, a composite of men, women and older teenagers. The buckets were being filled from a stand-pipe and passed down the line, to soak the wooden doors of the church. The church Bible with its irreplaceable history, never mind its religious significance, was safely below ground, in a vault, in the vicarage, as were the church valuables and the sacristy. What the vicar was now concerned about was the church itself. To see it burn was a monstrosity of previously unimagined hell. He found it hard to forgive the men who had done this wickedness.

Jack spotted Caroline Manners fifth or sixth in the fire-bucket line, perspiring beneath a tin helmet but readily recognizable in the light from the flames. The vicar had taken the responsibility of actually tossing the water on to the wooden doors. Which was how it should be, Jack considered. If a clergyman couldn't avoid a falling wall or shattering glass, no other bugger stood a chance. Short of something unforeseen, the fire-bucket squad was safe enough – for now.

Greyfoot identified the 'something unforeseen'.

'What about duds? I mean, what about something that looks like a dud but is actually a time-elapsed fuse? We could all be down the street outside The Wheatsheaf, and in a few pieces, if there's something in there no one knows about. According to the manual, we should withdraw a few hundred yards until the engineers have scouted the area.'

'Brew didn't send us here to abandon the church.'

'I don't know about that.' Greyfoot managed a grin. 'Unless it's got a painted face and is thirty feet high, I don't pray. Even then, it's to Manitou.'

'Maybe we'd better check the interior, as far as we can. Christ knows when the bomb-disposal guys'll get here. They've a lot on tonight.'

'You feeling heroic, Jack?'

'Not especially, I'm relying on your magic.'

'It's in my other pants.' Greyfoot studied the burning church. The fire-fighters were not exactly winning, but they were holding their own. A further detonation, however, would put paid to that. And half the fire-fighters too. 'It's going to be bloody warm in there. How far does our brief go?'

'I guess that's up to me.'

'So it's volunteers.'

'Right. You, me, Alphabet. Any more and we'll get in each other's way. Fewer and we could miss something. And I'll tell you another thing. It's in, a quick squint, and out. Anything that looks like it's got fins, I'll race you to the exit.'

'Porch door?'

'He's thrown enough water over it and it's not burning yet. We'd better move the fire-bucket line, though. I'll organize that. You tell the hose teams to switch off in, say, five minutes. It's going to be hard enough to see in there anyway without being soaked.'

Jack approached the vicar and explained what he proposed to do. The clergyman was concerned.

'Are you sure?'

'Far from it, but we don't have a lot of choice. When the hoses are turned off, I'd appreciate anything special you've got in the way of prayers. I'm not going to try and defuse anything I find. I don't have the expertise. But it'll help to know what's in there. Will you ask your team to back off? We may have to hit the doors a bit hard.'

'They're unlocked, but if the catches are jammed because of the heat, break them open. We can replace catches.'

Jack went across to Caroline Manners as the vicar herded his group away from the porch and explained what the Canadians planned to do.

'You father asked me to make sure you were okay, Mrs Manners.'

She recognized him immediately and, recalling the occasion of their previous parting, looked a little uncertain. Then she smiled wearily.

'Thank you, I am. Are you convinced this is a wise idea?'

'Not by a country mile, but the alternative's being kept in the dark.' He grunted irritably. 'If you see what I mean. Is that a tea urn over there?' She nodded. 'A hot cup would be handy when we come out. Make that three cups.'

Jack, Greyfoot and Alphabet donned gas masks. The moment they were through the double doors, which opened after a kick, the heat slammed into them with almost a physical force. The flames, however, were not as bad as they appeared from the outside. What they were getting was a steam bath caused by water from the hoses striking hot wood and metal. That steam, together with the dust raised by the original explosions, made it difficult to see, and seeing through the visor of a gas mask was hard enough at the best of times.

The church would not have held all the inhabitants of Chipping Saxonby had they elected to attend a service together. Maybe half that number could have been accommodated in the pews, which were in three rows, stretching much of the length of the church, each row separated by an aisle. From the porch doors at one end to the altar at the other measured in the region of two hundred feet. The transept was a hundred feet from the doors, perhaps a little more, and it was through the roof above it that the bombs had fallen. As well as could be seen that part of the stick that had done the damage had landed crosswise, damaging the pillars that held up the roof as well as the roof itself and at least one wall. In a way it was the church's smallness that had saved it, if indeed it could be saved. Many of the bombs in the stick had landed in the fields beyond the church. A larger building would have been hit from end to end.

The Chief and Jack took an aisle apiece, stepping gingerly around smouldering or burning pews, scrambling over rubble, and wincing involuntarily whenever a stain-glass window splintered or a piece of masonry fell. Alphabet stayed just inside the porch, keeping a close watch on both his friends, ready to help out if either was incapacitated, or summon assistance. No point in everyone being buried in a single fall.

There were no holes in the roof beyond the transept, though there was considerable blast damage to the altar. Logically, therefore, Jack calculated, finding it difficult to breathe even with the gas mask, if there were any UXBs awaiting an incautious intruder, they would be ticking away around the transept or be this side of it. One good thing – they'd constructed this church to last. The floor was flagstone. An unexploded bomb could not have buried itself its whole length. Parts would be visible.

None were. Short of something being out of sight under a mound of debris, there were no duds or delayed-action bombs in the church. The fire-fighters could go back and finish what they'd started.

Jack attracted Greyfoot's attention, gave him a thumbs-up, and pointed over his shoulder towards the porch, where they rejoined Alphabet. Outside they were gratified to hear the vicar lead a ragged cheer.

They peeled off their gas masks and wiped their foreheads. Mrs Manners appeared with three cups of tea on an old tin tray. 'There's a little whisky in it, compliments of my father.'

She hesitated.

'Go on,' encouraged Jack.

'It's just that he thinks you were mad too.'

The Canadians put themselves at the disposal of Colonel Charlton and made themselves useful wherever they were required for the rest of the night. There were no further raids, and by midnight it seemed as if the Luftwaffe had gone home from London, also. Of course, it would be back tomorrow.

In the small hours an AFS engine turned up. With its longer, more powerful hoses and turntable ladders, it made short work of what remained of the church fire, which in any case was largely out by then. The porch doors survived too, though the vicar was seen to be almost in tears when he emerged from them, after inspecting the church's interior. However, the church would be rebuilt, in time, and services could still be held once the inside was cleared and the tarpaulins thrown over the roof.

The Wheatsheaf fire had been extinguished before it could do major damage, but three houses at the south end of the High Street were destroyed by high-explosive. Providentially there were only two deaths, those of an elderly couple who refused to use their Anderson shelter. A Heavy Rescue crew who arrived at the same time as the bomb-disposal squad dug them out. Their bodies were taken to the vicarage.

After probing around the church rubble and anywhere else bombs had fallen, the engineers announced that there were no UXBs waiting to go off.

'But you were lucky,' the lieutenant in command admonished Jack, after being told what had happened at the church. 'Next time you might not be.'

By dawn there was very little else to be done, not by men and women and youths who were exhausted. The remainder of the clearing up could wait, or be left to the professionals. Those who had jobs prepared to change and go to them; those who didn't opted to grab some sleep – as soon as they'd eaten.

A mobile canteen had appeared from Godstone to serve tea and hot Bovril and sandwiches. Colonel Charlton wasn't at all convinced that non-alcoholic beverages were sufficient for people who had been through what Chipping Saxonby had, though he was prepared to concede that it was a mere bagatelle compared to what was happening in the big cities. Nevertheless, everything was relative.

He sought out the village bobby.

'I know this is probably against the law, Tom, but I wonder what you'd say if I wanted The Fox and The Wheatsheaf opened, even at this hour.'

The constable scratched his head and peered, as if seeking inspiration, into his tin helmet.

'Well, sir, it strikes me that you're a colonel and head of civil defence in these parts, and can doubtless do what you want, down to shooting looters if it comes to it. There's bound to be a regulation giving you permission to open pubs out of hours, somewhere.'

'Bound to be, Tom. Wouldn't surprise me if it's at the bottom of that pile of bumf I received yesterday. I'll see you're not the loser if anyone complains.'

No one did, not even the few teetotallers. God knows, they could all be dead, or occupied, by nightfall.

The colonel flitted from one inn to the other, to make sure that the Canadian infantrymen, at least, did not buy their own drinks. Not that anyone would have let them.

'You did a fine job, Sergeant Lambert.'

'Not just me, sir.'

'No, of course. I'll be talking to your commanding officer later in the day. If you've no objection, I'd like to tell him that your section's presence here was much appreciated.'

'That's fine with me, sir.' Jack cleared his throat. 'Has – er – Mrs Manners gone home, sir? The reason I ask, I wasn't exactly polite to her the day Private Kominsky was killed, and I haven't had a chance since to apologize.'

'I think you'll find her over by the mobile canteen. At least that's where she was when I came in.'

The colonel moved off, to talk to The Fox's landlord. Not a bad old bugger for an English brass hat, thought Jack, going across and handing what remained of his pint to Greyfoot, who was drinking lemonade. Clare Chappell, Jack noticed, was deep in conversation with one of the bomb squad, who wasn't making much attempt to keep his hand off her knee. Nor was Clare objecting. Well, it wasn't a relationship, his and Clare's, made in heaven anyway, and she'd be off to the Wrens shortly. The sailors would love her, and she them.

'Hang on to this, Chief. I'll be back.'

He joined Mrs Manners, looming alongside her so suddenly that she took a step backwards, startled. Those behind didn't object when they saw who it was queue-jumping.

'I forgot to ask you, what did you mean that your father thought we were mad too?'

'Just that we all did.'

'It's nice to know someone worries about you – especially in view of the way I snapped at you the day Kominsky died. I'm sorry about that, incidentally. I was out of order.'

'You don't have to apologize. I know from experience what it's like to lose someone close.'

The queue shuffled forward. When it was their turn to be served, Jack discovered to his embarrassment that he'd brought no money. There had been no need when the section had set off for Chipping Saxonby.

'I was going to buy you a cup of tea, but I'm afraid my pockets are empty.'

'Please allow me. Would you like a sandwich?'

'No, tea's fine.'

He carried both cups over to a low wall, where they sat. Either side of them other men and women were drinking and eating, but everyone was wrapped up in his or her own thoughts. The night had taken its toll mentally as well as physically, but few glanced nervously skywards. The sirens would tell them when the Luftwaffe was on its way.

She sipped her tea, holding the cup with both hands, shivering a little though the day promised to be a scorcher. She had removed her tin helmet and her dark hair was plastered against her skull. There were also smudges of soot and smoke on her cheeks and forehead, but he scarcely noticed them.

'You're staring, Sergeant Lambert. I suppose I look a wreck.'

In another woman he'd have considered that remark a trawl for a compliment. From her it was a genuine observation. Jesus, he thought, I've got it, or I'm about to get it, bad. Frigging biology.

'No, you look fine.'

She almost giggled. 'I think the heat's affected your brain. Or your eyesight. Where's the rest of your section, by the way?'

'In The Fox.'

'And you prefer tea to beer? My, for a soldier that makes you almost unique.'

'Let's just say you're prettier than that bunch of hoodlums.'

She blushed beneath the dirt and grime, and inclined her head away from him. But he sensed she was not offended, and followed up quickly. He might never get a better opportunity and, besides, in Canada what you didn't ask for, you didn't get.

'Back where I come from,' he said, 'we're a bit old-fashioned. If a woman buys a man a cup of tea, a man's expected to return the favour. Not necessarily with tea, of course. A drink, maybe, or a meal. Something, anyway,' he concluded lamely.

She turned to face him.

'Are you inviting me out? There could be objections in some quarters to that.'

Damn her, he thought. To hell with her. He'd been right in the first place. Without pips on his shoulders, she didn't consider him an equal.

68

Or her father wouldn't. Terrific for putting out fires, sure, but after that, back in your kennel.

He stood up.

'I'm sorry to have bothered you, Mrs Manners. It won't happen again.'

She read his thoughts.

'The objections I had in mind were the Luftwaffe. And Clare Chappell.'

Jack was astonished. How could she possibly know about Clare?

Again she surprised him.

'Sergeant Lambert, I've lived in this village all my life, and my family has been here for several generations. There isn't much goes on that I don't hear about sooner or later. In a small community people gossip. It's an ancient English pastime. For example, I know from the landlady in The Wheatsheaf that you've asked her about me, questioned her at length. I even know the nickname you have for me, though if I'm Snow White, which dwarf does that make you? In your present mood, I'd say it was Grumpy.'

It was Jack's turn to blush, something he'd thought he was beyond.

'And I also know a little about you,' she went on, 'because fair's fair. I suspect that you have some idea I wouldn't be seen out with an NCO. Well, let me tell you, my father joined the army in the ranks, in the Great War, and no one thought any the less of him then, or thinks any the more of him now. Frankly, I'm offended you view me in that light. It doesn't say much for your judgement of character. Perhaps that chip on your shoulder is getting in the way.'

'Ouch,' muttered Jack. 'Maybe I'd better start again.'

'And this time without the old-folks-back-home lines. Really, Sergeant, you've been seeing too many bad films. If you're asking me out, for heaven's sake say so.'

'I'm asking you out.'

'I accept. With a stipulation. This will be for a meal or a drink or a walk or a bicycle ride. What it's not going to be, what *I'm* not going to be, here or anywhere else, for NCOs, privates, or indeed major-generals, is the butt of a barrack-room joke. Remember, I have ears in this village. Nor do I expect you to stop seeing Clare Chappell. What your relationship is with her is between the two of you. What ours is, is between us.

'Now you can buy me a drink before my father, or Tom, decides

69

enough is enough. I'm sure your credit's good at either pub. After that, you can call me when your duties permit. If Hitler doesn't invade.'

Hitler didn't, though for a while it was a close-run thing.

Night after night and day after day, Goering's bombers hammered London and Britain's other major cities. The final total of civilian dead would amount to forty thousand with a further fifty thousand injured. A million homes were destroyed or damaged.

When the immediate threat of invasion was over, when aerial reconnaissance showed the landing barges being towed away, the Patricias struck canvas and moved into billets in the Godstone and Lingfield areas. A Company left the Chipping Saxonby vicinity because the village had no room to house them. Jack and Caroline Manners found it impossible to keep their date, though he telephoned Five Oaks as often as he could to stay in touch. At the beginning of October she informed him, without any trace of malice, that Clare Chappell had left for Plymouth, to begin her Wren training.

At the end of the first week in October, the lessening tension allowed the termination of the Patricias' daily stand-to. This was regarded as a two-edged sword. While leave was re-established, casualness of dress accepted during the invasion emergency was replaced by a return to spit-and-polish. Most of the troops moaned. They would rather have faced the Wehrmacht than the critical eye of the RSM.

It was the second week in October before Jack managed to wangle a day-pass and hitch a ride to Chipping Saxonby, where he met Caroline Manners in The Wheatsheaf. The landlord's wife was delighted to see him again, not least because her private prediction that he and Mrs Manners would get together appeared to be accurate. After two drinks and a short walk together, however, Caroline had WVS activities to attend to, and Jack, now that the nights were drawing in, had to hunt for a lift back to his billet.

When he found time he wrote home to Calgary. Clare Chappell had figured in earlier letters and now Caroline Manners was a feature. They wouldn't want to hear, his parents, his brother and sister, how Britain was getting bombed. In any event, they would already know that from radio broadcasts.

Between the middle of October and the first week in November, he managed to see Caroline half a dozen times, occasionally, with the help of a motor pool NCO, for no more than an hour. Only once did they make love, in her bedroom at Five Oaks, though afterwards she

70

seemed to regret it, as if somehow she had betrayed the memory of her dead husband. He resolved to remain patient, not push her. One day the past would be forgotten.

In the middle of November the battalion received orders to move to Sussex, to relieve the West Nova Scotia Regiment. From November 14 HQ would be at Roedean School and outlying companies at Lewes and Rottingdean. He telephoned Five Oaks to let her know, without revealing the battalion's destination, that it would be more difficult to see her after the 14th of the month, and was informed by her father that Caroline was in London, on WVS business.

'She's due back this evening, though. I'm picking her up at Godstone Station at seven. As she's on war work, I can use the car.'

'Perhaps I could come over later, sir. I can scrounge some transport, but I don't know what time it will be. It's pretty important that I see her.' He hesitated. It wouldn't be prudent to say too much to a colonel who was a frequent guest in the Patricias' officers' mess, especially not over the telephone. 'It might not be that easy in the near future,' he ventured.

'I think I know what you mean. Come over when you can. If you're here before eight, you're welcome to dine with us. Cold cuts, but better than nothing.' He attempted a mild joke. 'I hope your intentions are strictly honourable, Sergeant Lambert.'

'They are, sir.'

'I'm glad to hear it. My only concern is my daughter's happiness, and you seem to be having a beneficial effect.'

It was close on eleven before he made it to Five Oaks. The house was blacked-out, naturally, but Colonel Charlton's Austin 7 was parked in the drive. Unusual, that; he generally put it out of harm's way in the garage. They were both back, anyway. Jack hoped they hadn't gone to bed.

The colonel answered the bell, though the hall, because of air-raid precautions, remained in darkness until the front door closed. Then Caroline's father switched on the lights.

Jack was shocked at the sight of the older man's face. He looked a hundred.

'I should have called your billet. It would have saved you a trip. I'm sorry, it didn't occur to me.'

Over a whisky in the drawing-room, only the second time Jack had been entertained there, it came out slowly. London had been bombed the previous night. The flat where Caroline was staying with friends received a direct hit, by a land-mine it was thought. All the occupants were killed instantly, their bodies mutilated. It had taken the authorities fifteen hours to establish the identities of the deceased, sorting through the carnage for documentation. He had only heard himself late this afternoon. No, there could be no doubt about it. Caroline was another victim of the war.

For a week Jack walked around in a daze. He was offered compassionate leave and refused it. Being unoccupied was the last thing he needed. What he wanted most of all was to stick a Canadian bayonet in a German belly. And the bloody Patricias, almost the whole bloody British army, were stuck on this offshore fucking battleship. The invasion scare was over. Why the hell wasn't someone doing something? Apart from Bomber Command, no one was carrying the fight to the enemy.

He thought of asking for a transfer to the RAF, as an air-gunner if there was nothing else available, but recognized that he would get no further than a selection board.

He drove his platoon hard during the day and drank heavily in the evening. Brew worried about him, and spoke to the company commander.

'There'll be something coming through in Part Two Orders in a day or so that might appeal to him. Who are his friends?'

'He's closest to Corporal Greyfoot.'

'Yes, they'll be looking for men like Greyfoot if I'm any judge.'

'They, sir?'

'Wait for the orders, Brew. And talk to Greyfoot first. You'll see what I mean.'

The Chief approached Jack one afternoon as November was drawing to a close, after anti-invasion exercise.

'They're asking for commando volunteers, volunteers to undergo commando training. It's in Part Two Orders.'

'So?'

'So Alphabet, Kovacs, me – we're thinking of putting our names down. It's more money and it'll give us a crack at the Germans, Jack. No other fucker's going to be moving off this island for a year or two.'

'Where's the training?'

'A place called Achnacarry, in Scotland.'

'Brew going?'

'They're not taking officers, not yet. Maybe they're not mad enough.'

'But I am?'

'You're sure as hell not sane, these days.'

'Okay, so I'm mad. Maybe I'll volunteer. But why do you and Kovacs and that crazy Polack have to go?'

'We like it with you.'

'Who said I'm going?'

'I think you just did.'

FIVE

The taxi from Godstone Station dropped Ben outside The Wheatsheaf, which the driver informed him had accommodation, whereas The Flying Fox no longer took in guests. Hadn't for a year.

'It's the rationing, see. People don't want to spend good money staying at inns when they can't eat any better than they do at home. Meat, sugar, sweets for the kids. You can still get as much rabbit as you want, but me, I've given it up. I was starting to grow long ears. You wouldn't think we won the war, would you?'

Crossing London earlier, changing trains from the overnight Scottish express, Ben had experienced identical thoughts, being shocked by the bombed-out buildings which, two years after VE Day, showed little evidence of being reconstructed. When flying with 514 Squadron out of Waterbeach, he and his crew had managed quite a few overnight passes to the capital when they were stood down, and he didn't recall the devastation being that bad even when the doodlebug raids were at their height. The Londoners, too, now seemed subdued, lacking spirit, a far cry from their defiant attitude during the war. Perhaps it was his memory playing tricks or perhaps, as he and Jonathan had agreed, wars change people.

The British deserved better than they were getting, though.

The Wheatsheaf's landlord passed him the register and asked if he would be staying long.

'A day, maybe two.'

'Looking up old friends?'

'What makes you say that?'

'That accent and – well, there's something familiar about you.'

'I've never been here before. I was stationed in Cambridgeshire.'

'US Air Force?'

It was a common mistake. Ben no longer took offence at being taken for an American.

'Canadian.'

The landlord turned the register round.

'Calgary, eh. We had quite a few Canadians here at the beginning of the war. Mostly Yanks later.'

The landlord did not appear to recognize the name Lambert. Still, it was close on seven years since Jack left the area and Lambert wasn't an unusual handle.

'I'll show you to your room.'

Not having slept much on the train, Ben lay down for a couple of hours. When he awoke it was past three p.m. and the taste in his mouth was like the inside of an old flying gauntlet. He washed, shaved and cleaned his teeth in the communal bathroom, and felt slightly more human. The village church, he observed from his bedroom window, had received what were apparently direct hits from high-explosive and incendiary bombs. He'd seen enough photographs of similar damage to recognize the signs. Renovations were far from complete. Probably no one had thought it worthwhile starting until the Luftwaffe was beaten and then there'd be a shortage of skilled labour and materials.

Downstairs he found the landlord behind the bar, polishing glasses. There were no customers. Ben wondered why until he recalled the peculiar English licensing laws. There would be no food, either.

'You're a bit late for a hot meal, but I can make you a cheese sandwich if you like. And, as a resident, you're entitled to drink out of hours.'

Ben declined the sandwich but asked the landlord to join him in a beer. Over the drinks he said he was looking for a couple of people.

'Someone I know back home was billeted around here during the war. He asked me to pass on his regards if I was in the vicinity. To a Mrs Manners, Caroline Manners, and a Clare Chappell.'

After a moment, enlightenment spread across the landlord's face. He slapped the counter with pleasure.

'*Now* I know why your face is familiar. The name's the same too. It's been bothering me since you walked in, but mentioning Mrs Manners brought it back. You've got to be related to Jack Lambert.'

Ben admitted the fraternal connection. Also that he was impressed.

'That's quite a memory you've got.'

'It's a trick you learn in this business. I don't remember everyone, naturally, but Jack was one of my wife's favourites. She'll be furious having missed you, but she's staying with her mother for a week. The old girl's getting on now. How is Jack?'

Ben explained that his brother was dead.

'In a POW camp in 1943. Pneumonia. He was captured at Dieppe. I'm over here on business and decided to look up a few of his old haunts, and old friends. I should have come clean in the first place, but you know how it is.'

'Of course. For all you knew he could have sired half a dozen illegitimate children, leaving a mob of angry fathers ready to lynch him or any other Lambert. Right?'

Not quite, thought Ben, but it will do. He nodded.

The landlord pulled another two beers and waved aside Ben's offer of payment.

'Hell, I'm sorry to hear he didn't survive the war. My wife will be too. They used to sit exactly where we are now.' He frowned. 'But didn't he write to you about Mrs Manners? That she was killed in the Blitz?'

'No, he didn't.'

'Probably too shocked. They were getting very close. It was soon after her death we heard he'd joined some commando outfit. Colonel Charlton, Mrs Manners's father, mentioned it, I think, though maybe it was someone else. You know what it was like during the war. Half you heard was a rumour and half the rumours were wrong. All rumours were discouraged, of course, so perhaps it wasn't the colonel. The Patricias had moved away by then.'

'What about Clare Chappell?' asked Ben.

The landlord winked knowingly.

'There *was* something between those two at one time, but it came to an end when Clare joined the Wrens or the Patricias moved on, I don't remember which. She's Clare Beatty now, got two children and lives in Portsmouth. Married a chief petty officer. I can tell you where her parents live in the village. They'll have her Pompey address.'

'Maybe I'll leave it.' No point, thought Ben. If the landlord and his wife hadn't a bad word to say against Jack, Ben doubted few others would have, either. But he'd check out Colonel Charlton if Mrs Manners's father was still alive.

'He is, and spritely. It's not far. You can walk it in ten minutes.'

'Too many good men died,' Colonel Charlton was saying half an hour later. 'Far too many. Looking at the world today, I often ask myself whether it was worth it. It had to be done, of course, but . . . I really am very sorry about Jack, though I suspected he hadn't made it when I didn't hear from him after the war. He was the sort to keep in touch.'

They were in the Five Oaks library, the colonel standing, Ben in an armchair.

'I only saw him once after the night I told him my daughter had been killed. He called on me to say he'd volunteered for Achnacarry. It seemed like a good idea so far as I was concerned. I knew his commanding officer fairly well and kept in touch even after the Patricias moved to Sussex.'

'What do you mean, good idea, sir?'

'He was wasting his aggression, drinking too much. He wanted to get at the enemy and the poor old Patricias were doomed to spend three years in England. I believe Sicily was their first campaign. Mind you, he'd have seen action there. And in Italy.'

Colonel Charlton studied Ben curiously.

'Perhaps you'll forgive an impertinent question, Mr Lambert. Are you trying to contact everyone who knew him before he was taken prisoner-of-war?'

Ben had resolved flying over that he would fabricate an answer to this, if asked, as he would continue to lie about pneumonia being the cause of death. If he began explaining about the so-called suicide, the alleged collaboration and his own theory about Jack being executed, it would lead to all manner of complications.

'Not exactly, sir. But while I'm in England and possibly Europe for my brother-in-law, I thought I'd like to meet anyone who knew him if I found myself near where he was stationed.'

'Achnacarry's a few hundred miles away. I believe they closed it down after the war, in any case.'

'I might not bother with Achnacarry. According to Jack's letters, there wasn't much time for socializing. It seemed to be tough going from day one.'

'Yes, they weren't training Girl Guides up there.'

SIX

Because of processing and other delays the former Patricias did not reach Achnacarry, castle retreat of the Chief of the Camerons fourteen miles from Fort William in Inverness-shire, until January 1941, on a bitterly cold day of sub-zero temperatures. Flurries of snow added to the foot or so that was already lying on the ground.

Along with other volunteers, they debussed from the three-tonner that had brought them from the railway station and were marched along the castle drive by an NCO instructor. Every so often they were made to halt and read spoof epitaphs of imaginary recruits. 'He failed to take cover during an amphibious landing.' 'He thought he was invisible on the skyline.' 'He assumed the night would hide him.' 'He never saw the German who killed him.'

The NCO instructor, Halloran, was a menacingly huge sergeant, unlike many of the instructors they were to meet. He was so vast that Jack remarked, not exactly in his quietest voice, 'Jesus, the last time I saw something that big Captain Ahab was right behind with a harpoon.'

Those closest to Jack grinned, but unhappily Halloran heard the remark also. He didn't bawl or curse, however; he merely smiled and asked the comedian his name and number. Jack gave them.

'Right, Sergeant Lambert,' said Halloran, 'you'll find your stripes don't give you any privileges here. They mean nothing. Sergeants, corporals and lance-corporals are all recruits. We don't take them away because that would leave ugly patches on your battledress, wouldn't it? But you're all the lowest of the low and God knows, looking at you, I don't expect there'll be many of you left at the end of a week. Got it?'

Jack said he had. It seemed wiser not to argue. Then Halloran ordered every one of the new arrivals, packs on, to double-march through the snow for three miles, their rifles held at the high port, while he, rifleless and packless, trotted alongside. In spite of the cold, by the end of the run the trainees were sweating copiously. One or two were vowing to use Jack's head for a football. Had they not been some of the toughest individuals, mentally and physically, in the armed forces, their association with Achnacarry would have ended there and then. Because Halloran tormented them by saying that anyone who dropped by the wayside would be on the first three-tonner back to the station, RTU'd, Returned To Unit.

No one did drop out. To be RTU'd was the ultimate disgrace. But had there been a chance of any one of them falling at the first hurdle, they would not have got past the selection board to begin with. For the Patricias contingent down in Sussex, that board, consisting of two commando troop officers, a lieutenant and a captain, was far from the foregone conclusion they'd assumed when they put their names down.

Their physical condition was not taken for granted. What would pass muster in even a crack infantry battalion might not be good enough for the rigours of commando training. They got through, however; Jack, the Chief, Kovacs, Alphabet, four others from different companies. Initially twelve men had volunteered, but the CO put his foot down and only allowed the first eight to take the tests. He wasn't very keen on allowing more than four or five to transfer, but was confident that the board would weed out close on fifty per cent.

After the physical they were told the basic requirements of a commando. They had to be able to swim, be immune from sea and air sickness, have self-reliance and an aggressive attitude; be able to kill at close quarters; be able to live off the country for long periods. Much of what they needed to know would be taught at Achnacarry, but they had to be sure they could learn.

They were given a weapons proficiency test. They had to be marksmen with the .303 Lee-Enfield and at least one automatic weapon, preferably the Sten. Two of the Patricias failed at this juncture, one because his shooting was poor and one because of a cook-off when his Sten stuck on automatic and, panicking, he came close to taking the head of one officer from its shoulders.

The commando captain interviewed the six survivors one by one. Ostensibly it was to establish their attitude to the war and, more important, why they wanted to be commandos. But on the captain's desk was a huge bowl of fresh eggs, forty or fifty of them, and a bottle of Johnny Walker Red Label, three-quarters full and virtually unobtainable outside the black market or armed robbery.

Halfway through each interview, on one pretext or another, the captain left the room. When he came back he carefully counted the eggs, knowing full well that there were not forty or fifty in the bowl, but exactly forty-six. He also asked to see each interviewee's hands, because the scotch bottle was impregnated with an invisible dye which turned flesh bright green within a few minutes.

At this point any interviewee who had gone in for a little free enterprise during the captain's absence thought they were stuffed, destined for rejection at the very least and probably the guardhouse. But that was not the case. Only if a potential recruit hadn't stolen eggs or whisky was he viewed with suspicion, for that showed a definite lack of initiative. If a man couldn't take advantage of a situation when it was placed four-square in front of him, he stood precious little chance of surviving if he were on his own behind enemy lines. Thou Shalt Not Steal was not one of the Commandments to be obeyed to make a good commando. For that matter, few of them were.

The commando captain expressed himself satisfied when each Patricia stole at least one egg, but was less than happy with Kovacs, who'd had four away and could only hand three back. In the few minutes it had taken, Kovacs had eaten the fourth raw.

The whisky, too, had been well gargled, with only the Chief abstaining. Not the first Indian the captain had come across, it was accepted that Greyfoot couldn't, and wouldn't, touch hard liquor.

Kovacs very nearly didn't make it through the final interview in Rottingdean, which was again on a one-to-one basis but this time conducted by the lieutenant. Sex was the question. Senior commando officers understood that supremely fit men in the prime of life needed women, but any man who couldn't live without them could screw up an outfit by worrying about a girlfriend, or catch some disease from a whore. When asked about his sex life, Kovacs misunderstood the lieutenant's intention, believing it to be a test like the eggs. Be bold and you'd make it, timid you wouldn't. So he said, 'That's my fucking business, sir.'

The lieutenant turned an interesting shade of purple, and Kovacs realized he had pulled a boner. Racking his brains for a way out of the mess other than by direct apology, he feigned a fit, made a hideous noise in the back of his throat, rolled his eyes and fell to the floor, clutching his neck. Alarmed, the lieutenant came round the desk like a sprinter and bent over the moaning Canadian. Kovacs grabbed him by his tie. 'If you were a German, sir, you'd be dead by now.'

The lieutenant appreciated that Kovacs could think fast on his feet, and passed him.

Before boarding the train for Scotland one of the six Patricias, Don Seagrove, went down with appendicitis. That left the five the CO had predicted. The fifth was a slightly built D Company youngster, Ernie Kiley, from Maple Creek in western Saskatchewan. He didn't weigh more than ten stone soaking wet, but he was the best shot in the battalion and played a fierce game of Broom-i-loo, frequently brushing aside opponents twice his size. His other claim to fame was that he had seen *Gone With The Wind* twenty times and could quote from it by the yard. Whenever he was asked to do something that didn't appeal to him, he gave Scarlett O'Hara's usual response: 'I won't think about that today, I'll think about that tomorrow.'

At Achnacarry the new arrivals were surprised to learn that, after the first week, they would be allowed to live in civilian billets, which they could find for themselves wherever they liked and for which they received a daily allowance of 6s.8d., or about $1.60 Canadian. It was a small part of the process of teaching them to think and look out for themselves. The larger parts came at them thick and fast over the three-month course.

Physical fitness was very high on the list of priorities. In full combat gear and carrying a rifle, a trainee was expected to speed march at seven miles an hour, across some of the most rugged terrain in Britain, over a measured course of fourteen miles. The first time the new intake tried it, during their second week, it took them almost two and a half hours and a lot of blistered feet. Halfway through the march, Jack was longing to be back with the cosy old Patricias in dozy old Sussex.

'This is fucking ridiculous, Chief. I mean, Christ, are we going to kill the Germans or race them in the next Olympics?'

A speed march was part march, part run. After ten miles the squad was starting to dread hearing Halloran bellow, 'Break into double-time, double . . . march!'

Among the Patricias, only Ernie Kiley didn't seem to be having a problem, though he was damned near invisible under his gear and, by rights, should have been hammered into the road, like a nail into a plank, with every step he took. Rifle, pack and ammunition pouches weighed close on sixty pounds, and that wasn't far from half of what Kiley tipped the scales at. One place behind him in the same rank, Kovacs couldn't believe that the little guy from Maple Creek was real.

'You look like a mad fucking elf helping Santa,' he wheezed.

Kiley just grinned and said nothing. *He* wasn't puffing and panting. Kovacs sounded about on his last legs.

But they made it, the entire squad, and the next time was easier. Almost before they knew it they were down to as near two hours as made no difference, and just when they thought they had got this part of the course cracked, at least, Halloran produced The Sickener.

He announced that their next speed march would be over a different route, starting five miles from Achnacarry. Three-tonners would convey them to the start-line and bring them back.

The route took them in a figure of eight and Halloran seemed to be urging them along faster than usual. When they sighted the three-tonners again, they'd all had just about enough. Two hundred yards from the trucks Halloran ordered them to mark time. He went on ahead and climbed over the tailgate of the nearest vehicle.

'Jesus, he's human,' someone remarked. 'He's going to reverse the transport up to us.'

Except he wasn't. With a wave and a broad grin from Halloran, the three-tonners roared away, leaving the squad to do five extra miles. This was The Sickener.

When they weren't speed marching they were climbing hills and mountains until they were ready to drop, and then they climbed some more. They assaulted cliffs using hand-held rocket grapnels and learned how to abseil down.

They were taught bouldering, racing at top speed down a half-mile steep incline littered with large stones, leaping from one to the next. When the rocks were wet, and they generally were, not even their special SV boots (vulcanized rubber soles) were much use. You had to jump and hope for the best, but the casualty rate was surprisingly slight, just two broken ankles.

At the end of the bouldering course was the cat crawl, a slack rope fifty feet above a fast-flowing river and measuring two hundred feet from end to end. Crossing this in full fighting order, moving on their bellies hand over hand with one foot looped over the rope and the other dangling free, was never easy at the best of times, but it was invariably made harder by Halloran – and each and every man could have killed the bastard – jerking the rope when a trainee was in the middle, causing him to tumble sideways and hang on by his fingers only. The trick then was to regain the rope and continue the crawl. The alternative was that fifty-foot drop. If you didn't break your neck you'd probably drown, which was sufficient incentive for a man to get back up. Only two failed in the entire three months, and of that pair just one needed hospital treatment. They had a saying in the squad that God looked after the daft, the drunk, and commandos. Or maybe they were simply learning how to fall properly.

Someone was looking after them, anyway, for the dropout rate, whether from injury or merely an inability to hack it, was amazingly low. By the end of week six only three men had been RTU'd, and one of those went via Colchester military prison for getting drunk in Fort William and missing a night exercise.

The assault course sorted out several more. To begin with it was a piece of cake. Then the CO concluded he wasn't seeing enough blood and broken bones, that it was all a bit too easy. The new course was something dreamt up by Dante on one of his more wretched days. Thirty-foot walls to scale, high bars to walk across on tiptoe while instructors tossed thunderflashes, narrow, water-filled culverts to crawl through in pitch blackness. Penultimately a leopard crawl across two hundred yards of mud and slush, with fixed-position Brens firing live rounds above the exposed backs of the squad. And lastly, a ninety-foot rope to climb followed by a head-first cat-crawl death-slide down a hawser angled at forty-five degrees.

No one at Achnacarry had any difficulty getting to sleep at night, and the sex question everyone had been asked at their regiments became purely academic. They had a saying at the Depot: If you see a lot of guys walking around half-dazed with erections, they're commando trainees.

The flesh was willing but the spirit was weak.

One break from the physical activity was the offensive demolitions course, a favourite with everyone. They all liked to see something go bang, but unless the charges were handled carefully, the item in bits and pieces could well be themselves.

The demolitions instructor was a wiry Welshman named Jones and nicknamed Blow-up. He showed them how to handle the guncotton wet slabs that looked like dirty white Weetabix and how to insert the CE primer. How, also, to make for the hills at top speed if the charges became dry, because then they were unstable and dangerous. He demonstrated how '808' plastic explosive could be used underwater and, once primed, how the charge could be set off with rifle fire. He explained the difference between black powder number 11 fuses, which burnt at a rate of two feet a minute, and Cordtex, a white flexible fuse which burnt at two hundred *miles* a second. Mix them up, intoned Blow-up in his Welsh lilt, and the next thing you knew you'd be signing on in St Peter's big book.

In close combat training they were taught how to use the fighting knife, seven inches of carbon steel made by Wilkinson Sword; cheese wire, a length of wire stretched between two wooden toggles and capable, with very little wrist movement, of beheading an enemy instantaneously; and coshes, sometimes purpose built and spring loaded, sometimes nothing more than a sock filled with sand.

The emphasis here was on improvization. Use anything to hand. They might have been captured and disarmed, or they might have lost their weapons in an explosion or a botched amphibious landing. Therefore think quick. Thumbs could be used for gouging out eyes; you'd probably break your thumbs but the other guy would be blind. The blade of the hand sharply under a man's nose would thrust the nasal bone into the brain. Or put your fingers in an enemy's mouth and yank. If all else failed, or even if it didn't, a bloody good kick in the balls would send most men to the cleaners. Be silent if the operation called for it; if it didn't, make as much noise as possible. It was surprising how a few blood-thirsty yells could unnerve an opponent.

'Jesus,' Alphabet said one afternoon after a particularly gruelling session, 'if I'd known then what I know now, no bugger would have got me into Headingly.'

It occurred to a few others, too, that what they were being taught might save their lives against the Germans, but how the hell did you unlearn it when the war was over? For that matter, as it was becoming instinctive, how did you stop yourself using the various techniques if you got into a scrap with a fellow trainee?

Not that that happened very often. If it did and the perpetrators were caught, unless there were extenuating circumstances they were RTU'd. That was a good enough reason for a man to sit on his hands.

Throughout the course the officers and senior instructors kept meticulous files on all trainees, to be RTU'd if they were not coming up to scratch, but to be given further training as instructors if proving specially talented. Halloran put Jack in this category and recommended him to the troop commander.

'What would that entail exactly, sir?' Jack asked.

'Another four weeks here at the end of this course, doing more advanced training. Then, depending upon your own ideas and how we see you developing, perhaps a specialization: weapons, close combat, amphibious warfare, communications, demolition. Teaching others what we've taught you.'

'In other words, remaining in the United Kingdom.'

'Unless your speciality had a use elsewhere for a particular operation, yes.'

'I don't think so, sir. I'd rather join a unit.'

'I understand. But if you change your mind . . .'

Jack did not think he would. He wasn't looking to be a hero or win the Victoria Cross – for that matter, he didn't know a man in the outfit who was – and the image of Caroline Manners was fading as the months passed. But he didn't want to spend the war as a glorified school-master.

In the advanced weapons training cadre they learned how to fire the Bren from the hip and were introduced to what would become most commandos' favoured submachine gun, the 1928 model Thompson. Even though its cyclic rate of fire of 600 rounds per minute was only slightly greater than the Sten's, and its low muzzle velocity of 920 feet per second was actually less than the Sten's, the punch it packed from its .45 calibre ammunition gave everyone who fired one confidence. They were only a little disappointed, too, to be told they would be issued with box magazines and not the drums so familiar to most of them from Jimmy Cagney movies. Tracer would always be 1-in-5, higher than was customary elsewhere for the demoralizing effect it would have on the enemy to see death singling him out.

But there could come a time, Sergeant O'Malley, their weapons instructor, informed them, when all they might have would be firearms picked up from Germans, and it was therefore necessary to be familiar with the more common rifles and submachine guns. Few of them had seen German weapons close up before; there had not been many opportunities to capture any.

'This is the MP 38,' O'Malley told them, holding up a submachine gun approximately the size of a Sten, with a folding steel stock. 'That is, Maschinenpistole 38 made by Erma. You'll have seen it in the newsreels and no doubt heard it called a Schmeisser. That's wrong, though they make the same mistake in Germany. Hugo Schmeisser took a hand in the design of the MP 40, but not this. It fires 9mm rounds from this 32-round detachable magazine at a cyclic rate of 500 rpms with a muzzle velocity of 1250 fps, which is roughly the performance of the Sten. Its single-column feed makes it liable to jamming when you, or him, can least afford it. If it's you, run like hell while chanting the Lord's Prayer. If it's him, if you see Jerry pointing one of these things at you and leaping up and down and screaming *Gott in Himmel* because nothing's happening, take a chance and rush the bastard. The jams are hard to shift. Who wants to try it?'

Ernie Kiley's arm shot up. O'Malley tossed the MP 38 at him. Kiley caught it deftly, examined it, and slipped off the safety. The target was a German silhouette almost a hundred yards away.

'You're out of range,' said O'Malley. 'You'll have to get closer than that.'

Kiley squeezed the trigger. The machine pistol bucked in his hands. Then he steadied himself and tried again. The entire magazine was on target, neatly grouped in the upper half of the torso.

Kiley was one of O'Malley's favourites, but even he was surprised.

'According to the manual that's not possible.'

'I'll write and tell Erma, shall I, Sarge?'

When everyone had tried the MP 38, later in the session they examined and field-stripped the Mauser Kar 98K, the standard Wehrmacht rifle, which impressed none of them because, although it weighed a bit less than the Lee-Enfield, its magazine took only five 7.92mm rounds in an internal box compared to the Lee-Enfield's ten. It might just about make out as a club.

Neither the instructor nor the trainees were keen on the handguns, the P38 and the P08. Respectively Carl Walther and Georg Luger might be geniuses, but handguns were for girls to defend their honour, or the suicidally brave. And that went for Messrs Browning, Webley, and Smith and Wesson too.

Throughout the last three weeks of the course they concentrated on field firing exercises using live ammunition, the use of assault boats and scaling ladders, advanced demolitions with the Hawkins number 75 grenade and the Bangalore torpedo, night operations and survival techniques. This latter course involved, among other things, learning how to trap, skin and cook rats, and identify edible fungi. Then they were dropped off thirty miles from Achnacarry and told to survive unseen for seventy-two hours – individually or as groups, it was up to them. They were permitted no money and thieving from local farms or shops would be regarded, on this occasion, not as a test of resourcefulness but as an RTU offence. It was surprising just how quickly they all overcame their aversion to boiled rat and mushrooms when they couldn't snare rabbits.

'Though it's not something I'm going to make a habit of,' said Jack.

'Oh, I dunno,' mused Kovacs, 'tastes a bit like chicken to me.'

'He'd eat any fucking thing,' muttered Alphabet. 'Watch your legs.'

Their passing out test was one of uncompromising endurance, a sixty-three mile march in full battle order, which they accomplished in twenty-four hours with five casualties. These five, however, would not be RTU'd. They would be given another chance in a week. As for the remainder, it was all over.

The officers, Halloran, Blow-up Jones, Sergeant O'Malley all suddenly became human. It was no longer the staff and the trainees; they were all commandos. The only thing few of them had done was actually kill someone. That had to be taken on trust. As Halloran pointed out over several gallons of beer, it had been tough but the playing was over. Now they were ready for the real thing.

SEVEN

December 1941

The two LSIs (Landing Ships Infantry), HMS *Prince Charles* and HMS *Prince Leopold*, former cross-Channel ferries commandeered for the duration, were taking a fearful pounding in the Force 8 gales raging in the Norwegian Sea. Crammed below decks, the troops of 3 Commando held on to their stomachs and prayed there would be no repetition of the previous day's crisis, when the *Charles* took on fourteen feet of water in its for'ard hold. That had given them Christmas Day on Shetland, true, while one hundred and fifty tons of sea water were pumped out, but most of them would have foregone their Christmas dinner for flat seas and a landing ship that didn't leak.

Escorting the LSIs were the destroyers *Chiddingford*, *Offa*, *Onslow* and *Oribi* from the 17th Destroyer Flotilla, and the cruiser *Kenya*. The task force's destination was the tiny port of South Vaagsö on Vaagsö Island off the Norwegian coast. The secondary objective was enemy shipping; the primary, to destroy cod and herring oil factories, which were supplying the Germans with valuable sources of vitamins A and D, and glycerine for explosives.

They had trained hard for the operation, code named Archery, studying models of houses and factories and other buildings, and carrying out rehearsals at Scapa Flow in the Orkneys. In theory each man knew the terrain and his job as well as he knew his own name and service number, but few of them had participated in what was certain to be an opposed action, and this was to be their baptism. To assist the raiding party of almost six hundred officers and men, mostly regular members of 3 Commando but on this occasion reinforced by troops from 2, 4 and 6 Commandos, a diversionary assault against the Lofoten Islands, five hundred miles north, was to be carried out by 12 Commando, the second raid of the year against that target, although the first, in March, had been unopposed. If things were going according to plan,

12 Commando should be ashore by now, Boxing Day. H-hour for 3 Commando was first light, 0850, December 27.

After leaving Achnacarry in April, Sergeant Halloran's course were given two weeks' leave prior to joining their new units. Half went to 12 Commando, half to Lord Lovat's 4 Commando. Sticking to the belief that men who knew each other well were more likely to fight and protect each other's backs better, Combined Ops dispatched the Patricias contingent to 4 Commando. There they stayed and continued to train because there were few opportunities to do otherwise on a large scale.

The first Lofoten raid, Operation Claymore, had taken place while they were at Achnacarry, and the next operation, Chess, did not occur until July. This was against Ambleteuse on the French coast north of Boulogne, but only sixteen men of 12 Commando were involved. Just thirty men, of 5 Commando, participated in Operation Cartoon against Merlimont Plage in late August, and another handful, from 1 Commando, in Operation Chopper against Courselles, in September. True, every member of 4 Commando was refining, during the summer months, the skills learnt at Achnacarry, but that was not the same as being in action. On the only occasion 4 Commando was given the opportunity to mount a small nuisance raid against Normandy, the CO was overwhelmed by volunteers and the assault team had to be chosen by lot. None of the Patricias was amongst it, though in the event it didn't matter either way. The first sortie was called off due to poor weather, and the next attempt ran into a strong force of E-boats and had to flee for their lives. The raiders would have been sunk and machine gunned had not a squadron of low-flying Spitfires suddenly appeared to beat up the E-boats.

And that was the end of it until 4 Commando's CO received word of Operation Archery and was asked to provide personnel to bring 3 Commando up to strength. Thirty men were required and they would be returned when the operation was over.

A commando Troop comprised anything between fifty and sixty men, the Troop commander being a captain. A Troop's sub-units were sections and sub-sections commanded by, respectively, lieutenants, and sergeants or corporals. Thirty men made up a section.

For Archery the CO selected his most experienced officer, B Troop's commander, Bill Windus, but told him he could not go to Norway himself. Windus chose Lieutenant Mike Halliday's 2 Section as his surrogate, and the Patricias whooped with delight when they heard. They were all part of Halliday's 2 Section.

On their way to Scotland they stopped off in London for two days of learning how to roll a kayak in Marshall Street Baths, Soho. In the streets and doorways the whores were two and three deep, and 2 Section promised themselves a night of getting mightily drunk and laid. All they got was wet, and they didn't use kayaks on Archery, anyway. Alphabet Soup reckoned Mike Halliday knew that all along, that he just wanted to keep them occupied.

'And me, I haven't had a woman since Christ knows when. I'm even starting to like the looks of Kovacs.'

On arriving in Scotland they were informed by the adjutant that they were no longer 2 Section, B Troop, 4 Commando. Until the end of Archery they would form part of 2 Troop, 3 Commando.

Their final briefing was given below decks as the task force met the submarine HMS *Tuna*, patrolling as their navigation guide, at 0700 on December 27. The landing, they were reminded once again, would take the form of five assault groups. Group 1 would disembark at Hollevik on Vaagsö Island's south shore. Group 3 would storm and occupy Maaloy, a much smaller island measuring only five hundred yards by two hundred, but housing a barracks, an ammunition store, oil tanks and coastal defence guns. Maaloy was only a stone's throw from Vaagsö Island. Group 4 would act as a floating reserve, going where required when the balloon went up, and the fifth Group would be ferried upchannel by HMS *Oribi* for a landing north of the port to cut off reinforcements. Group 2 would be led by the CO, land just south of South Vaagsö, and capture it. Group 2 would comprise Troops 1, 2, 3 and 4.

Intelligence advised that South Vaagsö was defended by about one hundred and fifty men from 181 Division. It also possessed a solitary tank and some eighty men from a labour battalion. No German warships of any size were thought to be in the vicinity, and the nearest Luftwaffe fighter and bomber squadrons were at Stavanger and Trondheim. 3 Commando's air support would come from Coastal Command Blenheims and Beaufighters, as well as a flight of Hampdens out of Wick.

'Any questions?'

There were none, not even comments from the usual comedians.

The men were confident if tense, but had no time for jokes. Unlike the first Lofoten, it was an absolute certainty that some of them would not be coming back.

'Then let's get on with it. The sooner we get it all over with, the sooner we'll be home. For New Year's Eve, and you all know what a Scottish New Year is like.'

'What d'you think, Chief?' asked Jack.

They were on deck. It was damned cold. There were lights burning on shore because daybreak was still a few minutes off. No one was worried about the blackout up here. On either side of the fjord snow-covered mountains loomed eerily.

The *Kenya* was bombarding Maaloy and the destroyers engaging other targets. The troops were waiting to transfer to the smaller LCAs, their assault landing craft. Overhead the promised Hampdens were drawing flak from anti-aircraft batteries.

'Not a hell of a lot,' answered Greyfoot.

'I'm thinking I'd rather be in the army,' said Kovacs. 'The Swiss army.'

'Me, I'd settle for being in the reserve Group,' grunted Alphabet. 'I just hope the *Kenya* can keep their fucking heads down.'

'Ernie?' said Jack. The former Patricias were not really his responsibility now that 2 Section was part of 2 Troop and he was just another sergeant. Still, old habits died hard.

Kiley grimaced in the half-light. 'I'll think about that tomorrow.'

There was a tremendous racket going on, most of it from the *Kenya*'s 6-inch guns, as the LCAs were lowered from their davits. Apart from small arms fire, however, nothing much, for now, seemed to be coming from the Germans. At least, not at the assault craft. The main retaliation was from flak aimed at the bombers.

Rounding the headland for the run up to the landing zones, those closest to Group 3's LCAs could hear, even above the naval salvos, the Commando's 2 i/c, Major Churchill, playing his wretched bagpipes. To untutored ears 'The March of the Cameron Men' sounded like a couple of mad cats copulating in a steel dustbin, but one or two made mental notes that the pipes were doing wonders for morale.

While the *Kenya* fired starshells to illuminate Maaloy so that the *Onslow* and the *Offa* could join in the bombardment, the men in

Group 2's LCAs kept their heads down. Above them a Hampden dropping smoke canisters was hit by an armed German trawler and inadvertently jettisoned a phosphorus bomb short, pulverizing an LCA occupied by 4 Troop. Ammunition and grenades detonated. The landing craft split asunder, tossing burning and dying men into the icy fjord. A follow-up LCA with an RAMC commando captain aboard calmly picked up the injured, treated them, and ferried them back to the LSIs. For those who were unhurt, it was comforting to know that the medics were with them.

The *Kenya*'s bombardment lifted when Group 3 were only fifty yards from the shore. Maaloy's coastal batteries were either out of action or their crews dead, because they didn't fire back.

Leading Group 2, brushing burning phosphorus from his battledress, the CO fired red Very lights, the prearranged signal that his assault party was about to land and that the ships should find other targets. Blenheims and Beaufighters dropped more smoke to cover the landing zones.

More than the thought of sudden death lurking in the snow-covered hills, the noise was terrifying. Had the commandos not rehearsed time and time again at Scapa Flow and practised assaults with live ammunition at Achnacarry, the decibels alone would have rendered them immobile through fear. As it was, it was just another noisy exercise. That was how the majority thought of it, at any rate. There was nothing to be gained by worrying that the opposing machine guns were not firing on a fixed trajectory.

1, 2 and 3 Troops plus those of 4 Troop who had survived the Hampden's jettison headed for the sheer rocks between the lighthouse and the wireless station, scaling them with ladders. Intelligence had assessed correctly that the Germans would not cover such an unlikely beach-head with machine guns. They were then on the road running parallel to the shoreline and some three-quarters of a mile from the port.

Jack found himself next to the Chief and Ernie Kiley and right behind Lieutenant Halliday. It was becoming quite light now, although smoke drifting across from Maaloy hindered vision to a large extent. There was a house up ahead and it seemed possible it contained snipers or a machine gun nest. If it didn't, the next one surely must, or the garage or the Ulvesund Hotel.

Lieutenant Halliday was conferring with 2 Troop's commander.

Close by a wirelessman was trying frantically to raise control, without success. They had all been warned at Scapa Flow that radios would not work too brilliantly with the mountains around, and that meant it was unlikely they could call down an air strike or a naval bombardment on any building that looked suspicious. Each and every one of them would have to be taken out by the men on the ground.

In military theory the most difficult operations are amphibious landings in the dark or, worst of all, amphibious withdrawals without light. Sandwiched somewhere in between was street fighting, for at any given moment there was no telling where the bullets were coming from. All the rehearsals in the world couldn't second guess where the defender was going to be. 3 Troop's commander was already dead, killed while house clearing. The runner who reported that fact to the CO wasn't sure whether a German had shot him from within the house or whether he'd been hit from across the street. In any case, 3 Troop was now pinned down and pressure had to be taken off them so they could move.

'They've given it to us, Jack,' said Halliday, formerly an officer with the East Anglian Regiment. Like most junior commissioned ranks in the commandos, on active service or in the field he called his NCOs by their given names. He was a head shorter than Jack and, unusual for a British officer in Jack's view, had streetwise eyes. Nothing escaped him on the parade square and little elsewhere. He was also as hard as a Naafi sausage, frightened of nothing. Back at 4 Commando, on the firing ranges, his party trick was holding two live grenades at arm's length, releasing them, and burying his face in his arms while lying prone. As a demonstration it looked spectacular, and was. And bloody dangerous. All grenade explosions went upwards and outwards, but it only took one malfunction, one rogue grenade, to send the shrapnel into Halliday and not harmlessly into the air. It impressed the hell out of newcomers, though there were not many who took up his challenge of trying it for themselves.

'We'll use the whole section. Straight in and at the buggers.'

One hundred yards give or take a yard separated the wall behind which the section had taken temporary cover from the house. On Halliday's whistle thirty men charged forward, some firing Thompsons, some rifles. Before they had covered more than a few strides they came under defensive fire from the house's upper storey. Heavy stuff, automatic. Someone fell, but in the smoke and confusion it was impossible to see who. In any case, they were all well versed in the golden rule, that no one stopped to attend the fallen. That was someone else's job. The objective was everything, casualties nothing.

Running zigzags, fifty yards from the house Jack and Halliday were out in front of the main group. Greyfoot was ten yards behind it and way over to the right. Jack saw that the Chief wasn't shooting, that he was carrying what appeared to be two buckets full of liquid, some of which was sloshing over the rims. Buckets, he thought? *Buckets*, for Christ's sake.

The bulk of the defensive fire was coming from the right-hand upper window, that nearest the road. As if tied together by wire, Jack and Halliday veered left. Most of the section followed them. Only Greyfoot ploughed on, slower than everyone else, weighed down by his buckets.

Jesus, Chief, thought Jack.

Then a hosepipe of fire from the supporting section zoned in on the right-hand window, the 1-in-5 tracer making a pretty fairy bridge between the guns and the house. Abruptly the heavy machine gun fell silent. The Chief kept going.

Halliday reached the nearest groundfloor window, ducked and lobbed a grenade through the shattered glass. When the grenade detonated he put his Thompson through the empty frame and squeezed off a long burst.

Jack and three others – he couldn't see who – were already at the back door. Jack kicked it open and ran inside, finding himself in the kitchen. From the cover of an overturned table someone shot at him with a low-calibre automatic weapon. Crouching, he sprayed the room with his own Thompson, the .45 calibre rounds hacking chunks out of the table and the masonry. A scream of anguish told him he'd hit something, but he couldn't see what. Was there just one, he wondered?

There were two. The second German rose from behind the table. An ordinary infantryman might have accepted a surrender, for no one but a fool would leave cover to do anything other than hold up his hands and quit. But Achnacarry had taught the commandos not to accept anything at face value. For all Jack knew there might be a third defender waiting to take advantage of any lapse in concentration. Besides, Jack couldn't see whether or not the German's hands were empty. There was smoke and dust everywhere. So he shot him without a second's thought before heading for the door that led to the rest of the house.

He thought he heard someone call his name, but, glancing over his shoulder, he could see no one. The three who'd been with him outside were no longer in evidence. They were taking out another room, maybe, but it was suddenly getting bloody lonely.

Beyond the door was a narrow passage leading to a short flight of stairs. He knelt at the foot of them. There was a hell of a din coming from the upper storey, but whether that was from the attackers firing in or the defenders firing out was impossible to tell. It also occurred to him that he might be overdoing the aggression. If he were inside the house while the support section was still strafing it, he was in as much danger as the German occupants.

Then Ernie Kiley appeared behind him.

'Let's get the hell out, Jack!' bawled the little Canadian. 'The Chief's got a firecracker going.'

Jack didn't question Ernie's judgement. If Kiley said go he meant go.

Outside the mystery of the Chief's buckets became clear. Jack was just in time to see Greyfoot toss the contents over the woodwork and race away.

Petrol.

Thirty yards behind the Chief, Alphabet unpinned a grenade and let fly. The detonation ignited the petrol and the whole house went up in flames. Germans came out burning, and were shot. One bailed out of an upper storey window, turned a spectacular somersault, and was hit while falling by machine gun fire. The bullets seemed to keep him aloft for a fraction of a second, like a pingpong ball on a water spout at a funfair's rifle range.

'You're not supposed to burn me too, you mad bastard,' said Jack to the Chief, severely, a little later.

'You're not supposed to be trying to break the record for the hundred yards dash, either. Hell, I waited as long as I could before Halliday sent Ernie in after you. I carried that stuff all the way across no-man's-land. I wasn't about to hang on to what was left of it longer than necessary.'

'Where did you get it from, anyway?'

'It was sitting in a pump back there and it seemed like a good idea.' The Chief hadn't retreated far enough when the petrol ignited. His face was blacker than it had been when he landed from the LCA, and he'd lost his eyebrows. 'It's an old Cree trick we learned from John D Rockefeller and Standard Oil.'

'Oh, yes? Was that before or after you started putting air-conditioning in the tepees?'

'About the same time.'

'God spare me from old Crees and bullshitters. I liked you guys better when all you had were flaming arrows and feathered hats.'

'Yeah, but then we got wiped out in the last reel.'

The Ulvesund Hotel proved a tougher nut to crack than any of the houses, and by this time the commandos were taking casualities in worrying numbers. Here 4 Troop lost its Troop commander, plus a lieutenant and a Norwegian liaison officer while trying to storm the main door. The hotel was defended by seasoned troops who had seen action in the 1940 Norwegian campaign and who were well organized. There was no way in without suffering heavy losses, and the CO continued to be concerned about the tank known to be somewhere nearby. Two sergeants from 1 Troop were dispatched to locate it, which they did. One disabled it with a large satchel charge, but was killed in the premature explosion.

2 Troop were brought into the hotel battle, as well as reinforcements from 6 Troop, freed from the Maaloy Group now that the small island was occupied. But the hotel defenders resisted fiercely until Kovacs appeared lugging a 3-inch mortar and a case of bombs. Since the Commando did not possess any heavy weapons of this variety, Halliday asked him where it came from. Kovacs pointed to the markings. They were in German. And it wasn't exactly a 3-inch but 76mm. Converted, however, that was more or less the same thing. It was big enough, anyway, to make a mess of the hotel.

The mortar teams were trained to fire nothing bigger than a 2-inch but this didn't prevent an NCO from 1 Troop lining up the weapon and putting a bomb straight down the hotel chimney. He claimed it as accurate shooting, but everyone knew it was pure luck. Whichever, it became the turning point in the battle for the Ulvesund.

Since 4 Troop had lost officers and men in the original assault, they were given the privilege of finishing off the defenders with tommy-guns and grenades. Few prisoners were taken.

Two hours had passed since the first landings, and the CO was anxious to keep forward movement going for fear of the Germans breaking through from the north or the present defenders becoming more organized. As the radios, for the most part, were still useless, he left his command post and, with a small HQ group and ignoring the threat from snipers, walked up the road to see for himself how matters stood.

So far, so good, in spite of casualties.

Demolition teams were beginning to set their charges in a fish-oil factory and a very unhappy quisling, the owner, was under arrest, about to be taken to the rear for transportation to England. Those guarding him were warned to take extra care with the prisoner. He might try to bolt. In England he would be facing interrogation and probable execution. He had little to lose by making a run for it. Or the Norwegians might attempt to snatch him, to make an example of him as a warning to other would-be collaborators. No one much cared how he died, but he could have valuable information to pass on before doing so.

Away from the road a second demolition squad had blown up four 75mm field guns previously being used against the ships. Down the fjord the *Kenya* was exchanging salvos with a coastal battery not yet silenced, while anti-aircraft fire from the cruiser and the destroyers was being directed at newly-arrived Messerschmitts, which, logically, continued to attack the ships and leave the ground troops alone. If the Luftwaffe could knock out the escorts, the LSIs would have no protection when it came time to withdraw, and would be easy meat.

A minor lull in the battle took place towards midday. 2 Troop had just cleared a warehouse and were ordered, by CO's runner, to stay put while Blenheims bombed the steamship wharf up ahead. Apparently at least one channel of ship-to-shore communication was operational and messages from the aircraft were being relayed to the ground forces by the *Kenya*.

Now that they had time to draw breath, many of the troops, crouched behind walls or in shell or bomb craters, found that they had difficulty in stopping their legs from quivering, though few admitted the phenomenon to even their closest buddy. The shakes were part fatigue, part fear, part excitement. This was their first offensive action, and nothing in training had prepared them for the sight of so many dead and wounded. Quite a number lit their cigarettes with trembling fingers, holding the hand that held the match with the opposite hand and guiding the flame towards the tobacco gingerly. In training you had to be a damned fool or unlucky to get your head shot off by the fixed-trajectory Brens, but here it was all in the lap of the gods. The gaping masonry of burning or bombed houses could not be rebuilt tomorrow, either, for the next exercise. This was the real thing.

Ernie Kiley didn't smoke. He was beginning to wish he did, or should start. Fifty feet away a body in field-grey was sprawled supine over a wall, head and torso on one side, legs the other. The corpse was smouldering, and the smell of burning flesh, a sweet smell like pork and apple, assailed his nostrils and made him want to vomit. Macabrely, the limbs twitched every now and then.

To be able to do a speed march in less than the allotted time, or score a three-inch group at three hundred yards with a rifle against a cardboard target, was just playing games. Cardboard targets didn't bleed, and didn't stink. He'd get used to it, he thought, and maybe that was half the trouble. Who the hell wanted to get used to it?

Close to Kiley Alphabet Soup was drinking water from his canteen and wishing it was rum. Or whisky. He wondered where the hell the water went to. He'd been awake since the small hours, eaten breakfast, and, since landing, had emptied one water canteen and was three-quarters of the way through his second. But he hadn't relieved himself once, not even involuntarily when they were about to attack the last warehouse. Where the fuck did all the liquid go? It wasn't natural. He guessed he'd piss like a horse once they were back aboard the LSIs. Assuming they got back aboard. Some wouldn't. He'd heard scuttle earlier, before it was sharply jumped on by Halliday, that the Commando had lost a dozen dead and twice that number wounded up to now; and it wasn't over yet, not by a streak. Only one good thing, the medics weren't leaving anyone behind. That was somehow important. If he was killed, he wouldn't be buried in Canada, sure, but they wouldn't leave him in Norway, maybe just to be shoved in a hole without ceremony, a burial service. Although he'd been born and brought up a Catholic, he hadn't thought much about God until a few hours ago, though he suspected he wasn't alone in that. Bloody funny, really, all these big deal commandos. He'd seen more than one with a Bible in his kit.

Kovacs had come back from wherever with a dozen cans of peaches and a similar number full of sardines. Christ knows how, because there were no peaches in Norway and no sardines, either. The cans were unlabelled so there was no way of telling if they were German stock.

He wouldn't reveal to Halliday where he'd found them, saying no more than, 'Same place I got the 76 mortar.'

He kept a tin of each for himself and passed the rest around.

'These are going to cost you a pint apiece when we get back to the UK,' he warned. 'Let's see, that's twenty-two cans at eightpence a can. What the hell does that add up to, Chief?'

'Who the hell knows? What am I, your accountant?'

'Do you know how much a .45 calibre Thompson round costs?' asked Lieutenant Halliday, butting in. 'About sixpence, last I heard. And a grenade's ten bob.' He tossed Kovacs one full Thompson magazine and a 36 grenade. 'At the current rate of exchange, I reckon that means we're not only quits but you owe me one 76mm mortar bomb.'

'You're all heart, Lieutenant.'

'It comes with the rank.'

'You okay, Chief?' asked Jack.

'Sure. But it's a bit fucking grim, isn't it? I mean, have you counted the number of officers who've bought it?'

'Think yourself lucky. In an infantry regiment they'd be leaving most of the dirty work to us NCOs.'

'Not in the Patricias.'

'I didn't say the Patricias.'

Greyfoot rubbed his burnt eyebrows. He wondered if they'd grow back. He hadn't been afraid when he'd carried the petrol against the house, though he recognized now the cunning of the men who'd trained him. He'd simply seen the supply, understood it could be used, and let the rest happen. He could easily have been killed. Sure, Jack had pulled his leg, and he'd responded, but all that was just nerves. The thing was, no one in this outfit ever admitted to nerves. Training again, he supposed.

Carrying one of Kovacs's cans of peaches, Halliday haunched down beside Jack. Overhead a finger-four of ME 109s shot past at a thousand feet, heading out to sea. Halliday wondered how many more the Luftwaffe could produce from Trondheim and Stavanger. The Blenheims and Hamdens were only covered by Beaufighters, which were no match for 109s.

'Five minutes,' said Halliday. 'Damn, these peaches are good. Guys like Kovacs are going to rule the world when the war's over.'

'Do you want me to get them on their feet?' asked Jack.

'No, let them finish up. Then we'll have an O-group. There's some shit up front they're not going to like.'

'And just when they were starting to enjoy themselves.'

Halliday smiled. 'Sorry you volunteered?'

'Not me. I was a peacetime soldier.'

'Yes, I forgot. And you'll stay in when it's finished?'

'I reckon I might. My parents own a hotel in Calgary. After this, what the hell will I talk to the guests about? Apologize because their bath water's cold? That the soup's off, the central heating on the fritz?'

'You can tell them what it was like on Vaagsö.'

'Those who weren't here won't care, and those who were won't want to listen. Some choice, eh? The frying pan or the frying pan.'

'You'll think differently when we get home.'

'I know. First I'll take off my boots, then I'll screw my girlfriend, then I'll take off my pack.'

'Another girl? Well, it's about time.'

'Another? I'm not with you.'

'It's part of my job to read backgrounds on NCOs, Jack. I can't recall the details offhand, but I know why you volunteered for Achna-carry.'

A lifetime ago, thought Jack. A different world and, maybe, a different person. Shit, that was in 1940 and this was almost 1942.

He could hardly recall what Caroline Manners had looked like, not always, anyway. Sometimes the image was clear, sometimes less so, like an out-of-focus photograph. Had her death in the Blitz really brought him to this grim killing ground? If it had, how many others, German and British, were here because they had lost a girl or a wife or a parent?

Deep thoughts, Lambert, and out of place here.

In any case, Halliday had misunderstood the joke. There wasn't another girl, not on a regular basis, a correspondent whose letters and picture he carried. There were just one-night stands when he got leave.

'Get 'em up Jack,' said Halliday, finishing the last of the peaches and hurling away the empty tin like a grenade.

The southernmost buildings of South Vaagsö had been cleared or largely destroyed, but the Germans were far from finished up coast, where the Blenheims were peeling away from the steamship wharf. No one had been counting RAF losses, but at least one Blenheim had crashed after a set-to with ME 110s, and someone had seen two Beaufighters go down.

They'd studied the wharf area in detail from aerial reconnaissance photos and Norwegian Resistance reports back at Scapa Flow, recognizing that it would be heavily defended. If not to begin with, because of surprise, then surely as the Germans were driven back. It contained a factory or two, several warehouses, one bright red, stables, a shop, other buildings. These could be outflanked to reach the power station half a mile further north, but that would still leave armed defenders at the commandos' rear, and they had to get out again, down the fjord to the LSIs. One way or another, the wharf had to be neutralized, which meant factory- and warehouse-hopping. The bombers had done what they could, as had the ships, but all land battles involved occupying territory. Bombs and naval shells alone didn't win fights.

It was a bloody business, with no quarter given. It was also against the clock, because the Germans would certainly know by now that the Lofoten raid was a diversion and be looking for a means to wipe out the Vaagsö invaders, not least for the propaganda value; every room in every building had to be cleared before it became safe to move on. Leave a single German alive or uncaptured, and he could be the man who put a bullet between your shoulder blades.

Men of 6 Troop led the assault, and cleared a factory and store before being pinned down by snipers between a small shed and a wood pile. Every time the commandos tried to move, the snipers let loose, more often than not finding a target. Hitler's *Kommandobefehl*, the order that all commandos, whether in uniform or not, were to be subjected to *Sonderbehandlung* – special treatment, a Nazi euphemism for execution after torture – would not come into general usage for almost another year, but already the Vaagsö garrison had recognized that their attackers were not run-of-the-mill soldiers; that they were specialists who would more than likely kill them rather than take them prisoner. There was little point, therefore, in flying the white flag, surrendering to sit out the rest of the war in a British POW camp. It was better to fight, and fight hard, and hope for the best.

'Snipers are weird buggers, anyway,' grunted Halliday to no one in particular, while waiting his opportunity to attack some stables to the left of the red warehouse and distract the snipers, or offer them other targets, for long enough to allow 6 Troop a safe egress. He was a horse lover and hoped the stables were empty of animals of the equine variety. 'They live by themselves, train by themselves, eat by themselves. You've got to be a little crazy to be a sniper.'

'And we're totally fucking sane, of course,' said Kovacs, wondering why he'd allowed that 1 Troop sergeant to take his 76mm mortar, and where the bugger was now. Two bombs from that and the red warehouse would be history. 'Next time anyone asks for volunteers, they can go fuck themselves. After this lot, I'm not even joining a Christmas club.'

'I'm not even joining a queue,' agreed Alphabet.

Halliday knew neither of them meant it. All they were doing was exercising a soldier's right to complain. They'd be looking for more action, champing at the bit, three days after the Vaagsö raid was over.

'Hey, Chief,' he called, 'don't you have a copyright on that idea?'

Across the way someone had evidently considered that Greyfoot's trick with the petrol was a sound one. While 6 Troop, the CO among the people behind the wood pile, pumped in round after round at the snipers' windows, the Troop Sergeant Major ran forward and splashed liquid over the wooden walls. It had to be petrol. The TSM sure as hell wasn't trying to put a fire out.

'We'll go when it blows, Jack,' shouted Halliday, and waited until the follow-up grenade ignited the petrol.

'Fried sniper,' muttered Kovacs. 'Lovely.'

'Needs cabbage,' said Alphabet.

Halliday's section, screaming fit to wake the dead, hit the stable block like a fist in the face. Thirty men, maybe a few less now, against four or perhaps five. Except the four or five had wood and metal between themselves and instant death. There were no sounds of panicking horses, Halliday noted absently.

Grenades went first, smoke and fragmentation. Grenades would have been in short supply by now had not civilian volunteers from the town carried sacks forward from the LCAs to the men in combat. There wasn't one, among those who returned, who didn't come back filled with admiration for the Norwegians. How totally different they were from the spineless Swedes next door.

Crossing the open space between cover and the stables, Jack felt something bounce off his steel helmet. He looked down to see a stick grenade fall at his feet. Several thoughts crossed his mind in a microsecond. He could pick it up and throw it back. He could sprint away from it. He could hope that someone behind him would be courageous enough to throw himself on top of it, because he certainly wasn't about to. He could die where he was.

None of these things happened. The grenade failed to explode.

He wasn't alone in thinking that today was his lucky day. 6 Troop's commander, Captain Peter Young, found three stick grenades being hurled at him as the Troop attacked the red warehouse. Two exploded harmlessly, injuring no one, and the third's fuse fizzled out without detonating the charge.

Halliday was first into the nearer end of the stable block, blasting open the full-length door with his Thompson and diving headlong inside, to avoid giving a defender a perfect silhouette to aim at. Jack, Kovacs, Ernie Kiley and several others were right behind, while Greyfoot led the group racing for the next door, the one halfway up the block. From now on everyone was under orders not to use grenades. Stables weren't houses, with enclosed rooms. A grenade would just as likely wipe out an attacker as a defender. Submachine guns only, backed up by, for those equipped with rifles, bayonets. And fighting knives if it came to hand-to-hand combat.

It was almost pitch-black inside the stable. Jack cannoned into Halliday. From behind a bale of straw an MP 38 blasted the intruders. Momentum was everything, though, and while Halliday and Jack disentangled themselves, Ernie Kiley hurdled them both and went at the straw bale like a leopard at a tethered pig, screaming at the top of his lungs. Foolishly or terrified, the German with the machine pistol stood up, revealed himself to get a better angle and frame the attackers against the open door. Kiley shot the man's face to splinters at the same moment as the Chief and his back-up unit thundered in through the middle door.

'Torch the straw, Ernie,' bellowed Jack, but Kiley had already gone, running towards the Chief's sub-section, kicking open each stall as he passed it and raking the interiors, just to be on the safe side.

'I'll do it,' said Kovacs. 'He thinks carrying a light will encourage him to smoke and endanger his health.'

He loped forward and put a match to the bale. Smoke billowed. Anyone upstairs, on the platforms above each stall designed to hold winter feed, would have to suffocate, burn, or come out and be shot.

There didn't seem to be anybody on top, not at this end of the building. Not that that meant anything; the platforms ran from one end to the other, something Greyfoot had already deduced. He and his sub-section were shooting overhead, peppering the rafters.

The stable assault lasted five minutes, fifteen less than Halliday had anticipated. Four Germans were killed and one taken prisoner for the loss of two commandos, both fatalities, whom Halliday made certain were picked up by the medics. Two Germans got away, were seen running off through the smoke. They led charmed lives. Even Ernie Kiley couldn't hit them. Okay, thought Halliday, recalling the stick grenade that had bounced off Jack Lambert's steel helmet, maybe they deserved a slice of luck.

He gave orders to check the pockets of the dead Germans, before the stables became a ruin, for maps, papers, orders of battle. Jack led a team of three, who were all familiar with German rank insignia. None of the dead was higher than an *Unteroffizier* – corporal – and none had anything more in his pockets than personal papers, photographs, letters. Nevertheless, as none of them spoke more than a few words of German, they collected everything. The Intelligence people could sort it all out later.

One dead German lying among the rubble at the far end of the stable block, half-in, half-out of a stall, was wearing what appeared to be an expensive wristwatch. Which didn't seem consonant with his lowly rank. Even if he'd looted it, highly likely, someone higher up the pecking order should have taken it from him. He didn't appear marked, either. There was no obvious indication of how he'd died.

Jack knelt to search his pockets. Ernie Kiley shouted at him to freeze, not so much as blink.

'Booby-trap, Jack. Touch him and we all go up. You don't know he's not a Norwegian they killed and put in a Wehrmacht uniform. The wristwatch is bait. Now, if you were a greedy bastard . . .'

Carefully, Kiley tied a length of rope around the German's feet and, with Jack, left the blazing stables. From the cover of some oil drums, Kiley yanked at the rope. There was a massive explosion and the end of the stables caved in, feeding the flames. It didn't take a genius to figure out that the corpse had been lying on a grenade, probably more than one, from which the pins had been pulled. Shift the body and the fuses ignited. Several seconds later, the corpse and whoever moved it were in the same happy hunting ground.

'Jesus,' said Jack, 'I'm not thinking straight. Remind me to recommend you for a medal when we get back.'

'They don't give medals for saving the lives of sergeants,' said Kiley. 'Officers, maybe. Now if you can get Halliday to do it next time . . .'

Then came a house. *The* house, as they all thought about it later. Way over to the left of the red warehouse, which was still under siege though burning merrily, this house was bigger than any of the others they had come up against. And, being bigger, it would be defended by more troops.

Halliday called for a casrep while he sent a runner across to find the CO. Some of 6 Troop and the supporting Troops were already beyond the red warehouse, heading for the power station. Overhead, Luftwaffe fighters were trying to pick out ground targets, doubtless being called down on German-deserted buildings by wireless. The house wasn't being attacked, which seemed ominous, and Halliday wanted to know if he could expect any flanking help in taking it out. The answer came back: No – do what you can. The runner also reported that the CO had been wounded by a grenade that had fallen between his feet. His injuries were only superficial splinters in his hands, as he'd managed to dive out of the way before the grenade exploded. His personal runner hadn't been so fortunate, and was seriously wounded. The grenade thrower, who had attempted to surrender immediately afterwards, was dead, shot by an incensed friend of the injured runner. 'Sorry, sir,' he told the CO. 'I didn't realize his hands were up.'

Halliday totted up the casrep figures on a message pad, not trusting mental arithmetic, even though the sums were simple, with all the activity going on around him. He was six men down on his original strength. A few stragglers had joined the section, however, stray lambs who'd been left behind by other Troops, so that brought him up to establishment, more or less. Thirty blokes against what could be ten or a dozen. Not the kind of odds he liked, or had been trained for, but at least the Luftwaffe was chasing 6 Troop up the road towards the power station.

'Here comes our scavenger-in-chief,' said Jack, while Halliday was pondering the best way to assault the house.

'Come again?'

Jack pointed. Through the smoke came Kovacs and Alphabet, the former carrying the 76mm mortar across his shoulders, the latter pushing a caseful of bombs in a wheelbarrow.

'Don't those buggers ever tell you when they're about to disappear?'

demanded Halliday. 'Christ, they're like a couple of juveniles on a beach. Turn your back and they're gone.'

'Are you complaining?' asked Jack.

'Yes and no. Kovacs gets a Mention the second we get back, and right after that he goes to Colchester.'

'I'd forget both, if I were you. He's just as likely to take offence and sell the whole kit and caboodle to the Wehrmacht.'

'Maybe you're right. Where the hell did you get that lot from, Kovacs?' asked Halliday.

'Stole it from 1 Troop,' said Kovacs. 'Borrowed it, that is.'

'Borrowed it right after he'd given the sergeant who had it two cartons of German cigarettes and a few tins of fruit,' added Alphabet. 'And after he'd pointed out that all the bombs were faulty.'

'Mind you,' said Kovacs, 'the bombs I gave him a demonstration with only became faulty after I'd tampered with them.'

'Point the fucker,' said Halliday in disgust. 'Let's see if your aim's as good as your mouth.'

'I've always wanted to do this,' said Kovacs, grinning like a kid at Christmas. 'You load, Alphabet.'

It took Kovacs and Alphabet three bombs to understand how the weapon operated, and two of those landed too close for comfort. Straight up and down jobs that scared the hell out of everyone, what the 2-inch mortarmen called widow makers. But the fourth went right through the roof, and the fifth and sixth came close to making an acceptable group. There was suddenly enough shit coming from the other direction, in any case, to let Halliday know that the house was heavily defended.

The Chief crouched beside Jack and Halliday.

'I don't think that petrol gag is going to work again. Not with me doing Jack and Jill with the buckets, anyway. Someone else wants a try, they're welcome.'

'No, balls,' said Halliday. 'Let's try and do this properly, copybook, and get out without too many more casualties. Jack, organize the Bren teams . . .'

'I hope that doesn't mean I've got to stay with them. That's not my job, and I've done bugger all, already . . .'

'For Chrissake, I didn't say you were staying,' Halliday flashed back irritably. He was tired and it was showing. 'On my whistle, get them to pour everything they've got into the downstairs windows. Sixty

106

seconds of sustained fire. Forget upstairs. With any luck, Kovacs's mortar will soon have them evacuating the upper floors. What's the distance between us and them – a hundred yards?'

'Maybe a bit less. Eighty, say.'

'Right.' Halliday converted that to time in a swerving run. Between fifteen and twenty seconds. 'Tell Kovacs . . . No, scrub that, I'll tell him myself. I don't want the sod wandering off looking for a tank or maybe a spare Beaufighter the moment he gets fed up.'

Before going off to position the Brens, and check that the rest of the section knew what was expected of them, Jack nudged the Chief and inclined his head in Ernie Kiley's direction. Kiley was taping his fighting knife to his tommy-gun's stock, loosely but not that loose, where it would be handy if he suddenly ran out of ammo with no time to change magazines.

Greyfoot nodded to indicate he'd seen. Nothing ever seemed to faze the little guy from Maple Creek. Whatever made a commando, Kiley had it in abundance.

Forty-five seconds before Halliday was due to blow his whistle and launch the attack, a pair of Messerschmitts roared over at almost rooftop height. They banked to starboard before coming back for another look. Even with all the smoke around and at the speed they were travelling, they could hardly fail to see the assault group poised to strike, but they went away without firing a shot, recognizing that the attackers and the defenders in the house were too close to one another to add aerial warfare to the equation. No doubt, however, they had warned the house via their wireless that a sortie was imminent. Not that the defenders were likely to have missed the point. On Halliday's whistle the Bren teams let rip. Kovacs's 76mm added to the pandemonium almost immediately.

Sixty seconds, counted Halliday, checking each one off against the sweep-hand of his watch. He hoped everyone was remembering the commando rubric, instilled at Achnacarry and elsewhere. Had their lives not depended upon it, the words would have sounded ridiculously melodramatic. Probably did, anyway. But wars were melodrama as opposed to drama. Listen to Hitler, Goebbels, Mussolini, Lord Haw-Haw. Even Churchill. And to those who had invented the commando rubric.

Go in and batter the bastards until they didn't know Tuesday from Easter. This is what Hitler's panzers have done in Europe and Russia, bewildering opponents with their speed. This is what the Prime Minister is asking of you. Give no quarter and ask for less. Take the fight to the enemy before the enemy knows he's in a fight. Where there is no battle, begin one. Where there is calm, create a storm. When the enemy feels secure, terrorize him. Where he seeks sanctuary, let him find death.

Let him know, from the start, that he will never see his homeland or his loved ones ever again. Put him into a state of total fear. Let him perceive that his days are numbered. If he doesn't die today, he surely will tomorrow.

He cannot win this war, no matter what victories he has achieved up to now. His destiny is the destruction of his cities, the end of his chosen way of life. The best he can expect is ignominious defeat.

When in doubt, go forward. When all seems lost, attack. Wipe him out wherever he is. Annihilate him.

. . . Fifty-eight . . . fifty-nine . . . sixty . . .

Halliday put up a red flare. The Brens and the mortar stopped firing. The Bren teams plus Kovacs and Alphabet would now join in the attack, but would be some way behind the others. Kovacs wasn't sure he liked that, not when he saw guys going down. Still, as Joe Louis said, You can run but you can't hide.

'Let's go, Alphabet.'

Halliday led the charge, and was hit when only halfway across the snow-covered open ground that separated the section's cover from the house. He took several medium machine gun rounds in his legs, but it was a second or two before he realized he had been shot. There was no pain, not immediately, and he was not knocked off his feet the way others he'd seen wounded reacted. In fact, he managed a few more paces before he collapsed. But then he was down and stayed down. He shouted at Jack to take over. At least, he thought he shouted, but what actually emerged from his throat was unintelligible gibberish. Before he began to hurt, he wondered how long it would be before the medics got to him. It might be quite a while, all the shit that was flying.

He tried to drag himself out of harm's way, to the cover of an oil drum, but the effort was too great. In any case, it was probably a wiser tactic to lie doggo. To hell with it, he thought. I'll stay where I am.

Jack witnessed him fall. The man next to him fell also, caught by the same burst, but fell in such a manner that his body was in front of

Halliday's, shielding it, taking rounds meant for the section commander. Fuck, thought Jack, it was all going wrong in the first few seconds. And judging by the firepower coming from the house, there were bloody near as many defenders as attackers.

No one was stopping, though, seeking cover. Not that he was expecting anyone to do so. That was not how they'd been trained.

He was the first to reach the front door, astonished that he was unhurt. Still, that was how it went. Some died, others didn't. It was arbitrary whether you were hit or not.

He placed a satchel charge against the front door and sprinted round the corner of the house until the guncotton had reduced the door to so much matchwood. While waiting for the explosions he shot dead a German who foolishly poked his head through a downstairs window. It made him feel a whole lot better.

When he got back to the front door, Ernie Kiley was standing to one side of the opening, spraying whatever lay behind with his Thompson. Then Kiley tossed in two grenades. After they detonated, he led the way inside. Jack was about to follow when he caught sight of a Wehrmacht-issue steel helmet above sandbags at the head of a flight of stairs. Parts of the upper floor were ablaze thanks to Kovacs's mortars, so either this guy was foolhardily brave and ready to stick it out, or scared witless and unwilling to descend the stairs. Whichever, he was certainly armed, as he proved the moment after Jack flattened himself against the outside wall by firing a long burst. There was no answering fire from Kiley.

Jack peekabooed his Thompson around what remained of the jam and gave the stairs half a magazine. This done, he lobbed a grenade towards the top of the flight. Even in the tumult, he heard it strike the sandbags and come bouncing back down. Then Kiley came out of the door like a whippet, and hit the dirt just before the wayward grenade went off.

'Fuck me, Jack,' complained Kiley, picking himself up and dusting himself down, 'I'm on your fucking side, remember.'

'You didn't fire back. I thought you were a goner.'

'I had a jam. I was going to take him out with my knife.'

'Ernie, the guy's got a machine pistol.'

'Okay, I didn't say it was going to be easy. Cover me, I'll go and douse his lights.'

'No, hold it.'

Jack remembered that he was in command now that Halliday was down. It was a bit different from being a senior NCO. There were decisions to be made, and lives to be lost if he made the wrong ones.

Looking behind him, he could see that most of the section, those who had made it across the open ground, had all reached the house. Some were already heaving grenades through downstairs windows. The battle wasn't over yet, not by a long chalk because the Germans weren't surrendering, but fifty per cent of the danger was at an end. He'd lose a few more men, that was inevitable, but the Wehrmacht were going to lose the fucking lot. There was no reason why Ernie should be among the casualties, however.

He saw Kovacs lolloping towards him. It had to be Kovacs because only that crazy bastard would have a five-foot tube slung across his shoulders. And only Kovacs would have been able to persuade Alphabet to push his wheelbarrow full of mortar bombs across eighty yards of territory being riddled by German bullets. Trying to weave with the barrow, Alphabet looked like some insane gardener in a Keystone Kops movie.

'Kovacs, over here!'

Jack explained what he wanted. Kovacs beamed with pleasure.

'I knew I was right to bring this bugger.'

'He was just worried that that 1 Troop sergeant would try to pinch it back,' grumbled Alphabet, sweat pouring off him.

Jesus, thought Jack, Laurel and frigging Hardy.

There was still a lot of shooting coming from the top of the stairs. Kiley tossed in a grenade while Kovacs set up the mortar, anchoring it with rocks and aiming it like a field gun at the flight of stairs.

The bomb took out the German, the sandbags, the stairs, and most of that section of the house.

'Leave it behind this time,' said Jack to Kovacs. 'You won't be needing it inside.'

Kovacs positioned it carefully against the side of the house. He was coming back for it later. He thought he might like to try for the Heavy Weapons Troop when the commandos got round to including one in every unit.

The Chief loomed up as they were about to enter the house. His battledress was covered with a dark substance that Jack assumed to be oil until he realized it was blood. And not Greyfoot's judging by the state of his fighting knife. He was about to send the Chief packing because it was getting crowded down this end, until he recognized that he had all five former Patricias together. Shit, they'd see it through that way, though he wished he could remember what Halliday's orders had been for withdrawal. That couldn't be long now, if the LSIs and the LCAs were still afloat. Operation Archery was designed as a hit-and-run mission. Okay, they'd hit, and now, almost, it was time to run. He could damn near taste that tot of rum.

They moved from room to room, not always alongside one another, using stairs where they found them intact to explore the upper floors – though not really too worried about storeys other than the ground floor. What the 76mm hadn't destroyed would become hamburger before long.

The pattern rarely varied. This was stuff they'd practised at Achnacarry and Scapa Flow. You found a closed door and removed it with a Thompson or a grenade. Then you threw another grenade through the gap. After that you went in with tommy-guns or, if that was impracticable, with bayonets and knives. Much of the fighting was hand-to-hand, grim personal battles where you could see the eyes and smell the fear of the man you were about to kill, or who would kill you if he got the chance. No one came out of that house a virgin.

For most of the attackers time became meaningless. Later, none would be able to calculate with any accuracy just how long they were inside. Some guessed five minutes, others fifty, but it was actually less than thirty before resistance began to weaken. A few Germans were still in a downstairs back room, in which, someone said, there was a door that led outside. The moment had come to move out, anyway. Amscray. Burning timbers from the upper storeys would make staying any longer hazardous.

Jack passed the word along. Screamed it, rather. Men went by him, a few carrying dead or wounded comrades.

Jack found Halliday's runner and told him to warn the troops still in the open air to be fucking careful what they shot at when the house was finally evacuated.

'We wear khaki, they wear grey.'

He asked the runner how Halliday was.

'You got me, Sarge. Last I saw, the medics had him.'

For those who took part in the battle for the house, it was a major incident. For the CO it was a small engagement among other small engagements.

When they were outside, concealed behind cover to mop up any Germans who were not prepared to call it a day, Jack ordered Greyfoot to make a head count. The house was close to being an inferno. Anyone still inside was in big trouble. Someone shouted that a handful of Germans were legging it through the back door. Jack dispatched half a dozen men to deal with them.

The Chief came back to report that everyone was accounted for except Ernie Kiley. He was neither among the living nor the dead.

'Shit,' said Jack.

To make matters worse, two 109s came thundering in from the west, shooting up the blazing building. Whoever was on the German radio link was doing a good job. A bit late, maybe, but a good job. For everyone, that is, bar Ernie Kiley. If he was still inside. But where else could he be?

The 109s roared away, seeking other targets. Even from the air it must be apparent that the house was a goner.

'I'm going in for him,' said Jack, taking off his steel helmet and grounding his Thompson.

'Everyone's pulled out, Jack.'

Greyfoot pointed up the road. Commandos were streaming down it, some helping their wounded, others herding prisoners. Beaufighters were doing their best to keep the Messerschmitts occupied. It was 1345 hours and the short Arctic day was drawing to a close.

'Save me a place in the LCA.'

'Get someone else. I'll come with you.'

'Shut the fuck up and do as you're told. Organize the section. I won't need covering fire. There's no bugger in there.'

Except, maybe, Ernie. Possibly thinking that the 'tomorrow' he was always talking about had arrived a day early. Possibly dead, possibly trapped, possibly wounded. He mightn't get buried in Maple Creek, but he sure as hell wasn't going to be deep-sixed on Vaagsö.

'Get them down to the LCAs.'

Twenty yards from the house Jack realized he'd set himself an impossible task. This side, he couldn't get anywhere near because of the heat and smoke.

He sprinted round the back. Not so bad there. He bellowed Kiley's name at the top of his lungs.

Nothing.

He had no option but to go inside. He wished he'd brought the

Thompson. There was nothing to shoot at – he hoped – but the butt would have been useful for battering down anything that stood in his way.

He found Kiley in what was once the kitchen. Now it was a mound of rubble, some of it alight. The little guy from Saskatchewan was just recovering consciousness, shaking his head, which was bloody, and rubbing his ankle. Alongside him was the brickwork that had knocked him cold. Also there were two dead Wehrmacht.

'Thought you buggers had pissed off and left me. I was on my way out after getting rid of this pair when that lot fell on my fucking head.'

'Tell me later, Ernie. Can you walk?'

'Tell you what, Jack, I can fucking run.'

Except he couldn't. His ankle wasn't broken, but it was badly swollen.

'Okay, so I can hobble. Just give me a hand.'

'Be a lot easier if I carried you out. Jeez, you don't weigh much more than my sister. When are you going to start putting some meat on? You come across some big Kraut, he'll put your lamps out.'

Jack slung Kiley across his shoulders in a fireman's lift. 'What did your last slave die of?' The Chief was still outside. So too were Kovacs and Alphabet. So too was the Troop's OC, who had come to see what had happened to 2 Section. Lieutenant Halliday, he'd established, would certainly survive, and be back in action in a couple of months.

'I gave you an order,' Jack scowled at Greyfoot.

'He asked my permission, Sergeant Lambert,' the Troop commander said, 'but you can argue it out later. In the meantime, let us get the hell out of here.'

Two days after the Vaagsö raid Churchill addressed the Canadian Parliament. Scorning the French General Weygand's words earlier in the war – 'In three weeks England will have her neck wrung like a chicken' – he retorted, 'Some chicken, some neck.'

Operation Archery was judged by Lord Mountbatten, Chief of Combined Ops, and the War Cabinet to be a complete success. The Wehrmacht had received much more than a bloody nose. German dead were not known for certain but were estimated at one hundred and twenty. Prisoners taken were ninety-eight, and the Royal Navy had disposed of 16,000 tons of shipping. On top of that, 30,000 German troops were withdrawn from the Atlantic Wall and deployed in Norway, which Hitler announced to be a 'zone of destiny', and part of the German Navy's master code was captured aboard the armed trawler *Fohn*. On the minus side, the raiding forces lost twenty killed and fifty-seven wounded, plus several aircraft.

At an investiture in the New Year, 1942, Sergeant Jack Lambert received from the King the DCM – not for rescuing Ernie Kiley but for organizing the section and keeping the attack fluid after Halliday was shot. Kiley got the MM for taking out, as far as it could be judged, more Germans single-handedly than just about anyone else on the operation. Kovacs was pissed off to get nothing at all. It had been his sodding mortar, which some thief swiped and which he never saw again, after all. But there were only so many medals to be shared out without debasing the coinage. In any case, the question of who should have been awarded what was relegated to the back burner when the leave roster was posted.

EIGHT

March 1942

The former Patricias travelled up to London together. At King's Cross Station they stood impatiently in line for half an hour, queuing for a taxi, until Kovacs said, 'To hell with this,' and disappeared. He was back within five minutes in a cab driven by a middle-aged Cockney who seemed of the opinion he'd been hijacked.

Kovacs gave him the location of their billet, a commercial hotel off Russell Square that catered for servicemen from the Dominions, and whose address had been furnished by 3 Commando's billeting officer. They would not be seeing him again, for after their leave they were to report back to 4 Commando.

Now that the United States was in the war, there were many more Americans in evidence on the streets than they remembered seeing before leaving for Scotland. Most were USAAF personnel, but there were army uniforms too, advance parties, no doubt, for the tens of thousands of Yanks who were on their way.

'That means the whores' prices go up right away,' grumbled Alphabet. 'It'll have to be whores because we won't get a look in on regular women once the Yanks start waving their dollar bills.'

That was likely to be the least of their problems. If World War 1 tales were anything to go by, before long the Americans would be saying: 'Here we go again, pulling the Limeys' chestnuts from the fire.' Then blood would flow.

It damn near started before the cab had covered three hundred yards. At a red light, an American air force master sergeant, a good-looking redhead in tow, spotted the taxi and threw open the passenger door. There was a light drizzle and he and his girl were getting wet.

'I don't know where you guys are heading, but I hope you won't mind if we go via this lady's place. Cabs are scarcer than hen's teeth. It's not far and I'll settle the tab.'

'We mind,' said Jack.

'Now, that's not very friendly. If I was in your shoes . . .' Then the American caught sight of the commando shoulder flashes and five pairs of eyes drilling holes in him. 'On the other hand, babe,' he said to the redhead, 'maybe we'd be more comfortable in a cab of our own.'

'Come on, now, Jack,' said Kovacs unexpectedly, 'you're not being very fair to someone from our side of the pond. It's cold and miserable out there and the lady's ruining her hair-do.'

Jack caught Kovacs winking at the Chief and Alphabet, who were sitting opposite one another by the far passenger door, the Chief on the dicky seat alongside Kovacs on the second dicky.

'Have it your way, hero,' said Jack, twigging a scam.

'Look here, guv,' whined the cabby over his shoulder, 'I'm only licensed to carry four. I've already got five up and you want to make it seven.'

'The top kick will make it worth your while, won't you, top?' asked Kovacs, smiling like a cat with the condiments on the table and the canary in the oven. 'What do you say to ten bob?'

The cabby didn't have to think twice. Ten shillings was about four times the fare to Russell Square.

'Suits me, guv. But in advance.'

'Could we please make up our minds,' said the redhead, putting on a phoney middle-class accent. Now that she was close up they could see that her hair came from the same counterfeiter as her voice. She was eminently layable, but that was about all. She wouldn't be going home to meet too many mothers. 'It's freezing out here.'

'You heard the man,' said Kovacs. 'Ten bob, top. Up front.'

The American weighed it up. It was highway robbery, but there wasn't an unoccupied taxi in sight. Same as New York. The rain came down and the friggin' cabs ran for cover.

He handed over a ten shilling note. Kovacs passed it through the opening to the cabby. 'Ladies first,' he said.

There was nowhere for the redhead to sit except on someone's knee. Kovacs made sure that knee belonged to him, copping a free feel – beaming innocently – on the way.

'You next, top,' said Kovacs, nodding to the Chief and Alphabet.

The American climbed aboard as Alphabet opened the passenger door his side. He squeezed past Kovacs, who helped him on his way with a gentle push. Alphabet and Greyfoot finished off the manoeuvre

by assisting him out of the far door. One . . . two . . . three. In . . .
pause . . push . . . out. Piece of cake.

'Let's go, driver,' said Kovacs.

'But what about . . .'

'Forget him. Probably can't take the beer. Hit the gas.'

Through the rear window they saw the American pick himself up,
dust himself down, and dance on his hat with rage. Fare gone, cab
gone, girl gone. Except the girl didn't want to go. Adding it all up, she
reckoned she was better off with her Yank. She'd read about these
commandos.

She started yelling in top-C, all traces of middle-class accent gone.

'You bastards! I'll have you up for rape and abduction! You fucking
cheapskates!'

She couldn't exactly leap up and down in a cab, but she was
squirming plenty. Kovacs seemed to be enjoying it. The girl knew it.

'And you, you bastard,' she cursed, turning on him, 'have you got a
bayonet in your pocket or are you just pleased to see me?'

'Put her down, Kovacs,' said Jack. 'You don't know where she's
been.'

They dropped her at the next red light. 'Scummy commandos!' she
screamed after them. 'Bums!'

'Now that's what I missed up in Scotland,' said Kovacs. 'The
English rose.'

The famous commando green beret was not adopted officially until
the autumn of 1942. Before then, commandos wore regulation headgear and the cap badge of their parent regiment. Shoulder flashes
bearing the legend 'Commando' were also worn but, for security
reasons, the number of the unit to which an individual belonged was
not included, not until 1943. The government was justifiably concerned
that not all German agents and fifth columnists had been rounded up
and accounted for. If fifty or sixty men wearing the insignia of, say, 3
Commando were seen on the streets of London, chances were that 3
Commando wasn't going anywhere that week. It was useful information for the Abwehr to have.

There had been some talk of not allowing any man who was a
commando anything to show he was, though not for security reasons.
Just seeing the designation had a peculiar effect on other outfits, and
other services and nationalities. To some it was like a red rag to a bull.
These were the top guns, the so-called hard men of Lofoten and

Vaagsö and, more recently, Bruneval, and there were many who wanted to assay just how accurate the myth was. Others accepted the legend on hearsay and steered a course in sheltered waters.

'Frigging Yanks,' said Kovacs conversationally, without any malice.

'We're going to need them before it's all over,' said Jack. 'You'd better get used to it or be prepared to wear an arrowed suit.'

He'd wondered, on the train down, whether he should take time off to see Colonel Manners in Chipping Saxonby. He'd decided against. All that was over now, in the past. He didn't want Chipping Saxonby awakening painful memories. There'd be another day if he survived the war.

'Jesus, grab that,' said Ernie Kiley.

The taxi was moving slowly, to conserve precious fuel. In the doorway of a derelict shop, although it was still daylight, raining and cold, a soldier and a whore were humping away, standing up. If they weren't humping, he was indulging in a strange form of callisthenics and she, because her skirt was up around her hips, was getting some fresh air in the engine room. She was also smoking a cigarette with one hand while clinging to the guy's neck with the other. All in all, the scene was about as erotic as a week-old trawler catch.

'We don't get anything like that in Maple Creek.'

'They don't have doorways in Maple Creek,' cracked Alphabet.

'They're not allowed to smoke, either,' said Jack, joining in.

'I'd be amazed to learn they've got running water in Maple Creek,' said Kovacs. 'Sorry, Chief,' he apologized, deadpan. 'I know Running Water's your wife.'

'Up yours,' grinned Kiley, taking no offence.

'After you with Kovacs's,' said Alphabet.

At their billet the cabby put the flag up on his meter and held out his hand for the fare, more in hope than expectation. But you never knew. Some of these blokes from overseas hadn't got the hang of the currency yet. He'd managed to convince an American earlier in the week that the one-and-six registered on the meter meant seven – 'That's how we do it over here, guv. One and six added together, see' – and extract seven shillings from him. If he could pull something like that with these Canadians, he might be able to wrap it in for the day.

'You've had ten bob,' said Jack.

'But that was the Yank's ten bob. You haven't paid.'

'Tell you what I'll do,' said Greyfoot, drawing himself up to his full height, 'I'll spin you for it. Heads we pay you the meter, tails we tip the cab over with you in it.'

'I'll settle for what I've got.'

The woman behind the desk was forty and blowzy. In ten years, maybe less if the gin held out, she'd look like something from the first scene of Macbeth. She was also pissed off that her hotel – that is, the hotel she ran with her husband when the drunken bum could be sobered up – had been designated for British and Empire troops by the powers that be. She would have preferred Americans.

However, she took an instant shine to Kiley, probably because, according to Kovacs, he was the only one she thought she could outfight. She could give him thirty pounds, and then some. In any event, there were only three rooms available and he got the single. Jack and the Chief teamed up, as did Kovacs and Alphabet.

'She's got her eye on you, Ernie,' said Jack, as they went upstairs.

'Her eye and the rest of her,' said Kovacs. 'Jeez, we've only been in an hour and you've scored already.'

'Own goal,' grunted Alphabet. 'She'll lie on top of him and smother him.'

'I'll settle for that,' said Kiley. 'If it happens, means I don't have to go out and tangle with them hoors.'

It didn't work out that way, however. For the first three days they did little else but go out, have a few drinks, the odd scuffle when someone spotted the commando flashes, and 'tangle with them hoors'. Then they dropped down a gear and started taking in the sights and sounds: a piano recital at the National Gallery, an ENSA concert if they could get tickets, drinks or meals at one of the clubs that catered for overseas servicemen. The Luftwaffe came over at regular intervals, and then it was time to hit the shelters and listen to the ack-ack batteries in Hyde Park and Green Park trying to even up the score.

In the beginning they sortied as a quintet, but after a while they took to going out individually. Other occasions they'd sit in the hotel's tiny lounge, chew the fat with Canadians from other regiments, and Australians and New Zealanders, and write letters home. The Patricias, by all accounts, were still down in Sussex, and Kiley, for one, thought it would be a good idea to visit their old regiment. But non-priority travel was frowned upon, and they couldn't get clearance.

In Scotland, on first learning their lowly place in the pecking order for leave, they wouldn't have believed it possible that less than halfway through a fourteen-day pass they would be bored stiff. But they were.

Jack talked it over with the Chief.

'I'm missing the action.'

It was a couple of days before the end of March and news was filtering through about the successful raid on St Nazaire, where HMS *Campbeltown* with four and a half tons of explosives aboard had rammed the battleship dock. Men of 2 Commando and 12 Commando had also taken part in the operation and rumour had it that casualties had been heavy.

'You'll be getting plenty of that before long.'

'That's not what I mean.' They were in the bedroom they shared. Breakfast was over and the pubs wouldn't be open for another couple of hours, even if he felt like an early drink, which he didn't think he did. Outside it was a bright spring day; still cold, but at least not raining for once.

'Spell it out.'

'I'm not sure I can. Christ, I hope I'm not getting war-happy like that air force guy from Regina.'

Two days earlier they had spent part of an evening with a Canadian sergeant pilot serving with the RAF and flying Stirlings from somewhere in East Anglia. It wasn't until they were all, apart from Greyfoot, three-quarters drunk that they learned the flier had married an English girl just before Christmas. They lived in a rented cottage close to the bomber 'drome. He hadn't told his wife that he had been given a forty-eight hour pass. She thought he was on call and confined to base.

'But I didn't want to go home,' he confided. 'I can't explain it, but I just didn't. I didn't even want the fucking forty-eight, but the Groupie made me take it. And made me get off the base. I'd rather have flown another op or stayed there. I don't know how the hell I'll explain this to my wife if she ever finds out, but I'd rather be with other Canadian servicemen than with her. I'd rather fly most of all, but if the brass won't let me do that for a few days, I'd rather get shit-faced with guys who know what it's like.

'She's a beauty, too, my wife. Great to look at, great in the sack. Coming back from Hamburg on my last mission before this leave, I promised myself, next time I saw her, I was going to keep her in bed the whole time. But when the Groupie told me to take a hike, the last place I wanted to be was with her. Now how the hell do you figure that?'

Jack couldn't at the time, part booze, part mystification. If he'd been given forty-eight hours with an attractive wife, wild horses wouldn't have dragged him away. Or so he'd thought then. It might still hold true if he'd had someone special to spend the hours with. But he was beginning to doubt even that.

'Maybe he was just scared, the fly guy,' said Greyfoot. 'Scared of having to sit around some cottage while his friends were taking off over his head. He was the pilot. He got the forty-eight, not his crew. If they bought it with someone else at the controls – well, maybe he'd rather not think about it. I don't know anything about wives, but I'll bet his wouldn't have gone a bundle on him sitting around drinking beer instead of paying attention to her.'

'No,' said Jack thoughtfully, 'there was more to it than that. He wanted to talk to people who'd been at the sharp end of the war, though God knows I wouldn't be a bomber pilot for a million dollars. His wife wouldn't understand.'

'You can't know that, Jack.'

'I can guess. When I write to my parents, or to my brother and sister, I don't tell them much of what goes on. I tell them about the weather and maybe a girl I'm seeing. That's all. They wouldn't understand the rest. My dad might, but not the others. You must do the same.'

Greyfoot raised his eyebrows ruefully, and Jack recalled that the Chief never wrote home. No one to write to.

'Sorry, Chief. My mind's going. But, anyway, you've got to be involved to figure it all out. We can talk about what happened at Vaagsö because we were there. I couldn't write my sister about this lunatic Cree who was staggering along with a couple of buckets of petrol. It seems to me that if you're not in action, you've got to talk about it to someone. So you talk to those who were involved. The thing is, how involved am I getting? I probably wouldn't say this to anyone but you, but I don't enjoy killing Krauts. What I do enjoy is being there. *There.* What happens to the fly guy from Regina when there are no more targets to bomb? Maybe you get used to it. Not dropping bombs, but doing *something.* Christ, in the Depression I was a bum before the Patricias took me in.'

'So was I.'

'So you were.' Jack shrugged dismissively. 'I'm talking rubbish. Let's put it down to boredom.'

'It sounds a bit more than that, whichever way you look at it. I'd say you needed this leave.'

'Maybe. Come on, let's get out there and see what London has to offer today.'

'No, I'll pass.'

Jack thought he knew why. To his certain knowledge the Chief had seen the same whore, Tessa, three days running. They'd picked up Tessa and a friend their first night. She was a pretty little thing, dark and petite, about twenty years of age, with a room above an unoccupied shop in Soho. But she was still a whore. Jack forgot about his own troubles and concerned himself with Greyfoot. Sure, he was old enough and big enough to take care of himself, but Tessa, given a chance, would take him for every penny he had. Okay, that was par for the course. Whores sold sex to servicemen who wanted sex in exchange for money. But for the Chief to be wondering where she was now, or when he was going to see her, when it was still early, was unhealthy.

'She'll only stick around as long as you can pay, you know. And with the Yanks in town, that won't be long.'

'I know she'll be at it again once we're gone, but while we're here she's seeing no one but me.'

'Don't be a jerk.'

Greyfoot's jaw tightened aggressively.

'I'll take that from you, Jack, because I owe you, one way or another. But I'll take it just once. Understood?'

Okay, it was his problem. They'd all come on leave together, but that was as far as it went.

'Understood,' said Jack. 'I'll catch you later.'

Making sure he had his gas mask and identity papers, Jack walked as far as the Tottenham Court Road and turned left. At the end of the Charing Cross Road he turned into Shaftesbury Avenue and went as far as Piccadilly, where Eros was still boarded up and would probably remain that way until the Third Reich was yesterday's news. The French House would be open by now, and he made for it.

The first person he saw when he walked in was Lieutenant Brewerton, Brew from the Patricias, drinking with a couple of RAF types. After they'd pummelled each other a few times, Brew prodded a rather drunken finger at the ribbon of Jack's DCM. He was evidently a few drinks ahead of the game.

'We heard about it, and Ernie Kiley's Military Medal. You two are the first accredited Patricias heroes in this war.'

'About time we were on our way,' said one of the RAF types, a flight lieutenant with a regulation handlebar moustache. He obviously didn't think much of officers being too familiar with other ranks. 'Let the colonials get on with old home week.'

'Blow, then,' said Brew.

He and Jack had half a pint of beer apiece before Brew decided he'd better eat something before he fell over.

They lunched at one of the new British Restaurants, where a first-class subsidized meal – roast beef, two vegetables, treacle pudding, bread and butter and coffee – could be had for elevenpence.

While eating, Jack asked Brew what he was doing in London.

'We heard the Patricias were still in Sussex.'

'They are. I'm doing two weeks at the War Office. Not very secretive, but not something I can discuss, either. How about you? How was Vaagsö?'

'Cold.'

Brew wanted to know who was with Jack on leave, if leave was what it was. Jack told him.

'That rogue,' said Brew, when he heard that Kovacs had survived Vaagsö.

'Another twenty-four hours and he'd have owned the place. You know what the bugger's like.'

'I'm surprised they didn't offer you a commission to go with the gong,' said Brew. He was sobering up now, though still a bit pale round the gills.

'It never cropped up,' said Jack. 'Hell, I wouldn't want one, anyway. It doesn't matter so much in the commandos. Everyone's one of the boys from the CO down. A couple of pips don't mean a thing.'

'You might think differently after the war, if you stay on.'

'If. They'll disband a standing army quicker than you can say knife once the hostilities are over. Somebody had to squeeze Mackenzie King's balls pretty hard to get us this far. I was a regular before it all, sure, and maybe I'll stick around if I'm wanted. But I'm not interested in pips on my shoulders.'

'Couldn't get on for the chips, huh?'

'It's not that, believe me.'

Outside the restaurant they watched a patrolling tart arrange a bit of business with a sailor. Her face wasn't up to much, and she was wearing earrings that would not have been out of place on the front axle of a 3-tonner; but she had the most staggeringly beautiful breasts, which she was showing off to full advantage via a low-cut blouse in spite of the cold. As a selling point they were winners, and the sailor was hooked and landed.

'Bet you don't get many of those to a pound,' said Brew enviously.

At the corner of Shaftesbury Avenue Brew asked Jack what he was doing later in the day, around six.

'Not a lot, at a guess.'

'Why not meet me? I've had the morning off because the people I'm dealing with are doing something else, but I should show my face this afternoon in case something turns up. I'll be free after about five thirty, though, and I know this place in Mount Street. It's not a club. In fact, it's far from a club. It's a private house owned by a very beautiful lady called Katie Roth. She's an Englishwoman married to an American Jew, a very influential man if I'm reading between the lines correctly. He's hardly ever there, but when he is and if you keep your ears pricked, you'll hear half the War Cabinet mentioned.

'Anyway, from around six in the evening until the small hours, air raids permitting, she runs a kind of open house. If you've got an invite from a regular visitor – and I was lucky enough to get one from the people I'm liaising with at the War Office – you just turn up. There are tea and sandwiches always on tap, magazines to read if you want to relax. You're usually offered a drink or two as well, but the clincher is that there are always plenty of uniformed women around. It's a rare night when there aren't a dozen or more. It's not a knocking shop. Far from it, though I guess Mrs Roth – no one calls her Katie unless they've been around a while – doesn't object if a man and a woman make an arrangement to meet later. There's usually a lot of brass and red tabs on view, but they're human, most of them.'

Jack tapped his stripes.

'Maybe I'll skip it. Sounds like officer country to me. They'll get embarrassed if you turn up with an NCO.'

'An NCO with a DCM and commando flashes? The hell they will. You'll be the belle of the ball. The majority of these guys are chairborne infantry. Anyway, you won't be the only NCO there. As I said, it's open house. Mrs Roth's a beauty in more ways than one. Come on, God knows when we'll bump into each other again. I'll meet you at six on the corner of Mount Street, the Park Lane end. Do you now where it is?'

'I'll find it.'

Strolling back to Russell Square Jack wondered if the invitation extended to the Chief and Kovacs, Ernie and Alphabet. Probably not, or Brew would have mentioned it.

As it happened, it didn't matter. None of the four was in the hotel when he returned, and hadn't appeared when it came time for him to leave shortly before five thirty. He'd lay odds he knew where the Chief was, but the others could be anywhere. Kovacs was probably trying to buy Buckingham Palace. Steal it, rather.

Brew hadn't exaggerated, Jack was thinking a couple of hours later. Mrs Roth was some looker. About five five with shoulder-length blonde hair framing high cheekbones that would have had a sculptor turning cartwheels. Her eyes, he judged correctly from a distance, were on the grey side of blue, and her smile lit up the room. She curved in and out where it all counted too.

He had been expecting someone much older, but he doubted if she was thirty. Which made it all the more surprising when Brew pointed out her husband. He had to be in his sixties at least, and he wasn't much taller than she. He obviously adored his wife, however, but then so did most of the other men surrounding her. Men who didn't rank lower than major, squadron leader or lieutenant commander.

No matter what Brew said, this was no place for an NCO. There were pretty girls in evidence, to be sure, but each one had three or four men dancing attendance on her. The few other non-coms present seemed uneasy and tended to congregate in groups around the edges of the huge second-floor drawing-room, whose walls were hung with original oils. As was the hall outside. The place oozed money.

Mrs Roth hadn't put in an appearance until seven thirty, and then she was immediately surrounded by middle-ranking and senior officers. Jack hadn't been introduced. He did not expect to be. Nor did he anticipate staying long. When Mr Roth pecked his wife on the cheek and left the room, dressed for the street and carrying a briefcase – 'Off to tell Churchill what Roosevelt's thinking,' someone close by murmured – Jack took that as his own cue to leave. People were coming and going all the time. He'd had two glasses of delicious malt whisky, but now he'd also had enough.

He looked around for Brew, but Brew had joined the coterie surrounding Mrs Roth. Well, he'd see Brew another day. It was going to be a long war.

He'd left his headgear in the cloakroom on the ground floor. He retrieved it and washed his hands. The damned cloakroom, he thought incidentally, was twice the size of the room he shared with the Chief in the Russell Square hotel.

Mrs Roth was waiting for him outside, impatiently tapping a foot that peaked from beneath the hem of her long burgundy gown. She shooed away a wing commander who appeared and tried to engage her in conversation. The RAF officer went. What Mrs Roth wanted, apparently, Mrs Roth got.

'Leaving without saying goodbye, Sergeant Lambert? That makes you the first Canadian I've met who didn't have to be persuaded to leave.'

Her voice was everything he would have expected. Honey and spring rain and lazy summer days.

Jack felt his cheeks redden.

'I'm sorry, Mrs Roth, I – er . . .' He couldn't find the words.

She chuckled conspiratorially.

'I know, I know. Too much brass. It gets on my nerves, also, sometimes. When I first started these evenings it wasn't my intention to turn the house into an anteroom for the Imperial General Staff. I've already had several sharp words with Lieutenant Brewerton. He, and others who have been here before, have strict instructions to introduce me to newcomers, no matter who I'm talking to at the time.'

'I don't think it was Brew's – Lieutenant Brewerton's fault, exactly,' Jack defended his fellow Canadian loyally.

'Of course it was. He's my guest, you're his. Well, you were. Now you're mine. Come along, my husband's study is presently unoccupied. I want to hear all about Vaagsö. Oh, go away, Toby,' she scolded a Royal Navy captain.

'Sorry, Kate, but I'm afraid this just won't wait.'

'Don't run away, Sergeant Lambert.'

Mrs Roth and the Navy put their heads together. Jack remained where he was, far from comfortable. Finally, Mrs Roth heaved a long sigh.

'I'm afraid you'll have to tell me about Vaagsö another day,' she said to Jack, rejoining him. 'I'm needed elsewhere.'

Jack took it as a brush-off and managed a tight smile. She seemed genuine enough, but what the hell could he tell her about Vaagsö that she didn't already know? Mountbatten probably came for drinks twice a week.

'That's quite all right, Mrs Roth. Another day.'

She walked him to the front door.

'I mean it,' she said. She studied him. In her court shoes the top of her head came about level with his eyes. 'In fact, I mean it tomorrow. Here at four o'clock in the afternoon if you're not otherwise occupied. I'm interested. In Vaagsö, of course. Please say you'll be here.'

Now what the devil did she mean by that 'of course', Jack wondered, as he made his way home, occasionally colliding with other pedestrians because, even though it was nearly April, thick fog, what Londoners called 'smog' or a 'pea-souper', had descended during the short time he had been in Mrs Roth's house. Even the searchlights in Hyde Park, presumably part of an exercise because the sirens hadn't sounded, were having difficulty probing the choking muck.

He stepped aside at the last moment to avoid a group of American airmen, arms around each other's shoulders and slightly the worse for drink, singing a current popular song, tunelessly. Kay Kyser's 'Praise the Lord and Pass the Ammunition'. From a corner pub someone was also vocalizing, badly: a Donald Peers imitation of 'When They Sound the Last All-Clear'.

Of course. No, he was reading too much into it, just because she was a lovely, highly desirable woman. With a husband who had Churchill's ear, he reminded himself. Try anything on with her and he'd find himself facing a firing squad in the Tower of London. There'd be a bunch of others there, in any case, all talking about their own Vaagsös, be they bombing missions over Berlin or Atlantic convoys. Still, he'd turn up. It wasn't often a man got to see how the rich lived.

He arrived at two minutes to four. She opened the door herself, though the previous evening a maid had done so. In peacetime it would no doubt have been a butler or a footman, or whatever it was the wealthy called their flunkies in England.

On this occasion she was wearing a charcoal grey two-piece suit, the skirt shorter than was fashionable. She had excellent legs, unseen beneath her burgundy dress last night, though he would have put money on that.

She linked her arm through his and led him up to a first-floor sitting-room. There she poured him a whisky from a decanter, took a smaller one for herself, diluted neither, and indicated that he should sit beside her on the long sofa.

'Now, about Vaagsö. Only as much as you're permitted to tell, naturally.'

He didn't consider himself to be much of a raconteur, but she seemed fascinated and listened more or less in silence, interjecting only the occasional question, for forty minutes. Halfway through, when his glass was empty, she poured him a second drink, taking nothing for herself. He was acutely aware of her femininity, her refined delicateness. God knows, a non-com didn't come across her kind very often. She weighed, he estimated, about one hundred and fifteen pounds. Next to her he felt huge.

At a quarter to five she glanced openly at her wristwatch.

'We'll have to leave it there, I'm sorry to say. I have lots to do before this evening. It's going to be a very boring one, I'm afraid. A little like last night.'

He took that to mean that he should not put in an appearance, and was surprised by her next words.

'But tomorrow afternoon, at the same time . . .'

The third afternoon they ended up in bed together. *Her* bedroom, she pointed out, not one she shared with her husband. She made no bones about leading him directly to it, where she kicked off her shoes and unfastened her skirt. Standing there in her slip she said, 'There's a bathroom through there and a robe behind the door.'

When he returned she was already in bed, her head peeking above the sheets.

'If you're the slightest bit worried about my husband, please don't be. You'll have noticed that he is considerably older than I, twice as old, in fact. I owe him a great deal and he's a marvellous man, but we lead our own lives.'

They made love vigorously. She was a talker, a groaner. 'Ah . . . yes. Like that . . . That's marvellous . . . Oh Christ yes . . . that's beautiful. More . . . more . . . more. Oh yes yes yes . . .'

Somewhere in the middle of it all he felt sure he heard the door open. He sensed, anyway, that someone had been standing there, watching them, if only for a brief second.

He tackled her about it afterwards, when he was dressed. She was still in bed. She would have a bath, she said, when he left.

'It could have been my husband, I suppose. He sometimes comes home during the day.'

Jack was embarrassed.

'How am I supposed to look him in the face when I see him again?'

'Why would you be seeing him again?' She seemed genuinely surprised. 'You surely don't want to attend my soirees. We'll have our afternoons until your leave is over. And please don't tell me when that will be. I don't want to know. When it's time to go, just go.'

In the street he realized that not once during their love-making had he called her Kate, or even thought of her as Kate. The following day he did. And she called him Jack.

'I suppose you could say we've been introduced,' she giggled girlishly.

Several afternoons later he could not resist asking, 'Why me?'

It was a ham-fisted, unsophisticated question, he knew, but he couldn't help himself.

'Because you're beautiful.'

'Me?'

'Yes. A hard man is good to find.'

That was as much as he ever got out of her.

Making love was as much as he ever got, also. For roughly an hour each day. When he asked if he couldn't see her, meet up with her, outside the house, perhaps just to go for a walk in the park, she said no.

'I don't think that would be a good idea at all.'

He wasn't stupid enough to believe that he was the first to have shared her bed since her marriage, or that he would be the last. But he wanted more from her than she was willing to give. When they were making love they were as close, spiritually as well as physically, as any man and woman could be. He sensed she felt the same. But when it was all over, apart from a certain friendliness, she withdrew within herself.

Shortly before two o'clock on the penultimate day of his leave, everything went wrong.

He had been out to buy her a gift. There wasn't much available in wartime London, not that he could afford, but he had found her a

129

small bunch of flowers. He suspected she would guess the reason for the bouquet, that it was a farewell present, and be angry with him for letting her know that his leave was coming to an end. He didn't care. He was going to tell her that he would write while he was away. They couldn't just leave it like that. He'd want to see her next time he was in London, too. He would persuade her. Somehow.

When he returned to the hotel after buying the flowers, to clean up thoroughly before heading for Mount Street, he was accosted by the blowzy woman behind the desk.

'You'd better see to your friend, Sergeant Lambert. I know soldiers like a drink, but I keep a respectable establishment here, and he's had too much. Swearing and cursing and knocking over the furniture. It's in the regulations, you know, that I can call the Military Police if I'm given any trouble.'

Shit, thought Jack, now which one of those bastards could it be trying to mess up his last day? Kovacs, for a pound.

'Who is it?'

'Corporal Greyfoot.'

Jack took the stairs three at a time. Greyfoot was slumped in a chair, drunk out of his mind, though with the Chief that would have taken a maximum of three pints. He had been in a fight as well as a bar, judging by the scratches on his face.

'For Chrissake, Chief . . .'

Jack manhandled him to the bathroom and stuck his head under the cold tap. Then he made him drink two glasses of water. Then he stuck him in the lavatory and waited until Greyfoot had thrown up. But it was a while before he was sober enough to talk coherently.

Slowly it came out. This was their last full day of leave. After lunch he had gone to see Tessa in Soho. She never rose much before one o'clock, so he knew he'd be certain of catching her in. He wanted to spend the rest of the day with her.

Well, he'd caught her all right. In bed with a French matelot. They'd had a fight, he and the sailor, but then he'd turned on Tessa. The matelot didn't hang around. Nor did he come back with the police. The Chief reckoned he was AWOL or something like that.

'I didn't mean to hurt her, I swear to God, but I slapped her around a bit. I must have slapped her too hard because she fell over, cracked her head, and didn't get up. I panicked, I guess. I left her where she was and went to the nearest pub. I had three, maybe four pints. Christ knows how I got back here. I don't know myself.'

'You stupid bastard,' Jack swore at him. 'What did I tell you? She's a whore. She goes with guys for money. Did you think she was saving it all for you?'

But what was the difference between himself and the Chief? The Chief had fallen for a tart, a girl who had to make her living on her back because she had no other source of income. Kate didn't take money, true, and did everything with a lot of style, but were they so unalike?

Jack remembered the Blackfoot from the Reserve south of Calgary who had been topped in 1940 for killing an English girl. If Tessa was dead Greyfoot could expect no mercy. Even if she wasn't, he was likely to go into a military prison for a very long time and that, for someone like the Chief, was as good as being dead. Unless . . .

'She lives above that empty shop, doesn't she?'

'Yes.'

Okay, so far so good. It didn't sound as if it had been much of a fight, and in that part of Soho they were used to a few raised voices and chairs being knocked over. Thank God Tessa lived alone.

'Give me the exact address.'

'What are you going to do?'

'Never mind. Just give me the address and don't move out of this room until I come back.'

There were no police vehicles or policemen on foot outside the address, anyway, Jack thought thankfully half an hour later, but he still ascended the stairs cautiously, as if this were one of the houses on Vaagsö Island and not one in central London. The card in a metal slot on the door read 'Tessa – French practised' written in a childish hand.

Jack pressed the bell.

'Go away,' called a tiny voice.

She was alive, that was something. Otherwise the next step would have been tough. Now there was only one obvious move.

'I've got something for you,' said Jack. 'Money.'

'I'm not doing business today.'

'It's not business, honey. It's a gift from a friend.'

That brought her to the door, but when she opened it and saw who her visitor was, she tried to slam it in his face.

Jack easily prevented her from doing so, pushed her inside, and closed the door behind him.

She cowered in a corner, hands up to her face. She didn't appear to be badly hurt, but there was a nasty bump on her forehead, presumably where she'd fallen.

'If you've come to finish off what your friend started, I'll scream so loud every copper in the neighbourhood will be outside my window in half a minute.'

'I haven't come to do anything of the sort,' said Jack easily. 'As a matter of fact, I've come to apologize for him.'

'Apologize!' She spat the word out. 'The bastard bloody near killed me.'

'I know, I know, he told me. But he was jealous of that French guy, you see. He wants to make it up now. Have you got anything to drink around here?'

'Around here' consisted of a single room twelve feet by twelve containing a bed with a screen in front of it, a couple of hard chairs, a sideboard and a wash basin.

'You said something about money,' Tessa said cunningly. 'I could have that bastard put in prison for twenty years, you know. Look at my face. How the fuck can I work with my face like that?'

'That's what we're going to sort out,' said Jack. 'Now, about that drink.'

'There's some gin and a glass over there.'

Jack helped himself to a couple of fingers and topped up the glass with water from the basin tap. Now came the tricky bit.

'You put him in prison, you don't get a penny. Oh sure, you'll have had your revenge, but how does that pay the rent? In a way, you should be flattered. How many guys do you get fighting over . . .' Whoops, he thought.

'Go on, say it, over a jam tart. Thanks a lot, mister, but I'll tell you what. You keep your flattery and I'll keep the money.'

Twenty years of age, he thought, and already as hard as they come. She'd be able to take on a Panzer division single-handed before she was twenty-five, if someone hadn't, by that time, made a better job of seeing her off than the Chief had.

She knew how to drive a hard bargain. He had slightly over thirty pounds on him. He started the bidding with ten and increased his offer in twos, but at the end of an hour she'd taken the lot and his wristwatch. About two weeks' wages for her, in his estimation. He had another five pounds plus his accommodation money back at the hotel. If he'd brought it she'd have had that too. She had a whore's uncanny instinct for the size of a purse. In some respects it was a blessing the leave was over.

'And he's getting away with this bloody easy, if you want my opinion. A man like him shouldn't be let loose. He's crazy.'

'Come on, Tessa,' said Jack. 'It's not the first time you've taken a beating.'

'Maybe, but mostly I get paid for it.'

'Which is how we'll tell it if you change your mind and go to the police.'

He had to walk back to Russell Square. When he arrived there it had turned five o'clock. Far too late now, damn it, for his afternoon rendezvous with Kate. He would just have to go to Mount Street later, for the soiree. Get her to one side and explain it all. Try to arrange something for tomorrow. Before they left.

Greyfoot was still in the same chair, face ashen. He hardly dared look up when Jack came in.

'Tell me the worst.'

'She was alive if that's what you mean. She'll have a headache for a couple of days, but you were lucky.'

'And?'

'I squared it.'

'How?'

'Talk, Chief, just talk. And a few pounds we'll discuss another day. I persuaded her it wasn't in her interests to go to the police. But keep away from Soho until we're ready to leave. I wouldn't put it past her to whistle up the MPs if she saw you again.'

'Thanks, Jack. It was a bloody stupid thing . . .'

'Forget it.'

Jack took his last five pounds from the dressing-table. The flowers he'd bought earlier didn't look much now, but that was neither here nor there. He couldn't have given them to her while there were others around.

He arrived at Mount Street around seven. Kate hadn't put in an appearance yet, but he saw Brew in the second-floor drawing-room, deep in conversation with a Guards captain. The Patricias lieutenant came over when he spotted Jack.

'I was beginning to think this wasn't to your taste. Where have you been the last few evenings?'

'Things to do,' said Jack. 'You know how it is.'

Kate arrived at a quarter to eight. She was wearing the same burgundy dress as the first evening, and appeared tired. She did not see Jack at first, but when she did she stiffened and turned away. No smile, no acknowledgement of any sort.

It took him almost an hour to get her alone. Even then he had to break up a tête-à-tête and make it formal. 'I'm sorry to interrupt, Mrs Roth, but if I could have a few words with you.'

He tried to explain his earlier absence, keeping his voice down. She seemed to be only half-listening.

'One of the guys from my outfit got into some trouble. I had to bail him out. It took longer than I expected.'

She was smiling for her distant audience, as though their conversation was about something pleasant or trivial, but her words had an edge.

'I thought you'd gone. In fact, in my mind you have. That's the way it has to be.'

He recalled she'd made him promise not to tell her when his leave was over. When he hadn't turned up this afternoon, she must have assumed he'd left London.

'Kate . . .'

He reached out to touch her. She removed her arm as if stung.

'It's Mrs Roth, Sergeant Lambert,' she said coolly. 'And I really think it would be better if you left now.'

'We can't finish it like this.'

'Of course we can.' She turned her glittering smile on him, but her eyes weren't smiling at all. 'Goodbye, Sergeant Lambert,' she said in a normal voice. 'Goodbye, Jack,' she murmured.

Brew, curious, had witnessed the whole scene from close by.

'Mrs Roth seems upset,' he said, accosting Jack as he made for the door. 'Nothing you said, I hope.'

'What could I say that would upset an iceberg like Mrs Roth?'

'Iceberg? I'm not with you.'

'Of course you're not.'

'I didn't hear you call her Kate, did I?'

'Me? You said it yourself, you have to know her very well to be allowed to call her Kate. I hardly knew her at all. See you around, Brew.'

Back at the hotel, there was a letter he had written to his brother Ben propped up on the dressing-table, one he'd begun on his second day in London and had added to ever since. Kate Roth and the address in Mount Street were mentioned, because Ben was due for call-up any time now and might one day find himself in England. He had said nothing about his brief affair with Kate, however. In fact, when he'd first written the address the affair hadn't begun.

He was tempted to tear the whole thing up, but he knew it might be weeks before he got a chance to write again. Eventually he decided to let it go.

The Chief was asleep, but Jack didn't feel like bed. Nor did he feel like a drink, though he could just about have made last orders.

He sat in the hotel lounge, talking to a Canadian from Vancouver.

Around midnight Kiley bowled in, one sleeve hanging loose from his tunic. He was accompanied by two burly MPs, who had been ready to throw him in the can until they heard this was his last night of leave. He had got into a fight with some British troops who didn't believe anyone of his stature could be a commando. He had been holding his own until the MPs broke it up.

One of them said to Jack, as they left, 'But you're responsible for him. Any further trouble and he's for it.'

'Get to bed, Ernie.'

At one a.m. Kovacs and Alphabet returned, Kovacs furious. He and Alphabet had found what looked like a sucker card game, but had wound up losers.

'The fucking winner had a full house, aces over tens. I had two pair, aces and queens. That made five aces in the game. I couldn't say anything because I had another ace tucked up my sleeve, and I still don't know which ones were the phoneys. The cheating bastards. Eighty flaming pounds it cost us. Me losing eighty pounds. Me!'

Jesus, thought Jack, let's get back to the war. We're safer there.

NINE

After leaving Colonel Charlton in Chipping Saxonby, Ben's next port of call was his only other English lead, Mrs Roth in Mount Street. Jack's letter concerning Mrs Roth's soirees had reached him a few weeks before he was called up for basic training, but he'd left it in Canada when he was sent overseas and gradually forgotten about it. During his time in England, although he had visited London on a number of occasions, he had never bothered to establish whether Mrs Roth still held what Jack had called open house. Now it was time to meet the lady herself. She might remember his brother. There was always a chance.

When he called, he was informed by a maid that Mrs Roth was out of town and would be for a week. He booked himself into a hotel and opted to wait for her return.

In the meantime he telephoned Jonathan Margolis in Edmonton, but the transatlantic line was terrible. He managed to let Jonathan know that he would cable or write instead, update him, and this he proceeded to do.

What he had to say would have cost a fortune by telegraph, so he settled for a letter. This would take a lot longer, but he would be able to say a great deal more. He requested a reply by cable, however; otherwise, he wrote, he would be in England until the autumn.

In essence he apprised Jonathan that he had learned little in Chipping Saxonby except that Jack appeared to have been popular, and that he was seeing a Mrs Roth in a week. If Mrs Roth had nothing to offer, his English contacts were at an end. Probably for security reasons, Jack had been a poor correspondent during the pre-Dieppe exercises, and after Dieppe he was a POW. That left only Germany, but Germany, in any case, was doubtless where the answers lay, if answers could be found.

Could Jonathan therefore use his Ottawa contacts to establish the name or names of the senior officers who held command in the Stalag? That shouldn't be difficult. They had the number and location of the prison camp, after all. Had the German/Germans survived the war? Had they been incarcerated as war criminals, and were they still? If not, where were they now?

If papers were required for Occupied Germany, could Jonathan pull a few strings there? Having come so far, it would be foolish to quit now. He was much closer to Germany than to Canada.

Ben concluded by writing, 'I'm sorry the bills are mounting up but, as we agreed, I should see this through to the end for all our sakes.'

At the end of a week Ben telephoned Mrs Roth, obtaining her number from the London directory. He explained his business, that her name and address had been found in a letter written by his brother Jack during the war.

She did not appear to recognize his surname – 'My house was open to a great many servicemen during the war years, Mr Lambert' – but agreed to see him the following morning at eleven a.m.

When he presented himself, however, he was told that Mrs Roth was indisposed.

'I'm sorry to hear that,' said Ben to the maid. 'I'll make another appointment if I may.'

The maid hesitated. 'Mrs Roth will be indisposed for some time.'

Ben smelt a rat.

'How can you know that? She sounded all right yesterday.'

'Well, I'm afraid she's not today.'

'Five minutes is all I ask.'

'That won't be possible.'

Ben doubted he could barge in without inviting the attentions of a London bobby, but he hadn't travelled six thousand miles to be fobbed off by some lame excuse. If there was more here than met the eye, he wanted to know what it was.

He tried a bluff.

'Just tell Mrs Roth I have something she would be interested in seeing.'

'Wait there,' said the maid, and closed the door.

When it was opened again Mrs Roth was standing there. At least Ben assumed it was Mrs Roth. Jack had written something about her being a beautiful woman of around thirty, and that was five years ago. This woman was about thirty-five, and she was certainly beautiful.

'I'm Kate Roth. You'd better come in, Mr Lambert.'

In the first-floor sitting-room, she said: 'Now what could you have that I would be interested in seeing?'

'I made that up, I'm afraid.'

Far from being annoyed at the subterfuge, Mrs Roth appeared relieved.

'Because I changed my mind about meeting you?'

'Yes, though if you're ill . . .'

'I'm not, as you can see. I'm in perfect health.'

'Then why . . .'

'Because after you telephoned yesterday I remembered who Jack Lambert was. As a matter of fact, he once sat exactly where you're now sitting. I wondered if he had been indiscreet on paper and if I was to be subjected to a crude form of blackmail.'

Ben saw the light. Jack's relationship with Mrs Roth had been more than that of hostess and guest.

'I see you understand, Mr Lambert.'

Ben nodded, not quite sure how to react. But he said: 'If it's any comfort, Mrs Roth, my brother never wrote anything other than your name and address, and the fact that your house was open to servicemen.'

'I'm gratified to hear it. A great many things happened during the war, some pleasant, others less so. Had you been a blackmailer I would have dealt with you in my own way. Paid you off if necessary. You see, my husband is the one who's really ill. The latter years of the war undermined his health totally. I didn't want him worried by even a whiff of scandal.' She smiled. 'However, I can see I misinterpreted the reason for your visit. Please tell me how I can help.'

She was saddened to learn that Jack had died in a German POW camp, though not, she said, entirely surprised. 'I somehow knew you were going to tell me he was dead.'

Ben stuck to the fiction he had rehearsed on the flight over, that he was on business in England and Europe and, when he had time, was trying to meet anyone who had known Jack in the war years.

'He left Canada in 1939. I never saw him again.'

Mrs Roth rang for the maid, who brought in tea. 'I'm afraid coffee is still very hard to come by. Who would have thought it, two years after Hitler?'

Mrs Roth poured. Then she said, 'I'm not quite sure I understand the purpose of your visit. Wouldn't it be better to forget the past?'

Ben tried a shot in the dark.

'You're one of the few people I've met who saw my brother after I did, Mrs Roth. Would you think it conceivable that he could be a traitor, that he would betray his friends?'

'Is that what they're saying?'

Ben decided he could trust this woman.

'It's been suggested.'

'The answer's no, certainly not, but I'd hate to have to define treachery. Commonly, it's a violation of trust. Jack would have had his own views on that. But betray his friends? Never. However, the war changed all of us.

'Let me ask you a question. Would you believe that a woman of good character and background, one who respected her husband, could hurt him by sleeping with other men, even though she had done nothing of the sort before the war? That's a form of treachery. Ah, I see I'm embarrassing you.'

'Not really,' said Ben. 'It's just that I don't know the answer. It would depend on the woman. If my life depended upon answering, though, I'd say yes, it was possible.'

'Love is a primordial emotion, Mr Lambert, but so is hate. Who's to know which is the more powerful, or even if they're not different sides of the same coin? If you marry a man because he needs you, because you help him in his vital work, but then discover that you, personally, need more, and look for it, can he still love you and tell you not to hate yourself? Which emotion will win out?

'I'm giving nothing away that you don't already suspect, but for a time I loved your brother. For a time I'm certain he loved me. I know he loved the men who depended on him. He loved life too. If that altered because of his experiences in war or in the POW camp, he must have had a good reason. But that's the easy way out. The world requires absolutes. Every German was bad, every Allied soldier good. I wonder if it's that simple.'

At the front door they met an elderly man in a wheelchair just coming in. He was being pushed by a uniformed chauffeur. Mrs Roth kissed the elderly man on the forehead. 'Pleasant outing, darling?'

That this was Mr Roth, Ben guessed; and that Mr Roth had suffered a stroke, he assumed. What he couldn't define lay beyond Mrs Roth's eyes. Did she tolerate him, love him, because he was her husband, or did she loathe him because he lived and prevented her from doing so?

Had Jack experienced something at Dieppe, or in the Stalag, that had changed him from an NCO who cared for his men to one who didn't give a damn?

TEN

Breakfast for 4 Commando aboard the LSI *Prince Albert* was at 0130 hours. H-hour, when they hit the beach, would be 0455. Once transferred to the LCAs for the assault, the Commando would split into two groups. Group 1 would land just west of Vasterival on the beach designated as Orange One. Group 2 led by the CO, Lord Lovat, hereditary chieftain of Clan Fraser, would land a few hundred yards east of Quiberville on Orange Two. A little under two miles separated the two beaches. The Commando's major objective was a battery of six 150mm guns, codenamed the Hess Battery, set 1100 yards inland behind high cliffs four hundred feet above sea level, for these weapons, if not silenced, could destroy the ships standing offshore to protect the invaders during re-embarkation. Because this was a Reconnaissance in Force, Operation Jubilee against Dieppe.

The battle order read: 'The 2nd Canadian Division will seize Jubilee and vicinity. Occupy the area until demolition and exploitation tasks are completed. Re-embark and return to England.'

It all sounded very easy. A day out in the sun.

As well as ships and fighter aircraft, the Canadians would be supported by 4 Commando in the west, 3 Commando, on Yellow Beaches One and Two in the east, and by Royal Marines of A Commando, soon to be redesignated as 40 Commando RM. Fifty officers and men of a US Ranger Battalion would also take part.

Jubilee had originally been called Operation Rutter and planned for July, when it was cancelled due to bad weather. The overall objective was not to open a Second Front, much though this was being called for by the Russians and President Roosevelt, but to test at first hand the problems that would confront any large-scale amphibious force attempting to gain a foothold in the Continent.

It was also to blood previously untried Canadian infantry regiments and armoured troops. The Canadians were champing at the bit to be let loose. Many of them had garrisoned the United Kingdom for almost three years and they were anxious to see action. If any of them were worried that previously promised maximum-intensity bombing by Bomber Command had now been abandoned, they tried not to show it. It made sense, they argued, not to clutter up the streets with rubble. The Churchill Mark 1 tank had not been used before. Like the Canadians, this would be its debut. Better to see how it performed in its infantry support role than ask it to surmount piles of debris its first time out. Others suspected a political motive, that the War Cabinet was hoping to persuade the Vichy Government to hand over its large navy before Hitler got his hands on it. Saturation bombing of Dieppe was bound to have caused French civilian casualties, which would anger Vichy.

The former Patricias with 4 Commando, now back with Captain Bill Windus's B Troop, were disappointed not to see PPCLI in the battle order. The Royal Regiment of Canada was there, designated to hit Blue Beach, as was the Essex Scottish, Red Beach, and the Royal Hamilton Light Infantry, White Beach. The French-Canadian Fusiliers Mont-Royal would act as a floating reserve. Nearest 4 Commando, on their left flank, Green Beach, were the South Saskatchewans and the Queen's Own Cameron Highlanders. A Company of the Black Watch would land with the Royals and the tanks were in the capable hands of the Calgary Regiment. But no Patricias.

'They've got it in for them,' said Jack. 'We were right to get out when we did. Otherwise we'd still be in England.'

'What a bore,' drawled a listener. 'Just think of it. We're here and they're still in their pits. A few hours after we go ashore they'll be supping tea in the Naafi or grabbing a beer in the Pig and Whistle. Jeez, I'll bet they envy us.'

'They've got it in for us too,' grumbled Kovacs typically. 'I'd feel a flaming sight happier if I had something on my head other than hair.'

'You haven't got a hell of a lot of that,' said Jack.

'I've got tall skin.'

As each man in 4 Commando had been instructed to carry two mortar bombs ashore as well as his personal gear and weapons, to keep the weight down in what would otherwise be overloaded LCAs, no one would be wearing steel helmets or carrying water canteens or rations.

'And I'd feel a bloody sight happier if the Chief would get rid of

142

that damned drum and Jack that fucking chicken,' said Alphabet. 'Unless he's carrying dinner for the section, of course.'

'Yes, I was meaning to have a word with you about that, Jack,' said Lieutenant Halliday.

Halliday had completely recovered from the leg wounds received on Vaagsö and had been waiting for them when they returned to 4 Commando after their leave. He'd carry the scars for the rest of his life, but his injuries had not slowed him down any. He was still one of the fittest and toughest officers in the Commando.

The chicken in question was actually a Rhode Island Red hen, which Jack had christened Henry. It had attached itself to him during exercises for Operation Rutter on the Isle of Wight, and for some reason best known to hens refused to leave his side. Kovacs had wanted to wring its neck and pop it in the pot, but Jack vetoed that. 'You wring Henry's neck, I'll wring yours and no mistake. You'd eat your own mother.' When he tried to scoot it away after the exercises, Henry declined to go. So Jack had fashioned a small canvas sack for Henry, one he could attach to his webbing, and carried the hen everywhere Henry could not walk by herself. After a while he had begun to trust in her as a good luck charm, which was why she was now an honorary commando and the only hen on Jubilee. Captain Windus didn't object. Commandos, in his view, were meant to be a mite eccentric. That's what made them commandos.

The Chief's drum was a side-drum, a toy, a half-sized version of the real thing. He had found it in Lulworth Cove, Dorset, during rehearsals for Jubilee. Abandoned, or lost, by some child, it was filthy, marked by the sea and rusting in places. But he'd cleaned it up and made himself a harness. He had planned to leave it behind before they boarded the *Prince Albert*, but at the last moment he had elected to take it with him, for much the same reason that Jack was bringing Henry. He couldn't play it very well – 'Some fucking Indian you are,' Kovacs was fond of saying. 'All you guys are meant to wham that thing like Gene Krupa' – but he could batter out a tattoo with his fingers or one hand and his fighting knife. It made an agreeable noise.

'So say your word,' said Jack to Halliday.

'Hens make a noise, for one thing.'

'She's not now.'

'She's clucking, or whatever the fuck it is hens do.'

'You're making a bigger row than she is.'

'Wait till the shooting starts. They don't know we're here yet.'

'Christ, when the shooting starts no one's going to hear one bloody hen. Same goes for the Chief's drum.'

'Okay, her presence is turning Soames green,' tried Halliday.

Soames was one of B Troop's snipers. There would be a lot of green where he was going, and he was daubing his face and hands with camouflage cream of the same colour. Everyone else was blacked-up like minstrels. The black usually came off easily. The green was a bigger problem. They said you could always tell a sniper because he was the only guy in a bar who looked like an aspidistra.

'Seasickness,' said Jack.

'Ah, screw it,' said Halliday. 'Take the bloody chicken.'

'She's a hen,' Jack called after him.

'So why's she called Henry, then?'

'Because when I found her I'd given up women for the duration.'

'You're heading for a psycho discharge.'

'Why don't we get eggs if she's a hen?' Kovacs wanted to know.

'Christ, Kovacs, you're dumb,' said Jack. 'Let me tell you a few facts of life. Hens don't lay eggs just because they look like hens any more than cows give milk because they're cows. You've got the IQ of a radish. You need a bit of biology.'

'Maybe that'll come over in the second wave, huh?'

'There isn't a second wave, don't you listen? What you see is what you get.'

'Still,' said Ernie Kiley, 'I'm glad to be going back to France. At least it's warm. It could have been bloody Norway again.'

He was busy doing his usual trick of taping his fighting knife to the stock of his Thompson, his mind largely elsewhere. The others stared at him, and hooted.

Kovacs tossed a spring-loaded cosh at him.

'He thinks he's on a pleasure cruise.'

'For Maple Creek, read maple syrup. Which is what he's got between his ears.'

'You'll get warm, all right. Just wait till those 88s open up.'

Kiley grinned sheepishly.

'No, I mean . . . Aaagh, fuck it. I like France.'

Of which he had seen about half a square mile on several visits.

After they returned from leave and reported back to 4 Commando, they had fully expected to be training for a major operation immediately, because 4 Commando as an entire unit had barely seen any real action since its formation in July 1940. Instead, all that happened were small hit-and-run operations, section strength, against the French coast. This might have been a nuisance to the enemy and given them frequent headaches, but it was also a long way to go for what was frequently less than an hour ashore. It was a matter of going in under the cover of darkness, demolishing the radar aerials or radio beacon or whatever the target was, then skedaddling before the Germans sent out E-boats or fighters.

They had taken American Rangers with them on a couple of raids, men who had done the Achnacarry course and who could street-fight with the best of them, but even they came back pale and shaking when they saw how the commandos did things.

'Don't you guys ever get any naval gunfire cover?' one asked.

'Artillery?' said Halliday. 'You've got to be able to spell it to ask for it. We're all pretty thick in this outfit.'

But they were good guys, the Rangers, most of the commandos, especially the Canadians, prepared to dislike any American on sight, were surprised to find. Once they'd seen action and knew what to expect, they could hack it with the top-notchers.

Then came the rehearsals for Operation Rutter, during which many of them in 4 Commando, particularly Canadian nationals, were sent to the Isle of Wight to help train elements of the 2nd Canadian Division in commando tactics, for while the Canadians were going, commandos were not part of the original plan. Their place in the battle order, had the operation taken place, would have been occupied by airborne troops. Only when Rutter was cancelled did Lord Mountbatten elect to use commandos instead of Paras, for the very good reason that low cloud formations would no longer be a handicap.

'Just as well,' said Jack, exhibiting the customary, if occasionally phoney, dislike commandos had for airborne forces, who, the commandos thought, wouldn't know what feet were for if no one had shown them boots. Feet were just something to keep your ankles from fraying at the ends. 'They're great at bailing out of aircraft, but once they're on the deck you have to hold their hands and show them what to do next. The biggest danger in this war is not the Germans. It's a Para officer with a map. God speed the plough.'

Halliday topped that remark.

'To Paras, the Continent are those who can keep their bladders in check.'

When Rutter was cancelled and the commandos became part of the new operation, Lord Lovat's Commando did eight exercises over measured terrain in Lulworth Cove, which was as close as anyone could get to the conditions they would meet in Dieppe. The Clan Fraser chieftain decided early on to use only four of the six fighting Troops he had available. What he lost in strength he would gain in speed and manoeuvrability. In any case, the armada already comprised two hundred and thirty-seven vessels and looked like a bad day on the Solent. Add in another hundred and twenty men plus support units and there would be a traffic jam of monumental proportions. A German spy in Southampton, Portsmouth, Newhaven and Shoreham, the ports of embarkation, would not have to be a genius to divine that this was not a peacetime regatta.

They used scaling ladders and rocket-fired grappling-irons to get up the chalk of Lulworth. On one occasion Henry the hen led the way, flapping about and cockadoodling until she found an easy route.

'See,' said Jack to the disbelievers, who saw Henry only as ambulatory rations, 'we'd have been here for a week without Henry.'

Sergeant Lambert was losing his marbles was a generally held opinion.

Jack didn't believe he was, though as the time came to leave the *Albert* and board the LCAs, he was inclined to take a second opinion.

Cards and dice were put away, winnings pocketed or IOUs written. Half-finished letters were stowed. Lieutenant Halliday came along to make sure everyone had eaten, was well, and that all was shipshape. He couldn't tell 2 Section anything more. The CO had given his pep talk. So had the Troop commander. Like late revision on the morning of a vital exam, it was too late now if they didn't know their stuff. Except he was convinced they did.

Mike Halliday didn't expect to survive Dieppe. He just had that feeling. After convalescing from his Vaagsö wounds, he had refused a secure training job. He wanted to get back to B Troop. They were a bit special.

Take Soames there, the sniper, with his idiotic green face, now looking purple under the security lamps below decks. He was a married man with a small daughter, a farmer from some hick town in Somerset. He could take the skin off a fly's balls with a rifle, blindfold.

If you could ever rely upon a man to keep their bastard heads down, Soames was that man. He'd be twenty years of age in a month or two.

Then there were the Canadians who'd come thousands of miles to fight for their Mother country. God help the Krauts.

Take Corporal Kiley. Weighed nothing, looked less. A few crooked teeth and a grin that would not have been out of place on a ten-year-old truant. But a hell of a fighter, and one who took meticulous care with weaponry. The taped fighting knife loose on his Thompson; a heavy cosh strapped to his thigh in a frog that never came out of stores; a stick grenade, Wehrmacht issue, stuck down his boot. Every inch, about sixty-eight of them, the professional.

Take Alphabet Soup. Everyone thought, because he and Kovacs were usually inseparable, that Alphabet was low man on the totem pole. Believe that and a flat earth. A bit more schooling and he'd be looking at another stripe.

As for Kovacs, give him a few hours in Dieppe and he'd be peddling captured German weapons to the highest bidder. He'd already asked: 'Who gets the scrap metal if one of these ships gets hit?'

The dice and cards had now been stashed, but old Kovacs wasn't willing to let it go at that. He was trying to bet anyone who'd put up the ante, synchronizing watches, the precise hour and minute Lord Lovat's Group would hit Orange Two. Refusing markers and wanting cash. 'Some of you bastards might lose and get killed. Then how would I collect?' He'd make a great politician, Kovacs. If there was a dollar in it, he'd kiss wall-to-wall babies.

Then there was the Chief and his frigging drum, on which he was presently tapping out the opening notes of Beethoven's Fifth, the homophonous letter 'V' – for Victory – in Morse. Di-di-di-dah. Di-di-di-dah. On the BBC's European Service, broadcasting to the Resistance in various countries, that was how it always opened up.

'I hope you're not going to be banging that thing all the way up the beach,' Halliday heard Jack Lambert say. 'It'll bring down flak from every which way.'

'It'll scare the hell out of them.'

'It already scares the hell out of me. They'll think they're being attacked by the toytown fusiliers.'

Halliday knew quite a lot about David Greyfoot. In his personnel dossier against next-of-kin, there was written: None. Halliday had challenged him about it.

'So who do we telegraph if you get wounded or killed?'

'Why does it matter? If there's any pay coming, give the guys a drink.'

Because he was an officer who wanted the best for the men in 2 Section, Lieutenant Halliday had been concerned that the Chief never received any mail, or wrote any. Until he, Halliday, contacted one of the charitable organizations whose female members did little more than correspond with lonely soldiers. Then the letters poured in. The Chief never found out how it all began, but he wouldn't be short of people to write to and places to visit if he made it back from Jubilee.

Lambert helped him with some of the correspondence, the few difficult words the Chief couldn't handle. But that was Jack Lambert, anyway, over there fussing over his frigging chicken, putting Henry in the carrier. Part nanny, part martinet, part big brother.

Some of the senior NCOs and all of the officers had been briefed by MI9, the Escape and Evasion part of Military Intelligence, before Jubilee got on the road. The sea. What to do if taken prisoner. How to get information back to England. The escape lines down to Spain or up to Scandinavia. Lambert was one of the privileged few. As well as everything else he had to remember regarding the destruction of the Hess Battery, he had to keep codes in his head. Ways out. It wasn't the slightest use telling only the officers. If they were put in the bag, the officers would go to an Oflag, the other ranks to a Stalag. Geneva Convention. In war a man wasn't just a man. He was either a Gentleman or a Player. Crazy, but those were the rules. Everyone bled the same if hit, but there were those whose blood was designated as blue and those whose blood was the normal red variety. Total war might be insane, but the world was a damned sight loonier.

Hopefully it wouldn't come to capture, imprisonment. They would all be back in England for lunch. Yeah, even me, thought Halliday. Stuff this being the big blotto. They'll do their job and I'll do mine, and tonight we'll guzzle beer.

Jack Lambert was already doing part of his job. He'd seen the hour and knew that soon they would be climbing aboard the LCAs. This in mind, he was checking through the section, making certain no one was leaving anything behind, or taking anything that would overload the LCAs further. As usual, everyone had primed their grenades. Also as usual, most of the men had removed the pins and taped down the firing levers. It didn't save much time, fractions of a second, but that was how they chose to hit the beaches. Some of the buggers had even interfered with their fuses, shortening the detonation time from the regulation seven seconds down to four or five, and had marked the various grenades with coloured ink, numbering them four or five, just in case they forgot under pressure. It would take just one wayward piece of tape to come unravelled and the entire section, the entire *Prince Albert*, would be a floating coffin. There had already been an accident among the Black Watch aboard the *Duke of Wellington*. A man had primed a grenade, turned away when someone called to him, then absent-mindedly picked up the live grenade and started to prime again. After a moment he realized his error and tried to hurl the grenade out of a porthole. It hit a bulkhead and exploded, killing the thrower and seriously wounding nineteen others.

Captain Windus came by as 0300 approached, thumbing skywards. Time to get on deck, board the LCAs for the ten-mile run to Orange Two, and hope to Christ the davits hadn't chosen today to go on the blink, as had happened regularly outside Lulworth.

Further east, the fifty American Rangers were starting to like this method of disembarking, where the landing craft were lowered from their davits with the assault troops already aboard. In the years to come, in the Pacific, they would fight like mad to overrule the American way of hitting a beach, where the LCAs were put in the water first and the men scrambled down to them via nets. Then the assault craft would play chase-the-next-guy's-tail in a vast circle until the lead coxswain put them all in a straight line for the landing zone. Using the American method, the LCAs cleared the parent ship faster but were then sitting ducks for any stray fighter freelancing for glory.

There were five thousand-plus men in the assault group, ranging all the way from 3 Commando's Yellow Beach in the east, across the 2nd Canadian Division in the centre, to 4 Commando's Orange Beach in the west. Mine-sweepers had combed the seas ahead of the task force, and marauding gunboats were ready to take out anything that presented a threat. Eight destroyers and a sloop were on hand to deal with whatever the gunboats couldn't take care of, as well as helping provide smoke cover. The RAF would be over before long: fifty-six fighter squadrons, four tactical reconnaissance squadrons, and five smoke-laying and close support bombing squadrons. Upwards of two hundred and fifty fighter and fighter-bomber aircraft from 11 Group to make a less than polite mess of the Luftwaffe, tempt it into a scrap away from the landing beaches. Spitfires, Hurricanes, Typhoons, Mustangs, Blenheims, Bostons.

At 0300 hours exactly the LCAs from the *Prince Albert* were lowered into the water and formed up in two columns, heading for the beach ten miles away and approximately two hours off. No one was unaware of the formidable task facing them. The Hess Battery was protected by flak towers containing anti-aircraft guns, and around the perimeter were machine-gun emplacements, anti-tank guns, minefields, and double concertina coils of barbed-wire. Their best weapons were speed, stealth, surprise.

Weapons they were not to get.

Halfway across the run-in the Germans discovered that something was amiss. By an unfortunate accident the eastern flank of the task force stumbled across some armed German trawlers. Starshells illuminated 3 Commando's gunboats and the big secret wasn't so secret any longer.

'Shit,' said Mike Halliday. Although Yellow Beaches were ten miles east, and in the darkness it wasn't possible to ascertain precisely who or what was being hit, some instinct told him it was 3 Commando under the hammer. The unit they had fought with on Vaagsö.

'Our turn next,' he bawled.

Except it wasn't. Not yet. The lighthouse on the point at Ailly kept blinking as if nothing had happened.

Four miles out they had another stroke of luck. Three ships were spotted ahead, sailing without navigation lights. They could only be German and looked like more armed trawlers from their superstructure, but they failed to observe the LCAs' silhouettes, low in a sea that was as flat as a plate.

A mile out it all changed. The lighthouse doused its illumination. From nearby starshells soared skywards. Then enemy machine guns opened up. The LCAs' tiny escort, a converted landing craft, replied with a 5-inch gun and twin Vickers mounted port and starboard. A squadron of Spitfires came over low to see what it could do to help as the first creeping fingers of dawn approached. Bedlam raged.

'Told you,' said Kovacs. 'Knew we should have worn tin hats.'

Group 2 hit Orange Two at 0453, two minutes ahead of their e.t.a. There was now a hell of a lot of shooting coming from the shore, but Kovacs still found a moment to check his watch and note the time. At a rough guess he'd made about seventeen pounds from his book.

'Just in case anyone gripes later or doesn't believe the war diary,' he said to Alphabet, 'check me that it's 0453.'

'You're fucking barmy,' said Alphabet.

'Maybe, but I'm going to be the richest nutter in Civvy Street.'

'Shut the fuck up, Henry,' said Jack to his hen, still in her carrier, who was getting a bit alarmed by all the excitement.

The Chief was playing his drum as the bow door of the LCA dropped open. Doing his Victory 'V'. Di-di-di-dah. From now on he wouldn't have much opportunity. B Troop and F Troop and a section of A Troop on Orange Two were having it worse than the remainder of A Troop and all of C Troop on Orange One. From the clifftop heavy mortar fire and machine-gun fire were pouring down on the invaders. Several of the men first ashore were killed as they tried to cross the barbed-wire, and others were wounded.

Captain Windus had his head poked over the side. He could see the coils of barbed-wire, precisely where he had known they would be from recce photographs.

'Bangalores,' he yelled.

While half a dozen men inched forward and tried to blast gaps in the wire with the Bangalore torpedoes, the lieutenant in command of the A Troop section, using scaling ladders where possible, climbed the cliffs with a small squad and silenced the machine gunners in two pillboxes with grenades. Then he and his section set off east to join the remainder of A Troop on the cliffs above Orange One.

Meanwhile Lord Lovat, carrying his personal Winchester, directed B and F Troops through the holes blasted in the barbed-wire to the banks of the River Saane, which ran almost due south, inland. The ground here was heavy after recent flooding, but B Troop led the speed march, setting a cracking pace, along the river bank to a bend a thousand yards up-river, where the whole of Group 2 turned east and advanced in extended formation across open country. One sub-section covered another, and then the first moved through while being protected by the second. Thus the Group advanced in a series of leapfrogging manoeuvres towards the sanctuary of Blancmenil le Bas wood, which was, or would be if and when they reached it, only a few hundred yards from the Hess Battery. *Achtung Minen* signs obligingly warned them where it was hazardous to tread, but not before a forward scout had stepped on an anti-personnel mine and blown himself in half.

For the moment B and F Troops were getting away with the worst of it. Up front they could hear the reassuring sounds of battle as Group 1 engaged the battery defenders, keeping them fully occupied, their attention seawards. Just as well, for it was broad daylight before Group 2 entered the wood, where they paused to take stock and draw breath before launching their own attack.

In B Troop Captain Windus had received an arm wound from mortar shrapnel, but had had it treated by a medic and was in no manner hors de combat. The Troop had also lost several men killed on the beach and several more wounded and left behind for evacuation, but there was still enough of them to complete their part of the operation. Which was to attack the machine-gun posts and buildings to the right of the battery while F Troop charged across the open ground to assault the big gun emplacements.

Before that happened, as F Troop left the wood and moved north along a narrow road under cover of smoke, they came across a German patrol detrucking prior to mounting a counter-attack on Group 1. In a brisk and vicious firefight, shooting Brens and Thompsons from the hip, F Troop slaughtered the patrol but were then, in turn, engaged by a second squad of Germans unseen in nearby farm buildings. Among others, the Troop OC was killed and command passed to a liaison officer.

The timing of the final assault had been decided as 0630 hours many weeks earlier. Shortly before that A and C Troops of Group 1 proceeded to lay down smoke, a heavy cone of LMG fire, and mortars, whose bombs hit the dry ground and sent dirt up in a straight line like an angry cat's fur.

At 0620 RAF Spitfires from 129 Squadron came over at low level to strafe the battery. Back in England there had been considerable debate about the wisdom of using close support fighters this late on, since it was hoped, and proved to be the case, that the commandos would be very close to the battery by then, putting themselves at almost as much risk from the Spitfires' cannon as the Germans. As it happened, the RAF sorties were flawless, right on the money. The battery and the surrounding buildings were shot up time and time again, but not one of the invaders received as much as a scratch from a wayward shell.

At 0630 Lord Lovat put up a series of white Very lights, the signal for A and C Troops to stop firing, that the attack was about to begin.

Jack plucked Henry from her carrier. He was sorry to see her go, but she'd only get in the way now, hinder his running. She might get hurt too. She was safer in the woods. He wasn't sure he wanted to rid himself of his good luck talisman, but it was for the best.

'Go on, fuck off. Find a cockerel and set up house.'

She seemed bemused for a moment, but then began pecking the ground. Jack put a gentle boot behind her and she scuttled away, clucking irritably. She'd probably wind up in someone's pot, but that was her look out.

'Sure she can speak French, Jack?' asked Kiley.

'There's no language barrier for what she'll get up to.'

The Chief also grounded his drum. The speed march up the River Saane had convinced him that he couldn't run across three hundred yards of killing ground with that banging against his thigh. If he got lucky, he'd come back for it later.

Captain Windus gave the order to fix bayonets. A few seconds before the charge began, B Troop witnessed a heartening sight. One of their green-faced snipers from some position of concealment knocked a German sharpshooter from his gun platform in the flak tower.

'Saw a film like that once,' grunted Kovacs, 'only that time it was an Indian out of a tree. Randolph Scott got him, I think.'

'Watch your mouth,' said the Chief. 'That could have been a relative.'

'No, this guy was a Mohican.'

Firing a pistol with his good arm, Captain Windus led B Troop's charge in a straight line, directly for the barbed-wire, urging the Bangalore torpedomen to keep up with him. Screaming like banshees and uttering all kinds of oaths, B Troop hurled themselves at the battery defenders.

An athelete in running kit and spiked shoes can cover three hundred yards on a track in something under forty seconds. It took the commandos rather longer because they had machine guns trying to prevent them from reaching the finishing tape.

Lieutenant Halliday was killed in the first hundred yards. He was at the head of 2 Section, where he should be, and they all saw him fall, fall in that peculiar manner of a man who has taken many medium-calibre rounds in his body. In a way, it appeared as if he were surrendering – the very likelihood of such a thing from Mike Halliday! – because his arms went up. But that was how men who were hit from the front died, and there was no doubt he was dead. You got to learn what it looked like after a while. He had been right in his first premonition that he wasn't going home from Jubilee.

There was no time for Jack to shout that he was taking over 2 Section. They were now getting close to the wire. Everyone knew the chain of command, anyway.

Halliday wasn't the only one to get hit. Long before the Bangalore men primed their torpedoes and blew gaps in the wire, others were falling, caught in a murderous crossfire. It seemed impossible that B Troop, and F Troop over to their left, could get anywhere near the wire with anything like their number intact. This was crazy. They needed more men. It was roughly one-on-one as far as anyone could judge, while everyone knew, even with commandos, that three-on-one in favour of the attackers was only just enough.

Oh for some of those fucking Zombies back in their funkholes in Canada, Jack cursed, seeing a Bangalore man go down and Ernie Kiley stoop and scoop up the torpedo without breaking stride.

'Zombie' was a slang term for Canadian soldiers conscripted under the NRMA, the National Resources Mobilization Act. Because of Canada's peculiar attitude towards the military, no man who wasn't a volunteer could be sent to fight overseas. A conscript, a Zombie, could only be compelled to defend Canada. Just as if there was anyone close enough to attack Canada! Though there might be if some of those weasels didn't get off their butts and help defeat Hitler and Tojo.

In a recent plebiscite Mackenzie King had asked Canadians to relieve him of his pledge never to send NRMA men overseas. He'd received it from much of English-speaking Canada, but French-speaking Quebec had rejected him. He'd caved in, needing Quebec to stay in power, not polarize the country; or worse, attempt to secede. The majority of Canadian servicemen considered the Liberal Mackenzie King spineless, and knew full well what Churchill would have done facing a similar problem.

Not all French Canadians felt the same. Like the Fusiliers Mont-Royal, currently acting as a floating reserve on Jubilee, those who fought were some of the bravest men to be had. And not all of the Zombies were French Canadian. They were out-numbered in a ratio of two-to-one by English-speaking Canadians who had taken advantage of Quebec's 'Non', who were too chicken, or comfortable, to pick up a rifle, and were willing to see others do the dirty work. They'd get their comeuppance one day, but they were needed now. If not against the Hess Battery, elsewhere, on the Canadian beaches.

Knowing that he was now a Bangalore man and, in any case, being one of the fittest in the Commando, Ernie Kiley raced on ahead after he picked up the torpedo. There were machine-gun rounds coming at him in huge arcs from every direction, but he was within thirty feet of the nearest barbed-wire before he was hit the first time. From a flank. In the side. Unlike Halliday he didn't fall. His momentum carried him forward until he was hit again, on this occasion only a few feet from the wire. Dragging the eight-foot tube he crawled towards his objective, primed the Terryl ignitor, and detonated the torpedo. He didn't quite get out of the way in time. The explosion blew the necessary gap in the wire, but took part of Kiley with it.

Seeing the gap, Jack raced for it, knowing the remainder of the section wouldn't be far behind. He paused only momentarily. It wasn't his job to take care of Kiley but to obey the CO's orders: to take the battery at all costs. But Christ, he'd known Ernie for a hell of a long time.

Part of the little guy's side was blown away. Bits of viscera were mixed up with bits of battledress, webbing, wire. It was all over, and he knew it. He wasn't going back to Maple Creek. About all Maple Creek could expect was a cable from that lousy chicken-shit government.

'Fuck it, Jack,' he said before his eyes closed. 'Fiddle-de-dee.'

Then he was dead.

The Hess Battery defenders were beginning to realize they were in real trouble. They had had their chance over the three hundred yards of open killing ground, and had taken it as best they could. But now what remained of B Troop and F Troop were through the barbed-wire and slaughtering anyone who stood in their way with rifle butt, bayonet, Thompson and grenade.

Some of the Germans elected to stand and fight behind their sandbag breastworks, some withdrew to nearby buildings, and some retreated into a labyrinth of tunnels around the battery. Some tried to surrender, but few prisoners were taken. Four, someone counted at the end, including a cook. The commandos had seen their friends hacked to pieces by murderous gunfire and were in no mood to be merciful.

When it was over Lord Lovat sent a signal to Lord Mountbatten. 'All the gun crews finished off with bayonets. Okay with you?'

That said it for all of them.

In the meantime dozens of hand-to-hand battles took place, with 2 Section in the thick of it. For every Ernie Kiley and Mike Halliday who died, four or five Germans did. The order of the day was, No Quarter.

The Chief caught sight of a Wehrmacht Unterfeldwebel, a sergeant, in the act of bayoneting in the back a wounded commando who was endeavouring to give himself a shot of morphine. He couldn't save the injured man, but he could make damned sure the Unterfeldwebel didn't live to brag about his feat.

Bellowing maniacally, he chased the German into a nearby building and cornered him. When the sergeant saw he was trapped he turned and threw down his rifle, the bayonet covered in the blood of the man he had just killed. He also attempted to smile, and said, '*Kamarad*' – in a tone of voice that implied: 'Well, we're all soldiers in this together. I won the last one, you've won this. So let's call it quits.'

The Chief shot him dead before pinning him to the floor with the German's own bayonet.

Elsewhere other Germans were being butchered where they were found. Some were young and petrified, but Ernie Kiley hadn't lived to see his twenty-first birthday, either. Others were older. Sons, fathers, husbands; it was all the same to the commandos. This was what they had been trained for, why they were selected in the first place, partly because of their mental toughness.

While B Troop took care of mopping-up operations, F Troop, under their replacement OC, the liaison officer, a captain who had already been wounded three times but who was still leading from the front, stormed the battery's gun pits, killing anyone who got in their way. Although it seemed to most, later, that they had been in battle for hours, only fifteen minutes passed between the time the white Very lights were fired and the time the battery was in F Troop's hands.

The charges to spike the guns had been prepared in England and were now rammed down the barrels of each and detonated. Lord Lovat could see what was happening, but a runner was sent to him anyway. 'The Hess Battery is no longer a threat to the ships standing offshore.'

To finish it off the battery buildings were set alight.

Now it was time to withdraw, down to Orange One according to plan, before the Germans sent in reinforcements from the direction of Varengeville and cut off 4 Commando's escape route.

The CO ordered the Union Jack to be hoisted on the captured German flagstaff and the Commando's dead, insofar as they could be found, laid beneath the flag. There were twelve of them. Other casualties to date were estimated at thirty-five. 4 Commando had been ashore for a little over two and a half hours.

Captain Windus, his already wounded arm having been hit again during the assault on the wire, sent runners to round up B Troop, those who were still not actively fighting. Even those who were were told to break contact. The returning LCAs had a schedule to keep to.

In the tunnels part of 2 Section was engaged in the lethal pursuit of two German officers, who naturally knew every inch of the ground. This pair were the only two commissioned ranks anyone had seen and Jack Lambert was determined to finish them off before heading for Orange One. They were making it difficult for him, however, and they knew their stuff. While one sprayed the tunnel behind with submachine gun fire, the other ran on. Then he would hurl a stick grenade while his companion joined him. They were playing the leapfrog game to perfection. But they could not have an inexhaustible supply of grenades. Or ammunition. Then again, neither did the pursuers. A couple of clips apiece was about the size of it, and half a dozen grenades between them.

When the runner from Captain Windus informed him that everyone else was getting out and that German armour had been spotted, Jack gave the order for all of 2 Section to leave the tunnel bar himself and the Chief.

'This won't take long. There are only two of them.'

'There are a fucking sight more than that upstairs, Jack,' protested the runner.

Jack hesitated. The runner had a point. There was no way the Commando could have wiped out all the defenders, let alone the reinforcements. When he got back up top, he might find a whole host of Germans between himself and the sea.

To hell with it. He'd give it five minutes. If the Wehrmacht officers survived that, maybe it was their day.

'How close are the others to Orange One?'

'Well, they've got the wounded.'

'The Chief and me, then. The rest of you, clear out.'

He wasn't entirely surprised to find, when everyone else had gone, that Kovacs and Alphabet were still there. They'd known Ernie well, also, and he was too tired to enter into what would only be a futile argument. Besides, four would stand a better chance than two of getting down to Orange One if the route was blocked.

It took them ten minutes of deadly stalking to catch up with the Germans, who apparently didn't know the tunnels as well as they might. Or perhaps what they thought was an egress had been blocked by collapsing masonry when the big guns were spiked, because the tunnels led to underground magazines and were directly below the now useless 150mms.

In any event, they must have been out of ammunition except for their sidearms, because around a corner appeared an MP 38 with a white handkerchief tied to the muzzle.

'They must be fucking joking,' said Kovacs.

'And the joke's on them,' said Jack grimly. 'Stand back.'

They were calling something in German, the white flag still waving frantically, when Jack pulled the pins of two of the last grenades and threw them in tandem.

After the detonations, he ran forward. The officer with the white flag had taken most of the shrapnel and was dead or unconscious. His companion was on the ground apparently unhurt but stunned, and trying to crawl away. There was nowhere to go. Ahead was a heavy steel door, its hinges buckled. It wouldn't budge one way or the other by the looks of it.

Jack finished off the crawling man and, to be on the safe side, put a short burst into the officer with the MP 38.

'Let's get out of here.'

Now there was nothing to limit speed, they made it back to the surface in two minutes. There weren't many Germans around, and those that were there were firing towards the sea. But one glance was enough to tell Jack that there was no way through to Orange Beach One. They could with luck have got to Orange Two via Blancmenil le Bas wood, but that was no earthly use. There were no LCAs coming back to Orange Two and it would take too long, even if they didn't meet opposition and the tide was right, to go along the beach from Orange Two to Orange One. The LCAs couldn't and wouldn't wait. The Troop commander would assume that anyone who wasn't there wasn't coming. Their best chance was to skirt Varengeville and make for Pourville, Green Beach. 4 Commando's brief had been to move in, destroy the battery, then move out, which they had succeeded in doing magnificently in a little over two and a half hours. But the South Saskatchewans and the Queen's Own were not due to re-embark for some time yet. It was a long way to Green Beach, five miles or more with the route they'd be forced to take, and they'd have to avoid German patrols every yard. It was all they had. They couldn't wait until dark. Everyone would have gone by then.

'Sounds about right,' said the Chief.

Alphabet nodded, but Kovacs pulled a long face.

'Sounds more dicey than right.'

'Buck up,' said Jack with more optimism than he actually felt. 'The show isn't over 'til the fat lady sings.'

'We've got company,' said the Chief.

It was Henry, who had somehow made her way out of the wood and found them. Jack popped her in her carrier.

'Now I know we'll be okay.'

They succeeded in leaving the battery area without being seen. All the smoke around from blazing buildings and the RAF still flying protective sorties meant that it was easier than they had expected. Then they struck east, keeping well clear of the road.

There were hundreds of German troops milling about, many motorized, but there was also a great deal of confusion, especially up front, around Pourville and, further on, in the port of Dieppe itself. One hell of a battle was going on there.

4 Commando made a perfect withdrawal, with C Troop laying down smoke and covering the other Troops with LMG and rifle fire. A section from A Troop took out a German patrol threatening danger, and another accounted for a mortar crew which had zeroed in on the Goatley boats ferrying out the wounded. Off the beach the navy had deployed smoke-floats, which covered the commandos re-embarking on the landing craft. Two miles offshore the wounded were transferred to a destroyer while the landing craft made their own way home.

By 0830 hours 4 Commando had left French waters. At the same hour Sergeant Lambert and his companions were still four and a half miles from Pourville.

ELEVEN

If the four Canadians had suspected for an instant what was happening across the rest of the Front, they would have taken their chances and run the gauntlet down to Orange One. The destruction by 4 Commando of the Hess Battery was virtually the only success of Operation Jubilee.

On central Beaches Green, Blue, Red and White their fellow countrymen were being slaughtered wholesale. What appeared, from a distance, to be an equal battle, with the RAF taking on the Stukas – easy meat – and 109s – tough beef – was, close up, a one-sided affair. Many Canadians died sprawled across the barbed-wire barricades, some of them, heroically, having thrown themselves over the wire where it couldn't be cut, to act as a bridge for their comrades to walk over. Many others never even left their landing craft. Very, very few got off the beaches. After recovering from the initial shock that the Churchill Government had had the temerity to try something as bold and as foolhardy as this, for the Germans Jubilee became a turkey shoot.

The objectives for the South Saskatchewans and the Queen's Own Camerons on Green Beach were the twin targets of the heavily fortified Les Quatre Vents farm and the Hindenburg Battery of guns on the west headland. This achieved, troops were then expected to move through the valley of the River Scie, hook left, and capture the St Aubin airfield and a German divisional HQ at Arques la Bataille.

This achieved. Two words, and not the slightest chance of an all-round knock-out blow without armour support from the main Dieppe Beaches Red and White. Which never arrived.

Due to an error in navigation the LCTs carrying the tanks of the Calgary Regiment, briefed to land at the same time as the infantry of the Essex Scottish and the Royal Hamiltons, were fifteen minutes late. When the armour debouched, Red and White Beaches were already littered with Canadian dead and wounded, and the tankers that hadn't been hit on the way in foundered in the shallows or on the shingle, where they were hammered unmercifully, now it was light, by artillery fire and anti-tank guns. Only a handful made it across the sea wall, and none got much further than the Casino, into Dieppe itself. The South Saskatchewans and the Camerons would be receiving no help from that quarter.

Communications broke down rapidly. Where the wirelesses weren't hit and destroyed, the operators were, or the officers whose task it was to relay messages back. Senior officers, ashore and on board the ships standing off, had no means of knowing what was going on. Trying to direct the battle was hopeless. Apart from guesswork, which isn't much use when the enemy is alert and organized.

Every square foot of the beaches was covered by German forward observation officers, directing heavy artillery, 88s and captured French guns against the invader. The destroyers replied with 4-inch guns when a target could be identified. But 4-inch guns, valuable against other warships, were ineffectual against dug-in shore-based targets.

Before long there was no Allied chain of command. Regiments didn't fight as organized units. Men of different battalions and frequently different nationalities fought for each other where they found each other. They frequently died alongside men whose names they did not know.

All the time, because Lord Lovat's Commando had been successful, the brass considered the 'Reconnaissance in Force' to be going well. It didn't matter that a landing that should have taken place in darkness began in daylight. It was unimportant that Intelligence reports had been faulty, giving the height of the sea wall facing the Camerons, for example, as three feet instead of seven. The Canadians were tough. The Canadians could take it.

On White Beach shortly after 0830 hours the Royal Marines of A Commando were committed to the battle. Leading from the front in the first LCA, their CO quickly perceived, once through the smoke-screen, that White Beach was a shambles and that a landing would be a fiasco. It was not part of his function, he judged, to sacrifice men needlessly.

He donned a pair of white gauntlets, stood up in the LCA carrying him, and waved everyone else off. He was shot in the head almost instantly, though whether the fatal round emanated from an onshore sniper or from one of the marauding 109s, now getting the better of the fight with the RAF, was never established. The few Marines who got ashore died.

On Yellow Beach fewer than ten per cent of 3 Commando landed, though they succeeded in partly disabling the Goebbels Battery at Berneval. The other major batteries, however, were not silenced then or ever, and could fire at will. The Rommel and Bismarck above Blue Beach, the Hindenburg above Green Beach. What was already a death-trap now became an abattoir.

When Jack and his fellow Canadians got closer, they knew they were in trouble. It wasn't just that the big guns were still firing, although by this hour, if the landing was being judged a success, they should have been out of action. Worse, however, in their view, was that the Stukas were continuing to dive-bomb the warships and landing craft. If the RAF was winning the aerial battle, the Stukas would have fled by now, leaving it to the 109s. While they couldn't see the actual beach below Pourville from where they were, it must be a Holy Christ of a mess. A child of ten could have divined that Jubilee was a balls-up, in spite of the smoke and flames. Had it been the other way round, there would be Germans retreating inland. Instead they were all going the other way, and there wasn't a Churchill tank in sight. All the armour to be seen carried black crosses.

They had made it this far without encountering any opposition. Now they understood why. The Germans were not expecting any of the enemy to be behind them.

'Like I said earlier,' said Kovacs, 'dicey. I'll lay six-to-four that someone's already given the order to withdraw.'

It was now 0945 hours and, although Kovacs had no means of knowing it, the decision to pull out had been taken at 0900, it now being appreciated by the force commander that the operation was a failure. The remaining destroyers in the gun-line were to follow the rescue craft in and protect them as far as possible, beginning at 1020 hours. The only problem was, with communications being almost nil, how to tell the forward troops to get back to the beaches.

Jack could see Pourville in the distance even through the pall of smoke above it. The town was, he estimated, about a mile and a half away. He tried to visualize in his head the entire battle plan as drawn in the briefing room. As far as he could recall the first objective for the Camerons and the South Saskatchewans was Les Quatre Vents farm, which was approximately a mile due east of Pourville and across the River Scie. Okay, that was out of the question. Bridges over the Scie would be well guarded and there was no way he was going to attempt a river crossing with just four men in broad daylight. It had to be Pourville, which was at the end of the road they were presently on – or rather off, several hundred yards to the seaward side but using it as a marker. If the Camerons and South Saskatchewans were pulling out, they would do so through Pourville. Of course, there were probably a thousand German troops surrounding Pourville, but he'd face that when he had to. Certainly, trying to scramble down to the beaches before they were anywhere near Green Beach was no alternative. The clifftop was lined with pillboxes, and they were all doing good business by the sound of it.

They checked ammunition. About enough for a brisk fire-fight, which he hoped to avoid. He also thought briefly about Henry before deciding to take her. For now, anyway. The last time he let her go they weren't in this mess and Ernie and Mike Halliday had been alive.

The closer they got to Pourville, the more they realized the magnitude of the task facing them. There were grey uniforms everywhere up ahead, and more motorized infantry hurtling along the road to Pourville from Varengeville. They could see that the Germans were under attack too, presumably by the withdrawing Camerons and SSR, but there was little chance of reaching Canadians.

Then they encountered what seemed, at the time, to be a small miracle.

There were suddenly no more motorized columns coming from Varengeville. The roar of vehicles from the road to their right stopped. And in one of those remarkable happenings that occasionally occur in war, for a fraction of a second there were no planes overhead, no big guns firing. Silence. For a fraction of a second. Then they all heard, from the road, the sound of an auto engine turning over. And not catching.

'Take a look, Chief,' ordered Jack.

Greyfoot was away five minutes.

'A Kübelwagen,' he said when he returned. 'Stalled by the side of the road. Looks like a communications vehicle. Bristling with aerials, anyway. Two of them with their heads stuck under the hood. Not another fucking thing in sight.'

The K-wagen was the military version of the Volkswagen. An open-topped four-seater that functioned for the Wehrmacht the way the Jeep did for the Americans.

'I can drive it,' said Jack, 'but what I know about engines you could write on a fly's balls and still leave room for the National Anthem.'

'Leave it to me,' grinned Alphabet. 'They taught me a few things in Headingly. I knew that fucking prison would pay off one day.'

'Fighting knives,' said Jack. 'Me and the Chief. Distract them, Kovacs.'

'Give me Henry.'

The Germans could have been father and son. The one scratching his head while standing back from the hood was overweight and forty. The other, around twenty, smoking a cigarette, was leaning against the near-side of the K-wagen. From the cover of the trees Jack could see that they were wearing Signal Corps *Waffenfarbe*. And they didn't seem anxious to join their comrades in Pourville.

There was nothing else on the road. They were the last of the Varengeville reinforcements. Well, for now.

Both men were wearing sidearms and helmets. There would be a machine pistol in clips in the vehicle, Jack judged. Come on, Kovacs, where are you?

Kovacs appeared, came out of the trees twenty yards ahead of the K-wagen with his hands above his head. 'I'm surrendering.'

'Shit,' muttered Jack, 'who writes his lines?'

The two Germans froze, startled, while they absorbed the sight of this unshaven, bareheaded *Tommi*, a submachine gun in one hand and a hen dangling by its feet in the other. Then both fumbled for their sidearms, which was as near as made no difference the last move they ever made. The ultimate one was when they fell to the road, their throats neatly slit.

'Get rid of them,' snapped Jack, taking Henry and putting the frightened hen back in her carrier. 'Leave their helmets.'

Anxiously he glanced up and down the road. Nothing.

While the Chief and Kovacs disposed of the corpses, Alphabet fiddled under the hood.

'Try it now.'

Jack turned over the engine. It caught first time.

'Coil,' said Alphabet triumphantly. 'Just a wire. Dumb bastards.'

Jack put on the older man's steel helmet while Alphabet wore the younger's. These two occupied the front seats. The Chief and Kovacs climbed in behind, perching uncomfortably atop the radio equipment. Jack debated taking the dead German's tunics, but decided against. There was a chance they wouldn't make the beach. If so, he didn't want to be captured in enemy uniform. Nor, if they got through, did he want to be fired on by his own side. A helmet he could discard quickly.

'What's the plan, Boss?' asked Alphabet.

'We'll drive and see what happens. Keep the Thompsons out of sight.'

Like most miracles, this one promised more than it delivered, and wasn't a patch on turning water into wine or making a banquet out of a few trout and some bread. Since leaving the Hess Battery their luck had held. Outside Pourville it ran out.

Probably, although they never established this for certain, the field police at the roadblock were trying to wave them down because, further on, Canadians were fighting a delaying rearguard action. But a roadblock was a roadblock, and none of them had enough German to try and bluff their way through.

It wasn't much of a barrier – a red-and-white pole across two saw-horses – and, because the K-wagen was so far behind the convoy it had been part of, there were no other vehicles waiting in line.

'Ram it, Jack,' said Alphabet.

'I intend to. Hold on.'

A few hundred yards beyond the obstruction a fierce battle was taking place. That meant Canadians. Get through the obstruction and they were on their way to the beach. It might not be very pleasant down there, but it was superior to the alternative.

The field police could see that the K-wagen wasn't going to stop when it was fifty yards from the barrier. They couldn't know why, but they had their orders and opened fire.

If he'd kept going, Jack was to think later, he might have crashed through. But it was asking a lot when there were suddenly dozens of 9mm rounds heading in your direction. He yanked at the steering-wheel and went into a tail-spin. The K-wagen hit the barrier broadside and turned over, spilling out its passengers.

Jack lost consciousness. When he opened his eyes they were

staring into a rifle muzzle, the rifle being held by a tough-looking corporal. Nearby, another German had just finished wringing Henry's neck.

So she was going in the game-bag after all. For that matter, they were all going in the bag. A quick glance around told him that the Chief, Kovacs and Alphabet had suffered no more than a few minor cuts and bruises when the K-wagen turned turtle. One thing, though, about that bag. Wherever they were taking him, he wasn't staying. No, sir.

'About that fat lady, Jack,' said Kovacs. 'I think she just sang our number.'

Many reasons were given for the Dieppe débacle. Wrong timing. Unseasoned troops. Poor intelligence. Sheer bad luck.

Too many men, not enough men. Inadequate air cover. Beach-head too wide, beach-head too narrow. Wrong landing zones, wrong month, wrong commanders. They had learnt, the Allies said, that you couldn't support and supply invasion beaches from the sea. And the Mulberry Harbours on D-Day were part of the lessons learnt.

When the Canadians were being carted off to the POW cages, some of the French civilians called to them: 'They were ready for you. They knew you were coming three weeks ago.'

No one ever found out whether that was rumour or truth, but the casualty figures were the same either way.

The RAF flew 2617 sorties and lost 106 planes, including eighty-eight Spitfires. German losses vary according to sources, with the RAF claiming 170 planes and the Luftwaffe admitting to forty-eight destroyed and twenty-four damaged. Probably the real figure lies somewhere between the two estimates.

All twenty-eight tanks that managed to get ashore were lost. So too was the destroyer *Berkeley* and numerous landing craft, thirty-four ships in all. The Royal Navy lost eighty-one officers and 469 men killed, wounded or missing.

The total military lost was 494 officers and 3890 men killed, wounded or missing. Or POWs. The Commando losses were twenty-four officers and 223 men.

By far the greatest number of casualties were suffered by the Canadians: 215 officers and 3164 men, well over half the total strike force. Only one Canadian regiment, the Fusiliers Mont-Royal, brought back its CO. Two thousand Canadians became prisoners-of-war, and one thousand died on the beaches.

Black Wednesday, they called it. For those who survived to be taken to the Stalags, there were to be many more.

TWELVE

Christmas 1942

The camp they finally wound up in was numbered Stalag XIII K and situated a few miles east of Frankfurt-am-Main. It was small by German standards, having accommodation for a mere six hundred men, mostly Canadian but with a sprinkling of American and British troops, all army or commandos. All of the incarcerated Canadians and Americans, but only some of the British, had been captured at Dieppe. The remaining British had been in the bag since Dunkirk. The majority of prisoners taken after the ill-fated Operation Jubilee had finished up in a camp much further east, in Stalag VIII B at Lamsdorf in Upper Silesia, rumour had it. The Germans never explained why some were in one camp and others elsewhere, frequently men from the same regiment captured at the same hour. Whether it was a question of removing blankets or switching off the water supply, or holding a *Sonderappell*, a special rollcall, in the middle of the night, they seemed to do everything on a whim. The Kriegies – *Kriegsgefangenen* or prisoners-of-war – had few rights notwithstanding the Geneva Convention. To speak out of turn often meant a beating. To complain about conditions or treatment or the absence of mail or Red Cross parcels earned a man the cooler, solitary confinement. To do the unthinkable and strike a camp officer or NCO was to risk being shot. Or, worse, to be subjected to a refined form of the Nazis' *Nacht und Nebel* – Night and Fog – decree, whereby a man was spirited away during the small hours and was never heard from or seen again. Not to know whether a friend was dead or being tortured in some Gestapo cellar was worse than seeing him executed.

The Germans thought they could get away with being tough during these months. Although the invasion of England had failed, so too had Jubilee, and thus the invasion of the Continent was a long way off. El Alamein and Stalingrad, when the tide began to turn against the Wehrmacht, were still to come.

Stalag XIII K contained only other ranks – enlisted men, the Americans called them – from senior NCOs down to privates. The adjacent Oflag XIII K – officers' camp – held around one hundred commissioned ranks and was separated from the Stalag by high barbed-wire and two hundred yards of open ground covered by machine-gun posts in goon towers. It was one of these officers, a classics scholar, who nicknamed XIII K, Oflag and Stalag, Camp Calypso, after the nymph in Greek mythology who imprisoned Odysseus for eight years. Few understood the reference, but the name caught on. It had a pleasant ring to it, and there was very little pleasant about XIII K. Nor had there been for any of the inmates since August 19.

Directly after recovering consciousness, Jack saw two of the field police examining the K-wagon and jabbering excitedly to one another. One pointed back up the road towards Varengeville. He couldn't understand a word they were saying, but he could guess. Where had these four *Tommis* come from all by themselves? Where had they obtained the K-wagen? What had happened to the original occupants?

The corporal pointing the rifle at him, the senior rank at the roadblock as far as he could judge, joined in the discussion. Then he sent a dispatch-rider towards Varengeville. Uh-uh, thought Jack, hoping that the Chief and Kovacs had hidden the bodies well. They wouldn't have done, of course. There hadn't been time for that.

He exchanged glances with the Chief, Kovacs and Alphabet, sitting a few feet away, their hands, like his, clasped behind their heads.

While the motorcyclist was away, the field police corporal ordered them by gesture to empty their pockets. Everything went: documents, wallets, paybooks, coins, currency. Their personal weapons, fighting knives and spare ammunition magazines had already been taken, of course. Then they were instructed to remove their wristwatches, and finally individually hand-searched in case they were trying to conceal something. A strip-search would probably come later, if they weren't shot in the meantime. The loot all went on a pile. The Canadians had no doubt that it was *loot*, personal booty. The manner in which the corporal examined the wristwatches demonstrated that.

The dispatch-rider returned after forty minutes. He went up to the corporal, said something in German, and drew the blade of his hand across his throat, an unmistakable gesture.

'We'd better be ready, Jack,' said Kovacs.

Jack nodded briefly. They had been trained to use their hands against weapons, though under the circumstances hands were unlikely to be much use. Still, they weren't going quietly against a wall.

White-faced with rage at the death of two Germans, the corporal screamed at Kovacs for opening his mouth, and followed up by side-swiping him across the head with his rifle.

Jack, Greyfoot and Alphabet got to their feet as one man, and half a dozen rifle bolts clicked ominously.

Their war might have ended then and there if an officer had not at that moment driven up, standing on the running-board of a truck. He shouted something at the corporal, who sprang to attention and began, evidently, explaining what had happened to the original occupants of the K-wagen. Again the gesture of the hand across the throat.

The officer, an Hauptmann – captain, listened in silence before waving the corporal to one side. He walked over to the Canadians and peered at their unit flashes. Then he collected their paybooks from the pile of loot. Everything else remained there.

He handed the paybooks to Jack.

'You redistribute them, Sergeant,' he said in good if accented English.

Jack accepted them. He was in two minds whether or not to salute the German captain. That was the rule, after all. He decided against. He'd start the way he meant to go on.

'We're prisoners-of-war,' he said. 'We have some rights.' In those early days he really believed they had.

'You must consider yourselves fortunate you're still alive to make a protest,' said the Hauptmann mildly. 'The two signalmen you killed were not so lucky. It's the war, I understand that, but please do not try my patience.' He added a sentence that they were to hear frequently in the weeks and months to come: *'Für euch ist der Krieg zu Ende.'* He obligingly translated. 'For you the war is over. You would be advised to remember that. Now, you will go with these men.'

Hardened though they thought they were, the former Patricias were shocked to the core when, on being marched at bayonet point from Pourville to the centre of Dieppe, they saw how the remainder of the invasion force now in captivity had fared. At each street corner their small column grew in length as more prisoners coming up from the beaches were added to it, many of them with the most dreadful wounds. The ambulatory were being helped along by their comrades;

the more seriously injured being carried on stretchers. Some had lost limbs and should have been hospitalized immediately. Some had suffered appalling burns. A few, judging by their bandages, were blind or would go blind.

They had suspected that the 'Reconnaissance in Force' was a failure before hijacking the K-wagen, but were totally unprepared for the extent of the debacle. At worst they'd judged they had been unlucky in getting cut off from B Troop and failing to crash the roadblock, and had expected to be joined by no more than a few hundred others en route to a Stalag. But there had to be a thousand, maybe double that, being prodded along. Everywhere they looked there were men in khaki.

The walking wounded were faring no better than their unwounded comrades at the hands of the German escorts. It didn't matter if a man was faint through loss of blood and needed to rest or obtain a drink of water. If he faltered he was slapped back into line. So was anyone else who tried to help him. With the butt of a rifle if he was lucky or the point of a bayonet if he wasn't. And not just a jab, a pinprick. The Germans didn't give a damn if they inflicted another wound. Anyone who fell by the wayside and could not regain his feet was dragged out of the column and up a side street. Some were never seen again. To protest invited a beating.

Jack was enraged at the capricious punishment being handed out. The commandos had treated the prisoners they'd captured on Vaagsö without much gentleness, but they hadn't been vicious towards men who were no longer a threat. In England during the Blitz they had witnessed British soldiers, and British bobbies, intervene when Luftwaffe aircrew who had bailed out were in danger of being lynched by angry civilians. How the hell could a so-called civilized nation behave towards wounded men in such a manner? And these guys weren't even SS.

Had the French had to put up with this kind of treatment since 1940? If so, no wonder the Resistance wasn't as strong as some of its armchair critics in England claimed it should be.

But they'd pay for it, these bastards, some day and one way or another. They wouldn't pay because of Ernie Kiley or Mike Halliday or even for belting Kovacs around a skull a grenade couldn't dent. They'd pay for making wounded Canadians suffer.

Jack recalled telling the Chief, once, back in London during a leave, that he didn't hate Krauts and didn't enjoy killing them. Okay, cancel that. He'd break them before they broke him.

They were lining the sides of the roads as the prisoners entered the town, the Dieppoise, and in one respect they still had some fight left in them, men and women alike. Some guts. When men of the Fusiliers Mont-Royal started singing the 'Marseillaise', Frenchmen and Frenchwomen and even small children joined in. Anglo-Canadians didn't always know the words, but they knew the tune and could hum along. It was a heartening experience. It was also one of the last.

Thanks to the insistence of a medical officer and the chaplain from the Royal Hamiltons – who had allowed themselves to be captured, the Canadians learnt later, when both could have escaped in one of the last rescue boats – the more seriously wounded were attended to on arriving in Dieppe. For some it was far too late, and they died. Others became amputees because of the delays. At five p.m. outside the main Dieppe hospital, where they had been allowed to rest briefly, all those who were uninjured or whose injuries were regarded as slight were ordered to their feet, several thousand of them, an unbelievable and depressing sight. Not a single regiment that had taken part in Jubilee was unrepresented among the POWs, and few men had eaten for close on sixteen hours.

Some had lost much of their uniform during the landings, torn to shreds by the barbed-wire or blown off on the beaches. Many had lost their footwear. Men who were more fortunate made private pacts to go barefoot part of the way and allow their boots to be used by anyone who fit them. For it was now made clear by the Germans that they had a long march ahead of them and that there was no transport available for prisoners.

This was a lie, they found out later. There was transport, rail and road. The march was further punishment.

Their destination was certain to be Paris, some calculated, recalling a map of France and deducing that the Germans would be unable to resist displaying their prisoners to Parisians. Others couldn't believe Paris was where they were headed. Wasn't Paris over a hundred miles away? How the hell could anyone be expected to march a hundred miles without, for many of them, footwear and adequate clothing, even though some had now fashioned makeshift shoes out of Mae Wests and anything else they had managed to salvage. How the hell could they go a hundred miles without food and water, none of which was forthcoming as yet?

But Paris it was. Or rather, Verneulles, a transit camp twelve miles short of the French capital.

Whether it took them two days or three days or a week, and whether they stopped twice or a dozen times, few of them could remember when they arrived at Verneulles. All they had had to eat were small chunks of black bread and a little water, plus anything else they could beg from, or that was surreptitiously slipped to them by, the French civilians who lined the boulevards to see what they had hoped would be a liberating force taken into ignominious captivity. If these were the much vaunted *Tommis* about whom such a lot had been heard via clandestine radios, Hitler would be occupying France for many years.

The wounded were in a terrible state when they got to Verneulles, and the shoeless had developed abscesses that were likely to become gangrenous unless treated fast. The Canadian doctors taken into captivity did what they could, aided by German surgeons and orderlies who at least appeared to have heard of Hippocrates, but medical supplies were limited, or anyway not forthcoming, and amputation was the order of the day if there was no other solution.

A senior officer protested that the majority of the men could not walk a step further. He was informed they would not have to. From here on, after initial processing, they would be taken by train to their permanent camps. At the time a rail journey sounded like manna from heaven, though no one expected to be travelling Canadian Pacific.

Jack and his fellow Patricias, and some British troops who had been taken from 3 Commando, had fared, even after sharing boots, better than men from the infantry regiments. Thanks to the rigorous selection process for Achnacarry and the brutal training schedule there, they were more accustomed to enduring hardship. But even they were suffering from lack of nourishment.

It was a deliberate ploy, they understood now, not exclusively punishment, to keep them marching day and night with minimum sustenance. They all knew, and of course the Germans would too, that the best time to make an escape attempt was within the first few hours after capture, when morale was still high and they were strong. When confusion was their ally. But short rations, shared footwear and guards who made it abundantly clear that any recaptured escaper would be shot on the spot alongside the nearest six men, no questions asked and no appeal granted, meant that not a single man had tried to get away.

Before the first day was over it occurred to someone in authority that they had a fair number of commandos in Verneulles, who were likely to be a little more determined to get out than anyone else. The Germans did not underestimate the Canadian infantrymen, far from it, but as a matter of record they knew what 3 Commando had achieved on Vaagsö and how Lord Lovat's Commando had destroyed the Hess Battery.

Accordingly, when the initial processing took place and paybooks were examined, troops of 3 and 4 Commando and the few American Rangers taken into captivity were herded to one side. Close to a row of gallows, as it happened, though this appeared to be a coincidence, or a less than subtle reminder. In any event, the commandos and Rangers were kept apart from the other Kriegies and watched over day and night by heavily armed guards, some of them SS. There was no opportunity to escape and their daily rations were designed to sap their strength and weaken their will.

Morning and evening they were issued with a bucket of thin soup, little more than cabbage water in which an occasional dead rodent turned up, and 250 grams of black bread. In modern terms about five thin slices with a total daily nutritional value, soup and bread, of 550 calories. No butter, naturally, and no other animal fats. No vitamins, either.

To sustain life, except for someone dieting, and then only over a short period with extra vitamins thrown in to make up the deficit, takes around 1200 calories per day. In less than seventy-two hours the POWs' major enemy became hunger, not Germany. Not even Kovacs could solve the problem.

In many respects the starvation diet had a worse effect on the commandos and Rangers than on the ordinary infantrymen. Because of their specialist duties and the need to keep up an inordinate amount of mental vigour and physical strength, even in wartime commandos ate better than most other servicemen. Remove the food they were accustomed to and they would deteriorate faster.

If that was the Third Reich's theory, it didn't entirely work out, although inadequate rations and the presence of SS guards with itchy trigger fingers ensured that no one escaped from Verneulles. Those who did get out went in a pine box due to wounds or disease.

They were there five days. On the fifth day they were marched in columns to the railway station at Verneulles, where each man was given a loaf of black bread and, between two, a can of liverwurst. And warned that it would have to last them. The Fusiliers Mont-Royal and any other identifiable French-Canadians were handed apples and extra rations. A gift, the packages said, from Vichy France to non-European France.

The French-Canadians accepted the packages graciously and promptly split the contents half and half with non-French Canadians.

It took a while to get everyone lined up for the trains. Freight-cars, rather, which were labelled prominently: Forty men or eight horses.

'I'll go with the horses,' said Kovacs. 'You guys are starting to stink.'

'And you're the Queen of the May, of course,' said Alphabet.

It didn't take long to discern that there were two groups of trains and that the POWs were being divided up in a ratio of 3-to-1. Some were obviously heading one way, some another. The officers had already gone to their own Oflag.

The Chief did a quick check, wondering if the division was by regiments. That didn't seem to be so. Nor were all the commandos and Rangers in one bunch.

'Maybe our lot are going to Italy,' said Alphabet. 'It stays pretty warm in Italy all year round, I read somewhere. In the south.'

'You don't think this is warm, bugwit?' said Kovacs. It was around seventy degrees in the station. 'You sound like Kiley.'

'Shut up about Kiley,' said Jack.

Kovacs did not take offence. Jack had a lot on his mind. Kovacs knew – they all knew – that Jack had been given an escape-route briefing two days before Jubilee, although Jack had naturally not confirmed it. But if there were ways out of Germany, out of Europe, he might know them. Or how to interpret BBC broadcasts once they were in their permanent camp and could manufacture a radio. Or how to get information into the camp, or out. Or what anyone fortunate enough to make a 'home run' should look out for on the way. Troop concentrations. Effects of bombing on the morale of German civilians. Any obvious shortages of men and materials. Queues for food. Things like that. For the brass were not being entirely unselfish in wanting a man home. Sure they'd be glad to see him, and put out the red carpet; but what they mostly wanted him back in the UK for was to give them information that agents-in-place could not provide.

Kovacs could see Jack scanning the massed ranks of POWs, trying to establish, perhaps, who was going one way, who another. Who, if anyone, had been at the same briefing. From another regiment, of course. There could be no one from 4 Commando.

So much for looking forward to a rail journey, they were to think an hour later. Forty men or eight horses in a freight-car would have been a tight squeeze, but the Germans had crammed at least fifty men into each. There was only a tiny grille for fresh air and a single large pail to be used as a sanitation bucket – if a man could reach it, with forty-nine of his fellow Kriegies hemming him in. Many men didn't, and by far the worst aspect of the journey to Stalag XIII K was standing or lying in one's own filth.

The Germans made a serious mistake by transporting the Jubilee POWs from Verneulles to Frankfurt and Lamsdorf like the cattle or horses that normally occupied the freight-cars. They allowed the Canadians and the British and the Americans to see their nation for what it actually was, one that didn't give a damn about human dignity. When the Third Reich was finally overrun, there were many who were apologists for the Germans. 'Ah, it wasn't all of them, it was just the Nazis. There were crimes and atrocities, sure, but that was just the SS.'

No so. Emphatically not so. It was convenient to blame the Nazis and the SS because that, by implication, let everyone else off the hook. But there were ordinary soldiers on the trains, manning machine guns on the flat-cars, who could have shown a little humanity. Not overt. It didn't have to be that. No one was expecting a roast beef sandwich with all the trimmings or clean linen or a hot shower. But a glance, a look of sympathy for a fellow creature. 'I'm sorry about all this, but there's fuck all I can do about it.'

It never happened. The Wehrmacht was delighted to see the POWs from Jubilee humiliated.

The wounded going to Stalag XIII K fared hardly better than the unharmed. They travelled by freight-car too, if not quite so many to a carriage. But there was still only straw on the floor beneath their stretchers, straw fouled by the previous bovine or equine occupants. There was only the same large pail for sanitation, for those who could make it by themselves or be assisted there by the two medical officers travelling with them. There was only a milk-churn full of stale and unclean water for quenching thirst. And there were few stops for the sliding doors to be thrown open. When they were, when German Red Cross women tried to give food and drink to the occupants of the freight-cars, the sustenance was swept from their hands by ill-tempered guards and ground under jackboots. Precious food, life-giving and irreplaceable.

None of the men who emerged from the train east of Frankfurt and marched to the camp held anything but an abiding hatred for all things German. Many were bloodied and all were filthy, but all had a little pride left, and some hope. Until they saw Stalag XIII K.

They had been expecting something like Verneulles, but this was much worse. Even the cheering British troops who greeted them, in the bag since Dunkirk with few means of knowing who else was in the war and who was winning, did nothing to raise the newcomers' spirits. If Verneulles was the anteroom to hell, this was the real thing.

End to end the Stalag measured eight hundred yards, side to side three hundred and fifty. The inner perimeter fence was nine feet high and constructed of barbed-wire, of which they had seen more than enough. A yard in front of this was a trip-wire twelve inches off the ground. To cross this for any reason was to risk being shot.

Ten feet separated the inner wire from the outer, which was twelve feet high, again barbed-wire. At regular intervals there were elevated goon towers – 'goon' after Alice the Goon, a ridiculous creature in the Popeye comics. Each tower was also a machine-gun post and contained a searchlight. Between the towers at intervals of forty or fifty yards were boundary lights, less powerful than the searchlights but capable of illuminating the immediate area. The trees had been cut down for sixty yards in each direction beyond the compound on the three sides that did not face the Oflag. Anyone with immediate thoughts of tunnelling out was in for a hell of a long dig.

There were a dozen accommodation huts in the compound, each containing a tiny stove, a trestle table, and about half as many benches for seating as were needed. Each hut was capable of holding sixty men in two-tier bunks, but was split down the middle by a washroom served by just two cold-water taps. At the end of every hut was a latrine.

The commandant's quarters and the administration block, they would learn later, was the large building at the south end of the compound. Other huts served as general stores, kitchens, sick quarters, laundry and cell block. There was also a communal latrine for use when the prisoners were locked out of their huts as punishment or during a shakedown.

Among those most depressed was Alphabet. In Headingly, unpleasant though it was, he had known the length of his sentence. Here it could be years. Unless there was a swift Allied victory which, judging by the fuck-up at Dieppe, was unlikely. Or unless he got out.

To begin with on arrival they were lined up, searched for any useful implement they might have picked up on the way, photographed and given their POW numbers. They were told, by an officer who spoke English, that the camp rules were posted in each hut. The most important, however, were two, and would be given verbally. First, any escape attempt would be punished severely. Second, only private soldiers would be compelled to work. In accordance with the Geneva Convention, NCOs would not be forced to labour.

Many of them wondered at this. Up to now, the Germans hadn't shown much regard for the Geneva Convention. Then they cottoned on. Work, whatever the nature, would obviously take place outside the camp. By definition of achieving rank, NCOs were supposed to be more enterprising than private soldiers, and any escape attempt would stand a better chance of success if the barbed-wire did not have to be negotiated. It would be difficult, now they had all been photographed, for an NCO to change places with a private soldier and get on a work detail. Difficult, but not impossible. It was something to bear in mind.

They were allocated quarters by the guards, but it didn't take long, if close friends were separated, to arrange swaps. Jack and his fellow Patricias wound up in Hut 6B.

No clothes were issued, for the moment, to those unfortunates who were without them or in rags. No footwear, either, and there was only a single thin blanket given to each man. Plus a spoon to eat with. No knives or forks to devour what quickly came to be called *cordon gris* rations.

If anything these were worse than Verneulles and comprised, per day, a pint of weak cabbage soup which frequently contained dead, and sometimes demonstrably live, caterpillars and other creepy-crawlies, and four slices of black bread. The calorie count was still hovering around the 500 mark.

At weekends, if the Germans were in the mood and no one had upset them, there was a minute issue of cheese, which few could get as far as their mouths because of its foul smell, and even fewer keep down. A small piece of liverwurst was also on the menu.

Occasionally a few potatoes were added to the soup, but until the first of the Red Cross parcels arrived – and the Germans made clear, not bothering about the Geneva Convention on this occasion, that these parcels were a privilege and not a right – it was back to starvation rations or stealing from the kitchens. Jack put Kovacs and Alphabet to work on this, but it was several weeks before Kovacs got organized. Even then, the pickings were slim.

Jack Lambert took charge of Hut 6B from the beginning. He was a natural leader who knew what he wanted and how to get it, and he was one of the few peacetime NCOs in the compound. He was far from the senior NCO in the Stalag, however. There were several CSMs in another hut and a couple of WO2s around. The single RSM to be taken into captivity had been sent to Lamsdorf.

When it came to electing a Compound Leader at the end of the first week, most of the men wanted Sergeant Lambert. He turned them down.

'Give it to one of the WO2s.'

'Why, Jack?' Kovacs wanted to know. 'You're the best qualified for the job.'

'Maybe, but I don't want it. I'll look after 6B and maybe 6A, but that's as far as it goes.'

The WO2 who eventually accepted the job, Regimental Quartermaster Sergeant Maitland, understood Jack's reluctance. Unlike in the Oflags, where the senior officer automatically assumed command, regardless of ability and whether he wanted to or not, an elected Compound Leader, whose job it was to represent the men and pester the camp authorities if they stepped too far out of line, had taken on a voluntary responsibility. Complaints would be funnelled through him and he would become a marked man with the goons. He would find it harder to escape than most, not only because of having to leave behind the people who trusted him, and who had voted for him, to fend for themselves. In effect a Compound Leader was giving up his own crack at freedom.

Personally RQMS Maitland thought they all had about as much chance as a snowball in hell of getting out, but he rather suspected Sergeant Lambert wanted to try.

He did, but not yet. Escape wasn't priority number one. Survival was. They couldn't manufacture food out of thin air, the Kriegies, but the NCOs could make damned sure no one became wire-happy and tried something foolish like charging armed guards, or became a stool pigeon for the Germans to obtain better treatment.

With this in mind during the month of September, Jack kept a weather eye on the sixty men in Huts 6A and 6B, prepared to transfer out anyone he wasn't quite sure of. The Chief, Kovacs and Alphabet he would trust, had trusted, with his life. The rest were unknown quantities.

There was a guy from his home town of Calgary, Sergeant Tom Ross of the Calgary Tanks, who seemed to have what it took. He had almost fried when his Churchill tank was hit on Red Beach, but had managed to scramble out with only a few minor burns. The other four crew members hadn't been so lucky, and if Ross occasionally became nervous when someone struck a match near him, that was understandable. Hearing your pals being barbecued couldn't be pleasant. There would always be a thought, deep down, that perhaps you could have done more to get them out.

No one asked too many questions of their fellow Kriegies in Stalag XIII K or any other Stalag. Information was either offered freely or not at all.

Ross was the talkative sort. A married man two or three years Jack's senior, he obviously had some money. Or his wife did. It wasn't only his Mount Royal address that indicated wealth. One or two things he said showed he was not short of a dollar.

In some respects he didn't seem the type to have volunteered for overseas service, not without a commission, anyway. The fact that he had proved something. With a wife to worry about and money behind him, it wouldn't have taken much to wangle a home posting without being labelled a Zombie. Had Jack met him in civvy street he would have put him down as a lawyer or banker. When he found out that Ross was an accountant, Jack wasn't surprised.

He would do unless he blotted his copybook.

Two American Rangers, both Pfcs, would do too. Zeke Ryan and Jim Webb, both in their middle twenties. Lennie and George in Steinbeck's *Of Mice and Men*, Kovacs called them. Not that Kovacs had read the book, but he had seen the film with Lon Chaney and Burgess Meredith. The comparison wasn't strictly accurate because the Lennie character, Ryan, while a giant, was far from simple-minded.

And Webb wasn't a schemer–dreamer who kept him out of trouble. But the analogy was close enough. Ryan was a logger from Wyoming or Montana or somewhere like that, and Webb a sharp-faced New Yorker who'd lived on his wits since he was weaned. Both were thoroughly pissed off to have been captured, and both wanted out.

Jack wasn't at all sure what form, if any, escape attempts would take. Whether, when it came down to it, he would be trying a solo run from a work party or taking someone with him. But he reckoned the two Americans would be invaluable members of any breakout team.

Two British POWs in Hut 4A he wasn't sure about to begin with. They were both former infantry sergeants who had joined 3 Commando after Vaagsö. Both were in their late twenties. Harry Granger was a heavy-set Yorkshireman and Duncan McCann an Edinburgh Scot. They seemed totally humourless, but it wasn't this that worried Jack. What did was the manner in which they mixed with the men captured at Dunkirk, who were, until the Germans realized the impracticality of the arrangement, kept in a separate compound from the Jubilee Kriegies.

Jack was willing to concede that anyone who hadn't been a POW for over two years wasn't in much of a position to criticize the apparent apathy of those who had. But as far as he could ascertain, not one of the several hundred Dunkirk POWs had made any attempt at getting out. If Granger and McCann preferred the company of men who had evidently chucked their hands in, that was their business. But they weren't likely to be much use to him.

Then he had reason to change his mind. Far from sympathizing with the Dunkirk POWs, it transpired that every time Granger and McCann mingled with them, it was to berate them for being faint-hearted enough to accept their confinement.

One afternoon the Dunkirk Kriegies had had enough and the accusations of what amounted to cowardice turned into a fight. Granger and McCann flattened half a dozen before the goons broke it up. They received fourteen days in the cooler for their pains, and Jack quickly decided he'd made a mistake about them.

They were far from humourless, too. At least Granger was. On their release he was heard to complain that it wasn't only the miseries of solitary confinement a man had to worry about in the cooler.

'There's a guard in there who should be in the WAACS, or whatever they call the German women's service. As queer as a nine-bob note. He made it pretty obvious from Day One that McCann and me could do ourselves a favour by way of rations if we'd accommodate him – or if he could accommodate us. It was a bit tricky with none of us speaking more than a few words of the other's language. But he made his intentions clear. The bastard of it was, I was starting to like the look of him by Day Five. For Christ's sake let's get out of here before we all become beefers.'

Jack got Granger to point out the goon in question. He was a blond youngster not much more than twenty. Whether he was homosexual or bisexual, information like that was useful to have when it came down to blackmail. He remembered the MI9 Escape and Evasion officer lecturing them forty-eight hours before Jubilee.

'Some of you will be captured. That's inevitable. It's then up to you. But don't ever underestimate the Germans. Just because we're fighting them and they're doing one or two nasty things in Europe I'm not at liberty to reveal, don't believe all our propaganda. It's convenient for us for general consumption, for cartoons in the popular newspapers, for example, to try to show the Jerries as either inhuman or buffoons. Inhuman many of them certainly are. Buffoons most of them certainly are not. They're clever, crafty, well-trained, tough. Brilliant in some areas. Therefore it's a question, gentlemen, of knowing your enemy, finding his weakest spots and exploiting them.

'Most of that will have to be left to the man on the spot. I apologize for being blunt, but I mean for those of you who are caught. In one respect, however, we have a tiny advantage over the warriors of Hitler's Reich. That is, that they are disciplined to the point of regimentation. Apart from their top field commanders, they will always react in a predictable manner.

'So, to survive needs more than courage. It needs, perhaps, cunning. The tiger is often killed on a tiger-shoot, but few hunts ever catch a fox.'

Jack decided to put the theory to the test. For his guinea pigs he chose two corporals from the Royal Hamiltons who had travelled down in the same freight-car from Verneulles and who had proved themselves pretty resilient under the appalling conditions. Jem Turner was a fair-haired twenty-three-year-old from Ottawa who had boxed at middleweight for his regiment. Won most of his bouts, too, judging by his unmarked face. He was something of an engineer and had invented a device that he hoped to patent and make his fortune with after the war, one that could reduce petrol consumption in automobiles by up to a third. If all else failed, one of the big gasoline companies would buy him out to keep the invention off the market.

His constant companion, Bob Tucker, could have been his twin brother. Same clean-cut features and fairish hair. Tucker was also twenty-three and hailed from the border town of Sarnia at the foot of Lake Huron. He was one of those youngsters who had roamed the country during the Depression, even skipping across the line to the States in search of work at a very early age. But he'd never stuck at any job for more than a week or two until he finally found his niche in the army. He hoped to remain on when the war was over, but if Canada didn't want him he planned to enlist in the French Foreign Legion.

'Let's get this straight,' said Turner, when he, Jack and Tucker were walking round the exercise circuit. 'You want us to do something that'll get us thrown in the boob for fourteen days to test if Jean Harlow likes his meat sliced left to right. Correct?'

The goon's real name was Schultz, but everyone had taken to calling him Jean Harlow.

'That's about the size of it.'

'It's the size of it that's going to worry us,' cracked Tucker. 'Jesus, Jack, why us?'

'Because you two have got the looks.'

They had too. The buggers looked more German than the goons. Or as much as.

'Thanks very fucking much.'

That wasn't what Jack had meant, but he let it slide.

'What the hell happens if he doesn't take no for an answer this time?' asked Turner. 'We might not get as lucky as Granger, and that sod's got a rifle.'

'Don't call him a sod,' said Tucker deadpan. 'It's too close to home.'

'So you get some decent rations for fourteen days,' grinned Jack.

'Forget it. Find another couple of pigeons.'

'I'm not asking you to take him up on his offer, for Christ's sake,' said Jack. 'I just want to know if he propositions you. Come on, you know how valuable that sort of information would be. I don't know too much about discipline in the Wehrmacht, but I reckon Harlow would be on his way to the Eastern Front quicker than a blink if the commandant suspected he was a beefer. Or up against a wall.'

'So we're to start a fight and get tossed in the tank. What happens if the shift assignments are changed and Harlow doesn't turn up for a week?'

'It's not a fight you'll be starting. I've got something a bit special in mind. You'll get fourteen days at least.'

'You know, Jack, you're getting to be more fun by the minute.'

With the 'something a bit special' Jack proposed to kill two or three birds with one well-aimed stone, and perhaps raise morale in the Stalag at the same time.

The weather had been scorching hot for several weeks, summer's last throw before autumn set in. For reasons best known to themselves the Germans were switching on the cold water supply for only twenty minutes per day. Not enough time for every Kriegie to have a decent wash, let alone a shower to cool himself down. Men were becoming fractious, bad-tempered, snarling at one another. Arguments were too numerous to count and fights were commonplace. RQMS Maitland and the senior NCOs were having a hard time maintaining discipline.

The goons were enjoying every moment of it, not even bothering to break up the fights and throw the combatants in the cooler unless they became too serious. Watching Allied soldiers scrap among themselves was a pleasure.

Nor had any Red Cross packages turned up as yet, and men were permanently hungry. There was plenty of food in the kitchens and one of the storerooms, Kovacs reported, but either the cooks were always around or an armed guard. He had tried everything he knew to get all of the cooks away from the kitchens at the same time, but to no avail. They were not stupid. They knew what he was up to.

So the men were hot, dirty, combative and hungry, and morale was on the floor. Jack reckoned he could solve it all granted a minute slice of luck. They were about due some, the Kriegies, he considered. It had all been one-way traffic up to now.

On the Tuesday afternoon of September 29 the barometer hit the eighties and the water didn't appear at all. When RQMS Maitland demanded to see the commandant, Oberst Gessel, he was told that the Oberst was away for the day. So was his adjutant, Hauptmann Axheim. In any case, protests were forbidden, the junior officer in the Stalag, Oberleutnant Hoffmann, informed him. Hadn't the Compound Leader studied the rules? The water would remain off until the protests ceased.

It was a chicken and egg situation. If Maitland complained because of no water, the water would not be turned on. If he did not complain, it would stay off anyway. Maitland agreed with Jack that the time was ripe to move. Before they all had a riot on their hands.

'They're itching to shoot someone, the bastards.'

As headgear some of the goons wore the *feldmütze*, or field cap, and some peaked caps. The quickest way to get any of them hopping up and down with rage was to treat them with less respect than they considered their uniforms warranted. It was a risky business for it often meant a beating or seven days in the cooler. But if enough people did it . . .

One of the Kriegies who spoke fairly good German had taught fifty or sixty selected men, among them Turner and Tucker, a simple phrase. *Träger, legen Sie die Koffer in den Kofferraum und hier haben Sie Reichmark zwei*. Translated it meant: Porter, put the cases in the boot and here's two Marks.

Not all of the Kriegies had the accent perfect, but the German-speaker considered they were close enough. If fifty or sixty men treated a couple of the peak-capped goons like uniformed hotel or railway workers, the Germans would have a fit.

Jack chose five p.m. as the time to try it out, for at five the kitchen-shift workers were getting ready to pack up for the day. He collected his fifty or sixty volunteers and, casually, walked them in the direction of the laundry complex. It was close to the kitchens and storerooms and there were always a couple of goons in the vicinity, awaiting a chance to slip away for a crafty smoke or bum a cold drink. Jack made certain Tucker and Turner were prominent at the front of the crowd. Kovacs, Alphabet, the Chief and the New Yorker Webb were not part of it. They had another task elsewhere.

Sure enough there were two goons loafing near the kitchens. Through the open windows Jack could see the cooks putting away utensils and cleaning up.

The German guards paid little attention to the crowd. There was nothing formal about it, nothing sinister. Just a handful of men in loose formation passing the time until lock-up.

When Tucker and Turner got within a few feet of the goons, Turner snapped his fingers arrogantly, like an impatient and wealthy guest at a ritzy hotel anxious to get his car packed up and be on his way.

'*Träger, legen Sie die Koffer in den Kofferraum und hier haben Sie Reichmark zwei.*'

The nearer goon couldn't believe his ears. Was this cheeky bastard *Tommi* treating him like a servant?

Before he could react with more than astonishment, Tucker joined in, also with a flick of the fingers.

'Schnell, Träger, schnell!'

Then the crowd took up the chant.

'Schnell, Träger, schnell. Legen Sie die Koffer in den Kofferraum!'

Both goons reached for their sidearms. Now this next bit, thought Jack, could get a little tricky.

'Phase two,' he called out.

As one man the crowd began whistling and humming a burlesque bump-and-grind number while Tucker and Turner started taking off their clothes like strippers in a sleazy downtown show. Exaggerating their movements.

Wiggling their hips in a grotesque parody of seduction but one which wouldn't have raised a flicker of excitement in either Sodom or Gomorrah, Tucker and Turner proceeded to remove their uniforms.

The goons looked on open-mouthed until one of them screamed, in English, 'Stop this!'

At which point the rest of the crowd, still whistling and humming, joined in the act. Pretty soon fifty or sixty men were stripping down to their underwear. From all corners of the compound men came running to see what the excitement was all about. When they saw, they too started to strip. There were items of apparel flying in all directions.

Other goons came racing towards the bizarre scene. All had weapons drawn, but Jack was fairly confident they wouldn't shoot. Not even the Germans would let fly under the circumstances. He hoped.

One goon brighter than the rest, or so he thought, ran into the laundry and emerged with a hosepipe. Other goons fetched other hoses and switched them on. The Kriegies couldn't have been happier. As Sergeant Lambert had predicted, on a baking hot afternoon here they were getting a refreshing shower courtesy of the Germans.

The cooks from the kitchens came outside to see what all the shouting was about, and jeer at the soaking the *Tommis* were getting. The guard in front of the food store ran to help hold a snaking hose. While the Germans' attention was distracted, Kovacs and his hit squad went into action. The Chief and Alphabet held sacks fashioned out of blankets while Kovacs and Webb passed out of the kitchen windows anything they could lay their hands on, supplies the Germans retained for their own use. Tins of liverwurst, long loaves of bread, tins of butter, fresh fruit, eggs. Even knives and forks, for cutlery might be useful at a later date for digging or picking locks.

The padlock on the food store was a simple affair. Kovacs had it off in a few seconds. It was Aladdin's cave in there, and more booty went into the sacks until they could hardly be lifted. At that moment Kovacs called it a day. Judging by the noise outside the striptease was coming to an end.

'Let's get the hell out of here.'

Oberleutnant Hoffmann sprinted up, bellowing at the top of his lungs. A little way behind came Oberst Gessel, sleepy from an afternoon nap, and Hauptmann Axheim, neither of whom had been 'away for the day' after all.

Jack gave a prearranged signal and the crowd drifted away from the hoses, out of range, picking up their clothes as they went, scattering in all directions. Except for Tucker and Turner, who could have disappeared too, but whose task it was to remain where they were. The NCOs instructed everyone to lay out their sodden uniforms in the sunniest spots so that they would dry quickly.

Oberst Gessel ordered the hoses turned off and Tucker and Turner placed under arrest after one of the goons identified them as the ringleaders of the 'riot'. They were each sentenced on the spot to fourteen days' isolation.

Gessel suspected that it was all a carefully orchestrated put-up job when he discovered that the kitchens and storeroom had been ransacked. He called a *Sonderappell* and threatened to keep every POW in the Stalag standing to attention in the compound until the purloined food was returned. But the rations were *spurlos verschwunden*, vanished without trace, and he recognized after keeping the Kriegies out in the open for the remainder of September 29 and the night hours of September 30 that no one was going to tell him where they were hidden. Very well, he would try something else.

He would have liked to have thrown the entire camp into the cooler, but it wasn't big enough. He did, however, sentence four other men, selected at random, to join Tucker and Turner. The remaining POWs would receive no rations for three days nor have the water turned on for more than five minutes each day for the same seventy-two hours.

The Kriegies didn't care. They had all had marvellously cooling showers and the food they'd hijacked was more than enough to keep them going for twice seventy-two hours and better than anything they'd eaten since arriving at Calypso. What was more, Sergeant Lambert had made the Germans look complete fools. For the time being everyone was happy, and as if to make the conspiracy against the Third Reich complete, shortly afterwards the weather broke. Thunder and lightning preceded torrential rain. Summer was over.

When Tucker and Turner got out they confirmed that Harlow was as bent as a dog's hind leg. Jack filed the information for future use. It had to be in the future because long before Tucker and Turner were released from solitary, the Germans reached a new low in barbarity.

On October 8, the POWs stumbled from their huts shortly after six a.m. to find the entire compound filled with armed German troops. Fresh troops from outside, not Stalag guards. RQMS Maitland's immediate thoughts were that they had come for Lambert, because Lambert had been identified as the brains behind the rations ransack; how no one knew. It could have been a careless word spoken in front of a goon who understood English but pretended not to; it could have been a Kriegie trying to curry favour with Oberst Gessel. Maitland hoped not, not so soon after capture, but in a camp containing six hundred men there had to be one or two.

Whatever the reason, the previous morning Lambert had been rousted from his bunk long before *Appell* and frog-marched to the commandant's office in the administration block. Maitland was quickly informed and demanded to know what the authorities wanted with Lambert, to be present if Lambert was to be interrogated for some unspecified offence. His request was denied. What transpired in the commandant's office he heard later from Lambert himself.

The commandant spoke reasonable English, his adjutant a little more. But Oberleutnant Hoffmann was almost fluent. All three officers were present when Jack was marched in, his guard then dismissed with much clicking of heels.

The first thing he noticed was that they were immaculate in their uniforms. They had obviously been awake for at least an hour preparing for this interview. Their boots were polished, their uniforms freshly pressed, their faces pink and clean-shaven. The adjutant Axheim was even wearing cologne.

By way of contrast he felt like a street urchin. He was unshaven, naturally, and his close-cropped hair, cut almost to the scalp like everyone else's because of the danger of lice, was spikey. In the weeks since his capture he had also lost a stone, and his uniform hung on him like castoffs on a scarecrow. If they wanted to make him feel like an impoverished gatecrasher at a swell party, they were going the right way about it.

On Gessel's desk was a steaming pot of coffee that smelt as if it was the real McCoy. All three officers refilled their cups occasionally. The aroma was intoxicating, as was the smell of their cigarette smoke. Cigarettes were in short supply in the compound and would be until the Germans allowed the Red Cross parcels through. A few could be bought from venal guards, exchanged for fountain pens or wristwatches that the owners had managed to hide.

Jack remembered something else the MI9 officer had told them all before Jubilee.

'It's a silly trick but it works. I've tried it myself under different circumstances. Simply imagine your interrogator is stark naked. Imagine his fleshy belly, flaccid penis. Imagine him in a funny hat and a clown's red nose. It'll help you not to be intimidated.'

They tended to believe this man, those who were there. Rumour had it that he had been in and out of France on more than one occasion, and had even escaped from the Gestapo.

Jack tried it now, the strip-trick or ST as it was known.

Oberst Gessel was, in any case, a fattish man. No food shortages there. Colonel or not, his fighting days were over. Behind a desk, where he was now, was his milieu. He would have lasted about four seconds in a commando unit.

Jack stripped him from head to foot, saw the obesity, the limp dick. Without the jackboots and the rank, he was a bespectacled forty-year-old zero.

Hauptmann Axheim was a different kettle of fish who wore both Iron Crosses, First and Second Class. A tallish man with dark, gypsyish looks, he had seen combat. What he was doing here Jack had no idea. A wound, maybe. He was wearing a wound badge. The Krauts had a badge for everything. Cut yourself shaving and up came a medal.

Jack took Axheim's clothes off and put him in a dress. Polka dots. It worked, he was amazed to find. Axheim became less of a threat.

As befitted the junior officer, Oberleutnant Hoffmann stood a deferential pace or two behind Gessel's left shoulder. He was the youngest, twenty-five or so, blond like Harlow. It was a good image. Jack removed his uniform and put him with Harlow, in a compromising position.

'Coffee, Herr Lambert?' offered Oberst Gessel.

Jack was both surprised at the offer and the manner of address. Usually it was plain 'Lambert', occasionally 'Sergeant Lambert'.

'And a cigarette?'

Jack would have spilt blood for either, sold his soul for both. But he understood that this was a softening-up process. They probably had their own equivalent of MI9 psychologists in the Wehrmacht. First the velvet glove, then the iron heel.

'*Danke, nein, Herr Oberst,*' he answered politely.

'Don't antagonize them unnecessarily,' the MI9 man had said. 'They hold the whip hand. While you can, be compliant. And surprise them.'

'You speak German, Herr Lambert?'

'*Nein, Herr Oberst.*' Jack finished in English. 'A few words.'

Axheim pounced.

'Such as, *Legen Sie die Koffer in den Kofferraum?*'

'That, yes. Alongside sixty others.'

'Fifty-nine others and you,' said Gessel. 'Have you eaten our rations yet?'

'I know nothing about rations, Herr Oberst. I was outside the laundry that day, I admit, but I know nothing about the missing rations.'

'They didn't share them with you, with the man who planned it all with such military precision?' This from the Oberleutnant, speaking out of turn but evidently with Gessel's permission. This, thought Jack, was a well-rehearsed act. And so it should be. The Germans were renowned for their thoroughness. 'Well, well, that does seem unfair. I imagine you resent the thieves, then?'

'There are thieves everywhere, Herr Oberleutnant. It's a waste of energy to resent every one.'

Jack felt inclined to smash the supercilious sod's head in, but managed to overcome the desire. The tiger and the fox, he recalled. This was no time for martyrdom.

'That ribbon,' said Axheim unexpectedly, 'the first one on your breast.' He consulted the file he was holding. 'That is the Distinguished Conduct Medal, is it not?'

Jack saw no reason to deny it. They obviously knew, anyway.

'*Jawohl, Herr Hauptmann.*'

'Awarded for bravery.'

'Awarded for being lucky.'

'And where exactly were you lucky?'

'I don't have to answer that, Herr Hauptmann. Either you know or you do not.'

'Oh, we know, we know. During that criminal raid by 3 Commando. Before you returned to 4 Commando.'

How the bloody hell did they know about Vaagsö and the DCM, Jack wondered? He didn't have enough rank to be on file before he was captured, so the information had to have come from someone in the compound. He must have told a dozen people, those who'd asked, where the DCM was won. The Chief, Kovacs and Alphabet could have told another thirty-six when they were trying to get him to stand for Compound Leader. Any of that four dozen could have told another four dozen who could have told the goons. They couldn't have obtained the information anywhere else.

'May I ask why I've been summoned here?' he asked, still keeping his tone polite.

'We have already told you,' said Gessel. 'To answer for the missing rations. You see, their loss caused me a great deal of embarrassment. I had to indent for more.'

'And I have already told *you*,' emphasized Jack, 'Herr Oberst, that I know nothing about missing rations. You have the wrong man.'

'Perhaps.'

The three consulted in rapid German, far too fast for Jack to pick out more than the odd word except when his own name was mentioned.

Finally the commandant said: 'On this occasion we are inclined to believe you, Herr Lambert.'

Jack was astonished. What sort of bloody nonsense was this?

'But we would appreciate your assistance,' said Oberleutnant Hoffmann. 'The criminals who stole the rations were responsible for the entire Stalag going short for three days and three nights. It would be in your interest to tell us the names of these men. We will not arrest them immediately. We appreciate that that would point to you as the informer. We will leave it for several days, and during those days we will interview more men. No one will ever know who told us.'

They want me to be a stoolie, thought Jack, unable to believe his ears. They want me to rat. What the hell's given them the impression I'd go for a deal like that?

He took several deep breaths, scarcely able to contain his rage.

'I must emphasize again,' he said slowly, 'that I know nothing about missing rations or who stole them. Perhaps the goo . . . your guards did it. They had every opportunity.'

'You're suggesting that one German would deprive another of food?'

'You've just suggested that one Allied soldier would another.'

'Think about it carefully, Lambert,' said Oberleutnant Hoffman. The 'Herr' or 'Sergeant' were definitely missing this time. 'You would find it to your advantage to cooperate.'

'Dismiss,' said the commandant.

Hoffmann accompanied Jack to the colonel's door. On the verandah, surprisingly, he gestured Jack away in a friendly manner. There were about thirty Kriegies standing outside, in the mud now the compound was churning up after the rain. Not one of them failed to see Hoffmann's apparent amiability.

'What the hell was all that about?' demanded RQMS Maitland.

'They want to know who organized the striptease and the rations rip-off. Someone around here's got a big mouth.'

'Why was Hoffmann treating you like a blood brother?'

'You've got me. Trying to give the impression I'd talked, I guess.'

'It would have made more sense to kick you off the verandah.'

Maybe not, thought Jack. Never underestimate the bastards, the MI9 officer had said. Treating him like an old pal made as much sense as kicking him down the steps. More, in a way. No one would believe that the goons would treat an informant like an ally, in full view of thirty men. They'd see through the ruse. Probably, however, that was precisely how the goons would behave with a stool pigeon. Double bluff.

Whistles were blowing, the goons shouting that it was time for morning rollcall.

'We'll go over this with the Committee after *Appell*,' said Maitland. 'I want to know everything that went on in there. In the meantime, be careful, Jack. If they've got you marked down for some reason, they're going to watch you like a mother hen. Be a model prisoner for a while. Keep out of the limelight.'

Jack nodded, but he was still puzzled. The whole interview hadn't made sense. Nor had the commandant made an inspired guess regarding who had organized the rations ransack. The odds were six hundred-to-one against that. Gessel *knew*. And it wasn't like the Germans to let someone off the hook for the 'serious crime', in their book, of stealing food.

That was on the morning of October 7. Now it was October 8 and there were at least two companies of Wehrmacht troops, armed to the teeth, in the compound when the whistles went for *Appell*. But they weren't there for Jack Lambert. Before the day was out RQMS Maitland was beginning to wish they had been.

Except for the sick, every POW was lined up in front of the administration block. There had been no head count this morning for the first time ever, none of the customary little tricks the goons normally practised to make the Kriegies's lives more of a misery. Such as taking an hour over the first count, pretending it didn't tally with the records, and starting all over again. For another hour. Until the breakfast issue of soup was cold. It didn't matter to the goons. They had to be there, out in the open, anyway. Until the shifts changed and they could retreat to their own barracks.

Every machine gun in the goon towers was pointed at the serried ranks. The two companies brought in for the occasion surrounded the Kriegies on three sides at ground level. There were an awful lot of heavy automatic weapons in evidence, and some of the troops held primed stick grenades as though expecting trouble, or something worse. More than one POW thought a massacre was on the cards.

Then the commandant appeared on the verandah, pale with anger, a clipboard in his hands. Without preamble he read from a prepared statement. In German and at speed, as though deliberately to confuse or terrify. Even the German-speakers were catching only one word in three. If the text wasn't understood, however, the mood was. He wasn't wishing them the best of health.

When he had finished Oberleutnant Hoffman took over. There was no doubt that the commandant's anger was genuine, as was Hoffmann's.

'The Government of the Third Reich,' Hoffman began, 'has always shown due clemency to prisoners-of-war and afforded them the treatment due to soldiers captured in battle in accordance with the International Agreement. This is beyond dispute.'

Someone blew a Bronx cheer. Other POWs jeered the statement, still not knowing why it was being given. But if the short rations they were on and the conditions in the freight-cars was clemency, Christ help everyone if the Krauts decided to get harsh. A few choice epithets were tossed in Hoffmann's direction. He waited patiently until Maitland restored some sort of order. It took time, but eventually the RQMS got it across to the men that it was in their interests to hear what Hoffman had to say.

'After the abortive August 19 enemy invasion of Dieppe,' the Oberleutnant went on, 'when British, Canadian and American forces attempted a landing on the Continent, many German soldiers were found shot with their hands tied behind their backs.'

'Shit,' said Kovacs, 'here it comes.'

'I don't think so,' said Jack. 'They wouldn't bother to give us a speech if they were going to shoot us.'

'The following operations order was recently found on the person of a captured Canadian officer,' said Hoffmann. '"A prisoner-of-war cage will be established away from the invasion beaches and all German POWs will be assembled there for interrogation by the Canadian Provost Corps."' He paused dramatically. '"Their hands will be tied behind their backs to prevent them destroying any documents, movement orders or maps in their possession."'

Hoffmann had their full attention now. This was serious. There was no jeering on this occasion. One or two men claimed to have heard of the existence of such a document, which, if true, was a violation of the Geneva Convention. As for them being shot while tied by their captors, that was unlikely. But there were millions of rounds being exchanged on the beaches, and it wasn't impossible the Germans had been caught in the crossfire.

'The Government of the Third Reich,' intoned Hoffmann sombrely, 'has demanded an assurance from the British Government that such inhumane treatment will never occur again. It has also demanded an apology.

'No such apology having been received, the Government of the Third Reich has no alternative but to take reprisals against all officers, NCOs and men of the Dieppe Force.'

Now the silence was broken as men murmured mutinously to one another, the muttered, bitter, fearful conversations sounding like hordes of angry bees. If the Germans were talking about reprisals, which they

194

had never done before, that could only mean the punishment to be handed out was going to be worse than anything they had experienced up to now. As if that wasn't bad enough. Everyone remembered what had happened to the village of Lidice after Czech partisans killed SS General Heydrich, in June. German radio had made no secret of the fact that Lidice had ceased to exist, that all males over fifteen years of age had been shot.

'Stand fast in the ranks!' bawled Maitland, and the senior NCOs took up the cry, imposing their authority with a clenched fist when necessary.

This was a powder keg. It would take just one spark to ignite it, which could well be what the Germans were hoping for. 'Putting down a dangerous rebellion' they would call it then. It would be as well to wait and see what form the threatened reprisals were going to take.

They did not have to wait long.

Hauptmann Axheim gave the order for the first ten men at the extreme right of the front rank to be marched away, to the cell block. Everyone else tensed, waiting for the sound of automatic gunfire, prepared to turn on their captors if it looked like a massacre.

No shots came. When the men returned their hands were bound behind their backs with cord. There was some nervous laughter among the other five hundred-odd POWs. If this was to be the extent of the reprisals, they could handle it. Only a few senior NCOs realized that the situation was far from humorous, for it quickly became apparent that the Germans intended keeping them tied twenty-four hours a day.

As it happened, the cords were easily removed – by a fellow Kriegie fumbling behind his back or, more often, by the Dunkirk POWs, who were not restrained. But cord was only a stopgap measure. Afterwards came chains and handcuffs. For some, lengths of barbed-wire were interwoven in the chains. Now freeing one's hands wasn't so easy, not without occasioning cuts and gashes, for which there were no ointments or antiseptics.

The Germans could keep them bound for days, weeks, months, the senior NCOs concluded. Until the British Government issued the apology that had been demanded. While they were shackled there was presumably no question of work parties. Therefore no chance of getting out that way. Any tunnels in the pipeline, and there were some contemplated, could not be excavated, because the goons would make damned sure that every man handcuffed remained handcuffed. Spot checks would be stepped up, day and night.

Two men, both corporals from the South Saskatchewans, proved adept at freeing prisoners from handcuffs and chains, using homemade tools fashioned from the cutlery Kovacs and his hit squad had hijacked on the afternoon of the rations ransack. Ted Lucas was, providentially, a locksmith, from Wainwright in Alberta. He had the long fingers and studious air of a concert pianist and could, reputedly, manipulate a card deck like a magician. He was also totally unflappable, as cool as a cucumber under pressure. He certainly knew all about handcuffs. Corporal Andrew McKenzie was a blacksmith from North Battleford. A bull of a man, not tall but built like a brick blockhouse, he had spent fifteen of his twenty-eight years working with his father in the family smithy. What he didn't know about weak links in chains wasn't worth knowing. He could also put them back in a hurry if goons were spotted approaching.

It was never easy. Oberst Gessel made it clear from the start that any man caught without his fetters was in for trouble. And it wasn't until word got out of Germany about what was happening, and the Allies took their own reprisal measures by chaining selected German POWs in England and Canada, that conditions eased. Even so, there were POWs in Lamsdorf who remained bound for thirteen months. In Stalag XIII K they were slightly luckier, but even they were fettered day and night, except for a couple of days over Christmas, until early 1943.

While handcuffed and chained, a man had to do the best he could with his food, usually by teaming up with someone, the one feeding the other, helping him to soup, assisting him with his bread ration. This was placed on a hut's trestle table and devoured by a POW bending from the waist and gnawing at the crusts like an animal.

The worst thing was going to the lavatory. As some of the Kriegies, thanks to the poor rations and standards of hygiene, now had dysentery, for which there was no medicine, relieving oneself was demoralizing. A man couldn't clean himself afterwards, not without the help of an unfettered medical orderly or a friend, and McKenzie and Lucas could not be everywhere at once even when the goons weren't watching. Sick men were degraded to the point of despair, and half a dozen didn't make it to Christmas, choosing instead to cross the trip-wire, charge the main barricades, and be shot. Others died of so-called natural causes because their strength and spirit had left them.

It was a time of the utmost hopelessness, and only the strongest could survive.

Cunning, a few said to themselves, cunning. Not bravery.

Though maybe cunning and bravery were synonymous.

Jack got thrown in the cooler twice, the first time early in November, for fourteen days, after being found without his manacles feeding Alphabet, who appeared to be suffering the most of the former Patricias. There were those, Maitland among them, who swore Sergeant Lambert could have reshackled himself, as taught by Lucas and McKenzie, long before the goons appeared on the scene. That he had deliberately allowed himself to be discovered without his bonds. A few knew that Lambert wanted to test for himself just how blackmailable Harlow was. But attacking the goons who found him was lunacy. He was one man, they were three. He was weak after his months in captivity, they were fit and strong. They had weapons, he did not.

He was rifle-butted to the floor of Hut 6B and severely beaten all the way to isolation. When he came out he was still marked, some of the cuts and bruises fresh. A Kriegie in one of the adjacent solitary confinement cells, who finished his term before Jack, said that Sergeant Lambert had given his guards constant trouble.

On his release Jack said nothing about his ordeal. Not even to the Chief, Kovacs or Alphabet. They didn't press him. Harlow had been on duty for at least half of the fourteen days.

'If he's got that kind of guts,' said Kovacs with a kind of awe, saying aloud what they were all thinking, 'he'll either lead this camp into a rebellion the Krauts will never forget, or they'll break him.'

'Or he'll get us all shot,' someone remarked.

When Jack went into the cooler the second time at the beginning of December, it was because of the propaganda and rations posters.

The goons had them everywhere in the huts, and the rations posters were an insult. They purported to show what each POW received each day and week. Fat: 2.5 ounces; potatoes: 8 lbs; sugar: 6 ounces; meat: 5.5 ounces. Soup, peas, millet, sausage, cabbage, barley.

None of it had anything to do with reality.

Jack tore them down as fast as they were put up.

The propaganda posters seemed to incense him even more. One showed a German hand throttling John Bull, with the caption: *Wir brechen England Tyrannei*. (We are breaking England's tyranny.) Another depicted Hitler in a magisterial pose. *Adolf Hitler ist der Sieg*. (Hitler is victory.) Yet another portrayed Aryan youths with rifles and daggers and the legend: *Harte Zeiten, Harte Pflichten, Harte Herzen*. (Hard times, hard work, hard hearts.) The one that enraged everyone was a drawing of a mailed fist crushing caricatures of Frenchmen, Britons and Jews: *In den Staub mit allen Feinden Grosse-Deutschlands*. (Into the dust with all enemies of Greater Germany.)

All went on to a fire, to which Jack applied one of the hut's precious matches.

When he was released from isolation this time, both his eyes were half-closed because of the beatings he had received.

'They're going to kill him before long,' said the Chief to Kovacs.

But apparently not. He appeared to have learnt his lesson on this occasion. He made no further attempts to tear down the new posters, or antagonize the guards in any manner. Whenever they ordered him to his feet, or to stand to attention if he was already up, he complied instantly.

Some thought it was a bluff, that he had found out what he needed to know about Harlow and was now biding his time. His close friends were not so sure.

'Even Jack can only take so much,' said Kovacs shrewdly, though he was careful not to say it in Jack's presence.

In any case, he was not alone in being subdued. Winter was now upon them and it was bloody cold. Clothing parcels from home were not being allowed through, and the single thin blanket did nothing to keep them warm during the bitter nights. Nor did the 25 lbs of coal each hut was permitted for heating. They would all die before the spring, that was obvious. If not of malnutrition then of hypothermia. No one could survive this, though some, perversely, were encouraged by Sergeant Lambert's attitude, compliant though it seemed to be for now. At all events, he was worse off than most of them were, except for the chronically sick.

The only time he perked up was when the Compound Leader ordered a blitz on a few of the 'fat cats' who were making hay out of their fellow Kriegies' misery. This dozen, at least half of them Canadian, had cornered the market in bribery and corruption, but only for self-gain, not the common good. They had become the middlemen between the goons and the POWs, taking what the prisoners had to offer by way of personal belongings and bartering these with the goons for cigarettes or extra food. They were giving a poor rate of exchange too. If a secreted fountain pen or watch was worth ten cigarettes, the donor received only five. The other five went to the 'fat cats'.

Kovacs, because he would, knew what was going on from the beginning. He was even invited to join the consortium, but declined. Whatever he could wangle went into the common pot of Huts 6A and 6B.

When the 'fat cats' were beaten up by their fellow inmates and their loot confiscated, Jack smiled for the first time in days.

'Good. Keep after the bastards.'

The goons distributed Red Cross parcels on Christmas Eve and allowed each Kriegie to be unmanacled for two days. One parcel was given between four men, but it was more food and cigarettes than they had seen since the rations ransack.

Parcels differed according to whether they came from the Red Cross of Britain, Canada or America. Those from Britain contained biscuits, cheese, chocolate, dried fruit, margarine, cocoa, dried eggs, soap. And much more. Canada's contained corned beef but no mustard, cigarettes but no condensed milk. The Americans had just about everything, but there were few American prisoners in Stalag Calypso.

On Christmas Eve selected officers from the adjacent Oflag were also unchained and allowed into the Stalag. Carefully watched over by goons, they were permitted to mingle with the NCOs and privates. And permitted to join in the singing of Christmas carols.

To make everything seem particularly hopeless, on December 24 it snowed. The White Christmases of childhood – though partly imagined, maybe – became reality. Everyone thought of home and how to get there.

'Silent Night, Holy Night . . .'
'God rest ye merry gentlemen . . .'
'The Holly and the Ivy . . .'

Some camps, somewhere, were no doubt putting on a Christmas show. To ease the weariness and pain. That wasn't sanctioned in Stalag XIII K. Rehearsals wouldn't have been possible, in any case, thanks to the manacles.

In one of the parcels Alphabet had found a mimeographed message from the Canadian Prisoners-of-War Relatives Association. Part of it read:

> Our Christmas gift of chocolate and cigarettes has been dispatched to you . . . The thoughts of your friends and relations are with you at this time . . . The message we send you is one of hope and faith . . . May the coming year bring you back to us . . .

Alphabet began to cry. He didn't mean to, and neither was he alone in having tears in his eyes, but he could not help himself.

Jack went across and put an arm around Alphabet's shoulders.

'We'll get 'em next year, feller.'

'Some fucking soldier I am,' sniffed Alphabet, ashamed.

'You're the best. You've come a long way.'

'I can't take much more.'

'Sure you can. You'll get through.'

In another part of the compound the Germans were also celebrating, but with wine and beer and a larger rations handout. Some of them were also singing 'Silent Night', though in their own language. '*Stille Nacht, Heilige Nacht . . .*'

'Who's that?' asked a visiting officer of RQMS Maitland, pointing to Sergeant Lambert.

The Compound Leader told him.

'He looks like he's coping.'

'We're not sure. He's been through a lot.'

'I can see that. What do you mean, not sure?'

'He could be getting wire-happy.'

'Keep an eye on him. Come on, let's join the carols. God knows when we'll have another opportunity.'

It rang out, 'Silent Night', not tuneful but heartfelt. Many of the men stood up. It seemed somehow appropriate. Jack remained seated, keeping a tight hold on Alphabet.

THIRTEEN

March 1943

The shackles came off for good in Stalag XIII K in the middle of January. Oberst Gessel again made a speech in German and Oberleutnant Hoffmann in English. They were being freed, Hoffmann said, because the required apology had been given by the Churchill Government. Thanks to a wireless receiver several officers had constructed out of parts obtained by bribery, blackmail and pilfering in their Oflag, the entire camp knew this to be untrue. A more likely reason was that Oberst Gessel and his staff, with one eye on the future after the defeats of Rommel at El Alamein the previous November and Paulus at Stalingrad at the beginning of February, had decided, in case ultimate victory for the Third Reich proved illusory, to play within the rules as far as they dared. Or it could have been that Gessel could not provide the work parties requested by the local Gauleiter while the Kriegies' hands were tied.

Important messages came via a powerful BBC transmitter each Wednesday evening on the Forces programme, on a show called the 'Radio Padre', featuring Dr Selby Wright. Although German Intelligence monitored these broadcasts, and others, as a matter of course – suspecting that many POW camps now had wireless receivers and occasionally finding one – the contents of Dr Selby Wright's talks were so apparently innocuous that no attempt was ever made to jam them.

Not every broadcast contained a coded message. Only if the clergyman began his talk with the words, 'Good evening, Forces,' was the entire commentary taken down in shorthand for later deciphering by officers who were privy to the code. For if it began in that manner there was a hidden message, which not even Dr Selby Wright knew. He was simply given the text by MI9 officers and instructed to start his broadcast with that phrase. Thus news of the Red Army's victory at Stalingrad was circulating throughout the compound within a couple of days of Paulus surrendering. The Germans would certainly have jammed the transmission if the BBC had tried to broadcast in clear.

It was all one-way traffic, however, on the airwaves. There were no transmitters in any camps. A receiver could be the size of a biscuit tin and easily hidden. A transmitter would have been huge. Sending messages out had to be done by letter, and many came in this way. Selected officers and NCOs had their own codes, all different. It was a laborious business but almost foolproof, especially as the officers and NCOs who had taken part in the briefing by MI9 before Jubilee were under strict instructions not to discuss their private methods of communication, for security reasons. They knew who each other was because they had all been together in the same briefing room, but they studiously ignored one another. There were only a handful, in any case, and only three were NCOs. Some others had been killed on the beaches, some had avoided capture, many were in Lamsdorf. In XIII K apart from Jack Lambert there was a sergeant named Winterman from the Royal Regiment of Canada and another called Hayes from the Essex Scottish.

Without making it obvious, Jack kept an eye on Winterman and Hayes, as they were no doubt watching him and each other, waiting for the day when they were not there, when they had, like the rations, *spurlos verschwunden*, vanished without trace. He would then know that they had received coded instructions to make their escape attempts. Until that happened they couldn't make a move, as Jack couldn't. He didn't know what they had been told in their final private briefing. He only knew what the MI9 officer has instructed him to do.

'Make plans to get out but don't go until you get the word. When the time comes you'll be given a broad route to travel. Morale in the camps is going to be the biggest debilitating factor. Do what you can to keep everyone's up. No one knows yet how this war's going to turn out, but it would be an enormous fillip to the Allied cause if, even though they're POWs, there are thousands of Allied troops determined to make life difficult for the enemy.'

Jack wanted to know why he couldn't make an escape bid as soon as he was ready, God forbid that he should ever be captured.

'Because those are your orders, Sergeant Lambert. Prisoner or not, you're still subject to military discipline. As of today, August 16, we have a good idea of what is going on in most parts of France and quite a lot of Germany. There are vast areas of ignorance, however, and it might be essential, for example, that we know precisely what is happening in Stuttgart, say, next May.

'We don't know which camp you'll be taken to or even which part of Germany. Until we do we can't put you in touch with people who might be able to help you get home. Once out you'll know what to look for, or be told. If it's any consolation, everyone in that briefing room is being given the same, or similar, orders, even senior officers. You have been selected as one of a handful from 4 Commando because of your record. It goes without saying, naturally, that we hope not a sentence of your briefing will be necessary, that you will be back in England after a successful operation on the afternoon of August 19.'

So Jack sat it out, not able even to confide in his closest friends why he was uninterested in any plans for tunnels. He was not alone in being told to stay put. Apart from Winterman and Hayes in XIII K, in Lamsdorf senior NCOs Beesley, Sherriff and Lowe, among others, had been given identical instructions.

Now that the manacles were off and the camp authorities were permitting letters and parcels to be sent and received, Jack had two principal means of contacting London. They were communications to notional girlfriends, relationships formed, if the Abwehr ever took more than a passing interest, with women while he was in England. The two fictitious ladies were Dorothy Spencer and Gwen Taggart, one with an address in Surrey and one in Hertfordshire. The addresses were equally fictitious. Correspondence to Miss Taggart and Miss Spencer was intercepted by MI9 before it got into the postal system, by officers in all the major sorting depots. Female members of Nine wrote back, just in case the Germans were being extra diligent one day and opened a letter, for censorship purposes, signed by a woman but written in a man's hand. To add verisimilitude to the stratagem, not every letter contained information for Nine. It all depended upon how it was dated. If, for example, the date was in figures, 26/2/43, the letter could be junked unread. If the month was spelt out, 26th February, 1943, then there was something contained therein for the decoders.

Also to keep up the pretence, Jack wrote home to his parents, brother and sister whenever he was allowed, though he guessed by now Ben would be in England. These communications naturally contained nothing secret.

Apart from the letters from Dorothy Spencer and Gwen Taggart, MI9 had another method of reaching him, via fictitious organizations invented by MI9y, the coding sub-section. These were The Licensed Victuallers' Sports Association and the Prisoners' Leisure Hours Fund, which purported to be philanthropic establishments concerned with the welfare of prisoners-of-war. Occasionally a gift of table tennis balls would be received, or a dartboard. The message would either be on the wrapping or somewhere on the gift. Or in it, because sometimes the present was of clothes. It was all so intricately worked out that there was never a balls-up, such as sending a cricket bat to a Canadian, who probably didn't know what cricket was.

When Jack wrote back to thank the philanthropists for their kindness, within the text of the letter was whatever MI9 wanted to know. Frequently it was no more than asking, for instance, what happened to camp security when the air-raid sirens went, or whether any unusual brutality took place after a raid. If work parties were being forced to help clear up the debris or the average age of camp staff. If old men were replacing young men that could mean that Hitler had a manpower problem.

Snatches of information from camps all over Germany. By themselves they meant little. Added together they could tell Allied Intelligence a lot. Jack often wondered if Nine had any intention of giving him the green light to escape.

The code Jack used to both send and receive messages was a simple affair. After the date had indicated that there was something within the text to be deciphered, the mode of greeting told the cryptanalyst how many words to look for. 'Dearest Gwen' – eleven letters – meant eleven words. 'My darling' – nine letters – nine words. And so on.

The opening sentence advised the cryptanalyst where to look. 'I miss you desperately' – four words – meant that the key lay in every fourth word starting with the next sentence. It had been decided in England that the first and last letters of the key words would be used alternately. Thus in the message 'POWs manacled reprisals Dieppe' 'POWs' could be coded, every fourth word, as – Please . . . go . . . where . . . events . . . No questions were ever asked that involved the use of awkward letters such as Z or X, because zebras and Zulus were not the sort of subjects a POW would be likely to write to his best girl about. MI9 had a good thing going, and they didn't want to spoil it.

It all took time, in any case, and was only effective when the Germans were not being bloody-minded about mail, but it was better than nothing.

Maps and compasses and occasionally currency came in via parcels from organizations like the Licensed Victuallers' Sports Association. Miniature compasses were often jacket buttons, sometimes draughtsmen, checkersmen. Maps of Germany or specific areas of it came on gifts of handkerchiefs – handkerchiefs that appeared plain until the material was exposed to heat. Other maps were drawn from memory by British officers from Oflag who had known Germany before the war.

One brilliant MI9 ruse got several thousand Marks into Stalag XIII K in a Chinese puzzle of a chessboard, sandwiched between the upper and lower layers, which could only be separated if one knew where to apply pressure. That information, in code, was contained in a letter from 'the kindly old lady' donor. In reality, the kindly old lady sported a handlebar moustache and held the rank of major.

The Germans were not fools. In various sorting depots they had X-ray machines to photograph suspect parcels. But in the case of the chessboard a thin sheet of lead covered each side of the currency hoard, and nothing showed up on the plates.

Currency was needed not only to help an escaper once he got out, but to bribe selected goons into turning a blind eye when, for instance, civilian clothing was being appropriated by a member of an outside work party. Fortunately for the Kriegies of Stalag XIII K, and elsewhere, the master plan for the Master Race had not succeeded in eradicating venality.

Civilian clothing, essential for a Kriegie on the run, was the second hardest item to come by. It wasn't impossible to obtain. It could be manufactured by remodelling uniforms, dyeing them different colours with berries. Or ink supplied by a crooked guard. It could be, and was, regularly bought from German civilian labour gangs, who often worked alongside POWs clearing up last night's bombing raid. These TENO platoons – *Technische Nothilfe* – usually consisted of men too old or unfit for combat, and were always short of cigarettes or chocolate. Stealing clothing was very difficult from the TENOs, because there were few places a Kriegie could hide a jacket once the loss was discovered.

The hardest item to obtain was papers. The Germans had documents for everything. A man posing as a worker in the Third Reich needed a whole hatful of passes and permits to cover a few miles. Every civilian, under threat of a fine or imprisonment, had to carry his *Ausweis*, his identity card, at all times. To work he needed an *Arbeitskarte*. When travelling he had to be able to show, on demand, his *Bescheinigung*. In special cases a *Polizeiliche Erlaubnis*, a police pass, was required.

The work parties confirmed that the Kriminalpolizei as well as the Gestapo stopped citizens at random for a documents check. Not looking for escaped POWs – as yet no one had got out of Stalag XIII K – but hunting for deserters from the Wehrmacht or young men who had conveniently avoided the call-up by being unavailable when the summons came.

Kriegies who had been printers or commercial artists before the war were in demand for their skills at copying passes obtained from corrupt guards, or stolen, as were those who spoke decent German. The Situations Vacant columns of newspapers and magazines, obtained by bribery, were scoured. An advertisement would often state not only the position to be filled and the company requiring help, but the name of the manager or supervisor to whom applications should be made. So-called responses to a non-existent application could then be forged.

Every document a man could carry might help. No one underestimated the task of escaping from a hostile country, and few thought they would make it all the way. But the attempt was the important thing.

A major drawback was that few of the Kriegies spoke German, and those who did were imperfect. They might be able to pass for Dutch if they were lucky. The POWs from the Fusiliers Mont-Royal would stand a reasonable chance, for there were many Frenchmen of the Vichy persuasion in Germany. Their peculiar patois would be immediately identifiable as non-Continental French if they happened to be stopped by a Gestapo officer who understood the language, but that was a risk they would have to take.

If and when they, or anyone else, got out.

Four officers – three Canadians and an Englishman – made a dash for it in the middle of February, from a tunnel they had been excavating, apparently, since the previous September, only stopping when they were manacled. They were all recaught within forty-eight hours and spent the next twenty-eight days in their version of the cooler. They were paraded in Oflag and Stalag prior to their solitary confinement, and Oberst Gessel made another of his speeches.

'It is useless to try to escape.'

Their recapture rocked the confidence of XIII K. All four men, it came across the grapevine, spoke excellent German.

In the Stalag two tunnels were started as soon as the manacles were off, in late January, despite the freezing weather and the ground being hard as iron. One went north from the latrine abutting Hut 1A, the second east, from the central washroom, from Huts 5A and 5B. It was a hell of a long way to the nearest trees, but the men involved at least considered they were doing something positive.

Every man who wanted to get out – and not everyone did, some considering it a mug's game – did his share of digging or shoring up. Or stooging, keeping watch for wandering ferrets, the name the Kriegies had given to the German NCOs whose task it was to establish where, if at all, tunnels were being excavated.

Jack Lambert observed it all, occasionally stooging, with some envy but otherwise total disinterest. He wasn't going, that was the sum of the cards, though even if he had been advised by London to get out instantly, he wouldn't have chosen one of the tunnels as his method of egress. In his view they were far too risky. The escape would be discovered at the six a.m. *Appell* and then all hell would be let loose. With only a tiny percentage of the tunnellers speaking any kind of acceptable German, everyone would be swept up so fast their heads would spin. If four German-speaking officers couldn't make it, non-linguists were stuffed from the off. In a mass escape.

One man, perhaps two, stood a better chance, and he had his own long-term plan for that, just waiting for the signal. It would not involve a break from a work party. He couldn't even get on one, substitute himself for a private soldier, because his face was too well known to the goons as a troublemaker.

With bribes of cigarettes, however, he had managed to acquire some civilian clothes from outside work parties, private soldiers who had no interest in escaping themselves and simply used whatever they bought from the TENO platoons as a means of barter. These clothes were carefully stashed. Two sets, for that matter, in case he decided to take someone with him. He was also stockpiling rations from his Red Cross parcels, non-perishables, because he doubted he'd be able to walk into a shop and buy food with the few Marks that had been allotted him. He had practised his German, but he still had only a few sentences. And a lousy accent. He'd be lost if someone came back at him rapid-fire. For the same reason he wasn't worried about documents. To be challenged was to be caught. The most perfect forgeries wouldn't save his skin once he opened his mouth. He had a handkerchief map of the

Frankfurt area, but if he was to get back to England, or contact anyone MI9 put him in touch with, it would not be on public transport. He would have to live off his own rations and the land, as he had been trained to at Achnacarry.

The Chief and Kovacs were diggers in the tunnel starting from Hut 1A's latrines. Alphabet was in the one under the washroom of Huts 5A and 5B. To simplify matters for general discussion they were known by the initials of latrine and washroom in the phonetic code: London and William, two words that might easily crop up in any Kriegies' normal conversation. The way things were going London would be finished several days before William, be under the nearest trees. If that proved to be the case, the diggers who had participated in William would move into London. Thirty-six men were to be involved in the breakout and the most likely day for their exit was March 24, a Wednesday, in the small hours. Four days off.

Jack was concerned about Alphabet, who appeared even closer to the end of his tether than he had at Christmas, though the tunnel did seem to have given him a new lease of hope. He was concerned about the Chief, too, and Kovacs. And Turner and Tucker, the Americans Ryan and Webb, the blacksmith McKenzie. But it was mainly Alphabet who troubled him, and the chances of success of the venture. It puzzled him that the two excavation teams had been working for weeks without any sign that the goons knew what was going on. It didn't seem logical that they hadn't stumbled on at least one of the tunnels, though to safeguard against both being found was why they had been placed so far apart and heading in different directions. Still, an awful lot of timber was missing, for shoring-up purposes, from bunks and the rafters of huts. It would have been more except Canadian gift parcels came in plywood containers, which were used in the shafts.

However, something wasn't right. Something stank. The goons must at least suspect that digging was taking place, but the ferrets hadn't stepped up their vigilance. Maybe he was getting paranoid or wire-happy. *Stacheldrahtkoller*, the Germans termed it: barbed-wire madness.

He kept out of any discussions the escape teams had, even when they took place in 6B, when travel rations were being counted or civilian clothes distributed. On those occasions he would volunteer for a stooge patrol, hunting ferrets. That was how it should be. He wasn't going. What they had to say to one another wasn't his business. It was the business of McKenzie, Turner, Tucker, Ross, Granger. The others.

But on March 22 he took the Chief and Kovacs to one side. Alphabet was doing a digging stint in William. He gave them each about an ounce of chocolate and three cigarettes.

'For the trip. For luck. I'll see Alphabet before he goes.'

'You should be coming with us,' said Greyfoot.

'No.'

'Orders?'

'Now why would you think that? Maybe I think you don't stand an earthly and I'm looking after my own neck.'

'Thanks for the vote of confidence,' said Kovacs sharply.

'Somebody's got to say it.'

'Just don't say it in front of the others. One or two of them aren't happy with you as it is.'

'Because I don't want to go?'

'Something like that.' Kovacs softened his tone. 'You forget, Jack, they hardly know you from Adam. The Chief and I guess you've got your reasons. Alphabet, too. But to lots of these guys you're a stranger who spends half his life causing trouble.'

'They've known me since August last year, for Christ's sake.'

'Some of them. And some of *those* don't go a heap of horse pucky on you believing the tunnels can't make it.'

'I haven't made it that obvious.'

Kovacs and Greyfoot exchanged glances.

'It's been discussed,' said Kovacs.

'You mean you've told them what I think.'

Kovacs shrugged.

'If it's not just that you don't like the odds,' said the Chief, 'what else is there?'

They'll be picked up, thought Jack. They'll be picked up before noon on March 24 and be in a Gestapo cellar by three p.m. By midnight they'll have told the Gestapo everything I've told them.

'Don't say anything even to your closest friends about what occurred in that briefing room, or here,' the MI9 officer had said to him. 'In fact, this conversation never took place. It will not appear on your service record. You may believe they're tough and loyal, but no one's tough enough to withstand Gestapo treatment. Trust me, I know. You

209

need luck, and luck is something we try not to budget for in this department.'

Jack was inclined to take this officer's word. If Oberst Gessel and his miserable bunch could behave as they had since Jubilee, God know what the Gestapo or the SS would be like.

'Have you had your escape numbers drawn yet?' he asked casually.

'What's that got to do with a hill of beans? We haven't, as it happens.'

'Take late numbers if you can manage it. It's a feeling I have.'

'Maybe it's a feeling you should communicate to the rest of the guys.'

'They wouldn't listen to me. But you can tell them one thing if you get the chance. Ask them why the goons haven't tried any sudden shakedowns, blitzes. There has to be a reason.'

'We've already discussed that. We've been craftier than they are, that's all. They don't suspect a thing.'

'I see,' said Jack. 'All the brainy guys are on our team and all the dumb ones on theirs, is that it?'

'Those beatings are going to your head, if you see what I mean,' said Kovacs.

Jack tackled Alphabet separately.

'The hazards are enormous. You don't speak a word of German and you're going to walk out of here dressed as some kind of labourer. Even if your papers are okay – and I don't want to know – you're buggered the minute someone stops you.'

'Better than being buggered by Harlow in the cooler,' sniffed Alphabet resentfully. He didn't want to be told, not even by Jack Lambert, that his escape shot stood no chance of success.

Jack stared at him.

'Is that what they're saying, in London and William?'

Alphabet hesitated.

'A few, maybe.'

'I ought to break your neck.'

'You'd be doing me a favour, if I don't get out.'

Jack took a couple of deep breaths and calmed down. Whatever was being said wasn't Alphabet's fault.

'What's your escape number?' he asked Alphabet. 'Have you been told?'

'Just now, drew them out of a hat. It's two. We're moving into London. William's three days behind.'

'Change it, you jerk off. Don't ask me why, just change the bastard, Zgerbzwsky.'

Alphabet was startled by Jack's use of his family name.

'Why change? First out, first away.'

'Just do it. Get to the back of the line. Someone else will want to go ahead, you mark my words.'

The escapers went into Tunnel London like clockwork soldiers shortly before nine p.m. on March 23. At twenty minutes after midnight on March 24 they broke through the earth's surface, fifteen feet into the trees, within a yard of what had been predicted. At twenty-six minutes after midnight the German machine guns opened fire.

The Krauts, it was agreed later, hadn't rushed matters. From their machine-gun trenches they had permitted two men to get past the cordon, in order to get more into the clearing. These two were picked up before two o'clock in the morning heading for Frankfurt. Picked up by a Wehrmacht patrol that knew where they were going and handed over to the Gestapo for interrogation. They never came back to Stalag XIII K. Rumour had it that they were hanged with piano wire. One of them, anyway. The other was said to have faced a firing squad while his companion looked on, being strangled.

Apart from those who were shot on exiting, everyone else in London scampered back down the tunnel, panic-stricken. They were arrested by grinning ferrets as they emerged from the trapdoor. The Chief and Kovacs were among the survivors.

So too was Alphabet. He had accepted Jack's advice and exchanged his number two for number twenty-four.

The survivors were tossed into solitary for twenty-eight days. The Krauts used the Oflag cooler, also, because there was not enough room in that belonging to the Stalag. London was filled in by the Kriegies, as was William. The goons had known about them both.

Oberst Gessel displayed the bodies of the six men 'shot while trying to escape' on the morning of March 24, during *Appell*. They were covered by tarpaulins, but each sheet was lifted to reveal the dead men's faces.

Jack was relieved to see that Alphabet was not among the corpses. Nor was the Chief or Kovacs. Nor anyone he knew closely. They'd lived as strangers and, now, they would be buried as strangers.

The poor bastards.

In the postmortem that followed the failed escape, Jack was called before a committee headed by RQMS Maitland, and grilled. Why had he been so certain the attempt would fail? Why had he advised Zgerbzwsky to swap a low number for a high one, because the fact that he had was common knowledge? Someone had tipped off the goons and not a hell of a lot could happen in the compound until the committee found out who.

He managed to convince his interrogators that it was just an instinct, a gut feeling, that their security was lousy. Convince some of them, anyway. A few remained sceptical, felt that he had somehow betrayed them. This handful was not willing to go as far as saying that Sergeant Lambert was a stool-pigeon for the goons, but he must have, they insisted to one another, let something slip. Maybe to save himself from another beating.

They would let it slide for now because they had no proof, but a handwritten note, unsigned, left Jack in no doubt that he would be watched carefully in the future.

FOURTEEN

March–May 1943

Two of the major escape and evasion routes run by MI9 in Western Europe were known as the PAO, or Pat, line and the Comet line. PAO were the initials of a man who, when first coming to the attention of MI9, called himself Patrick Albert O'Leary and who claimed to be an evading Canadian flier. ('Evaders' were men who, like aircrew, had been shot down but never taken into custody; 'escapers' had been captured but had made a successful break.) Nine quickly established that he was actually Albert-Marie Guérisse, a Belgian doctor who had served with a cavalry regiment before Belgium was overrun and he escaped to England. The reason he gave for his nominal subterfuge was that he did not wish to spend the rest of the war tending the sick in some secure British hospital. He wanted to take a more active part in the hostilities than that. Later he became so valuable that MI9, many of whose officers did not trust Continental exiles now sitting it out in London, insisted he never be referred to by his true name for fear of betrayal when he was back in Europe. Thus everyone always called him Pat, and the name stuck as a soubriquet for th- e escape route he operated.

From collecting centres in Lille, Amiens, Rheims and Paris, among others, escapers were passed hand to hand down Pat through Vichy France, one route going via Clermont-Ferrand to Arles, a second via Lyons to Marseilles. A third took in Limoges and Toulouse. All routes led to Barcelona, a delivery centre. From Barcelona the escapers went via Madrid to Gibraltar. Anyone who got that far, naturally, was almost home and dry.

Until he was betrayed in March 1943 and disappeared under Hitler's *Nacht und Nebel* decree, Guérisse was responsible for moving to safety six hundred people. (Guérisse did, however, survive his concentration camp and the war.)

The Comet line began at the Paris collecting centre and skirted

Vichy France to the west, travelling south-west to San Sebastian and Bilbao, thereafter Madrid and Gibraltar. The leading light in Comet was the twenty-five-year-old daughter of a Brussels schoolmaster named Andrée de Jongh, at first suspected of being a Nazi plant. She soon proved otherwise, however, and afterwards her bravery and ingenuity were never again questioned. She was tough, too. Before being captured by the Gestapo early in 1943 she personally escorted over one hundred people across the Pyrenees into Spain.

Like Guérisse, Andrée de Jongh survived her concentration camp, in this case Ravensbrück, and later used her nursing training with refugees in Ethiopia and Senegal. Her schoolmaster father wasn't so fortunate. The Gestapo shot him.

Pat and Comet were slowly replaced by other evasion lines, most notably Shelburne operating from Paris to Britanny and then Cornwall. But Shelburne, and Pat and Comet before they were destroyed, were only active outside Germany's borders. In order to utilize their services, therefore, an escaper from Germany had first of all to get out of the Third Reich.

MI9, its sister service MI6, and the American equivalent of Nine, MIS-X, had many agents-in-place in Germany, in the major cities, quite a few since well before the war. Most of these men and women, naturally, were German nationals, either Communists or just plain anti-Nazis. All had taken great care for many years to conceal their true sympathies. To all intents and purposes they were model citizens, frequently in positions of some authority. They took enormous chances with clandestine wirelesses and were often picked up by the Gestapo, tortured and shot.

For the most part men and women working in the same city did not know of the existence of one another. All they had were some code words, recognition signals, and perhaps the location of a street corner in a nearby town or city to which any escaper who contacted them and could prove his identity should be delivered, on specific days at specific times.

Frankfurt's sole agent-in-place was codenamed Cupid. His real name was Hans-Dieter Biber, age thirty-five, a teacher of higher mathematics at the Schillerschule on Gartenstrasse, half a mile south of the River Main. He lived alone in a two-room apartment on Cranachstrasse, just a few yards from the school.

Unmarried, thin and bespectacled, he was a most unlikely looking agent, which is how it should be. Thanks to chronic asthma, the Wehrmacht hadn't wanted his services. He was, in any case, a valuable member of the faculty and strings could have been pulled to get him deferment even if he'd been one hundred per cent fit.

A socialist, but never a Communist, since his university days, he had been scouted by a talent spotter for British Intelligence soon after Hitler's Anschluss of Austria. When he proved amenable he was given a radio and taught how to use it; Morse only, since in the event of war Frankfurt would be out of range for voice communications without a massive antenna.

He was told in the middle of May to expect an escaper some time towards the end of June. The password would be Strudel. No other details were given. Jack Lambert was also informed, in a series of coded letters from the Licensed Victuallers' Sports Association, that his password was Strudel, where and to whom to report in Frankfurt, and to make his escape attempt, as he'd said he could when ordered, between 20th and 30th of June, as near to the first date as possible. It had to be a series of communications from the LVSA because there was too much information to go in one coded letter without it being of vast, and therefore suspicious, length.

Sergeant Lambert was not instructed to look out for anything in particular, just keep his eyes open for troop movements. If anything else was required, he would be informed of it by one of his contacts somewhere down the line. He would be debriefed in full in England.

Late in May, due to the high spring pollen count and the air being filled with choking dust as a result of a heavy bombing raid on Frankfurt, Cupid took to his bed with a severe asthma attack, scarcely able to move or breathe let alone keep his weekly wireless rendezvous with Bletchley Park in Buckinghamshire. For seventy-two hours he sweated and coughed and thought he was going to die. Concerned at his non-appearance, his landlady, Frau Blessing, brought him soup and other hot drinks, about the only nourishment he could take. Several of his students came to see him, as did the head of the mathematics department. Wheezing piteously, he thanked them as best he could, but said there was nothing to be done. He had medication always available. With it and rest, the attacks would eventually subside. They understood and left him in peace.

On the fourth day he felt better and on the fifth he was able to move around. He should, he accepted, communicate with Bletchley Park immediately. If they didn't hear from him they would jump to the wrong conclusion, assume he'd been caught, and inform Strudel accordingly. For all he, Hans-Dieter Biber, knew, Strudel might be vitally important in the fight against Hitler's evil.

So he broke his golden rule and set up his radio on a non-scheduled day. Hitherto it had always been a Wednesday afternoon, when Frau Blessing left the house as regularly as clockwork for four hours. She said, when he joked with her about it, that every Wednesday she played bridge with three girlfriends on the other side of the river. He suspected she had a married lover who was only free on Wednesday afternoons.

He set up his wireless and aerial, and donned his headphones. Then he tapped out his call sign. It took a little while for Bletchley Park to answer, and he suspected what was happening. Probably his regular operator, one who would recognize his Morse 'fist', was not on duty, and someone had gone to fetch the Duty Officer. Whatever it was, he was sitting there, headphones on, for ten minutes before Bletchley responded positively.

In that ten minutes, it not being a Wednesday, Frau Blessing appeared at his apartment door, a bowl of soup and some black bread on a tray, and knocked softly. She was a maternal soul, a widow no longer in the first flush of youth, and she rather liked Herr Biber. Certainly he was not much to look at, but he was an educated man with a good position and absolutely no chance of being taken away to war. (Cupid was wrong in believing she had a lover; she did, as she said, play bridge on Wednesday afternoons.)

When she received no reply to her first rapping, she knocked again, louder.

Again nothing, and she began to worry. Perhaps he'd had a relapse. He had seemed better yesterday, true, but her husband had appeared as fit as a flea two hours before he suffered a fatal heart attack. Apart from her personal interest in Herr Biber, he was an excellent tenant, always paying his rent on time. He might, even now, be lying dying on the floor, waiting for someone to help him. He might also, of course, be semi-naked in the middle of having a wash.

She put the tray on a small table and produced her pass key. Gently she opened the door, calling, 'Herr Biber, Herr Biber.'

He didn't hear her, couldn't. He was sitting facing the window, facing away from her, headphones on, Morse key on his lap, pencil and pad on a high-backed chair.

Frau Blessing withdrew, shocked. Radios like that were absolutely forbidden under the war regulations. Surely that nice Herr Biber wasn't a spy? Surely not. But if he was . . .

She knew her duty, Frau Blessing. There was a sub-police station on Schneckenhofstrasse, three minutes away. Within five minutes she was telling her story. Within fifteen Hans-Dieter Biber was under arrest, a uniformed policeman guarding the entrance to his apartment. Within an hour Cupid was in Gestapo HQ at 22 Bürgerstrasse.

It didn't take rubber truncheons or pliers or lighted matches to break him. He was a dedicated anti-Nazi but quite an ordinary man beneath all that. And a sick one. After he was punched a few times, he told the Gestapo all he knew.

They promised him his life if he would cooperate with them, if he continued to stay in touch with British Intelligence, sending what he was told to send. The sudden cessation of his recent transmission could easily be explained. He had seen a detection van in the street below. Or he had lost power owing to an electricity supply cut. Simple.

Still far from well after his asthma attack, he pretended to agree, knowing they would shoot him, or worse, when they had no further use for him. They wanted Strudel, whoever Strudel might be. They wanted this Strudel and every other Strudel who came through. That was no way to beat Hitler.

He had been told by his doctor that he was unlikely to live beyond the age of forty, due to the strain put on his heart and lungs when he had one of his spasms. So be it. If only they would shoot him they would probably be doing him a service. But he couldn't take a lot of pain.

There was an automatic cutout warning signal agreed with Bletchley from the start. If he began his transmission by keying in that Bletchley's carrier wave was being received strength five, then amended that to strength one, he was sending under duress.

When he tried it he was caught out immediately by the Gestapo radio expert sitting next to him and wearing a duplicate headset. The signal had obviously not changed from strength five to strength one, and the Gestapo man pulled the plug.

Biber was returned to Bürgerstrasse and again grilled, this time not so gently. When he was discovered to be asthmatic they blew cigarette smoke in his face and laughed when he coughed and spluttered.

Who was Strudel?

He couldn't tell them because he didn't know. Strudel was expected at Cranachstrasse some time before the end of June; that's all he had.

After a few hours the Gestapo accepted they had bled him clean. They would catch Strudel when Strudel turned up.

They sent Biber to Buchenwald with specific instructions to put him in a cell no bigger than a small cupboard. He was not to be permitted the easy death of a bullet. In the cell, because of his asthma, he died in dreadful agony within two weeks.

Knowing the cipher and Biber's codename, the Gestapo continued trying to stay in touch with England. But not for long. The operator at Bletchley, never mind the cutout, recognized that the sending fist was not that of Hans-Dieter Biber. Station Cupid went off the air for good before the end of May.

But now MI9 had a problem. Strudel had been instructed to get out between June 20 and June 30, preferably nearer June 20. Should they use the Radio Padre to tell Strudel to abandon his escape attempt until other arrangements could be made?

They decided against it. The Radio Padre already had enough messages to get through without adding to them, some more vital than Strudel's breakout. Looking at the thing as a whole, there was more involved than the possible capture of one Canadian commando. If that was tough, so was the war. Guérisse was missing, possibly dead. Andrée de Jongh had gone too. They would do their best, but . . .

Anyway, the earliest date Strudel would be making his attempt was three weeks off. There was plenty of time to warn him via the LVSA provided a letter was dispatched immediately.

Which would have been fine had Jack Lambert not learned early in June that Harlow was due to be transferred to a fighting unit before the middle of the month, at least a week before the first date Jack could make his break. All his patient planning would have been for nothing if Harlow went to the Eastern Front or wherever. He would just have to go off his own bat whenever the opportunity arose, either contact Cupid early or lie low, live off the land until he could.

FIFTEEN

June 1943

His friends noticed a change in Jack Lambert starting around the middle of May. Where before he had been surly and morose much of the time, now he was almost jovial. As if he had accepted prison camp life and was going to stay within the system rather than buck it. He no longer taunted the goons or tried to make trouble. He was no longer a loner. He joined in conversations with his fellow Kriegies, talked enthusiastically about participating in the next tunnel venture, though agreeing that it would be unwise to begin one until the stool pigeon who betrayed London was unmasked. When someone produced a volley ball, he became a keen member of one of the scratch teams. If someone wanted an opponent for a chess game or a checkers game, he was among the first to offer his services. A fifth for a poker hand, cigarettes as chips? Ask Jack Lambert. He was, in short, a model prisoner.

His friends were not the only ones to witness the metamorphosis. Sergeants Winterman and Hayes did also.

'Lucky bastard,' grunted Winterman. 'He's got the word.'

'Either that or he's taken one beating too many.'

'Not him, I'll lay you eight-to-five.'

'I'd like to see how he manages it,' said Hayes. 'Without a tunnel or a work party it's going to be a neat trick.'

'My money's on Lambert. The crafty sod's got something going for him.'

It had taken months to work out and the linchpins were Harlow and the cooler.

As Jack knew from bitter if self-imposed experience, once in solitary a Kriegie became virtually a non-person. He was stuck in a tiny cell, one of a row of six, in which a single naked bulb burned day and night. His meagre rations, the cabbage soup and black bread, were thrust through a tiny flap in the door once a day. There was no way out through the flap. He'd examined it. A man would have to be half the size of Ernie Kiley to stand anything of a chance, and then he was in a corridor that ran the length of the six cells. At the end of the corridor was a massive iron door, locked from the outside. Even Lucas the locksmith could not have cracked it.

Because it was considered impossible to escape from the cooler, and because solitary, intended as a punishment, meant exactly that, no outside human contact, no permanent guard was placed in the cell block. Instead the duty goon appeared once an hour on the hour during his shift and opened a grille set high in the cell door. Just to make sure the prisoner hadn't despaired and opened a vein, or tried to dispose of himself in some other manner. Not that the goons from Gessel down cared much about their charges' fate. They just didn't want a Kriegie to get out of it that easily.

Guard duties were in eight-hour periods, changing at six a.m., two p.m., and ten p.m. Before the new guard took over it was customary for the old one to make his final inspection a quarter of an hour before the end of his watch. Then the relieving goon made his usual on-the-hour inspection of the cells.

Jack had made a study of Harlow's routine when he came off the late watch, at ten p.m. Although by that hour the Kriegies were always locked up, it was a simple matter to get out of a hut. A length of hooked wire through a forced transom, and the latch was lifted. It was always dangerous because sometimes the dogs were loose, but the prisoners did it regularly if for no other reason than to see friends in other huts or continue a card game. There were also the searchlights from the goon towers to be taken into consideration, but these usually played the length of the perimeter fence.

Harlow's habits hardly ever varied, winter or summer. He came off watch, dumped his machine pistol and *stahlhelm* in the guardroom, donned his walking-out cap, and jumped into the K-wagen standing close to the cell block. Then he drove out through the main gates, always alone. Jack guessed he was never accompanied because of his peculiar sexual tastes. He probably headed for a homosexual club or bar in Frankfurt. Or maybe he had a male lover in a nearby village.

Jack suspected, because petrol was doubtless rationed, that it was strictly speaking against regulations for off-duty goons to use the K-wagen for private motoring. But other goons did it too, sometimes. Either Gessel and Axheim didn't know about it or chose to turn a blind eye. Whichever, the K-wagen was never stopped at the barrier. Harlow tooted the klaxon, gave a wave, and then he was through.

Jack supposed other Kriegies had observed the routine also, but had found no way to exploit it. The goons could leave the key in the ignition for all the good it would do. It wouldn't be much use waiting in the shadows for Harlow or any other guard, battering him senseless and then attempting to drive the K-wagen through the gate. Just because the goons were dumb didn't mean they were idiots. The barrier guard would immediately spot a stranger behind the wheel. There were a hell of a lot of lights at the gates. As for overpowering a guard while in solitary and forcing him to do the driving, that was impossible. The cell doors were never opened except once every forty-eight hours, during the day, for the prisoner to slop out his latrine pail.

Impossible? Well, not quite.

Jack had thought long and hard, way before he heard from MI9, about who, if anyone, he would take with him when he made his break. Ideally it should be someone who spoke reasonable German; that would give him more of a chance. But someone had ratted to the goons about Tunnel London, and that someone could be any one of six hundred souls. About the only people he would really trust were the Chief, Alphabet and Kovacs.

Since his time in the cooler after the Tunnel London fiasco, Alphabet had become more withdrawn and disconsolate. The day was coming when he would do something stupid and get shot for his pains. If anyone it had to be Alphabet. The Chief would make out okay even if he was forced to stay behind barbed-wire for the rest of the war. He hated it, of course, but he was tough. So too was Kovacs. Kovacs would make it and go home to earn a fortune. Or run Canada.

So Alphabet it would be. The only question remaining was: did two stand a better chance than one? On balance Jack thought they did. When he heard from London he decided that Strudel would have to have an Apfel to go with it, and London could either like it or lump it.

But he said nothing to Alphabet. Alphabet would learn all about it when the day came.

One other man was needed for the scheme. Well, probably not essential but useful. And in selecting a guy named Munroe, Jack proposed to kill two birds with one stone.

Munroe, a ferret-faced individual from Timmins in Ontario, was one of the 'fat cats', the racketeers who operated as middlemen between the goons and the Kriegies, exchanging cigarettes or anything else marketable from Red Cross parcels for extra food, and keeping much of the barter for themselves. They weren't even beaten up regularly any longer since many of the POWs accepted that it was better to get a little extra, even at a price, than nothing at all. Moreover, the Germans with whom they traded acted as their protectors.

Jack had had a set-to with Munroe in May, when Munroe had given a prisoner from Hut 6B two small potatoes for fifteen cigarettes. The going rate was four for ten. Jack had been ready to beat the daylights out of the Ontario man when Munroe took to his heels. Thirty minutes later two goons appeared in 6B and gestured Jack outside at bayonet point. There he was warned, in broken English but with the meaning demonstrably clear, that if anything happened to Munroe the goons would know who to look for. Sergeant Lambert would then find himself in the cooler for a considerable period.

Since Sergeant Lambert had just learned that his breakout was imminent, he decided that discretion was the order of the day. He couldn't afford any trouble.

It did cross his mind that Munroe or one of the other 'fat cats' was the man who had ratted on Tunnel London, but then he dismissed the thought. The goons wouldn't be that obvious. The stool pigeon was someone the other Kriegies would never suspect.

Once Jack knew he was to escape somewhere close to June 20, he began to let his hair grow. Attempting a home run was going to be difficult enough without looking like a convict. Hair was still kept very short because of the threat of lice, but now the POWs cut their own. The goons didn't seem at all concerned that there were several pairs of scissors in the camp. Alphabet couldn't be warned to grow his also, not without letting him know that something was in the wind.

Jack also began exchanging what remained of his 'soft' rations from his last Red Cross package for 'hard' stuff: cigarettes, tea, dried milk for chocolate and biscuits. These he buried, during the dark hours, behind 6B's latrines, with the rest of his rations and the two sets of civilian clothes. The cache would have to be unearthed and reburied closer to the cooler in due course, but it was safe enough where it was for now.

In spite of himself he found it hard to conceal his excitement throughout the first days of June. Kovacs tackled him about it during a game of poker in which the other players were Tucker, Turner and McKenzie, when Jack gambled foolishly with only two tens in his hand and lost ten hard-won cigarettes to McKenzie's three sevens.

'If I didn't know better, Jack, I'd say you'd been drinking some of Munroe's potato wine.'

'I'll go blind in my own way, thanks. Put it down to the weather.'

The temperature was in the low eighties. 'As hot as a whore's box,' as Tucker termed it.

Two hands later, with twenty cigarettes in the pot, Jack was holding two pair, queens and fours, with only Kovacs and Turner still in the game. He was concentrating now and pretty certain he had both of his opponents beaten. He would get back what he'd lost and a few more cigarettes as a bonus. Translated, that meant two bars of chocolate or a packet of biscuits. Enough to sustain life for twenty-four hours if used sparingly.

Then the Chief came in and dropped his bombshell.

'Something to make us laugh, for once. Harlow's got his marching orders. In two weeks he's heading for the Eastern Front. In three, with a bit of luck, he'll be dead. Christ, they must be running short of manpower if they're conscripting the Girl Scouts.'

Jack fought to keep the tremor from his voice.

'Where did you hear that?' he asked casually.

'Maitland. He got it from some goon or other.'

Jack played out the hand, and won as he'd predicted, but then announced that he was cashing in his chips. Today was June 3. A fortnight away was June 17, three days before the first day he'd been instructed to make his break. What rotten bastard luck!

It took him another day to catch up with Harlow, doing a stint as a patrolling compound ferret. They each had a little of the other's language by now. Not much and mostly ungrammatical, but enough to communicate in either pidgin German or English, or a combination of both. Private Schultz looked as if he'd been asked to take on the whole Russian army by himself. Life expectancy was measurable in days out there, and he knew it.

'*Ost Frontur?*' said Jack. '*Russland?*'

'*Ja,*' answered Harlow miserably. 'East.'

'*Wann?*'

'*Vierzehn Tage. Siebzehn Juni.* June seventeen. Dead soon.'

Oh no you fucking don't, thought Jack. Oh no you don't.

Jack sought out Maitland. What he had to say was taking a chance, but he needed the answer.

'I've got something in mind that I'd rather not explain, but I need to know who's on cooler duty for the next couple of weeks.'

'Not thinking of getting yourself thrown in the boob again, are you, Jack?'

'You never can tell. Can you do it?'

'It means I'll owe someone a favour or two. I'd like to know a bit more.'

Jack had his lie ready.

'The fat cats are starting to rip off some of my lads again, and I'm thinking of doing something about it. But that might earn me fourteen days' solitary and it'd help to know who's on. Some of those bastards get their rocks off by putting the boot in, and I don't fancy another whacking.'

'Sure it's worth it?'

'This war will run and run as they used to say on the movie marquees. Until it's over there's no real way of settling Munroe and his gang's hash. But they've got to be shown once in a while that they're not invulnerable.'

'Give me a day.'

Twenty-four hours later he had the list. Jack scrutinized it anxiously. Schultz's name was there, on the two-till-ten watch, between June 8 and June 15. After that he'd probably be given a forty-eight before reporting to his new unit.

Okay, to hell with June 20. It had to be between June 8 and June 15. And it still needed a great deal of planning.

On June 7, during the hours of darkness, he slipped out of Hut 6B and dug up his cache of rations and civilian clothes. He could hear dogs in the distance, but they seemed to be penned up. Or on the leash.

It took him two hours because he had to avoid patrolling sentries and the occasional searchlight that shone in his direction, but by four a.m. he had reburied his supplies and clothing, using a homemade trowel, ten feet from the cooler on the blind side and four feet deep. He was in no danger from the duty guard checking the cell block. It was unoccupied at present. He just hoped to God the dogs didn't have a nose for chocolate.

On the morning of June 7 he persuaded Alphabet to take a stroll round the compound. Earlier he had already spotted Munroe, surrounded by some of his fat cat cronies, over by the kitchens, smoking and laughing among themselves. Fair enough, the bastard would be laughing on the other side of his ugly face in a few minutes.

Munroe saw them coming, but reckoned there was little chance of trouble. They were eight to Lambert's two, and not even Lambert would fancy those odds. Nor was there anything threatening in Lambert's attitude.

Jack made sure it remained that way, as he made sure that Alphabet was between himself and Munroe's group. When they were level he gave Alphabet a sudden push, sending him sprawling through the men surrounding Munroe. A moment later he was among them himself, moving very fast. He managed to clip Munroe and deck him. Munroe's friends suddenly deserted him, not wanting anything to do with a situation that could land them all in the cooler, deprive them of the relatively comfortable life they enjoyed in the compound.

By the time the goons arrived to break up the fight there were only three people mixing it, and Alphabet, protesting, wasn't at all sure what was going on anyway. Jack worked it that Munroe had him pinned to the earth, apparently the aggressor, when the guards pulled them apart. For good measure Jack swung a punch at the nearest goon.

In front of Oberst Gessel twenty minutes later, Munroe protested volubly that Lambert had been the cause of the fracas and wanted to call his friends as witnesses. But they'd gone to ground, unwilling to speak in case Gessel was in one of his fouler tempers and decided to punish everyone. There was no honour among this particular den of thieves.

The commandant was hot and sticky, and not in the mood to be lenient. Nor interested in excuses. Three men had been caught fighting and three men would go to the cooler. Fourteen days apiece starting at once.

Alphabet stared at Jack in bewilderment as they were marched off. It was forbidden to speak now they had been sentenced, but his expression said it all. What the hell are you doing, Jack, getting me shoved in the slammer too?

Sergeants Winterman and Hayes watched them go. Winterman shook his head.

'He's fucked himself now, the silly bastard. What a waste.'

Kovacs was inclined to agree.

'He's flipped his lid again. I thought he was over all that.'

'Munroe deserves all he gets,' said the Chief.

'You'll get no argument from me on that score, but Jack could have done it by himself. Why drag Alphabet into it? Fourteen days'll be like fourteen years to him.'

Jack had no means of informing Alphabet that neither of them would be serving their full term. The solitary confinement cells were little more than small rooms and solidly built. It was possible to hear someone calling through the walls, but Jack was in the middle of the three occupied cells. Anything he said to Alphabet would be heard by Munroe also. And Munroe would spill it to the goons double quick.

Prisoners in the cooler received no food or water on their first day, or Red Cross parcels or mail ever. Thus Jack would not learn in the coded letter from the Licensed Victuallers' Sports Association that the escape attempt was off, even though the letter reached Stalag XIII K on June 11.

Before then, on their first day, he waited patiently for two o'clock to arrive and for Harlow's face to appear at the grille. He planned to get out that night if it was humanly possible. It was taking something of a chance because it would mean he and Alphabet having to lie low for almost two weeks, until June 20, but now he was so close he couldn't wait any longer.

When two p.m. duly arrived and the grille was opened, the face there was not that of Private Schultz. Because he had no wristwatch Jack thought at first that he had made a mistake with the hour and that it was only one p.m. But that couldn't be. The grille had opened fifteen minutes earlier for the retiring guard to make his final check. Where the hell was Harlow? What was Gefreiter Hornick doing on duty?

Three p.m. came and went and it was still Hornick making the hourly check. Jack fought down a surge of panic. Surely Harlow's movement order hadn't been brought forward? That would be too ironic for words.

At four p.m., when Hornick again opened the grille, Jack was ready for him.

'*Wo ist Shultz?*' he asked.

'*Er hat Halsschmerzen.* Sore throat.'

The grille slammed shut.

I do not believe it, groaned Jack, holding his head in his hands. I do not fucking believe it.

But at least it was only a throat infection, not a broken leg or the clap. Two or three days at the most.

For the first time in a long time Jack said a silent prayer.

Harlow turned up for duty again on June 12, just when Jack was beginning to despair. His blond head appeared in the grille opening and he grinned delightedly when he saw who the prisoner in the middle cell was. Jack smiled back, equally happy. Harlow would no doubt misinterpret his pleasure, but that was neither here nor there. Tonight was the night.

In one of the adjacent cells Munroe passed the time plotting his revenge on Sergeant bloody Lambert. Whatever the consequences, Lambert was going to get the worst beating of his life or a knife between his ribs as soon as the fourteen days were up. Munroe was so enraged at being incarcerated that he spent many of his waking hours screaming abuse through the walls. He was ignored, which angered him even more.

In the other adjacent cell Alphabet spent his days pacing up and down, counting his steps, trying to figure out how many made a mile. At an average walking speed of four miles per hour he could tell within a few yards when the grille would open again. It was a silly game, like children avoiding cracks in the pavement, but it stopped him from going insane. Or maybe, he thought, just doing what he was doing meant he'd gone mad. It was hard to tell. The dividing line between the normal and the abnormal was a fine one in Stalag XIII K.

The nights were worst. Or rather, as night approached and the shifts changed. Between eight o'clock and ten o'clock he felt at his lowest, because as soon as the night guard came on he knew, though tired, that it was time for sleep he wouldn't get.

On the evening of June 12, when Harlow opened the grille to make his final inspection, at nine forty-five, before going off duty, Alphabet sat on the blanketless straw palliasse that was his bed and wondered if he would be strong enough to see out the fourteen days. On the outside a man sometimes forgot what it was like on the inside: the bugs in the palliasse, the lack of fresh air or the sight of blue sky, the stench from the sanitation pail. Hut 6B was a palace compared to this.

Then something odd happened. In the next cell, instead of the grille opening, the door itself was unlocked. There was no mistaking the sounds, the rattle of keys, the hinges squeaking. What the hell was going on?

It didn't take long for Alphabet to find out. Those sounds, too, were easily recognizable, whether between a man and a woman or two men. In Jack's cell some kind of homosexual act was taking place.

Alphabet felt sick to his stomach.

In the cell on the other side Munroe also correctly deduced what was happening. He thumped one fist into the palm of the other hand with exultation. The mighty incorruptible Jack Lambert a beefer! What a turn up for the book. The bastard would never be able to hold his head up in the compound again once word got around. This was better, far, far better, than sticking a shiv in his ribs.

Then came another noise, one he couldn't identify. Like something heavy falling to the floor.

Alphabet scrambled to his feet at the sound of a key turning in the lock of his cell door. When it opened Jack was standing there, a fierce smile of triumph on his face.

'Come on, old son, we're getting out.'

Alphabet was totally bemused.

'I don't get it.' He stared at the keys in Jack's fist. And at the Mauser 98K rifle slung over one shoulder, bayonet gleaming. Harlow's rifle. 'How the hell . . .?'

'No time for questions now. The relief guard will be along in a few minutes. We've got to dispose of him. That'll give us at least an hour, maybe longer.'

'But the keys . . .'

'Harlow wasn't going to open the door unless I made it worth his while to come in, was he? It's been planned for months, laddie. Like they used to tell us at Achnacarry, there are more ways of breaking down a wall than hitting it with a battering ram.'

'Fucking incredible,' breathed Alphabet, awed. 'Absolutely fucking incredible. But Jesus, the gates, the guards . . .'

'It'll all be explained when I've got time. At the moment we're short of it.'

Alphabet followed Jack into the corridor. Passing Jack's cell he saw Harlow lying in a crumpled heap.

'Is he dead?'

'He'd better not be. He's our ticket out. I had to clobber him a bit hard to make sure, but he should be coming to in a couple of minutes. Keep an eye on him. Sit on him if you have to, but don't damage him any further.'

228

'What about Munroe?'

'Ah yes, Munroe. Mustn't forget Munroe.'

Jack selected a key and opened Munroe's cell door. The man from Ontario backed off when he saw who his visitor was. But he wasn't slow to comprehend what was going on. Or foolish enough, in his view, to participate in an escape.

'Forget it,' he snarled. 'Count me out. You'll get us all killed, you crazy bastard.'

'Nobody invited you to the party, Munroe. You'd be excess luggage.'

Munroe saw how he could make some capital out of this for himself. All he had to do was raise his voice, summon one of the guards, and Gessel would owe him. At the very least he would not be made to serve out the rest of his sentence in this stinking fleapit. Whatever happened to Lambert and the Polack, he couldn't give a shit.

He opened his mouth to yell. Jack took three quick steps towards him.

'I kind of gathered you'd try something like that,' he said, and sideswiped Munroe across the head with the muzzle of the Mauser. Munroe hit the dirt floor like a felled ox, blood pouring from the wound.

'Munroe's not coming I take it,' said Alphabet, standing over Harlow.

'You take it right. I've got other plans for him, just in case Harlow doesn't want to cooperate.'

Jack bent down and removed Harlow's watch. It was a British make, he noticed, doubtless taken from some poor bugger in exchange for an extra slice of bread. He slipped it over his own wrist. It was three minutes to ten.

'And you planned that too,' asked Alphabet, 'with Munroe? The fight and everything?'

'I've had a lot of time to think, old lad. Bloody near ten months. Make sure he doesn't make a noise while I deal with this new bastard.'

Jack stood just inside the cell block main door. It was open, of course, because Harlow had seen no reason to lock it when he came in. Unless they'd altered the duty roster from the list RQMS Maitland had obtained, the relief goon should be Gefreiter Grell, with whom

229

Jack had had dealings before, last time in solitary. Grell took particular pleasure in slamming a pistol butt into a prisoner's testicles.

When Grell came in, on the stroke of ten o'clock, the first thing that met his eyes were three open cell doors. He slipped his sidearm, a P38 Walther, from its holster and charged forward. That was his first mistake, not checking behind the cell block door. His second was not immediately calling for help. It was also his last.

Holding the Mauser by the muzzle, Jack swung it like a club. The butt caught Grell across the back of the neck and he went down without a whimper. His *stahlhelm* fell off and bounced away down the corridor like tumbleweed.

'Stick him in with Munroe,' Jack called, locking the main door just in case a patrolling goon got nosey. 'How's Harlow doing?'

'Coming round.'

Jack picked up Grell's Walther and pocketed it. He'd take that too, as well as the Mauser, though he wasn't planning on starting a Second Front all by himself. The rifle and the pistol would have to be ditched once they were clear of the Stalag. If he and Alphabet were captured they might just about get away with a lengthy spell in the cooler if they were found unarmed. With weapons it would mean a firing squad.

'He's conscious, Jack.'

Conscious and scared, not so much by two *Tommis*, one of them armed, as by the magnitude of his sin. There was only one way the cell door could have been opened and that was by him. He'd be lucky ever to see the Eastern Front. Gessel would have him shot or handed over to the Gestapo.

'Now listen to me,' said Jack, squatting on his haunches, 'and listen carefully.'

In a mixture of pidgin English and German he managed to convey to Harlow what he wanted from the guard. In a few minutes Harlow was going to get into the K-wagen as he usually did when coming off duty. And no fucking nonsense about not having the keys. They were in his pocket, that had already been checked. His two passengers would be crouched in the back, down behind the front seats. The Walther would be pointing at Harlow's spine. If anything went wrong, if he tried to warn the barrier guard, it would be the last move he made on this earth.

'I'll blow your balls of, *Ich verspreche Ihnen.*'

Most of the instructions were given in two-word sentences and monosyllables. 'K-wagen. You drive. Us. Out. Frankfurt.' But their meaning was unmistakable, especially when Jack drew the blade of his hand across his own throat.

Harlow shook his head in horror. He had already committed an unpardonable crime, but there was still a chance, just a chance, that he would only draw a weighty prison sentence or be sent to a suicide unit and not be put up against a wall. But to assist two *Tommis* to escape was certain death.

'*Nein, nein,*' he spluttered. 'No.'

Okay, thought Jack, there was no time to argue the toss. Harlow had to be made more frightened of him than of Gessel's wrath or the Gestapo. That too was part of Achnacarry.

'Bring him next door.'

Alphabet dragged Harlow to his feet and frog-marched him into the adjacent cell, where Grell and Munroe were lying unconscious. Harlow stared at the two men in terror. In just a few short minutes the whole world had gone insane.

Jack felt Grell's pulse. It was still there, but weak. That was one hell of a crack on the head he'd taken, but it hadn't broken his neck.

Jack ran a finger along the Mauser's bayonet. He looked Harlow straight in the eyes.

'You. Us. K-wagen. Out.'

'No,' said the German.

Jack bayoneted Grell through the heart. The blade went in like a hot wire through cheese. Then he planted one foot on the dead man's chest, twisted the rifle, and removed the bayonet. A sigh of air escaped like that from a punctured beachball. Jack wiped the blood off the blade on Grell's tunic.

'Jesus Christ,' said Alphabet. Killing a goon was a capital offence, no question, no appeal.

Harlow looked as if he were about to faint or be sick. Or both.

'You – us – out,' repeated Jack.

'No,' said Harlow, but there wasn't much resistance left.

There was none when Jack quickly reversed the rifle and crushed Munroe's skull with a single savage blow. Bone fractured like broken biscuits.

'The bastard deserved it,' said Jack, glaring defiantly at Alphabet, wondering if the Pole was about to give him a hard time.

'Check.'

'And we're covered. We escaped but left Munroe behind. When Grell came on duty he and Munroe got into a scrap. He clobbered Munroe, but Munroe got the rifle away before he hit the deck and bayoneted Grell. Perry Mason could tear holes in it, but it's all we've got going for us.'

'He knows different,' said Alphabet, indicating Harlow.

Jack spoke very fast so that Harlow would not be able to follow.

'But he's not going to be telling anyone.'

Jesus, thought Alphabet, you're a hard bastard, Lambert. Though if Harlow wound up dead, he wondered, what was the point in making it appear as if Grell and Munroe had iced each other?

'Now,' said Jack, jabbing the bayonet in Harlow's groin hard enough for it to hurt, 'you, us, K-wagen, out. *Verstehen Sie?*'

'*Ja,*' said Harlow, wincing at the pain. 'Not kill me, please.'

'Keep an eye on him,' said Jack. 'I'll get our civilian gear. Belt him if he as much as coughs out of turn.'

Jack removed the bayonet from the Mauser and took it with him, to use as a digging implement. It was just about dark outside, being close to the longest night of the year.

Because there was no longer any reason to cover his tracks, he unearthed his cache of clothing and rations in a few minutes. And the precious handkerchief map of Frankfurt city and the surrounding area. No time to change into civvies now. The clothes would have to go in the back of the K-wagen – parked, he was relieved though not surprised to see, in its customary place – and put on later. Harlow hadn't got his walking-out cap, which was doubtless in the guardroom, but that couldn't be helped. In any army many soldiers drove bareheaded, especially when it was hot.

He let himself back into the cell block and replaced the bayonet on the rifle. The Mauser would have to stay behind now that it had been used to kill Grell.

'Remember,' he said to Harlow, pointing the pistol menacingly.

Harlow nodded.

Jack locked the cell block from the outside and took the keys along. The goons would have spares, of course, but it would probably take some time to hunt them out. And time was life.

They made the K-wagen easily without being seen. There were no patrols around, the goon tower searchlights were concentrating on the perimeter fence, and even the dogs were quiet. They'd had a fair slice of luck up to now, thought Jack, and it was still with them. About bloody time the fates decided which side they were on.

He and Alphabet crouched down in the back, keeping as low as possible. If the gate guard looked inside they were dead men. But the duty sentry never had in the past and there was no reason for him to do so now. Harlow was going out to get laid or blow somebody's tubes. Situation normal.

Jack kept the Walther pressed up against Harlow's spine.

'Move,' he ordered.

Harlow turned the engine over. It misfired then caught. Jack sweated. Beside him Alphabet sweated, his heart beating like a tomtom, loud enough, he considered, to be heard in Berlin. The next ninety seconds were going to be the most dangerous.

It wasn't far to the main gates. Half a minute. Jack wondered if Harlow would go through with it, or if he'd leap out of the K-wagen and yell for help. If he did, he was history.

Harlow was aware of that. He had just witnessed the lunatic Sergeant Lambert kill two men, one of them a fellow *Tommi*. He had no doubt he would be the third victim if he didn't do as he was told. Another death would mean nothing to Lambert. They could only execute him once.

Jack felt the K-wagen slow down. That would be for the cantilevered barrier, the red-and-white pole fifteen yards from the gates. Nine-tenths of him wanted to poke his head up. Not being able to see what was happening was excruciating. The other tenth won out. He remained absolutely motionless apart from increasing the pressure on Harlow's spine.

The K-wagen kept rolling. Harlow called out something to the gate guard, but his tone was normal. The guard shouted something back.

The K-wagen continued on its way, at a snail's-pace. Then there was a clatter as the main gates swung open. A moment later Harlow put his foot down on the accelerator. The K-wagen gathered speed.

Jack counted to ten before sitting up and peering over his shoulder. The lights of Stalag XIII K were receding. He couldn't resist thumping Alphabet on the shoulder and letting loose a war whoop.

They were out.

Back in the Stalag guardroom they were playing cards and no one was much concerned about Grell's non-reappearance until a quarter to eleven. No one worried at all about Schultz. His cap was still on its peg, but he'd probably been in a hurry to hit Frankfurt and one of the queer bars. Still, good luck to him. He was heading east in a few days and that would be the end of him, the way the war was going out there.

At ten forty-six the guard commander sent a private named Riesel to look for Gefreiter Grell. Riesel returned after a few minutes to report that he couldn't find Grell but that the cooler was locked up and secure.

'I'll have that bastard's nuts,' growled the guard commander.

He was not bothered that Grell might be goofing off somewhere having a smoke or getting his head down. Grell's only duty was to make the hourly inspection of the solitary confinement prisoners, a soft number apart from having to be awake every hour on the hour. But the key-ring he was carrying, passed over by Schultz, held not only the keys to the cooler, but, among others, those to the kitchen. It was customary, at midnight, to send someone across there to prepare fresh coffee. The spare sets were in Oberst Gessel's quarters, and the colonel would not take kindly to being woken up because the guardroom's coffee-pot was empty.

At five minutes to twelve, when Grell had still not reappeared, the guard commander went to see for himself. He rattled the cell block door. Locked, as Riesel had said. Okay, he'd hang around. Grell was due to make his midnight inspection round about now.

But he hadn't at twelve o'clock. Nor at ten past, and now the guard commander began to worry.

By twenty past midnight he knew he had no option. Much though he dreaded the confrontation, he had to wake the commandant.

Long before that Jack had instructed Harlow to pull over to the side of the road. They had to ditch the K-wagen, preferably where it would not be found for a while, at least until daybreak. It was a shame because riding was better than walking, but they could be stopped by a mobile patrol at any time. Besides, there were still eight days to June 20. It was no use reaching Frankfurt too soon. The countryside was safer than the city. Easier to hide in, more to steal, fewer people.

He kept the pistol pointing at Harlow's head and gestured up front.

There were some trees there, the beginning of a forest by the look of it.

'*Immer gerade aus.*'

Shaking almost uncontrollably, Harlow drove until they were level with a road that led into the forest, a woodman's road, where he was ordered to turn off and keep going.

They went deep into the forest until they could drive no further, until their route was blocked by huge mountains of logs. This was as far as the timber cutters had penetrated.

'Halt,' said Jack. Harlow did so. Jack gestured. '*Motor.*' Harlow switched off the ignition.

'We're a bloody long way from Frankfurt, Jack,' said Alphabet, even now unable to believe he was out of the Stalag.

'About fifteen miles due east would be my guess. Crosscountry, that is. Longer by road, but we're not going by road.'

Jack glanced across at Alphabet. Though it was difficult to make out his companion's features in the darkness, Alphabet thought he could guess what was coming next. Maybe he was no longer the man who had stormed ashore on Orange Beach, but he felt squeamish about cold-blooded murder. Harlow wasn't much more than a kid.

'We could tie him up and gag him, or knock him cold.'

'And when they find him he tells them everything that happened in the cooler *and* what time we left him. Grow up, for Christ's sake! There's no pleasant way of doing this job and you'd better get used to it. *Face front!*' he shouted at Harlow who, sensing they were discussing his fate, turned round.

Alphabet shrugged. What the hell. Lambert was a realist and right.

Jack still had the Walther pressed against the back of Harlow's skull. Now he placed the pistol against the German's right temple. He remembered the phrase he'd heard over and over again since Dieppe.

'*Für euch ist der Krieg zu Ende,*' he said, and squeezed the trigger.

The explosion was deafening. Bits of bone and gristle and brains spattered the interior of the K-wagen. Harlow slumped in his seat. Alphabet stumbled from the vehicle and was immediately sick.

Jack placed the pistol in the German's right hand, sorry to see it go. Then he joined Alphabet and waited until the Pole had finished throwing up.

'He couldn't face the music after helping two Kriegies escape, see. He took the easy way out. The powder burns will show it was suicide.'

'You were probably doing him a favour,' said Alphabet dully, wiping the vomit from his mouth with his sleeve. 'He'd have been for the high jump either way, Eastern Front or Gestapo.'

'Fuck doing him a favour, the bastard. If I'd thought I was I'd have let him live. That was for everything he's put me through these past months.'

Jack hurled the cell block keys into the trees.

'Come on, let's get into the civilian stuff. After that we'll shove the vehicle off the track and camouflage it. It's Sunday tomorrow.' Jack squinted at Harlow's wristwatch. 'In about an hour, as a matter of fact. With any luck the lumberjacks don't work Sundays.'

'Then you'll tell me what the next step is?'

'Right. Then I'll tell you what the next step is.'

The *Sonderappell* began at one a.m., ten minutes after the cooler was unlocked with the commandant's keys and the bodies of Grell and Munroe discovered. Every guard in the camp was woken up, every Kriegie rousted from his bunk, every light in the camp switched on. Until a head-count was made, Oberst Gessel had no idea whether two men had escaped or two dozen.

Sleep-sodden prisoners were lined up in ranks while German NCOs took the tally. To start with no one knew what was going on, but gradaully word spread. Lambert and Zgerbzwsky had legged it. They'd done the impossible, got out of the cooler and away through the gates, taking a K-wagen and Schultz with them.

'The bastard,' said Winterman to Hayes. 'The ingenious bastard.'

The British began singing 'Rule Britannia', the French-Canadians the 'Marseillaise'. The Anglo-Canadians had a few songs of their own, mostly about Hitler having only one ball. Not even threats could shut them up. Two of their own guys had beaten the system and the goons were pig-sick.

In his office, even when it finally became clear that only two men had got out, Gessel's complexion went from purple to white and back again. His blood pressure hit the red mark. Two or two hundred, this was a disgrace. If he wasn't careful he could be joining Schultz, wherever that swine was, on the Eastern Front.

There seemed to be a dozen people present. Axheim. Hoffmann. The guard commander. Riesel. Sentries who had been patrolling, guards who had been playing cards. The only absentees were the dogs.

In between raging at all and sundry Gessel was on the telephone. To the police, the Frankfurt Gestapo, the local SS commander. Every call made him angrier because whoever he spoke to said more or less the same thing: Sure you're up to the job, Herr Oberst?

Finally he cleared the office of everyone bar Axheim and Hoffmann, with instructions that the prisoners were to be kept standing where they were, all night.

'How can this happen?' he screamed at Axheim. 'How can an escape like this take place? What about our informant? Bring him in.'

'Would that be wise, Herr Oberst?' asked Axheim diplomatically. 'At this moment? Better, surely, to talk to him in our own time.'

'*Why didn't he tell us?* As with the tunnel.'

'Perhaps he didn't know,' offered Hoffman.

'It's his damned job to know!' Gessel hammered his desk with a clenched fist. 'I'll throw him to the wolves, blast him! To the wolves! To his own comrades!'

He slumped in his chair, silent for a moment.

'They can't get far,' suggested Axheim. 'Sunrise is at 0440 hours. We'll mount a full-scale search then. When we recapture them . . .'

'When we recapture them they will be shot! Instantly!'

Axheim glanced at Hoffmann, but there was no help coming from the junior officer.

'We can surely do better than that, Herr Oberst. Much better.'

'Explain.'

Axheim did so. Gessel nodded, slowly.

'It's possible, possible. But find them,' he hissed. 'For God's sake find them!'

They were deeper in the forest as Gessel spoke, building themselves a hide the Achnacarry instructors would have been proud of. Better to keep away from farms and the like until the heat died down. A farm would be the first place the Krauts searched. They had more than enough food and there was water nearby. In a day or two it might be possible to make for Frankfurt, chance the rendezvous before June 20. In the meantime they were free. It was a bloody good feeling.

SIXTEEN

June 13–20 1943

Although mail and other privileges had been suspended until further notice by the commandant as a collective punishment, coded letters were already being written to England about the escape. MI9 would be delighted to learn, eventually, how many men had to be taken off other duties to search for just two Kriegies. It was a drop in the ocean as far as the war as a whole was concerned, but a few more drops would make a cupful, and a few cupfuls a bucket. Troops hunting prisoners on the run couldn't be employed elsewhere.

From sun-up scores of them, SS as well as Wehrmacht, scoured the countryside in all directions, from bases, as well as Frankfurt and Stalag XIII K, as far south as Darmstadt and as far north as Giessen. Specialist units with dogs were drafted in, together with a company of Hitler-jugend under the command of a Stammfuehrer, a rank peculiar to the Hitler Youth and the equivalent of a major. Roadblocks were set up and motorists stopped and questioned, asked to produce proof of identity. Travellers were hours late for Sunday appointments with their families and Wehrmacht convoys delayed. The two Canadians had unwittingly succeeded in enraging hundreds of individuals, civilian and military like.

In his office, low on sleep and high on nicotine and caffein, Oberst Gessel had already received a severe drubbing from the commanding general of the Wehrkreis, Military District, and had been ordered to report progress every two hours by phone.

'How can I do that?' he wailed at Axheim, seeing his career ending somewhere in the Ukraine. 'I'm not responsible for the SS and the Hitler Youth.'

Axheim wisely kept his own counsel. The commandant was about ready to bite someone's head off and he didn't want it to be his.

The Frankfurt Gestapo out of 22 Bürgerstrasse were all on the streets, stopping pedestrians at random and demanding papers. Because it was only June 13, they did not connect the two escapers with Hans-Dieter Biber and Strudel. That rendezvous was not due to take place until June 20 at the earliest.

The first priority for the troops and the HJ was to locate the Kubelwagen. It was obviously not on the road or it would have been found by now. Once they'd established its whereabouts they would have a rough idea how far the *Tommis* could have travelled. Without it they were working in the dark.

The petrol tank had been almost full, as far as anyone could recall. The *Tommis* could be a hundred kilometres away or five. And in any direction.

It was six o'clock in the evening before the vehicle was discovered, and then only by happenstance. A sharp-eyed dog handler, one of a small team scouting the forest, spotted some rooks circling. Curious, he investigated, and found Schultz's corpse. And the K-wagen. Schultz was no longer a pretty sight. Flies and ants and other insects had been at work on his face all day, attracted by the congealed blood surrounding his head wound and the eminently devourable viscera covering the dashboard and door frame.

The dog-handler raised a shout. Within minutes the Feldwebel i/c the dog section was on the wireless in the control vehicle.

Before a senior officer could arrive, however, the air-raid sirens sounded in Frankfurt. Wherever they were vehicles pulled off the road. The troops took cover, even those fifteen miles away from the city centre, in the forest. It was unlikely that the bombers were interested in destroying woodland, but overshoots and jettisons were commonplace. Better to be safe than sorry.

The daylight sortie by a dozen squadrons of USAAF B 17s began at six thirty and lasted forty-five minutes. The city itself was the target. Focke-Wulf 190 and ME 109 fighters were scrambled to beat off the raiders. The Americans lost seven Flying Fortresses that were seen to crash for only five Luftwaffe aircraft. But by the time the last of the bombing stream turned for home and the all-clear sounded it was seven thirty. It was almost eight o'clock before a Wehrmacht Oberst-leutnant appeared at the scene of Schultz's killing, accompanied by a doctor. In the interim a further search of the immediate area unearthed the uniforms the escapers had buried. They were now, obviously, in civilian clothes.

The doctor estimated Schultz had been dead for less than twenty-four hours, not much of a deduction as it was less than twenty-four hours since Schultz drove through the Stalag gates. He could not say for sure whether it was a suicide or faked to look like one.

Using a large-scale map to calculate the distance from the Stalag to the K-wagen and guessing at an average speed, the Oberstleutnant reckoned the vehicle had been abandoned around eleven the previous evening. He doubted if the Canadians would have risked moving during the day, but they'd still had almost six hours before sun-up. In pitch blackness over unfamiliar terrain, call that one mile an hour at the outside.

But then of course they had tonight as well, because it was almost too late to conduct more than a perfunctory search now. By dawn on Monday they could be ten or twelve miles from this spot. But in which direction? West through Frankfurt towards Belgium, or south-west towards France? Or due south towards Switzerland? Damn them to hell.

He gave orders to search all farms and isolated houses within a fifteen-mile radius, for signs of a break-in. That was his best bet. One thing was absolutely certain: they'd be many a mile from the K-wagen come sun-up tomorrow.

But that was where the Oberstleutnant was wrong. Jack and Al-phabet were in their hide not two miles from where the Wehrmacht officer was standing, determined not to move until the Germans were convinced they must be halfway to the border.

Their brushwood-and-branch shelter was deep in a thicket and so perfectly camouflaged that a herd of deer, coming down to the water for their evening drink, had passed within a few feet without taking fright. If that most nervous of animals could not sense their presence, it was doubtful any human would. Tracker dogs might be a problem – they'd heard some barking in the distance earlier – but they'd cross that bridge when they came to it. In any case, the Krauts must surely believe, once they found the K-wagen, that the escapers would have gone like bats out of hell to get as far away as possible. They knew nothing of Strudel and Cupid and the Frankfurt rendezvous.

Alphabet now did. Jack had told him during the night. Not all of it, just the password, the code name of their contact, and the location and time of the meeting: any date from June 20 onwards, at nine p.m. on the dot, on the corner where Cranachstrasse met Schneckenhofstrasse.

They — or rather Jack alone, since Cupid might take fright if he observed more than one person — would be approached. Jack had not been informed of Cupid's precise address for security reasons, though he guessed it would be close by.

Alphabet was astonished by it all.

'Jesus, and I thought we were going to take pot luck, try to get to Switzerland on our own. How the hell did you get all this information?'

'It's better you don't know.'

It was, too. Although Jack had shoved the possibility of recapture to a far corner of his mind, it had to be faced. If it happened, however, what Alphabet did not know he could not reveal. About the letter codes and the LVSA.

Alphabet had another question.

'How come I'm included in the deal? From what you're telling me, it sounds as if this Cupid guy is expecting only you. If two, why me and not the Chief, say?'

'Let's just say I thought you'd had about as much as you could swallow of prison life.'

Hell's teeth, thought Alphabet, I wouldn't have done that for my own mother.

'Thanks, Jack,' he mumbled. 'You reckon we can avoid the Krauts until the twentieth?'

'I reckon, but we'll see how it goes, play it by ear. We're pretty safe here, for the moment. The Krauts'll think we're miles away and the loggers won't be anywhere near this location until Christmas. It'll start to get hairy when we have to break cover. Cupid knows he's expecting an escaped prisoner-of-war and most of Frankfurt will be aware by now that two Kriegies have legged it. If he's bright, Cupid, he'll put two and two together. That could mean he'll turn up at the rendezvous from tonight, but that's too early for us. We'll leave it a few days before we move, or until we're low on rations. If we're careful we can last the whole week. It may come to that anyway, travelling only a couple of miles a night once the heat's off. Cupid could have added it up wrongly and I wouldn't give much for our chances if we have to hang around Frankfurt for more than a few hours. We haven't got any papers and my German accent wouldn't fool a six-year-old. We look the part in our civilian duds, but we're finished the moment we're challenged.'

Jack had on a collarless shirt, an old grey jacket and dark-blue trousers. For headgear he had a workman's cap and for footwear wellingtons. Alphabet wore a blue-and-white check shirt, a plaid lumberjacket, and brown cord trousers. Although Jack had brought wellingtons for him, also, they had proved to be far too large, making him resemble a circus clown. He was stuck with the boots he had been captured in. At least they didn't appear very military now, not after ten months without being polished. On his head he sported a railwayman's cap. Unshaven as they were, they could pass for labourers of the lowest class.

At least they wouldn't stink to high heaven after a week. They could certainly risk bathing in the stream after nightfall. They could keep their teeth reasonably clean by using the chewed end of a twig as a brush. Hygiene and general health were important. Their diet was going to be very basic as it was, and it wouldn't help their cause in the least if one or both became ill through neglect.

Through a narrow chink in the hide's foliage Alphabet spotted several rabbits as dusk approached on June 13. They were oblivious to the presence of man.

'Pity we can't snare a couple of them.'

'Oh, we could snare them, all right, but I don't fancy raw rabbit and a fire's out of the question.'

Alphabet had a gloomy thought before they turned in for the night. 'Those B 17s.'

'Beautiful sight, weren't they?'

'That's not what I meant. I just hope to God Cupid wasn't standing under one of them.'

'Don't,' said Jack, 'not even as a joke.'

'I wasn't joking.'

They remained in the hide for three more days. Not trusting his memory, Jack made a notch on a stick with his thumbnail each sun-up. No one came anywhere near them, neither tracker dog nor human. The hunters had gone elsewhere.

Although they had eaten sparingly, Jack had seriously miscalculated how long the accumulated rations would last two men. By the evening of June 16 they had only a single day's supplies remaining, which it would be wise to keep for emergencies. It was time to move on, find a farm or at least a farmer's field to raid. Risky but not too much providing they did nothing stupid like breaking windows or forcing locks.

They should, in any case, get on their way. Frankfurt was fifteen miles due west. Three or four miles a night would put them somewhere on the outskirts of the city by dawn on June 20.

It was with some reluctance that they left the hide after dark that night. The shelter represented safety, security. Now they were heading for the unknown. The forest would cover them part of the way, but they would soon have to abandon that too. There were no farms in forests.

By two a.m. they were walking across open fields, keeping tight to the hedgerows. The night was brilliantly clear. Jack used the tail of the Great Bear, the two stars Merak and Dubhe, to find Polaris, and set his course from that. The fires from the B 17s' bombing raid had been extinguished and Frankfurt, of course, was blacked out; as was every village and hamlet and even single houses. For a moment he thought nostalgically of home, of Canada. Unless Mackenzie King was still playing silly buggers, it would be possible to see the lights of Winnipeg or Calgary from miles away. Maybe they'd send him and Alphabet back across the herring-pond for a spell as instructors if they made it to England. Fat chance! In any case, he wouldn't accept even if it was offered. Crazy though it must sound, he wanted to get back in the fight. He owed Germany a bruise or two. It was the Stalag he couldn't stand, not the war.

At two thirty they were frightened out of their wits when something extremely large loomed up in front of them. And moved. But it was only an inquisitive horse that wanted to be friendly. Jack shooed it away and it galloped off, whinneying disappointedly.

At the far side of the same field a herd of cows was lying down, left in the open and not byred-up now the weather was so fine. Where there were cows there would be a farm, because the beasts would need milking at dawn, two and bit hours off. Time to find something to eat and also to take cover. Farm workers were early risers and they didn't want to be caught far from shelter as daybreak approached.

They left the field where it ended and chanced the road, ready to dive into the hedge at the sound of an approaching vehicle. After a few hundred yards they came across the farm buildings they were looking for. The farmhouse itself stood off the road and was in darkness. Further on was what appeared to be a barn. That would do. They had to keep clear of stables and cowsheds, anything to do with livestock, which would need attention during the day.

In the barn their luck held. Once their eyes were accustomed to the gloom they found, stacked in one corner, a mound of turnips and a sack of potatoes. Winter fodder for the animals, no doubt, or summer feed for pigs. Raw they would taste horrible, but they would be filling and nutritious. Escaping POWs could not expect five-star cuisine.

Close to the potatoes was a milk churn with a metal ladle dangling from a piece of string on one of the handles. Alphabet rocked the churn. It was half-full – of something. He dipped in the ladle and sampled the liquid. Milk. Almost-fresh milk. The first either of them had tasted for nearly a year. They had to use extraordinary willpower to restrict themselves to roughly a pint apiece. Too much richness would make them sick.

When they had drunk and eaten their fill – chewing the turnips with distaste and washing down the pulp with milk – they looked around for somewhere to hid out during the daylight hours. They finally found a tiny corner behind a small mountain of straw-bales, between the straw and a side of the barn. They had to move a column of bales a fraction before they could squeeze through, and then they were in a space no larger than a broom cupboard, with just enough room to curl up on the floor. There was no point in one of them sleeping while the other remained awake, keeping watch. If someone decided to move the bales they were dead meat. Besides, they were both exhausted.

They slept uneasily in fits and starts. The day seemed endless. Every so often Jack consulted the wristwatch he had liberated from Schultz and, when he was convinced an hour had elapsed, was amazed to find only fifteen minutes had.

Worst was not being able to move their bowels or urinate, but they gritted their teeth and suffered. As an anti-laxative a farmer with a pitchfork backed up by a company of SS troops took some beating.

From time to time throughout the day men, and sometimes women, came into the barn. They could hear them talking. But no one attempted to move the straw-bales, and when darkness fell they slipped noiselessly from the farm and continued heading west.

That night their fortunes were mixed. In the early hours, now on the road and outside a tiny hamlet, they came across a sack of apples standing beside a gate. Maybe for a morning caller. Maybe for someone to feed his pigs or horses. But standing there, anyway. Last year's, obviously, since it wasn't yet the season for apples, but nevertheless delicious for all that. They ate two or three each and crammed their pockets with a dozen more. Then a dog began barking. A dog with extra-sensory perception, apparently, for within seconds air-raid sirens started to wail and searchlights probe the skies.

'Shit,' said Jack. 'Go home.'

These were probably RAF Lancasters doing a follow-up raid in the wake of the B 17s. Whatever, there would be a lot of activity on the streets for the next few hours.

They took to their heels and found a wood. Not the best of funkholes, but all they could do in the time available.

They waited for the inevitable bombs. None came. The raid didn't reach Frankfurt, though something was happening further west. The RAF was plastering Mainz or Wiesbaden, somewhere around there.

They spent the whole of the day, June 18, in the wood, and lit out again in the evening.

Dawn of June 19 found them in the ruins of a bombed-out church four miles east of the Frankfurt suburb of Sachsenhausen. They were down to their final few apples now and opted to eat their last precious chocolate and biscuits, their emergency supplies. Although they were meant for a rainy day, in Jack's view it was coming down in torrents. They needed their strength for the last four miles. If the fates were being generous, the following morning would find them as close to the city of Frankfurt as made no difference. A few hours more and they would be meeting Cupid.

But the fates elected that time to withdraw their benevolence. Shortly after daybreak on June 20, disaster struck.

They had found another farm at three a.m. It must have been the last one east of Frankfurt, from which they were now no more than a mile. They were tired beyond belief and staggered gratefully into a Dutch barn.

There was a ladder there, a ladder leading to a platform on which bales of hay were stacked. They climbed it and debated the wisdom of pulling up the ladder behind them. This was rejected as untenable. A farmer finding it missing would become curious, and a farm would have more than one ladder. Their safest bet was to retreat to a corner and bunk down behind the furthermost hay-bales.

Jack slept fitfully, dreaming monstrous dreams, and sweating copiously. When he awoke, it was to the sound of someone climbing the ladder, singing softly. The sun was up.

He clamped a hand over Alphabet's mouth. The Pole struggled unwillingly to consciousness. Jack put the forefinger of his other hand to his lips.

The girl was dark-haired and about sixteen. Young, anyway. She was wearing a white peasant blouse that had seen better days, and working trousers. She had a lovely face, heart-shaped, and perfect teeth. She was singing because she was happy, in spite of the hour, and because she was at the start of her life and the world wasn't all that foul. But she was also moving the hay-bales, dragging them one by one to the edge of the platform and pushing them over.

When she saw Jack and Alphabet, after a few bales had gone, she froze. They must have looked a sight, Jack thought later, unkempt as they were. No wonder she tried to run.

But she didn't try to scream, and that was her mistake.

He raced after her as she made for the ladder. She was no sailor, who would have slipped down it with her back to the rungs. She had to turn and face him. He had a momentary glimpse of terrified bright-blue eyes as he grabbed her. She fought her way out of his grip, lost her footing, and fell twenty feet. When she hit the floor of the Dutch barn she lay perfectly still.

Jack scrambled down the ladder. She was out cold, concussed or worse. Her breathing was shallow; there was a pulse, but it was faint. He put her across his shoulders in a fireman's lift and hauled her back up to the platform.

Alphabet stared at her in horror.

'Is she dead?'

'No.'

Alphabet knelt beside her, raised an eyelid.

'But she will be unless she receives attention.'

'That can't be helped.'

'She's only a kid. We can't just let her die.'

'What do you suggest, fetch an ambulance? Get a hold of yourself,' snarled Jack. 'It's her or us. We're in a war, for Christ's sake. Civilians get hurt. Do you think every bomb from those Lancasters landed on a munitions factory? No babies dead, no young girls, no hospitals destroyed? Give me a hand with her.'

Alphabet knew Jack was right, but it didn't make it any easier.

They put her behind the furthest hay-bales, where they remained also. Occasionally she groaned, but she did not recover consciousness. Jack wondered what he would do if she did. Did her life matter any more than the lives of Schultz and Munroe and Grell?

Around eight a.m. they heard a woman's voice called, 'Anneliese, Anneliese.'

Somehow it made it worse to know her name.

Later on in the morning and many times during the afternoon a man's voice joined in, angrily.

'Anneliese! Anneliese!'

The owner of the farm, no doubt, wondering where his daughter was. Whether she was shirking work to see her boyfriend, lying in a field chewing a grass stalk, watching the sun, listening to the skylarks.

Jack recalled Snow White, from England, a thousand years ago when the world was innocent. Caroline Manners. The Luftwaffe bomber pilot who had killed her hadn't thought a lot about Colonel Manners's feelings.

The same voices, the man's and the woman's, were heard throughout the rest of the day. They were joined by others on occasions. But no one climbed the ladder.

By eight p.m. Jack knew they had to move. Otherwise there was no chance he and Alphabet could make the rendezvous with Cupid. But people were still searching for Anneliese and it was also far from dusk. They would be seen if they tried to get out now.

He had no right to ask for a miracle, but he offered up a silent prayer anyway. His second, he recalled wryly, in recent memory.

Someone was listening. It started raining stair-rods. Huge drops. A thunderstorm preceded by lightning.

'We can get out now,' he said to Alphabet.

Anneliese was still unconscious when they left, but still breathing also. Jack hoped someone would find her before it was too late.

They stayed on the roads, getting drenched. A few vehicles passed them, some of them military. The troops jeered at the 'labourers'.

Jack knew the map by heart. Just beyond the Fischer and Kastner factory on Offenbacher Landstrasse they had to cross the railway line east of Frankfurt South station. Then it was north until they hit Gutzkowstrasse, which led into Schneckenhofstrasse. Two hundred yards along there was where Cranachstrasse and Schneckenhofstrasse met.

And they were on time. It didn't matter that they were hurrying. Any fool would, in the rain. They were soaked to the skin, but it was within minutes of nine p.m. that they were in sight of the rendezvous.

Frankfurt had taken a pasting from the B 17s and probably earlier raids. There was a hell of a lot of damage. No doubt photo-reconnaissance Mosquitoes had recorded the results, but it was something to file away for MI9 anyway. There was no substitute for first-hand info.

'Wait here,' said Jack. 'Get in a doorway. Just in case.'

It was precisely nine p.m. according to Schultz's wristwatch when Jack reached the corner of Cranachstrasse. There was no one there except a stray dog, a mongrel, tail down and very wet. It wanted to be pally.

'Get lost,' said Jack.

He felt as conspicuous as Joe Louis at a Ku Klux Klan meeting, standing there in the rain, but of one thing he was sure: he wouldn't be killed by bombs. It was too late for the USAAF, who couldn't hit a bull's ass with a banjo in the dark, to be making a raid with any hope of getting home to England, navigating by night. And too early for the RAF to be targeting Frankfurt.

Were any of the scurrying passers-by Cupid? Was Cupid still alive?

A man approached him, in plainclothes.

'Strudel?'

'Cupid?'

'Ja.'

Jack raised an arm, beckoning Alphabet.

'You are English?' asked the man.

'No, Canadian.'

'And is he the other one?'

Alphabet was sidling along the pavement.

Jack was suddenly suspicious.

'You were expecting two of us?'

'No, but two of you escaped. I assumed there would be two. Answer my question, we haven't much time. Is he the other one?'

Alphabet joined them.

'Yes,' said Jack. 'Where are we going? For God's sake let's get off the streets.'

The man put a hand in his raincoat pocket – and withdrew a whistle. Which he blew.

Within seconds they were surrounded by troops and other men in plainclothes. SS, Jack noted dully, and Gestapo. For the first time in a long while he experienced fear.

SEVENTEEN

June–September 1943

They separated them in the Bürgerstrasse cells and, to begin with, the interrogation was mild. The Gestapo was disappointed that Strudel had turned out to be two POW escapers. Although expecting it, they had been hoping for bigger fish. Still, the Canadians were killers. The postmortem had proved beyond doubt that Schultz had not committed suicide. The angle of the shot was wrong and there were no traces of powder burns on his fingers. The only question remaining was, how had Lambert and Zgerbzwsky learned of the Cranachstrasse rendezvous while incarcerated? Somehow London was getting messages into, and presumably out of, Stalag XIII K. And other Stalags too, no doubt. The method would be useful information to have. Nail it here, in Frankfurt, and there was a good chance of nailing it elsewhere.

Jack studied his interrogator calmly. Though handcuffed to a heavy chair that was bolted to the floor, his earlier terror at being taken by the Gestapo had, temporarily, vanished.

The man had introduced himself as Herr Seiffert. No rank, although Jack knew that the Gestapo, as Amt IV of the RSHA, the Reich Main Security Office, came under Himmler, who Seiffert resembled to an uncanny degree, and were therefore SS officers. That the SS themselves were involved was beyond dispute. They had been present at the arrest and there were two of them in the interrogation room, which was below ground. One wore the insignia of an Hauptsturmfuehrer, the equivalent of a captain, and he deferred to Seiffert. Which made the man in plainclothes a Sturmbannfuehrer, a major, at the very least. The second SS man was an Oberscharfuehrer, a staff sergeant. Ugly as hell and the size of a bear.

Jack had been under arrest for four hours. It was now early morning of June 21. He had given his name, rank and serial number, as required by the Geneva Convention. Other than that he had said nothing. He had turned down a cigarette and a cup of coffee, fearing either could be drugged. If they were going to get anything out of him, they would have to beat it out.

He remembered what the MI9 officer had said to him before Jubilee.

'No one can withstand the Gestapo, no matter how hard they believe they are. Just don't get caught.'

Well, he was caught. He wondered if they could break him. He could take physical punishment and maybe a certain amount of mental torture, but he'd never been put to a severe test.

'Sergeant Lambert,' said Seiffert, in faultless English, 'be reasonable. You were recaptured wearing civilian clothing. Now *I* accept that you are a serving soldier who has done an extremely daring thing by escaping from a prisoner-of-war camp, but my superiors are going to want a little more than that. They are going to suggest that you are a spy whose job it was to get back to England and report to Military Intelligence. Why else would you be trying to contact another spy, the traitor Hans-Dieter Biber?'

'I've never heard that name,' said Jack, truthfully.

'Of course, of course. I mean the man you knew as Cupid. Roman god of love, if I remember correctly.'

'I don't know what you're talking about. I was heading west, via Frankfurt, that's all.'

'Our man said Strudel, your password, you answered Cupid, Biber's code name.'

'He misheard.'

Seiffert shook his head.

'Lambert, Lambert,' he intoned sorrowfully, 'are you determined to make it difficult? All we want to know is how you learned of Cupid after being ten months in a camp. Tell us that and you can go back there. You and Zgerbzwsky.'

'He knows nothing.'

'But you do. Why be hard on yourself? Give us your method of communication and sit out the remainder of the war in peace.'

'Eat it.'

Seiffert inclined his head at the Oberscharfuehrer. The NCO stepped forward and battered Jack about the face with a short truncheon. Twice. Left and right. Jack felt a tooth crack and spat blood.

'If my hands were free . . .'

'Of course, of course,' agreed Seiffert. 'And if the Fuehrer had invaded England in 1940 this would be no interrogation. But I'm afraid it is. I'm also afraid you'll have to answer me. You will eventually, so why not now? How did you learn of Cupid? What are your means of communication?'

'Go to hell.'

The Oberscharfuehrer thrashed Jack into unconsciousness. He was relieved to find himself going. While he was out, they could not ask any questions.

When he came to, with a bucket of water in his face, he found he was naked. There were also two more SS men in the cellar. They had taken Schultz's wristwatch, so he had no idea whether he had been cold for sixty seconds or sixty minutes. Nearer the former, he conjectured. The blood on his lips was still warm and sticky.

'You look like a cocksman,' said Seiffert. 'Isn't that the Canadian expression? Or am I thinking of America? Whichever, your equipment will not be of any use to you after the war unless you answer my questions. Oberscharfuehrer Veit, here, is a specialist. He can make a man wish he was dead.'

'So shoot me.'

'I might consider that, when I learn what I wish to know.'

'I was very lucky, that's all. Your man misunderstood. I didn't say Cupid.'

'You're being very foolish.'

'I've given you my name, rank and serial number. That's all you're entitled to.'

'Veit,' said Seiffert.

Grinning hugely, Veit beckoned the two SS men, who spread Jack's legs. He tried to struggle, but it was impossible in the bolted-down chair.

Veit swung the truncheon at Jack's testicles. Jack screamed with pain.

'Again,' said Seiffert.

Veit obeyed.

Jack was violently ill, vomiting over himself before passing out.

'Leave him there,' said Seiffert. 'We'll talk to the other one.'

When they came back Jack was conscious. He had never known such pain. His testicles were on fire. Tell them what they want to know, a private, inner voice whispered. It's only a matter of time.

'Now, Sergeant Lambert.'

'Take a hike.'

They had discussed this at Achnacarry, torture. The trick was, hold out until life becomes meaningless. He wasn't sure he could do it.

Veit hit his penis with the truncheon, and he lost consciousness again.

'Put him in a holding cell,' said Seiffert. 'It's early days and the Pole looks easier.'

They left him by himself, naked and in total darkness, for forty-eight hours, though he had no means of assessing time. No one came to tend his injuries, nor was he fed or given anything to drink. There was not even a sanitation bucket in the cell, and soon it began to stink.

In a nearby cell Alphabet had told them nothing because he knew nothing. Except that they had hurt, by accident, a young girl, which the Gestapo was now aware of anyway.

'But not hurt,' said Seiffert, 'murdered. The girl died.'

Zgerbzwsky was therefore of no further use to them unless as a stick with which to beat Lambert, who, Seiffert was convinced, did know something. About codes.

On the third day the holding cell was suddenly flooded with light. Then the door was flung open. Outside stood Oberscharfuehrer Veit. Behind him Herr Seiffert. Flanking them two SS troopers.

Jack backed into a corner. Seiffert wrinkled his nose in disgust at the smell.

'You are to be cleaned up,' he said. 'Go with these men. And no trouble, please.'

They took him to a washroom and hosed him down. Then he was handed a towel and instructed to dry himself. He was not permitted to shave for fear he would use the razor as a weapon – on himself.

Afterwards he was given his clothes, the civilian clothes he had been wearing when captured. They had been washed and dried.

'Dress,' commanded Veit.

When dressed he was led, again handcuffed, along a corridor and into an office. On a table stood a bowl of soup, a plate of bread, and a mug of steaming coffee.

'Eat,' said Veit.

The SS troopers stood by the door, machine pistols at the ready.

Seiffert was using the good guy/bad guy routine, playing both parts himself. They had tried the heavy stuff and that hadn't worked. Now they would apply the soft soap, allowing the prisoner to choose which was preferable.

Although it was difficult wearing the handcuffs and he still feared drugs, Jack set about the food with a vengeance. Starved, his will to resist would weaken very quickly. Fed he might hold out a little longer. Every day – every hour – was a small victory.

When he had finished eating Veit pressed a buzzer. A moment later Seiffert came in and took a chair behind a desk.

'Where's Zgerbzwsky?' asked Jack.

'That is not your concern,' answered Seiffert. 'Or perhaps it is. Zgerbzwsky lacks your mental toughness. He saw the advantages very quickly of telling us what we wanted to know.'

'I don't see how. He doesn't have anything to tell.'

The soup and bread had helped. He could feel his strength returning.

'Not even about Anneliese Weiss?'

'Who the hell's Anneliese Weiss?'

'A young girl, Herr Lambert. Fifteen years of age. Her parents are distraught at her death. Did you really believe her body would not be found or that, when it was, her parents would not tell the police? Who would inform us.'

So Anneliese had died of her injuries, thought Jack. Christ.

'The Pole says it was an accident,' said Seiffert. 'I'm not so certain he didn't kill her deliberately, perhaps with some sexual motive in mind. Pretty, adolescent girl, two men who have had no contact with females for almost a year. It must have been tempting.'

'A medical examination would prove she had not been interfered with.'

Seiffert smiled.

'Who, Lambert? This Anneliese Weiss you've never met?'

Jack said nothing. They had all the advantages, he had none. If he did not talk, though, he could not betray himself unwittingly.

'Strictly speaking, of course,' said Seiffert, 'you are both guilty of murder, since it doesn't really matter who struck the blow that killed her. You were both there. However, I am willing to accept that Zgerbzwsky did the actual deed.'

'Zgerbzwsky said that?'

'With a little persuasion from the Oberscharfuehrer,' Seiffert lied easily. 'That should, of course, mean the death penalty, and I'm not even bothering to count in Grell and the unfortunate Schultz. There is a way out of this dilemma, however. Simply tell us how you communicate with London and you will both be returned to the Stalag. Failing that, Zgerbzwsky will be shot.'

'You're bluffing,' scoffed Jack.

'I really wouldn't place a large wager on that, Lambert. I grant that Zgerbzwsky knows nothing of codes, but the same cannot be said about you. You have five minutes to tell us, or your friend will face a firing squad.'

Jack counted off the seconds. Seiffert would shoot them both anyway, once he had what he wanted, so there was really no decision to make.

'Well, Lambert?'

'I have nothing to say.'

'Bring him.'

They went out to a floodlit courtyard. It was night or early morning. Alphabet was bound to a stake with ropes, fully clothed but bruised and battered. He had taken some fearful beatings too. His face was in a terrible state. Twenty feet from the stake was a squad of SS men toting rifles.

'Bring Lambert forward,' said Seiffert, 'where the friend whose life he considers to be so valueless can see him. But keep him out of the firing line. This is a single execution, not a double.'

Alphabet held Jack's eyes with his own. They were full of hurt. And hopelessness. A whipped dog. Is this what it's all come down to after all these years? Was it worth it? Why did we bother?

'Now, Lambert,' said Seiffert, 'I shall repeat my question for the last time. Tell me all you know about how you communicate with London and you will both be returned to the Stalag. Refuse and Zgerbzwsky will be executed immediately.'

Surely it was a bluff, thought Jack. Jesus, I don't want another death on my conscience.

'I can't do it, Alphabet, you know that.'

The Pole nodded and lowered his eyes.

Bear up, old son, pleaded Jack silently. Hold your head up, please. Don't leave me with this one as well.

Seiffert gestured to Veit, who bellowed an order. Six rifles came to six shoulders. Seiffert glanced at Jack, but Jack was watching his friend.

At the last moment Alphabet's head came up. He stared his executioners in the face, defiantly.

'*Feuer!*'

A fusillade rang out. Alphabet's body shuddered under the impact. Then he slumped forward, held up only by the ropes.

They set about Jack seriously then, from that hour onwards, sometimes in the holding cell, sometimes in the chair bolted to the floor.

Most of the torture was physical. They rammed sharpened toothpicks under his fingernails and pulled out others with pliers. When he passed out from the pain they revived him with ice-cold water and started again.

They attached electrodes to his testicles, penis and nipples and shot an electric current through him, increasing the voltage gradually, wracking his body with agony. They put a metal bucket over his head and pounded it with truncheons until he knew for certain he was going insane. He prayed for death on more than one occasion.

When the torture wasn't physical it was mental. He was rarely fed and never allowed to clean himself up until the stench became so unbearable that even the Gestapo couldn't stand it. Then he was hosed down with freezing water.

One afternoon – or morning or night – Seiffert produced a handful of photographs. Of Anneliese Weiss.

'This was Anneliese at age five. A pretty little child, don't you think? This was her at ten, at her birthday party. This is her at twelve, on her pony. There is talk of her mother being confined to a mental institution. The poor woman is quite beside herself with grief. You did that, Lambert.'

Finally he broke. There were no early-warning signals. One moment he was taking a beating, strapped to the chair, from Oberscharfuehrer Veit, the next he was sobbing uncontrollably. He didn't know where the tears had come from. Or whether they were of pain or shame or hopelessness. All he knew was that he was mortal and he couldn't take any more. Tell them everything they wanted to know, that was all he had to do. They would kill him then, but at least he'd be out of it. He had done his best and it just hadn't been enough.

Seiffert took it all down in longhand. The LVSA, The Prisoners' Leisure Hours Fund, his personal code for communicating with MI9. All he knew and all they wanted.

He felt relieved when it was all over, like a Roman Catholic baring his soul in the confessional. For better or for worse, he'd cast off his burden.

'You see how easy it was, Lambert,' said Seiffert finally. 'If you had done this in the first place your friend would still be alive and you would have saved yourself a great deal of pain. Everyone talks, sooner or later.'

They allowed him to wash himself, under supervision, and get dressed. Then they fed him. Still no shave, though. There were few places his face could have taken a razor, in any case. He was a mass of cuts and bruises. His left eye was fully closed, his right one half so. He ached all over, mostly in his groin. His hands, particularly his finger-nails, looked as if they had been through a meat-grinder.

He wondered when they'd shoot him.

'I thought we'd never crack him,' said Seiffert to the SS Hauptsturm-fuehrer. 'He's close to the hardest man I've ever come across.'

They had given him a cell with a mattress now. He lay on it for thirty-six hours, hardly moving, rejecting food. Trying not to think.

A day later he had a visitor. Oberst Gessel. Jack automatically stood to attention when the commandant entered the cell. He was scarcely aware he had done so until much later, until he realized just how thoroughly he had been broken.

'We shall be glad to have you back, Sergeant Lambert,' said Gessel. 'In a few weeks when your face has healed, of course.'

Jack did not understand. Have him back? To the Stalag? They were not going to shoot him? What new sadism was this?

For a month he remained in Bürgerstrasse, until he no longer resembled a creature from an abattoir. He was examined daily by an SS doctor. The physical wounds mended. He doubted the inner scars would ever get better. Nor did he want them to, in some strange manner. He had to be punished for his weakness.

But why were they sending him back to the Stalag?

He was returned to XIII K in the dead of night, some time during the early weeks of August, he calculated later, placed directly in the cooler. Where he would serve thirty extra days' solitary, Oberleutnant Hoffmann informed him. Without any outside contact. No exercise periods. His sanitation bucket would be slopped out after dark.

'Of course,' smirked Hoffmann, 'you may write to London as often as you wish.'

So they all knew.

Word soon got around that Lambert was back among the Kriegies, who had already had it announced to them, by Gessel, that Zgerbzwsky was dead. 'Shot while escaping.' There was also a rumour being circulated that Jack and Alphabet killed a schoolgirl while on the run, but that was just a rumour. What was undisputed fact was that Schultz had died and so had Grell, and no one believed the tale about Munroe and Grell killing one another. Or Schultz deep-sixing himself, for that matter.

So why the hell were the Gestapo being so generous with Lambert? The late Munroe's fat-cat cronies had a theory.

'Because he's sold out, that's why.'

But they kept it to themselves.

Jack sweated out his time in solitary, not bothering to notch up the days. They would end when his confinement was over and not before. What did it matter? Where was he going? In some respects the Gestapo and the SS and the commandant had done him a favour, putting him away like this. He couldn't have faced the others, not yet. Not ever, maybe. Nor could he tell Wintermann and Hayes that they were compromised. He should, because they were in danger, but he didn't know how.

He wondered if he was going out of his mind. It was a possibility. He found it increasingly difficult to distinguish between what was real and what was imaginary. He also feared sleep, would do anything to avoid it, until he was exhausted through the lack of it. He had broken. That's all there was to it.

His dreams were demons. He had killed Anneliese Weiss, a young girl who would never see her sixteenth birthday. Her pretty face haunted him. He had witnessed Alphabet die, and for what? To promote Jack Lambert's toughness, which had turned out to be non-existent anyhow? Everything was an illusion, maybe life itself. A clever trick perpetrated by a master magician.

Could he have done any more, held out for another day, another hour, another sixty seconds? He would never know.

Like a boxer who has taken a severe beating at the hands of a superior opponent, it was doubtful if he would ever step into the ring again, even though he could whip most of the others.

When he was released the Kriegies knew it almost as soon as the goons. Many gathered outside the cooler to greet him, the Chief and

Kovacs included. They were shocked by his appearance. Not the physical scars – though evident they had mainly healed – but his demeanour. He seemed smaller than either the Chief or Kovacs recalled. Not necessarily in stature, though starvation had taken its toll, but in presence. This wasn't the Jack Lambert who had once been able to hack it with the best. Who was pretty damn near the best, if not the Man. The fire had gone, the driving force. The balls, although they did not know, literally, how close to the truth that was.

They had looked up to Jack as being extraordinary, and now he was human.

He knew it better than they did.

'Gestapo?' asked Kovacs.

'Just leave me alone. I don't want to talk about it.'

'What happened to your hands?'

'I had a fight with a tractor.'

'What happened to Alphabet?' asked the Chief.

'A Gestapo firing squad.'

'We were told he was shot while trying to escape.'

'Then that's about the size of it.'

'What about this schoolgirl who's supposed to have died?'

'She died, all right.'

The old Jack Lambert would have shaken a throat at such a question, cracked a skull or two. This one's eyes were empty, vacant, staring into the distance at something only he could see.

'Christ,' said Kovacs, watching Jack shuffle off, his gait that of an old man. 'Christ.'

EIGHTEEN

September–December 1943

Sergeants Winterman and Hayes had suspected they were in trouble the second they learned that Lambert was back in the cooler having spent some time in the hands of the Gestapo, and when they saw Lambert they were sure. He would neither confirm nor deny that he had talked, however; in fact, he did not appear to understand half the questions put to him. But they, Winterman and Hayes, closed down communications with London immediately. Their letter codes were different from Lambert's if only marginally, but if the Germans now knew about the LVSA and the other fake organizations, and individuals, they would be watching for mail to and from those addresses. There was nothing they could do to let MI9 know they were discredited; they could simply hope that London would read between the lines. Or rather, between no lines since there were no letters.

They were not surprised to escape a spell in the cooler, or worse; the goons weren't stupid. Now that they knew who, and what, to look out for, they simply had to wait until, and if, the two-way traffic started up again.

The wireless receiver in the Oflag was never found. The officers over there always moved it around, in any case, as a matter of general security.

Curiously no one blamed Jack Lambert for cracking, and everyone assumed he had because there was no other explanation for his eccentric behaviour. As long as that's all it was, breaking under terrible torture, they could forgive him and even understand. After a year, and for some a great deal more, of captivity, there were few heroes remaining in Stalag XIII K.

But there still seemed to be no reason for returning him to the camp, unless it was to act as a spy, a fifth-columnist, among his former comrades. If that turned out to be the case, well, it became a different ballgame. People were still trying to get out. There was another tunnel three-quarters dug, codenamed Yorker, which started under Hut 2B's washroom. They were taking their time on this one, but hoped to be getting a dozen men out early in December. To the best of anyone's knowledge Lambert knew nothing about Yorker, and that was the way they intended it to stay. No one could believe that he had been responsible for the debacle in Tunnel London last March, but anything was possible.

Not that Lambert seemed at all interested in tunnels or much else. He kept himself very much to himself. He hardly spoke to anyone and mostly just toyed with his food. If anyone approached him, even old friends like the Chief and Kovacs, he would get up and walk away.

He appeared terrified of Germans in uniform, something the goons quickly tumbled to. It became a standing joke among them to creep up behind him, one or more of them, and bellow his name at the tops of their voices. Then he would tremble while the Germans hooted with derisive laughter. Whatever trouble he had caused them in the past, they were repaying him tenfold.

Once when an SS Mercedes pulled up in front of the commandant's office, he literally ran away. Took to his heels. The Mercedes was only carrying several RAF fliers shot down the previous night, who were to be held in the Stalag until they could be sent to an airmen's camp, but he thought the SS had come for him. They found him later in 6B's latrine, on his haunches, skulking in a far, dark corner.

Those who had been closest to him in the past felt unutterably sorry for him. If he wasn't out of his mind by now, it couldn't be long. Every man had a limit beyond which he could not be pushed, and Jack had reached his. There was no way back.

In Hut 6B, where he was naturally no longer regarded as leader, he would lie awake for much of the night. When he did manage to sleep, he would toss and turn and moan. Sometimes whimper. It began to get on everyone's nerves and no one was too unhappy when, towards the end of October, he became physically ill, thanks largely to scarcely ever eating more than the bare minimum.

He collapsed at morning *Appell*. Just folded.

The camp had a small sickbay used mostly for minor ailments such as influenza. There he was placed and kept under guard for the entire month of November. They had to force-feed him when he refused to take nourishment, a fact that came out when another prisoner spent a couple of days there with suspected appendicitis. This force-feeding made a few of the Kriegies very suspicious. The goons customarily didn't give a damn about POWs, but here they were clucking over Lambert like a mother hen.

While he was in the sickbay the Stalag received one of its periodic visits from representatives of the International Red Cross, whose function it was to protect the basic human rights of all prisoners-of-war whose governments had signed the Convention, Allies and Axis. These inspections were always looked forward to because for a day or so beforehand victuals improved and clean blankets were issued. The blankets were confiscated as soon as the men from Geneva departed, of course, and the rations went back to the usual slop. But for a few hours the Kriegies were treated as human beings.

Complaints regarding mistreatment were always asked for by the Red Cross, but it wasn't wise to state grievances too vigorously. The men from Geneva would be gone in a few hours, whereas the Kriegies were inside for the duration. The Germans had ways of making life thoroughly unpleasant for any would-be barrack-room lawyer.

RQMS Maitland did take the opportunity to plead Sergeant Lambert's case, however, although the plea had to take place in front of Gessel, Axheim and Hoffmann. Private conversations were not permitted and Gessel, as commandant, could terminate the interview any time he chose. Thus it was not possible to say that Sergeant Lambert had escaped and been recaptured, and tortured by the Gestapo. In any event, the Swiss knew all about the Gestapo.

'He's a sick man. In his head. He should be repatriated.'

The Red Cross representative wanted to interview Lambert. This Gessel refused.

'He's in isolation.'

'In the sickbay?'

'For his own good. We look after our prisoners, you see.'

A furious row developed, but Gessel wouldn't shift an inch. The senior Geneva man finally shook his head in resignation. His powers were limited and Gessel knew it. It wouldn't take much for the Third Reich to ban his organization from German and German-occupied territory, and there were many lives at stake, not just one.

But he was allowed to take Lambert's name and serial number, and promised Maitland that he would look into the question of repatriation.

Always tricky because it required medical certificates and God knows how much other documentation. Plus a cast-iron guarantee that a repatriate was unfit for further combat.

Usually it was only the severely mutilated who went home. Few were released from POW camps because they would be able to report, officially, what conditions were like.

'It will take time,' said the man from Geneva. 'Months, perhaps longer.'

When Lambert was released from the sickbay at the beginning of December and a cold north-east wind brought the first flurries of snow that heralded the onset of another winter, he appeared much better. Certainly he hadn't lost any more weight and might even have put on a couple of pounds, but his eyes were unnaturally bright, the pupils pinpoints. He had the look of a man who has been a castaway for a very long time but doesn't know where he's been, or even that he's been gone.

He was taken under guard directly to Hut 6B and was there, occupying his usual bunk, when the others came in from a *Sonderappell*.

'Hi, Chief, Kovacs, you guys,' he said cheerily. 'Can someone do something about that damned stove? It's freezing in here.'

He was holding something in his hands, sitting cross-legged on his bunk with a blanket around his shoulders.

'What have you got there, Jack?' asked Kovacs.

He showed them. It was a hen's egg, something few of them had seen for over a year. He produced another from his tunic pocket. They could only have come from the goons, but Kovacs asked the question anyway.

'Where did you get them, Jack?'

'These? Christ knows. Somebody gave them to me, I forget who. Maybe they were here already. Take one.'

He tossed an egg across. Kovacs caught it deftly.

'More to the point,' Tom Ross was heard to mutter, 'what did he give for them?'

Jack heard that comment and for a moment was lucid.

'I got them regularly in the hospital. I think.'

A few men were seen to swap worried looks.

'Come on,' scoffed Kovacs later, 'we all know the goons aren't dumb. If Jack had changed sides, whatever the reason, do you think they're going to hand out eggs as a reward? So that we can see them' Makes sense.'

'Then where did he get the fucking eggs?' someone asked.

Kovacs couldn't answer that one, but he did have an answer of sort to another unspoken question.

'We all know Jack's been through a lot. We'll probably never know how much. But if you're seriously suggesting that the goons would recruit a stoolie who can't remember where his payment came from you're off your trolleys.'

'No one's exactly saying that,' retorted McKenzie, 'but if he doesn' know where the eggs came from, how the hell does he know what he' saying? The goons may be relying on the fact that he's half-looped That makes him dangerous, in my book.'

'There's something else we're missing,' said Tom Ross thoughtfully 'Let's give him the benefit of the doubt, that somehow he came by those eggs honestly, or that he stole them. He used to be a good thief Lambert, let's not forget that.'

'Get to the point, for Chrissake.'

'I'm getting there. Maybe bribes are not what the goons have hanging over his head. Maybe it's threats. "Do what we tell you or it': back to the Gestapo."'

'Crap,' said the Chief.

The following day Jack had two dozen cigarettes he could no account for. Some of the men were playing poker. Jack wasn' involved, merely a spectator. Kovacs had just lost heavily, cleaning himself out of the currency they were using, tobacco.

'Shit,' he swore. 'You'll have to deal me out.'

Then Jack said brightly, 'I'll stake you. I've got some spares.'

He produced the cigarettes from somewhere in his bunk, and now men were seriously concerned. Those involved in Tunnel Yorker were due to crash out in a few days, seven at the outside.

'Where did you get the butts, Jack?' asked one of the Americans Zeke Ryan.

'I've had them for ages.' Jack furrowed his brow. 'Haven't I?'

He hadn't had them yesterday, when he'd been trying to bum a couple. 'Until the next parcel arrives.'

'We've got to put him to the test,' said Harry Granger, later in the day when Jack was out of the hut. 'Otherwise I'm not going near Yorker.'

'How do we do that?' asked Kovacs.

Ross suggested a scheme he thought might work.

'Let him in on the tunnel. No, not Yorker,' he hurried on when he was almost drowned out with cries of protest. 'A fictitious tunnel in a fictitious location and the wrong date. How far are we from completing Yorker?'

'Four or five days would be my guess,' answered Lucas the lock expert.

'Then tell him there's a break on for tomorrow night from, say, 5B's latrine. A long way from 2B's washroom, anyway. Invite him along. Then watch and see what happens. If nothing, Lambert's in the clear.'

Kovacs was nominated to put the 'escape attempt' to Jack, who professed not to be interested.

'I've had a bellyful of that. Anyhow, I was never keen on tunnels.'

'I wouldn't be anxious to go, either,' growled Bob Tucker, 'if I thought there was a machine-gun squad waiting outside the wire.'

But there wasn't. Several men kept an all-night vigil, but there were no signs of any goon activity around 5B's latrine or beyond, outside the perimeter fence, where any tunnel could be expected to exit.

They watched until dawn. If there were Germans out there they would be visible packing up their machine gun.

Nothing.

'He's clean,' said one of the other Americans, Jim Webb, and that was the consensus until Jack made them all think again.

'You decided against it last night, did you?' he asked, in one of those rare moments when his eyes had lost their haunted look and his voice sounded absolutely normal. 'I thought you might. Can't say I blame you. Yorker from 2B is a much better bet than 5B.'

'You know about Yorker?' asked Jem Turner pleasantly. 'We thought we'd kept it a pretty good secret except for those immediately involved. Who told you?'

'*You* did, didn't you? Or Kovacs or Ross. Someone, anyway. Or maybe I just heard you talking. You can't keep much to yourself in a camp this size.'

That decided it for most of them. Yorker was too dangerous. They all had vivid memories of what had happened with Tunnel London, when half a dozen of the low numbers, those first out, had been shot in the clearing. Two others were taken by the Gestapo and never seen again.

Ross was the first to quit. His number was 1.

'Someone else can have it.'

The two British sergeants, Granger and McCann, followed suit, as did Ryan and Webb. The remaining Canadians – Tucker and Turner, Lucas and McKenzie, the Chief and Kovacs – debated the dilemma at length. They were joined by another British sergeant, Martinson, who would have made up the round dozen.

Martinson was all for taking a chance, but there were still four further days' digging to be accomplished, minimum, which he could not possibly do alone. No one was willing to sweat and slave in a tunnel if there was nothing in it for him.

'It's still all fucking guesswork,' complained Turner. 'I mean, what the hell have we got? A couple of eggs, a few cigarettes, the Gestapo not shooting Lambert the way they shot Alphabet? A heap of horse pucky. If Lambert's guilty, why didn't the goons turn up for the phoney 5B tunnel? If he's a stoolie, why would he tell us he knows about Yorker? The obvious thing to do would be to pretend he'd never heard of the bugger.'

'You're overlooking,' said McKenzie, 'that he's not right in the head. Half the time he doesn't know what he's talking about. Gessel could get him into his office on some pretext – Jesus, we've all been in there at one time or another because he's pissed off with something we did – ask him a few seemingly harmless questions, and he'd be spilling the beans without knowing what he's doing.'

'Or maybe knowing exactly what he's doing,' said Ross.

'We could put a guard on him,' offered Lucas. 'Watch him day and night until we're ready to go. If he doesn't talk to Gessel or Axheim or Hoffmann, we'll know we're safe. If he does, we call the deal off.'

'You're forgetting,' said Kovacs, reluctant to condemn his old friend but trying to be realistic, 'that since he knows that Yorker starts from 2B, he probably also knows just how far along we are. He could already have told Gessel. All the goons have to do is post a machine-gun team outside the wire from now till Christmas. So they get cold or frost-bitten, so what? It's a damn sight worse in Russia.'

'And if no one tries a break soon,' said Tucker, 'they'll know they've been rumbled and just "find" the tunnel during a routine shake-down.'

'You're not contributing much to this kaffeeklatsch, Chief,' said Kovacs.

'I haven't got a hell of a lot to say, except that you all seem to be assuming that Jack's a collaborator without an ounce of proof. I'm not ready to do that, not yet.'

'So you'll take your place in the tunnel, then, is that it?'

The Chief hesitated.

'I didn't say that. Okay, so someone ratted to the goons about London, but I'd stake my life it wasn't Jack. If it was, why did the Gestapo try to turn him into mincemeat? Where's the sense in that? And if London can't be laid at Jack's door, it must have been someone else. Someone who's still around. Think it over.'

The Chief got up and left the hut.

'He's got a point,' admitted Ross.

'Which still doesn't explain the eggs and the cigarettes, why the Gestapo set him free, the force-feeding,' persisted McKenzie. 'Too many coincidences, for my money. I'm not saying he's been informer since we were all captured and maybe London wasn't down to him, but the Gestapo or Gessel or both have bought him off somehow, now, whether his brains are scrambled or not.'

'Fucking goddamit!' swore Martinson. 'All that bastard work for nothing! And what happens next time, or the time after that?'

'He's right, you know,' said Ross. 'This can't go on. Whether we cancel Yorker or not, we've got to do something about Lambert, one way or another.'

Martinson rose to his feet. He was a tough ex-coal miner with a Military Medal to his credit.

'Cancel Yorker nothing! If you guys don't want to go, that's fine. I'll round up a few others to help with the digging and they can go instead.'

He managed to recruit four more. While not knowing all the details – because Martinson, fearing he would frighten off volunteers, told them nothing of the conversations concerning Lambert – the rest of the camp other than those four saw that the original tunnel team had backed away from the project and wondered why.

Five people to do the digging were barely enough. But, working in relays until they were exhausted, they managed to get under the trees only two days behind schedule. Breakout was timed for the small hours of December 14 and, before then, Lambert was shadowed closely. He was not called in by the commandant or approached by Axheim or Hoffmann. Now that the weather was so cold and it was snowing practically every hour of every day, even the compound goons had given up playing their games with him. For captors and captives alike, it was hard enough just trying to keep warm.

On the night of December 13/14 everyone went to bed as normal, except those due to make the break. Few slept, however. Lambert did, for once. Nightmareless, too, by the sound of it.

Two a.m. came and went, the time Martinson and his crew should be breaking through the earth's crust. No noises at all bar several of the dogs barking. Of course there were two feet of snow on the ground so that could delay matters. But not to a huge extent. The earth wasn't freezing. Allow thirty minutes for the snow and perhaps another thirty in case there had been a hitch in the tunnel. If nothing was heard by three a.m., three thirty at the outside, Martinson and his men were out. And everyone had made a mistake about Jack Lambert.

The machine guns opened up, it was judged later, a minute or two short of three forty-five. From inside the huts it was impossible to tell from which direction the shots came, or even if Martinson's escape team was the target. But everyone knew.

One or two of the men would have killed Jack Lambert, shaken roughly awake, there and then if Kovacs and the Chief hadn't intervened and said: No, this has got to be done properly if it's going to be done at all. And if the goons hadn't turned on every light in the camp and crashed open every hut door for a *Sonderappell*.

But it was all an act on Lambert's part, this apparent breakdown. Certainly Oberscharfuehrer Veit and the other SS thugs had smashed him bodily and mentally for a time, and he had told them everything because, then, he had genuinely cracked up. He would also have to live for ever with the memory of Alphabet's execution, but at least he had not been responsible for Anneliese Weiss's death. Anneliese hadn't died; she'd been found in time and saved. Seiffert had lied. Axheim had let it slip one afternoon, taunting him.

'The girl lived you'll be happy to hear,' he said, smirking. 'The Gestapo asked me to pass that on.'

He could have destroyed the arrogant bastard right then, but that would have been foolish, earned him a firing squad. There was a traitor somewhere in the camp, someone very close if he were any judge. The man had to be found and eliminated. It would be easier to establish the identity of the Judas if everyone thought he had never recovered from his treatment at the hands of the Gestapo. People were much more inclined to drop their guard in the presence of someone they suspected was not quite right in the head.

But he had recovered. It had taken time, but he hadn't come through the Depression, Vaagsö and Dieppe through lack of backbone. Let them all think he was a walking corpse that the goons could slip eggs and cigarettes to. Let the goons themselves think they were succeeding in framing him while protecting their real informant. It suited him, for now, to play the broken reed. One way or another he would make up for Alphabet's execution.

He could tell no one what he was up to, that was the hardest part, not even the Chief or Kovacs. Captivity had changed everyone. For all he knew, the traitor could be either of them.

NINETEEN

December 1943

Even the Chief finally agreed, a day later, that there had to be some
sort of trial, though he would have preferred the word enquiry. Still, it
was going to be a kangaroo court, a drumhead court martial, whatever
the label said. Five men had died, their corpses displayed by Gessel, and
someone had to pay for it or some answers found. At least at a trial,
crazy though he might be, Jack would have a chance to defend
himself, maybe even prove beyond any shadow of doubt that he had
not informed on his fellow Kriegies. Without a trial several of the
men, Tucker and McKenzie in particular, were likely to take the law
even further into their own hands. And to hell with the consequences.

Kovacs argued persuasively that only the original members of
Yorker should sit as the court.

'We're the ones immediately concerned. If Jack's guilty we've got to
say so and not pass the buck. Besides, what we're doing is illegal. If
RQMS Maitland gets wind of it he'll put a stop to it whatever the
verdict. If anyone else gets wind they may want to jump the gun.
Some of Munroe's fat cats would get a kick out of sticking a knife in
Jack's ribs, guilty or not. So we keep it to ourselves.'

It would be an informal hearing, question and answer, in Hut 6B.
Two men would always be on guard just inside the door, allowing no
one to enter regardless of the weather. With the snow it was unlikely
the goons would venture out to make snap inspections. Besides, there
were no other tunnels being dug. If the goons were paying an informer
as they must be, they would know that.

The two guards would be inside as opposed to outside because
they, too, had to participate in the tribunal, listen to the evidence and
join in the verdict. If anyone asked, the failed escape was being
discussed by those who had helped dig Yorker. And it was being done
in secret.

'Depending on how far Jack cooperates, it shouldn't take more than a couple of hours. The other guys from 6B can bed down in other huts for that length of time. Any questions?'

'Shouldn't there be something about him being innocent until proved guilty?'

'Can it, Chief,' snapped Kovacs. 'That goes without saying. None of us wants it to be Jack, but we need answers. Don't forget, that could be you lying out there, not Martinson.'

'When do we start?' asked Ross.

'I've spread the word around that we'll want the hut from midday tomorrow. Mac,' said Kovacs to McKenzie, 'I'd like you and Ryan to stick close to Jack throughout the morning. Have him here by noon. Then we'll see.'

McKenzie and Ryan took the door. The others either squatted on the floor or leaned against their bunks. Jack sat on his own. Kovacs opened the proceedings.

'There are a couple of questions we'd like to ask you, Jack, a few things that have been bothering some of the guys.'

'So Mac told me. Fire away. Anything I can do to help.'

Kovacs and the Chief exchanged glances. This was going to be difficult.

Kovacs tried it several ways. Some of the guys were still wondering why the Gestapo hadn't disposed of him the way they'd disposed of Alphabet. Some of the guys were wondering about the eggs and the cigarettes. Some of the guys were wondering how the goons had known about Yorker.

'Bastard Krauts. They know everything.'

'Yeah, but how?'

'You got me. Someone tipped them off would be my guess.'

'One of us?'

'Who else? You want my opinion, talk to everyone who knew about Yorker, even if it's half the camp.'

'You knew about it,' said Jim Webb.

'Of course I did. So did everybody in this hut.'

'But nobody else in this hut, apart from you, has been found with extra supplies,' said Ryan, from the door.

'I guess that's true.'

They couldn't figure him. He was answering their questions but he wasn't. He didn't appear to realize at all that he was in the dock, no

271

one else. He seemed to believe that he was an equal participant in a friendly discussion to get to the bottom of it all.

'If I had to lay money on it,' he said, 'I'd bet on Munroe.'

'You mean one of the fat cats?' asked Jem Turner.

'That's possible, but Munroe personally would be where I'd put my five dollars.'

Jesus, thought Kovacs.

'Munroe's dead, Jack,' said Ross.

'Munroe is? Serves the bastard right.'

'You killed him,' said Ryan.

'I did?' Jack frowned, then smiled. 'That's right, I did, didn't I? The night Alphabet and I got out.' The smile disappeared like chalk being wiped from a blackboard. 'They shot Alphabet you know. He wouldn't talk so they shot him.'

This was better, on the right track.

'Did *you* talk, Jack?' asked Harry Granger.

Jack examined his hands, his fingernails. Some had healed, some would never heal.

'They had this big guy, SS. Big as a house. And another guy in plainclothes. Gestapo. He kept asking the questions. The big guy did the damage, not just with a truncheon. They tried electrodes. Seiffert did the interrogations. Bloody cold in those cellars.'

'This is getting us nowhere,' said Sergeant McCann.

'Was Seiffert the Gestapo guy?' asked Kovacs.

'Mean little bastard. Looked like Himmler. Yeah, he was Gestapo.'

'Then why did he let you go?' Kovacs threw a curve. 'After he'd proved you'd killed the girl?'

Jack stared at Kovacs for a full fifteen seconds. So they still thought Anneliese had died, did they? Better to leave it like that, otherwise they might wonder how he knew she had survived. And that would complicate matters if the Judas was in the room, which Jack felt sure he was. Everything pointed to him being one of the original members of the Yorker breakout squad.

'They told me she was fifteen,' said Jack dully, continuing to act the part of a man who was never more than a hair's breadth away from total mental collapse. 'Showed me pictures of her when she was even younger.'

'But did you kill her?' persisted Kovacs.

'It was an accident. She came up the ladder, saw us. I ran after her and she fell. Jesus Christ, fifteen years of age!'

Jack buried his head in his hands. The others misunderstood the gesture, thought he was breaking down. The Chief passed Jack a handkerchief, a piece of dirty rag in actuality.

'Take it easy, boss.'

Jack hung on to the handkerchief, twisting it into knots.

Kovacs looked around for help. But no one was going to assist him on this one. The question had to be asked and he had been nominated to pose it.

'We have to know this, Jack. Martinson and four others were killed trying Yorker. The goons were waiting for them outside the wire. Did you tell Gessel about the tunnel?'

Time to change tack slightly, thought Jack. He feigned anger.

'You're calling me an informer? Me!'

'For Christ's sake . . .' began Ross.

'Shut it!' bellowed Kovacs. 'Shut it or I'll deck you like you've never been decked before. Did you tell Gessel, Jack?'

'No, I didn't.'

'Then where did you get the cigarettes and why did the Gestapo let you live?' demanded McKenzie.

'I don't know, for God's sake!' More cunning needed now, to keep the Judas off balance. 'Maybe I did tell Gessel. I don't remember.'

'That's good enough for me,' said Lucas.

'Think, Jack, think,' urged Kovacs.

'They told me Anneliese's mother was going to an asylum. Then they beat me up again. Look, I'm tired. I have to lie down.'

He stretched out on his bunk and closed his eyes, pretending to retreat behind the protective shield of sleep. He had done as much as he could for the moment. Now was the time to listen; see, if at all, which one of them wanted his head on a plate more than the others.

'He's bughouse,' said Kovacs. 'Round the bend.'

'He's also a collaborator,' said Ryan. 'You heard him, he just about admitted it. Martinson and the others are dead because of him. And who's next? You, me, the Chief? All of us? Who gets the chop at the end of the next tunnel? Because there'll be another one dug before this war's over and Lambert'll still be getting paid out in eggs and cigarettes whether he knows what he's doing or not. He said it himself, you can't keep tunnels a secret.'

Ross joined in the indictment.

'Ryan's right. Crazy or not, and maybe not always crazy, he's a menace to everyone in the camp. The thing is, what do we do about him?'

The Chief could see that quite a few had already made up their minds.

'You don't execute lunatics. You isolate them.'

'In a place this size?' scoffed Jem Turner. 'Don't be a jerk.'

The Chief went for Turner, fists clenched. Ryan and McKenzie pulled them apart. Okay, thought Jack, count the Chief out of the running. Not that he was ever a likely candidate in the first place.

'And there you have it in a nutshell,' said Ross, 'you two getting at each other's throats because of Lambert.'

Kovacs bawled for everyone to calm down.

'Nobody's talking about executing anyone. Not yet. Not until we're agreed on a verdict.'

It was a formality. Even the Chief, who was the last to deliver his, had to accept that the odds were that Jack, wittingly or otherwise, had informed Gessel about Yorker. That he had also talked to the Gestapo was virtually beyond dispute.

'Now we decide what to do,' said Kovacs.

I'm doing this too well, thought Jack uncomfortably, still faking sleep but listening carefully to every word, in case 'what had to be done' proved to be a crack over the skull with the nearest blunt instrument. Why the hell didn't the Judas say something to give himself away, so that he could jump down the bastard's throat?

They debated it backwards and forwards for several hours. Once someone hammered on the door and demanded to know how much longer the discussion was going on. McKenzie and Ryan, now back on guard, told the would-be intruder to go forth and multiply. Later Jack sat up on his bunk, feeling that he had to remind them of his presence, chivvy the discussion along. He said, 'Christ, you guys still at it?' — then promptly turned over and simulated sleep again. As he had hoped, that convinced the jury that he had forgotten everything that had transpired earlier.

There were only two possible sentences. They either disposed of him or let him go free. If they disposed of him, that was an end to it except insofar as their consciences were concerned. If they let him live, he would always be a threat to any future escape attempts, or anything else the inmates did to confound and confuse the goons. They would all be spending some time in the cooler, or worse, before the end of the war. Most of them had been there at least once and didn't want a second helping.

Ross, Kovacs and the Chief were the last to hold out against execution. Ross argued, quite cleverly thought one or two, that it might be possible to get Lambert transferred to another Stalag.

'You think the goons are going to stand for that?' sneered Lucas. 'Let someone be transferred who's invaluable to them here? Be your age. Besides, that's just dumping the problem on some other poor sucker, who won't know what the hell to expect. Just because you're from Calgary . . .'

'That's got nothing to do with it,' retorted Ross.

'Maybe, maybe not.'

It was eight-to-three in favour of execution at that moment. Ross shrugged and made it nine-to-two.

'Come on, Kovacs,' said Turner. 'You've had enough to say for yourself up to now.'

'Look at it this way,' said Webb. 'You'll be doing him a favour. He's as nutty as a fruitcake. Never mind that he killed Martinson, what kind of a life do you think he's going to have for the rest of the war? Which could go on for ten years. Or after the war. That kid, Anneliese whoever. He's never going to forget her. He can forget Schultz and Grell and that bastard Munroe. He might even get over the beating he took at the hands of the Gestapo and that Alphabet got shot and he didn't. But the German girl, fifteen years old? Not a chance.'

Interesting, thought Jack. Chalk up a strike against Webb.

Although Webb was right, of course, Kovacs reflected; for that matter he too, Kovacs, had something to forget: about Jack Lambert of the Patricias, of Achnacarry, of Vaagsö. This was just a shell of that man. It would be like putting down an old dog, one you'd tramped many a mile with, because of a festering and incurable disease.

He nodded.

'If that's a yes say it out loud, for Christ's sake,' said Tucker. 'Just so there's no mistake later.'

'It's a yes.'

Ten-to-one.

Maybe it's Kovacs, thought Jack. It didn't feel right, but feelings counted for very little at this stage of the game. If it could be termed a game. If he called the plays wrongly there wouldn't be a rematch. The loser forfeited more than a trophy.

'Just you, Chief,' said McKenzie, 'and we haven't got all day. It'll be dark soon and the goons'll be locking up for the night.'

The Chief thought that, when this poxy war was over, he was going to take to whisky like there was no tomorrow. Jack Lambert was the best friend he'd ever had, or would have. Jack had brought him into the Patricias, taught him to read and write properly, saved his bacon when he'd beaten up that hooker in London. Okay, so he'd collaborated, almost certainly without knowing what he was doing. But condemn him to death and form part of the execution team?

'I can't do it, guys.'

He got up to leave the group. McKenzie and Lucas barred his way.

'Oh no you don't, Chief,' said Lucas. 'You agreed with the verdict. Now you've got to show some balls and agree with the sentence. We can't have you walking around after the war saying that it was nothing to do with you. That it was the rest of us. You'll get us all topped.'

And maybe a strike against Lucas too, Jack decided.

'A minute, Chief,' said Kovacs, and led him to one side.

They went into a huddle, Kovacs and the Chief, Kovacs whispering fiercely, the Chief arguing his side of things.

But finally David Greyfoot's shoulders slumped. He nodded once and strode out of the hut, into the snow.

'It's eleven-to-nothing now,' said Kovacs.

'He didn't say so aloud,' grumbled McCann. 'He's supposed to tell us so that we can all hear.'

'Believe me, he's in favour.'

'How did you convince him?' asked Ross.

'I told him you, we, were going to get rid of Jack anyway, and that Jack might need a friend close by when it happens.'

'Clever,' said Lucas admiringly.

And bloody chilling, thought Jack, for a man to listen to his own death warrant.

'I'll pretend I didn't hear that,' said Kovacs.

'Okay, okay. I take it back.'

'So all that's left,' said Granger, 'is how and when.'

'I know the when,' said Kovacs. 'The when is tonight. I'm not going to sit here for another twenty-four hours looking at that poor mad bastard.'

The others agreed. The sooner the better. Jack breathed a little easier. He had a few more hours, though he was still no closer to unmasking the Judas. It was all guesswork. He'd better come up with a few answers pretty damned quick, however, before the charade got to the point of no return.

'It shouldn't look like an execution,' said Ross. 'Never mind our own various governments at the end of the war, if Gessel suspects we killed his informant it'll be the Gestapo for the lot of us. That leaves an accident or suicide. An accident's almost out of the question, so we're left with suicide.'

'Which figures,' put in McKenzie. 'He wouldn't be the first POW to top himself, and he's got more reason than most.'

'You know, Mac,' said Kovacs slowly, 'there's something about you that makes me feel just a bit ill.'

Jack sweated out the first of the dark hours, ready to spring into action if anyone so much as even coughed anywhere near him. Then he would tell them, because he would have to, that he had been play-acting. It would be unfortunate if it came down to that, because he was still no closer to the truth. Suspicions, yes, but no proof. No one had given himself away.

They had all left the hut to debate the manner of his 'suicide', presumably to prevent him overhearing their conversation during one of his so-called moments of lucidity. He thought he could guess the method, anyway. They'd put a rope round his neck, or a knotted shirt-sleeve. That was how those who'd had enough usually chose to exit.

McCann, Granger, Lucas, Webb, Ross, Kovacs. He'd narrowed it down to those six on no more than instinct. It could still be any of the others, except the Chief. It was probably time now, right now, to reveal his hand. He'd gambled for high stakes and they hadn't paid off. The identity of the Judas was still cloaked.

Ah well, without a gamble life was meaningless, a few score years of playing it safe before an eternity in a grave. If he'd thought otherwise he'd never have volunteered for anything hazardous.

In a corner someone stirred. Kovacs, he noticed. The goons always left a couple of bulbs burning all night, for security reasons. They could be extinguished by a master switch in the guardroom if the RAF came over and the Kriegies opted to tear down the blackout blinds and illuminate the whole camp. But the prisoners had found out long ago how to unscrew individual lamps, protected by what the Germans believed to be immovable wire mesh, without short-circuiting the entire system.

So, the time had come.

'Listen,' he said, sitting up.

'Clobber him,' said a voice.

Christ, he was getting slow, he thought, before something very heavy hit him on the head and he lost consciousness. He hadn't even heard anyone creeping up on him. Kovacs had distracted him for that very reason.

When he came round his hands and feet were bound, and he was gagged. Fear set in. He hadn't expected the gag. You didn't muffle a crazy man who didn't know what was happening anyway.

He tried to shout, and kick out, but it was hopeless. Wait a minute, he thought. For Christ's sake wait a minute.

The lamps were removed, the hut door opened, his foot fetters taken off.

The more he fought, the tighter they held him, heading him for the main latrines. Searchlights made hard work of penetrating the blizzard.

Jesus, he thought, I'm going to die.

'Let's get it over with before a wandering ferret stumbles in out of the snow,' said McCann, once they were inside the latrines.

He saw Ross fetch a bench, McCann and Ryan rebind his feet, Granger uncoil the rope, which went around his neck, the other end over a crossbeam. One of them, he thought in spite of his panic, one of the bastards was making sure.

Who, though? Who, for Christ's sake?

Then he knew, saw it in the man's eyes; not triumph but relief.

He tried to shout the name from behind the gag, tell the rest. But it was all far too late.

The last thing he saw was Turner kicking over the bench, and then there was nothing.

In May 1944 four men tried a break from Hut 3B's Tunnel Freddie. The goons allowed all four to get into the clearing before opening fire. Three died instantly, the other later from his wounds. Kovacs said it for them all.

'Did we execute the wrong guy or was there more than one?'

TWENTY

The first cable from Jonathan Margolis was relatively short. It was proving very difficult trying to trace any of the officers staffing Stalag XIII K for the years in question. However, doubtless they would get a break before long. In the meantime, Ben was to charge everything up to expenses and sit it out in London.

Ben did so for two weeks. Then the second cable arrived. This was much longer.

Of Oberst Karl Gessel, the former commandant, nothing was known after September 1944, when he was seconded to an active service detachment on the Eastern Front. The chances were he had either perished or was now a prisoner of the Russians. The adjutant, Hauptmann Werner Axheim, had been killed in an air-raid while on furlough in Munich in December of that same year, 1944. But one of the camp's junior officers, Oberleutnant Paul Hoffmann, had survived the war, served a term of one year's imprisonment for his part in the manacling of Canadian POWs after Dieppe, and was now living in the city of his birth, just fifteen miles from the Stalag in which he had spent much of his war service: Frankfurt. Exact details to follow as available.

There was further good news.

Margolis had not been idle while trying to track down the Germans. The addresses of Ross, Greyfoot and Turner they already knew, but Margolis, by using private detectives as well as his Ottawa contacts, had established the whereabouts of the four other Canadians mentioned in McCann's original letter, the one that had opened up this whole can of worms. Tucker, Kovacs, McKenzie, Lucas. He, Margolis, would see about them while Ben was pursuing Hoffmann.

'Stick it out,' Margolis concluded. 'It will all be worth it.'

Ben checked with the Canadian High Commission while waiting, though he was fairly sure he knew the answer. He was correct. Frankfurt lay in the American Zone of Occupation. Had Hoffman lived in the Russian Zone or, to a lesser extent, in the French Zone, obtaining papers for transit might have proved tough. In the case of the Russian Zone it would have been impossible. But the Americans would surely cooperate with Margolis.

They did. A week later Ben received Hoffmann's last known address, almost certainly his current address since the Americans did not allow ex-Wehrmacht officers, even junior ones, to move around at will. Nor would any German wish to do so since jobs were at a premium.

Ben should therefore present himself to a Colonel Mortimer at the US Embassy in Grosvenor Square, where he would receive travel documents, a temporary residential permit, and a priority two-way air warrant London–Bonn–Frankfurt. Also Colonel Mortimer would present him with two cartons of Lucky Strike cigarettes and five pounds of coffee, both virtually unobtainable for Germans outside the black market, where few could afford to venture. If Hoffmann proved reluctant to cooperate, four hundred cigarettes and five pounds of coffee should change his mind.

TWENTY-ONE

July 1947

Frankfurt had taken a far worse pasting than even London, though Ben, when he thought about it, realized that he should not be surprised at that. His own squadron had bombed the target often enough and it had naturally come under land artillery attack as the Allied armies began punching holes in the Third Reich. Patton's tanks had done the rest.

Almost half the city had been destroyed and much of the civilian population, two years after the war, was still living in makeshift camps on the outskirts of the city, provided by the Americans, or where they could, among the rubble. A fortunate few had a room in what remained of an apartment block or small hotel.

Hoffmann was one of the lucky ones. That should not have surprised Ben, either. Any man of combat age who managed to sit out his war in a POW camp had a knack of finding cushy numbers.

At the American Embassy before Ben left London, Colonel Mortimer had furnished him with more information than just Hoffmann's address, sent to the Embassy from Margolis. The cable was datelined just an hour after Margolis's last to Ben's hotel, Margolis assessing correctly that Ben would waste no time in checking out and getting on his way.

Last heard of, Hoffmann was working as a steward in an hotel requisitioned as a US officers' club. Mortimer gave Ben a typed letter on Embassy paper, instructing 'whom it may concern' to afford Ben every facility and courtesy.

Margolis could certainly turn on the taps when it came down to it.

Enquiring at the hotel desk, Ben produced his Embassy document and was asked by a corporal to wait where he was. When the corporal returned he was accompanied by a combat major with a chest full of fruit salad. He introduced himself as Major Courtney and he and Ben shook hands.

'Heavy wood, this,' said Courtney, waving the Embassy document. 'We like to think they've forgotten about us in London and Washington in case some desk jockey decides we're having it easy and wants to transfer one or two of us to Berlin to play footsie with the Russians.' His accent was cornpone, deep South. Ben wondered if he exaggerated it for strangers. 'What can I do to help?'

Ben kept it simple, saying no more than he had business with a former Oberleutnant Hoffmann, a steward here.

'Is this official?' asked Courtney curiously. 'You're a Canadian it says here.'

'It's official,' said Ben deadpan.

Courtney's expression said he doubted it, but he studied the document again.

'Well, it also says every facility and courtesy and it's signed by a bird colonel. That's good enough for me. I'm regular army so I don't get into beefs with colonels. Yeah, we employ him, Hoffmann. He's not here now, though. Went off duty about an hour ago. Can't say I like the bastard myself. Typical Kraut. Lost the war but can't take working as a servant. Tough shit. If you're out to nail him, good luck. He's a shifty sonofabitch.'

'I didn't say I was out to nail him,' said Ben.

Courtney eyed him carefully.

'That's right, you didn't. But you're a Canadian and Hoffmann served a year in the joint for what happened to a bunch of Canadians after Dieppe. I'm just putting two and two together.'

'Do you know where I'll find him?'.

Courtney took the hint. No more questions.

'At home. Where else can these bastards go? Most places are off limits. They're going to stay that way until the guys on our side of the fence are convinced that the guys on their side haven't got something else in mind. Like another Reich. You know where home is?'

'Elbestrasse.'

'Right. Across the river over what used to be called the Hitler Bridge. Just north of what was once the Gestapo HQ on Bürgerstrasse. What's left of that we turned into a jail. Cool, huh? Now we stick any Nazis we find still in the woodwork into the place the Nazis used to run. But you'd know all about that. Says here you were a flier.'

'Never heard of Bürgerstrasse, though. We had soft targets.'

'Tell that to Aunt Jemima. Would you like a ride to Elbestrasse?'

'If there's one on offer.'

Courtney escorted Ben to a Jeep in the club's car pool. Half a dozen duty drivers were shooting craps.

'If you get anything on Hoffmann I wouldn't mind knowing.'

Ben shook hands again.

'If I get anything, you'll know. Does he speak English?'

'Fluently. Wait for him,' said Courtney to the Jeep driver. 'He'll tell you when.'

Hoffmann's apartment block, three storeys, was virtually intact. Some job we did on this area, thought Ben.

There was no concierge, but there were names and numbers on a board at the entrance. Handwritten. Hoffmann was on the second floor, a walk-up.

Ben rang the bell. It didn't work. Then he knocked.

Ben did not know Hoffmann from Adam, but he recognized the type. About thirty years of age and fair-haired. An arrogant swine. Small wonder that he missed the power he'd wielded in the Stalag. Flunkeying for the conquerors would not go down well with him.

'*Bitte?*'

'Herr Hoffmann?'

'*Ja.*'

Ben continued in English.

'Major Courtney gave me your address. From the US officers' club.'

Hoffmann studied Ben's civilian clothes.

'Major Courtney needs me back?'

Hoffmann's English was as good as it had ever been, though now with a slight American accent. There was also anxiety in his tone. Ben heard it and grabbed at it.

'No, but I have his permission to talk to you. My name's Lambert. I'm from Canada. There might be something in this for you.'

Ben flashed the cigarettes and coffee. Hoffmann's eyes lit up. It would take him three months to earn enough to buy even the cigarettes.

'Please come in, Herr Lambert.'

But it wasn't easy.

Since Hoffmann had served time for his part, junior though it had been, in the administration of Stalag XIII K, anyone reminding him about that part of his history had better have a damned good reason. He didn't want the Military Government pouncing on him again.

The cigarettes and coffee were on what passed as a table. They were on offer, though Ben hadn't offered them yet. Instead he tried a little bit of blackmail coupled with a straight lie.

'Major Courtney is checking your credentials. I'm liaising with him on behalf of the Canadian Government, and I don't intend to beat about the bush. Let's have a talk about December 1943. About the Stalag and Sergeant Jack Lambert.'

The room itself was the pits. A put-up bed, a couple of rickety chairs, a wash-basin shielded by an old curtain. No heating of any description. It was going to be cold come the winter.

Hoffmann remembered Sergeant Lambert. Even though his death had taken place almost four years earlier, no one who had served in Stalag XIII K would ever forget Lambert. But the man opposite him was evidently his brother or some other close relation, and Hoffmann had no wish to reopen old wounds, not if it was dangerous.

But why should it be? He had served his prison sentence, unfair though that was, and it was probably better to cooperate with this Canadian on a voluntary basis than have him involve Major Courtney and make it official. God knows, then, what other trumped up charges would be laid against him, especially with Axheim dead and Gessel vanished, doubtless dead also.

'It was the war, you understand.'

'I'm familiar with the war,' said Ben.

'May I have a cigarette?'

Ben could have kicked his head in there and then. How many times might Jack have asked that sort of question? And not just for a cigarette. For an extra slice of bread or a clean blanket. Still, he held on to his temper. He needed to learn whatever Hoffmann knew.

'You can have a carton. In a minute. Maybe the other and the coffee too. But first I want some answers regarding Sergeant Lambert.'

'How much do you know?'

Ben played it straight. Jonathan would have handled it much better, as a negotiator, but Ben recognized he was not in Jonathan's league.

'The information I have is that he was a collaborator. He was found out and hanged himself. I don't happen to believe any of it, but the truth is what you're going to tell me.'

'Perhaps that is the truth.'

'Then the cigarettes and the coffee go back where they came from.'

Greed overcame Hoffmann. He stared at the two cartons of Luckies and reached out for the nearest. Ben let him take it.

'What I have to say is off the record,' said Hoffmann. 'If any of it is repeated outside this room, I shall deny our conversation ever took place. Is that understood?'

Ben nodded.

'Sergeant Lambert had been causing us, the camp authorities, a great deal of trouble almost from the day he arrived,' began Hoffmann. 'If there was a demonstration in the camp, you could guarantee that Lambert was the ringleader or one of them. If food was stolen from the kitchens, Lambert would be behind it. Again, I must emphasize that this was wartime and that periods in solitary confinement for breaches of discipline were not unknown. In England as well, I learned later.

'But isolation proved a useless punishment with Lambert. He was no sooner released than he was plotting something else. Discipline in the camp was a shambles.

'Then, in the middle of 1943 – June, I believe it was – Lambert escaped from the Stalag, along with another POW whose name I've forgotten. A Pole. A Canadian of Polish extraction, that is.'

Ben had to pinch himself to make sure he had heard Hoffmann correctly. There was nothing about an escape in Jack's dossier.

'Escaped? You mean he actually got away?'

'Clean away, both of them. The commandant was furious, beside himself with rage. Prior to that the Stalag had a perfect record. Several officers had made breaks from the adjoining Oflag, but in the Stalag we had always known when an escape was being planned.'

'Wait a minute, wait a minute.' Ben held up his hand. This was all going too fast for him. 'How did you know?'

'We had an informer on the inside, another Canadian. We never mentioned him by name, even in private conversations, in case we were accidentally overheard. We called him *Der Umhang*. Do you speak German?'

'Not enough to understand that.'

'*Der Umhang* means Cloak. That's what we called him, the Cloak. Considering his activities, it seemed appropriate.'

Ben kept his excitement under control with difficulty. If the commandant had been furious because Jack got away and the Germans already had a Canadian informer in the camp, it was only logical that Jack wasn't that man. Therefore no collaborator.

'What was the Cloak's real name?'

Hoffmann's eyes narrowed cunningly, sensing he had his interrogator on the hook. If he were clever he would receive both cartons of cigarettes *and* the coffee. There was a little blonde on the next floor who would do just about anything for even half a cup.

'I'll come to that, Herr Lambert. In due course.'

Hoffmann broke open a carton of Luckies, extracted a pack, unsealed it, and took out a cigarette. He lit it from a book of matches and inhaled deeply.

'You have no idea . . .' he sighed.

Ben cut him short.

'And that will be the only one you get unless I hear more than I'm hearing now.'

'Be patient, Herr Lambert. As I say, the commandant was furious when Sergeant Lambert escaped. When they were recaptured – and there was very little doubt that they would be – Oberst Gessel promised he would have Lambert and the Pole shot. But the adjutant, Hauptmann Axheim, claimed he had a better idea . . .'

June 1943

'We can surely do better than that, Herr Oberst,' said Axheim.

'Explain yourself.'

'Lambert has been a constant source of frustration to us, I think you'll agree.'

'Don't be a damned fool, Axheim,' barked Gessel. 'What the hell do you think we've been discussing for the last three hours? Get to the point.'

'Had he ever attempted an escape via a tunnel, as the others tried, we could have shot him legitimately and that would have been an end to it. But he's been much cleverer than that and I believe we should use his cleverness against him.

'The escapers will be picked up sooner or later, of that we can be certain. Then they will be handed over to the Gestapo. If the Gestapo is running true to form, after interrogation they will be executed. We must prevent that, at least as far as Lambert is concerned. We need him back here, whatever condition he's in. The other POWs will ask themselves why he has been released, particularly as he obviously killed Grell and is therefore a murderer. They will wonder what price he paid for his liberty.

'It shouldn't be too difficult to make him appear a collaborator. He can be found with a few more cigarettes than he should have, perhaps an extra egg or loaf. In the long run his fellow POWs will become even more suspicious of him.'

Gessel was still not following the strategy.

'So?'

'So, in a month or two – especially if another tunnel is started and is found thanks to *Der Umhang* – it would not surprise me in the least if the other Canadians decided to dispose of Lambert.'

Even Gessel could not miss the beautiful irony of that. Canadians executing a fellow Canadian. And an innocent one at that.

'And while they are assuming Lambert to be our informant,' concluded Axheim, 'they will not be looking for *Der Umhang*. He can operate as he always has and Lambert will be blamed.'

'It's possible, possible,' agreed Gessel. 'But let's find him first. Find *them*. We'll worry about talking to the Gestapo later.'

July 1947

You bastards, thought Ben, but kept his emotions to himself. He was getting close now and he didn't want to scare Hoffmann off. He was also curious about this business of Jack killing someone called Grell.

'Who was Grell?'

'A camp NCO, on cooler duties the night Lambert escaped. Lambert killed him and another Canadian, one of the chief blackmarketeers in the Stalag. He, Lambert, tried to make it appear as if they had killed one another in a fight, but the postmortem evidence was against that.'

Ben didn't like the sound of this, Jack killing a fellow Canadian.

'Still,' he said, 'there were no eyewitnesses.'

'Herr Lambert, be sensible. Had there been eyewitnesses Sergeant Lambert could hardly have escaped. There were none to the other murder, either, but there is no doubt Lambert committed it. Or the Pole. Or both.'

'What other murder?' asked Ben with trepidation.

'He shot the private who had driven him and the Pole through the camp gates. In cold blood,' added Hoffmann.

'You're lying!' said Ben angrily.

'I have no reason to lie to you.'

Ben believed him, reluctantly. Okay, he had begun his investigation to determine whether or not the war had changed Jack. It obviously had, but he was no collaborator. And probably no suicide.

'Go on, what happened when he was recaptured?'

'He was interrogated by the Gestapo, he and the Pole. The Pole was shot, but Lambert was returned to the Stalag. He was not, shall we say, in the best of health.'

Ben didn't need to second-guess what that meant. The bastards had tortured him. Seeing his expression, Hoffmann looked alarmed.

'You have to remember,' the German jumped in quickly, 'that the Gestapo and the SS were laws unto themselves. A state within a state. We in the Wehrmacht despised them, and feared them, but there was little we could do.'

Ben had heard it all before, and read about it, during the Nuremberg Trials. The swine of it was, some of it was undoubted fact.

'So the Gestapo agreed with the scheme put forward by – what was his name? Axel?'

'Axheim. Yes, they agreed. Lambert, in any event, was of no further use to them. They had learned all they wanted to know.'

'And what the hell does that mean?'

'That Lambert had talked, of course. What else? He may not have collaborated with us, the camp staff, but he did with the Gestapo.'

'With the help of rubber truncheons and thumbscrews,' said Ben bitterly. Poor bloody Jack.

Hoffmann shrugged his shoulders.

Ben took a hold of himself. It would get him nowhere to blame Hoffmann for something that wasn't Hoffmann's fault. For other things, yes, but not a Gestapo cellar. Besides, he wanted to know how they had put their plan into action.

'Hauptmann Axheim's plan, Herr Lambert. I was a junior officer, a lieutenant. I could not have influenced events in any manner.'

'Even if you'd wanted to.'

Hoffmann did not answer.

The bastard couldn't have done, anyway, thought Ben, and that was the truth. Many had been the times in Bomber Command when

Lancaster crews had known with an absolute certainty that the targets they were being briefed to bomb were not only poison gas factories and munitions works; that civilians' houses would be smashed also. But few had stood up and said they weren't going. He knew he hadn't.

It was the war. It didn't make it any easier, but it was a fact of life. And they, the Stalag officers, would have wanted to protect their informant, *Der Umhang*. If anyone deserved a bullet, it was the Cloak. He, and only he, would have known that Jack was being unjustly accused. Framed.

'Keep talking,' said Ben.

'There isn't a lot more to tell. Axheim's strategy was carried out to the letter. Lambert was found with eggs that could only have come from us, with more cigarettes than he could account for. Another escape attempt was tried, the tunnel discovered, the participants shot. Everything pointed to Lambert being the informant.'

December 1943

It was the morning Jack Lambert's corpse was discovered hanging in the latrines. The camp officers had been expecting something of the sort but had not known how, or when, it would happen. The commandant wanted details, but could not summon his real informant exclusively without arousing suspicion. Instead he had several dozen POWs in his office, one at a time. Finally it was *Der Umhang*'s turn.

'What happened?'

Der Umhang explained. About the trial, the verdict, the execution.

'We had to make it look like suicide.'

'Of course,' said Gessel, 'I understand that. You will be rewarded in the usual manner.'

'Don't make it too obvious.'

'We never have, have we? It will be an extra Red Cross parcel, diverted from someone else and relabelled with your name. Though I sometimes wonder,' said Gessel to Axheim and Hoffmann after *Der Umhang* had left, 'why the other Canadians are never concerned that he seems to receive more than his fair share.'

'They only see what they're looking for,' said Axheim. 'And they've been looking for Lambert.' Axheim stared at the now-closed door. 'A weak man, that one.'

'But useful,' said Gessel, 'so very useful. Did I ever tell you I once asked him why he collaborated with us?'

Axheim and Hoffmann looked at one another. Gessel had told the same story a dozen times, but he was a colonel and they were far junior. It paid to listen to colonels.

'Sir?' said Axheim politely.

'He said, "I shouldn't have volunteered for overseas service at all, but I knew it would help me politically to have a good war record behind me. I didn't expect to become a POW."' Gessel laughed uproariously. 'Imagine, gentlemen, that man a candidate for high office. If we lose this war, God forbid, we shall certainly win the next with men like him in power.'

'We should be grateful, Herr Oberst, that he found the regime in the Stalag too harsh to tolerate.'

'If we hadn't unearthed him we'd have unearthed another,' said Gessel. 'There's always one.'

July 1947

Ben was not sure whether to feel gratified or revolted. As he had suspected all along, Jack had neither been a traitor, nor had he killed himself. He had been executed by some of his fellow POWs for a crime he had not committed.

Of course he had committed other crimes, if crimes they could be called. He had killed without compunction, to escape, and he had broken under Gestapo torture, revealed things he should not have revealed. But he had not ratted on his nearest companions. *Der Umhang* had done that.

He could almost forgive the execution team because they had believed the evidence, false though it was. Only one man had known it to be a foul lie, a series of foul lies. The Cloak.

'Who killed Sergeant Lambert?' he asked Hoffmann. 'Who took part in the so-called suicide?'

'I can't remember,' answered Hoffmann. 'It's all so long ago. I'm not sure I ever knew, if any of us did.'

'But you'll remember the name of *Der Umhang*, all right.'

'Oh yes, I recall that.'

Ben waited. So did Hoffmann. Ben pushed across the second carton of Luckies and the tin of coffee.

'Tell me who it was.'

Hoffmann told him.

Ben called on Major Courtney after leaving Hoffmann.

'Get what you wanted?' asked the American.

'Yes, thanks, I got that.' Ben thought for a moment. 'About Hoffmann.'

'Yes.'

'If you sent a couple of MPs along to his room right now, you might find he's concealing two cartons of Lucky Strikes and a large tin of coffee. In my view he's stolen them from somewhere, probably here.'

Ben felt better after that.

Back in London, before arranging for a civilian flight to Canada, Ben telephoned Margolis, getting through after waiting three hours. The transatlantic cable was far from free of static, but he managed to get his message across.

He asked Margolis to telegraph six of the seven Canadian names contained in Sergeant McCann's original list. The seventh name was *Der Umhang*, and they would learn that from Ben's own lips. Margolis would guess anyway, by process of elimination.

The message was to be signed Ben Lambert and would be the same in all instances.

I know who the traitor in Stalag XIII K was.

'Put your own phone number at the end of the text, Jonathan,' said Ben, shouting the way people do with a poor connection. 'Get them to call you, then arrange a meeting.'

'When for? And where?' Margolis was also shouting.

'About a week from now. Your place, in Edmonton. I should be home in three days, but you never can tell. You might have trouble with David Greyfoot. Even if he's sober enough to read, he probably won't have any money.'

'Leave it to me.'

Ben replaced the receiver. A week and they'd all know.

TWENTY-TWO

August 1947

It took a few days longer than a week.

Some of the addressees had had business or other commitments, but out of the six five had called Margolis within twenty-four hours of the cables being received. On hearing what he had to say, each man promised to be in Edmonton as soon as he could, which wasn't good enough for Margolis. He wanted them all there at the same time, not turning up piecemeal. Finally a mutually acceptable date was agreed.

During every conversation, each caller wanted to know what Ben Lambert had discovered. Who, in fact, was the Stalag XIII K traitor? Margolis gave them all the same answer.

'You'll find out in good time.'

As Ben had predicted, Greyfoot hadn't responded. Nor would he have any truck with the private detective Margolis dispatched from Saskatoon to Foam Lake to persuade him. The man was driven off with a hunting rifle and he wasn't inclined to risk his neck a second time. Not without a brigade of tanks.

In the end Ben went to fetch him.

'He knows me as Jack's brother,' he told Margolis. 'He might listen.'

'And he might blow your head off. We're getting five, why do we need six?'

'Because he deserves to be there.'

'If your assessment is correct, he was one of those who killed Jack.'

'Even more reason.'

On this occasion Ben approached no closer than one hundred yards of the cabin. If the last time was anything to go by, Greyfoot would have been watching him for quite a way up the trail. Maybe that's all the poor bastard had to do, study the trail and drive off trespassers.

Ben just sat down and waited. Way over to the west geese were circling over Big Quill Lake. Too early for them to be skeining and flying south, though maybe they knew something he didn't. Saskatchewan had hellish winters.

An hour passed. Then two. Eventually Greyfoot came out. He seemed far from drunk and appeared much cleaner than Ben remembered. He also had on footwear, high boots.

He obviously recognized his visitor.

'I told you before,' he called, coming nearer, 'you're not welcome here.'

There was no slur in his words. He was sober. He wasn't carrying his rifle either, Ben was encouraged to notice. Maybe he had half-believed the message in the cable. Or wanted to believe it.

'It wasn't Jack, you know.'

'So your wire said.'

'It's the truth. I'm recently back from Germany. I spoke to Hoffmann there, in Frankfurt. Remember Hoffmann? He told me the whole story.'

Greyfoot came nearer still, within twenty yards, and squatted on his hunkers. He was as wary as a small animal with a predator on the prowl. He'd 'gone bush', as they said in this part of the country. Ben wondered how many people he spoke to during the course of a year.

'So tell it to me.'

Ben did just that, relating it slowly and carefully. All he left out was the identity of *Der Umhang*.

'And you believed Hoffmann?' asked Greyfoot, when Ben indicated he had finished.

'He had no reason to lie. He had nothing to gain.'

'Then who was it?' demanded Greyfoot, standing upright. 'Who was the bastard? Kovacs, Ross, Turner, McKenzie. You said it was a Canadian.'

'That's right. You'll find out the rest in Edmonton. The others involved are due there tomorrow. If you're interested.'

'We driving there?'

'That's about the size of it.'

'I'll put a few things together.' Greyfoot hesitated. 'I don't have much.'

'You've got enough.'

'You can come inside and wait if you like.'

The cabin was a dump. There were bottles everywhere, unwashed crockery, the smell of decay. It was difficult to believe that Greyfoot had once been a fighting soldier with several famous units.

Greyfoot took his time putting his 'few things' together and Ben sensed he had something on his mind, something he wanted off it before they left.

Finally it came out and the guilt was palpable.

'It was us, you know,' he said, and named names. 'We killed Jack.'

Ben had already come to that conclusion, the names on McCann's original list. Seven Canadians, two Americans, two Brits. One short of the Last Supper. And one Judas.

Ben planned to drive all night. He telephoned Margolis from a gas station, reversing the charges.

'We're on our way.'

Between them, Ben, Maggie and Margolis had concluded it was better if the former POWs, who had not seen each other for two years, had a sitting-room to themselves for an hour or so. To get reacquainted. It was going to be hard enough, Ben saying what he had to, without the others having to break the ice during it. These men had spent three years in a prison camp together. If you hadn't been there, you didn't know what it meant.

Ben didn't want Maggie present at all when he spoke to Jack's one-time friends. Nor did Margolis. But Maggie insisted.

She had heard the story first-hand from Ben on his return from Germany, and she found it hard to forgive the men in the sitting-room for executing her brother.

To begin with she had wanted to go public.

'We should go to the authorities. Or the newspapers.'

'Mags, Mags,' Ben had pleaded. 'If we do that they'll be forced to defend themselves. That's human nature. And then it will all come out. How Jack broke under Gestapo torture, said things he shouldn't. Is that how you want him remembered? He's a hero now, it said so in the *Calgary Herald* the day you and Jonathan were married. He always was a hero until he couldn't take any more. Let's leave it like that.

'Those guys thought they were being betrayed and acted the way most of us would have acted given the circumstances. They'll feel as guilty as hell when they know the truth. Greyfoot already does. Maybe between us we can do something about the real culprit. It isn't perfect, but it's the best we can hope for.

'Look at it positively. A couple of months ago we were told Jack was a traitor to his friends and a suicide. We now know he was neither.'

'You sound as if you're on their side,' said Maggie bitterly.

'I'm on Jack's side. That's why I've been halfway across the world.'

'They've had their hour,' said Margolis.

Only Greyfoot appeared uncomfortable in Margolis's near-palatial home. Only Greyfoot wasn't drinking, Ben was happy to see. The others were cradling whiskies or beers.

Ben addressed them formally, facing them in their chairs. The six, his sister and brother-in-law. Though it was still speculation, the six had already assumed, by the absentee, who the informer was.

'I've just returned from Germany,' Ben began, and proceeded to tell them everything that had transpired.

'You finished?' asked Kovacs, when Ben obviously had.

Kovacs looked prosperous. As Lieutenant Halliday had predicted on Vaagsö a lifetime ago, guys like Kovacs were going to run the world one day. Kovacs had not quite achieved that, but he was already a wheel in the Canadian film industry. If he was not yet Stuart Legg or George Dunning, he was still a force to be reckoned with. His enemies reckoned he also had underworld connections, which he never bothered to confirm or deny.

He had evidently been elected spokesman, or elected himself, which was more likely. Before they went any further, he said, it was his duty, on behalf of everyone, to apologize for the injustice Jack Lambert had suffered.

'It's little enough, I know, but it's all we can do.'

A few moments passed in absolute and embarrassed silence. Then Lucas the locksmith broke in.

'If we're here to decide what to do about the bastard, I vote we kill him. Somehow. I hope you'll forgive my language, ma'am.'

Maggie said nothing.

'Let's not talk about killing in this house, or in this company,' said Andrew McKenzie. The blacksmith from North Battleford had put on a few pounds round his middle since the war, but he was still as strong as an ox. 'Anything that has to be done in that direction is private. Forget you ever heard that comment, Mrs Margolis.'

Again, Maggie said nothing. These were the sort of men she had never met before in her life. Tough men. Hard as nails. Her husband was tough in business, but he was a pussycat compared with these people.

'Mac's right,' said Turner, the inventor from Ottawa. Like Kovacs, his career had evidently paid off. Money oozed from every pore. 'Killing's a mug's game.'

Turner had a lot to lose.

Tucker was still in the Canadian army. It had kept him on after the war and he had never had to join the Foreign Legion, as he had promised himself if it all went wrong. He had been promoted from the ranks and was now a lieutenant with his eyes on a captaincy. He was on furlough for the present and could ill-afford paying off old debts by becoming involved in a killing. Whoever organized it.

Jesus, what the hell was this, Murder Inc?

'There's got to be a different way.'

'Chief?' said Kovacs.

Greyfoot sat up in his chair. No one had called him 'Chief' in years. He had been without a serious drink for twenty-four hours and it didn't feel that bad. His head was clear for once. Maybe he could contribute.

'Ben Lambert said something to me coming up in the car from Foam Lake. He asked "How do you make amends for what you did?" I'm sorry, Mrs Margolis, I really am. I didn't have the answer then and I don't say I've got it now. But what that bastard did is worth more than a nugget through the head.'

'Carry on,' said Kovacs.

'They conned us,' said the Chief. 'The goons and the other swine. I'm not an educated man and there's probably a better word, but it still amounts to a con. What we did to Jack we can never undo. I reckon you've got to repay like with like.'

'Old Cree logic, huh, Chief?' said Kovacs.

'Something like that.'

'This is getting out of hand,' murmured Margolis to Ben.

'Let's start to control it, then.'

Margolis stood up.

'Gentlemen, I know something that perhaps you do not. The man in question is a potential candidate for the Federal Parliament in Ottawa. Not yet, of course. The last Parliament was not summoned until September 1945 and under statute need not be dissolved until 1950. It is likely to be before then, however.

'He has designs on a Calgary seat, Calgary West is my current information, which he is being groomed for and which he will almost certainly succeed in obtaining because of connections and personal wealth. Perhaps we can do something to prevent him achieving his lifelong ambition.'

'Perhaps we can do more than that,' said Kovacs. 'Hell, that's easy.'

'Cut to the chase, for God's sake,' said Turner.

Kovacs hesitated.

'I wonder if Mrs Margolis wants to hear this.'

Maggie dug her toes in.

'Mrs Margolis does.'

'Right,' said Kovacs, 'then I suggest we don't do anything as stupid as killing Tom Ross. Or spread so much dirt around that he'd become an unlikely candidate for Ottawa. I suggest we drive the man out of his mind. As he, in part, drove Jack Lambert. With a bit of luck, Ross'll do the job for us. Listen . . .'

TWENTY-THREE

Margolis had his private detectives following Ross everywhere. There was no way the man could escape.

The Rideau Club in Ottawa, on the corner of Wellington and Metcalfe Streets and directly opposite Parliament, was the most exclusive club in the capital, which meant it was the most exclusive in the whole of Canada. The food was reputed to be the best anywhere. Potential members needed four sponsors and were thoroughly investigated before being permitted to join. In any of the rooms at any one time it was possible to see the rich and mighty, men who ruled the country by virtue of their wealth or their political position. Guests could be signed in by a member. Naturally Margolis had entree.

Women were not allowed. Nor were scruffy Indians. Greyfoot stayed outside. He didn't mind.

Ross was sitting at a table, surrounded by political bigwigs. Margolis and Ben remained in the background. They were not needed here. The others walked over to Ross's table. And simply stood there.

The conversation at the table gradually faded. Puzzled, Ross glanced up. And then behind him. He paled when he saw Kovacs, Lucas, McKenzie, Tucker, Turner. They were all older, of course, than Ross remembered, but he recognized them.

They said nothing, just looked at him. After a moment they turned on their heels and left.

'What the devil was that all about?' asked one of Ross's companions.

'Damned if I know,' said Ross, but he kept his hands under the table. They were shaking.

Later the same day Ross was walking with his wife in Major's Hill Park, the earlier incident almost forgotten, when ahead of him, on the same path, he saw Kovacs and Lucas. Taking his wife by the arm he changed direction – to find the Chief and Andrew McKenzie strolling towards him.

He left by the nearest exit. No one followed him.

In the late afternoon he was being escorted around Parliament by one of the power brokers of the Party he hoped to serve. In the Commons Chamber with its magnificent stained glass window he thought: This is where I'll be sitting before long.

But in the Confederation Hall, the rotunda at the main entrance, he saw Tucker and Turner.

This couldn't go on. What the hell were they after?

He went up to them.

'Okay, so what is all this?'

Tucker and Turner stared straight through him as if he weren't there. Then they left the building.

Ross thanked God Ruth wasn't with him.

But she was that evening when they were both dining at the Chateau Laurier. Only Kovacs and McKenzie appeared on this occasion. Ruth Ross was dressed to the nines.

Jesus, thought Kovacs, it wouldn't exactly make me ill to take her to bed.

Ross tried to bluff it out.

'Hey, fellers. Mac, Kovacs.'

'Your number's up, Ross,' said McKenzie. 'It's just a question of how long the count lasts.'

'Who were they?' asked Ruth Ross, when she and her husband were alone again.

'Guys I knew in the war,' said Ross. 'From the POW camp.'

'What did the big one mean, your number's up?'

'Look, Rufus, it doesn't matter.'

'Don't call me Rufus in public. And it matters. Anything that affects your career matters.'

'Those days are long gone.'

'Tell me anyway.'

'It's a hell of a long story and I don't want to go into it now.'

'But you will. You certainly will.'

Ruth Ross had raised her voice. Others in the dining-room looked at her. She was certainly something to look at.

'Keep your voice down, for God's sake. We'll own this city in a few years. They're nothing. They don't count. Believe me.'

'Then they'll go away?'

Ross glanced around. McKenzie and Kovacs were not lurking anywhere. Nor were any of the others.

'Of course they will. They have.'

In their rooms at the Chateau Laurier, shortly before midnight, their telephone rang. Ross had just made love to his wife, highly satisfactorily to his way of thinking, and was in the bathroom. She answered the phone.

'Mrs Ross?' asked a male voice.

'Yes. Who is this?'

'Just a friend. An old friend. Why don't you ask your husband about Stalag XIII K? About Hoffmann and Axheim and Gessel. About the Cloak.'

'About the *what*? Look, who . . .'

But the caller had hung up.

Ross emerged from the bathroom.

'Was that the phone? Who the devil was calling at this time of . . .' Then he saw his wife's expression. 'What is it?'

'It was a man telling me to ask you about Stalag XIII K. About Hoffmann and some other German names. About something called the Cloak.'

'Oh, Jesus,' said Ross, and sat on the edge of the bed.

'We'd better have that talk,' said his wife. 'I've invested an awful lot of time, money and patience in your political career. If there's something that can blow it apart before you even get as far as the House of Commons, I want to know about it. We may be able to stop it happening. You wouldn't be the first would-be politician to have a skeleton in the closet.'

She was the stronger of them, he'd known that for years. Perhaps all political wives were stronger than their husbands. Preferred it that way. The power behind the throne.

But Christ, it was difficult. How did you tell the woman you'd married that you'd sold out to the enemy, been responsible for the deaths of others? Of *one* other in particular, because it could be no coincidence that the six men he had seen today were part of Jack Lambert's execution squad. Sold out for a little more food because starvation and deprivation were more than you could stand.

'As I told you earlier,' he said, his voice barely audible, 'it's a long story.'

'We've got all night,' said Ruth Ross.

'So far so good,' said Kovacs to the others. 'About time we headed back to Calgary, I reckon, because that's where the bastard'll run to next if I'm any judge.'

'First thing in the morning,' said Margolis. 'Though I'll keep my detectives on, just to make sure.'

It was almost dawn before Ross finished his story, though he'd told it, in different ways, a dozen times.

Ruth Ross felt disgusted with him and sorry for him simultaneously. This was the man whose bed she shared, who had made love to her not five hours earlier. She'd known he was weak, but she had seriously underestimated how weak.

Still, he was her husband, after all. Her child, too, in some ways. The one she would never have. It was her duty to protect him and advance his career.

'What do we do?' he asked her.

She had thought about it at length while he was talking.

'We sit it out. We can't have them arrested because they've committed no crime. We can't make any sort of fuss whatsoever because that could be what they're waiting for. Then it will be in the newspapers and you'll be finished. You might even go to prison. Maybe they've done what they set out to do, scare you. They won't want publicity, either, if everything you've told me is true.'

'It is.'

'Then maybe they'll go away.'

And for a few days, in Calgary, it seemed as if they had.

Ross was fearful every time he left the house, jumpy in case the Chief or Kovacs or one of the others appeared. In the street. At his office. In a restaurant.

But nothing happened.

On an evening in the middle of August, the fifth anniversary of Dieppe, he was to recall later, he received a phone call at his home in Mount Royal. From a man he didn't know, but one who claimed he was a supporter of Ross's political Party. Who would back his campaign when it came down to it. Who would put funds into it. Cash.

He gave his name as Jackson.

'But I don't want our arrangement generally known. In case you lose, you understand. The nomination, that is.'

Ross said he understood. The phone call was not unique. Since he had become the leading contender as the Calgary West nominee for the Federal Parliament, he had met many businessmen who wanted to support his candidacy. All were looking for eventual favours. Few wanted to poke their heads above the parapet.

'Where?' asked Ross.

The caller named a location thirty miles west of Calgary, a few miles beyond Cochrane on the Trans-Canada Highway. Ross said he'd be there. It didn't matter that it was late at night. That was how politics worked.

'I'll come with you,' said his wife.

She was looking especially attractive tonight, dark hair cropped close, short black dress, matching stockings and shoes. An asset to any man on his way.

Ross shook his head.

'Can't be done. That wasn't the deal. It's just me.'

'It's never been just you, you fool. I'll feel a lot more secure if I'm with you. For your sake.'

'You'll have to wait in the Buick.'

'That won't hurt.'

Ross drove. The location was a warehouse. Jesus, he thought, politics. But that was the system. You black-bagged money, you gave consideration. It was probably the same the world over.

Ross parked the Buick.

'Now remember, wait here.'

There was no illumination outside the warehouse. Not that Ross had expected any. Using a flashlight he walked towards the doors and pushed them open.

The sight that greeted him froze him into horrified immobility. What he faced was an exact replica of Hut 6B, Stalag XIII K. The bunks, the stove, the lousy table. And on the bunks were the Chief, Kovacs, McKenzie, Lucas, Tucker and Turner. On one of them lounged a figure that could only be Jack Lambert or his twin brother.

'Come in,' said Kovacs.

Ross fled.

There could be no doubt about it now if there'd been any before. The bastards knew.

302

'What's happening? What's the matter?' demanded his wife as Ross threw open the driver's door and leapt inside the Buick.

He gunned the motor, not answering. Okay, so they knew. What the hell could they do about it? He was an Ottawa candidate. He was safe.

His wife was shrieking at him to slow down. He paid no attention. Calgary was only thirty miles away. Half an hour. They'd be home then. Home and dry.

Six miles down the road, his wife hanging on for dear life, he saw the searchlights, probing. He thought he was imagining things. Searchlights, for Christ's sake.

Then he saw the barrier, the red-and-white pole across the road. The coils of barbed-wire. And two uniformed guards. Wehrmacht guards. Men dressed in German uniforms, anyway.

He couldn't stop. That would have been foolish. Nor could he ram the barrier. Someone was trying to send him out of his mind, or kill him.

He wrenched the wheel to the right. Then he saw the drop, the canyon. Ruth Ross screamed. But it was all too late.

The explosion, it was said later, was seen for ten miles. But the Buick was totalled, the driver and his passenger dead. Anyway, by the time the police arrived, apart from the blaze, there was nothing to see.

Kovacs paid off his crew. The props and uniforms were his, the men people he knew from the seamy side of life.

'Thanks, guys. There'll be other jobs.'

Epilogue

'We're not going to meet once a year,' said Kovacs, 'like some sort of club. Got that, Ben?'

Ben said he had. He was still shaken twenty-four hours later. Acting the part of his dead brother in the mock-up of Hut 6B had proved an unnerving experience, and Ruth Ross's death had not been part of the plan at all.

'Tough,' Kovacs had remarked, when they learned that Ross had been carrying a passenger and who it was. 'It's damned near a certainty she knew what Ross got up to during the war. If not before, she must have quizzed him after I spoke to her on the phone. But she didn't go running to the authorities, did she? It's better this way. The slate's clean.'

They were in Margolis's Edmonton house: Kovacs, the Chief, Ben, Margolis himself. Maggie was elsewhere. The others had all gone, back home, back to the rest of their lives.

'We did wrong,' said Kovacs, 'and we tried to put it right. Now we go our separate ways.'

East of Edmonton the Chief asked to be let out of Kovacs's big limousine.

'It's a hell of a long way back to Foam Lake, Chief. About five hundred miles.'

'Never mind, I'll walk.'

Crazy bastard, thought Kovacs.

Then he thought again. What the hell. He had nothing to do that wouldn't keep.

He switched off the ignition and pocketed the keys.

'Wait for me.'

'You know what that is,' said the Chief, nodding up ahead.

'Sure. Alberta, Saskatchewan, Manitoba.'

'No,' said the Chief, 'it's ours. And if it wasn't for Jack we probably wouldn't be here to see it.'

'Christ, you can't carry that monkey on your back for ever.'

'Maybe not.'

The Chief halted and faced Kovacs.

'Listen, there's no point in you coming with me. It'll mean sending someone for the car, anyway.'

'That's why I pay them. I could find a place for you, if you want a job.'

'No, thanks.'

They looked at one another. Kovacs thought of offering his hand, but something decided him otherwise.

'Take it easy, Chief.'

'You too.'

Although it was a long straight road on which a walker could be seen for miles, Kovacs remained where he was until the Chief vanished in the heat haze.

WALTER WINWARD

MUSIC OF A DISTANT DRUM

Since the last century, the Camerons had been part of Malaya. But first their tranquil colonial existence was shattered by the Japanese invasion. And now a bloody uprising threatened to destroy their way of life for ever.

And within the family and their social set, there were passions and scandals that could destroy everything they had built up – just as surely as the guerillas who lurked in the jungle . . .

'A superbly woven sequence of events, together with flesh-and-blood people, whose lives are over-shadowed by inexorable changes beyond their control, make it a memorable book'

The Evening News

Post·A·Book

A Royal Mail service in association with the Book Marketing Council & The Booksellers Association.
Post-A-Book is a Post Office trademark.

DAVID MORRELL

THE BROTHERHOOD OF THE ROSE

They were orphans – Chris and Saul – raised in a Philadelphia school for boys, bonded by friendship and devoted to a mysterious man called Eliot.

He visited them and brought them sweets. He treated them like sons.

He trained them to be assassins.

Trusting in him completely, they had never questioned their orders.

Now he is desperately trying to have them killed.

'Impossible to put down'   *San Francisco Chronicle*

'Riveting . . . Crackling . . . It really moves'
                                              Washington Post

HODDER AND STOUGHTON PAPERBACKS

DAVID MORRELL

THE FRATERNITY OF THE STONE

Each single cell was punitively plain, barely furnished. Each inmate, uniformly dressed, stripped of all personal possessions, was there for life. Yet each had volunteered.

A monastery.

In each cell: a monk — and all but one, dead. Poisoned. In the kitchens were the two lay brethren, also dead, shot in chest and head. A coldblooded massacre.

Drew MacLane, penitent, former professional assassin, now the one chance survivor, knew that he and only he had been the target, knew that his past had finally caught up with him.

With sickening certainty he understood now that he would have to revert, relearn his old killing instincts and go out into the world he had renounced in self-disgust. Would have to hunt down and destroy the men and the organisation that had destroyed his last hope of peace.

HODDER AND STOUGHTON PAPERBACKS

DAVID MORRELL

THE LEAGUE OF NIGHT AND FOG

In the Vatican, Cardinal Pavelic celebrated mass privately in his own living quarters. It was Sunday evening.

No one saw him again.

In St Paul, Minnesota, an old man, collar turned up against the driving snow, left his bridge evening to drive home.

He never arrived.

In Mexico City, near Toronto, outside Sydney, from Vienna, others disappeared. There were no accident reports, no bodies, no ransom notes. Just silence and the anguish of knowing nothing but fearing the worst.

Terror. A pattern of half-seen connections. The chilling premonition of more terror to come. A threat that would draw both the Brotherhood of the Rose and the Fraternity of the Stone into the search for an answer.

Whilst in Rome the agents of death had just arrived.

'One of the most compulsive and weirdly original thriller writers around'
The London Evening Standard

HODDER AND STOUGHTON PAPERBACKS

MORE FICTION TITLES AVAILABLE
FROM HODDER & STOUGHTON PAPERBACKS

WALTER WINWARD

☐	49732	1	Music of a Distant Drum	£3.50

DAVID MORRELL

☐	05892	1	The Brotherhood of the Rose	£3.99
☐	50933	8	First Blood	£2.99
☐	39746	7	The Fraternity of the Stone	£2.95
☐	42467	7	The League of Night and Fog	£3.99
☐	42476	6	Rambo: III	£2.50

All these books are available at your local bookshop or newsagent, or can be ordered direct from the publisher. Just tick the titles you want and fill in the form below.

Prices and availability subject to change without notice.

Hodder & Stoughton Paperbacks, P.O. Box 11, Falmouth, Cornwall.

Please send cheque or postal order, and allow the following for postage and packing:

U.K. – 80p for one book and 20p for each additional book ordered up to a £2.00 maximum.

B.F.P.O. – 80p for the first book, plus 20p for each additional book.

OVERSEAS INCLUDING EIRE – £1.50 for the first book, plus £1.00 for the second book, and 30p for each additional book.

Name ....

Address ....

....